CHILTON'S GUIDE TO
AIR CONDITIONING
REPAIR and SERVICE

Sr. Vice President	Ronald A. Hoxter
Publisher and Editor-In-Chief	Kerry A. Freeman, S.A.E.
Managing Editors	Peter M. Conti, Jr. □ W. Calvin Settle, Jr., S.A.E.
Assistant Managing Editor	Nick D'Andrea
Senior Editors	Richard J. Rivele, S.A.E. □ Ron Webb
Director of Manufacturing	Mike D'Imperio
Manager of Manufacturing	John F. Butler

CHILTON BOOK COMPANY

ONE OF THE **DIVERSIFIED PUBLISHING COMPANIES,**
A PART OF **CAPITAL CITIES/ABC, INC.**

Manufactured in USA
© 1985 Chilton Book Company
Chilton Way Radnor, Pa. 19089
ISBN 0-8019-7580-8

9 0 1 2 3 4 5 6 7 8   1 9 8 7 6 5 4 3 2

CONTENTS

SAFETY NOTICE

Proper service and repair procedures are vital to the safe, reliable operation of all motor vehicles, as well as the personal safety of those performing repairs. This manual outlines procedures for servicing and repairing vehicles using safe effective methods. The procedures contain many NOTES, CAUTIONS and WARNINGS which should be followed along with standard safety procedures to eliminate the possibility of personal injury or improper service which could damage the vehicle or compromise its safety.

It is important to note that repair procedures and techniques, tools and parts for servicing motor vehicles, as well as the skill and experience of the individual performing the work vary widely. It is not possible to anticipate all of the conceivable ways or conditions under which vehicles may be serviced, or to provide cautions as to all of th epossible hazards that may result. Standard and accepted safety precautions and equipment should be used when handling toxic or flammable fluids, and safety goggles or other protection should be used during cutting, grinding chiseling, prying, or any other process that can cause material removal or projectiles.

Some procedures require the use of tools specially designed for a specific purpose. Before substituting another tool or procedure, you must be completely satisfied that neither your personal safety, nor the performance of the vehicle will be endangered.

PART NUMBERS

Part numbers listed in this reference are not recommendations by Chilton for any product by brand name. They are references that can be used with interchange manuals and aftermarket supplier catalogs to locate each brand supplier's discrete part number.

Although information in this manual is based on industry sources and is as complete as possible at the time of publication, the possibility exists that some car manufacturers made later changes which could not be included here. While striving for total accuracy, Chilton Book Company cannot assume responsibility for any errors, changes, or omissions that may occur in the compilation of this data.

AIR CONDITIONING SYSTEMS

Manually Controlled Systems

The automotive air conditioning systems are basic in design and operation, but many different components are used by the vehicle manufacturers to operate and control the systems to their specifications. Improvements have been made through the years, to control the refrigerant movement through the system, by improved pressure and temperature components, which has greatly improved the interior cooling capacity. Many of the components are now made of lighter, but more durable materials, due to a mandated vehicle weight reduction program.

To assist service personnel to recognize the different air conditioning systems, an explanation of each is outlined.

BASIC SYSTEM

The basic air conditioning system utilizes all or some of the following components: the compressor, condensor, evaporator, receiver-drier, expansion valve and a thermostatic or ambient type switch to control evaporator freeze-up. The controls are manually operated and the unit is basic in design. This system is usually installed as an add-on or aftermarket unit. A sight glass may be used in the system.

E.P.R. SYSTEM

The E.P.R. (evaporator pressure regulator) system includes the condensor, muffler, low pressure shut off valve, receiver-drier, expansion valve, evaporator and a V-block, reciprocating crank type compressor. The E.P.R. valve is mounted on the suction side of the compressor and operates in conjunction with the expansion valve assembly, to regulate the flow of refrigerant from the evaporator to the compressor, under light air conditioning loads. By regulating the refrigerant flow, the evaporator temperature is controlled and freezing of the evaporator is prevented.

In contrast to other systems, the E.P.R. system uses the reheat procedure to control the temperature of the air, after it is cooled by passing through the evaporator fins. A manually controlled operating lever is connected to the heater water flow control valve and to a blend air door and the opening of the blend door proportions the amount of air around and through the heater core to control the mix of the cool and hot air for the desired inside temperature. A sight glass is used with this system.

Two types of expansion valves are used with this system. The first type has a capillary tube, mounted in a well on the suction line. The second type has no capillary tube, but senses the need to meter refrigerant into the evaporator by an internal sensing tube. This type of expansion valve is called the "H" type.

"H" VALVE SYSTEM

As was described in the E.P.R. system, the "H" expansion valve can be used with the E.P.R. valve, located in the V-block, reciprocating crank type compressor, to control the amount of refrigerant metered into the evaporator and to control the temperature of the evaporator coils to prevent freeze-up of the condensed moisture. However, when the "H" valve is used with the three piston, axial compressor, a cycling switch is used to control the temperature of the evaporator to prevent freeze-up, rather than the E.P.R. valve, as used with the reciprocating crank type compressor. This can be called the "H" valve system for explanation purposes only and should be recognized as such. The "H" system uses the same components as the other systems, basically the compressor (axial type), condenser, evaporator, expansion valve without a capillary tube ("H" type), receiver-drier, muffler and a low pressure shut off valve. The cycling clutch switch uses a capillary tube, attached to the surface of the suction line, to sense the need for refrigerant movement and compressor operation, therefore, causing the elec-

and coil to operate the compressor on demand from ... and to open the circuit to the coil when the demand ... sight glass is used with this system.

CCOT SYSTEM

... (cycling clutch orifice tube) system includes the compressor, ..., evaporator, an accumulator-drier, a clutch cycling switch ... without a capillary tube, and a fixed orifice tube, mounted to ... vaporator, replacing the expansion valve.

... clutch cycling switch with or without a temperature probing ... pillary tube, cycles the compressor clutch off and on as required to maintain a selected comfortable temperature within the vehicle, while preventing evaporator freeze-up. Full control of the system is maintained through the use of a selector control, mounted in the dash assembly. The selector control makes use of a vacuum supply and electrical switches to operate mode doors and the blower motor. A sight glass is not used in this system and one should not be installed. When charging the system, the correct quantity of refrigerant must be installed by measurement.

STV/BPO SYSTEM

The STV/BPO (suction throttling valve/by-pass orifice) system uses either two types of external expansion valves or a mini-combination valve assembly. The mini-combination valve assembly contains an expansion valve, suction throttling valve and a service port. The expansion valve is of the "H" block design and is used to regulate the flow of refrigerant into the evaporator core. It is also the dividing point for the high and low pressure within the system. The suction throttling valve is used to control the evaporator pressure and to prevent coil freeze-

up. The suction throttling starts when the compressor suction pressure decreases below the valve setting. The compressor suction pressure can continue to drop, but the evaporator pressure is held steady by the controlling or throttling action of the STV. A pressure differential valve is used within the combination valve assembly, to allow oil laden refrigerant to by-pass the restriction formed when the STV assembly is closed, to assure oil return to the compressor during times of reduced heat loads on the system. The by-pass valve remains closed under high heat loads since ample oil is moving through the system and compressor.

Evaporator pressure can only be measured on this system and a special type connector must be used to attach the high pressure gauge line to the service gauge port.

When either of the external type expansion valves are used, separate suction throttling valves are used. The operation of each is basically the same as the components of the combination valve assembly.

The type of external expansion valve used with the system will dictate either low suction or evaporator pressure measurements from the gauge service ports. To determine the pressure measurement that may be obtained from the system, examine the external expansion valve for one of the following conditions:

　　a. Should the expansion valve have one capillary tube and one equalizer line, it is of the conventional externally equalizer type and low pressure suction would be measured at the service port, normally located on the suction line. A second gauge port may be located on the POA valve body and an evaporator pressure reading can be obtained from this port.

　　b. If the expansion valve has only one capillary tube, it is the by-pass orifice (BPO) type and only evaporator pressure will be measured at the service port valve, located on the STV assembly. To assist the repair-person in the diagnosis of the two external expansion valve systems, two troubleshooting charts have been prepared and are located in the Troubleshooting Section of this manual.

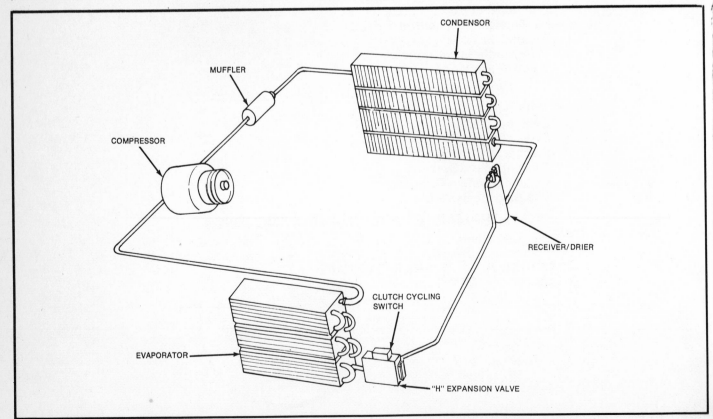

Typical 'H' type expansion valve air conditioning system

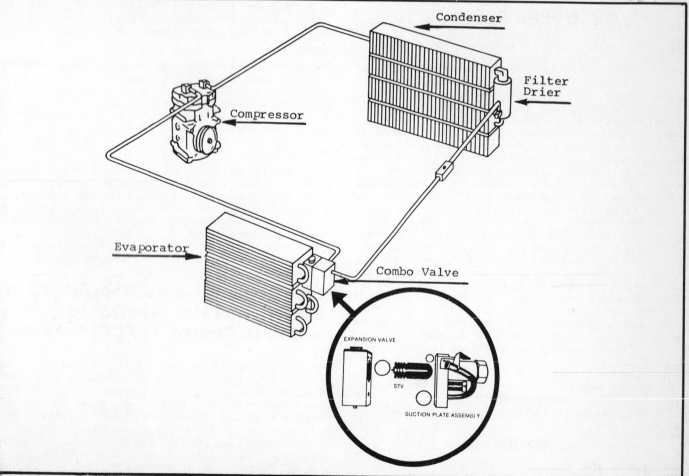

Typical Suction Throttling Valve/By-pass Orifice (STV/BPO) system

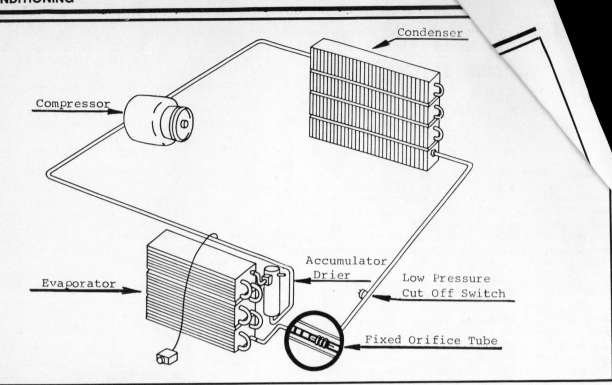

Typical Clutch Cycling Orifice Tube (CCOT) system

Automatic Temperature Controlled Systems

The automatic temperature control system will automatically control the temperature, blower speed and reduce the relative humidity of the vehicle's inside air. Upon setting the desired temperature and putting the system into operation, the system will maintain the set comfort level automatically and requires little or no change in the settings to compensate for changes due to the outside weather conditions. The system uses what is known as REHEAT to provide the comforting and conditioned air inside the vehicle. All blower air passes through the evaporator coils where it is cooled. The reheat system uses a temperature blend door to control the percentage of cooled air that flows through and around the heater core to provide the desired temperature of the air at the air outlet ports, after being mixed in the distribution plenum.

Different types of controls are used by the vehicle manufacturers and may vary from model year to model year in their application. Certain controls allow the vehicle operator, in addition to setting the desired temperature, to control the blower speeds when the system is in certain other operating modes other than the automatic mode. Certain other models control the blower speeds automatically, but have an automatic HI and LO operating mode on the control panel. The temperature control may be a rotating numbered dial wheel, electronically controlled or a sliding control lever, corresponding to temperature degree markings on the control panel face.

To understand the operation of the automatic temperature control system in general, three major control systems are used, with a description of the various components used in each major section. The major sections are:
1. Temperature control.
2. Blower control.
3. Electrical and vacuum functions.

The three major sections are all interconnected during the system operation.

COMPONENTS

IN-CAR SENSORS

Sensors are actually thermisters, which are a special resistors with a value that will change quickly with temperature changes. They also differ from ordinary resistors in that their resistance decreases as they get hotter. Two sensors are used, one sensing outside air temperature and the second sensor sensing vehicle interior temperature.

ASPIRATOR

The inside sensor is normally mounted in a box near or around the top of the dash panel, with an air hose connecting the sensor box to an aspirator. The aspirator is a tube within a tube arrangement and has blower air moving through the inner hose, which causes a suction and draws air into and past the sensor mounted in the box. The air is then directed through the hose and into the aspirator housing.

PROGRAMMER

A programmer is used on most automatic temperature control systems to control the operation of the electrical and vacuum systems, necessary for the correct operation of the automatic temperature control system. The programmer will contain such control units as the potentiometer, amplifiers, circuit boards, power modules, and control switches for the electrical and vacuum systems.

New electronically controlled automatic temperature programmers have been developed and are now being used in late model vehicles.

Electronic Climate Control (ECC) System and the Electronic Touch Climate Control (ETCC) System

The Electronic Climate Control system has a programmer that differs from the earlier models in that the main vacuum motor has been replaced by a reversible DC electric motor, which adjusts the air mode door position. Vacuum solenoids, mounted within the case, controls the vacuum to the actuators which open and close the hot water valve, the recirculating door, the mode door and the defroster door.

The Electronic Touch Climate Control system has no programm or vacuum motors as it is a totally electric system. Actuators are equipp with small DC electric motors to position the temperature door, defroster mode doors and the hot water valve.

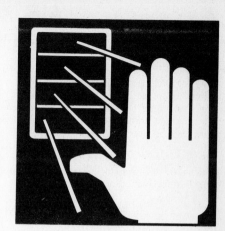

SECTION 1
General Information

INDEX

COMPONENTS

POTENTIOMETERS

Potentiometers also vary their resistance with conditions. The difference is that they vary resistance with the position of a lever by causing contacts mounted on the lever to carry current through a greater or lesser portion of the potentiometer resistance wire. A potentiometer allows the driver to vary the temperature setting through adjustment of a wheel or lever mounted on the temperature dial on the dash. Another permits the position of the programmer—the mechanism which actually operates the dampers and switches controlling system output—to feed back to the system's amplifier. The word "feedback" refers to the return of information to a controlling component, in effect telling that component its orders have been carried out.

AMPLIFIERS

An amplifier multiplies the strength of an incoming electronic signal by a constant factor. If resistance in a thermistor drops because of a sudden temperature change, there will be a change in the flow of power to the amplifier. This change will result in a proportional change in the power flow at the amplifier output. The amplifier will receive the extra energy required for the output circuit from the vehicle's electrical system.

TRANSDUCERS (SOLENOIDS)

Transducers also increase the amount of power available for control, but they change the signal from an electronic one to a pneumatic one. The source of power for a transducer is intake manifold vacuum. The transducer then throttles the intake vacuum down to a lower level for effective control. It converts the electronic signal to a vacuum signal by using a solenoid type of magnetic coil. The vacuum throttle inside the transducer consists of a pin whose position in an orifice is controlled by the intensity of the solenoid's magnetic field. An increase in the field strength tends to seat the pin in opposition to the pressure of a spring connected between the transducer housing and an armature assembly that positions the throttling pin. Spring pressure opposes the effect of the magnetic field on the armature in order that the throttle

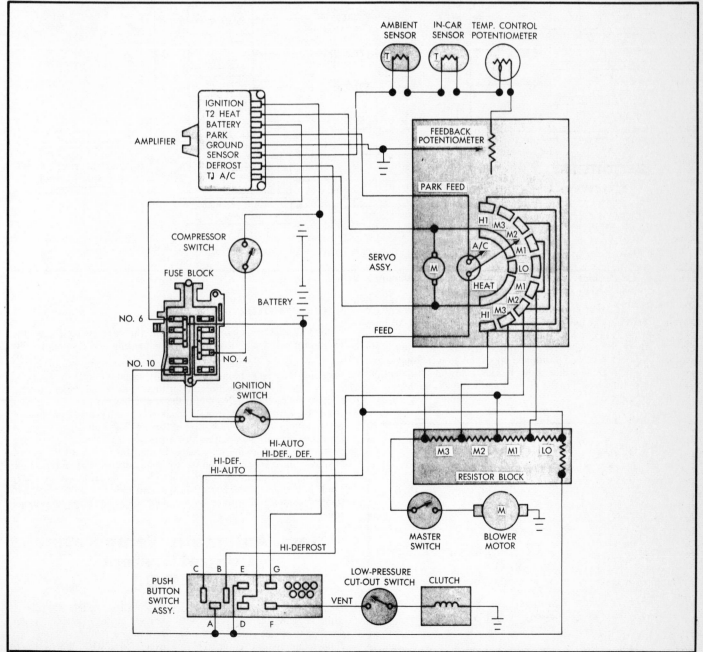

Non-micro type electrical schematic of automatic air conditioning system

5

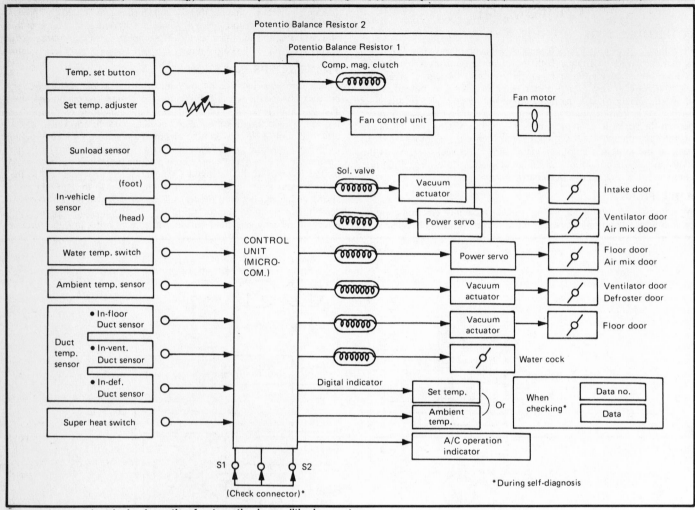

Electronic type electrical schematic of automatic air conditioning system

pin will respond gradually to changes in the amount of current the amplifier sends through the solenoid coil, so it will find a stable position. Gradual increases in amplifier output will produce gradual increases in the strength of the magnetic field. This will move the throttle pin gradually toward the closed position in opposition to increasing spring pressure. Closing off the orifice allows less air to flow into the manifold vacuum hose, thus reducing the vacuum the transducer applies to the system.

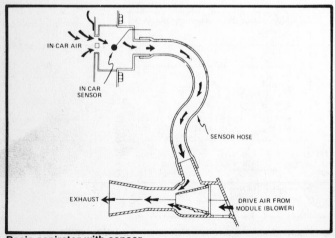

Basic aspirator with sensor

VACUUM MOTORS

NOTE: Electric motors operate on the same principle as the vacuum motors to control the various heating and cooling modes.

Vacuum motors are the limbs of the automatic temperature control systems. They take the final signal—the vacuum output of the transducer—and use it to position the air mixing door and the other components which ultimately control the temperature of the vehicle's interior. They are airtight housings containing vacuum operated diaphragms whose actions are opposed by spring tension. The diaphragm is pierced by a tiny hole at one point so that air flows in constantly, increasing pressure as soon as the transducer throttle moves toward the closed position. Since spring tension increases and decreases with the length of a spring, a slight change in the vacuum signal's value will generally result in a slight movement of the vacuum motor to a different, and stable, position where force on the diaphragm and spring tension are equal.

Semi Automatic Temperature Control System (S.A.T.C.)

This system maintains a selected temperature level within the vehicle while allowing the operator to select various modes of operation, depending upon the interior temperature, ambient temperature and the temperature control setting. The one exception is when the system is in the MAX A/C mode. At this time the water valve is closed and air

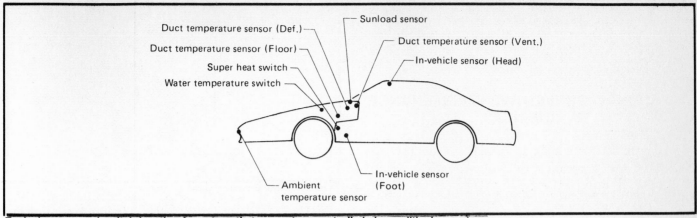

Duct temperature sensor (Def.)
Sunload sensor
Duct temperature sensor (Floor)
Duct temperature sensor (Vent.)
Super heat switch
In-vehicle sensor (Head)
Water temperature switch
Ambient temperature sensor
In-vehicle sensor (Foot)

Typical sensor and switch location for automatic temperature controlled air conditioning system

is stopped from passing through the heater core while the air is recirculated inside the vehicle. A bi-metal sensor is used instead of the thermistor type, to respond to the inside and outside vehicle temperature changes, so that the desired inside temperature can be maintained. The bi-metal sensor is actually a bi-metal spring which controls the vacuum supplied to the vacuum servo actuator by responding to the varying temperatures. The comfort control functions basically as a house thermostat by having five numbers on the front face of the control panel. This allows the operator to select a desired comfort range. Also included is a color band of blue, white and red to give the operator an idea of the comfort range.

Each automatic temperature control section contains a theory section that relates these basic principles to actual system operation. Each also describes the actual design of the ducting, control doors and other system components.

GENERAL SERVICING PROCEDURES

The most important aspect of air conditioning service is the maintenance of a pure and adequate charge of refrigerant in the system. A refrigeration system cannot function properly if a significant percentage of the charge is lost. Leaks are common because the severe vibration encountered in an automobile can easily cause a sufficient cracking or loosening of the air conditioning fittings; as a result, the extreme operating pressures of the system force refrigerant out.

The problem can be understood by considering what happens to the system as it is operated with a continuous leak. Because the expansion valve regulates the flow of refrigerant to the evaporator, the level of refrigerant there is fairly constant. The receiver-drier stores any excess of refrigerant, and so a loss will first appear there as a reduction in the level of liquid. As this level nears the bottom of the vessel, some refrigerant vapor bubbles will begin to appear in the stream of liquid supplied to the expansion valve. This vapor decreases the capacity of the expansion valve very little as the valve opens to compensate for its presence. As the quantity of liquid in the condenser decreases, the operating pressure will drop there and throughout the high side of the system. As the R-12 continues to be expelled, the pressure available to force the liquid through the expansion valve will continue to decrease, and, eventually, the valve's orifice will prove to be too much of a restriction for adequate flow even with the needle fully withdrawn.

At this point, low side pressure will start to drop, and severe reduction in cooling capacity, marked by freeze-up of the evaporator coil, will result. Eventually, the operating pressure of the evaporator will be lower than the pressure of the atmosphere surrounding it, and air will be drawn into the system wherever there are leaks in the low side.

Because all atmospheric air contains at least some moisture, water will enter the system and mix with the R-12 and the oil. Trace amounts of moisture will cause sludging of the oil, and corrosion of the system. Saturation and clogging of the filter-drier, and freezing of the expansion valve orifice will eventually result. As air fills the system to a greater

and greater extent, it will interfere more and more with the normal flows of refrigerant and heat.

From this description, it should be obvious that much of the repairman's time will be spent detecting leaks, repairing them, and then restoring the purity and quantity of the refrigerant charge. A list of general precautions that should be observed while doing this follows:

1. Keep all tools as clean and dry as possible.
2. Thoroughly purge the service gauges and hoses of air and moisture before connecting them to the system. Keep them capped when not in use.
3. Thoroughly clean any refrigerant fitting before disconnecting it, in order to minimize the entrance of dirt into the system.
4. Plan any operation that requires opening the system beforehand, in order to minimize the length of time it will be exposed to open air. Cap or seal the open ends to minimize the entrance of foreign material.
5. When adding oil, pour it through an extremely clean and dry tube or funnel. Keep the oil capped whenever possible. Do not use oil that has not been kept tightly sealed.
6. Use only refrigerant 12. Purchase refrigerant intended for use in only automatic air conditioning systems. Avoid the use of refrigerant 12 that may be packaged for another use, such as cleaning, or powering a horn, as it is impure.
7. Completely evacuate any system that has been opened to replace a component, or that has leaked sufficiently to draw in moisture and air. This requires evacuating air and moisture with a good vacuum pump for at least one hour.

If a system has been open for a considerable length of time it may be advisable to evacuate the system for up to 12 hours (overnight).

8. Use a wrench on both halves of a fitting that is to be disconnected, so as to avoid placing torque on any of the refrigerant lines.
9. When overhauling a compressor, pour some of the oil into a clean glass and inspect it. If there is evidence of dirt or metal particles, or both, flush all refrigerant components with clean refrigerant before

Air conditioning system contaminants

evacuating and recharging the system. In addition, if metal particles are present, the compressor should be replaced.

10. Schrader valves may leak only when under full operating pressure. Therefore, if leakage is suspected but cannot be located, operate the system with a full charge of refrigerant and look for leaks from all Schrader valves. Replace any faulty valves.

ADDITIONAL PREVENTIVE MAINTENANCE CHECKS

ANTIFREEZE

In order to prevent heater core freeze-up during A/C operation, it is necessary to maintain permanent type antifreeze protection of +15 degrees F. or lower. A reading of −15 degrees F. is ideal since this protection also supplies sufficient corrosion inhibitors for the protection of the engine cooling system.

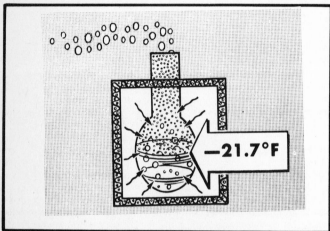

Remember -- R-12 refrigerant boils at 21.7 degrees F.

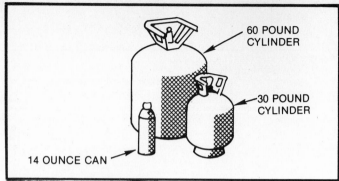

Typical refrigerant containers

NOTE: The same antifreeze should not be used longer than the manufacturer specifies.

RADIATOR CAP

For efficient operation of an air conditioned car's cooling system, the radiator cap should have a holding pressure which meets manufacturer's specifications. A cap which fails to hold these pressures should be replaced.

CONDENSER

Any obstruction of or damage to the condenser configuration will restrict the air flow which is essential to its efficient operation. It is therefore a good rule to keep this unit clean and in proper physical shape.

NOTE: Bug screens are regarded as obstructions.

CONDENSATION DRAIN TUBE

This single molded drain tube expels the condensation, which accumulates on the bottom of the evaporator housing, into the engine compartment.

If this tube is obstructed, the air conditioning performance can be restricted and condensation buildup can spill over onto the vehicle's floor.

SAFETY PRECAUTIONS

Because of the importance of the necessary safety precautions that must be exercised when working with air conditioning systems and R-12 refrigerant, a recap of the safety precautions are outlined.

1. Avoid contact with a charged refrigeration system, even when working on another part of the air conditioning system or vehicle. If a heavy tool comes into contact with a section of copper tubing or a heat exchanger, it can easily cause the relatively soft material to rupture.

2. When it is necessary to apply force to a fitting which contains refrigerant, as when checking that all system couplings are securely tightened, use a wrench on both parts of the fitting involved, if possible. This will avoid putting torque on refrigerant tubing. (It is advisable, when possible, to use tube or line wrenches when tightening these flare nut fittings.)

3. Do not attempt to discharge the system by merely loosening a fitting, or removing the service valve caps and cracking these valves. Precise control is possible only when using the service gauges. Place a rag under the open end of the center charging hose while discharging the system to catch any drops of liquid that might escape. Wear protective gloves when connecting or disconnecting service gauge hoses.

4. Discharge the system only in a well ventilated area, as high concentrations of the gas can exclude oxygen and act as an anesthesia. When leak testing or soldering, this is particularly important, as toxic gas is formed when R-12 contacts any flame.

5. Never start a system without first verifying that both service valves are backseated, if equipped, and that all fittings throughout the system are snugly connected.

6. Avoid applying heat to any refrigerant line or storage vessel. Charging may be aided by using water heated to less than 125 degrees to warm the refrigerant container. Never allow a refrigerant storage

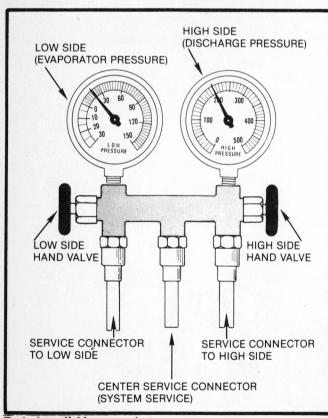

Typical manifold gauge set

container to sit out in the sun, or near any other source of heat, such as a radiator.

7. Always wear goggles when working on a system to protect the eyes. If refrigerant contacts the eyes, it is advisable in all cases to see a physician as soon as possible.

8. Frostbite from liquid refrigerant should be treated by first gradually warming the area with cool water, and then gently applying petroleum jelly. A physician should be consulted.

9. Always keep refrigerant drum fittings capped when not in use. Avoid sudden shock to the drum which might occur from dropping it, or from banging a heavy tool against it. Never carry a drum in the passenger compartment of a car.

10. Always completely discharge the system before painting the vehicle (if the paint is to be baked on), or before welding anywhere near refrigerant lines.

Air Conditioning Tools and Gauges

TEST GAUGES

Most of the service work performed in air conditioning requires the use of a set of two gauges, one for the high (head) pressure side of the system, the other for the low (suction) side.

The low side gauge records both pressure and vacuum. Vacuum readings are calibrated from 0 to 30 inches and the pressure graduations read from 0 to no less than 60 psi.

The high side gauge measures pressure from 0 to at least 600 psi.

Both gauges are threaded into a manifold that contains two hand shut-off valves. Proper manipulation of these valves and the use of the attached test hoses allow the mechanic to perform the following services:

1. Test high and low side pressures.
2. Remove air, moisture, and contaminated refrigerant.
3. Purge the system (of refrigerant).
4. Charge the system (with refrigerant).

NOTE: Chrysler Corp. requires the use of a third gauge on those units that have an evaporator pressure regulator (EPR) valve mounted on the suction side of the compressor.

The manifold valves are designed so they have no direct effect on gauge readings, but serve only to provide for, or cut off, flow of refrigerant through the manifold. During all testing and hook-up operations, the valves are kept in a closed position to avoid disturbing the refrigeration system. The valves are opened only to purge the system of refrigerant or to charge it.

When purging the system, the center hose is uncapped at the lower end, and both valves are cracked open slightly. This allows refrigerant pressure to force the entire contents of the system out through the center hose. During charging, the valve on the high side of the manifold is closed, and the valve on the low side is cracked open. Under these conditions, the low pressure in the evaporator will draw refrigerant from the relatively warm refrigerant storage container into the system.

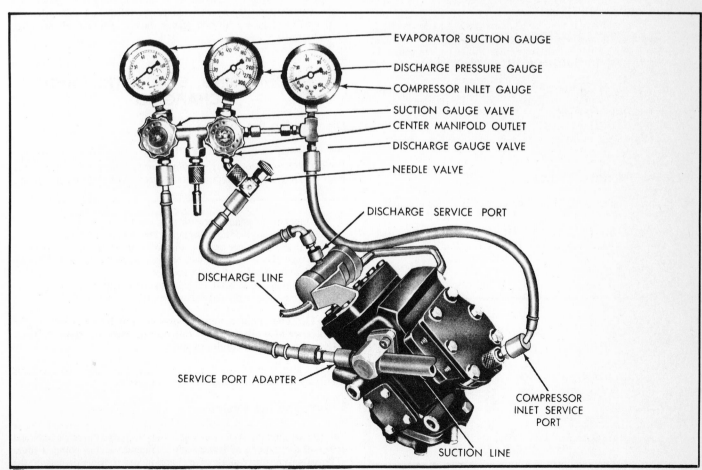

EVAPORATOR SUCTION GAUGE
DISCHARGE PRESSURE GAUGE
COMPRESSOR INLET GAUGE
SUCTION GAUGE VALVE
CENTER MANIFOLD OUTLET
DISCHARGE GAUGE VALVE
NEEDLE VALVE
DISCHARGE SERVICE PORT
DISCHARGE LINE
SERVICE PORT ADAPTER
COMPRESSOR INLET SERVICE PORT
SUCTION LINE

Use of third gauge for compressors equipped with the EPR valve

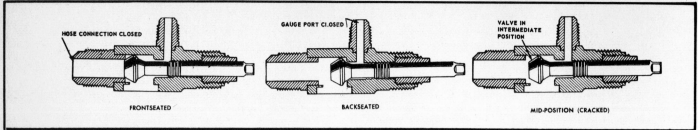

Manual service valve positions

SERVICE VALVES

For the mechanic to diagnose an air conditioning system he must gain "entrance" to the system in order to observe the pressures. There are two types of terminals for this purpose, the hand shut-off type and the familiar Schrader valve.

The Schrader valve is similar to a tire valve stem and the process of connecting the test hoses is the same as threading a hand pump outlet hose to a bicycle tire. As the test hose is threaded to the service port the valve core is depressed, allowing the refrigerant to enter the test hose outlet. Removal of the test hose automatically closes the system.

Extreme caution must be observed when removing test hoses from the Schrader valves as some refrigerant will normally escape, usually under high pressure. (Observe safety precautions.)

Some systems have hand shut-off valves (the stem can be rotated with a special racheting box wrench) that can be positioned in the following three ways:

(1) FRONT SEATED—Rotated to full clockwise position.

(a) Refrigerant will not flow to compressor, but will reach test gauge port. COMPRESSOR WILL BE DAMAGED IF SYSTEM IS TURNED ON IN THIS POSITION.

(b) The compressor is now isolated and ready for service. However, care must be exercised when removing service valves from the compressor as a residue of refrigerant may still be present within the compressor. Therefore, remove service valves slowly observing all safety precautions.

(2) BACK SEATED—Rotated to full counter clockwise position. Normal position for system while in operation. Refrigerant flows to compressor but not to test gauge.

(3) MID-POSITION (CRACKED)

Refrigerant flows to entire system. Gauge port (with hose connected) open for testing.

Using the Manifold Gauges

The following are step-by-step procedures to guide the mechanic to correct gauge usages.

(1) WEAR GOGGLES OR FACE SHIELD DURING ALL TESTING OPERATIONS. BACK SEAT HAND SHUTOFF TYPE SERVICE VALVES.

(2) Remove caps from high and low side service ports. Make sure both gauge valves are closed.

(3) Connect low side test hose to service valve that leads to the evaporator (located between the evaporator outlet and the compressor).

(4) Attach high side test hose to service valve that leads to the condenser.

(5) Mid-position hand shut-off type service valves.

(6) Start engine and allow for warm-up. All testing and charging of the system should be done after engine and system have reached normal operation temperatures (except when using certain charging stations).

(7) Adjust air conditioner controls to maximum cold.

(8) Observe gauge readings. When the gauges are not being used it is a good idea to:

(a) Keep both hand valves in the closed position.

(b) Attach both ends of the high and low service hoses to the manifold, if extra outlets are present on the manifold, or plug them if not. Also, keep the center charging hose attached to an empty refrigerant can. This extra precaution will reduce the possibility of moisture entering the gauges. If air and moisture have gotten into the gauges, purge the hoses by supplying refrigerant under pressure to the center hose with both gauge valves open and all openings unplugged.

DISCHARGING, EVACUATING AND CHARGING

Discharging the System

——————— CAUTION ———————

Perform operation in a well-ventilated area. When it is necessary to remove (purge) the refrigerant pressurized in the system, follow this procedure:

(1) Operate air conditioner for at least 10 minutes.

(2) Attach gauges, shut off engine and air conditioner.

(3) Place a container or rag at the outlet of the center charging hose on the gauge. The refrigerant will be discharged there and this precaution will avoid its uncontrolled exposure.

(4) Open low side hand valve on gauge slightly.

(5) Open high side hand valve slightly.

NOTE: Too rapid a purging process will be identified by the appearance of a oily foam. If this occurs, close the hand valves a little more until this condition stops.

(6) Close both hand valves on the gauge set when the pressures read 0 and all the refrigerant has left the system.

Evacuating the System

Before charging any system it is necessary to purge the refrigerant and draw out the trapped moisture with a suitable vacuum pump. Failure to do so will result in ineffective charging and possible damage to the system.

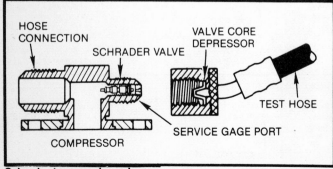

Schrader type service valve

Use this hook-up for the proper evacuation procedure:

(1) Connect both service gauge hoses to the high and low service outlets.

(2) Open high and low side hand valves on gauge manifold.

(3) Open both service valves a slight amount (from back seated position). Allow refrigerant to discharge from system.

(4) Install center charging hose of gauge set to vacuum pump.

(5) Operate vacuum pump for at least one hour. (If the system has been subjected to open conditions for a prolonged period of time it may be necessary to "pump the system down" overnight. Refer to "System Sweep" procedure.)

NOTE: If low pressure gauge does not show at least 28″ hg, within 5 minutes, check the system for a leak or loose gauge connectors.

(6) Close hand valves on gauge manifold.

(7) Shut off pump.

(8) Observe low pressure gauge to determine if vacuum is holding. A vacuum drop may indicate a leak.

Flushing a Badly Contaminated A/C System

A badly contaminated system presents a special problem and is the result of either using the wrong refrigerant oil, the compressor continuing to run during a refrigerant system failure, or improper cleaning following a previous failure. It may also be the result of prolonged operation with excessive moisture or water in the system.

If preliminary inspection shows that the system is badly contaminated with water, carbon and other decomposition products from the failure, it will be necessary to remove all these contaminants as well as clean and service or replace the compressor, replace the orifice tube and the suction accumulator/drier.

Flushing Agents

A number of refrigerants may be used as flushing agents for cleaning a badly contaminated refrigerant system or the individual components. However, not many of them can easily be used. Some are more toxic to humans than others and serious side effects may result from exposure to them. The safety precautions should always be observed with any refrigerant.

Refrigerant as a flushing agent, must be in its liquid state in order to effectively wash the inside surfaces of the components. In its vaporized state, the vapor will not flush away the contaminant particles.

The Refrigerant Flushing chart should be used to aid in the selection of the refrigerant to be used as a flushing agent. Of the four types of refrigerants shown in the chart, two (R-12 and F-114) are better for usage when flushing equipment is not available for two important reasons: (1) Greater pressure at a given ambient temperature and (2) Least toxic to humans.

Remember, however, that as the ambient temperature increases, they become more difficult to use as a flushing agent because of their increase tendency to vaporize rather than remain a liquid.

The remaining two refrigerants (F-11 and F-113) listed in the Refrigerant Flushing chart are better suited for usage with Special Flushing (continuous circulation) equipment. The lower pressure/temperature relationships will keep the closed system pressure lower and should reduce the danger of accidental discharge. F-11 is also available in pressurized containers. This makes it suitable for usage when special flushing equipment is not available; however, F-11 is more toxic than R-12 and F-114.

CAUTION

Extreme caution and adherence to all safety precautions governing the use of refrigerant are necessary when flushing a system.

After the system or individual components have been cleaned, the excess flushing refrigerant should be removed. This is done by blowing out with Refrigerant-12 or nitrogen. Be sure to use a pressure regulator on the nitrogen supply tank if nitrogen is used. The nitrogen supply tank pressure is extremely high and serious damage can result if the supply tank is not regulated.

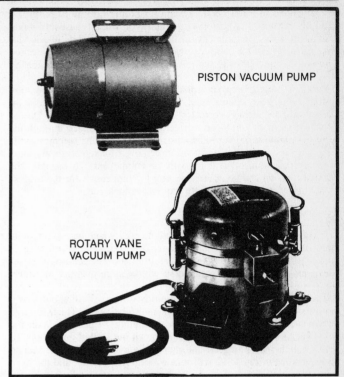

PISTON VACUUM PUMP

ROTARY VANE VACUUM PUMP

Two types of vacuum pumps

CLEANING SYSTEM COMPONENTS

Cleaning the refrigerant system component requires removal and replacement of some of the components and back flushing the condenser assembly. Periodic cleaning of the exterior surface of the condenser is helpful to permit good air circulation through the condenser fins.

The Safety Precautions should be observed at all times. If the components in the following procedure are flushed with a refrigerant other than R-12, it is necessary to remove the excess flushing refrigerant by blowing out with Refrigerant-12 or with nitrogen. If nitrogen is used, a pressure regulator should be installed on the nitrogen supply tank to reduce the extremely high nitrogen supply pressure.

Flushing the System
With Special Flushing Equipment

Special Refrigerant System Flushing Equipment is available from various air conditioning equipment manufacturers. This equipment provides a faster method of cleaning the major refrigerant system components without removing them from the vehicle. All restrictive components, however, such as the fixed orifice tube and the suction accumulator/drier must be removed. A temporary replacement for the removed suction accumulator can be made by using tubing such as neoprene or plastic garden hose. This allows for continuous circulation of a refrigerant system flushing agent so that all system contaminants can be washed out of the major refrigerant system components and hose assemblies, to be trapped in an external filter/drier assembly.

CAUTION

Always check to be sure the flushing refrigerant is compatible with the hose material being used. Some hose materials may dissolve, swell or become brittle when used with certain refrigerant.

When cleaning a contaminated refrigerant system using the continuous circulation method, follow the method as recommended by the manufacturer of the special flushing equipment.

Adding Refrigerant Oil

It is imperative that the specified type and quantity of refrigerant oil be maintained in a refrigerant system for proper operation. A surplus of oil, the wrong oil viscosity or insufficient oil will all cause refrigerant system problems. Insufficient oil or the wrong oil results in poor lubrication and possible compressor damage. A surplus of oil allows too much oil to circulate with the refrigerant causing the cooling capacity of the system to be reduced.

When it is necessary to replace a component of the refrigeration system, certain procedures must be followed to assure that the total oil charge on the system is correct after the new part is installed. During normal A/C operation, some refrigeration oil is circulated through the system with the refrigerant and some is retained in the compressor. If certain components of the system are removed for replacement, some of the refrigeration oil will go with the component. To maintain the original total oil charge, it is necessary to compensate for the oil loss by adding oil to the system with the replacement part.

System Sweep

The triple evacuation procedure should be used when there are definite indications of moisture in the system. This procedure is effective in removing small amounts of moisture from the refrigeration system. However, if system is contaminated with a large quantity of water, complete system flushing will be required.

The principle of the three evacuations is simple. The first pull-down removes about 90 percent of the air and moisture vapors. The first purge with new, dry R-12 mixes with the remaining 10 percent. With the next evacuation, this mixture will be drawn out so that only about 10 percent of the remaining air and moisture vapors remain. The second purge with new, dry R-12 will mix with this 10 percent and the third evacuation will finish the job by drawing out practically all the remaining vapors.

But, if any water was present in the system at the start of this procedure, most of it will still be there; because a short period of vacuum is not long enough to boil and vaporize the water. The R-12 purges, in passing over the liquid, will absorb only a relatively small amount of water.

This procedure is effective only when no water is in the system and should not be used if there is any indication of water in the system.

Charging the System

CAUTION

Never attempt to charge the system by opening the high pressure gauge control while the compressor is operating. The compressor accumulating pressure can burst the refrigerant container, causing severe personal injuries.

BASIC SYSTEM

In this procedure the refrigerant enters the suction side of the system as a vapor while the compressor is running. Before proceeding, the system should be in a partial vacuum after adequate evacuation. Both hand valves on the gauge manifold should be closed.

(1) Attach both test hoses to their respective service valve ports. Mid-position manually operated service valves, if present.

(2) Install dispensing valve (closed position) on the refrigerant container. (Single and multiple refrigerant manifolds are available to accommodate one to four 14 oz. cans.)

(3) Attach center charging hose to the refrigerant container valve.

(4) Open dispensing valve on the refrigerant can.

(5) Loosen the center charging hose coupler where it connects to the gauge manifold to allow the escaping refrigerant to purge the hose of contaminants.

(6) Tighten center charging hose connection.

(7) Purge the low pressure test hose at the gauge manifold.

(8) Start car engine, roll down the car windows and adjust the air conditioner to maximum cooling. The car engine should be at normal operating temperature before proceeding. The heated environment helps the liquid vaporize more efficiently.

(9) Crack open the low side hand valve on the manifold. Manipulate the valve so that the refrigerant that enters the system does not cause the low side pressure to exceed 42 psi. Too sudden a surge may permit

the entrance of unwanted liquid to the compressor. Since liquids cannot be compressed, the compressor will suffer damage if compelled to attempt it. If the suction side of the system remains in a vacuum the system is blocked. Locate and correct the condition before proceeding any further.

NOTE: Placing the refrigerant can in a container of warm water (no hotter than 125 degrees F) will speed the charging process. Slight agitation of the can is helpful too, but be careful not to turn the can upside down.

Some manufacturers allow for a partial charging of the A/C system in the form of a liquid (can inverted and compressor off) by opening the high side gauge valve only, and putting the high side compressor service valve in the middle position (if so equipped). The remainder of the refrigerant is then added in the form of a gas in the normal manner, through the suction side only.

SYSTEMS WITHOUT SIGHT GLASS, EXCEPT CCOT SYSTEM

The following procedure can be used to quickly determine whether or not an air conditioning system has the proper charge of refrigerant (providing ambient temperature is above 70 degrees F. or 21 degrees C.) This check can be made in a manner of minutes, thus facilitating system diagnosis by pinpointing the problem to the amount of charge in the system or by eliminating this possibility from the overall checkout.

1. Engine must be warm (thermostat open).
2. Hood and body doors open.
3. Selector lever set at NORM.
4. Temperature lever at COLD.
5. Blower on HI.
6. Normal engine idle.
7. Hand-feel temperature of evaporator inlet and outlet pipes with compressor engaged.

  (a) Both same temperature or some degree cooler than ambient—proper condition: check for other problems.

  (b) Inlet pipe cooler than outlet pipe—low refrigerant charge. Add a slight amount of refrigerant until both pipes feel the same. Then add 14 oz. (1 can) additional refrigerant.

  (c) Inlet pipe has frost accumulation—outlet pipe warmer; proceed as in Step b above.

If during the charging process the head pressure exceeds 200 psi, place an electric fan in front of the car and direct the turbulent air to the condenser. If no fan is available, repeatedly pour cool water over the top of the condenser. These cooling actions may be necessary on an extremely warm day to help dissipate the heat emitted by the engine during idle. If this fails and pressure on the discharge side continues

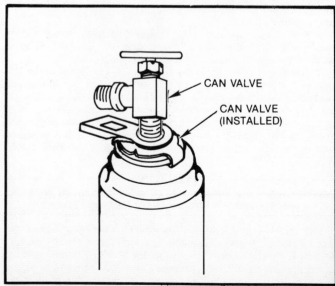

CAN VALVE

CAN VALVE (INSTALLED)

Use of single can valve for charging system

to rise, the system may be overcharged or the engine might be overheating. Never allow head pressure to go beyond 240 psi. during charging. If this condition occurs, stop engine, find and correct the problem.

(10) Continue dispensing refrigerant until container is no longer cool to the touch. On a humid day, the outside of the container will frost. When the frost disappears the can is usually empty. To detach dispensing can:

(a) close low pressure test gauge hand valve.

(b) crack open low pressure test hose at manifold until remaining pressure escapes.

(c) tighten hose coupler.

(d) loosen hose coupler connected to refrigerant can.

(e) discard empty can and repeat Steps 2 to 10.

(11) Continue to add refrigerant to the required capacity of the system. (Usually marked on the compressor).

─────────── CAUTION ───────────

DO NOT OVERCHARGE. This condition is usually indicated by an abnormally high side pressure reading and a noisy compressor resulting in ineffective cooling and damage to the system.

SYSTEMS WITH A SIGHT GLASS

The air conditioning systems that use a sight glass as a means to check the refrigerant level, should be carefully checked to avoid under or over charging. The gauge set should be attached to the system for verification of pressures.

To check the system with the sight glass, clean the glass and start the vehicle engine. Operate the air conditioning controls on maximum for approximately five minutes to stabilize the system. The room temperature should be above 70 degrees.

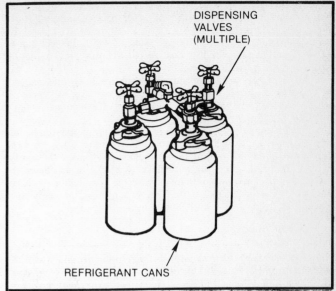

DISPENSING VALVES (MULTIPLE)

REFRIGERANT CANS

Use of multi-can despensing valve assembly to charge the air conditioning system

Check the sight glass for one of the following conditions:

1. If the sight glass is clear, the compressor clutch is engaged, the compressor discharge line is warm and the compressor inlet line is cool, the system has a full charge of refrigerant.

Check item / Amount of refrigerant	Almost no refrigerant	Insufficient	Suitable	Too much refrigerant
Temperature of high pressure and low pressure lines.	Almost no difference between high pressure and low pressure side temperature.	High pressure side is warm and low pressure side is fairly cold.	High pressure side is hot and low pressure side is cold.	High pressure side is abnormally hot.
State in sight glass.	Bubbles flow continuously. **Bubbles will disappear and something like mist will flow when refrigerant is nearly gone.**	The bubbles are seen at intervals of 1 - 2 seconds.	Almost transparent. Bubbles may appear when engine speed is raised and lowered. **No clear difference exists between these two conditions.**	No bubbles can be seen.
Pressure of system.	High pressure side is abnormally low	Both pressure on high and low pressure sides are slightly low.	Both pressures on high and low pressure sides are normal.	Both pressures on high and low pressure sides are abnormally high.
Repair.	**Stop compressor immediately** and conduct an overall check.	Check for gas leakage, repair as required, replenish and charge system.		Discharge refrigerant from service valve of low pressure side.

User of sight glass to aid in charging the air conditioning system

2. If the sight glass is clear, the compressor clutch is engaged and there is no significant temperature difference between the compressor inlet and discharge lines, the system is empty or nearly empty. By having the gauge set attached to the system, a measurement can be taken. If the gauge reads less than 25 psi, the low pressure cut-off protection switch has failed.

3. If the sight glass is clear and the compressor clutch is disengaged, the clutch is defective, or the clutch circuit is open, or the system is out of refrigerant. By-pass the low pressure cut-off switch momentarily to determine the cause.

4. If the sight glass shows foam or bubbles, the system can be low on refrigerant. Occasional foam or bubbles is normal when the room temperature is above 110 degrees or below 70 degrees. To verify, increase the engine speed to approximately 1500 rpm and block the airflow through the condenser to increase the compressor discharge pressure to between 225 to 250 psi. If the sight glass still shows bubbles or foam, the refrigerant level is low.

CAUTION

Do not operate the vehicle engine any longer than necessary with the condenser airflow blocked. This blocking action also blocks the cooling system radiator and will cause the system to overheat rapidly.

When the system is low on refrigerant, a leak is present or the system was not properly charged. Use a leak detector and locate the problem area and repair. If no leakage is found, charge the system to its capacity. (Refer to the individual vehicle section or to the refrigerant capacity chart at the end of this section).

CAUTION

It is not advisable to add refrigerant to a system utilizing the suction throttling valve and a sight glass, because the amount of refrigerant required to remove the foam or bubbles will result in an overcharge and potentially damaged system components.

CCOT SYSTEM

When charging the CCOT system, attach only the low pressure line to the low pressure gauge port, located on the accumulator. Do not attach the high pressure line to any service port or allow it to remain attached to the vacuum pump after evacuation. Be sure both the high and the low pressure control valves are closed on the gauge set. To complete the charging of the system, follow the outline supplied.

1. Start the engine and allow to run at idle, with the cooling system at normal operating temperature.

2. Attach the center gauge hose to either a multi-can dispenser or to a drum of refrigerant.

3. If a drum of refrigerant is used, it must be weighed before charging and during charging, to monitor the amount of refrigerant being placed into the system.

4. With the multi-can dispenser or the drum inverted, allow one pound or the contents of one or two 14 oz. cans to enter the system through the low pressure side by opening the gauge low pressure control valve.

5. Close the low pressure gauge control valve and turn the A/C system on to engage the compressor. Place the blower motor in its high mode.

6. Open the low pressure gauge control valve and draw the remaining charge into the system. Refer to the capacity chart at the end of this section for the individual vehicle or system capacity.

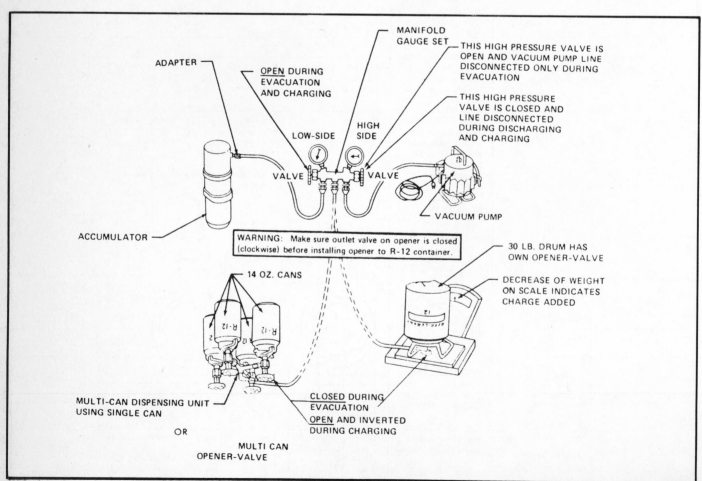

Use of muti-can despensing valve assembly or drum to charge the CCOT system

7. Close the low pressure gauge control valve and the refrigerant source valve, either on the multi-can dispenser or the drum. Remove the low pressure hose from the accumulator quickly to avoid loss of refrigerant through the Schrader valve.

8. Install the protective cap on the gauge port and check the system for leakage.

9. Test the system for proper operation as outlined under performance data in the Trouble Shooting Section.

Leak Testing the System

There are several methods of detecting leaks in an air conditioning system; among them, the two most popular are (1) halide leak-detection or the "open flame method," and (2) electronic leak-detection.

The halide leak detection is a torch like device which produces a yellow-green color when refrigerant is introduced into the flame at the burner. A purple or violet color indicates the presence of large amounts of refrigerant at the burner.

An electronic leak detector is a small portable electronic device with an extended probe. With the unit activated the probe is passed along those components of the system which contain refrigerant. If a leak is detected, the unit will sound an alarm signal or activate a display signal depending on the manufacturer's design. It is advisable to follow the manufacturer's instructions as the design and function of the detection may vary significantly.

NOTE: Caution should be taken to operate either type of detector in well ventilated areas, so as to reduce the chance of personal injury, which may result from coming in contact with poisonous gases produced when R-12 is exposed to flame or electric spark.

AFTERMARKET AIR CONDITIONING UNITS

Aftermarket air conditioning units are available for installation in both the domestic and import vehicles. Before installation, the BTU rating of the aftermarket unit should be compared to the vehicle manufacturer's recommended specifications for the particular vehicle model, to be assured of satisfactory cooling. The radiator should be examined and if necessary, a heavy duty assembly should be installed to help dissipate the heat build up from the a/c condenser and the engine cooling system. Fans with more blades are available, either in the a/c kit or can be gotten separately, to help move the air through both the condenser and the radiator. If the vehicle is equipped with an electrically operated radiator fan, a second fan with an auxiliary radiator core may have to be installed to help dissipate the heat build-up. In all cases, follow the aftermarket air conditioning installation instructions for the components to provide trouble free installation and operation.

BULK CONTAINERS

Many service people prefer to use the refrigerant bulk containers. In

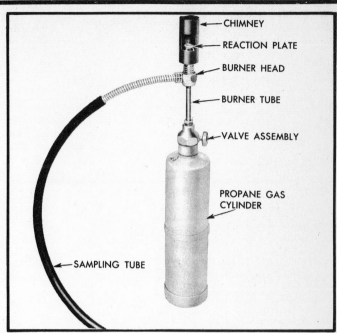

CHIMNEY
REACTION PLATE
BURNER HEAD
BURNER TUBE
VALVE ASSEMBLY
PROPANE GAS CYLINDER
SAMPLING TUBE

The Halide Leak Detector

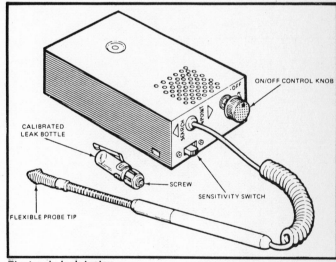

ON/OFF CONTROL KNOB
CALIBRATED LEAK BOTTLE
SCREW
SENSITIVITY SWITCH
FLEXIBLE PROBE TIP

Electronic leak tester

NORMAL FLAME — CHERRY RED

MINOR LEAK — LIGHT GREEN/YELLOW

MAJOR LEAK — PURPLE/BLUE

Appearance of the flame during leak testing and the effect R-12 would have on the flame

this charging procedure a weighing scale, graduated in pounds and ounces, is used to meter the refrigerant that enters the system. The compressor must be turned on as the refrigerant vapor is drawn into the low side service valve port.

ADJUSTING BELT TENSION

Different methods of air conditioning compressor belt tensioning is used by the varied vehicle manufacturers. The adjustment involves the movement of one or more of the components within the belt span, such as the A/C compressor, alternator, power steering pump or an idler pulley.

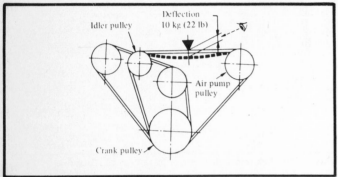

Typical belt deflection method

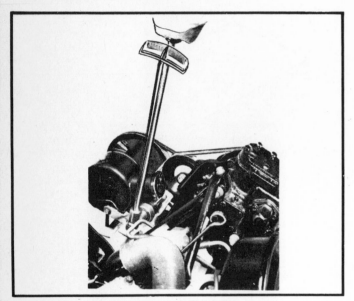

Use of a torque wrench to adjust belt tension

Caution must be exercised to avoid missing hidden retaining bolts/nuts before adjusting and to apply tensioning pressure on the component without causing internal damage or misalignment of the pulleys.

CAUTION

Do not, under any circumstances, attempt to adjust belt tension while the engine is running.

The methods for belt tension adjustments are as follows.

Deflection Method—A predetermined location on the belt span or the center of its longest span between pulleys are used in the deflection method adjustment. A straight edge or an imaginary line is used between the two pulleys involved, along the belt top surface. Either a predetermined pressure or a moderate thumb pressure is used to depress the belt in the center of its span. The amount of movement is measured and compared to specifications. Corrections are made as required by moving the adjusting component. All measurements are given in inches or millimeters.

Torque Method—Brackets are supplied on the adjusting component to accept a ½ inch drive torque wrench. With the adjusting component retaining bolts loosened, the torque wrench is inserted into its bracket hole and a tightening torque is applied against the component and belt until the specification is reached. Tighten the adjusting component retaining bolts while holding the specified torque with the wrench. All measurements are given in ft. lbs. or Nm.

Tensioning Gauge Method—A tensioning gauge is placed on the A/C belt at its center, between its longest span between pulleys. The adjusting component retaining bolts are loosened and forced outward against the belt. When the specified belt tension is reached on the gauge dial, the adjusting component retaining bolts are tightened without loss of tension. An alternate name for this method is the strand tension adjustment. All measurements are given in pounds or Newton.

The following precautions should always be observed.

1. Use only the belt which is specifically recommended for the application.

2. Check all mountings and pulleys for cracks, looseness. Check for, and, if necessary, correct misalignment.

3. Never pry a belt on. Always loosen the adjustment so that the belt can be installed without force.

4. Applying pressure in a manner that will not damage any of the components, adjust the belt to factory specifications.

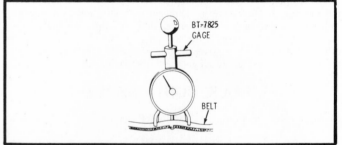

Gauge position on belt to measure belt strand tension

REFRIGERANT FLUSHING INFORMATION CHART

| Refrigerant | Vaporizes °C(°F)① | Approximate Closed Container Pressure① kPa (psi)② | | | | | Adaptability |
		15.57°C (60°F)	21.13°C (70°F)	26.69°C (80°F)	32.25°C (90°F)	37.81°C (100°F)	
R-12	−29.80 (−21.6)	393 (57)	483 (70)	579 (84)	689 (100)	807 (117)	Self Propelling
F-114	3.56 (38.4)	55.16 (8)	89.63 (13)	131 (19)	172 (25)	221 (32)	
F-11③	23.74 (74.7)	27 (8 in Hg)	10 (3 in Hg)	7 (1)	34 (5)	62 (9)	
F-113	47.59 (117.6)	74 (22 in Hg)	64 (19 in Hg)	54 (16 in Hg)	44 (13 in Hg)	27 (8 in Hg)	Pump Required

①At sea level atmospheric pressure.
②kPa (psi) unless otherwise noted.
③F-11 is also available in pressurized containers. This makes it suitable for usage when special flushing equipment is not available. However, it is more toxic than R-12 and F-114.

HOW TO SPOT WORN V-BELTS

V-Belts are vital to the efficient cooling system operation—they drive the fan and water pump. They require little maintenance (occasional tightening) but they will not last forever. Slipping or failure of the V-belt will lead to overheating. If your V-belt looks like any of these, it should be replaced.

Cracking

This belt has deep cracks, which cause it to flex. Too much flexing leads to heat build-up and premature failure. These cracks can be caused by using the belt on a pulley that is too small. Notched belts are available for small diameter pulleys.

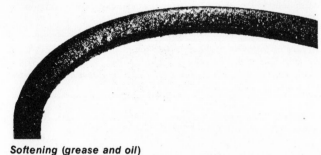

Softening (grease and oil)

Oil and grease on a belt can cause the belt's rubber compounds to soften and separate from the reinforcing cords that hold the belt together. The belt will first slip, then finally fail altogether.

Glazing

Glazing is caused by a belt that is slipping. The more the belt slips, the more glazing will be built up on the surface of the belt. The more the belt is glazed, the more it will slip. If the glazing is light, tighten the belt.

Worn cover

The cover of this belt is worn off and is peeling away. The reinforcing cords will begin to wear and the belt will soon break.

Separation

This belt is on the verge of breaking and leaving you stranded. The layers of the belt are separating and the reinforcing cords are exposed. It's just a matter of time before it breaks completely.

TROUBLESHOOTING THE AIR CONDITIONING SYSTEM

Careful visual inspection of the components can often uncover faults within the system or enable the service man to foresee eventual failures. The following sequence should be followed before any further tests are made:

1. Check the drive belts for tension within specifications.
2. Inspect the compressor brackets for looseness or breakage.
3. Examine the hoses and lines for wear or leak indications. Visual leak indications are often in the form of oil deposits on the faulty component.
4. Check for oily streak across the underside of the engine compartment hood, which could indicate a leaking compressor seal.
5. Check to make sure the condensor is fastened securely and positioned to obtain the maximum air flow. Bugs, dirt and foreign material must not clog the cooling fins. A bug screen is considered to be an obstruction to proper air flow through both the condensor and the radiator.
6. Operate all duct and louver mechanisms to make sure they operate freely.
7. Check the evaporator coil for accumulations of foreign material, particularly animal hair, which would retard the cooling efficiency of the unit.
8. Operate the blower motor at all speeds to insure proper response. If the blower motor operates in some of the speed settings, but stops or does not change its speed in others, check the blower motor resistor for short or open circuits.
9. In systems employing vacuum controlled heater coolant shut-off valves, the system must be checked for proper operation and correct adjustment. The vacuum supply must be routed correctly to the valve, be present when required and shut off when not needed. Check for pinched or restricted lines, should a problem be encountered.

After completing the check list, if no failures are evident, proceed by checking the refrigeration portion of the air conditioning system.

Manifold Gauge Set

The manifold gauge set is used to monitor the air conditioning high and low pressures during the discharge, evacuation, charging and operation of the system. The left hand gauge is a compound gauge, registering 0 to 60 psi and 0 to 30 inches of vacuum. This gauge is connected to the low pressure (suction) side of the system.

CAUTION
Never connect the compound gauge to the high pressure (discharge) side of the system. The high pressure of the system could be transferred into the charging containers and cause them to explode.

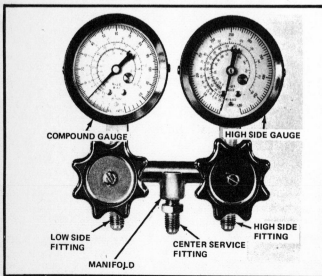

Manifold gauge set

The right hand gauge is the high pressure (discharge) gauge and is calibrated 0 to 600 psi. Three connections are provided in the gauge manifold. The left connection is used to connect the compound gauge to the suction (low pressure) side of the system by a hose, normally colored coded BLUE. The right hand connection is used to connect the high pressure gauge to the discharge (high pressure) side of the system by a hose, normally colored coded RED. The center connection is used for the servicing operation and is connected to the servicing unit by a hose, normally color coded WHITE.

The hand shut-off valves open or close the respective gauge connections to the center service connection or to each other. Pressure will be indicated on the gauges, regardless of valve positions. A third gauge is used with the manifold gauge assembly when servicing Air Conditioning systems having compressors equipped with the Evaporator Pressure Regulator (EPR) valve, such as the RV-2 Compressor, used on earlier Chrysler Corporation vehicles. This gauge is a duplicate of the compound low pressure gauge and is used to measure compressor inlet pressure.

CAUTION
Before installation of the manifold gauge assembly to the A/C system, be sure both hand valves are closed. Wear face and eye protection, along with gloves, when connecting or disconnecting the service hose connections to the service valve ports.

NOTE: The gauge and hose arrangement is basically the same when using an Air Conditioning Charging Station.

MECHANICAL SERVICE VALVES

This type valve assembly is used with the reciprocating crank type compressors and must be mechanically opened, closed or placed in mid-position for service.

SCHRADER TYPE SERVICE VALVES

This type of service valve is similar to a tire air valve. The hose connection must be screwed onto the valve stem, which in turn depresses the valve core, opening the system to either release pressure or allows pressure to be admitted into the system. A protector cap is used on the stem when the port is not in use.

QUICK CONNECTING TYPE SERVICE VALVES

Because of excessive pressure encountered when working with the discharge (high pressure) side of the air conditioning system, a quick disconnecting type hose connector is used to prevent excessive escape of refrigerant during the connection and disconnection of the high pressure service hose.

MANIFOLD GAUGE HOOK-UP FOR TESTING

Procedure

1. Close both gauge valves. Back seat both service valves, if mechanical.
2. Attach the hose leading from the low side gauge to the suction side service port and the high side hose to the discharge side service port.
3. If the mechanical type service valves, mid-position the valves.
4. Start the engine, turn the air conditioner control to maximum cooling and observe the reading on the gauges. It is not feasible to list an ideal combination of low and high pressure readings specifically because the pressure will vary according to environmental temperature,

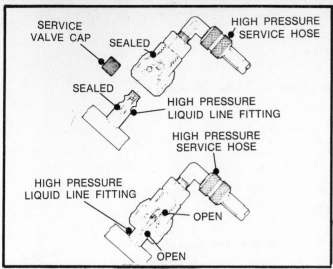

Schrader sevice port with manifold gauge hose attached

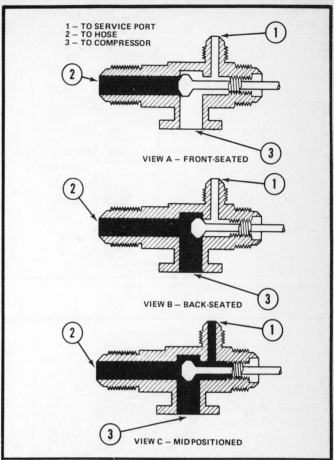

1 — TO SERVICE PORT
2 — TO HOSE
3 — TO COMPRESSOR

VIEW A — FRONT-SEATED

VIEW B — BACK-SEATED

VIEW C — MID POSITIONED

Mechanical service valve positioning

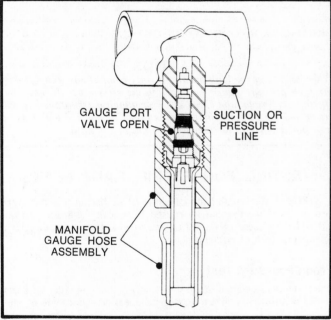

GAUGE PORT VALVE OPEN

SUCTION OR PRESSURE LINE

MANIFOLD GAUGE HOSE ASSEMBLY

Quick coupling connections and service port

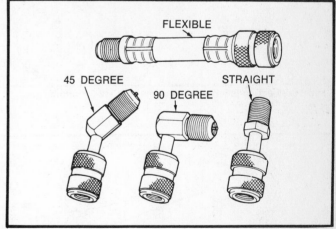

FLEXIBLE

45 DEGREE   90 DEGREE   STRAIGHT

Special coupling adapters needed for the quick coupling connector

relative humidity and atmospheric pressure. Generally, a system that has the following characteristics is considered normal and requires no immediate service.

a. No bubbles in the sight glass, if equipped.

b. Low pressure reading of 15 to 35 psi, depending upon the ambient temperature.

c. High side pressure reading between 150 and 200 psi depending upon ambient temperature.

Approximate high pressure readings at ambient temperatures are as follows:

80 degrees F.	150–170 psi
90 degrees F.	175–195 psi
95 degrees F.	185–205 psi
100 degrees F.	210–230 psi
105 degrees F.	230–250 psi
110 degrees F.	250–270 psi

d. High side of system should be hot to the touch before the condensor, warm to the touch after the condensor and the low side evenly cool.

e. The vehicle interior should cool down rapidly.

TEST GAUGE CONNECTION LOCATIONS FOR THE VARIOUS AIR CONDITIONING SYSTEMS

Procedure

Gauge port connector locations for most air conditioning systems are illustrated to guide the repairman when connecting the service gauge hoses to the high or low pressure sides of the system. As a guide to the locations of the high and low side connection ports, remember, LOW PRESSURE GOES TO THE INSIDE OF THE VEHICLE WHILE

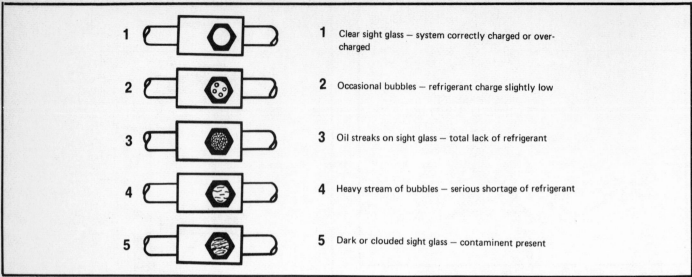

1 Clear sight glass — system correctly charged or over-charged

2 Occasional bubbles — refrigerant charge slightly low

3 Oil streaks on sight glass — total lack of refrigerant

4 Heavy stream of bubbles — serious shortage of refrigerant

5 Dark or clouded sight glass — contaminent present

Sight glass examination of refrigerant flow

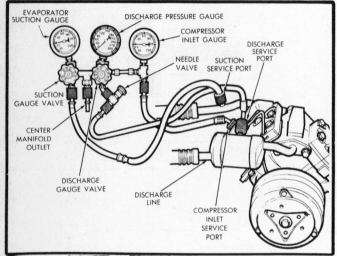

Gauge Connection location on systems with RV-2 compressor, typical

HIGH PRESSURE GOES TO THE OUTSIDE. With this in mind, the service gauges can be connected to any system that is not illustrated.

CAUTION

When unsure of the high or low pressure connections, connect only the high pressure gauge and hose to the service port in question. Operate the system and either a low or a high pressure reading will result and the correct connection can then be made. Never make a test connection with the low pressure gauge and hose.

TESTING FOR REFRIGERANT LEAKS

NOTE: A very small leak, causing system discharge about every two or three weeks, can be caused by a leaky Schrader service valve. Check these valves with extra care when testing the system for a small leak of refrigerant.

Freon Pressure Test

The system must contain some R-12 under pressure in order for a leak test to be effective. Therefore, begin the leak test procedure by con-

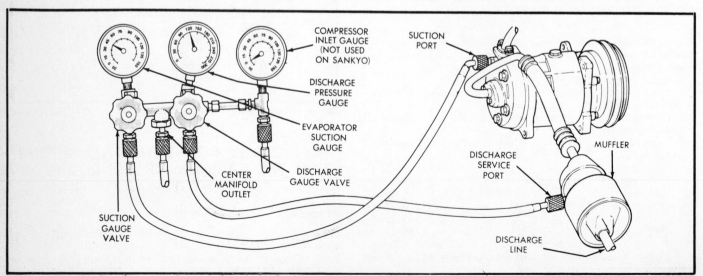

Gauge connection location on systems equipped with Sankyo compressor, typical

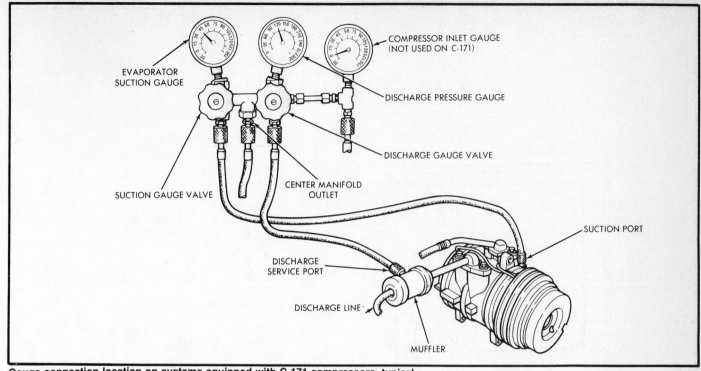

Gauge connection location on systems equipped with C-171 compressors, typical

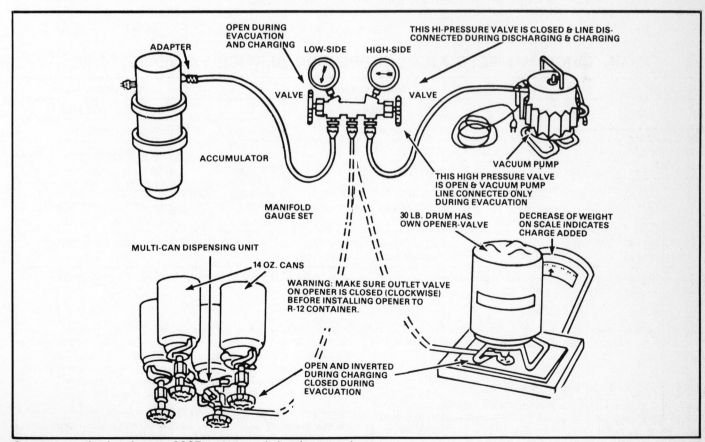

Gauge connection locations on CCOT systems and charging procedures

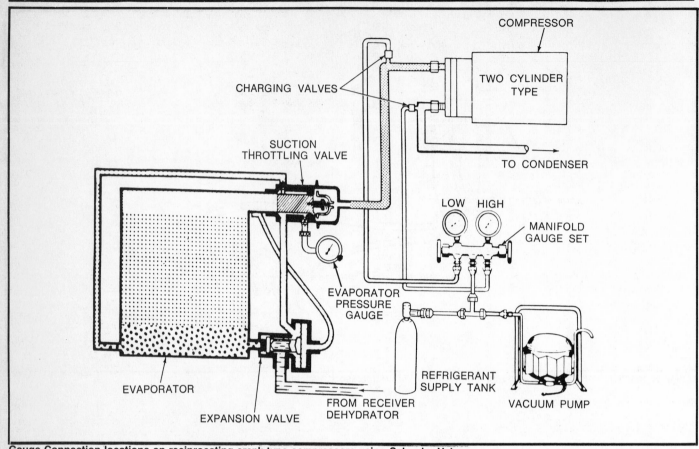

Gauge Connection locations on reciprocating crank type compressors using Schrader Valves

BAR GAUGE MANIFOLD AND COMPRESSOR SERVICE VALVE SETTINGS

Condition	Manifold Valves	Compressor Valves
Testing System	Both fully closed	Both cracked off backseat
Depressurizing System	Both cracked open	Both at mid position
Evacuating the system	Both wide open	Both at mid position
Charging in gas form with compressor running	High pressure valve closed	High pressure valve cracked off backseat
	Low pressure valve cracked	Low pressure valve at mid position
Charging in liquid form with compressor off	Low pressure valve closed High pressure valve wide open	Both valves mid positioned

Note: A very small leak, causing system discharge about every two weeks, can be caused by a leaky Schrader type service valve. Check these valves with extra care when testing for a small leak.

necting the test gauges and checking the system for pressure. If the pressure is not well over 5 psi, charge the system with at least 14 ounces of refrigerant.

Halide Flame Type Leak Detectors

Light the Halide leak detector according to the manufacturer's instructions. The flame should be adjusted until it is almost a colorless pale blue. Move the pick-up hose of the leak detector slowly over the entire system, being especially cautious at tube and hose connections. Hold the pick-up hose below the systems fittings or components, as freon (R-12) is heavier than air and will move to lower levels. The color of the flame will turn green when a small leak is detected. Large leaks will be indicated when the color of the flame turns to a brilliant blue or purple. When the pick-up tube is moved away from the leak, the flame will clear to an almost colorless pale blue again.

CAUTION

Do not breathe the fumes and black smoke that are produced as a leak is found. THEY ARE POISONOUS!!!!

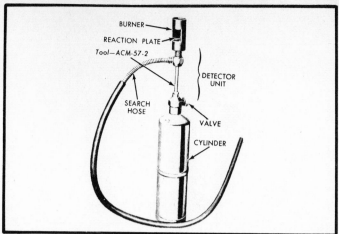

Flame leak detector

Electronic Leak Detectors

Electronic refrigerant leak detectors are available to the A/C repair shops. Instructions for the correct operation of this type of detector is supplied with the unit.

Liquid Leak Detectors

There are a number of locations throughout the air conditioning system where leak detecting solutions may be used to pinpoint leaks. Apply the solution to the suspected area with a brush or other applicator. Bubbles will form within seconds if a leak exists.

Colored Dye Refrigerant

Colored dye refrigerant is usually packaged in the 14 ounce can. It is a color dye substance, compatible with the refrigerant and will not contaminate the air conditioning system. Leaks, even sight seepages, will show up in the dye color at the point of leakage. If a leak is located and it becomes necessary to remove a component of the systems for repairs, the system must be discharged, the repairs made, the system evacuated and recharged. Add the necessary refrigerant oil to the system, dependent upon the unit being repaired or replaced.

Detecting Compressor Shaft Seal Leaks

The compressor shaft seal lubricates its self by leaking a tiny amount of oil. Therefore, a small amount of oil on the front of the compressor does not necessarily indicate an excessive leak. If oil has leaked over

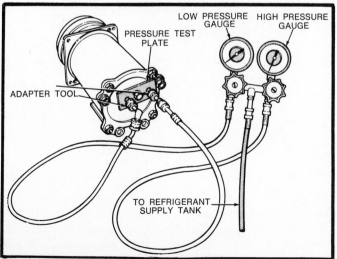

Compressor shaft seal leak test connections

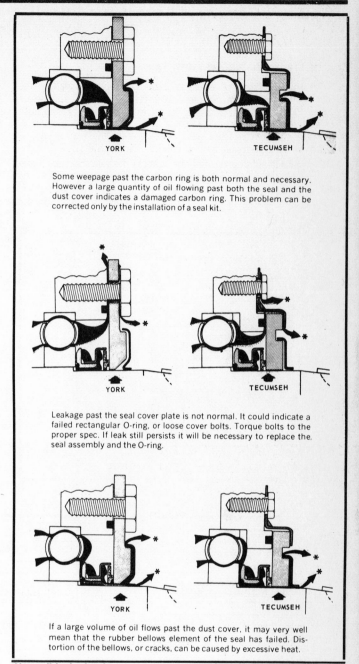

Some weepage past the carbon ring is both normal and necessary. However a large quantity of oil flowing past both the seal and the dust cover indicates a damaged carbon ring. This problem can be corrected only by the installation of a seal kit.

Leakage past the seal cover plate is not normal. It could indicate a failed rectangular O-ring, or loose cover bolts. Torque bolts to the proper spec. If leak still persists it will be necessary to replace the seal assembly and the O-ring.

If a large volume of oil flows past the dust cover, it may very well mean that the rubber bellows element of the seal has failed. Distortion of the bellows, or cracks, can be caused by excessive heat.

How oil leaks begin

an area much larger than the compressor clutch, or if there is evidence of oil seepage past the seal cover plate or the seal its self, replacement of the seal may be necessary. Careful examination will indicate the need to replace the seal or the need to inspect the compressor for more extensive damage or wear.

Leak Repair

Generally, leaky components of an automobile air conditioning system should be replaced. Welding, brazing or soldering is not recommended for two reasons. One, most automobile air conditioning systems are subjected to continuous, severe vibrations. Second, most systems, in the interest of weight reduction, employ components and tubing of minimum size, which in most cases will not accept welding of any type. If required, restore the system to its full efficiency and reliability by replacing the offending part. DON'T TRY TO SHORTCUT REPAIRS.

Compressor Leak Testing

COMPRESSOR REMOVED FROM VEHICLE

Compressor Shaft Seal Leak Test

1. With a pressure test plate tool and ''O'' rings installed on the compressor in place of the hose assembly block, connect the manifold gauge set to the high and low Schrader valves. Connect the center hose to a supply of refrigerant.

2. With the high pressure valve closed and the low pressure valve open, allow the refrigerant to flow into the compressor.

3. Loosen the high pressure hose fitting at the gauge set and allow air to exhaust until the refrigerant vapors starts to flow from the loosened fitting.

4. Tighten the high pressure hose fitting and open the high pressure

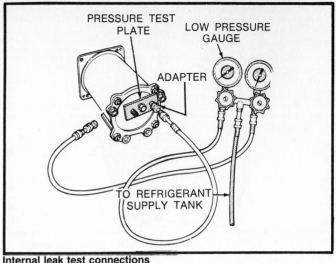

Internal leak test connections

valve on the gauge set to allow the container pressure to stabilize in the compressor.

5. Rotate the compressor shaft several times in the direction of normal operation and leak test the seal area with a leak tester. Correct any leakage found as required and retest.

6. Close the refrigerant supply and release the pressure slowly and safely. Remove the test plate tool and reinstall the hose block assembly.

Compressor External Leak Testing

1. Install the test plate tool and ''O'' rings in place of the hose assembly block. Rotate the clutch hub several times in the direction of normal operation. This also lubricates the rings and oil seals with oil from the compressor.

2. Connect the high and low pressure lines to their respective fittings on the test plate. Connect the center hose to a refrigerant supply. Do not invert the supply container.

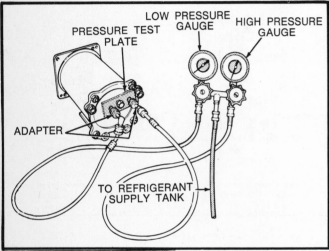

External leak test connections

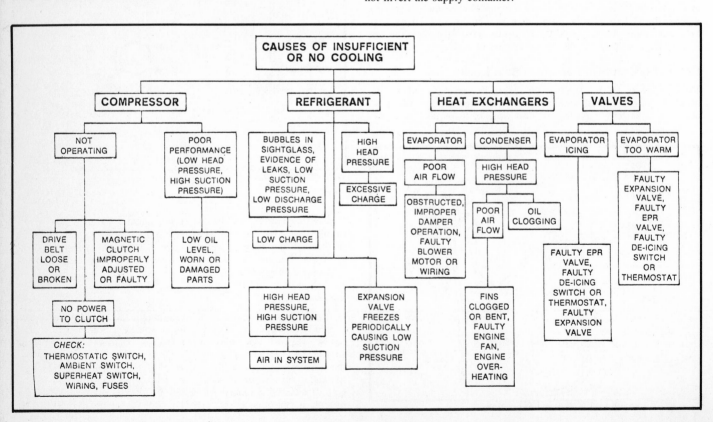

3. Open the high and low pressure gauge valves. Open the refrigerant container valve and allow the pressure to stabilize.

4. Using a leak detector, check for leaks at the oil drain fitting, if equipped, compressor front head seal and the compressor shaft seals.

5. Close the manifold gauge valves, release the pressure and make the necessary repairs. Retest as required and remove the test components.

Compressor Internal Leak Test

1. Disconnect the manifold gauge hoses from the test plate, if connected from a previous test.

2. Connect the low pressure hose to the high pressure fitting on the test plate.

3. Open the low pressure control valve to allow the refrigerant vapors to flow into the compressor.

4. Observe the pressure reading on the gauge and close the control valve. If the gauge readings drops to 10 psi or under in 30 seconds or less, indications are that the compressor is leaking internally. Correct as required and retest.

Abnormal Gauge Readings and Possible Causes

The following gauge readings are encountered when the various components of the air conditioning system fail to function properly. Both hand valves are closed, the test hoses are attached to their respective service ports and the system has been stabilized. All gauge readings illustrated are for an engine compartment temperature of 95 degrees. If the temperature of the testing area is not the same, refer to the accompanying temperature relationship chart for equivalent readings.

Gauge Reading Indications

LITTLE OR NO COOLING

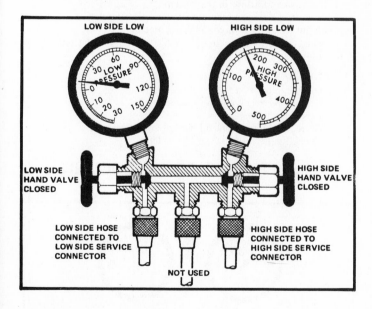

CONDITIONS

1. Low side pressure too low. Gauge should read 15–30 psi.
2. High side pressure too low. Gauge should read 185–205 psi.
3. Bubbles in the sight glass.
4. Evaporator discharge air not cold.

CAUSE

1. Refrigerant low in system through possible leak.
2. Air or moisture present in system.

CORRECTION

1. Leak test the system.
2. Repair the leak as required.
3. Evacuate the system.
4. Check the system refrigerant oil to assure no loss. Install oil as required if components were replaced.
5. Evacuate the system.
6. Charge the system and test performance.

INSUFFICIENT COOLING

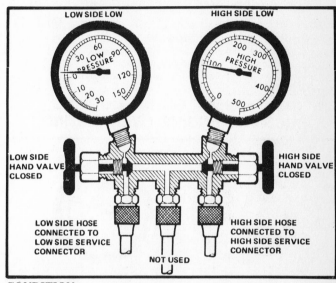

CONDITION

1. Low pressure side gauge very low. Gauge should read 15–30 psi.
2. High side pressure too low. Gauge should read 185–205 psi.
3. No liquid or bubbles in the sight glass.
4. Evaporator discharge air warm.

CAUSE

1. Refrigerant excessively low due to leakage.

CORRECTION

1. Leak test the system.
2. Discharge the system and repair the leak.
3. Evacuate the system.
4. Check the system refrigerant oil to assure no loss. Install oil as required if components were replaced.
5. Charge the system.
6. Check the performance of the system.

INSUFFICIENT COOLING AND POSSIBLE COMPRESSOR NOISE

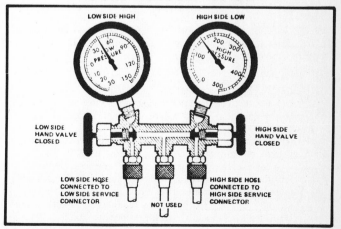

CONDITION

1. Low side pressure reading too high. Should read 15–30 psi.
2. High side pressure gauge reading too low. Should read 185–205 psi.
3. No bubbles present in the sight glass.
4. Evaporator discharge air not cold.

CAUSE

1. Compressor malfunction.
2. Possible internal leakage in compressor.
3. Defective compressor pistons, rings or cylinders.

CORRECTIONS

1. Repair or replace the compressor.
2. Verify correct level of refrigerant oil is used.
3. Evacuate and recharge the system.
4. Check the operational performance of the system.

INSUFFICIENT OR NO COOLING, POSSIBLE ENGINE OVERHEATING

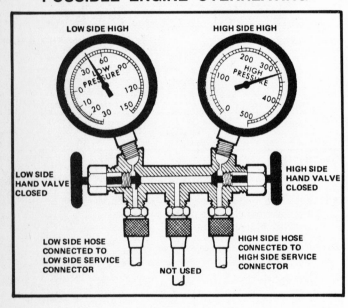

CONDITION

1. Low side pressure gauge too high. Should read 15–30 psi.
2. High side pressure gauge reading too high. Should read 185–205.
3. Occasional bubbles in the sight glass.
4. Evaporator discharge air warm.

CAUSE

1. Lack of cooling caused by too high pressure on the high side resulting from improper operation of the condensor. The refrigerant charge may be normal or excessive.

CORRECTION

1. Check the belt tension and correct as required.
2. Check for obstruction in the condenser core, use of a bug screen or other obstructions that would reduce the air flow through the condenser and radiator.
3. Check the engine for proper radiator fan, pressure cap or cooling system capacity. Be sure correct coolant is being used.
4. Check for overcharge of refrigerant and correct as required.
5. If necessary, check the condenser being plugged. Flush as required.
6. Replace the receiver/drier assembly.
7. Evacuate, recharge the system as required. Add sufficient refrigerant oil to the system and check for proper operation.

INSUFFICIENT COOLING DURING HOTTEST PART OF THE DAY

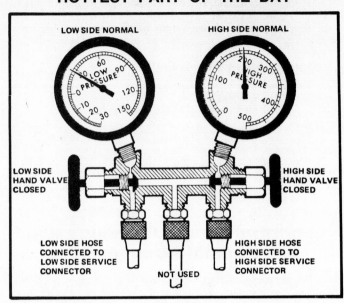

CONDITION

1. Low side pressure reading is normal at 15–30 psi, but drops to a vacuum during testing.
2. High side pressure reading is normal at 205 psi, but drops when low side reading shows a vacuum.
3. Bubbles present in sight glass.
4. Evaporator discharge air is sufficiently cold until low side pressure gauge shows a vacuum reading, and then the air becomes warm.

CAUSE

1. Excessive moisture in the system.
2. The drying agent in the receiver/drier is saturated and releasing moisture during times of high outside temperatures.
3. The moisture is freezing in small orifices, causing restrictions to the flow of refrigerant.

CORRECTION

1. Discharge the system.
2. Replace the receiver/drier assembly.
3. Evacuate the system.
4. Correct the refrigerant oil needed and recharge the system.
5. Check the performance of the system.

INSUFFICIENT OR NO COOLING

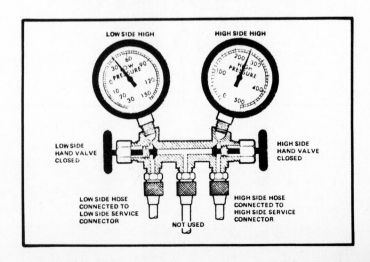

CONDITION

1. Low side pressure too high. Should read 15–30 psi.
2. High side pressure too high. Should read 185–205 psi.
3. Occasional bubbles in the sight glass.
4. Evaporator discharge air not cool.

CAUSE

1. Large amount of air in system.

CORRECTION

1. Discharge the system and replace the receiver/drier assembly.
2. Evacuate the system.
3. Recharge the system and verify the refrigerant oil supply is correct.
4. Verify the system performance is correct.

INSUFFICIENT OR NO COOLING, SYSTEMS WITH THERMOSTATIC EXPANSION VALVE

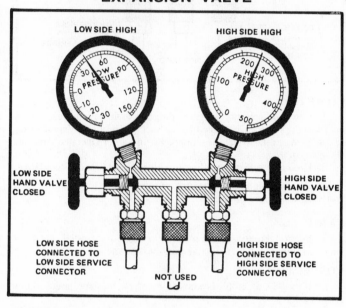

CONDITION

1. Low side pressure gauge reading too high. Should read 15–30 psi.
2. High side pressure gauge reading too high. Should read 185–205 psi.
3. Evaporator discharge air warm.
4. Evaporator and suction hose (to compressor) surfaces show considerable moisture.

CAUSE

1. Sticking expansion valve.

CORRECTION

1. Check for a sticking expansion valve or incorrect mounting of the temperature sensing bulb.
   a. Operate the system at maximum cooling.
   b. Spray the head of the expansion valve and/or the sensing bulb with refrigerant.
   c. Check the low side gauge which should show a vacuum reading.
2. If the preceding test indicates the expansion valve is operating properly, proceed as follows:
   a. Clean the surface of the evaporator outlet pipe and the temperature sensing bulb and clamp the bulb to the pipe.
   b. Operate and check the performance of the system.
3. If the test indicate the expansion valve is defective, discharge the system, replace the expansion valve, evacuate the system, recharge and test the operation of the system.

INSUFFICIENT COOLING, SYSTEMS WITH THERMOSTATIC EXPANSION VALVES

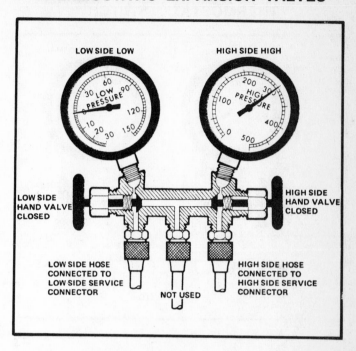

CONDITION

1. Low side gauge reading low at 0 psi or in a vacuum mode. The gauge should read 15–30 psi.
2. High side pressure too high. Should read 185–205 psi.
3. Evaporator discharge air cool, but not cold.
4. Expansion valve inlet pipe surface shows considerable moisture or frost.

CAUSE

1. Expansion valve stuck, not allowing sufficient refrigerant flow.
2. Screen clogged.
3. Insufficient amount of refrigerant in the temperature sensing bulb.

CORRECTION

1. Place finger on the expansion valve inlet, if cold to the touch, proceed as follows:
   a. Operate the system at maximum cooling.
   b. Spray refrigerant on the head of the valve and/or temperature sensing bulb, if possible.
   c. Check the low side gauge which should show a vacuum reading.
2. If the previous test indicates the expansion valve is operating satisfactory, clean the surface of the evaporator outlet pipe and the temperature sensing bulb and clamp the bulb to the pipe.
3. If the expansion valve inlet surface shows signs of frost or heavy moisture, proceed as follows:
   a. Discharge the system.
   b. Disconnect the inlet line from the expansion valve and inspect the screen.
   c. Clean the screen or replace it and reconnect the inlet line to the valve.
4. If step one indicates the expansion valve is defective, proceed as follows:
   a. Discharge the system.
   b. Replace the expansion valve.
5. Be sure the temperature sensing valve is positioned properly to the evaporator outlet pipe.
6. Evacuate the system, recharge and test the performance of the system.

COMPRESSOR CYCLES TOO RAPIDLY OR IMPROPERLY ADJUSTED THERMOSTATIC SWITCH

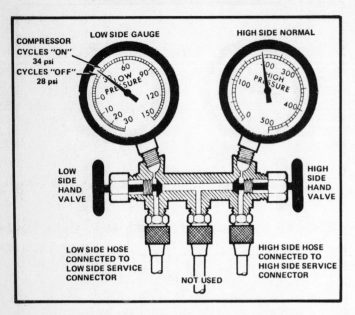

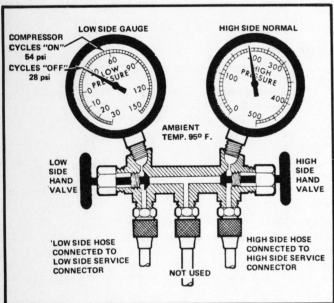

CONDITION

1. Low side pressure readings are too high during both the ON and OFF compressor cycle and between cycles.

2. The gauge readings should be 12–15 psi during cycle OFF, 36–39 psi during cycle ON, with a range of 2428 psi between cycles.

3. The high side gauge should read 185–205 psi.

CAUSE

1. The thermostatic switch is defective or adjusted too high.

CORRECTION

1. Either replace the thermostatic switch or adjust the assembly, if possible.

NOTE: If the switch does not have an adjustment screw, the switch must be replaced.

INSUFFICIENT COOLING, STV OR POA SYSTEMS

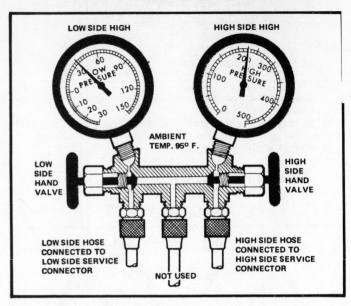

CONDITION

1. Low side pressure gauge reading too high. Should read 29–3i psi when the system is equipped with a Suction Throttling Valve (STV), or 28–31 when the system is equipped with a Pilot Operated Absolute (POA) system.

2. High side pressure reading too high. Should read 185–205 psi.

NOTE: The high side pressure reading being high could result from high low side pressure.

CAUSE

1. Suction throttling valve may not be properly adjusted. The POA valve assembly may be defective and must be replaced.

CORRECTION

1. If the STV assembly is adjustable, refer to the appropriate section for procedures.

2. If the POA valve assembly is defective, the assembly must be replaced.

INSUFFICIENT COOLING, WITH EVAPORATOR PRESSURE REGULATOR (EPR) SYSTEM

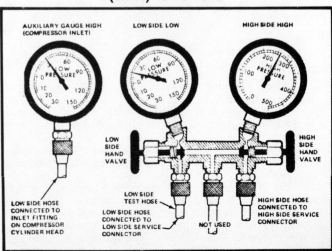

NOTE: Testing the EPR system requires the use of three gauges, consisting of the high and low pressure gauges of the manifold gauge set, plus an auxiliary low pressure compound gauge. The auxiliary gauge is used to measure the pressure drop across the EPR valve control device. The gauges should be connected as follows:

a. The manifold low pressure gauge hose must be connected to the low pressure service fitting where the low pressure line enters the compressor. This reads evaporator outlet pressure before the EPR valve.

b. The auxiliary low pressure compound gauge hose must be connected to the service fitting on the compressor head. This reads the compressor inlet pressure after the EPR valve.

c. The manifold high pressure gauge hose must be connected to the high side service fitting at the compressor or the muffler of the system. This reads compressor outlet pressure.

CONDITION

1. Low side manifold gauge reading too low. Should read 22–31 psi.
2. Auxiliary low pressure gauge reading too high. Should read 17 psi or less.
3. High side pressure too high. Gauge should read 185–205 psi.

CAUSE

1. Evaporator Pressure Regulator (EPR) valve stuck open.

CORRECTION

1. Discharge the system and remove the EPR valve.
2. Clean, install new "O" Ring and re-install or replace with new valve assembly.
3. Evacuate the system.
4. Verify refrigerant oil level and charge the system with refrigerant.
5. Check the performance of the system.

NO COOLING, EVAPORATOR FREEZE-UP, WITH EVAPORATOR PRESSURE REGULATOR VALVE SYSTEM

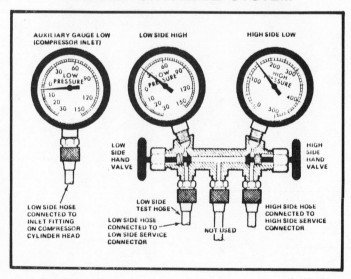

NOTE: The manifold gauge set and auxiliary must be connected to the air conditioning system as in the past test.

CONDITION

1. Low side manifold gauge reading too high. Should read 22–31 psi.
2. Auxiliary low pressure compound gauge very low, 0 or partial vacuum reading. Should be 17 psi or less.
3. High side pressure too low. Should read 185–205 psi.

CAUSE

1. Evaporator Pressure Regulator valve stuck closed.

CORRECTION

1. Discharge the system and remove the EPR valve.
2. Clean, replace the valve "O" ring and re-install or replace the EPR valve with a new assembly.
3. Evacuate the system.
4. Check the refrigeration oil level and recharge the system.
5. Verify the performance of the system.

Troubleshooting Air Conditioning Systems Without Specific Specifications

Troubleshooting air conditioning systems without specific specification may be encountered by the diagnostician. The following procedures can be used as a rule of thumb to determine approximate pressures needed for the systems to operate satisfactorily.

HIGH SIDE

Since the high side gauge reading depends entirely upon the temperature of the day, a rule of thumb is to record the temperature of the day, add one hundred (100) degrees and the total should be the approximate high side pressure reading. This reading can vary twenty (20) degrees, plus or minus, depending upon various conditions.

LOW SIDE

The pressure reading will vary on the low side. Approximate low side readings for various systems are as follows:

a. 5 Basic Component system—(Used by AMC, Ford, Chrysler, Aftermarket Units, trucks, buses, farm equipment and certain import vehicles) Approximately 15–30 psi.

b. Ford Units with FOTCC Units—22–48 psi.

c. Ford Units with Combo valve—28–32 psi.

d. General Motors with CCOT and Thermostatic Switch—15–30 psi.

e. General Motors with CCOT and Cycling Pressure Switch—22–48 psi.

MANIFOLD GAUGE PRESSURE INDICATIONS

Conditions and Probable Cause

LOW SUCTION PRESSURE

Filter or Screen Plugged
Liquid Line Plugged
Expansion Valve Super-Heat Setting too High
Expansion Valve Thermal Bulb Charge Lost
Expansion Valve Plugged with Dirt or Moisture
Blower Fan Inoperative
Temperature Control Thermostat Does Not Cut-out
Moisture or Freeze-up Expansion Valve

HIGH SUCTION PRESSURE

Leaky or Broken Compressor Valves
Low Charge
Clutch Slipping
Loose Belts
Expansion Valve

LOW HEAD PRESSURE

Low Charge
Leaky or Broken Compressor Valves

HIGH HEAD PRESSURE

Condenser Air Passages Clogged
Air in System
Radiator Fan Belt Slipping
Excessive Charge
Engine Over-Heating
Restriction in Discharge Line
Restrictions on Outlet Lines of Condenser
Restriction in Check Valve
Restriction in Receiver
Expansion Valve Super-Heat Setting too Low
Filters or Screens Plugged

COMPRESSOR NOISY WITH LOW SUCTION PRESSURE

Excessive Oil

GLOSSARY OF TERMS

ABSOLUTE HUMIDITY—the actual amount of water vapor in a given volume of air; for example, grams of water per cubic foot of air.

ABSOLUTE PRESSURE—a pressure scale having as its zero point the complete absence of pressure. Atmospheric pressure on the absolute scale is 14.7 psi or 29.92 inches of mercury (Hg).

ABSOLUTE ZERO—the complete absence of heat which would occur at zero degrees absolute or minus 460 degrees Fahrenheit.

ACCUMULATOR—a unit which separates liquid retainer from vapor, retains the liquid and releases the vapor to the compressor.

AIR INLET VALVE—a vacuum operated door which allows selection of inside or outside air.

AIR OUTLET VALVE—a vacuum operated door which directs air flow into the heater core or ducts, usually located in the plenum blower.

AMBIENT SENSOR—a device which samples and detects changes in temperature of the surrounding air.

AMBIENT SWITCH—a double pole switch which prevents operation of the compressor and recirculating air mode below an outside temperature of 40°F.

AMBIENT TEMPERATURE—the changing temperature of an existing given area.

AMPLIFIER—a device which increases the strength of an electrical impulse.

ASPIRATOR—air intake of a sensor.

ATMOSPHERIC PRESSURE—the pressure on all objects in the atmosphere due to the weight of the air which makes up the atmosphere. Atmospheric pressure at sea level is 14.7 psi absolute and decreases as altitude increases.

AXIAL COMPRESSOR—a compressor wherein the pistons are arranged horizontally around and parallel to the crankshaft.

BACK-SEAT—turning the valve completely counterclockwise.

BLOWER—electric fan unit which directs air through the duct work.

BOILING—conversion from the liquid to vapor state which takes place throughout the liquid and is accompanied by bubbling as the vapor below the surface rises.

BRITISH THERMAL UNIT (BTU)—the amount of heat necessary to raise the temperature of one pound of liquid water one degree Fahrenheit. The measure of heat quantity. 1 BTU = 778 pound feet or 252 calories.

BOWDEN CABLE—a wire or cable encased in a metal or rubber sheath used for remote control of a component.

CAPILLARY TUBE—a tube with a very small inside diameter.

CHARGING STATION—a portable assembly consisting of a vacuum pump, refrigerant supply, gauges, valves and a five pound metering refrigerant charging cylinder.

CHECK VALVE—a one way valve in a line permits flow in one direction only.

COEFFICIENT OF EXPANSION—the percent of increase in length per degree of temperature rise. An aluminum bar lengthens 13 millionths percent of the original length for each degree (F.) of temperature rise.

COMPRESSION—reducing the volume of gas by squeezing it into a smaller space. Increased pressure and temperature always accompany compression.

COMPRESSOR—a unit which pumps and increases the pressure of the refrigerant vapor.

CONDENSATION—conversion from the vapor to the liquid state.

CONDENSER—a heat exchanger in which a vapor is changed to the liquid state by removing heat from the vapor.

CONDUCTION—the transfer of heat between the closely packed molecules of a substance or between two substances that are touching.

CONTROL HEAD—a unit consisting of three parts: the mode selector, the blower switch, and the temperature control lever.

CORROSION—chemical action, usually by an acid, that decomposes a metal.

DEHUMIDIFY—to remove water vapor from the air.

DESICCANT—a substance which removes moisture from a vapor.

DISCHARGE AIR—conditioned air which is forced into the passenger compartment.

DISCHARGE LINE—connects the compressor outlet and the condenser inlet.

DISCHARGE PRESSURE—pressure of the refrigerant being discharged from the compressor.

DISCHARGE VALVE—a device used to check high side pressures.

DRIER—a unit containing a desiccant, located in the liquid line.

ELECTRO VACUUM RELAY (EVR)—a combination solenoid vacuum valve and electrical relay, which locks out blower operation and closes the fresh air door in cold weather, and switches the system to the recirculating air mode during maximum A/C use.

EQUALIZER LINE—a line which obtains required operation from any given valve.

EVACUATE—to pump the system clean of foreign material with a vacuum pump.

EVAPORATION—conversion from the liquid to the vapor state at the surface of the liquid only. It can occur at temperatures below the boiling point.

EVAPORATOR—unit in which refrigerant evaporates at a reduced pressure, thereby cooling the air blown through it.

EVAPORATOR PRESSURE REGULATOR (EPR)—a temperature control device for the evaporator regulated by back pressure.

EXPANSION TUBE—a filtering device wherein high pressure liquid refrigerant becomes low pressure liquid refrigerant.

EXPANSION VALVE—a device consisting of a metering valve and a temperature sensing capillary tube and bulb which meters refrigerant into the evaporator according to cooling requirements.

FEEDBACK POTENTIOMETER—a variable resistance unit which reports the position of the shaft to which it is mounted, to the control head.

FLOODING—the overcharging of the system.

FLUSH—removal of solid particles from the system by pressurized refrigerant.

FOAMING—the forming of bubbles in the oil and refrigerant due to rapid boiling of refrigerant dissolved in the oil when the pressure is suddenly reduced.

FRONT-SEAT—turning the valve completely clockwise.

GAUGE SET—a device which incorporates low and high pressure controls and gauges as well as a vacuum control and refrigerant control.

HEATER CORE—a finned unit through which water from the engine flows and over which air entering the passenger compartment passes.

HIGH PRESSURE RELIEF VALVE—a safety valve located in the discharge line with six cylinder compressors and in the compressor block with two cylinder compressors.

HOT WATER VACUUM VALVE—vacuum actuated valve controlling the flow of water through the heater core.

ICING SWITCH—cuts off the compressor when the evaporator temperature falls too low.

IN–CAR SENSOR—dual bi-metallic strip which samples passenger compartment air and controls a vacuum modulator.

LATENT HEAT—hidden heat required to change the state of a substance without changing the temperature. Latent heat cannot be felt or measured with a thermometer.

LIQUID LINE—line connecting the drier outlet and the expansion valve inlet.

LOW REFRIGERANT PROTECTION SYSTEM—a system which permanently stops the flow of power to the compressor in the event of a refrigerant loss.

MANIFOLD GAUGE SET—a manifold complete with gauges and charging hoses.

MODE DOOR—unit which directs the flow of air at a given time.

MUFFLER—a sound deadener on the discharge line.

PLENUM—contains air ducts, air valves, and blower.

POWER SPRING—extends from a retainer at the edge of the programmer housing to the vacuum motor mechanism and serves to position the vacuum motor in the full A/C position when the vacuum motor diaphragm is vented.

PRESSURE—force per unit area or force divided by area. Usually measured in pounds-per-square-inch (psi).

PROGRAMMER—controls the blower speed, air mix door, and vacuum diaphragms.

PURGING—a thorough evacuation of the system.

RECEIVER-DEHYDRATOR—a combination container for the storage of liquid refrigerant and a desiccant.

RECIPROCATING COMPRESSOR—a unit which pumps and compresses refrigerant vapor and in which the pistons travel in cylinders perpendicular to the crankshaft.

REED VALVES—thin layers of screen located in the valve plate of the compressor to act as suction and discharge valves.

REMOTE BULB—a sensor connected to the expansion valve by a capillary tube.

RESISTOR—a device which controls blower speeds by reducing voltage.

RESTRICTOR—a porous device located in vacuum lines to delay vacuum applied to diaphragms.

RELAY—an electrical switch which transmits impulses from unit to unit.

RHEOSTAT—a variable resistor used to control blower speeds.

SCHRADER VALVES—spring loaded valves located in the service valves, used to hold refrigerant in the system.

SERVICE VALVE—a device used to check side pressures at the compressor.

SERVO—a calibrated vacuum motor with an attached electrical switch.

SIGHT GLASS—a glass port in the top of the drier used to check refrigerant flow.

SOLENOID—an electro-magnetic relay.

SUCTION LINE—connects the evaporator outlet to the compressor inlet.

SUCTION THROTTLING VALVE—a device regulated by back pressure which prevents evaporator core freeze-up.

SUPERHEAT SWITCH—activated by a thermal fuse, this is the main component of the low refrigerant protection system.

SUPERHEATED VAPOR—a vapor that is not in contact with the generating liquid, and that has a higher temperature than the saturated vapor at the same pressure.

TEMPERATURE—the measure of heat intensity or concentration in degrees. Temperature is not a measure of heat quantity.

TEMPERATURE DIAL—a calibrated control lever or wheel used to regulate ATC modes.

THERMAL—of or pertaining to heat.

THERMISTOR—a heat activated resistor.

THERMOSTATIC SWITCH—same as icing switch.

TRANSDUCER—a vacuum relay coupling.

VACUUM—a condition of pressure less than atmospheric pressure. Vacuum can be measured by psi, but is more commonly measured in inches of mercury (Hg). A perfect vacuum is 29.92 inches of Hg. This is based on the fact that a perfect vacuum above a column of mercury will support the column to a height of 29.92 inches.

VACUUM MOTOR—a vacuum actuated device used to operate doors and valves.

VALVES-IN-RECEIVER UNIT (VIR)—combines in one unit the thermostatic expansion valve, the POA suction throttling valve, the receiver-dehydrator, and the sight glass.

VOLATILE—readily vaporizable.

WATER VALVE—a valve used to shut off flow of water to the heater.

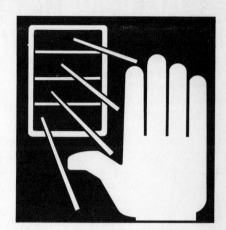

SECTION 2
American Motors

INDEX

AMERICAN MOTORS CORPORATION SPECIFICATIONS

Car Models by Year

1982   Eagle (30 Series–Sedan, Station Wagon)
        Eagle (50 Series–Kamm Back, SX)
        Concord

1983   Eagle (30 Series–Sedan, Station Wagon)
        Eagle (50 Series–Kamm Back, SX)
        Concord
        Spirit
1984–85 Eagle (30 Series–Sedan, Station Wagon)

REFRIGERANT CAPACITIES—AMERICAN MOTORS CORP.
Passenger Cars 1982–85 Models
Refrigerant given in ounces, Refrigerant oil given in fluid ounces

1982			1983			1984			1985		
	Recharge Capacities			Recharge Capacities			Recharge Capacities			Recharge Capacities	
Models	R-12	Oil	Models	R-12	Oil	Models	R-12	Oil	Models	R-12	Oil
Eagle	32	①	Eagle	32	①	Eagle	32	①	Eagle	32	①
Concord			Concord								
Spirit			Spirit								

①Compressor requires dipstick check. Between 4 to 6 increments must be covered on the dipstick. Add one ounce of refrigerant oil for each component being replaced.

BELT TENSION CHART
1982–85 American Motor Corp.

	New Belt		Used Belt	
Engine	Ft. Lbs.	Newtons	Ft. Lbs.	Newtons
	Serpentine Drive Belt			
Four and Six Cylinder Engines	180–200	800–890	140–160	616–704
	Alternator Drive Vee Belt			
Four and Six Cylinder Engines	125–155	556–689	90–115	400–512
	Air Condition Compressor Vee Belt			
Four and Six Cylinder Engines	125–155	556–689	90–115	400–512
	Air Pump Vee Belt			
Four Cylinder Engine	125–155	556–689	90–115	400–512
Six Cylinder Engine W/O P.S.	125–155	556–689	90–115	400–512
Six Cylinder Engine W/P.S.	65–75	289–334	60–70	267–311
	Power Steering Vee Belt			
All Engines	125–155	556–689	90–115	400–512

Blower Motor

Removal and Installation

ALL MODELS

NOTE: The blower and fan wheel are accessible in the engine compartment.

1. Disconnect the blower motor electrical wire connector.

2. Remove the three retaining nuts from the blower mounting plate.

3. Remove the blower and fan wheel assembly.

4. Remove the fan wheel from the motor shaft for access to the motor attaching nuts.

5. When installing the fan wheel back onto the motor shaft, a clearance of 0.350 inch must exist between the fan cage and the mounting plate.

6. The installation of the motor and fan wheel assembbly is the reverse of the removal procedure.

Compressor

ISOLATING THE COMPRESSOR PRIOR TO REMOVAL

NOTE: It is not necessary to discharge the air conditioning system for the compressor removal. The compressor can be isolated from the remainder of the system, eliminating the need to recharge the system when performing compressor service.

1. Connect the manifold gauge set to the air conditioning system.

2. Close both manifold gauge hand valves and mid-position (crack) both service valves.

3. Start the engine and operate the air conditioning system.

4. Turn the suction service valve slowly clockwise towards the front-seat position. When the suction pressure is reduced to zero or less, stop the engine and compressor. Quickly finish front-seating the suction service valve.

5. Front seat the discharge service valve.

6. Loosen the oil check plug slowly to release any internal pressure in the compressor.

7. The compressor is now isolated from the remainder of the system

and the service valves can be removed from the compressor.

NOTE: Refer to the Compressor Overhaul Section for overhaul information and procedures.

Removal

1982–83 SPIRIT, CONCORD, EAGLE WITH FOUR CYLINDER ENGINE

1. Disconnect the negative battery cable.
2. Isolate the compressor as previously outlined.
3. Remove the discharge and suction hoses from the compressor. Immediately plug or cap all openings.
4. Remove the drive belts by loosening the idler pulley. Remove the air pump and lay aside, if equipped.
5. Remove the compressor from the mounting bracket and lift from the engine compartment.

Installation

1. Install the compressor on the mounting bracket.
2. Install the drive belts.
3. If equipped, install the air pump.
4. Tighten the drive belt to specifications.
5. Remove the plugs or caps from the hoses and install onto the compressor.
6. Connect the negative battery cable. Check the compressor oil as required.
7. With the manifold gauge set attached, mid-seat (crack) the suction and discharge service valves, start the engine and verify the air conditioning operation.
8. Back-seat the service valves and remove the manifold gauge set.

Removal

1982–83 SPIRIT, CONCORD, EAGLE WITH SIX CYLINDER ENGINE

1. Disconnect the negative battery cable.
2. Isolate the compressor as previously outlined.
3. Remove the discharge and suction hoses from the compressor. Immediately cap or plug all openings.
4. Remove the drive belts by loosening the alternator and idler pulley.
5. Remove the alternator from the mounting bracket and lay aside.
6. Remove the compressor from the mounting bracket and lift from engine compartment.

Installation

1. Install the compressor onto the mounting bracket.
2. Install the alternator onto the mounting bracket.
3. Install the drive belts and tighten to specifications.
4. Remove the caps or plugs from the discharge and suction hoses and install onto the compressor.
5. Connect the negative battery cable. Check the compressor oil as required.
6. With the manifold gauge set attached, mid-seat (crack) the suction and discharge service valves, start the engine and verify the air conditioning operation.
7. Back seat the service valves and remove the manifold gauge set.

Removal

1984–85 EAGLE WITH FOUR OR SIX CYLINDER ENGINE

1. Disconnect the negative battery cable.
2. Isolate the compressor as previously outlined.
3. Remove the discharge and suction hoses from the compressor. Cap or plug all openings immediately.
4. Remove the dirve belt(s) by loosening the idler pulley, or loosen the alternator for engines equipped with a serpentine belt.

5. Remove the compressor from the mounting bracket and remove the compressor from the engine compartment.

Installation

1. Install the compressor onto the mounting bracket.
2. Install the drive belt(s) and tighten to specifications.
3. If equipped with a serpentine belt, tighten to specifications.
4. Remove the caps or plugs from the discharge and suction hoses and attach the hoses to the compressor.
5. Connect the negative battery cable. Check the compressor oil as required.
6. With the manifold set attached, mid-seat (crack) the suction and discharge service valves, start the engine and verify the air conditioning operation.
7. Back-seat the service valves and remove the manifold gauge set.

Expansion Valve

Removal and Installation

NOTE: Add one fluid ounce of approved refrigerant oil to the air conditioning system when replacing the expansion valve.

1. Safely discharge the system as previously outlined.
2. Remove the package tray and steering column finish panel.
3. Remove the insulation wrapped around the expansion valve, thermal bulb and fittings.

NOTE: Care should be exercised when removing the insulation for re-use purposes, unless new insulation is available.

4. Mark the thermal bulb location on the suction line.
5. Remove the thermal bulb clamp and move the bulb away from the suction line.
6. Disconnect the inlet and outlet connections and remove the expansion valve.
7. Cap or plug the openings on the air conditioning system until the replacement expansion valve is ready to be installed.
8. Install the replacement expansion valve and tighten securely.
9. Attach the thermal bulb to the marked location where the original bulb was installed.

NOTE: It is important that the bulb be clamped securely so that a clean, firm contact with the suction line exists.

10. Install the insulation by wrapping it around the bulb and suction line. Be sure the bulb and line are properly covered.
11. Install the package tray and steering column finish panel.
12. Evacuate, leak test and charge the system as previously outlined. Verify that the system if operating properly.

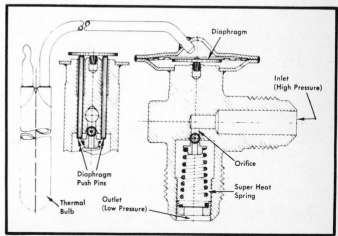

Cross section of typical expansion valve assembly
(© American Motors Corp.)

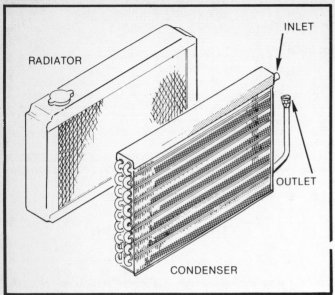

Typical condenser unit mounted in front of radiator (© American Motors Corp.)

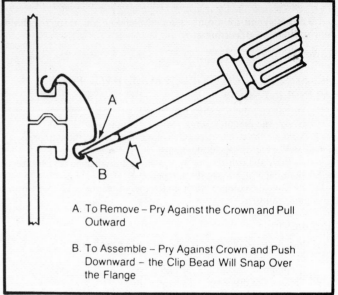

A. To Remove – Pry Against the Crown and Pull Outward

B. To Assemble – Pry Against Crown and Push Downward – the Clip Bead Will Snap Over the Flange

Evaporator housing retaining clip (© American Motors Corp.)

Condenser

Removal and Installation

ALL MODELS

1. Allow the cooling system to cool down and drain the system of coolant. Save the coolant for re-use, if acceptable.
2. Safely discharge the air conditioning system as previously outlined.
3. Remove the hoses from the radiator outlets.
4. Disconnect and plug the oil cooler lines, if equipped with automatic transmission.
5. Four cylinder models—disconnect and remove the charcoal canister and its bracket from the radiator.
6. Four cylinder models—disconnect the ambient air inlet duct from the radiator.
7. Remove the fan shroud and radiator retaining bolts. Remove both the shroud and radiator from the vehicle.
8. Disconnect the compressor discharge-to-condenser line.
9. Disconnect the receiver/drier-to-evaporator line.
10. Plug or cap all openings to prevent moisture and dirt from entering the system.
11. Remove the retaining screws and remove the condenser and receiver/drier assembly.

NOTE: Upon installation of the condenser and receiver/drier assembly, add two fluid ounces of approved refrigerant oil to the components, one fluid ounce for the condenser and one fluid ounce for the receiver/drier.

12. The installation of the condenser and the receiver/drier components are in the reverse of the removal procedure.
13. Add either new coolant or the coolant that was drained from the cooling system originally. Bring the engine to normal operating temperature and verify that the cooling system if functioning correctly.
14. Evacuate, leak test and recharge the air conditioning system. Verify that the system is operating properly.

Evaporator

Removal and Installation

ALL MODELS

1. Disconnect the negative battery cable.

2. Safely discharge the air conditioning system as outlined previously.
3. Remove the package tray and air duct assembly from under the instrument panel.
4. Remove the instrument panel center housing, the steering column finish panel and the ash receiver assembly.
5. If equipped with a radio, remove the assembly.
6. Remove the center air outlet and duct.
7. Remove the insulation and disconnect the inlet and discharge hoses at the evaporator connections.
8. Disconnect the control cables and remove the temperature sensing capillary tube.
9. Remove the evaporator housing-to-dash panel retaining screws in the passenger compartment and the housing-to-dash retaining nuts in the engine compartment.
10. Remove the evaporator housing from the interior of the vehicle.
11. Remove the evaporator housing cover retaining clips and the evaporator core attaching screws.
12. Remove the evaporator core from the housing.
13. The installation of the evaporator core into the housing is the reverse of the removal procedure.
14. With the cover installed onto the housing and the clips in place, install the evaporator housing back into the vehicle's interior.
15. Install the retaining screws and nuts to hold the housing in place.
16. Complete the assembly in the reverse of the removal procedure.

NOTE: When installing the capillary tube into the tube guide mounted on the front of the evaporator case, carefully make a 90° bend at the colored tape before installing it between the evaporator core fins.

17. Evacuate, leak-test and recharge the air conditioning system. Verify that the operation of the system if correct.

Heater Core

Removal and Installation

ALL MODELS

1. Disconnect the negative battery cable.
2. Drain at least two quarts of coolant from the cooling system
3. Disconnect the heater hoses from the heater core tubes and plug or cap both the hoses and the tubes.

4. Disconnect the electrical wire connectors for the blower motor and fan. Remove the blower motor and fan from the housing.

5. Remove the housing attaching nuts from the studs. Disconnect the resistor wire.

6. On the 1982–83 Spirit, Concord and Eagle, remove the instrument panel center housing, the air outlet and the air duct.

7. Disconnect the recirculating air door cable.

8. Remove the right door scuff plate.

9. Remove the right side windshield pillar moulding, the upper instrument panel attaching screws and the instrument panel-to-right A-pillar attaching screw.

10. Remove the housing attaching screw.

11. Pull the right side of the instrument panel slightly rearward and remove the heater core and blower housing assembly.

12. Remove the heater core from the housing.

13. Being sure all seals are in place, install the heater core into the housing.

14. Installation of the heater and blower housing assembly back into the vehicle is the reverse of the removal procedure.

15. Fill the cooling system, bring to normal operating temperature and verify the cooling system operation.

Control Panel

Removal

ALL MODELS

1. Disconnect battery negative cable.
2. Remove instrument panel center housing.
3. Remove control panel attaching screws.
4. Remove center upper discharge duct.
5. Remove radio, if equipped.
6. Remove attaching screws and lower control and disconnect cables from control levers.
7. Disconnect vacuum hose assembly from vacuum switch.
8. Disconnect electrical connectors.
9. Remove control panel.

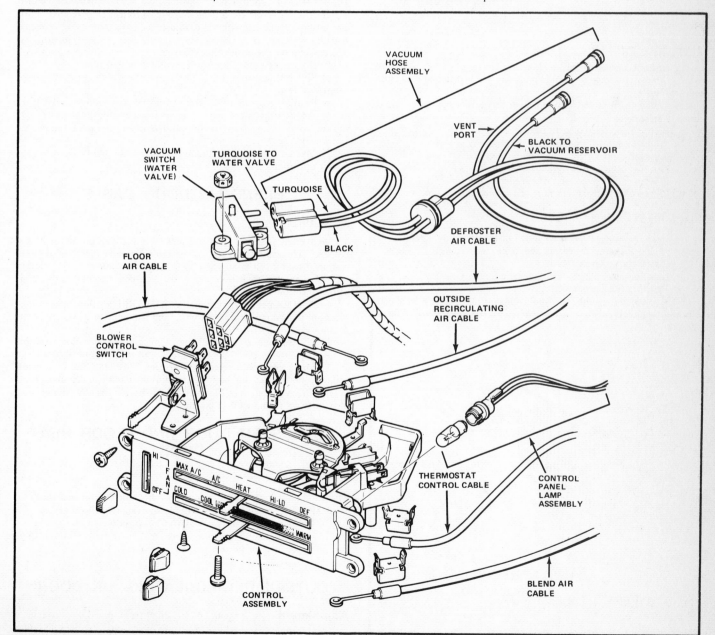

Control panel—typical of all models (© American Motors Corp.)

NOTE: The blower control switch attaching screw is accessible from the bottom of the control assembly after removal.

Installation

1. Connect electrical connectors.
2. Connect vacuum hose assembly to vacuum switch.
3. Connect cables to control levers.
4. Position control panel and install attaching screws.
5. Install center upper discharge duct.
6. Install radio, if equipped.
7. Install instrument panel center housing.
8. Move control levers to full travel in both directions to adjust cables.
9. Connect battery negative cable.
10. Check system operation.

Temperature Control Thermostat

Removal

ALL MODELS

1. Disconnect battery negative cable.
2. Remove package tray outlet assembly and instrument panel center housing.
3. Remove screw and clip attaching thermostat capillary tube to evaporator housing.
4. Remove capillary tube from tube guide.
5. Remove radio, if equipped.
6. Remove control panel attaching screws.
7. Remove center discharge duct.
8. Lower control panel and disconnect thermostat wiring.
9. Remove thermostat attaching screws and thermostat.

Installation

1. Install thermostat on bracket and install attaching screws.
2. Connect thermostat wiring and cable.
3. Install center discharge duct.
4. Install control panel attaching screws.
5. Install radio, if equipped.
6. Route capillary tube to evaporator housing. Make a 90 degree

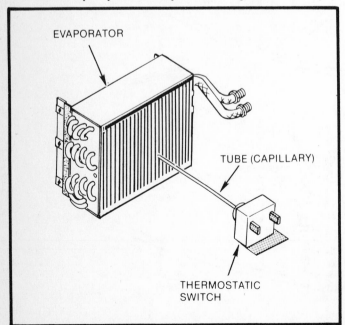

EVAPORATOR

TUBE (CAPILLARY)

THERMOSTATIC
SWITCH

Typical thermostatic switch (© American Motors Corp.)

bend (at colored tape) in capillary tube and insert end into tube guide mounted on front of evaporator housing between evaporator core fins.

7. Install clip and screw attaching capillary tube to evaporator housing.

CAUTION

Do not kink tubing.

---

8. Install instrument panel center panel and package tray outlet assembly.
9. Connect battery negative cable.
10. Check system operation.

Control Cables and Control Doors

TEMPERATURE CONTROL

Adjustment

The temperature control lever operates the A/C temperature control thermostat. The cable from the control lever to the temperature control thermostat is equipped with a self-adjusting clip to simplify adjustment. The clip is located at the temperature control thermostat crank arm and is accessible on the front of the housing.

1. Hold temperature control lever in the midposition.
2. Slip self-adjusting clip, approximately 1/2 in. toward end of control cable wire.
3. Position temperature control thermostat crank arm in cold detent.
4. Move temperature control lever from mid-position to COLD, causing control cable wire to slip through self-adjusting clip to proper adjustment.
5. Check operation of the temperature control thermostat to assure proper operation.

BLEND-AIR DOOR CABLE

Adjustment

The temperature control lever operates the blend-air door in the heater housing. The cable from the control lever to the blend-air door is equipped with a self-adjusting clip to simplify adjustment. The clip is located at the blend-air door crank arm and is accessible on the front of the heater housing.

1. Hold temperature control lever in WARM position and position blend-air door crank arm in extreme right hand end of travel (full heat position).
2. Slip self-adjusting clip, approximately 1/2 in., along control cable wire moving blend-air door crank arm toward control panel.
3. Move temperature control lever from WARM to COLD, causing control cable wire to slip through self-adjusting clip to proper adjustment.
4. Check operation of blend-air door to assure positive door closing at both WARM and COLD positions.

DEFROSTER DOOR AND FLOOR HEAT DOOR

Adjustments

The air control lever controls door operation for Defrost and Heat.
1. Remove cable retaining clips from evaporator housing.
2. Hold air control lever in MAX A/C position.
3. Hold defroster door firmly closed and install cable retaining clip. Repeat procedure for floor heat door.

OUTSIDE/RECIRCULATING AIR DOOR

Adjustment

The cable to the outside/recirculating air door is equipped with a self-adjusting clip to simplify adjustment. The clip is located at the door crank arm and is accessible on the top right hand surface of the heater/blower housing.

1. Hold air control lever in MAX A/C position.
2. Slip self-adjusting clip, approximately 1/2 in., along control cable wire, moving door crank arm away from control panel.
3. Move air control lever from MAX A/C to HEAT, causing control cable wire to slip through self-adjusting clip to proper adjustment.

Heater Water Valve

SPIRIT, CONCORD, EAGLE MODELS WITH FOUR CYLINDER ENGINE

The Spirt, Concord, Eagle models with four cylinder engine and air conditioning are equipped with a bypass heater water valve. When the heater valve is closed, coolant flow to the heater core is bypassed back to engine. When heater water valve is open, coolant is directed through the heater core and back to the engine.

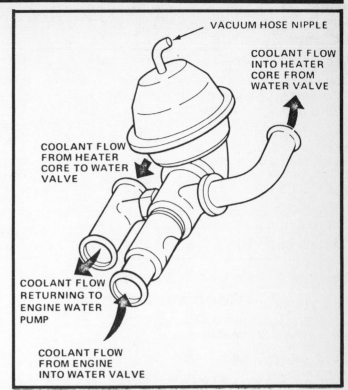

Heater water valve used with six cylinder engines (© American Motors Corp.)

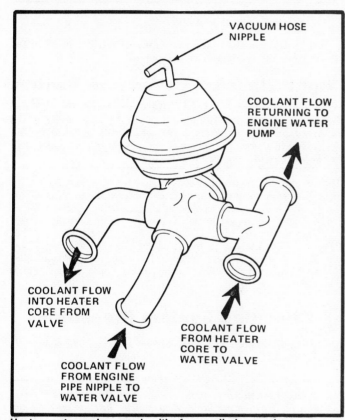

Heater water valve used with four cylinder engines (© American Motors Corp.)

1982-83 SPIRIT, CONCORD, EAGLE MODELS WITH SIX CYLINDER ENGINE 1984-85 EAGLE MODELS

The heater water valve regulates coolant flow to the heater core. The inlet and outlet heater hoses are attached to it. It requires vacuum to close and bypass flow to the heater core.

Vacuum is applied to the valve when the mode control lever is in the OFF or VENT position.

WATER VALVE

Test

A vacuum gauge and tee are required for this test.

1. Disconnect turquoise vacuum hose from heater water valve vacuum motor.
2. Using tee, connect vacuum gauge between vacuum hose and water valve vacuum motor nipple.
3. Start engine.
4. Move temperature control lever to WARM and air control lever to HEAT. No vacuum should be indicated on gauge.
5. Observe water valve while moving temperature control lever to COOL and/or air control lever to A/C. Water valve should close and manifold vacuum should be indicated on gauge.

Removal

1. Drain approximately two quarts of coolant from radiator.
2. Disconnect turquoise vacuum line from heater water valve vacuum motor.
3. Disconnect water valve attaching clamps and slide clamps up heater hose away from valve.
4. Disconnect heater hoses from heater water valve.

Installation

1. Connect heater hoses to water valve with arrow on valve pointing toward heater core.
2. Slide attaching clamps back over valve nipples
3. Connect turquoise vacuum line to water valve vacuum motor.
4. Replace coolant.
5. Check operation of water valve.

WATER VALVE DIAGNOSIS

Condition	Cause	Correction
Water Valve Does Not Close With Applied Vacuum	1) Defective water valve.	1) Replace water valve.
No Vacuum Applied to Water Valve When Temperature Control Lever is at Extreme Left Position	1) Vacuum hose off intake manifold.	1) Correct as required.
	2) Defective check valve.	2) Replace check valve.
	3) Blocked or leaking vacuum hose from check valve to switch.	3) Replace hose.
	4) Vacuum hose not connected to switch.	4) Correct as required.
	5) Switch not adjusted properly or defective.	5) Adjust or replace switch.
	6) Blocked or leaking vacuum hose from switch to water valve.	6) Replace hose.

Receiver/Drier

Removal and Installation

ALL MODELS

NOTE: The condenser must be removed to gain access to the receiver/drier attaching screws.

1. Safely discharge the air conditioning system.
2. Remove the condenser and receiver/drier as an assembly.
3. Disconnect the receiver/drier inlet line.
4. Remove the receiver/drier from the condenser.

NOTE: Cap or plug all openings on components that will be reinstalled.

5. Install the replacement receiver/drier. Connect the receiver/drier inlet line and fasten securely.
6. Install the condenser and receiver/drier as an assembly.
7. Evacuate, leak test and recharge the system. Verify that the operation of the air conditioning is correct.

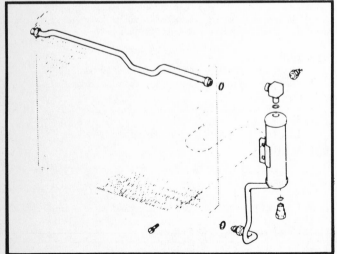

Receiver/drier location on condenser (© American Motors Corp.)

NOTE: Add one fluid ounce of approved refrigerant oil to the system when the receiver/drier is replaced.

Sight Glass/Low Pressure Switch

CAUTION

The rotary compressor used with this system is a high speed unit and requires lubrication at all times. Do not override or bypass the low pressure switch when the system is not capable of maintaining sufficient pressure to circulate the lubricant.

The low pressure switch does not change what is visually seen in the sight glass when there is a partial or complete charge of refrigerant in the system. If the system has lost its charge, the low pressure switch will disengage the magnetic clutch. If the system is partially charged a continuous stream of bubbles will be seen in the sight glass. When there is a complete charge in the system, bubbles will appear and disappear when the magnetic clutch cycles on and off. During the time the clutch is off, bubbles will appear and then disappear when the clutch comes on.

Checking System Pressures

The pressure developed on the high side and low side of the compressor indicate whether the system is operating properly.

CAUTION

Use extreme caution when engine is operating. Do not stand in direct line with fan. Do not put hands near pulleys, belts or fans. Do not wear loose clothing.

1. Attach pressure gauge and manifold assembly.
2. Close both hand valves on gauge and manifold assembly.
3. Set both service hand valve stems to midposition.
4. Operate air conditioning system with engine running at 1500 rpm and controls set for full cooling but not into the MAX or COLD detent.
5. Insert thermometer into discharge air outlet and observe air temperature.
6. Observe high and low side pressures and compare with those shown in the Normal Operating Temperatures and Pressures Chart. If pressures are abnormal, refer to Pressure and Performance Diagnosis Charts.

NORMAL OPERATING TEMPERATURES AND PRESSURES

Relative Humidity (percent)	Surrounding Air Temperature (°F)	Engine Speed (RPM)	Maximum Desirable Center Register Discharge Air Temp. (°F)	Suction Pressure PSI (REF)	Head Pressure PSI (+25 PSI)
20	70	1500	40	11	177
	80		41	15	208
	90		42	20	226
	100		43	23	255
30	70	1500	40	12	181
	80		41	16	214
	90		42	22	234
	100		44	26	267
40	70	1500	40	13	185
	80		42	18	220
	90		43	23	243
	100		44	26	278
50	70	1500	40	14	189
	80		42	19	226
	90		44	25	251
	100		46	27	289
60	70	1500	41	15	193
	80		43	21	233
	90		45	25	259
	100		46	28	300
70	70	1500	41	16	198
	80		43	22	238
	90		45	26	267
	100		46	29	312
80	70	1500	42	18	202
	80		44	23	244
	90		47	27	277
	100		—	—	—
90	70	1500	42	19	206
	80		47	24	250
	90		48	28	284
	100		—	—	—

Note: Operate engine with transmission in neutral. Keep car out of direct sunlight.

PRESSURE DIAGNOSIS

Condition	Cause	Correction
Low Side Low-High Side Low	1) System refrigerant low.	1) Evacuate, leak test, and charge.
	2) Expansion valve clogged.	2) Replace expansion valve.
Low Side High-High Side Low	1) Internal leak in compressor—worn.	1) Remove compressor cylinder head and inspect compressor. Replace valve plate assembly if necessary. If compressor pistons, rings, or cylinders are excessively worn or scored replace compressor.
	2) Head gasket leaking	2) Install new cylinder head gasket.

PRESSURE DIAGNOSIS

Condition	Cause	Correction
Low Side High-High Side Low	3) Expansion valve.	3) Replace expansion valve.
	4) Drive belt slipping.	4) Set belt tension.
Low Side High-High Side High	1) Clogged condenser fins.	1) Clean out condenser fins.
	2) Air in system.	2) Evacuate, leak test, and charge system.
	3) Expansion valve.	3) Replace expansion valve.
	4) Loose or worn fan belts.	4) Adjust or replace belts as necessary.
Low Side Low-High Side High	1) Expansion valve.	1) Replace expansion valve.
	2) Restriction in liquid line.	2) Check line for kinks—replace if necessary.
	3) Restriction in receiver.	3) Replace receiver.
	4) Restriction in condenser.	4) Replace condenser.
Low Side and High Side Normal (Inadequate Cooling)	1) Air in system.	1) Evacuate, leak test, and charge system.
	2) Moisture in system.	2) Evacuate, leak test, and charge system.

PERFORMANCE DIAGNOSIS

Condition	Cause	Correction
Compressor Noise	1) Broken valves.	1) Replace valve plate.
	2) Overcharged.	2) Discharge, evacuate, and install correct charge.
	3) Incorrect oil level.	3) Isolate compressor and check oil level. Correct as necessary.
	4) Piston slap.	4) Replace compressor.
	5) Broken rings.	5) Replace compressor.
	6) Accessory drive pulley bolts loose.	6) Tighten to torque specifications.
Excessive Vibration	1) Incorrect belt tension.	1) Set belt tension. Refer to Compressor Belt Tension.
	2) Clutch loose.	2) Tighten clutch.
	3) Overcharged.	3) Discharge, evacuate, and install correct charge.
	4) Pulley misaligned.	4) Align pulley.
Condensation Dripping in Passenger Compartment	1) Drain hose plugged or improperly positioned.	1) Clean drain hose and check for proper installation.
	2) Insulation removed or improperly installed.	2) Replace insulation on expansion valve and hoses.
AC Airflow Stops on Acceleration	1) Defective vacuum storage tank.	1) Check tank. Replace if necessary.
	2) Vacuum line separated or defective.	2) Check vacuum lines. Replace as required.
	3) Vacuum switch defective.	3) Replace switch.
	4) Vacuum leak.	4) Check vacuum motors and lines.

PERFORMANCE DIAGNOSIS

Condition	Cause	Correction
Frozen Evaporator Coil	1) Faulty thermostat.	1) Replace thermostat.
	2) Thermostat capillary tube improperly installed.	2) Install capillary tube correctly.
	3) Thermostat not adjusted properly.	3) Adjust thermostat.

TROUBLE SHOOTING CHART

Symptom	Problem Diagnosis and Inspection	Cause and Remedy

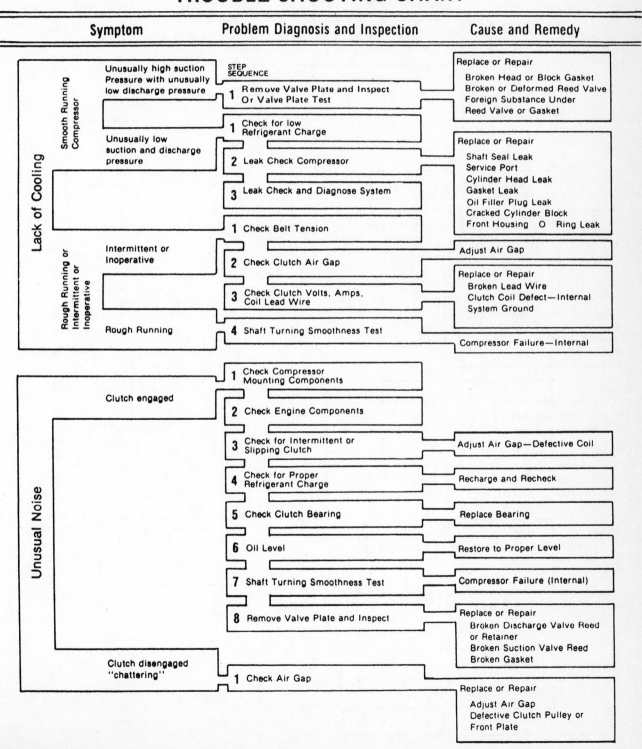

STEP SEQUENCE

Lack of Cooling

Smooth Running Compressor

Unusually high suction Pressure with unusually low discharge pressure
1 Remove Valve Plate and Inspect Or Valve Plate Test
→ Replace or Repair
  Broken Head or Block Gasket
  Broken or Deformed Reed Valve
  Foreign Substance Under
  Reed Valve or Gasket

Unusually low suction and discharge pressure
1 Check for low Refrigerant Charge
2 Leak Check Compressor
3 Leak Check and Diagnose System
→ Replace or Repair
  Shaft Seal Leak
  Service Port
  Cylinder Head Leak
  Gasket Leak
  Oil Filler Plug Leak
  Cracked Cylinder Block
  Front Housing O Ring Leak

Rough Running or Intermittent or Inoperative

Intermittent or Inoperative
1 Check Belt Tension
2 Check Clutch Air Gap → Adjust Air Gap
3 Check Clutch Volts, Amps, Coil Lead Wire
→ Replace or Repair
  Broken Lead Wire
  Clutch Coil Defect — Internal
  System Ground

Rough Running
4 Shaft Turning Smoothness Test → Compressor Failure — Internal

Unusual Noise

Clutch engaged
1 Check Compressor Mounting Components
2 Check Engine Components
3 Check for Intermittent or Slipping Clutch → Adjust Air Gap — Defective Coil
4 Check for Proper Refrigerant Charge → Recharge and Recheck
5 Check Clutch Bearing → Replace Bearing
6 Oil Level → Restore to Proper Level
7 Shaft Turning Smoothness Test → Compressor Failure (Internal)
8 Remove Valve Plate and Inspect
→ Replace or Repair
  Broken Discharge Valve Reed or Retainer
  Broken Suction Valve Reed
  Broken Gasket

Clutch disengaged "chattering"
1 Check Air Gap
→ Replace or Repair
  Adjust Air Gap
  Defective Clutch Pulley or Front Plate

Magnetic Clutch Troubleshooting

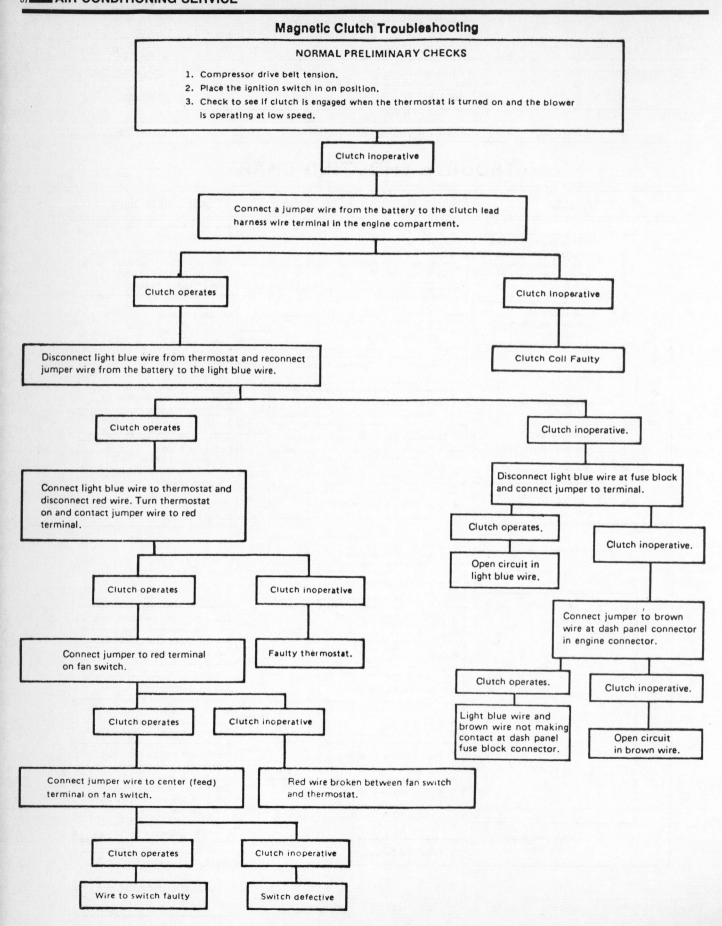

NORMAL PRELIMINARY CHECKS

1. Compressor drive belt tension.
2. Place the ignition switch in on position.
3. Check to see if clutch is engaged when the thermostat is turned on and the blower is operating at low speed.

Clutch inoperative

Connect a jumper wire from the battery to the clutch lead harness wire terminal in the engine compartment.

Clutch operates

Clutch inoperative

Clutch Coil Faulty

Disconnect light blue wire from thermostat and reconnect jumper wire from the battery to the light blue wire.

Clutch operates

Clutch inoperative.

Connect light blue wire to thermostat and disconnect red wire. Turn thermostat on and contact jumper wire to red terminal.

Disconnect light blue wire at fuse block and connect jumper to terminal.

Clutch operates.

Open circuit in light blue wire.

Clutch inoperative.

Clutch operates

Clutch inoperative

Faulty thermostat.

Connect jumper to red terminal on fan switch.

Connect jumper to brown wire at dash panel connector in engine connector.

Clutch operates.

Clutch inoperative.

Light blue wire and brown wire not making contact at dash panel fuse block connector.

Open circuit in brown wire.

Clutch operates

Clutch inoperative

Connect jumper wire to center (feed) terminal on fan switch.

Red wire broken between fan switch and thermostat.

Clutch operates

Clutch inoperative

Wire to switch faulty

Switch defective

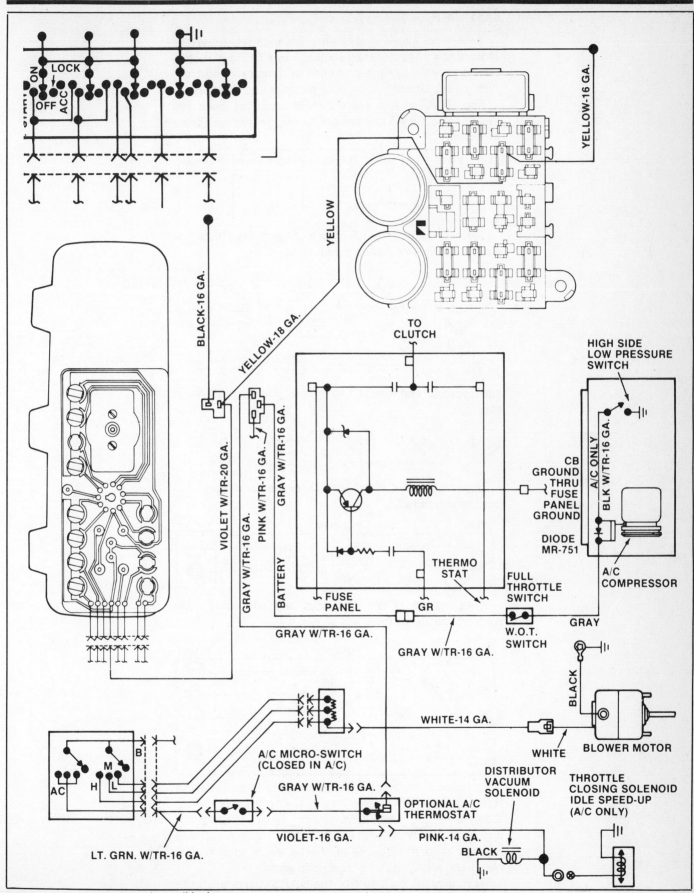

Wiring schematic of heater/air conditioning system—typical of all models (© American Motors Corp.)

DARS Charts

In several places throughout this manual, American Motors new Diagnosis and Repair Simplification(DARS) charts provide a graphic method of diagnosis and troubleshooting through the use of pictures and symbols.

The DARS charts are different from the ones you have used before. They are not "go-no go" decision trees or tables.

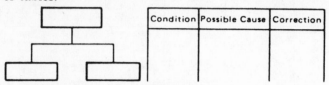

Instead,the new DARS charts use pictures plus a few words to help you solve a problem. . .

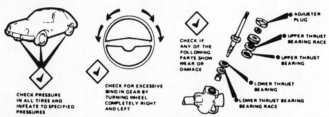

and symbols and words help guide you through each step. . .

The charts are divided into three sections: **step, sequence** and **result**.

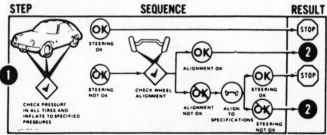

Always start at the first step and go through the complete sequence from left to right.

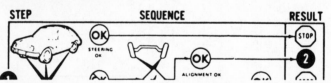

A sequence could be checking pressure in all tires and inflating to specified pressures. If the problem is solved, the symbol (OK) will send you to (STOP) . If the problem is not solved, the symbol (OK) will send you through another sequence of checks which ends with a result and tells you the next step to go to.

Work through each step of the DARS charts until the system is repaired (STOP)

DIAGNOSIS AND REPAIR SIMPLIFICATION CHART

PROBLEM: SYSTEM DOES NOT COOL PROPERLY

Chart 1

STEP	SEQUENCE	RESULT

1 — TURN IGNITION ON

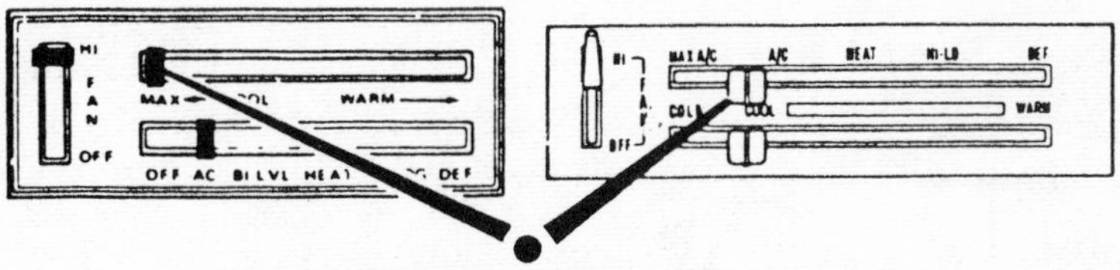

SET THERMOSTAT AT MAX. COOL
BLOWER SWITCH ON HIGH

LISTEN FOR "CLICK" AT CLUTCH

OK CLICK → **3**

OK NO CLICK → **2**

---

2 — CHECK • MAGNETIC CLUTCH | REFER TO MAGNETIC CLUTCH DIAGNOSIS CHARTS

3

RPM x 100

SET ENGINE SPEED AT 1500 RPM

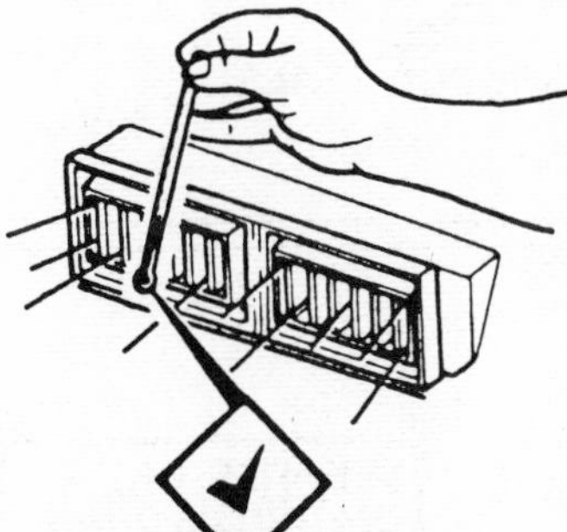

CHECK DISCHARGE TEMPERATURE WITH THERMOMETER

NOTE:
DISCHARGE AIR TEMPERATURE MUST CORRESPOND TO AMBIENT AIR TEMPERATURE AS SHOWN IN NORMAL OPERATING TEMPERATURE AND PRESSURE CHART

● SYSTEM COOLS AND CYCLES PROPERLY → **10**

● DISCHARGE AIR COOL BUT SYSTEM DOES NOT ADEQUATELY COOL INTERIOR → **4**

● SYSTEM DOES NOT COOL OR CYCLE → **7**

● SYSTEM CYCLES AT INCORRECT TEMPERATURE → **8**

4

CONTROLS

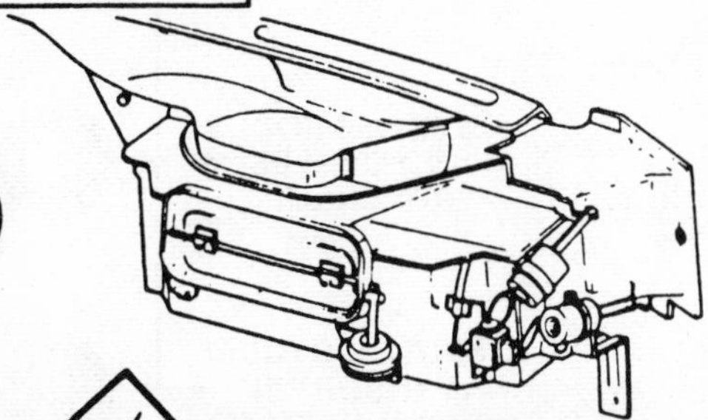

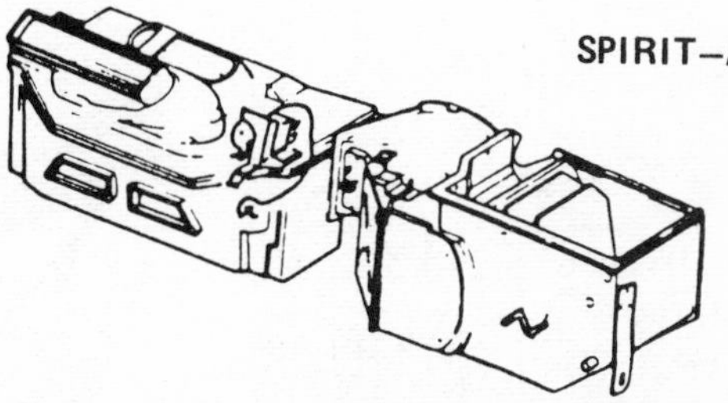

SPIRIT—AMX—CONCORD

REPAIR IF NECESSARY

→ **5**

CHECK • ADJUSTMENTS • DAMPER DOORS • CABLES • VACUUM MOTORS • WATER VALVE

STEP	SEQUENCE	RESULT

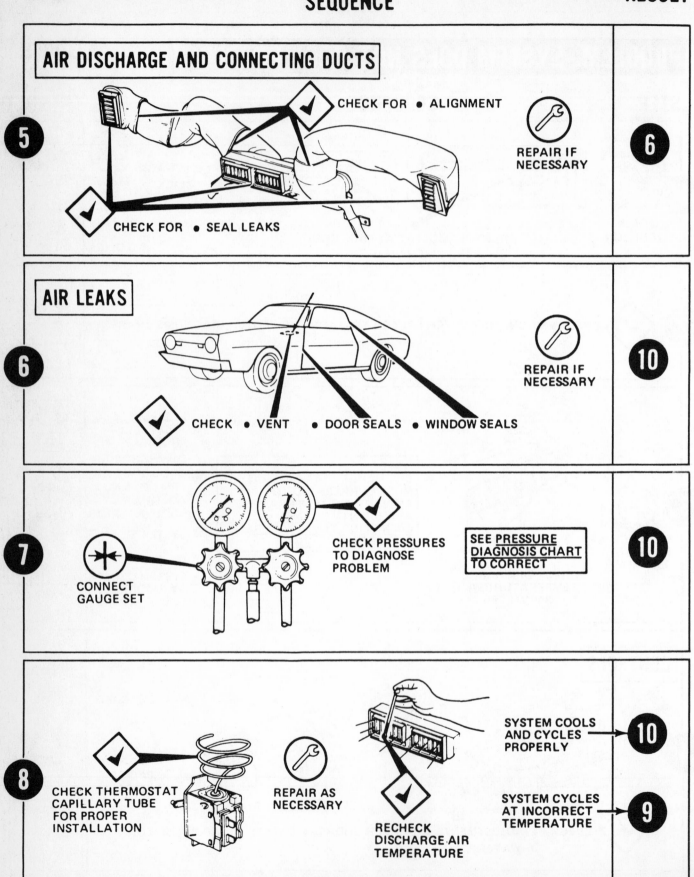

AIR DISCHARGE AND CONNECTING DUCTS

5

CHECK FOR • ALIGNMENT

CHECK FOR • SEAL LEAKS

REPAIR IF NECESSARY

6

AIR LEAKS

6

CHECK • VENT • DOOR SEALS • WINDOW SEALS

REPAIR IF NECESSARY

10

7

CONNECT GAUGE SET

CHECK PRESSURES TO DIAGNOSE PROBLEM

SEE PRESSURE DIAGNOSIS CHART TO CORRECT

10

8

CHECK THERMOSTAT CAPILLARY TUBE FOR PROPER INSTALLATION

REPAIR AS NECESSARY

RECHECK DISCHARGE AIR TEMPERATURE

SYSTEM COOLS AND CYCLES PROPERLY → 10

SYSTEM CYCLES AT INCORRECT TEMPERATURE → 9

STEP	SEQUENCE	RESULT

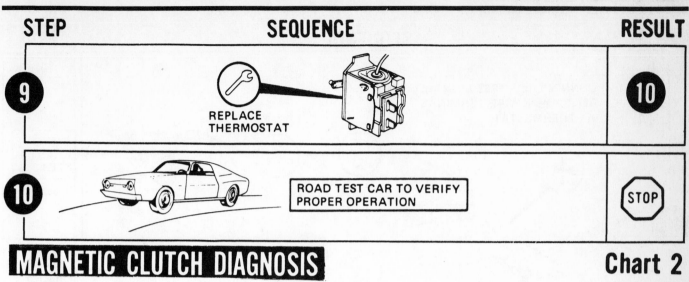

9 — REPLACE THERMOSTAT → **10**

10 — ROAD TEST CAR TO VERIFY PROPER OPERATION → **STOP**

MAGNETIC CLUTCH DIAGNOSIS

Chart 2

STEP	SEQUENCE	RESULT

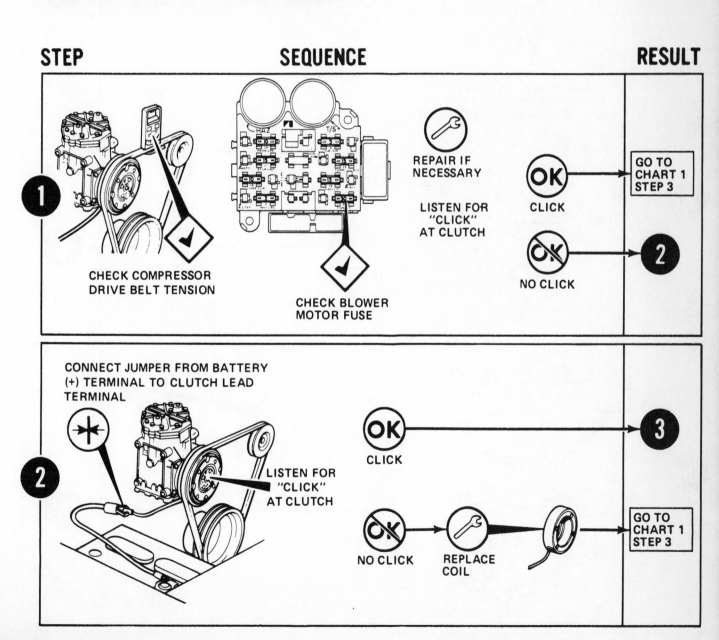

1 — CHECK COMPRESSOR DRIVE BELT TENSION — CHECK BLOWER MOTOR FUSE — REPAIR IF NECESSARY / LISTEN FOR "CLICK" AT CLUTCH

OK CLICK → GO TO CHART 1 STEP 3

NO CLICK → **2**

2 — CONNECT JUMPER FROM BATTERY (+) TERMINAL TO CLUTCH LEAD TERMINAL / LISTEN FOR "CLICK" AT CLUTCH

OK CLICK → **3**

NO CLICK → REPLACE COIL → GO TO CHART 1 STEP 3

STEP	SEQUENCE	RESULT

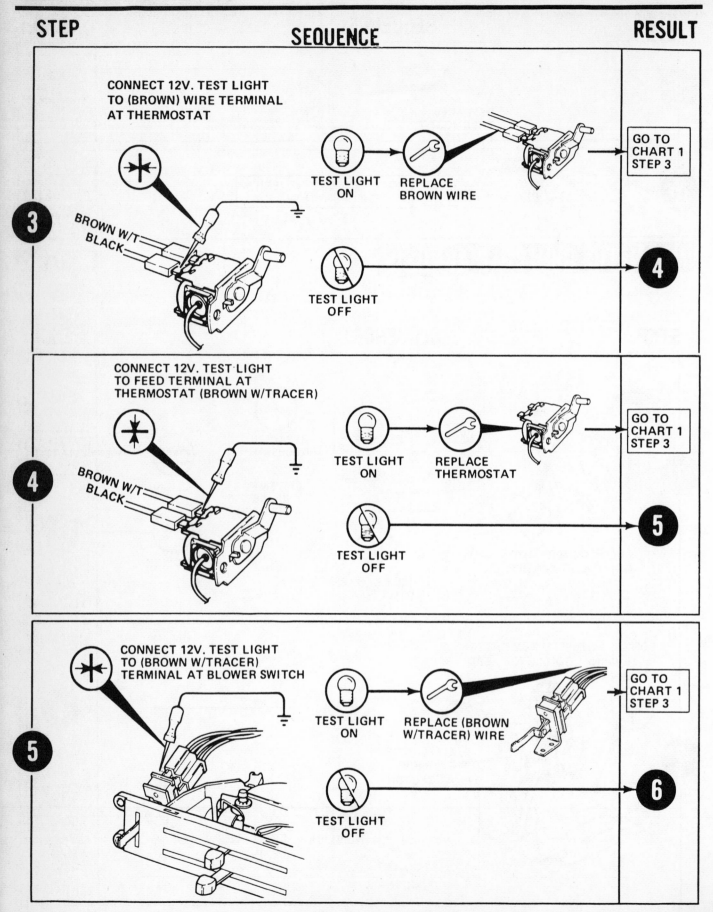

Step 3

CONNECT 12V. TEST LIGHT TO (BROWN) WIRE TERMINAL AT THERMOSTAT

BROWN W/T BLACK

TEST LIGHT ON → REPLACE BROWN WIRE → GO TO CHART 1 STEP 3

TEST LIGHT OFF → 4

Step 4

CONNECT 12V. TEST LIGHT TO FEED TERMINAL AT THERMOSTAT (BROWN W/TRACER)

BROWN W/T BLACK

TEST LIGHT ON → REPLACE THERMOSTAT → GO TO CHART 1 STEP 3

TEST LIGHT OFF → 5

Step 5

CONNECT 12V. TEST LIGHT TO (BROWN W/TRACER) TERMINAL AT BLOWER SWITCH

TEST LIGHT ON → REPLACE (BROWN W/TRACER) WIRE → GO TO CHART 1 STEP 3

TEST LIGHT OFF → 6

STEP	SEQUENCE	RESULT

6

CONNECT 12V. TEST LIGHT TO (BLUE) WIRE TERMINAL AT BLOWER SWITCH

TEST LIGHT ON → REPLACE BLOWER SWITCH → GO TO CHART 1 STEP 3

TEST LIGHT OFF → **7**

7

CONNECT 12V. TEST LIGHT TO (BLUE) WIRE TERMINAL AT FUSE PANEL

BLUE

TEST LIGHT ON → REPLACE (BLUE) WIRE → GO TO CHART 1 STEP 3

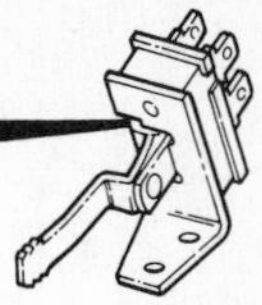

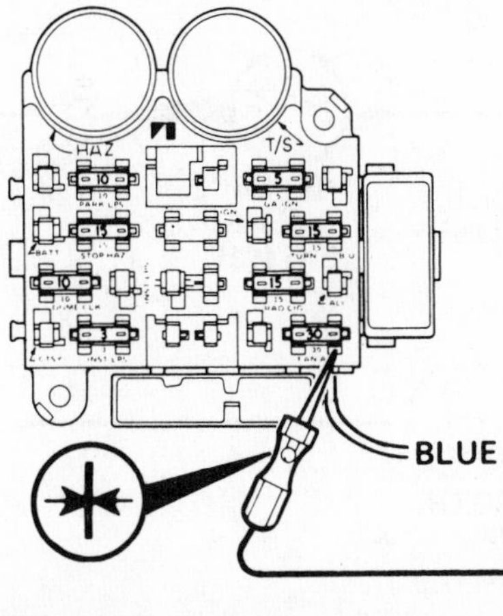

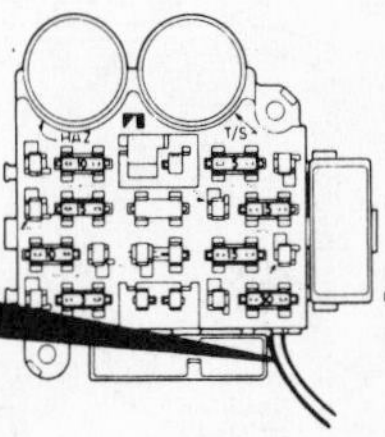

MAGNETIC CLUTCH DIAGNOSIS

Chart 3

STEP	SEQUENCE	RESULT

1

CHECK COMPRESSOR DRIVE BELT TENSION

CHECK BLOWER MOTOR FUSE

AMP

REPAIR IF NECESSARY

LISTEN FOR "CLICK" AT CLUTCH

OK CLICK → GO TO CHART 1 STEP 3

OK NO CLICK → **2**

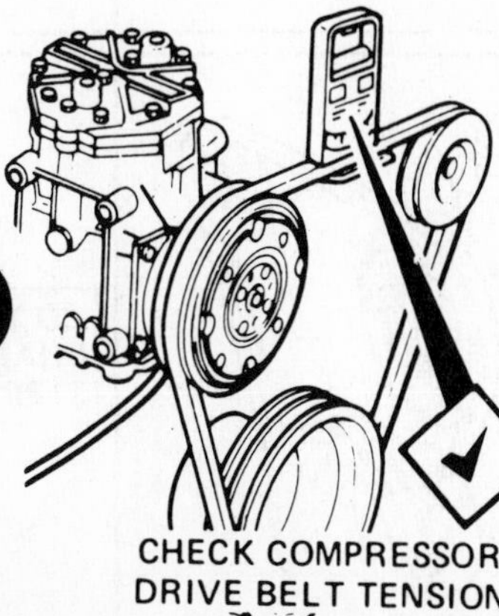

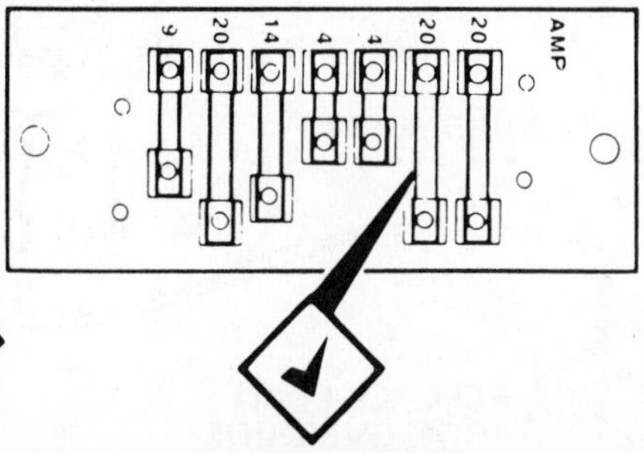

STEP   **SEQUENCE**   **RESULT**

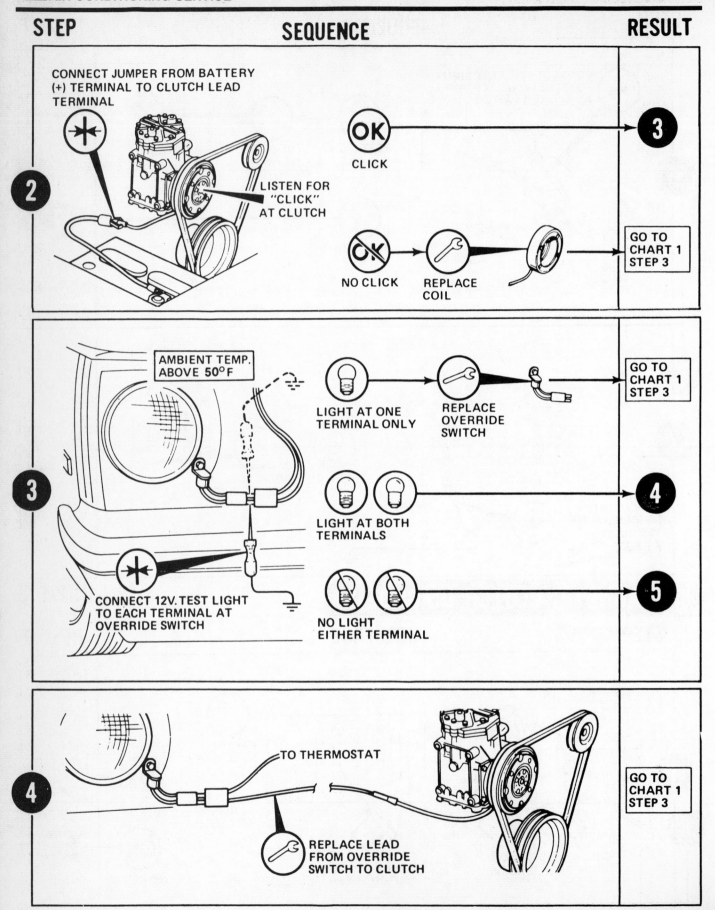

2

CONNECT JUMPER FROM BATTERY
(+) TERMINAL TO CLUTCH LEAD
TERMINAL

LISTEN FOR
"CLICK"
AT CLUTCH

OK CLICK → **3**

NO CLICK → REPLACE COIL → GO TO CHART 1 STEP 3

3

AMBIENT TEMP.
ABOVE 50°F

CONNECT 12V. TEST LIGHT
TO EACH TERMINAL AT
OVERRIDE SWITCH

LIGHT AT ONE TERMINAL ONLY → REPLACE OVERRIDE SWITCH → GO TO CHART 1 STEP 3

LIGHT AT BOTH TERMINALS → **4**

NO LIGHT EITHER TERMINAL → **5**

4

TO THERMOSTAT

REPLACE LEAD FROM OVERRIDE SWITCH TO CLUTCH

GO TO CHART 1 STEP 3

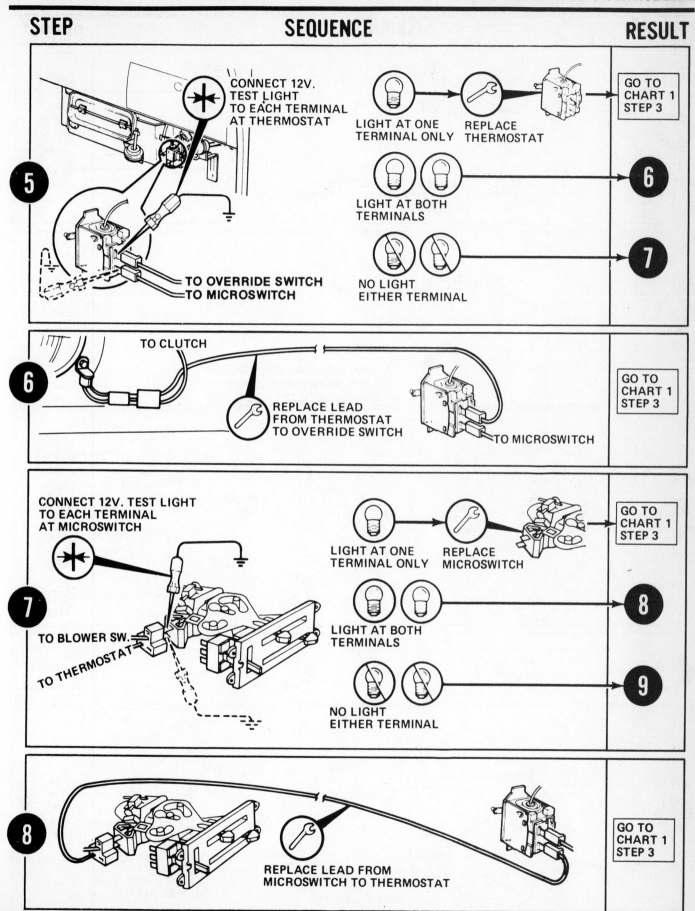

STEP | **SEQUENCE** | **RESULT**

5

CONNECT 12V. TEST LIGHT TO EACH TERMINAL AT THERMOSTAT

TO OVERRIDE SWITCH
TO MICROSWITCH

LIGHT AT ONE TERMINAL ONLY — REPLACE THERMOSTAT → GO TO CHART 1 STEP 3

LIGHT AT BOTH TERMINALS → **6**

NO LIGHT EITHER TERMINAL → **7**

6

TO CLUTCH

REPLACE LEAD FROM THERMOSTAT TO OVERRIDE SWITCH

TO MICROSWITCH

GO TO CHART 1 STEP 3

7

CONNECT 12V. TEST LIGHT TO EACH TERMINAL AT MICROSWITCH

TO BLOWER SW.
TO THERMOSTAT

LIGHT AT ONE TERMINAL ONLY — REPLACE MICROSWITCH → GO TO CHART 1 STEP 3

LIGHT AT BOTH TERMINALS → **8**

NO LIGHT EITHER TERMINAL → **9**

8

REPLACE LEAD FROM MICROSWITCH TO THERMOSTAT

GO TO CHART 1 STEP 3

STEP	SEQUENCE	RESULT

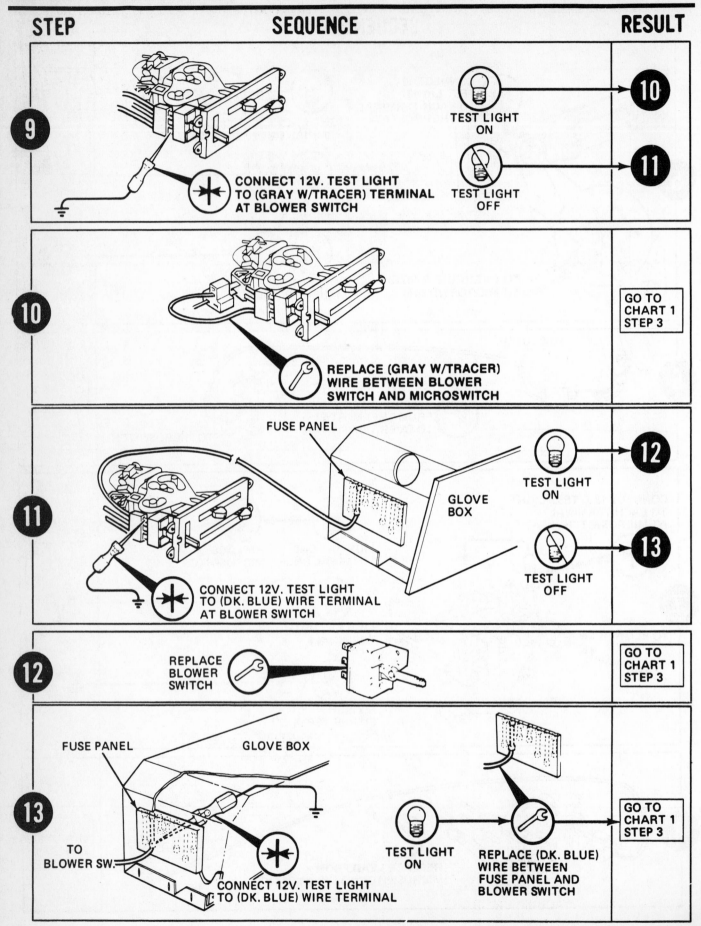

9 CONNECT 12V. TEST LIGHT TO (GRAY W/TRACER) TERMINAL AT BLOWER SWITCH

TEST LIGHT ON → **10**

TEST LIGHT OFF → **11**

10 REPLACE (GRAY W/TRACER) WIRE BETWEEN BLOWER SWITCH AND MICROSWITCH

GO TO CHART 1 STEP 3

11 FUSE PANEL

GLOVE BOX

CONNECT 12V. TEST LIGHT TO (DK. BLUE) WIRE TERMINAL AT BLOWER SWITCH

TEST LIGHT ON → **12**

TEST LIGHT OFF → **13**

12 REPLACE BLOWER SWITCH

GO TO CHART 1 STEP 3

13 FUSE PANEL GLOVE BOX

TO BLOWER SW.

CONNECT 12V. TEST LIGHT TO (DK. BLUE) WIRE TERMINAL

TEST LIGHT ON → REPLACE (D.K. BLUE) WIRE BETWEEN FUSE PANEL AND BLOWER SWITCH → GO TO CHART 1 STEP 3

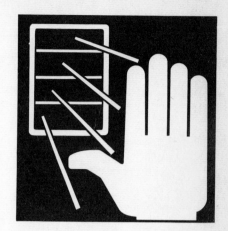

Chrysler Corporation

INDEX

CHRYSLER CORPORATION
Front Wheel Drive Models

Vehicle Code	1982	1983	1984	1985
C	LeBaron —	LeBaron —	LeBaron Laser	LeBaron Laser
D	Aries —	Aries —	Aries Lancer	Aires Lancer
E	—	600	600	—
J	—	Caravelle	Caravelle	Caravelle
M M M	TC-3 Miser Horizon Turismo	Horizon Turismo —	Horizon Turismo —	Horizon Turismo —
P	Reliant	Reliant	Reliant	Reliant
T T	— —	E-Class New Yorker	E-Class New Yorker	New Yorker —
V V	400 —	400 —	600 Daytona	600 Daytona
Z Z Z Z	Omni Miser O24 O24-Charger 2.2	Omni Charger — —	Omni Charger Shelby Charger —	Omni Charger Shelby Charger —

Note: For 1984–85 there is a FWD Limousine with a 2.6 liter engine.

CHRYSLER CORPORATION FRONT WHEEL DRIVE MODELS
Freon and Refrigerant Oil Capacities

Year	Vehicle	Refrigerant Capacity (oz.)	Refrigerant Oil Capacity (oz.)	Compressor Oil Level Check (in.)
1982–84	All Vehicles Except, Horizon, Omni, Charger, Turismo, 024 and TC-3	38	10	①
1982–84	Horizon, Omni, Charger, Turismo, 024 and TC-3	34	10	①
1985	All Vehicles	34	8	①

Note: The oil used in the C-171 compressor is a 500 SUS viscosity, wax free refrigerant oil. When adding oil to the compressor use only refrigerant oil of the same type, do not use any other type of oil.

① = The compressor used on all the FWD vehicles in this section, is the C-171 compressor. Refer to the text for more information on the compressor oil level.

CHRYSLER CORPORATION
Rear Wheel Drive Models

Vehicle Code	1982	1983	1984	1985
B	Gran Fury	Gran Fury	Gran Fury	Gran Fury
B	Caravelle	Caravelle	—	—
F	New Yorker	New Yorker	Fifth Avenue	Fifth Avenue
F	—	—	Newport	—
G	Diplomat	Diplomat	Diplomat	Diplomat
S	Cordoba	—	—	—
X	Mirada	—	—	—
X	Imperial	—	—	—

CHRYSLER CORPORATION REAR WHEEL DRIVE MODELS
Freon and Refrigerant Oil Capacities

Year	Vehicle	Refrigerant Capacity (oz.)	Refrigerant Oil Capacity (oz.)	Compressor Oil Level Check (in.)
1982–85	Gran Fury, Caravelle, New Yorker, Fifth Avenue, Newport, Diplomat, Cordoba, Mirada, Imperial	42	14	①

Note: The oil used in the C-171 compressor is a 500 SUS viscosity, wax free refrigerant oil. When adding oil to the compressor use only refrigerant oil of the same type, do not use any other type of oil.

① = The compressor used on all RWD vehicles in this section, is the C-171 compressor. Refer to the text for more information on the compressor oil level.

BELT TENSION ADJUSTMENTS

There are different methods of air conditioning compressor belt tensioning adjustments used, involving the movement of one or more of the components within the belt span. These components are the, air conditioning compressor, alternator, power steering pump and or an idler pulley if so equipped. When making belt adjustments be careful not to avoid any hidden bolts or nuts, so as not to cause any internal damage or misalignment of the pulleys, when applying tension pressure on the components.

— CAUTION —

Do not attempt to adjust the belt tension while the engine is running.

The methods for belt tension adjustments are as follows:

Deflection Method

A predetermined location on the belt span or the center of its longest span between pulleys are used in the deflection methods adjustment. A straight edge or an imaginary line is used between the two pulleys involved, along the belt top surface. Either predetermined pressure or a moderate thumb pressure is used to depress the belt in the center of its span. The amount of movement measured and compares to specifications. Corrections are made with a wrench and all measurements are given in ft. lbs. or Nm.

NOTE: Refer to the Belt Tension Chart for the proper belt tension specifications.

Tension Gauge Method

A tension gauge is placed on the air conditioning belt at its center, between its longest span between pulleys. The adjusting component retaining bolts are loosened and forced outward against the belt. When the specified tensions on the belt is reached on the gauge dial, the adjusting components bolts are tighten with out loss tension. All measurements are given in pounds or Newton. The following precautions should always be observed.

1. Use only the belt which is specially recommended for the application.
2. Check all mountings and pulleys for cracks, looseness. Check for, and, if necessary, correct misalignment.
3. Never pry a belt on to its pulley, always loosen the adjustment bolts enough so that the belt can be installed with out force.
4. Applying pressure in a manner that will not damage any of the components, adjust the belt to factory specifications.

NOTE: The proper belt tension specifications can be found in the Belt Tension Specification Chart in this section.

Chrysler Rear Wheel Drive Models 1982–85
Torque Method

All Measurements in Ft. Lbs.

Component		Gauge	Deflection	Torque
1.6L ENGINE				
Air Pump	New	95 lb.	5.558mm (7/32 in.)	37 ft. lbs. (50 Nm)
	Used	70 lb.	7.938mm (5/16 in.)	28 ft. lbs. (39 Nm)
Alternator-Water Pump	New	95 lb.	6.35mm (1/4 in.)	—
	Used	60 lb.	7.398mm (5/16 in.)	—
Power Steering	New	95 lb.	9.525mm (3/8 in.)	—
	Used	70 lb.	11.113mm (7/16 in.)	—
1.7L ENGINE				
Air Conditioning Compressor	New Belt	—	8mm (5/16 in.)	90 ft. lbs. (122 Nm)
	Used Belt	—	9mm (7/16 in.)	45 ft. lbs. (61 Nm)
Air Pump/Water Pump	New Belt	—	4mm (3/16 in.)	70 ft. lbs. (95 Nm)
	Used Belt	—	5mm (3/16 in.)	40 ft. lbs. (54 Nm)
Alternator/Water Pump	New Belt	—	3mm (1/8 in.)	65 ft. lbs. (88 Nm)
	Used Belt	—	6mm (1/4 in.)	40 ft. lbs. (54 Nm)
Power Steering Pump	New Belt	—	6mm (1/4 in.)	80 ft. lbs. (108 Nm)
	Used Belt	—	8mm (5/16 in.)	50 ft. lbs. (68 Nm)
2.2L ENGINE				
Air Conditioning Compressor	New	95 lb.	8mm (5/16 in.)	40 ft. lbs. (54 Nm)
	Used	80 lb.	9mm (7/16 in.)	30 ft. lbs. (41 Nm)
Air Pump	New	—	5mm (3/16 in.)	45 ft. lbs. (61 Nm)
	Used	—	6mm (1/4 in.)	35 ft. lbs. (47 Nm)
Alternator/Water Pump	New	115 lb.	3mm (1/8 in.)	110 ft. lbs. (149 Nm)

Chrysler Rear Wheel Drive Models 1982–85
Torque Method
All Measurements in Ft. Lbs.

Component		Gauge	Deflection	Torque
		2.2L ENGINE		
"V" Belt and Poly "V"	Used	80 lb.	6mm (¼ in.)	80 ft. lbs. (108 Nm)
Power Steering Pump	New	95 lb.	6mm (¼ in.)	75 ft. lbs. (102 Nm)
	Used	80 lb.	11mm (⁷⁄₁₆ in.)	55 ft. lbs. (75 Nm)
		2.6L ENGINE		
Power Steering Pump	New	95 lb.	6mm (¼ in.)	110 ft. lbs. (194 Nm)
	Used	80 lb.	9mm (⅜ in.)	75 ft. lbs. (102 Nm)
Alternator	New	115 lb.	4mm (³⁄₁₆ in.)	—
	Used	80 lb.	6mm (¼ in.)	—
Alternator/Air Conditioning	New	115 lb.	6mm (¼ in.)	—
Compressor	Used	80 lb.	8mm (⁵⁄₁₆ in.)	—
Water Pump	New	—	8mm (⁵⁄₁₆ in.)	—
	Used	—	9mm (⅜ in.)	—

Chrysler Rear Wheel Drive Models 1982–85
Torque Method

Component	New Belt●		Used Belt ▲	
	225 CID	318 CID	225 CID	318 CID
ALTERNATOR				
With A/C	60 (81 Nm)	75 (101 Nm)	40 (54 Nm)	50 (68 Nm)
Without A/C	60 (81 Nm)	75 (101 Nm)	40 (54 Nm)	40 (54 Nm)
AIR PUMP				
With A/C	40 (54 Nm)		25 (34 Nm)	
Without A/C	75 (101 Nm)		50 (68 Nm)	
POWER STEERING				
With A/P①		120 (163 Nm)		60 (81 Nm)
Without A/P		50 (68 Nm)		40 (54 Nm)
AIR CONDITIONING				
Without A/P②	35 (48 Nm)		20 (27 Nm)	

● Gauge Method: 120 lbs. (530 N)
▲ Gauge Method: 70 lbs. (310 N)

①Initial orientation of torque wrench is approximately horizontal.
②Adjusted at idler pulley bracket.

Blower Motor

Removal

1982–85 IMPERIAL, NEW YORKER, DIPLOMAT, GRAN FURY, CARAVELLE, FIFTH AVENUE

NOTE: All service to the blower motor is made from inside the vehicle, under the right side of the instrument panel.

1. Disconnect the battery ground cable.
2. Remove the blower motor feed wire and ground wires at the connector.
3. Remove the blower motor mounting nuts from the bottom of the recirculation housing or separate the lower blower housing from the upper housing.
4. Remove the blower motor assembly from the recirculation housing.
5. Remove the blower motor mounting plate screws.

6. Separate the blower motor housing from the blower motor fan assembly.

Installation

1. Position the grommet on the feed wire into place on the blower motor housing.
2. Set the blower motor and fan assembly into the blower motor housing and install the housing to mounting plate screws.
3. Position the blower assembly up into the recirculation housing and install the retaining nuts.
4. Install the blower motor feed and ground wire connector.
5. Install the battery ground cable.
6. Test the blower motor operation on all fan speeds.

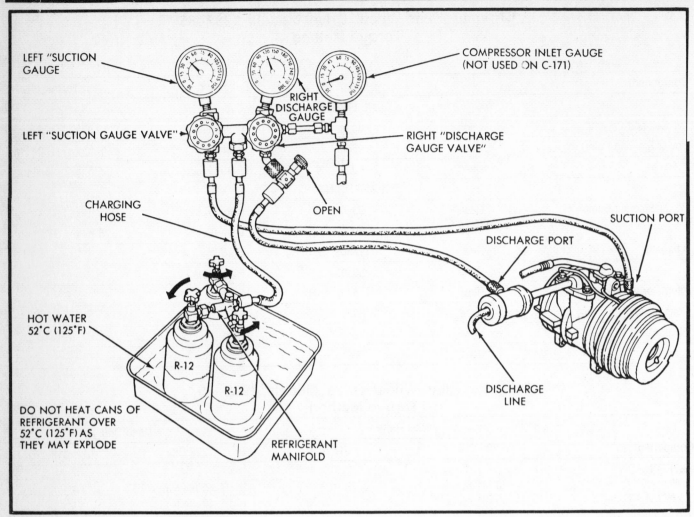

Recharging the system (© Chrysler Corporation)

Removal

1982–85 CORDOBA, MIRADA, NEWPORT

NOTE: All service to the blower motor and blower motor fan must be done inside of the vehicle from the passenger side of the instrument panel.

1. Disconnect the negative battery cable.
2. Remove the glovebox assembly.
3. Disconnect the blower motor feed and ground wires at the resistor block.
4. Remove the rear heater assembly to the plenum mounting brace.
5. Remove the screws holding the blower motor assembly to the heater housing.
6. Remove the blower motor assembly.

Installation

1. Before installing the blower motor assembly, be certain that the blower fan bottoms on the motor shaft and is fastened securely.
2. Position the fasten blower motor assembly into the heater housing.
3. Install the brace from the heater assembly to the plenum.
4. Install the blower motor feed and ground wires on to the resistor block.
5. Install the glovebox assembly.
6. Install the negative battery cable and check the operation of the blower motor.

Compressor

Removal

1982–85—ALL REAR WHEEL VEHICLES

1. Discharge the system and disconnect the suction and discharge lines from the suction and discharge ports. Cap the lines and ports immediately to prevent moisture and dirt from entering the system.
2. Disconnect the clutch wire and remove the compressor-to-bracket attaching bolts and remove compressor. It may be necessary to loosen the bracket-to-engine attaching bolts.
3. Drain the oil from the compressor suction and discharge ports.

NOTE: To service the compressor, it will be necessary to remove the compressor clutch assembly. Refer to the compressor overhaul section in this manual.

Installation

1. Adjust the oil level through the compressor suction ports to 5 fluid ounces if necessary.
2. Install the compressor on the vehicle and tighten the drive belts to specifications. Torque the compressor mounting bolts to 40 + or − 10 ft. lbs.

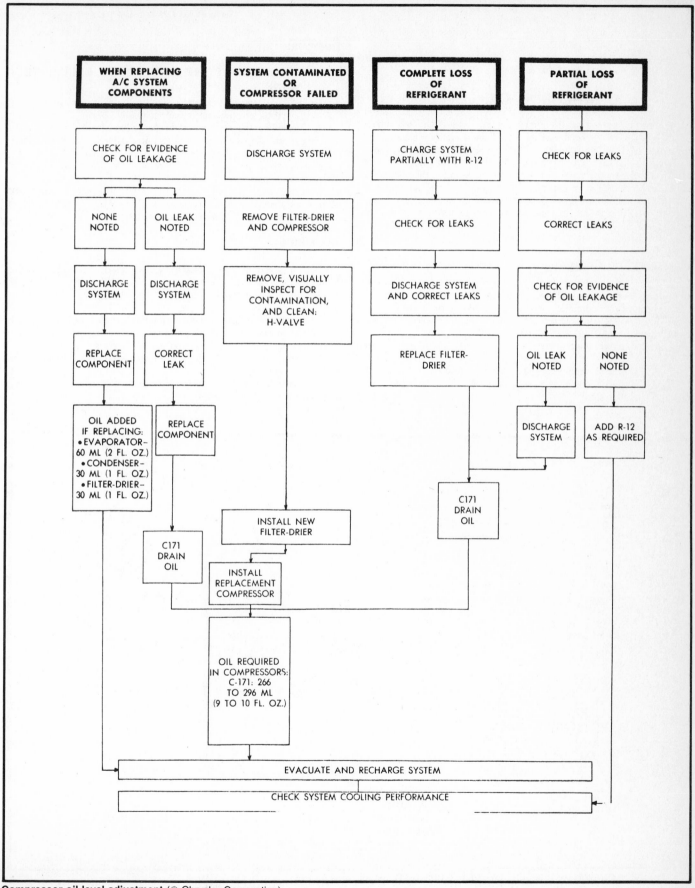

Compressor oil level adjustment (© Chrysler Corporation)

3. Reconnect the clutch wire and remove the caps from the suction and discharge lines and suction and discharge ports.

4. Using a new gaskets, install lines onto compressor and tighten to 170 to 230 in. lbs. (19 to 26 Nm).

5. Evacuate the system and charge the system, check the operation of the system and also check for refrigerant leaks.

COMPRESSOR OIL LEVEL

When a new compressor is installed at the factory, it contains 8 ounces (1985 vehicles) of a special wax free 500 SUS viscosity refrigerant oil (10 ounces in 1982–84 vehicles). While the air conditioning system is in operation, the oil is carried through the entire system and returns to the compressor by the way of the suction port. Some of the oil will be trapped and retained in various parts of the system. So once the system has been in operation, the amount of oil left in the compressor will always be less than the original amount. So when replacing a compressor measure the amount of the oil in the failed compressor and add that same amount of oil to the new compressor.

Checking The Compressor Oil Level

1. Slowly discharge the system and once the system is discharged, remove the suction and discharge lines from the compressor.

2. Remove the compressor and clutch assembly from the vehicle.

3. Remove the compressor oil by turning the compressor over and letting the oil drain from the suction and discharge ports.

4. Add five fluid ounces of the specified refrigerant oil through the suction port.

5. Reinstall the compressor and clutch assembly.

6. Using new gaskets reinstall suction and discharge lines and evacuate and charge system.

Compressor

Removal

1982–85—ALL FRONT WHEEL VEHICLES EXCEPT THE 2.6L ENGINE

1. Discharge the system and cover up the alternator with a shop rag to prevent oil dripping on the alternator.

2. Disconnect the suction and discharge lines from the suction and discharge ports. Cap the lines and ports immediately to prevent moisture and dirt from entering the system.

3. Disconnect the clutch wire and remove the compressor-to-bracket attaching bolts and nuts.

4. Remove the compressor and drain the oil from the compressor suction and discharge ports. Refer to the Compressor Overhaul section before performing any services to the compressor.

Installation

1. Adjust the oil level through the compressor suction port to five fluid ounces if necessary.

2. Install the compressor on the vehicle and tighten the drive belts to correct torque specifications.

3. Torque the compressor mounting bolts to 40 + or − 10 ft. lbs.

4. Reconnect the clutch wire and remove the caps from the suction and discharge lines and suction and discharge ports.

5. Using new gaskets, install the lines onto compressor and tighten to 170 to 230 in. lbs.

6. Evacuate and charge the system, make a systems operation test and check for refrigerant leaks.

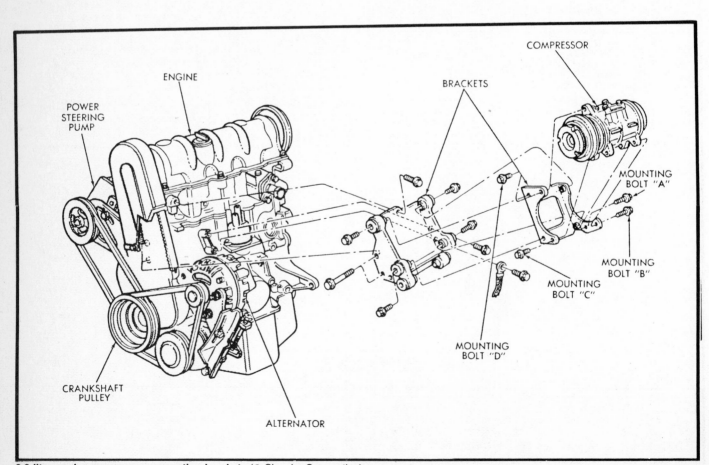

2.2 liter engine compressor mounting brackets (© Chrysler Corporation)

Removal

1982–85 2.6 LITER ENGINE

NOTE: Because the compressor is mounted on the lower end of the 2.6 liter engine, the vehicle must be raised off the ground in order to remove the compressor properly.

1. Remove the negative battery cable, raise and support vehicle safely and discharge the system.
2. Disconnect the suction line from the suction port and cap the line to prevent any moisture or dirt from entering the system.
3. Release the belt tension and remove the belts from the compressor. Disconnect the clutch lead wire, remove the clevis and clamping screw.
4. Remove the right front tire and wheel assembly, also the shipping tie down if it is still in place.
5. Remove the three mounting screws and remove the dust shield.
6. Remove the three mounting screws that hold the front support bracket to the engine.
7. Remove all compressor mounting bolts and brackets.
8. Raise the compressor slightly and hook the rear mounting ears over the rear mounting bracket.
9. Tip the nose of the compressor down and remove mounting bolt and front bracket.
10. Disconnect discharge line from discharge port and cap the line to prevent moisture or dirt from entering the system and remove the compressor.

Installation

1. Adjust the oil level through the compressor suction port to five fluid ounces if necessary.
2. Install the compressor on the vehicle and tighten the drive belts to correct torque specifications. Torque the compressor mounting bolts and bracket bolts to 40 + or − 10 ft. lbs.
3. Reconnect the clutch wire, clevis and clamping screw. Remove the caps from the suction and discharge lines and suction and discharge ports.
4. Using new gaskets, install the lines onto the compressor and tighten to 170 to 230 in. lbs.

5. Install the front support bracket and torque down the three mounting screws.
6. Install the dust shield and its three mounting screws.
7. Reinstall the front tire and wheel assembly.
8. Lower the vehicle, reconnect the negative battery cable and evacuate and charge the system. Check for any refrigerant leaks.

NOTE: After installing a compressor the compressor clutch should be cycled off and on with the engine at fast idle, 15 to 20 times to ensure clutch parts reseat with each other after installation, before the clutch engages with high head pressure at the compressor.

Expansion Valve

The H-valve is used for all vehicles and its function is to meter refrigerant into the evaporator in accordance with cooling requirements. The low pressure cut-off switch is part of the H-valve assembly.

EXPANSION H-VALVE

Removal

1982–85—ALL VEHICLES

NOTE: The system must be completely discharged before opening any refrigerant lines.

1. Disconnect the wires from the low pressure cut-off switch.
2. Remove the bolt in the center of the plumbing sealing plate.
3. Carefully pull refrigerant line assembly towards the front of the car, be careful not to scratch the valve sealing surfaces with tube pilots.
4. Remove the two allenhead cap screws.

Installation

1. Replace the aluminum gaskets on the evaporator and plumbing sealing plates. Carefully position the new gaskets over the plate pilots and push them firmly against each plate.

CAUTION
Be careful not to scratch the gasket surfaces while installing.

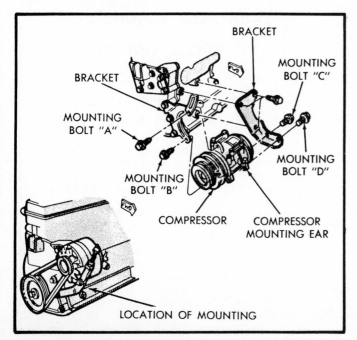

2.6 liter engine compressor mounting bracket (© Chrysler Corporation)

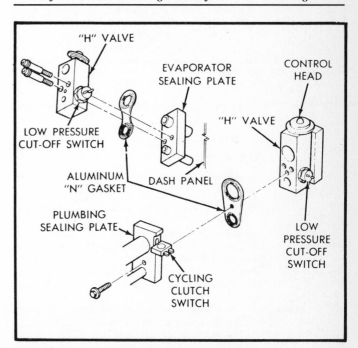

Typical H–valve assembly (© Chrysler Corporation)

2. Remove the sealing cap from the H-valve control head side sealing surface only and position the valve surface recesses on the evaporator plate pilots.

3. Hold valve firmly in place and install the two allen head screws, torque the screws to 100 + or − 30 in. lbs. (11 + or − 3 Nm).

4. Remove the sealing cap from the H-valve plumbing side sealing surface. Insert the bolt in the center of the plumbing plate straight through to the threaded hole in the valve. Align the plate pilots with the valve surface recesses and hold the plate firmly against the valve. Torque the bolts to 200 + or − 30 in. lbs. (23 + or − 3 Nm).

5. After the expansion valve is installed and the system has been charged, check for any refrigerant leaks and perform a systems operation test. Connect the wires to the low pressure cut-off switch.

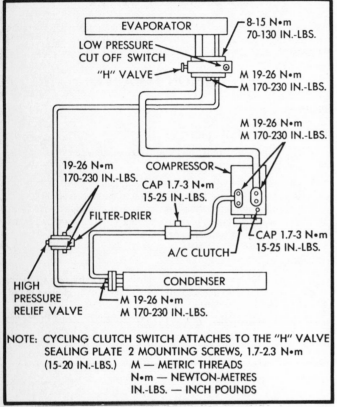

Refrigerant line torque specs (© Chrysler Corporation)

H-VALVE TEST

1982–85—ALL VEHICLES

NOTE: The ambient temperature must be between 70 and 85 degrees F.

1. On the SATC systems, close the windows and operate the engine at 800 rpm.

2. Set the air conditioning controls for Max-A/C, high blower, temperature control lever in full reheat position, with cycling clutch switch and low-pressure cut off switch electrically by-passed.

3. The blend door must be locked in the full heat position. Refer to the blend air door positioning procedure in the SATC diagnosis section.

4. Operate the system for at least 5 minutes in order to obtain partial stabilization and sufficient reheat to load the system.

5. Pressure at the discharge service port should reach 115–240 psig (793–1656 kPag). If head pressure of the same reading as above can not be obtained, check the system charge level.

6. Spray the H-valve control head with liquid freon for 10 to 15 seconds. Be extremely careful when handling freon.

7. The evaporator suction port pressure must drop to below 15 inches of vacuum, if this condition is not met, the H-valve is stuck open and should be replaced.

8. Stop spraying the control head with freon and watch the evaporator suction pressure, it should increase and stabilize at a pressure of 20 to 35 psig (140 to 240 kPag).

9. Any H-valve that does not produce this response is stuck closed and should be replaced.

NOTE: The alternate method is to use dry ice on the H-valve control head, instead of liquid freon. Protective gloves should be worn when handling dry ice as skin injury can occur.

10. Set the engine speed at 800 rpm and switch the blower to hi, the evaporator suction pressure should be in the range of 20–35 psig (140 to 240 kPag). If the compressor discharge is higher than 240 psig (1656 kPag), check for a restricted discharge line, radiator overheating, air in the system or a faulty viscous fan drive.

11. Reconnect the A/C water valve vacuum hose (gray) and set the temperature control to the cool position.

12. Reconnect the electrical wires to the cycling clutch switch.

Condensor

Removal

1982–85—ALL VEHICLES

1. Discharge the system of refrigerant.
2. Disconnect the inlet and outlet connections at the condensor.
3. Remove the bolts retaining the mounting brackets to the radiator assembly.
4. Lift the condensor straight up and out from the vehicle.

Installation

1. Position the condensor onto the condensor mounting surface.
2. Install the condensor retaining bolts.
3. Connect the inlet and outlet connections to the condensor.
4. Evacuate, leak test and charge the system.

Evaporator Assembly

FRONT WHEEL VEHICLES

Removal

1982–85 CARAVELLE, 400, 600, E CLASS, NEW YORKER, RELIANT, ARIES, LEBARON, DAYTONA, LASER, LANCER

1. Discharge the system before opening any lines and drain the engine coolant, disconnect the battery fusible link.
2. Disconnect the heater hoses at the heater core and plug the heater core tube openings to prevent coolant from spilling out when assembly is removed.
3. Disconnect the vacuum lines at the engine intake manifold and at the water valve.
4. Remove the right scuff plate and the cowl side trim panels.
5. Remove the glovebox and remove the heater A/C control head (see the Chrysler heating section).
6. Remove the console if so equipped and remove the forward console mounting bracket if so equipped.
7. Remove the center distribution duct and remove the demister adapter on the vehicles equipped with demisters.
8. Pull the defroster adapter out from under the dash panel and remove clamp and condensate drain tube.
9. Disconnect unit from wiring harness.

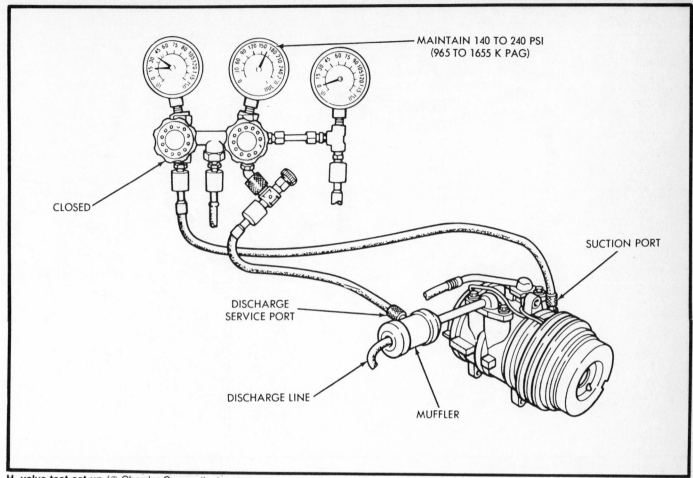

MAINTAIN 140 TO 240 PSI
(965 TO 1655 K PAG)

CLOSED

SUCTION PORT

DISCHARGE
SERVICE PORT

DISCHARGE LINE

MUFFLER

H—valve test set up (© Chrysler Corporation)

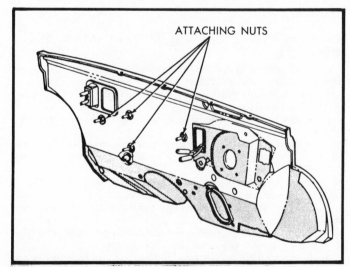

ATTACHING NUTS

Removing the mounting nuts (© Chrysler Corporation)

10. Remove the control cable by depressing the tab on the flag and then pull the flag out of the receiver on the evaporator heater assembly.

11. Remove the right side cowl to plenum brace and pull the carpet back from under the unit.

12. Remove the four nuts in the engine compartment which attach the A/C unit to the dash panel.

13. Pull the unit rearward until the A/C unit studs clear the dash liner. Drop the unit vertically until it comes in contact with the converter tunnel.

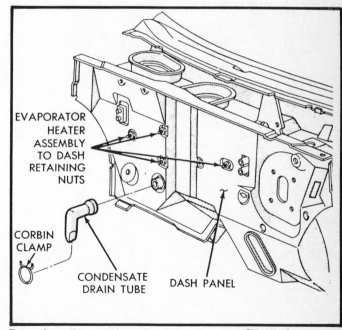

EVAPORATOR
HEATER
ASSEMBLY
TO DASH
RETAINING
NUTS

CORBIN
CLAMP

CONDENSATE
DRAIN TUBE

DASH PANEL

Removing the condensate drain tube (© Chrysler Corporation)

14. Rotate the unit out of the lower instrument panel on to the floor, being sure not to let the unit slide either to the right or the left.

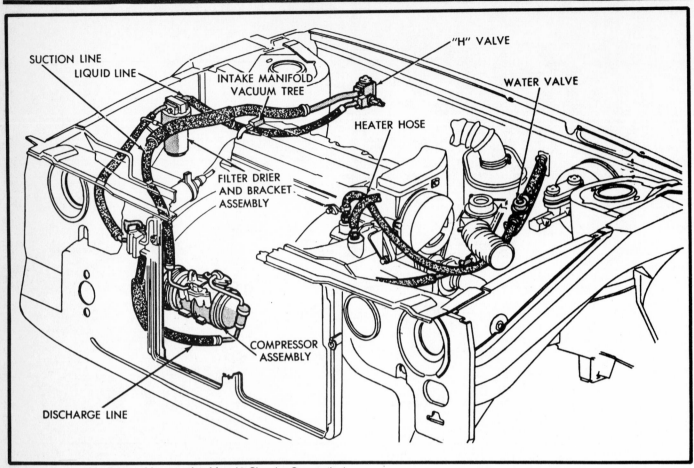

Typical air conditioning and heater plumbing (© Chrysler Corporation)

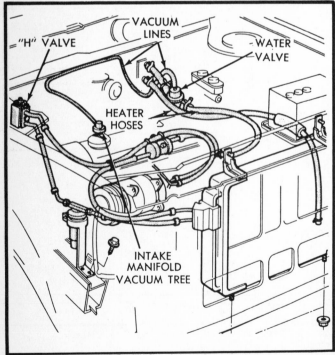

Air conditioning and heater plumbing (© Chrysler Corporation)

Removal

1982–85 HORIZON, TURISMO, OMNI, CHARGER, TC-3, MISER, 024

1. Discharge the system before opening any lines, drain the engine coolant and disconnect the battery fusible link.

2. Disconnect the blend air door cable and disengage from the clip on the heated air duct.

3. Remove the glove box, disconnect the center bezel and remove the center bezel.

4. Remove the defroster duct adapter and disconnect the heater and A/C lines at the dash panel. Plug the heater tubes to prevent coolant leakage.

5. Disconnect the vacuum lines at the engine water valve and remove the four retaining nuts to the dash panel.

6. Remove the right side cowl trim panel and the right instrument panel pivot bracket screw.

7. Remove the two screws securing the lower instrument panel at the steering column and remove the panel top cover.

8. Remove all but the left panel to fenceline attaching screws and pull the carpet back from under the A/C unit as far rearward as possible.

9. Remove the support strap nut and the blower motor ground cable, while supporting the unit, remove the strap from its plenum stud.

10. Lift and pull unit as far rearward as possible to clear the dash panel and liner. At the same the dash panel will also have to pulled rearward to allow unit clearance and this operation will probably require two people.

11. Lower the unit and be sure nut to let the dash attachment studs get hung up in the dash liner.

12. When the unit is lowered to the floor, slide the unit rearward and remove the unit from the vehicle.

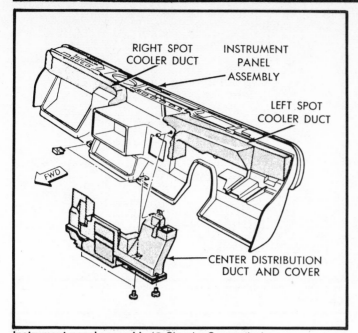

Instrument panel assembly (© Chrysler Corporation)

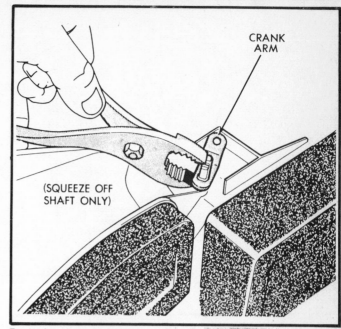

Removing the actuator arm (© Chrysler Corporation)

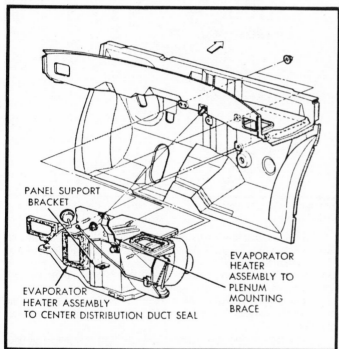

Evaporator heater assembly (© Chrysler Corporation)

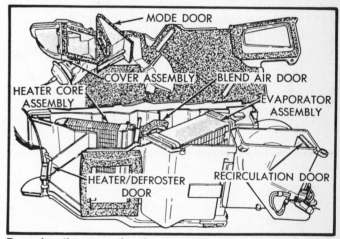

Removing the cover for the evaporator assembly (© Chrysler Corporation)

Disassembly

1982–85—ALL FRONT WHEEL VEHICLES

1. Place evaporator assembly on a work bench in the position as would be viewed by the front seat passenger.

2. Remove the nut from the mode door actuator arm on the top cover on the Horizon, Turismo, Omni, Charger, TC-3, Miser, 024 vehicles.

3. On the Caravelle, 400, 600, E Class, New Yorker, Reliant, Aries, LeBaron, Daytona, Laser, Lancer vehicles, remove the mode door actuator arm by squeezing it off of its mounting shaft.

4. Remove the two retaining clips from the front edge cover and to remove mode door actuator, remove the two mounting screws holding the actuator to the cover.

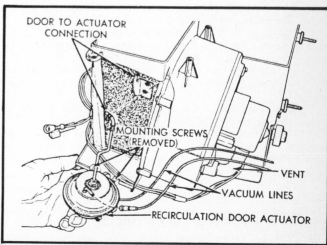

Removing the recirculating door actuator (© Chrysler Corporation)

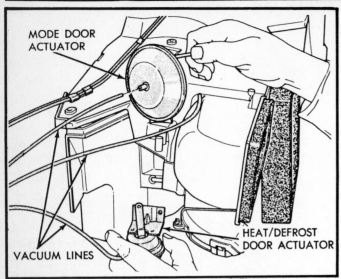

Removing mode and heater defrost door actuators (© Chrysler Corporation)

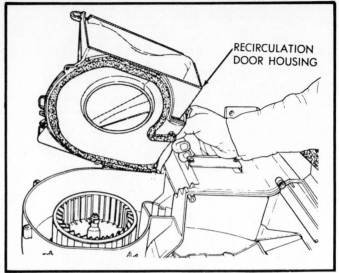

Installing recirculating door housing (© Chrysler Corporation)

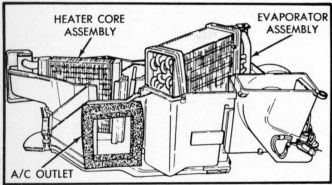

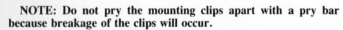

Removing the heater core and evaporator coil (© Chrysler Corporation)

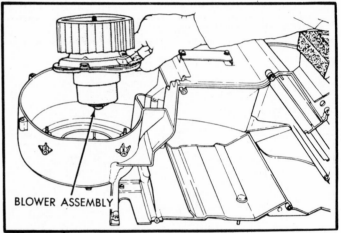

Installing the blower motor assembly (© Chrysler Corporation)

NOTE: Do not pry the mounting clips apart with a pry bar because breakage of the clips will occur.

5. Remove the 15 screws attaching the evaporator assembly cover to the assembly and lift off the cover, also remove the mode door from the unit.

6. Remove the screw from the heater core tube retaining bracket and remove the heater core.

7. Remove the H-valve, seal and sealing bracket screw from under the H-valve sealing plate and lift the evaporator coil out of the unit.

8. Disconnect the actuator linkage from the recirculation door and vacuum lines from actuator. Remove two screws attaching the actuator to housing and remove actuator and recirculation door.

9. Remove five screws attaching recirculation housing to unit and lift off the housing, remove the vent tube from the evaporator heater housing.

10. Remove the three screws holding the blower motor assembly into the unit and remove the blower motor.

11. Remove the heater/defrost door, disconnect the linkage from the door and vacuum line from the actuator. Remove the two attaching screws holding the actuator to the unit and remove the actuator with the heater/defrost door.

Assembly

1982–85—ALL FRONT WHEEL VEHICLES

1. Place the evaporative coil and the heater core into position in the unit and fasten them with attaching screws.

2. Position the blower motor assembly into the unit and fasten with the three mounting screws. Reconnect vent tube to evaporator housing.

3. Install the recirculation housing with its five mounting screws and place the recirculation door into place. Mount the recirculation door actuator on the housing and reconnect the linkage and vacuum line.

4. Place heater/defrost door in its proper position and mount the heater/defrost actuator onto the housing. Reinstall the linkage and vacuum line.

5. Place mode door into housing and carefully position cover onto housing, fasten the cover to the housing with the 15 mounting screws.

6. Mount mode door actuator onto the cover and reconnect the linkage and vacuum line.

7. Fasten the actuator arm to mode door on all models in the reverse order of the removal. Install the retaining clips on the front edge cover.

CAUTION

When installing the evaporator unit, be sure that the vacuum lines to the engine compartment do not hang up on the accelerator, or become trapped between the assembly and dash. If the vacuum lines are kinked it will be necessary to remove the evaporator unit again to free the vacuum lines. The proper routing of the vacuum lines as the unit is positioned to the dash may require two people. The portion of the vacuum harness which is routed through the steering column support, must be positioned before the distribution housing is reinstalled. The vacuum harness is routed above the temperature control cable.

Evaporator Assembly

Installation

1982–85 CARAVELLE, 400, 600, E CLASS, NEW YORKER, RELIANT, ARIES, LEBARON, DAYTONA, LASER, LANCER

1. Place unit on the floor of the vehicle and as far forward as possible, raise the unit taking care not to catch the studs in the dash liner and at the same time pull the lower instrument panel rearward as far as possible.
2. Position the assembly into place and install the four nuts in the engine compartment which attach the unit to the dash panel.
3. Install the screw which fastens the hanger strap to the unit and reinstall the carpet.
4. Replace the right side cowl to plenum brace and install the control cable by snapping the flags back into receivers unit.
5. Install the condensate drain tube and clamp.
6. Install the defroster adapter under the dash panel and install center distribution duct.
7. Install forward console mounting bracket and console if so equipped.
8. Install the A/C heater control head, (see the Chrysler heating section).
9. Install the right scuff plate and cowl side trim panel, connect vacuum lines at engine intake manifold and at water valve.
10. Connect the heater hoses at the heater core after unplugging the lines.
11. Connect the battery fusible link and refill the cooling system.
12. Evacuate and recharge the system, check the operation of all controls and performance of the A/C system.

Installation

1982–85 HORIZON, TURISMO, OMNI, CHARGER, TC-3, MISER, 024

1. Place the unit on the floor as far forward under the instrument panel as possible, raise the unit being careful not to catch the studs on the dash liner and at the same time pull the lower instrument panel rearward as far as possible.
2. Position the assembly in place and attach mounting brace to stud, reinstall blower motor ground cable onto stud and tighten nut.
3. Reinstall panel top cover, install two mounting screws holding the lower instrument panel to the steering column.
4. Install the right instrument panel pivot bracket screw and install the right side cowl panel.
5. Install the four unit to dash panel retaining nuts and connect the vacuum lines at the engine and water valve.
6. Connect the heater hoses and A/C lines at the dash panel.
7. Install defroster duct assembly and center distribution duct.
8. Install the center bezel and glove box.
9. Connect blend air door cable and engage clip on heater air duct.
10. Connect the heater hoses to the heater core after unplugging the lines.
11. Connect the battery fusible link and refill the cooling system.
12. Evacuate and recharge the system, check operation of all controls and performance of the A/C system.

Evaporator Assembly

REAR WHEEL VEHICLES

Removal

1982–85—ALL MODELS

1. Discharge the refrigerant system completely before opening any refrigerant lines.

2. Disconnect the negative battery cable, drain the cooling system, remove air cleaner and disconnect the heater hoses. Plug the heater core tubes to prevent the coolant from spilling out.
3. Remove the clamp and the condensate tube, remove the H-valve, cap all refrigerant openings to prevent entrance of dirt or moisture.
4. Slide the Front seat rearward to allow room to remove the unit from the vehicle.
5. Remove the cluster bezel and the instrument panel upper cover.
6. Remove the steering column cover and the right intermediate side cowl trim panel.
7. Remove the lower instrument panel and instrument panel center. If vehicle is equipped with a floor console it must be removed.
8. Remove right center air distribution duct and disconnect the locking tab on the defroster duct.
9. Disconnect the blower motor resistor block wiring.
10. Disconnect vacuum lines from engine compartment water valve and vacuum source tree.
11. Remove wiring from evaporator housing, remove vacuum lines from inlet air housing and disconnect the vacuum harness coupling.
12. Remove rubber drain tube in engine compartment and remove nuts from housing mounting studs in the engine compartment.
13. Remove the hanger strap from plenum stud above evaporator package.
14. Roll evaporator package back so plumbing pipes clear dash panel and remove the unit from the vehicle.

Installation

1. Position the evaporator housing on the front floor of the vehicle under the instrument panel.
2. Place the housing up under the instrument panel and press mounting studs through dash panel being sure the defroster duct and A/C distribution duct is properly seated on unit and the gasket is seated properly.
3. Connect the locking tab on the defroster duct and while holding the housing in position, install the nut on mounting bracket, the top of the unit and the plenum stud.
4. In the engine compartment install the retaining nuts and tighten securely. Install the condensate drain tube.
5. Connect the electrical connectors to the resistor block and connect the vacuum lines in the engine compartment, making sure the rubber grommet is seated properly.
6. Connect the vacuum lines to inlet air housing and vacuum harness coupling and install the right center air distribution duct.
7. Install the instrument panel center to the lower reinforcement and install the lower instrument panel.
8. Install the right intermediate side cowl trim panel and install the steering column cover.
9. Install the instrument panel upper cover and the cluster bezel assembly.
10. Remove the plugs from the heater core tubes and connect the hoses to the core. Install the condensate tube and clamp.
11. Install the H-valve and the refrigerant lines going to the valve and replace the gaskets.
12. Refill the cooling system and inspect for leaks, install the air cleaner and connect the negative battery cable.
13. Evacuate and recharge the system, check the operation of all controls and performance of the A/C system.

Low Pressure Cut-Off Switch

1982–85—ALL VEHICLES

The low pressure cut-off switch, is located on the H-valve and is wired in series with the compressor magnetic clutch. The function of this switch is to cut off the electrical power to the clutch, when ever the refrigerant pressure drops below the control point of the switch. The switch itself, is a sealed factory calibrated unit and no attempt should be made to adjust or repair the switch. If the switch is defective the switch should be replaced.

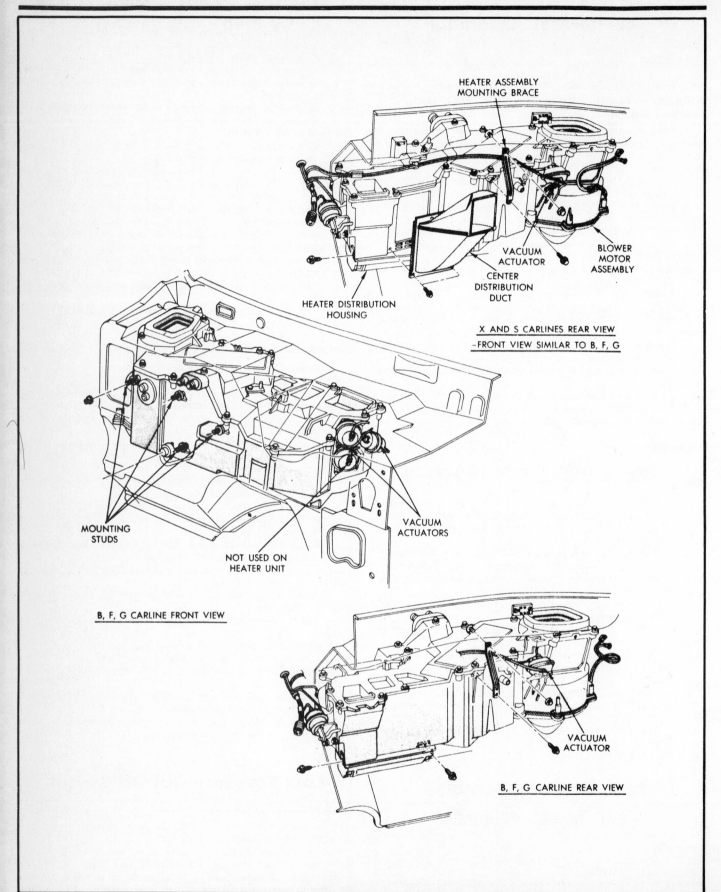

HEATER ASSEMBLY
MOUNTING BRACE

VACUUM
ACTUATOR

BLOWER
MOTOR
ASSEMBLY

CENTER
DISTRIBUTION
DUCT

HEATER DISTRIBUTION
HOUSING

X AND S CARLINES REAR VIEW

-FRONT VIEW SIMILAR TO B, F, G

MOUNTING
STUDS

VACUUM
ACTUATORS

NOT USED ON
HEATER UNIT

B, F, G CARLINE FRONT VIEW

VACUUM
ACTUATOR

B, F, G CARLINE REAR VIEW

Exploded view of the evaporator heater assemblies (© Chrysler Corporation)

Low Pressure Cut-Off Switch

TEST

1. With the engine off remove the protective rubber boot from the low pressure cut-off switch. Jump the leads together.

2. Move the control lever to the A/C position and momentarily turn the ignition switch on (do not crank over the engine), listen for the compressor clutch to engage.

3. If the clutch does not engage, the cycling switch, wiring or fuse could be defective. Check the clutch circuit and clutch.

4. If the clutch engages, connect the manifold gauge set and read the evaporator suction pressure. At any pressure of 18 psig. (125 kPag) and above, the switch must actuate the clutch.

5. If the evaporator suction pressure is below 25 psig (172 kPag), the refrigerant system is low on freon or empty due to a leak.

6. Check for refrigerant leak and recharge the system, after the system has been recharged perform step number 3 again.

7. If the clutch does not engage, discharge the system, replace the switch, and recharge the system.

High Pressure Relief Valve

This relief valve is located on the filter-drier and its function is to prevent damage to the air conditioning system, in the event that excessive pressure developes due to condensor air flow being restricted, for example; by leaves, newspaper, or an overcharge of refrigerant. The relief valve will only vent a small amount of refrigerant to reduce system pressure and then reseats itself. The relief valve is calibrated to vent at a pressure of 450 to 5550 psig (3100 to 3790 Kpag), so the fact that the valve vented refrigerant, does not mean that the valve is defective. The valve is part of the filter-drier assembly and must not be removed or disturbed.

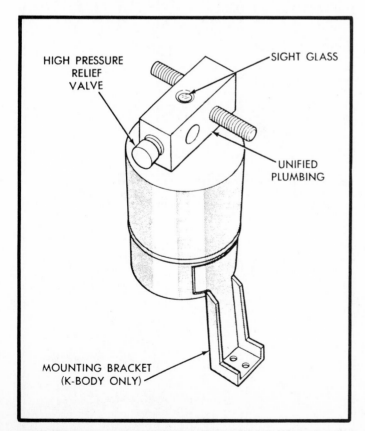

Typical filter drier (© Chrysler Corporation)

Cycling Clutch Switch

1982–85—ALL VEHICLES

The cycling switch is an on-off switch situated in series with the magnetic clutch coil. Its operation depends on the suction line temperature, which is transmitted to the cycling switch through a freon-charged capillary tube, attached to the suction line with a clamp and is insulated.

Cycling Clutch Switch

TEST

1. Remove the wires from the switch and check for continuity of the cycling clutch switch. The switch contacts are closed at temperatures above 45 deg. F. (7 deg. C.), if there is no continuity replace the switch.

2. If the contacts are closed, verify switch operations as follows:

   a. Reconnect the wires to the switch and set the control lever to the full cool position.

   b. Set the A/C blower motor on low speed and set the control lever to the A/C position.

   c. Run the engine at 1300 rpm for approximately 5 minutes to stabilize the A/C system.

   d. If the compressor clutch cycles on and off two to three times per minute with the temperature between 68 deg. to 90 deg. F (20 deg. to 32 deg. C.), the cycling switch is normal.

   e. If the compressor fails to engage, check for a short in the electrical circuit.

NOTE: When the temperature is above 90 deg. F (32 deg. C) the compressor clutch may be continuously engaged due to the high heat load; this is a normal conditon.

Removal

1. Remove the electrical wires to the switch and remove the two screws at the plumbing sealing plate.

2. Wrap a shop rag or equivalent around the capillary tube at the well opening.

3. Pull the tube out of the well while holding the rag firmly around the tube so that the grease stays in the well. Take care not to bend the tube during this procedure.

NOTE: It is important for the proper A/C performance that the grease remains in the well.

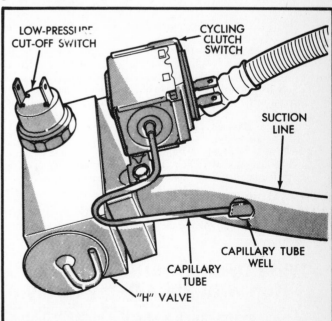

Typical cycling clutch switch (© Chrysler Corporation)

Installation

1. Insert the capillary tube into the grease filled well.
2. Attach the cycling clutch switch to the refrigerant plumbing plate with two screws and torque the screws to 15 to 20 in. lbs. (1.7 to 2.3 Nm).
3. Reconnect the wires and check the operation of the switch.

Anti-Diesel Relay

1982 (1983—1.7 L ENGINE) ALL FRONT WHEEL VEHICLES

The anti-diesel relay energizes the air conditioning clutch for 4–20 seconds after the ignition is turned off. This puts a load on the engine and prevents any dieseling that might occur. The relay is located on the evaporator heater housing on the 1982 TC-3, Miser, Horizon, Turismo, 024, and the Charger 2.2. On all the other 1982 FWD vehicles the relay is located in the engine compartment. The relay is located in the engine compartment on the 1983 1.7 liter engine also.

TEST

1. Remove mounting screw from the relay and remove the relay from the vehicle.
2. Connect a 12 volt test light to terminals 1 and 5 and leave terminal 2 open.
3. Apply 12 volts to terminals 3 and 4 and ground terminal 5.
4. Place a 60 ohm carbon resistor between terminal 4 and ground.
5. Apply 12 volts to terminal 2 and the test light should come on.
6. Remove the 12 volts from terminal 2 and the test light should go out.
7. Remove the 12 volts from terminal 4 and the test light should come on and stay on for 5 to 12 seconds, then time out.

Wide Open Throttle Cut-Out Switch

1982–83 1.7 AND 2.2 LITER ENGINES

The function of this switch is to open the A/C clutch circuit when the carburetor throttle is 10 degrees before wide open. This switch is mounted on the carburetor.

TEST

1. Disconnect the wire going to the wide open throttle cut-out switch.
2. Making sure the throttle is in the closed position, check the continuity of the switch with an ohmmeter or a continuity tester. If there is no continuity, replace the switch.
3. Place the throttle in the position of 10 degrees before wide open, and bring up to the wide open position, check the continuity of the switch.
4. If there is continuity, push the actuator arm with a suitable tool and check the continuity.
5. If there is no continuity adjust the switch so that the circuit is wide open in the throttle position of 10 degrees before wide open, to wide open. If continuity still is present, replace the switch.

SWITCH ADJUSTMENT

1. Loosen the mounting screws and move the switch so that the A/C circuit is open with the throttle position 10 degrees before wide open throttle.

Wide Open Throttle Cut-Out Switch with Time Delay Relay

1984–85 SHELBY CHARGER ONLY

NOTE: This wide open throttle cut-out switch is the same as the one used in the 1982–83 vehicles. The test and the adjustment for the switch is also the same as the 1982–83 vehicles. The major difference in the two switches is the time delay relay in the 1984–85 Shelby Charger models. The job of the time delay relay is to prevent the A/C clutch from re-engaging for 4 to 8 seconds after a wide open throttle is released.

Time Delay Relay

TEST

1. Be sure that the wide open throttle cut-out switch is operating properly.
2. With the key in the on position, the A/C on and the engine not running, open the throttle wide and hold it for at least 5 seconds.
3. Close the throttle and note the time delay until the A/C clutch re-engages. It should be 3 to 9 seconds.
4. If there is no delay or excessively long delay, replace the relay.

WIDE OPEN THROTTLE CUT-OUT RELAY

Turbo Automatic

1984–85

The wide open throttle cut-out relay opens the A/C clutch circuit when the throttle position sensor, senses a wide open throttle condition. The A/C clutch will not re-engage until the engine speed drops below 4000 rpm.

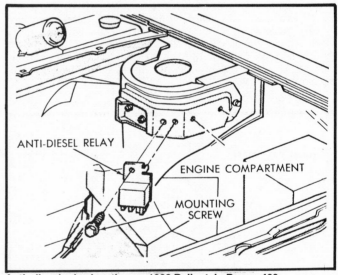

Anti–diesel relay location on 1982 Reliant, LeBaron, 400, Aries and 1983 1.7 liter engine (© Chrysler Corporation)

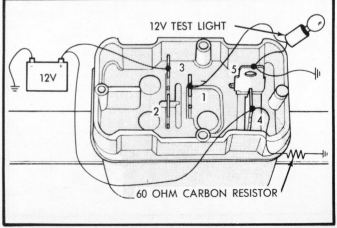

Anti–diesel relay test (© Chrysler Corporation)

Semi-Automatic Temperature Control (SATC)

1982–85—ALL REAR WHEEL VEHICLES

The SATC system is designed to maintain a selected temperature level, and also allows for a selection from among the various modes of temperature regulating operations. This system of temperature control is functional in all modes and blower speed combinations except for Max-

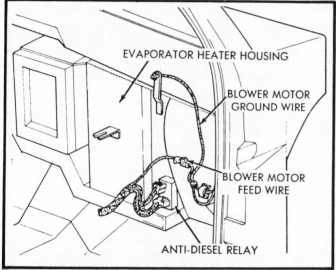

Anti–diesel relay location on 1982 Horizon, E–Type, TC–3, Miser, 024 (© Chrysler Corporation)

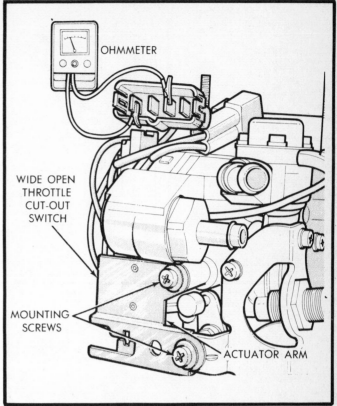

Typical wide open throttle cut–out switch (© Chrysler Corporation)

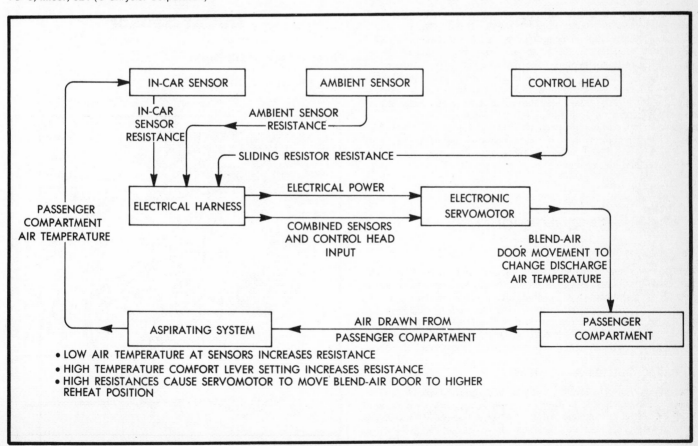

- LOW AIR TEMPERATURE AT SENSORS INCREASES RESISTANCE
- HIGH TEMPERATURE COMFORT LEVER SETTING INCREASES RESISTANCE
- HIGH RESISTANCES CAUSE SERVOMOTOR TO MOVE BLEND-AIR DOOR TO HIGHER REHEAT POSITION

Control system component relationship (© Chrysler Corporation)

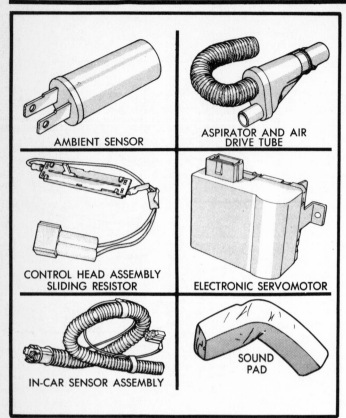

SATC components (© Chrysler Corporation)

A/C. In the Max-A/C position the water valve is closed thereby restricting the flow of engine coolant to the heater core. The result is a reduction in temperature in the heater core. A combination of controlled temperature reduction in the heater core and recirculated inside air allows for maximum cooling. The SATC controls, situated on the instrument panel, consists of a temperature control lever, a pushbutton mode switch, and a 4 speed blower switch. Operations of the temperature control lever is transmitted through a cable to an operating arm on the SATC control head sliding resistor. Mode selection is accomplished through pushbutton operated vacuum and electric switches. The vacuum switch controls the water valve operation and the positions all doors except the blend air door. The electrical switch controls the compressor and blower motor.

SATC COMPONENTS

In Car Sensor

This sensor assembly is connected to the aspirator suction nipple and the instrument panel. Air from the passenger compartment is drawn through the instrument panel opening past a temperature sensing thermistor located in the sensor assembly. The electrical resistance of the thermistor increases when in car air temperature decreases. The electrical resistance decreases when the in car temperature increases, this reaction enables the system to detect the in car temperature changes.

Ambient (Outside Air) Sensor

The ambient sensor is located inside the rear surface of the evaporator heater assembly. Outside air is drawn into the ventilation system plenum, is blown across the ambient sensor. The sensor's electrical resistance increases when ambient air temperature decreases and decreases when temperature increases, this reaction allows the system to detect the outside air temperature.

Electrical Harness

The SATC system is equipped with a special electrical harness to supply power to the systems components. This harness is mounted on the evaporator heater assembly.

Sound Pad

The sound pad is a plastic covered, bar shaped, sound absorbing pad that is wrapped around the servo motor. The job of this sound pad, is to act as a sound barrier which reduces the noise emitted by the servomotor.

Aspirator and Air Drive Tube

The aspirator is located on the rear surface of the blower motor housing. Pressurized air from the housing is fed through the air drive tube to the aspirator and the evaporator heater assembly. The air passing through the aspirator creates a slight vacuum which draws the air from the passenger compartment through the in-car sensor assembly.

Comfort Control Sliding Resistor

The resistor is mounted on the control head assembly and is mechanically linked to the control lever. The resistor electrical resistance increases when the lever is moved to the right or the high temperature settings. Moving the control lever to the left will decrease resistance. This control allows the user to select a desired comfort level.

Electronic Servo Motor

This servo motor is located on the evaporator heater assembly above the blend air door shaft. The function of this servo motor is to measure the resistance of the sensors and the control head resistor and moves the blend air door to a position which relates to a certain electrical resistance. High sensor or control head resistor resistances cause the servo motor to move the blend air door to a higher (more heat) position.

In-Car Sensor

Removal and Installation

1982–85—ALL VEHICLES

1. Remove the glovebox and disconnect the in car sensor assembly

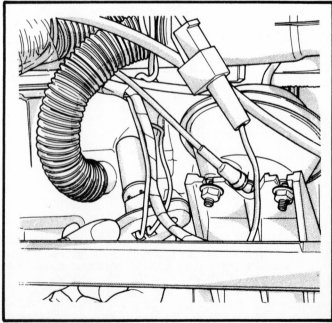

Removal and installation of the ambient sensor (© Chrysler Corporation)

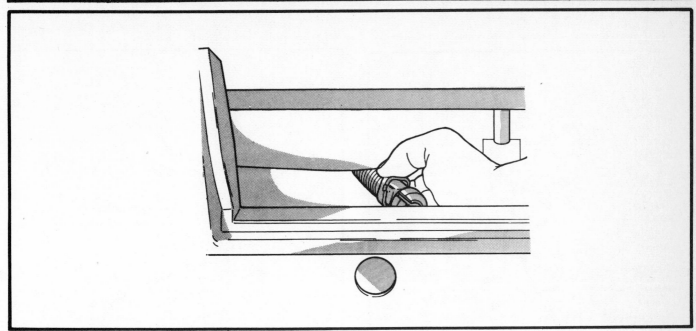

In–car sensor removal (© Chrysler Corporation)

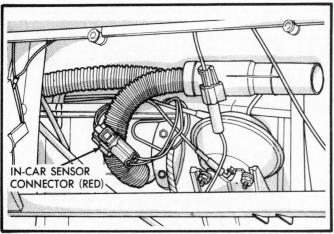

IN-CAR SENSOR
CONNECTOR (RED)

Installation of the aspirator (© Chrysler Corporation)

from instruction panel by pulling and slowly rotating the sensor assembly plastic housing to unsnap it from the panel.

NOTE: Do not pull on the tube to remove the sensor.

2. Disconnect the in-car sensor assembly from the aspirator tube.
3. Separate the sensor wiring connector from the harness connector and remove the sensor.
4. The installation is the reverse order of the removal procedure.

Ambient Sensor

Removal and Installation

1982–85—ALL VEHICLES
1. Remove the glovebox and the two mounting screws holding the ambient sensor socket in place.
2. Pull the socket and the ambient sensor out of the heater-A/C housing.
3. If the sensor pulls out of the socket and falls inside, remove the blower scroll assembly for retrieval.
4. Installation is the reverse order of the removal procedure.

Sound Pad

Removal and Installation

1982–85—ALL VEHICLES
1. Remove the right side distribution duct.
2. Remove the sound pad.
3. Installation is the reverse order of the removal procedure.

NOTE: When installing the sound pad, carefully wrap the material around the servo motor so that open gaps are not formed which allows sound to radiate past the pad.

Aspirator Assembly

Removal and Installation

1982–85—ALL VEHICLES
1. Remove the glovebox and slide the air drive tube off of the aspirator air drive nipple.
2. Slide the in-car sensor tube off of the aspirator suction nipple.
3. Remove the air recirculation door actuator, to gain access to the aspirator mounting screws.
4. Remove mounting screws and aspirator.
5. Installation is the reverse order of the removal procedure.

Control Sliding Resistor

Removal and Installation

1982–85—ALL VEHICLES
1. Remove the instrument panel center bezel and remove the control head mounting screws.
2. Pull the control assembly out of the dash panel towards the rear of the vehicle and disconnect it from the wiring harness.
3. Depress the comfort lever retaining clip and remove it. Lower the retaining pin and slide the lever away from the resistor.

4. Straighten the mounting tabs and remove the resistor from the control.

5. Installation is the reverse order of the removal procedure.

4. Install the mounting screw, wiring harness and sound pad.

5. Check the operation of the assembly and install the air distribution duct or instrument panel components.

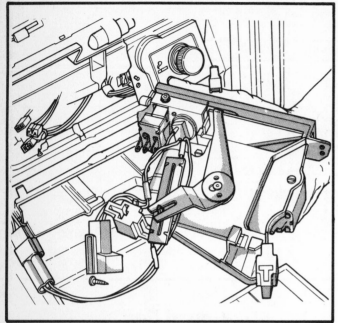

Control head sliding resistor removal (© Chrysler Corporation)

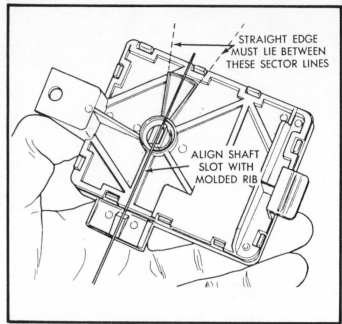

Servo motor shaft alignment (© Chrysler Corporation)

Electronic Servo Motor

Removal

1982–85—ALL VEHICLES

1. Remove the right side air distribution duct and remove the sound pad.

2. Separate the wiring harness connector from the servo motor and remove the servo motor mounting screws.

3. Rotate the servo motor until the forward tab on the motor housing clears the retaining clip on the heater-A/C unit cover.

4. Lift the servo motor off of the blend air door shaft and remove it from the vehicle.

Installation

NOTE: Before installing the servo motor, be sure that the shaft is properly positioned by checking the alignment of the shaft flats. When using a straight edge held against the shaft flat side, the straight edge should lie within the molded sector lines so the motor can be installed. It may be necessary to move the motor shaft to the proper position using the procedure described in the servo motor test section.

1. Align the key on the end of the blend air door shaft with the slot in the motor shaft.

2. Gently, press down on the servo motor until both motor housing legs touch the heater-A/C unit cover. The two shafts should engage without need for excessive force.

NOTE: If there is a need for excessive force to install the servo motor, check the length of the blend air door shaft. The shaft should extend less than one inch above the A/C heater unit. Repair the shaft if necessary and too much excessive force can damage the servo motor.

3. After the blend air and the servo motor shafts are engaged, rotate the motor until the tab fits under the retaining clip and the mounting screw holes align.

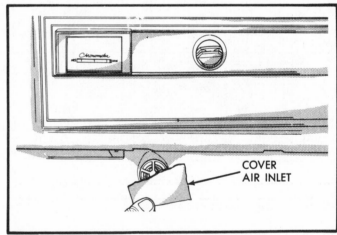

Aspirator paper test (© Chrysler Corporation)

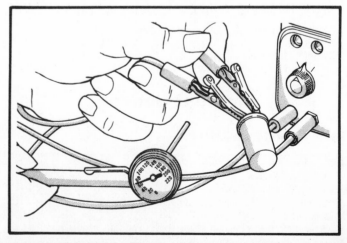

Ambient sensor test (© Chrysler Corporation)

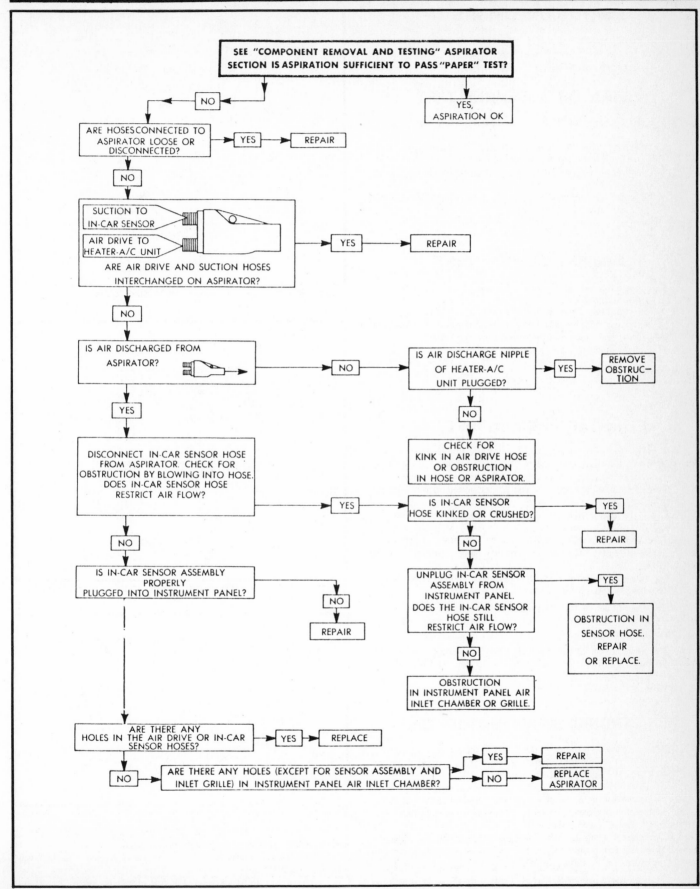

SEE "COMPONENT REMOVAL AND TESTING" ASPIRATOR SECTION IS ASPIRATION SUFFICIENT TO PASS "PAPER" TEST?

— NO →

YES, ASPIRATION OK

ARE HOSES CONNECTED TO ASPIRATOR LOOSE OR DISCONNECTED? — YES → REPAIR

NO

SUCTION TO IN-CAR SENSOR

AIR DRIVE TO HEATER-A/C UNIT

ARE AIR DRIVE AND SUCTION HOSES INTERCHANGED ON ASPIRATOR? — YES → REPAIR

NO

IS AIR DISCHARGED FROM ASPIRATOR? — NO → IS AIR DISCHARGE NIPPLE OF HEATER-A/C UNIT PLUGGED? — YES → REMOVE OBSTRUCTION

YES

NO

DISCONNECT IN-CAR SENSOR HOSE FROM ASPIRATOR. CHECK FOR OBSTRUCTION BY BLOWING INTO HOSE. DOES IN-CAR SENSOR HOSE RESTRICT AIR FLOW?

CHECK FOR KINK IN AIR DRIVE HOSE OR OBSTRUCTION IN HOSE OR ASPIRATOR.

— YES → IS IN-CAR SENSOR HOSE KINKED OR CRUSHED? — YES → REPAIR

NO

NO

IS IN-CAR SENSOR ASSEMBLY PROPERLY PLUGGED INTO INSTRUMENT PANEL? — NO → REPAIR

UNPLUG IN-CAR SENSOR ASSEMBLY FROM INSTRUMENT PANEL. DOES THE IN-CAR SENSOR HOSE STILL RESTRICT AIR FLOW? — YES → OBSTRUCTION IN SENSOR HOSE. REPAIR OR REPLACE.

NO

OBSTRUCTION IN INSTRUMENT PANEL AIR INLET CHAMBER OR GRILLE.

ARE THERE ANY HOLES IN THE AIR DRIVE OR IN-CAR SENSOR HOSES? — YES → REPLACE

NO → ARE THERE ANY HOLES (EXCEPT FOR SENSOR ASSEMBLY AND INLET GRILLE) IN INSTRUMENT PANEL AIR INLET CHAMBER? — YES → REPAIR

— NO → REPLACE ASPIRATOR

Aspirator system diagnosis (© Chrysler Corporation)

SATC COMPONENTS

Test

1982–85—ALL REAR WHEEL VEHICLES

ASPIRATOR ASSEMBLY TEST

1. Set the controls for high blower speed in the heat mode of operation.
2. Completely cover the air inlet to the in-car sensor with a piece of paper big enough to cover the air inlet.
3. The aspirator system suction should hold the paper against the air inlet grille.
4. If the paper does not stay in place, check the system as described in the aspirator system diagnosis chart.

AMBIENT SENSOR TEST

1. Pull the ambient sensor out of the socket and measure its resistance at room temperature.
2. Do not hold the sensor with the bare hand or apply a meter test for more than 5 seconds, because body heat and ohmmeter current both affect the sensor resistance and measurement of accuracy.
3. The ambient sensor resistance should read between 225 and 335 ohms, with the room temperature between 70 deg. and 80 deg. F. (21 deg. and 27 deg. C.).

IN-CAR SENSOR TEST

1. Remove the glovebox and disconnect the in-car sensor wiring connector from the harness connector. Be sure not to disconnect the aspirator tubes or remove the sensor from the instrument panel.
2. Perform the aspirator paper test as performed in the aspirator sensor test.
3. Place the entire stem of a test thermometer into the air inlet grille near the in-car sensor.
4. Set the blower motor speed on the second notch, depress and then pull out the Max-A/C button to turn off compressor and close the water valve.
5. Operate the blower and connect ohmmeter leads to sensor wiring terminals, quickly measure the in-car sensor resistance.

NOTE: Do not leave the ohmmeter connected for more than 5 seconds, because the ohmmeter current can affect resistance, and measurement accuracy.

6. Resistance of the in-car sensor should be between 1100 and 1800 ohms when the thermometer reads between 70 deg. and 80 deg. (21 deg. and 27 deg. C.).

ELECTRONIC SERVO MOTOR TEST

1. Remove the servo motor as described in the removal procedure.
2. Using a blend air door operating crank from a manual heater-A/C unit, check the door for free movement.
3. Using a fully charged 12 volt battery, two test leads one positive and one negative and an ambient sensor, the positive lead should have a series connected instrument panel lamp to indicate current flow. Just use a plain wire for the negative lead.
4. Once the test leads are connected, the motor should run smoothly and the test lamp will glow dimly as the shaft turns and brightens when the internal stops of the motor are reached.

NOTE: The test lamp will also glow brightly if the motor jams between stops.

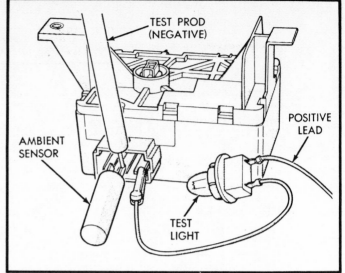

Connection to turn the servo motor shaft clockwise
(© Chrysler Corporation)

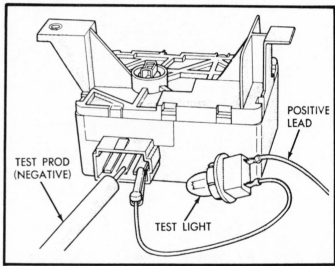

Connection to turn the servo motor shaft counterclockwise
(© Chrysler Corporation)

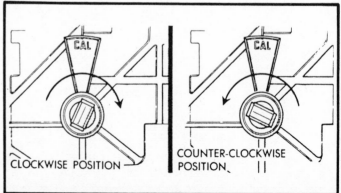

Full travel position of the servo motor shaft (© Chrysler Corporation)

5. If the motor shaft does not turn, check the battery connections and check to see if all the connections are secure.
6. Check the ambient sensor if the motor only moves to the counterclockwise position.
7. The motor must move to the full clockwise position and full counterclockwise position, to be acceptable.

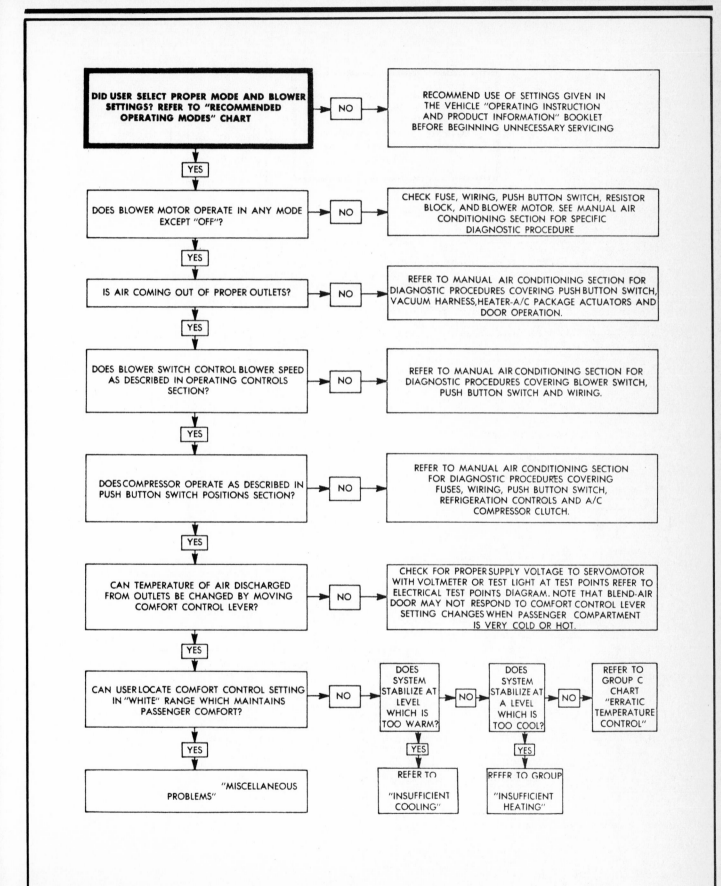

DID USER SELECT PROPER MODE AND BLOWER SETTINGS? REFER TO "RECOMMENDED OPERATING MODES" CHART — NO → RECOMMEND USE OF SETTINGS GIVEN IN THE VEHICLE "OPERATING INSTRUCTION AND PRODUCT INFORMATION" BOOKLET BEFORE BEGINNING UNNECESSARY SERVICING

YES ↓

DOES BLOWER MOTOR OPERATE IN ANY MODE EXCEPT "OFF"? — NO → CHECK FUSE, WIRING, PUSH BUTTON SWITCH, RESISTOR BLOCK, AND BLOWER MOTOR. SEE MANUAL AIR CONDITIONING SECTION FOR SPECIFIC DIAGNOSTIC PROCEDURE

YES ↓

IS AIR COMING OUT OF PROPER OUTLETS? — NO → REFER TO MANUAL AIR CONDITIONING SECTION FOR DIAGNOSTIC PROCEDURES COVERING PUSH BUTTON SWITCH, VACUUM HARNESS, HEATER-A/C PACKAGE ACTUATORS AND DOOR OPERATION.

YES ↓

DOES BLOWER SWITCH CONTROL BLOWER SPEED AS DESCRIBED IN OPERATING CONTROLS SECTION? — NO → REFER TO MANUAL AIR CONDITIONING SECTION FOR DIAGNOSTIC PROCEDURES COVERING BLOWER SWITCH, PUSH BUTTON SWITCH AND WIRING.

YES ↓

DOES COMPRESSOR OPERATE AS DESCRIBED IN PUSH BUTTON SWITCH POSITIONS SECTION? — NO → REFER TO MANUAL AIR CONDITIONING SECTION FOR DIAGNOSTIC PROCEDURES COVERING FUSES, WIRING, PUSH BUTTON SWITCH, REFRIGERATION CONTROLS AND A/C COMPRESSOR CLUTCH.

YES ↓

CAN TEMPERATURE OF AIR DISCHARGED FROM OUTLETS BE CHANGED BY MOVING COMFORT CONTROL LEVER? — NO → CHECK FOR PROPER SUPPLY VOLTAGE TO SERVOMOTOR WITH VOLTMETER OR TEST LIGHT AT TEST POINTS REFER TO ELECTRICAL TEST POINTS DIAGRAM. NOTE THAT BLEND-AIR DOOR MAY NOT RESPOND TO COMFORT CONTROL LEVER SETTING CHANGES WHEN PASSENGER COMPARTMENT IS VERY COLD OR HOT.

YES ↓

CAN USER LOCATE COMFORT CONTROL SETTING IN "WHITE" RANGE WHICH MAINTAINS PASSENGER COMFORT? — NO → DOES SYSTEM STABILIZE AT LEVEL WHICH IS TOO WARM? — NO → DOES SYSTEM STABILIZE AT A LEVEL WHICH IS TOO COOL? — NO → REFER TO GROUP C CHART "ERRATIC TEMPERATURE CONTROL"

YES ↓   YES ↓ (too warm)   YES ↓ (too cool)

"MISCELLANEOUS PROBLEMS"   REFER TO "INSUFFICIENT COOLING"   REFER TO GROUP "INSUFFICIENT HEATING"

General diagnosis (© Chrysler Corporation)

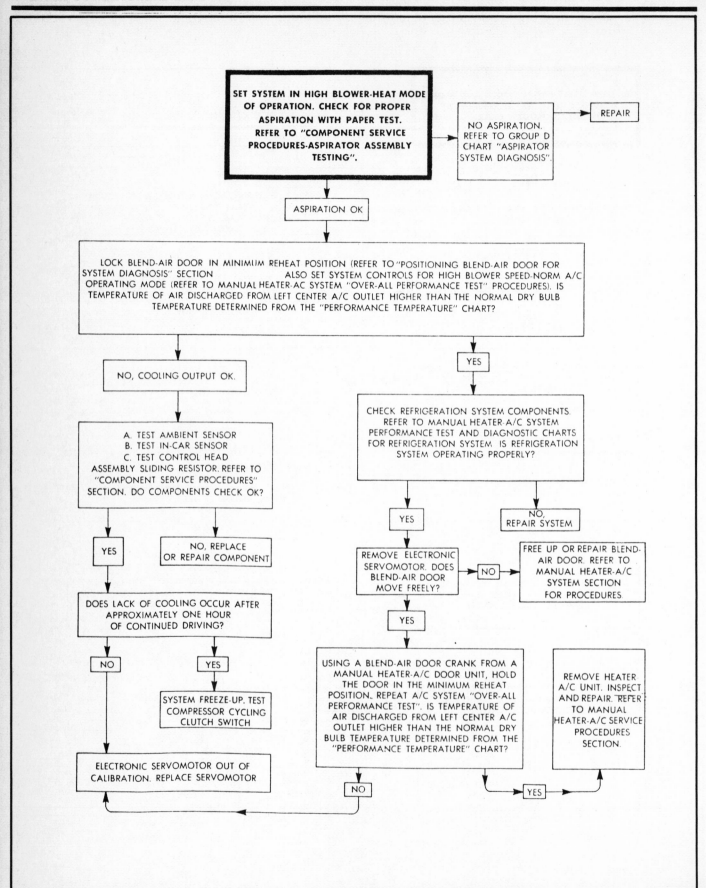

Insufficient cooling diagnosis (© Chrysler Corporation)

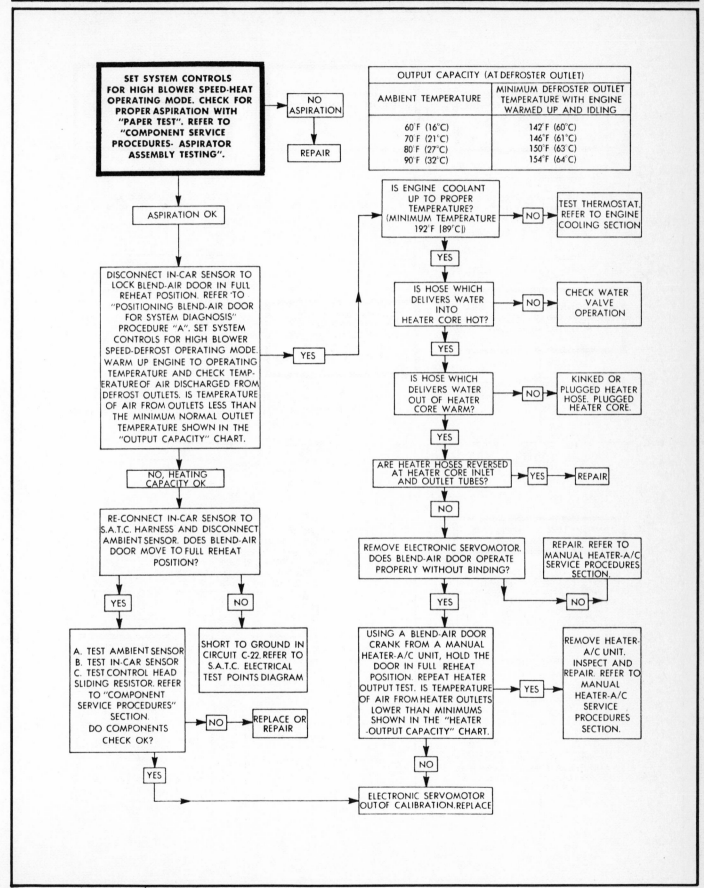

OUTPUT CAPACITY (AT DEFROSTER OUTLET)	
AMBIENT TEMPERATURE	MINIMUM DEFROSTER OUTLET TEMPERATURE WITH ENGINE WARMED UP AND IDLING
60°F (16°C)	142°F (60°C)
70°F (21°C)	146°F (61°C)
80°F (27°C)	150°F (63°C)
90°F (32°C)	154°F (64°C)

SET SYSTEM CONTROLS FOR HIGH BLOWER SPEED-HEAT OPERATING MODE. CHECK FOR PROPER ASPIRATION WITH "PAPER TEST". REFER TO "COMPONENT SERVICE PROCEDURES- ASPIRATOR ASSEMBLY TESTING".

NO ASPIRATION → REPAIR

ASPIRATION OK

DISCONNECT IN-CAR SENSOR TO LOCK BLEND-AIR DOOR IN FULL REHEAT POSITION. REFER TO "POSITIONING BLEND-AIR DOOR FOR SYSTEM DIAGNOSIS" PROCEDURE "A". SET SYSTEM CONTROLS FOR HIGH BLOWER SPEED-DEFROST OPERATING MODE. WARM UP ENGINE TO OPERATING TEMPERATURE AND CHECK TEMPERATURE OF AIR DISCHARGED FROM DEFROST OUTLETS. IS TEMPERATURE OF AIR FROM OUTLETS LESS THAN THE MINIMUM NORMAL OUTLET TEMPERATURE SHOWN IN THE "OUTPUT CAPACITY" CHART.

YES

IS ENGINE COOLANT UP TO PROPER TEMPERATURE? (MINIMUM TEMPERATURE 192°F [89°C]) — NO → TEST THERMOSTAT. REFER TO ENGINE COOLING SECTION

YES

IS HOSE WHICH DELIVERS WATER INTO HEATER CORE HOT? — NO → CHECK WATER VALVE OPERATION

YES

IS HOSE WHICH DELIVERS WATER OUT OF HEATER CORE WARM? — NO → KINKED OR PLUGGED HEATER HOSE. PLUGGED HEATER CORE.

YES

ARE HEATER HOSES REVERSED AT HEATER CORE INLET AND OUTLET TUBES? — YES → REPAIR

NO, HEATING CAPACITY OK

NO

RE-CONNECT IN-CAR SENSOR TO S.A.T.C. HARNESS AND DISCONNECT AMBIENT SENSOR. DOES BLEND-AIR DOOR MOVE TO FULL REHEAT POSITION?

REMOVE ELECTRONIC SERVOMOTOR. DOES BLEND-AIR DOOR OPERATE PROPERLY WITHOUT BINDING? — NO → REPAIR. REFER TO MANUAL HEATER-A/C SERVICE PROCEDURES SECTION.

YES

YES / NO

A. TEST AMBIENT SENSOR
B. TEST IN-CAR SENSOR
C. TEST CONTROL HEAD SLIDING RESISTOR. REFER TO "COMPONENT SERVICE PROCEDURES" SECTION.
DO COMPONENTS CHECK OK?

SHORT TO GROUND IN CIRCUIT C-22. REFER TO S.A.T.C. ELECTRICAL TEST POINTS DIAGRAM

NO → REPLACE OR REPAIR

YES

USING A BLEND-AIR DOOR CRANK FROM A MANUAL HEATER-A/C UNIT, HOLD THE DOOR IN FULL REHEAT POSITION. REPEAT HEATER OUTPUT TEST. IS TEMPERATURE OF AIR FROM HEATER OUTLETS LOWER THAN MINIMUMS SHOWN IN THE "HEATER -OUTPUT CAPACITY" CHART. — YES → REMOVE HEATER-A/C UNIT. INSPECT AND REPAIR. REFER TO MANUAL HEATER-A/C SERVICE PROCEDURES SECTION.

NO

ELECTRONIC SERVOMOTOR OUT OF CALIBRATION. REPLACE

Insufficient heating diagnosis (© Chrysler Corporation)

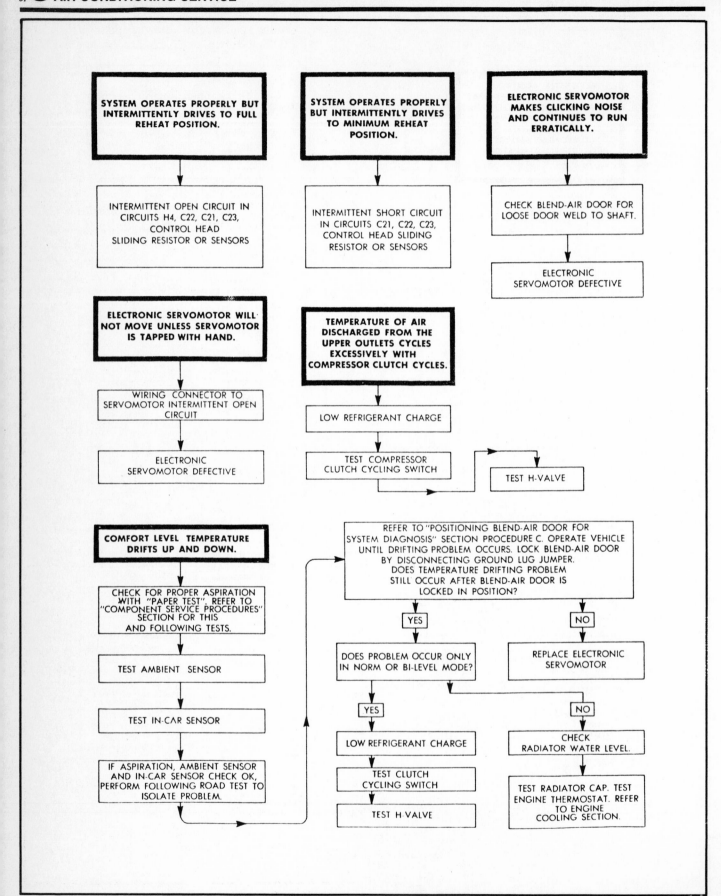

Erratic temperature control diagnosis (© Chrysler Corporation)

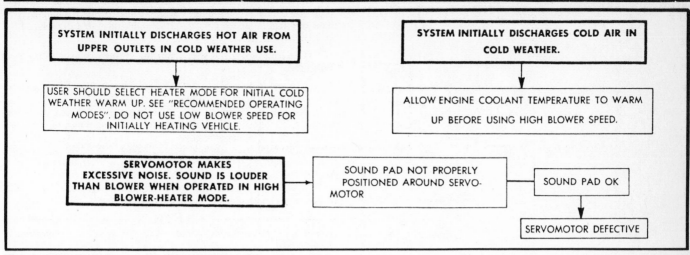

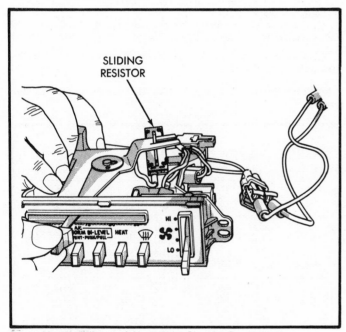

CONTROL SLIDING RESISTOR TEST

1. Attach ohmmeter leads to resistor connector terminals, position the comfort control lever at the 65 digit setting. The resistance reading should be less than 390 ohms.

2. Slowly move the control lever toward the right until the ohmmeter reads 930 ohms.

3. The reading should increase smoothly and the control lever should be near the 75 digit reading.

4. Move the comfort lever to the extreme right at the 85 digit reading, the resistance should increase smoothly to at least 1500 ohms.

SATC SYSTEM DIAGNOSIS

The blend air door may need to be set in one of three different positions, in order to diagnosis the system. When locking the door in the full and minimum positions, set the controls for low blower speed and bi-level mode of operation.

1. To set the blend air door in the full reheat position, disconnect the in-car sensor from the wiring harness and switch on the system.

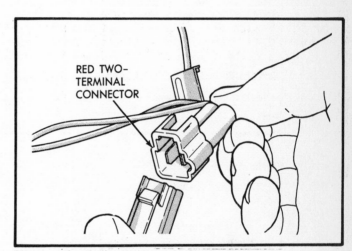

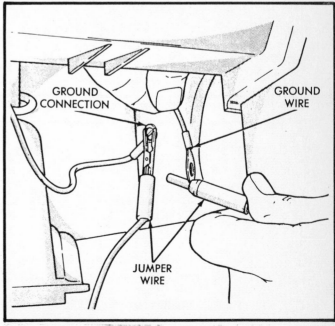

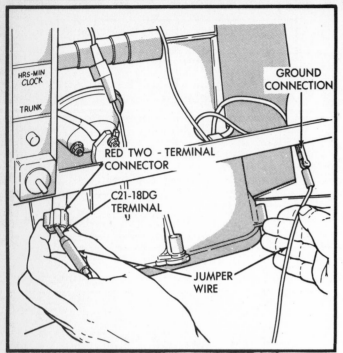

Setting the blend air door to the minimum reheat position in order to test the SATC system (© Chrysler Corporation)

2. To obtain the minimum reheat position connect a jumper wire to the terminal in the red connector that holds the wire from the control head sliding resistor.

NOTE: Do not use the wire from the ambient sensor to the red connector.

3. Ground to the other end of the jumper wire at the harness ground connection. Switch on the system.

4. To set the blend air door in between the full and minimum positions, disconnect the negative battery cable and remove the ground screw on the passenger side cowl.

5. Take the harness ground wire (18 gauge black wire with tracer) from the ground screw and reconnect the blower ground wire to the cowl.

6. Connect a jumper lead from the harness ground to any good body ground and reconnect the battery ground cable.

─── CAUTION ───
Do not apply power to the system when the blower motor ground is disconnected.

7. Move the temperature control lever to operate the servo motor until the blend air door moves to the desired mid position and disconnect the harness ground jumper.

8. The door will remain in this position until the harness ground lead is reconnected to the cowl ground screw.

NOTE: These blend air door positions may be called for in the troubleshooting charts.

NOTE: Refer to the heater section for control head and cable removal.

Garage Ambient Temperature	70°F (21°C)	80°F (26.5°C)	90°F (32°C)	100°F (37.5°C)	110°F (43°C)
Discharge Air Temperature	38-48°F (3-9°C)	38-48°F (3-9°C)	40-50°F (4-10°C)	46-56°F (8-13°C)	54-60°F (12-16°C)
Compressor Discharge Pressure	140 180 psig / 965 1241 kPag	170 210 psig / 1172 1448 kPag	200 240 psig / 1379 1655 kPag	220 260 psig / 1517 1792 kPag	250 290 psig / 1724 2000 kPag
Evaporator Suction Pressure	10 17 psig / 69 117 kPag	12 22 psig / 83 152 kPag	17 27 psig / 117 186 kPag	22 32 psig / 152 221 kPag	26 36 psig / 179 248 kPag

Performance temperature chart for, Gran Fury, Caravelle, New Yorker, Fifth Avenue, Newport, Diplomat (© Chrysler Corporation)

PUSH BUTTON	OFF	A/C MAX	A/C NORM	A/C BI-LEVEL	HEAT	DEFROST
Inlet Air Door (Open to)	Inside	Inside	Outside	Outside	Outside	Outside
Heat-Defrost Door (Open to)	Heat	Heat	Heat	Heat	Heat	Defrost
Upper Bi-Lev Door (Open to)	Bi-Lev-A/C	Bi-Lev-A/C	Bi-Lev-A/C	Bi-Lev-A/C	Heat	Heat
Lower Bi-Lev Door (Open to)	A/C	A/C	A/C	Bi-Lev/Heat	Bi-Lev/Heat	Bi-Lev-Heat
Compressor Clutch	Off	On	On*	On*	Off	On**
Blower	Off	On	On	On	On	On
Water Valve	Off	Off	On	On	On	On

* Pulling out NORM button provides VENT mode with refrigeration off. BI-LEVEL button pull-out works same way.
** Pulling out DEF button provides DEFROST mode with refrigeration off.

Temperature control chart (© Chrysler Corporation)

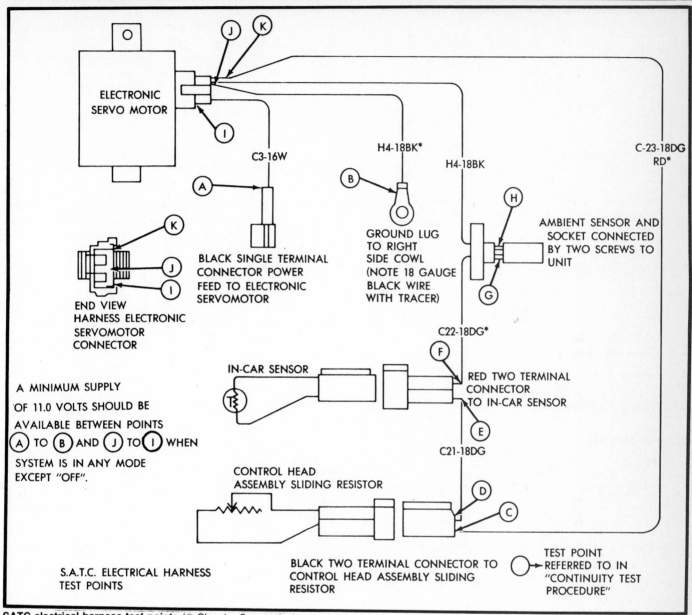

SATC electrical harness test points (© Chrysler Corporation)

ELECTRONIC SERVO MOTOR

C3-16W

BLACK SINGLE TERMINAL CONNECTOR POWER FEED TO ELECTRONIC SERVOMOTOR

END VIEW HARNESS ELECTRONIC SERVOMOTOR CONNECTOR

H4-18BK*

H4-18BK

GROUND LUG TO RIGHT SIDE COWL (NOTE 18 GAUGE BLACK WIRE WITH TRACER)

C-23-18DG RD*

AMBIENT SENSOR AND SOCKET CONNECTED BY TWO SCREWS TO UNIT

A MINIMUM SUPPLY OF 11.0 VOLTS SHOULD BE AVAILABLE BETWEEN POINTS Ⓐ TO Ⓑ AND Ⓙ TO Ⓘ WHEN SYSTEM IS IN ANY MODE EXCEPT "OFF".

IN-CAR SENSOR

C22-18DG*

RED TWO TERMINAL CONNECTOR TO IN-CAR SENSOR

C21-18DG

CONTROL HEAD ASSEMBLY SLIDING RESISTOR

S.A.T.C. ELECTRICAL HARNESS TEST POINTS

BLACK TWO TERMINAL CONNECTOR TO CONTROL HEAD ASSEMBLY SLIDING RESISTOR

TEST POINT REFERRED TO IN "CONTINUITY TEST PROCEDURE"

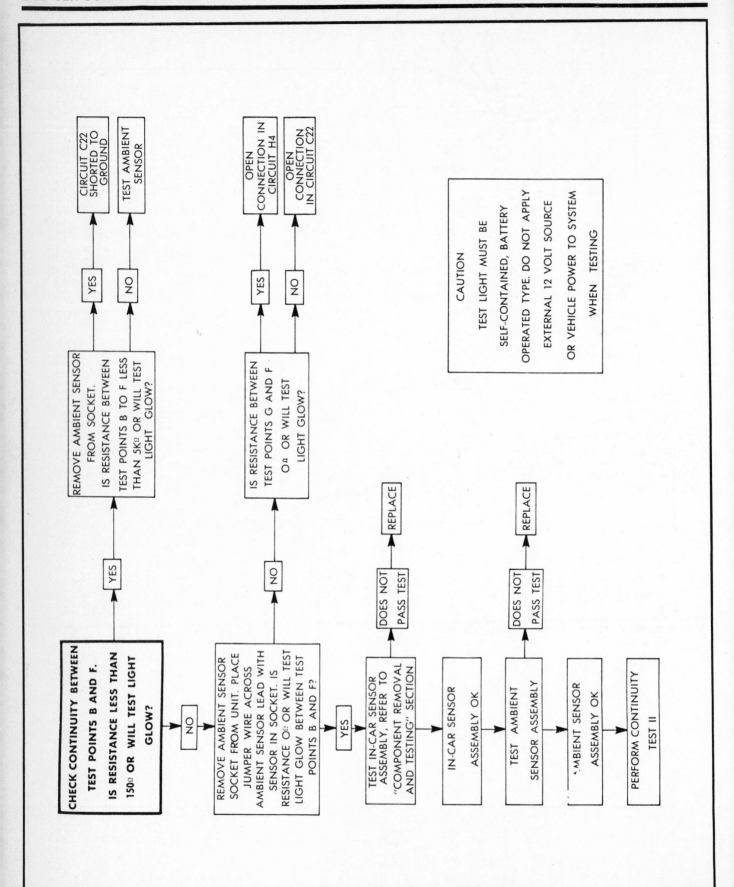

SATC system continuity test procedure no. #1 (© Chrysler Corporation)

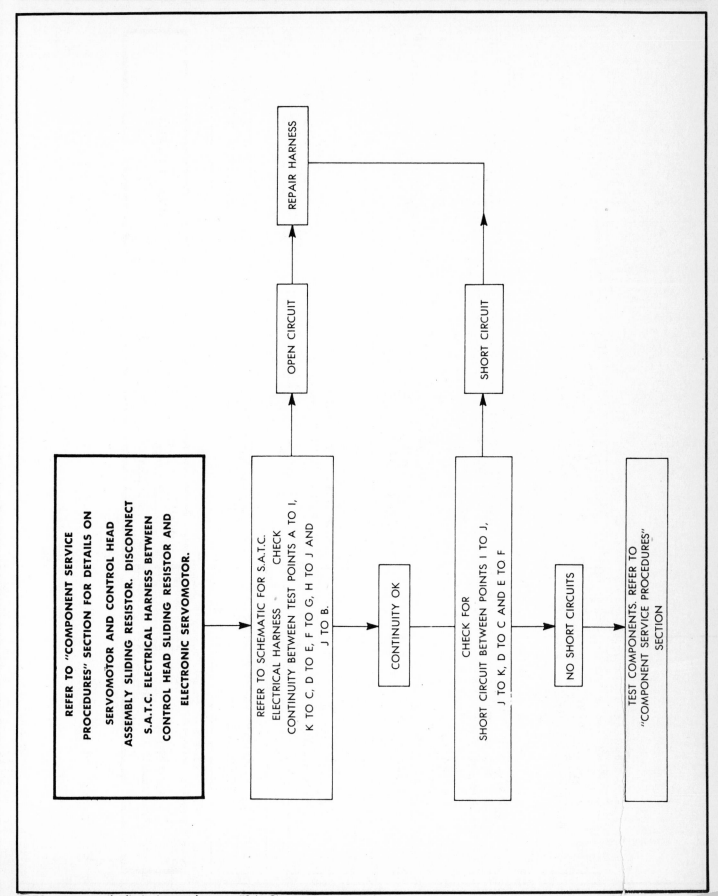

SATC system continuity test procedure no. #2 (© Chrysler Corporation)

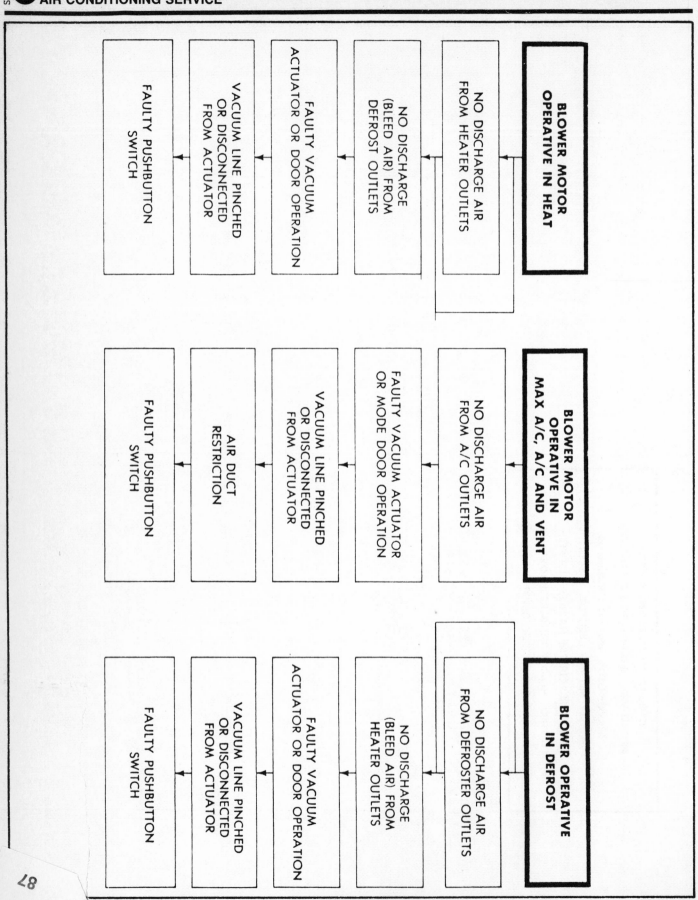

BLOWER MOTOR OPERATIVE IN HEAT

→ NO DISCHARGE AIR FROM HEATER OUTLETS → NO DISCHARGE (BLEED AIR) FROM DEFROST OUTLETS → FAULTY VACUUM ACTUATOR OR DOOR OPERATION → VACUUM LINE PINCHED OR DISCONNECTED FROM ACTUATOR → FAULTY PUSHBUTTON SWITCH

BLOWER MOTOR OPERATIVE IN MAX A/C, A/C AND VENT

→ NO DISCHARGE AIR FROM A/C OUTLETS → FAULTY VACUUM ACTUATOR OR MODE DOOR OPERATION → VACUUM LINE PINCHED OR DISCONNECTED FROM ACTUATOR → AIR DUCT RESTRICTION → FAULTY PUSHBUTTON SWITCH

BLOWER OPERATIVE IN DEFROST

→ NO DISCHARGE AIR FROM DEFROSTER OUTLETS → NO DISCHARGE (BLEED AIR) FROM HEATER OUTLETS → FAULTY VACUUM ACTUATOR OR DOOR OPERATION → VACUUM LINE PINCHED OR DISCONNECTED FROM ACTUATOR → FAULTY PUSHBUTTON SWITCH

or and control system diagnosis all vehicles (© Chrysler Corporation)

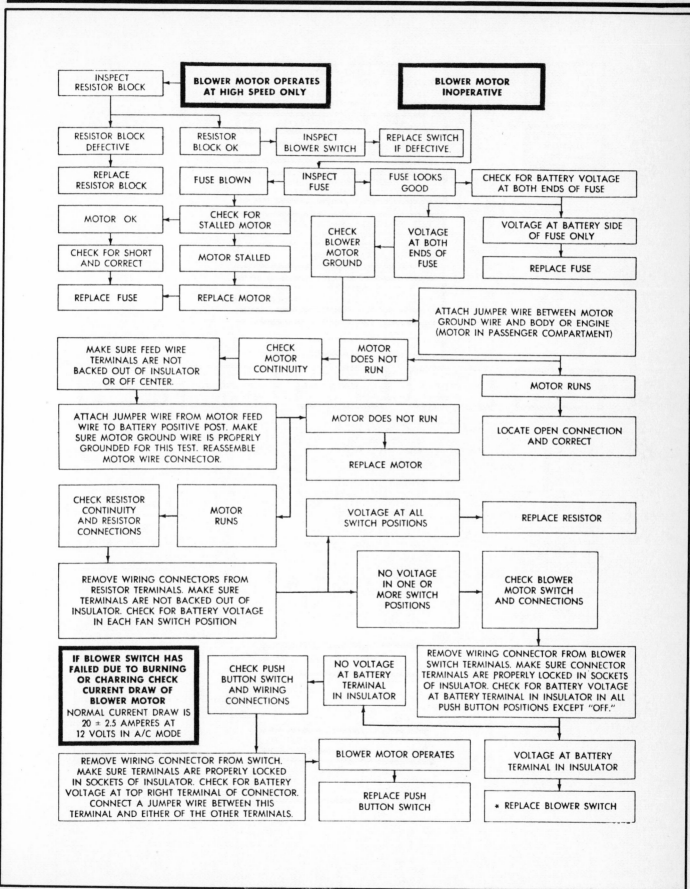

Electrical A/C blower motor and control system diagnosis all vehicles (© Chrysler Corporation)

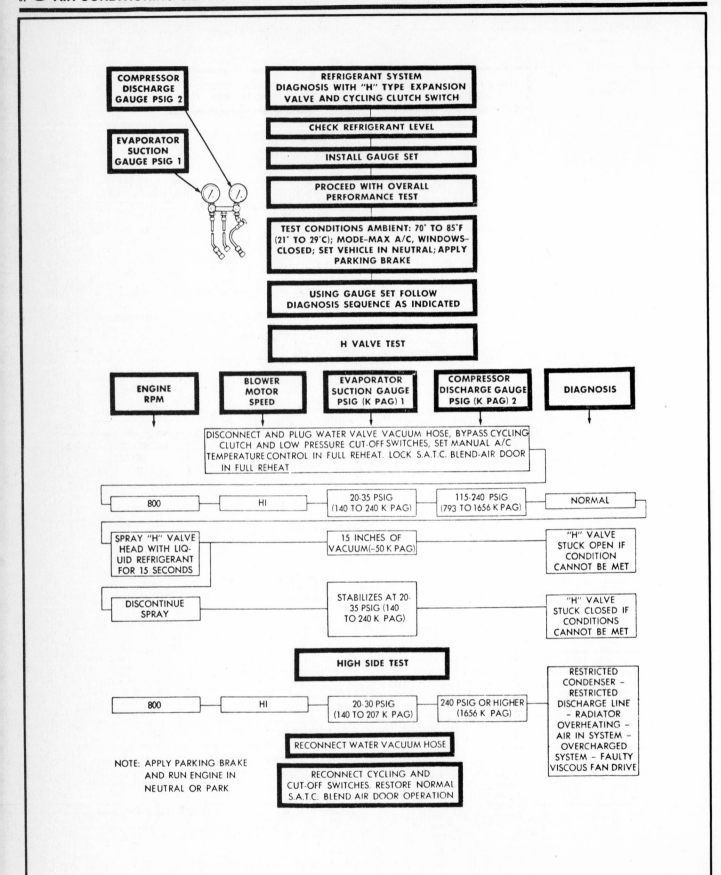

A/C refrigeration system diagnosis all vehicles (© Chrysler Corporation)

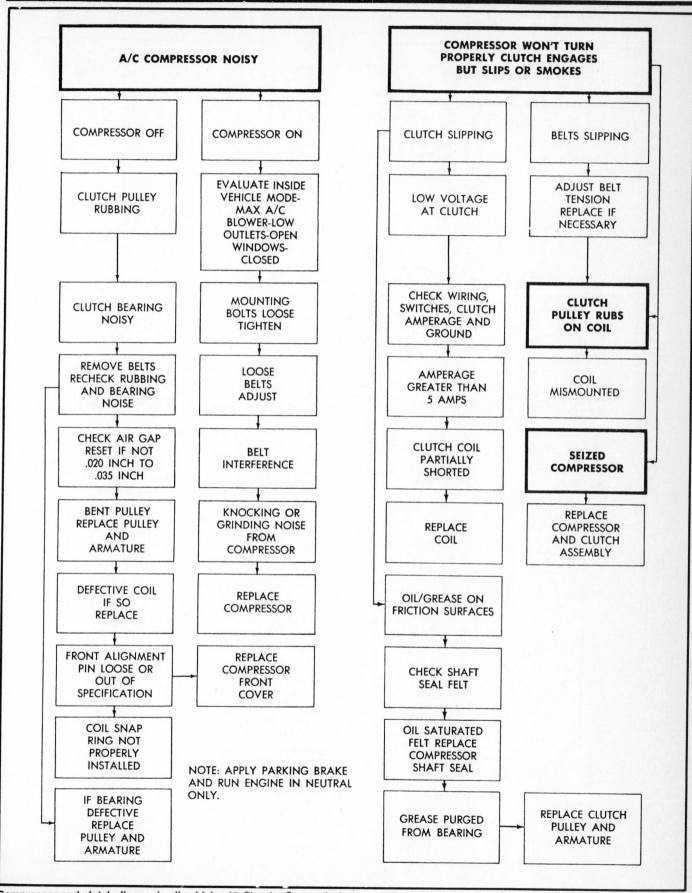

A/C COMPRESSOR NOISY

COMPRESSOR OFF

CLUTCH PULLEY RUBBING

CLUTCH BEARING NOISY

REMOVE BELTS RECHECK RUBBING AND BEARING NOISE

CHECK AIR GAP RESET IF NOT .020 INCH TO .035 INCH

BENT PULLEY REPLACE PULLEY AND ARMATURE

DEFECTIVE COIL IF SO REPLACE

FRONT ALIGNMENT PIN LOOSE OR OUT OF SPECIFICATION

COIL SNAP RING NOT PROPERLY INSTALLED

IF BEARING DEFECTIVE REPLACE PULLEY AND ARMATURE

COMPRESSOR ON

EVALUATE INSIDE VEHICLE MODE-MAX A/C BLOWER-LOW OUTLETS-OPEN WINDOWS-CLOSED

MOUNTING BOLTS LOOSE TIGHTEN

LOOSE BELTS ADJUST

BELT INTERFERENCE

KNOCKING OR GRINDING NOISE FROM COMPRESSOR

REPLACE COMPRESSOR

REPLACE COMPRESSOR FRONT COVER

NOTE: APPLY PARKING BRAKE AND RUN ENGINE IN NEUTRAL ONLY.

COMPRESSOR WON'T TURN PROPERLY CLUTCH ENGAGES BUT SLIPS OR SMOKES

CLUTCH SLIPPING

LOW VOLTAGE AT CLUTCH

CHECK WIRING, SWITCHES, CLUTCH AMPERAGE AND GROUND

AMPERAGE GREATER THAN 5 AMPS

CLUTCH COIL PARTIALLY SHORTED

REPLACE COIL

OIL/GREASE ON FRICTION SURFACES

CHECK SHAFT SEAL FELT

OIL SATURATED FELT REPLACE COMPRESSOR SHAFT SEAL

GREASE PURGED FROM BEARING

BELTS SLIPPING

ADJUST BELT TENSION REPLACE IF NECESSARY

CLUTCH PULLEY RUBS ON COIL

COIL MISMOUNTED

SEIZED COMPRESSOR

REPLACE COMPRESSOR AND CLUTCH ASSEMBLY

REPLACE CLUTCH PULLEY AND ARMATURE

Compressor and clutch diagnosis all vehicles (© Chrysler Corporation)

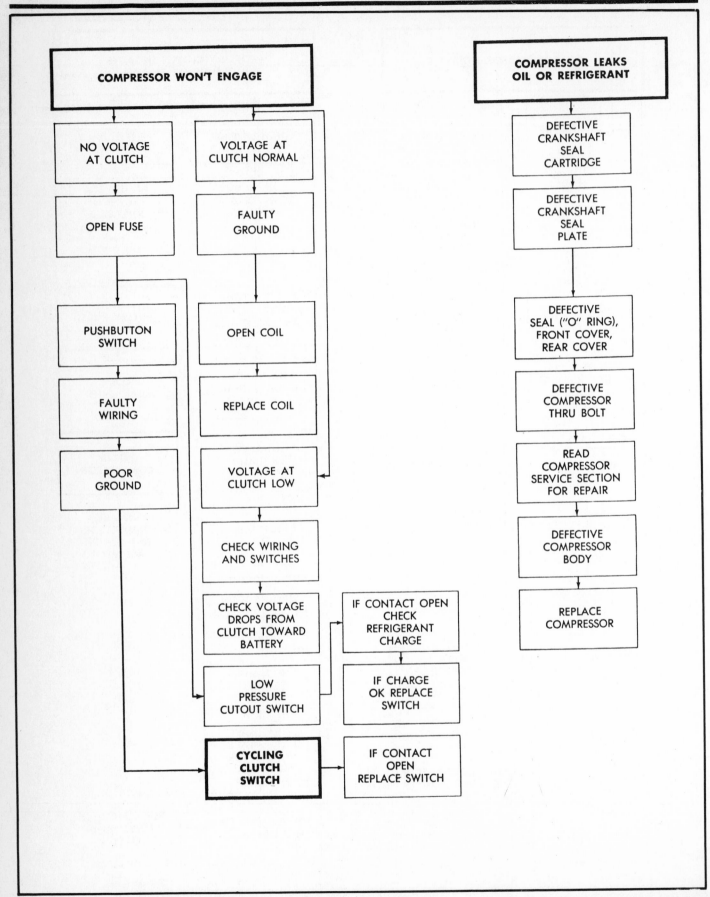

COMPRESSOR WON'T ENGAGE

- NO VOLTAGE AT CLUTCH
  - OPEN FUSE
  - PUSHBUTTON SWITCH
  - FAULTY WIRING
  - POOR GROUND

- VOLTAGE AT CLUTCH NORMAL
  - FAULTY GROUND
  - OPEN COIL
  - REPLACE COIL

- VOLTAGE AT CLUTCH LOW
  - CHECK WIRING AND SWITCHES
  - CHECK VOLTAGE DROPS FROM CLUTCH TOWARD BATTERY
  - LOW PRESSURE CUTOUT SWITCH
    - IF CONTACT OPEN CHECK REFRIGERANT CHARGE
    - IF CHARGE OK REPLACE SWITCH
  - CYCLING CLUTCH SWITCH
    - IF CONTACT OPEN REPLACE SWITCH

COMPRESSOR LEAKS OIL OR REFRIGERANT

- DEFECTIVE CRANKSHAFT SEAL CARTRIDGE
- DEFECTIVE CRANKSHAFT SEAL PLATE
- DEFECTIVE SEAL ("O" RING), FRONT COVER, REAR COVER
- DEFECTIVE COMPRESSOR THRU BOLT
- READ COMPRESSOR SERVICE SECTION FOR REPAIR
- DEFECTIVE COMPRESSOR BODY
- REPLACE COMPRESSOR

Compressor and clutch diagnosis all vehicles (© Chrysler Corporation)

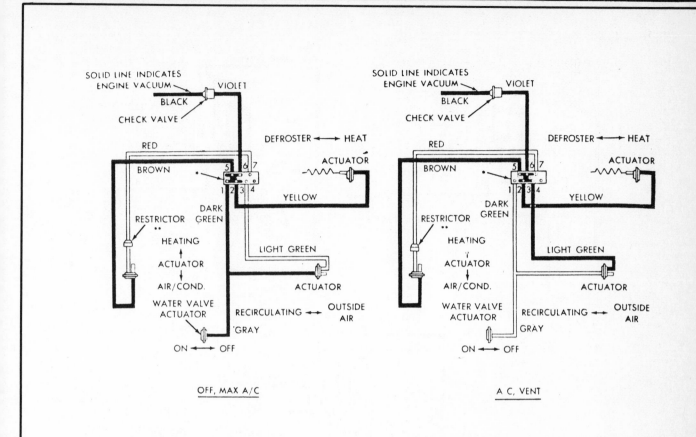

OFF, MAX A/C

A C, VENT

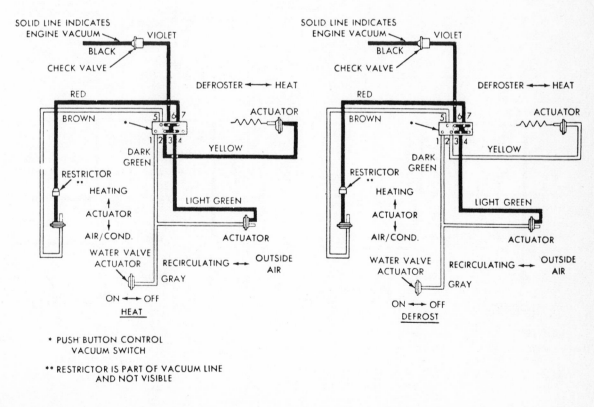

HEAT

DEFROST

* PUSH BUTTON CONTROL
  VACUUM SWITCH

** RESTRICTOR IS PART OF VACUUM LINE
  AND NOT VISIBLE

1982–85 A/C and heating vacuum circuits for, Horizon, Turismo, Omni, Charger, TC–3, Miser, 024 (© Chrysler Corporation)

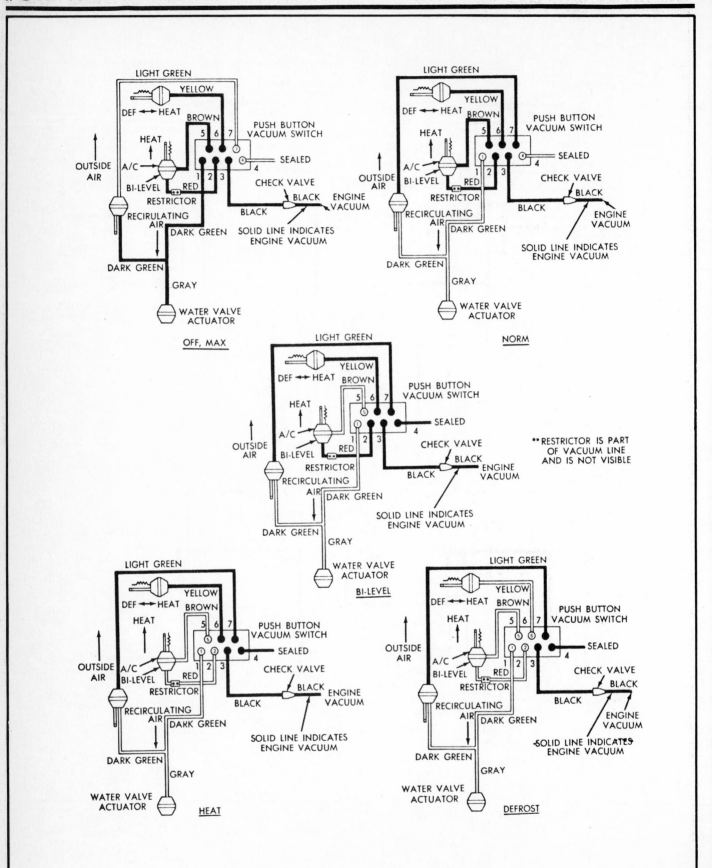

1982–85 A/C and heating vacuum circuits for, Caravelle, 400, 600, E, Class, New Yorker, Reliant, Aries, LeBaron, Daytona, Laser, Lancer (© Chrysler Corporation)

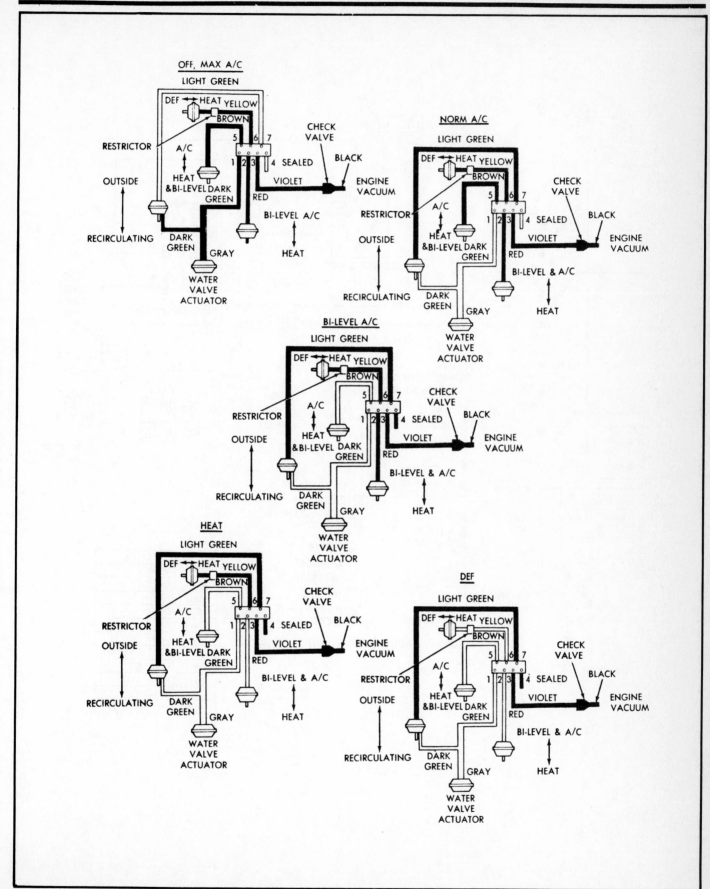

1982–85 A/C vacuum circuits SATC all rear wheel drive vehicles (© Chrysler Corporation)

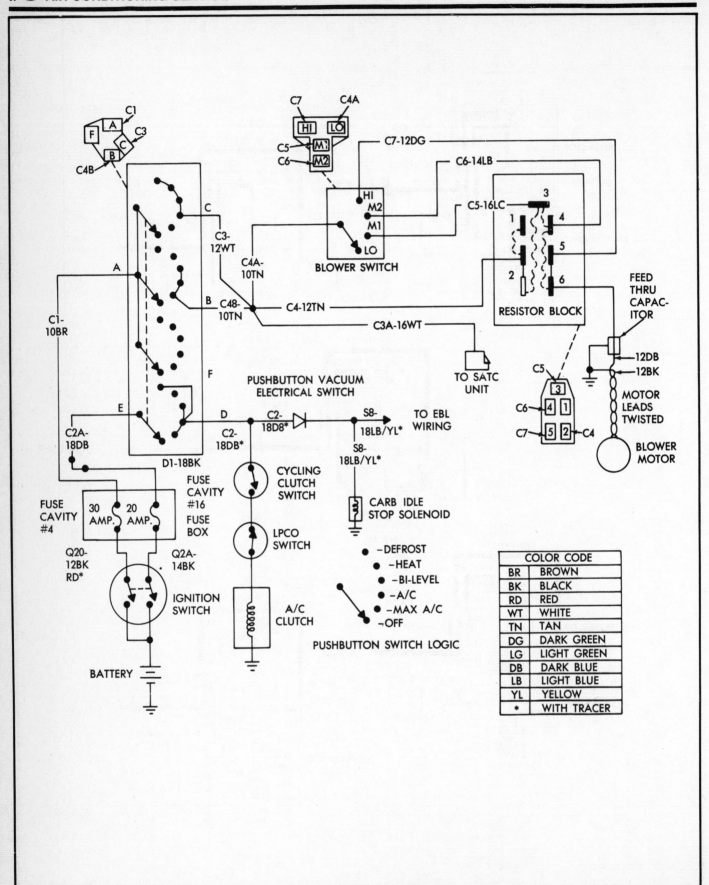

1982 SATC electronic control circuit all rear wheel drive vehicles. (© Chrysler Corporation)

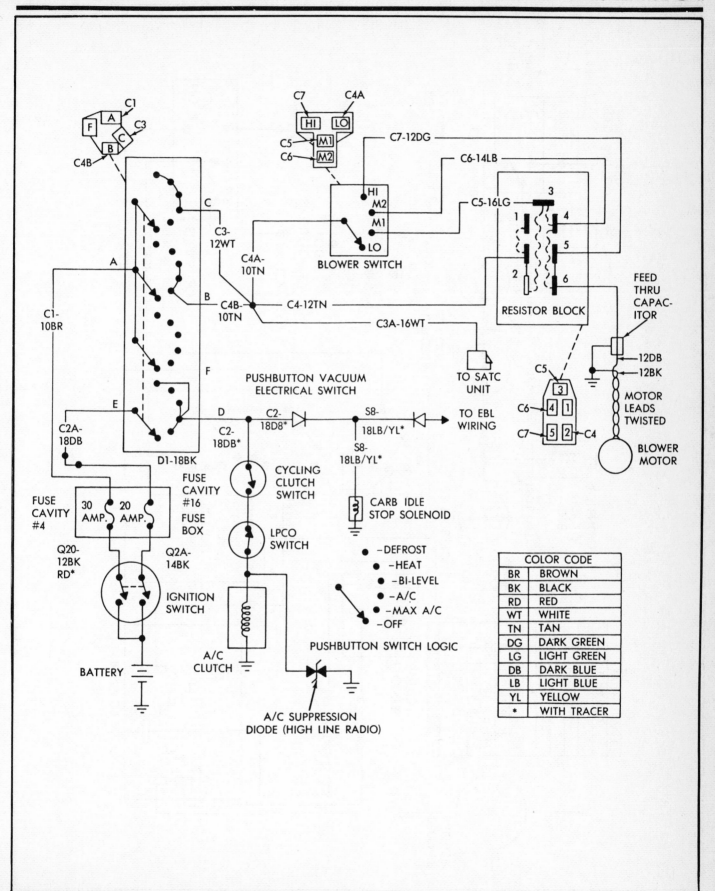

1983–85 SATC electronic control circuits all rear wheel drive vehicles (© Chrysler Corporation)

COLOR CODE	
BR	BROWN
BK	BLACK
RD	RED
WT	WHITE
TN	TAN
DG	DARK GREEN
LG	LIGHT GREEN
DB	DARK BLUE
LB	LIGHT BLUE
YL	YELLOW
*	WITH TRACER

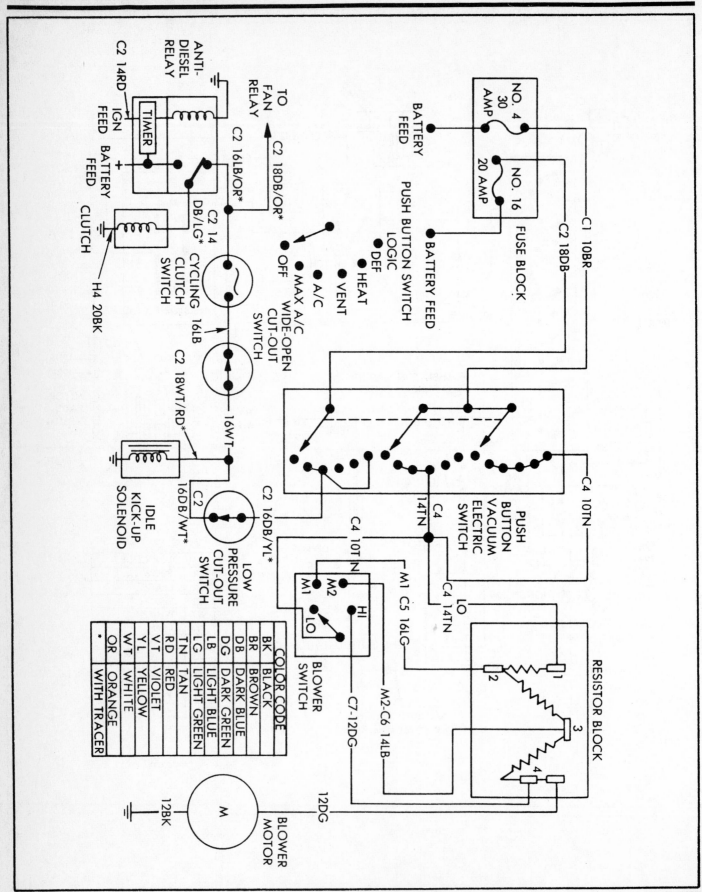

1982–83 FWD 1.7 and 2.2 liter engine electrical control circuits (© Chrysler Corporation)

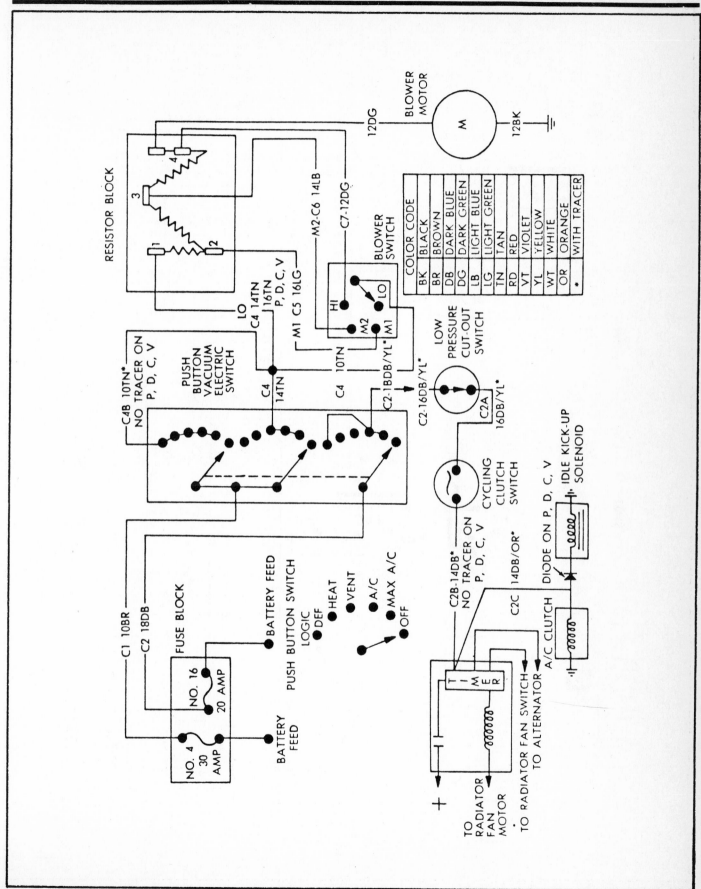

1982–83 FWD 2.6 liter engine electrical control circuits (© Chrysler Corporation)

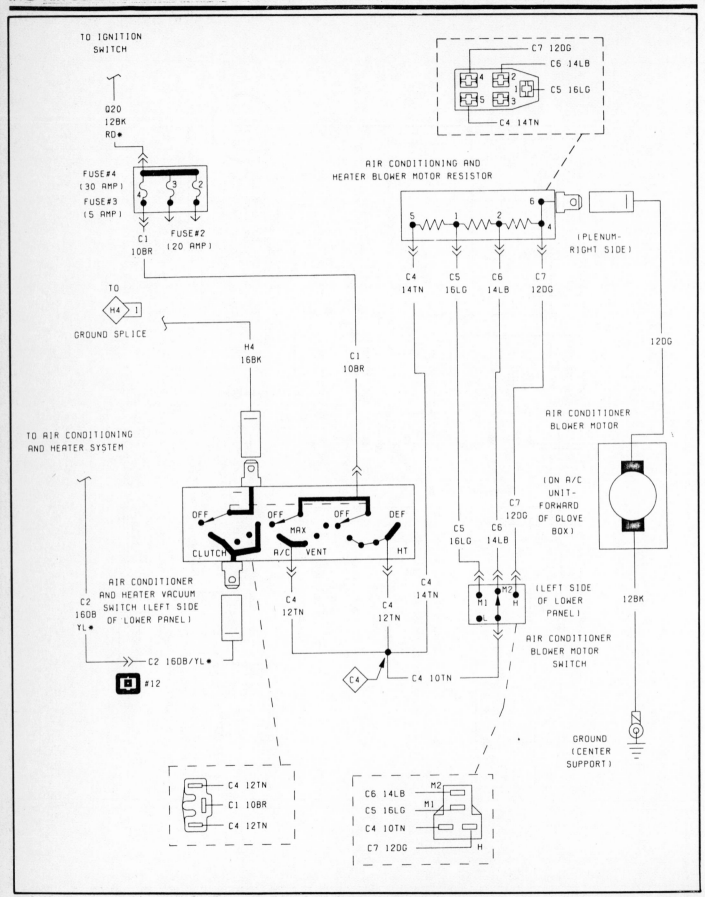

1984–85 A/C and heating schematic for, Horizon, Turismo, Omni, Charger (© Chrysler Corporation)

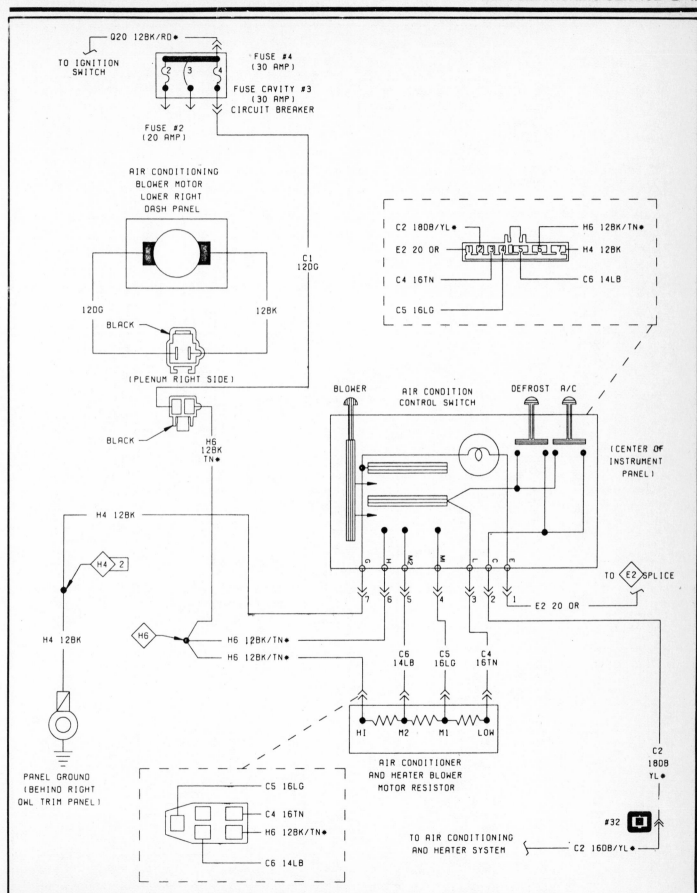

1984–85 Air conditioning schematic for, Caravelle, 600, E, Class, New Yorker, Reliant, Aries, LeBaron, Daytona, Laser, Lancer
(© Chrysler Corporation)

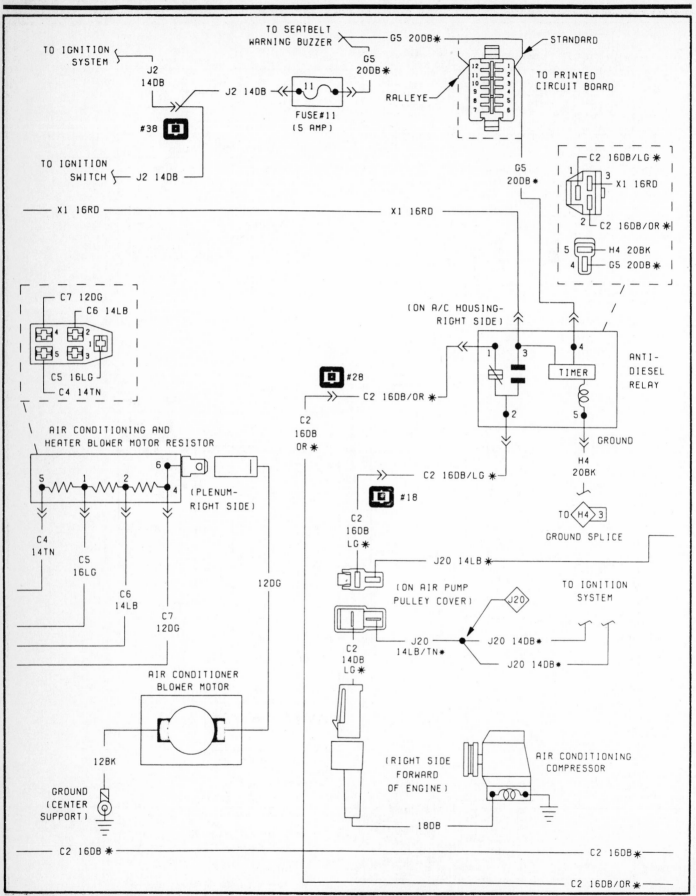

Electrical schematic for 1982-83 A/C and heating systems - 2.2 Liter engine (© Chrysler Corp.)

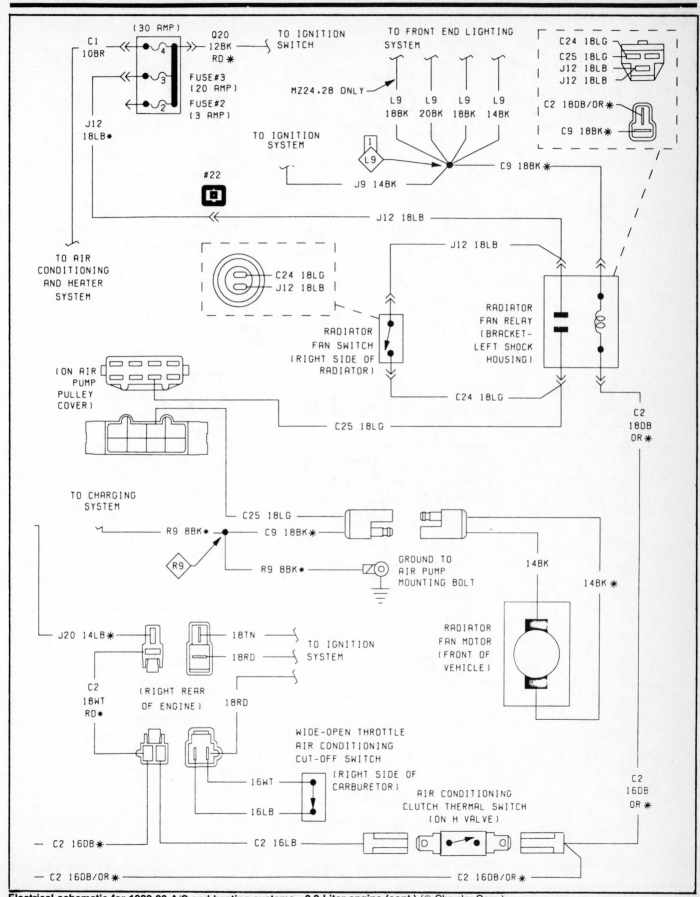

Electrical schematic for 1982-83 A/C and heating systems - 2.2 Liter engine (cont.) (© Chrysler Corp.)

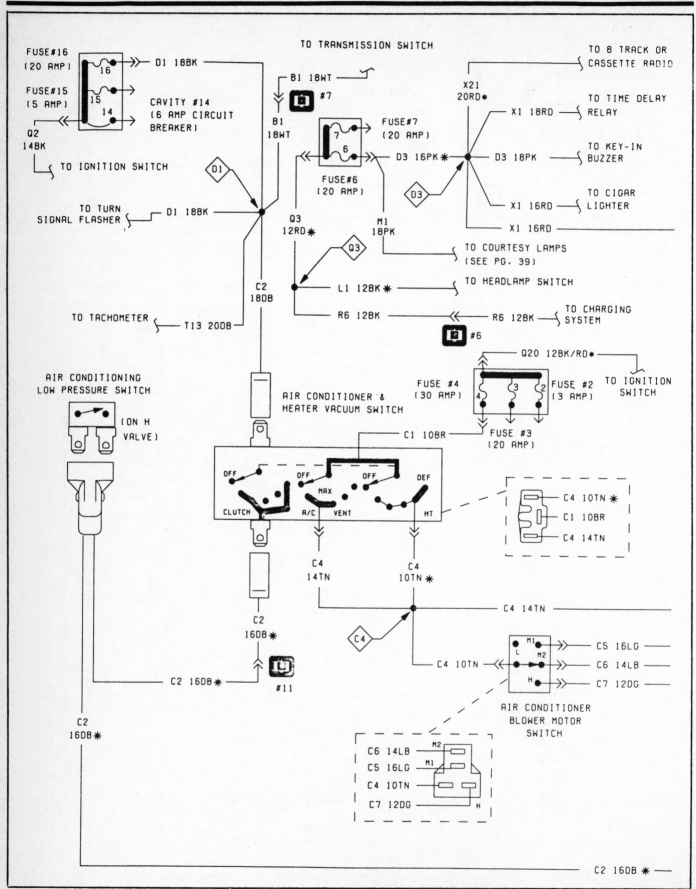

Electrical schematic for 1982-83 A/C and heating systems - 2.2 Liter engine (cont.) (© Chrysler Corp.)

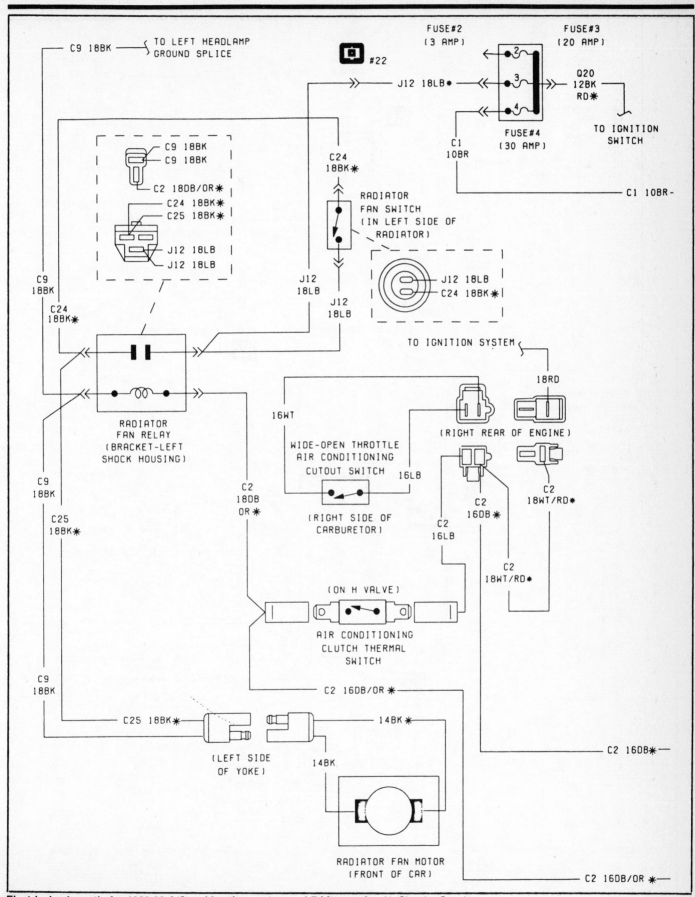

Electrical schematic for 1982-83 A/C and heating systems - 1.7 Liter engine (© Chrysler Corp.)

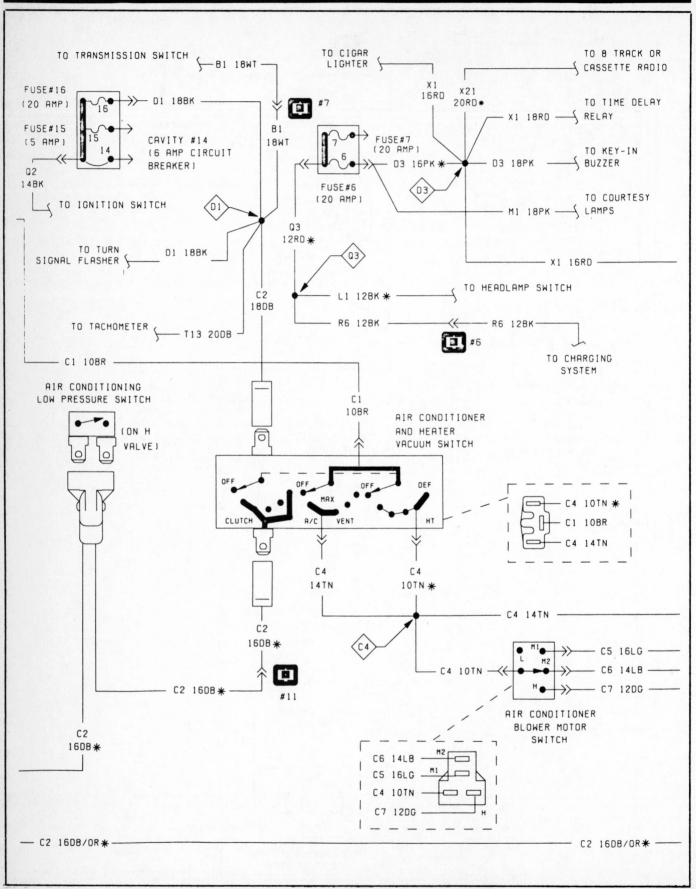

Electrical schematic for 1982-83 A/C and heating systems - 1.7 Liter engine (cont.) (© Chrysler Corp.)

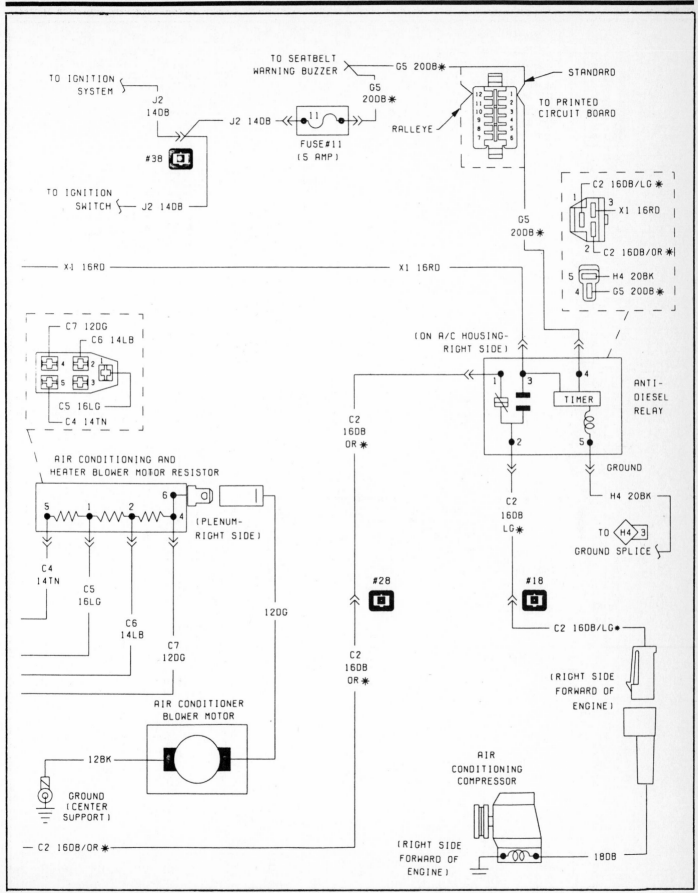

Electrical schematic for 1982-83 A/C and heating systems - 1.7 Liter engine (cont.) (© Chrysler Corp.)

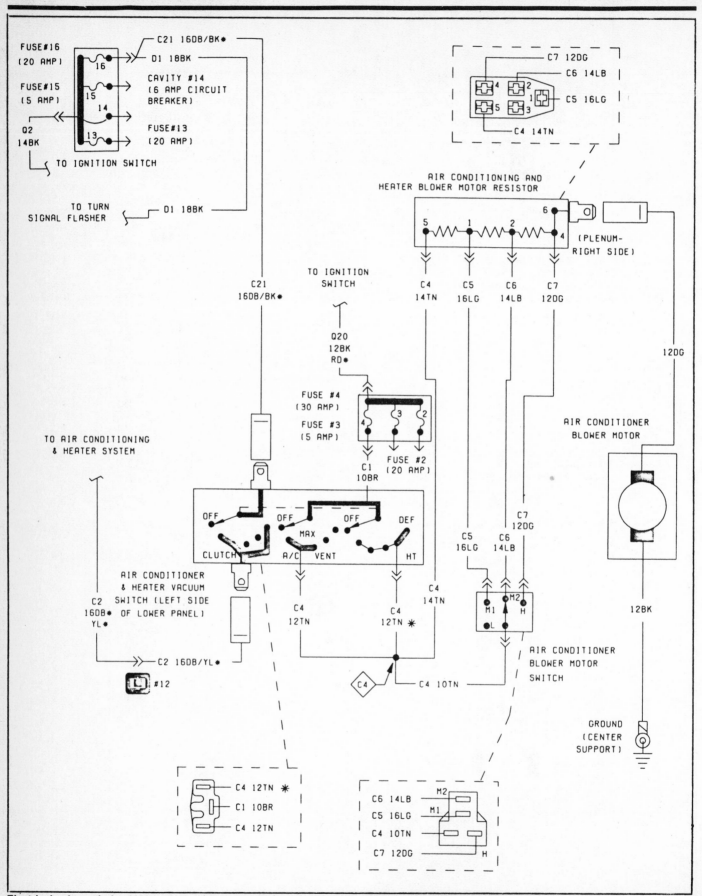

Electrical schematic for 1984 and later A/C and heating systems - Basic 1984 and later (© Chrysler Corp.)

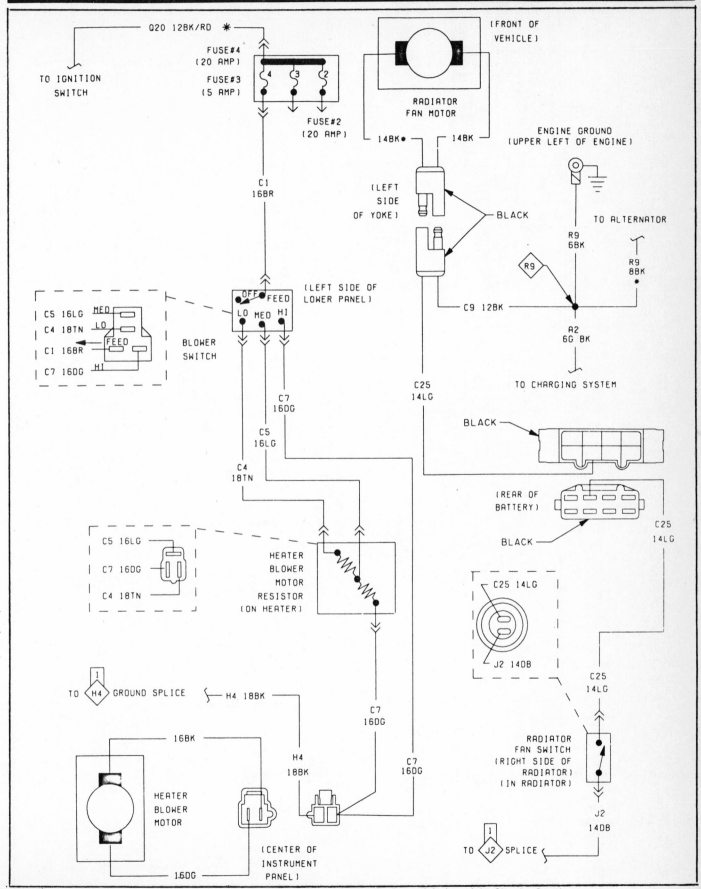

Q20 12BK/RD ✱

TO IGNITION SWITCH

FUSE#4 (20 AMP)
FUSE#3 (5 AMP)
FUSE#2 (20 AMP)

(FRONT OF VEHICLE)

RADIATOR FAN MOTOR

ENGINE GROUND (UPPER LEFT OF ENGINE)

C1 16BR

14BK✱   14BK

(LEFT SIDE OF YOKE)

BLACK

TO ALTERNATOR

R9 6BK

R9

R9 8BK ✱

C9 12BK

A2 6G BK

TO CHARGING SYSTEM

(LEFT SIDE OF LOWER PANEL)

OFF   FEED
LO MED HI

C5 16LG   MED
C4 18TN   LO
C1 16BR   FEED
C7 16DG   HI

BLOWER SWITCH

C7 16DG

C5 16LG

C4 18TN

C25 14LG

BLACK

(REAR OF BATTERY)

BLACK

C25 14LG

C5 16LG
C7 16DG
C4 18TN

HEATER BLOWER MOTOR RESISTOR (ON HEATER)

C25 14LG

J2 14DB

C25 14LG

TO ⟨H4⟩ GROUND SPLICE

H4 18BK

C7 16DG

RADIATOR FAN SWITCH (RIGHT SIDE OF RADIATOR) (IN RADIATOR)

16BK

HEATER BLOWER MOTOR

H4 18BK

C7 16DG

J2 14DB

TO ⟨J2⟩ SPLICE

(CENTER OF INSTRUMENT PANEL)

16DG

Electrical schematic for 1984 and later A/C and heating systems - Shelby Body models (cont.) (© Chrysler Corp.)

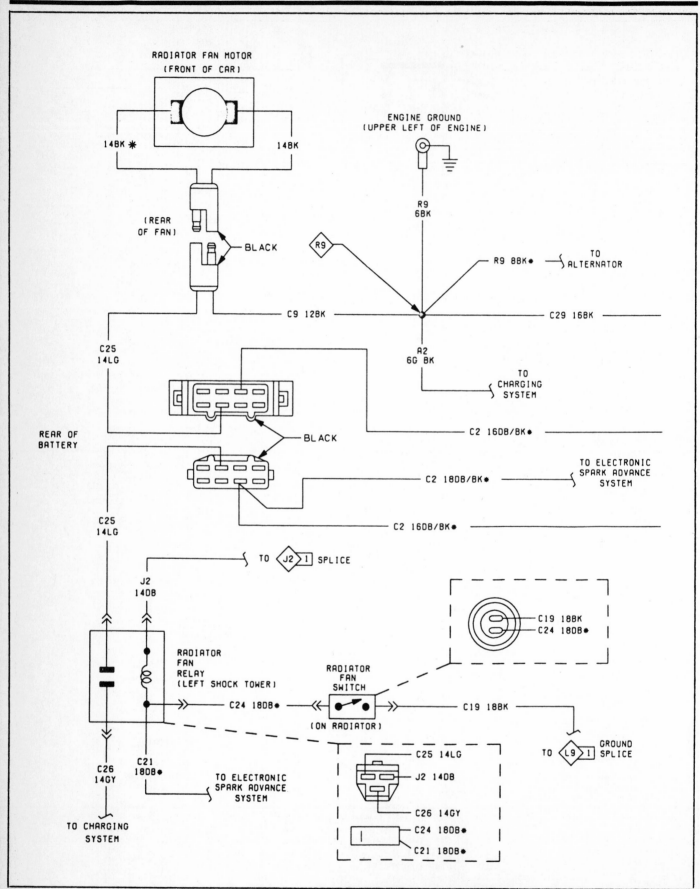

Electrical schematic for 1984 and later A/C and heating systems - All except Shelby Body models (© Chrysler Corp.)

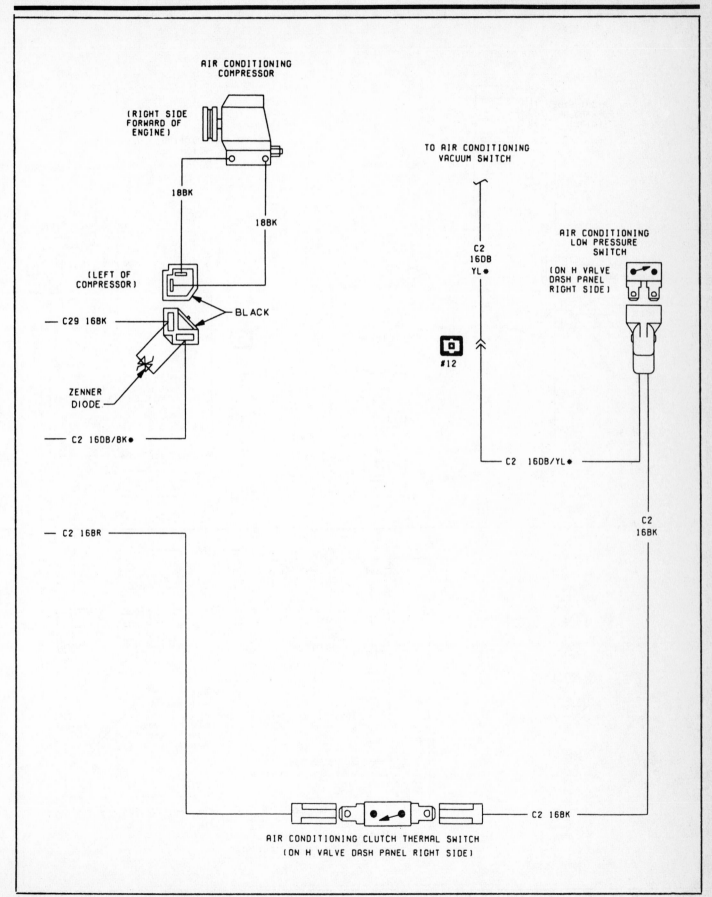

AIR CONDITIONING
COMPRESSOR

(RIGHT SIDE
FORWARD OF
ENGINE)

18BK

18BK

TO AIR CONDITIONING
VACUUM SWITCH

C2
16DB
YL*

AIR CONDITIONING
LOW PRESSURE
SWITCH

(ON H VALVE
DASH PANEL
RIGHT SIDE)

(LEFT OF
COMPRESSOR)

— C29 16BK

BLACK

ZENNER
DIODE

#12

— C2 16DB/BK*

— C2 16DB/YL*

C2
16BK

— C2 16BR

C2 16BK

AIR CONDITIONING CLUTCH THERMAL SWITCH
(ON H VALVE DASH PANEL RIGHT SIDE)

Electrical schematic for 1984 and later A/C and heating systems - All except Shelby Body models (cont.) (© Chrysler Corp.)

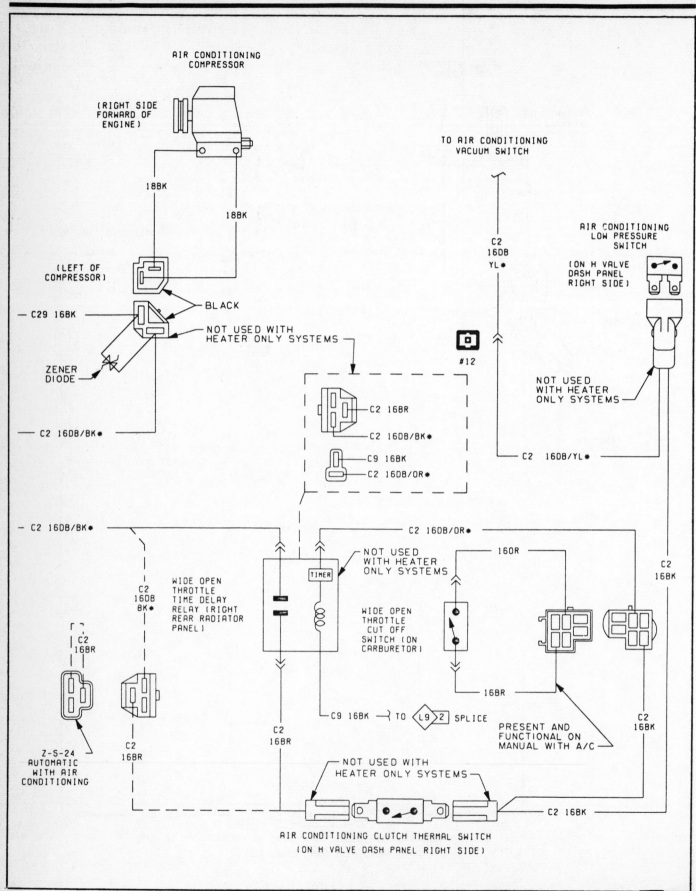

Typical electric fan circuit - 1984 and later (© Chrysler Corp.)

SECTION 4
Ford Motor Company

INDEX

FORD MOTOR COMPANY

Year	Ford Vehicles	Lincoln/Mercury Vehicles
1982	Escort/EXP	Lynx/LN7
	Mustang	Capri
	Fairmont Futura	Zephyr
	Granada	Cougar
	Thunderbird	Continental XR-7
	LTD	Marquis
	—	Marquis
	—	Town Car
	—	Mark VI
1983	Escort/EXP	Lynx/LN7
	Mustang	Capri
	Fairmont Futura	Zephyr
	LTD	Marquis
	Thunderbird	XR-7
	Crown Victoria	Grand Marquis
	—	Continental
	—	Town Car
	—	Mark VI
1984–85	Escort/EXP	Lynx
	Tempo	Topaz
	Mustang	Capri
	LTD	Marquis
	Thunderbird	Cougar
	Crown Victoria	Grand Marquis
		Continental
	—	Mark VII
	—	Town Car

REFRIGERANT CAPACITIES
FORD MOTOR COMPANY—1982–85 MODELS

Refrigerant given in ounces, Refrigerant oil given in fluid ounces

Year	Models	Recharge Capacities	
		R-12	Oil
1982	Escort/Lynx EXP/LN7	40	15

REFRIGERANT CAPACITIES
Ford Motor Company—1982–1985 Models

Refrigerant given in ounces, Refrigerant oil given in fluid ounces

Year	Models	Recharge Capacities	
		R-12	Oil
1982	Granada/Cougar Fairmont/Zephyr Mustang/Capri	40	15
	Thunderbird/XR-7 Lincoln Continental	40	15
	Ford/Mercury	52	15
	Lincoln Mark VI	48	15
1983	Escort/Lynx EXP/LN7	37	15
	Mustang/Capri w/ 3.8 or 5.0L Engine	40	15
	Thunderbird/XR-7 LTD/Marquis Lincoln Continental Fairmont/Zephyr	40	15
	Crown Victoria Grand Marquis	52	18
	Lincoln Mark VI	48	15
1984	Tempo/Topaz Escort/Lynx EXP	48	15
	Lincoln Town Car	48	15
	Crown Victoria Grand Marquis	52	18
	Mustang/Capri Continental Thunderbird/Cougar XR-7 LTD/Marquis Mark VI	40	15
1985	Tempo/Topaz Escort/Lynx	41	15
	EXP	37	10
	Lincoln Town Car	48	10
	Crown Victoria Grand Marquis	52	13
	Mustang/Capri Continental Thunderbird/Cougar LTD/Marquis Mark VI	40	10

BELT TENSION CHART
1982-85 Ford Motor Company

Year	Model	Belt Type	
1982	Escort/Lynx Exp/LN7	5 Rib Type Belt New Used Reset Used Min.	 110–140 lbs. 110–130 lbs. 75 lbs.
	Granada/Cougar Fairmont/Zephyr Mustang/Capri Thunderbird/XR-7 Lincoln Continental Ford Mercury Lincoln/Mark VI	6 Rib Type Belt New Used Reset Used Min. 'V' Type Belt New Used	 140–170 lbs. 140–160 lbs. 90 lbs. 120–160 lbs. 90–120 lbs.
1983	Escort/Lynx EXP/LN-7	6 Rib Type Belt New Used Reset Used Min. 5 Rib Type Belt New Used Reset Used Min.	 110–140 lbs. 110–130 lbs. 75 lbs. 110–140 lbs. 110–130 lbs. 75 lbs.
	Mustang/Capri W/3.8L or 5.0L Engines W/2.3L Engine	5 Rib Type Belt New Used Reset Used Min. 6 Rib Type Belt New Used Reset Used Min. 'V' Type Belt New Used	 110–140 lbs. 110–130 lbs. 75 lbs. 140–170 lbs. 140–160 lbs. 90 lbs. 120–160 lbs. 90–120 lbs.
	Thunderbird/XR-7 W/Auto Overdrive W/out Auto Overdrive or w/Auto Temp. Control W/Manual A/C and 2.3L or 3.8L Engine W/5.0L Engine	'V' Type Belt (Ribbed) New Used 'V' Type Belt New Used 'V' Type Belt New Used 6 Rib Type Belt New Used Reset Used Min.	 110–140 lbs. 75–130 lbs. 120–160 lbs. 90–120 lbs. 110–140 lbs. 110–130 lbs. 140–170 lbs. 140–160 lbs. 90 lbs.
	LTD/Marquis Lincoln Continental Fairmont Futura/Zephyr	'V' Type Belt New Used 6 Rib Type Belt New Used Reset Used Min. 'V' Type Belt (Ribbed) New Used Reset Used Min.	 120–160 lbs. 90–120 lbs. 140–170 lbs. 140–160 lbs. 90 lbs. 110–140 lbs. 110–130 lbs. 75 lbs.

BELT TENSION CHART
1982-85 Ford Motor Company

Year	Model	Belt Type	
1983	Ford Crown Victoria	5 Rib Type Belt	
	Mercury Grand Marquis	New	110–140 lbs.
	Lincoln/Mark VI	Used Reset	110–130 lbs.
		Used Min.	75 lbs.
		6 Rib Type Belt	
		New	140–170 lbs.
		Used Reset	140–160 lbs.
		Used Min.	90 lbs.
1984	Tempo/Topaz	6 Rib Type Belt	
	Escort/Lynx/EXP	New	110–140 lbs.
		Used Reset	110–130 lbs.
		Used Min.	75 lbs.
	Lincoln Town Car/	6 Rib Type Belt	
	Ford Crown Victoria/	New	140–170 lbs.
	Mercury Grand Marquis	Used Reset	140–160 lbs.
	Mustang/Capri	Used Min.	90 lbs.
	Thunderbird/Cougar	'V' Type Belt	
	LTD/Marquis	New	120–160 lbs.
		Used	90–120 lbs.
		'V' Type Belt (Ribbed)	
		New	110–140 lbs.
		Used Reset	110–130 lbs.
		Used Min.	75 lbs.
	Mark VII/Continental	6 Rio Type Belt	
		New	120–160 lbs.
		Used	90–120 lbs.
1985	Tempo/Topaz	6 Rib Type Belt	
	Escort/Lynx/EXP	New	110–140 lbs.
		Used Reset	110–130 lbs.
		Used Min.	75 lbs.
		Used Min.	75 lbs.
	Lincoln Town Car/	5 Rib Type Belt	
	Ford Crown Victoria	New	110–140 lbs.
	Mercury Grand Marquis	Used Reset	110–130 lbs.
	Mustang/Capri	Used Min.	75 lbs.
	Thunderbird/Cougar	6 Rib Type Belt	
	LTD/Marquis	New	140–170 lbs.
		Used	140–160 lbs.
		'V' Type Belt	
		New	120–160 lbs.
		Used	90–120 lbs.
		'V' Type Belt (Ribbed)	
		New	110–140 lbs.
		Used Reset	110–130 lbs.
		Used Min.	75 lbs.
	Mark VII/Continental	6 Rib Type Belt	
		New	120–160 lbs.
		Used	90–120 lbs.

Blower Motor

Removal

1982 GRANADA AND COUGAR

1. Remove the right ventilator assembly and disconnect the blower lead wire (orange and black strip) connector from the spade terminal of the resistor assembly and push it back through the hole in the case.

2. Remove the right side cowl trim panel for access to the blower ground terminal lug (black) and remove the ground terminal lug retaining screw.

3. Remove the three blower motor flange retaining screws from inside the blower housing (The blower wheel can be removed for easy access).

4. Remove the blower motor from the housing.

Installation

1. Insert the blower motor wires through the opening at the back of the housing and position the blower motor mounting flange onto the two locator pins of the blower housing.

2. Install the blower flange retaining screws and install the blower wheel onto the blower motor shaft.

3. Position the ground terminal lug, install the ground terminal lug retaining screw and install the right side cowl trim panel.

4. Run the blower motor power lead wire through the hole in the center of the case and install the connector on the spade terminal of the resistor assembly.

5. Install the right ventricular assembly and test the blower for proper operation.

Blower motor

Removal

1982-85 ESCORT, EXP, LYNX, LN7, TEMPO AND TOPAZ

1. Remove the glove compartment door, disconnect the blower motor wires from the blower motor resistor.

2. Loosen the instrument panel at the lower right hand side before removing the blower motor through the glove compartment opening.

3. Remove the four mounting screws, holding the blower motor and the mounting plate to the evaporator housing.

4. Rotate the motor until the mounting plate flats clear the edge of the glove compartment opening and remove the blower motor.

5. Remove the hub clamp spring from the blower wheel hub. Then remove the blower wheel from the motor shaft.

Installation

1. Place the blower motor wheel on the motor shaft and install the hub clamp spring.

2. Position the blower motor assembly onto the evaporator case install the four mounting screws.

3. Connect the blower motor wires to the harness at the hardshell connector.

4. Check the blower motor for proper operation and install the glove compartment door.

Blower Motor

Removal

1982-85 FORD/MERCURY, TOWN CAR, CROWN VICTORIA AND GRAND MARQUIS

1. Disconnect the blower motor lead assembly from the main wiring

harness and remove the blower motor cooling tube from the blower motor.

2. Remove the four attaching screws, two upper and two lower from the blower motor mounting plate.

3. Turn the blower motor assembly to the right so that the bottom edge of the mounting plate follows the contour of the wheel well splash panel.

4. While still in the blower housing, lift the blower motor assembly up and maneuver it out of the housing assembly.

NOTE: The blower motor wheel can be removed by simply removing the hub clamp spring from the wheel hub and sliding the hub off of the motor shaft.

Installation

1. Tilt the blower motor assembly to the right so that the bottom edge off the mounting plate follows the contour of the wheel well splash panel.

2. Maneuver the assembly past the wheel well splash panel and into the top portion of the housing opening, then down into position.

3. Install the four attaching screws and the blower motor cooling tube.

4. Connect the blower motor wire connector to the main wiring harness and check the system for proper blower motor operation.

Blower Motor

Removal

1982-85 THUNDERBIRD, COUGAR/XR-7, LTD, MARQUIS, CONTINENTAL, MARK VI AND MARK VII

1. Remove the air inlet duct and blower motor housing from the vehicle.

2. Remove the four blower motor mounting plate screws and remove the blower motor assembly from the blower housing.

NOTE: Do not remove the blower motor mounting plate from the blower motor.

3. Remove the blower wheel from the motor shaft.

Installation

1. Install the blower wheel on the blower motor shaft until the outside edge of the blower wheel is 3-3/4 inches from the blower motor mounting plate. Now install the new retaining clip on the blower wheel.

2. Position the blower motor and wheel assembly to the blower housing with the flat side of the flange near the blower outlet.

3. Install the four attaching screws.

4. Tape the blower motor power lead the air inlet duct to keep the wire away from the blower outlet during installation.

5. Install the air inlet duct and blower housing assembly in the vehicle.

Blower Motor

Removal

1982-85 FAIRMONT/FUTURA, ZEPHYR, MUSTANG AND CAPRI

1. Remove the right ventilator assembly and remove the hub clamp spring from the blower wheel hub.

2. Pull the blower wheel off of the blower motor shaft and remove the three blower motor flange attaching screws located inside the blower housing.

3. Pull the blower motor out from the blower housing and disconnect the blower motor wires from the motor.

Installation

1. Connect the wires to the blower motor and position the motor in the blower housing.

2. Install the three blower motor attaching screws and place the blower wheel on the blower motor shaft with the hub clamp spring.

3. Install the right ventilator assembly and check the system for proper operation.

Compressor

1982-83 GRANADA/COUGAR, FAIRMONT/FUTURA, ZEPHYR, AND MUSTANG/CAPRI

TWO-CYLINDER COMPRESSOR

Removal

1. Discharge the refrigerant from the A/C system at the low pressure service access gauge port valve, located on the suction line.

2. Energize the magnetic clutch and remove the clutch retaining bolt.

3. Install a 5/8-11 bolt in the compressor shaft hole of the clutch and, with the clutch energized, tighten the bolt to push the clutch from the compressor shaft.

4. Loosen the idler attaching screws and release the drive belt tension. Then, remove the drive belt from the compressor clutch.

5. Disconnect the clutch field wire at the connector.

6. Remove the refrigerant lines from the compressor and plug the lines and compressor ports to prevent the entrance of dirt and excessive moisture.

7. Remove the compressor mounting bolts and remove the compressor.

8. Remove the clutch field coil from the compressor if the compressor is to be replaced.

Installation

1. If the compressor is to be replaced, drain the oil from the cold compressor into a suitable measuring container. Record the amount of oil drained from the compressor. Then, discard the oil.

2. Drain all the oil from the new service compressor. Then, add the same amount of clean refrigerant oil to the drained service replacement compressor that was drained from the removed (old) compressor.

3. Position the compressor to the compressor mounting bracket(s) and install the attaching bolts and lockwashers. Tighten the bolts to specification.

4. Install the clutch field coil on the compressor if it was removed or if the compressor was replaced.

5. Connect the refrigerant lines to the compressor. Use new O-rings lubricated with clean refrigerant oil.

6. Install the pulley and clutch drive assembly on the compressor shaft. Connect the clutch field coil wire at the connector and energize the clutch. Then, tighten the clutch retaining bolt to specification.

7. Install the drive belt on the compressor clutch pulley and tighten the belt to specification.

8. Leak test, evacuate and charge the refrigeration system following the recommended procedures and safety precautions.

SIX CYLINDER (6P148) COMPRESSOR

Removal

3.8L AND 5.0L ENGINES

1. Discharge the system following the recommended service procedures. Observe all safety precautions.

2. Disconnect compressor clutch wires at the field coil connector on compressor.

3. Disconnect the discharge and suction hoses from the compressor manifolds. Cap the refrigerant lines and compressor manifolds to prevent the entrance of dirt and moisture.

4. Remove two screws attaching brace to rear mounting bracket.

5. Remove two screws attaching bracket to compressor lower front mounting lugs.

6. Remove one screw attaching bracket to compressor upper mounting lug.

7. Remove compressor/clutch assembly and rear support from vehicle as unit.

8. Remove two screws attaching compressor to rear support and remove rear support.

9. If the compressor is to be replaced, remove the clutch and field coil assembly from compressor.

Installation

1. A new service replacement compressor contains 10 fluid ounces of the specified refrigerant oil. Before installing the replacement compressor, drain four fluid ounces of refrigerant oil from the compressor. This will keep the total system oil charge within specifications.

2. Reverse removal procedure.

3. Using new O-rings lubricated with clean refrigerant oil, connnect the suction and discharge lines to the compressor manifolds. Tighten each fitting to specification.

4. Connect the clutch wires to the field coil connector.

5. Install the drive belt. Adjust the drive belt to specification.

6. Leak test, evacuate and charge the system following the recommended service procedures. Observe all safety precautions.

7. Check the system for proper operation.

SIX CYLINDER (FS-6) COMPRESSOR

Removal

3.3L ENGINE

1. Discharge the system following the recommended service procedures. Observe all safety precautions.

2. Disconnect compressor clutch wires at the field coil connector on compressor.

3. Disconnect the discharge and suction hoses from the compressor manifolds. Cap the refrigerant lines and compressor manifolds to prevent the entrance of dirt and moisture.

4. Remove one screw attaching brace to compressor upper mounting lug.

5. Remove two screws attaching bracket to the compressor lower front mounting lugs.

6. Remove two screws attaching bracket to compressor lower rear mounting lugs.

7. Remove compressor/clutch assembly and rear support from vehicle as a unit.

8. Remove two screws attaching compressor to rear support and remove rear support.

9. If the compressor is to be replaced, remove the clutch and field coil assembly from compressor.

Installation

1. A new service replacement FS-6 compressor contains 10 fluid ounces of the specified refrigerant oil. Prior to installing the replacement compressor, drain four fluid ounces of refrigerant oil from the compressor. This will maintain the total system oil charge with the specified limits.

2. Reverse removal procedures.

3. Using new O-rings lubricated with clean refrigerant oil, connect the suction and discharge lines to the compressor manifolds. Tighten each fitting to specification.

4. Connect the clutch wires to the field coil connector.

5. Install the drive belt. Adjust the drive belt to specification.

6. Leak test, evacuate and charge the system following the recommended service procedures. Observe all safety precautions.

7. Check the system for proper operation.

FOUR CYLINDER (HR-980) COMPRESSOR

Removal

1982-85 WITH 2.3L ENGINE

1. Discharge the system following the recommended service procedures. Observe all safety precautions, refer to

2. Disconnect compressor clutch wires at the field coil connector on compressor.

3. Disconnect the discharge and suction hoses from the compressor manifolds. Cap the refrigerant lines and compressor manifolds to prevent the entrance of dirt and moisture.

4. Remove screw and washer assembly from the adjusting bracket.

5. Rotate compressor outboard and remove drive belts.

6. Remove compressor mounting bolt attaching bracket to compressor lower mounting lug.

7. Remove compressor and adjusting bracket intact.

8. Remove clutch field coil and adjusting bracket from the compressor if the compressor is to be replaced.

Installation

1. Install the clutch field coil and adjusting bracket if it was removed or if the compressor was replaced.

2. Reverse the removal procedure and connect the refrigerant lines to the compressor.

3. Connect the clutch wires to the field coil connector.

4. Evacuate, charge and leak test the system following the recommended service procedures. Check the system for proper operation.

SIX CYLINDER (FS-6) COMPRESSOR

Removal

1984-85 MUSTANG/CAPRI WITH 3.8L ENGINE

1. Discharge the system following the recommended service procedures. Observe all safety precautions.

2. Disconnect compressor clutch wires at the field coil connector on compressor.

3. Disconnect the discharge and suction hoses from the compressor manifolds. Cap the refrigrant lines and compressor manifolds to prevent the entrance of dirt and moisture.

4. Remove one screw attaching brace to compressor upper mounting lug.

5. Remove two screws attaching bracket to the compressor lower front mounting lugs.

6. Remove two screws attaching bracket to compressor lower rear mounting lugs.

7. Remove compressor/clutch assembly and rear support from vehicle as a unit.

8. Remove two screws attaching compressor to rear support and remove rear support.

9. If the compressor is to be replaced, remove the clutch and field coil assembly from compressor.

Installation

1. A new service replacement FS-6 compressor contains 10 fluid ounces of the specified refrigerant oil. Prior to installing the replacement compressor, drain four fluid ounces of refrigerant oil from the compressor. This will maintian the total system oil charge with the specified limits.

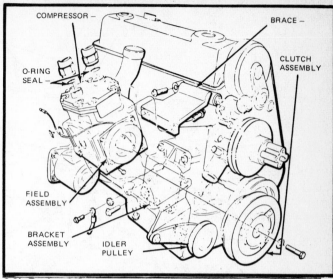

2.3L Engine A/C compressor installation (© Ford Motor Co.)

2. Reverse removal procedures.

3. Using new O-rings lubricated with clean refrigerant oil, connect the suction and discharge lines to the compressor manifolds. Tighten each fitting to specification.

4. Connect the clutch wires to the field coil connector.

6. Install the drive belt. Adjust the drive belt to specification.

6. Leak test, evacuate and charge the system following the recommended service procedures. Observe all safety precautions.

7. Check the system for proper operation.

SIX CYLINDER (6P148) COMPRESSOR

Removal

1984-85 MUSTANG/CAPRI WITH 5.0L ENGINE

1. Discharge the system following the recomended service procedures. Observe all safety precautions.

2. Disconnect compressor clutch wires to the field coil connector on compressor.

3. Disconnect the discharge and suction hoses from the compressor manifolds. Cap the refrigerant lines and compressor manifolds to prevent the entrance of dirt and moisture.

4. Remove two screws attaching brace to rear mounting bracket.

5. Remove two screws attaching bracket to compressor lower front mounting lugs.

6. Remove one screw attaching bracket to compressor upper mounting lug.

7. Remove compressor/clutch assembly and rear support from vehicle as unit.

8. Remove two screws attaching compressor to rear support and remove rear support.

9. If the compressor is to be replaced, remove the clutch and field coil assembly from compressor.

Installation

1. A new service replacement compressor contains 10 fluid ounces of the specified refrigerant oil. Before installing the replacement compressor, drain four fluid ounces of refrigerant oil from the compressor. This will keep the total system oil charge within specifications.

2. Reverse removal procedure.

3. Using new O-rings lubricated with clean refrigerant oil, connect the suction and discharge lines to the compressor manifolds. Tighten each fitting to specification.

4. Connect the clutch wires to the field coil connector.

5. Install the drive belt. Adjust the drive belt to specification.

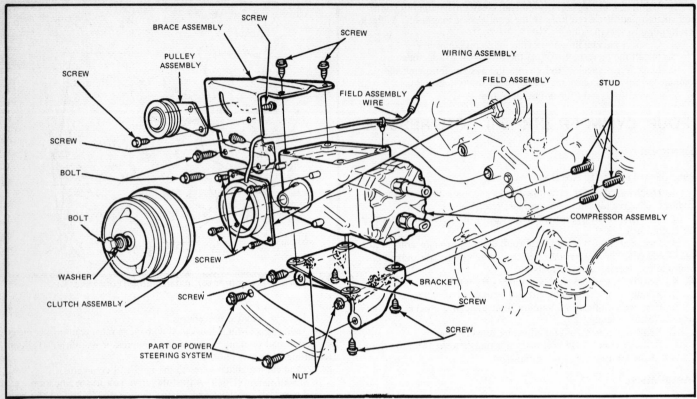

5.0L Engine A/C compressor installation (© Ford Motor Co.)

6. Leak test, evacuate and charge the system following the recommended service procedures. Observe all safety precautions.

7. Check the system for proper operation.

SIX CYLINDER (6P148) COMPRESSOR

Removal

1982-83 ESCORT/EXP AND LYNX/LN7

1. Discharge the system following the recommended service procedures. Observe all safety precautions.

2. Disconnect the alternator wires at the multiple connector.

3. Remove the carburetor air cleaner and the air intake and tube assembly from the radiator support.

4. Disconnect the alternator air tube from the air inlet on the radiator support.

5. Remove the alternator from the engine.

6. Disconnect the compressor clutch wires at the field coil connector on the compressor.

7. Disconnect the discharge hose and the suction hose from the compressor manifolds. Cap the refrigerant lines and compressor manifolds to prevent the entrance of dirt and moisture.

8. Raise the vehicle and remove two bolts attaching the front legs of the compressor to the mounting bracket.

9. Remove two screws attaching the heater water return tube to the underside of the engine supports.

10. Remove two bolts attaching the compressor bracket assembly to the compressor bracket.

11. Lower the vehicle and remove one bolt attaching the top of the compressor to the mounting bracket.

12. Tilt the top of the compressor toward the radiator to disengage the top mounting tab from the compressor bracket. Then, lift the compressor from the engine compartment, rear head first.

13. If the compressor is to be replaced, remove the clutch and field coil assembly and the compressor bracket assembly from the compressor.

Installation

1. If the compressor is to be replaced, drain the oil from the removed compressor into a calibrated measuring container. Record the amount of oil (fluid ounces) drained from the old compressor. Discard the oil.

2. Drain all the oil from the new service replacement compressor.

3. If the oil drained from the old compressor measured less than three fluid ounces, pour six fluid ounces of new clean refrigerant oil in the drained replacement compressor.

4. If the oil drained from the removed compressor measured between three and six fluid ounces, the oil is properly distributed throughout the system. Pour an equal amount of new clean refrigerant oil in the drained service department compressor.

5. If the oil drained from the old compressor measured more than six fluid ounces, pour only six fluid ounces of new clean refrigerant oil in the drained service replacement compressor.

6. Install the compressor bracket assembly on the compressor rear legs if the compressor is being replaced.

7. Position the compressor to the vehicle and the compressor bracket.

8. Raise the vehicle and install four bolts to attach the compressor and bracket assembly to the compressor bracket.

9. Install two screws to attach the heater core return tube to the engine supports.

10. Lower the vehicle and install one bolt to attach the top tab of the compressor to the compressor bracket.

11. Using new O-rings lubricated with clean regrigerant oil, connect the suction and discharge lines to the compressor manifolds. Tighten each fitting to the specified torque.

12. Connect the clutch wires to the field coil connector.

SIX CYLINDER (6P148) COMPRESSOR

Removal

1984-85 ESCORT/EXP AND LYNX

1. Disconnect the alternator wires at the multiple connector and remove the alternator from the engine.

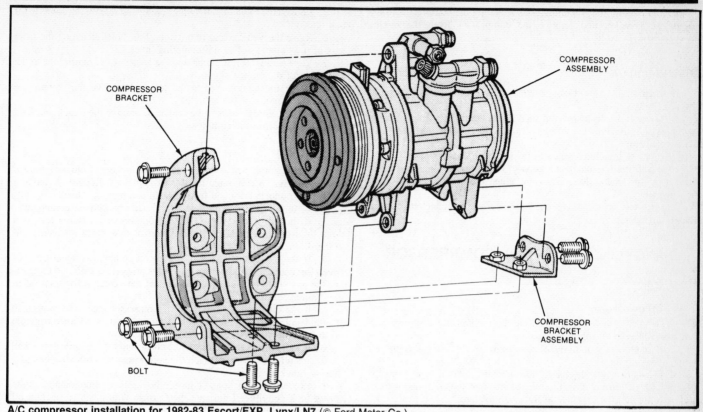

A/C compressor installation for 1982-83 Escort/EXP, Lynx/LN7 (© Ford Motor Co.)

2. Discharge the A/C system and disconnect the compressor clutch wires at the field coil connector on the compressor.

3. On the 1.6L EFI and HO engines, remove the discharge and suction hoses at the compressor manifolds.

4. On the 1.6L Turbo and the 2.0L Diesel engines, remove the discharge hose from the manifold tube with a ½ inch lock coupling tool (#T81P-19623-G2 or equivalent). Use a ⅝ inch spring lock coupling tool (#T83P-19632-C or equivalent) to remove the suction hose.

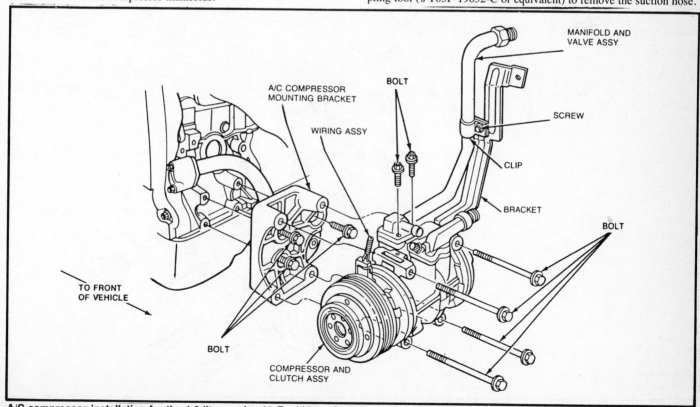

A/C compressor installation for the 1.6 liter engine (© Ford Motor Co.)

5. Remove the four retaining bolts attaching the compressor to the compressor bracket and remove the compressor from the engine compartment.

Installation

1. Position the compressor onto the compressor bracket and install the four bolts.

2. Connect the discharge and suction lines to the manifold and tube assembly. On the threaded fittings, install a new O-ring lubricated with clean refrigerant oil.

3. Connect the clutch wires to the field coil connector.

4. Install the alternator and connect the multiple connector to the alternator. Install the drive belts and adjust the belts to the specified belt tension.

5. Leak test, evacuate and charge the system and check the system for proper operation.

SIX CYLINDER (6P148) COMPRESSOR

Removal

1983-85 Tempo/Topaz

1. Discharge the system following the recommended service procedures. Observe all safety precautions.

2. Disconnect the compressor clutch wires at the field coil connector on the compressor.

3. Disconnect the discharge hose and the suction hose from the compressor manifolds. Cap the refrigerant lines and compressor manifolds to prevent the entrance of dirt and moisture.

4. Separate the discharge refrigerant line at the spring lock coupling above the compressor with Tool T81P-19623-G or equivalent and remove the lower end of the discharge line.

5. Loosen the two idler attaching screws and release the compressor belt tension.

6. Raise the vehicle and remove the four bolts attaching the front legs of the compressor to the mounting bracket.

7. Remove two screws attaching the heater water return tube to the underside of the engine supports.

8. Move the compressor to the left and remove the compressor from the underside of the vehicle.

9. If the compressor is to be replaced, remove the clutch and field coil assembly from the compressor.

Installation

1. If the compressor is to be replaced, drain the oil from the removed compressor into a calibrated measuring container. Record the amount of oil (fluid ounces) drained from the old compressor. Discard the oil.

2. Drain all the oil from the new service replacement compressor.

3. If the oil drained from the old compressor measured less than three fluid ounces, pour six fluid ounces of new clean refrigerant oil in the drained replacement compressor.

4. If the oil drained from the removed compressor measured between three and six fluid ounces, the oil is properly distributed throughout the system. Pour an equal amount of new clean refrigerant oil in the drained service replacement compressor.

5. If the oil drained from the old compressor measured more than six fluid ounces, pour only six fluid ounces of new clean refrigerant oil in the drained service replacement compressor.

6. Position the compressor to the vehicle and the compressor bracket.

7. Install four bolts to attach the compressor assembly to the compressor bracket.

8. Lower the vehicle and connect the discharge line together at the spring lock coupling. Lubricate the O-rings with clean refrigerant oil prior to assembly.

9. Install one bolt to attach the top tab of the compressor to the compressor bracket.

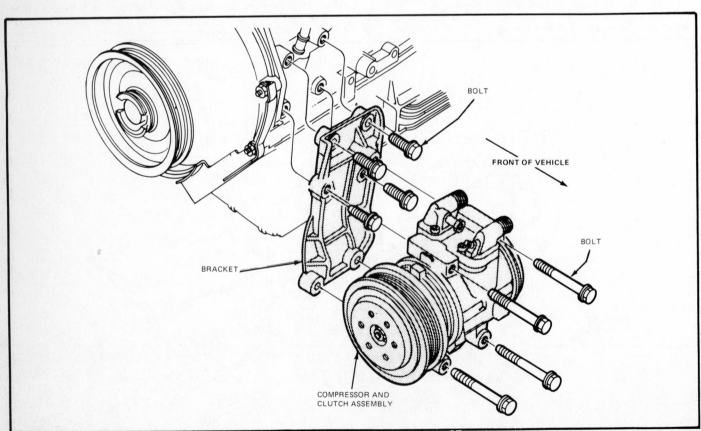

A/C compressor installation for 83-85 Tempo/Topaz (© Ford Motor Co.)

10. Using new O-rings lubricated with clean refrigerant oil, connect the suction and discharge lines to the compressor manifolds. Tighten each fitting to specification.

11. Connect the clutch wires to the field coil connector.

12. Install the drive belts on the pulleys and adjust the belt tension to specification.

13. Leak test, evacuate and charge the system following the recommended service procedures. Observe all safety precautions.

14. Check the system for proper operation.

SIX CYLINDER (FS-6) COMPRESSOR

Removal and Installation

1982-85 FORD/MERCURY, TOWN CAR, CROWN VICTORIA AND GRAND MARQUIS

1. Discharge the refrigerant from the system following the recommended service procedures.

2. Loosen the idler pulley to remove the tension from the compressor drive belt, and remove the drive belt from the clutch pulley.

3. Remove the refrigerant lines from the compressor manifolds.

4. Disconnect the clutch wires at the wire connector.

5. Remove one bolt attaching top of the compressor to the compressor front bracket.

6. Remove the locknut and stud from the compressor front lower inboard attachment at the front bracket.

NOTE: If the stud does not come out with the lock nut, install a stud remover or equivalent and remove the stud.

7. Remove the three compressor lower attaching bolts and remove the compressor.

8. Installation is the reverse order of the removal procedure. Leak test, evacuate and charge the system, also check the system for proper operation.

Two Cylinder Compressor

Removal and Installation

1982-83 THUNDERBIRD/XR-7 AND LTD/MARQUIS

1. Discharge the refrigerant from the A/C system at the low pressure service access gauge port valve located on the suction line near the compressor following recommended service procedures.

2. Energize the magnetic clutch and remove the clutch retaining bolt.

3. On 3.3L (200 CID) engines, loosen alternator attaching bolt and the adjusting arm bolt. Then, release the compressor and alternator belt tension.

4. Remove the drive belt from the compressor clutch pulley.

5. Install a ⅝-11 bolt in the compresor shaft hole of the clutch and, with the clutch energized, tighten the bolt to push the clutch from the compressor shaft.

6. Disconnect the clutch field wire at the connector.

7. Remove the refrigerant lines from the compressor and plug the lines and compressor ports to prevent the entrance of dirt and excessive moisture,

8. Remove the compressor mounting bolts and remove compressor.

9. Remove the clutch field coil from the compressor if the compressor is to be replaced.

10. Installation is the reverse order of the removal procedure. Leak test, evacuate and charge the system. Check the system for proper operation.

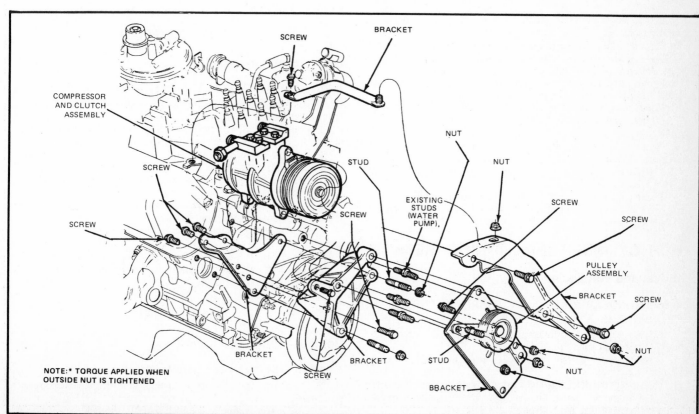

NOTE:* TORQUE APPLIED WHEN OUTSIDE NUT IS TIGHTENED

4.2L and 5.8L engine—A/C compressor installation (© Ford Motor Co.)

SIX CYLINDER (FS-6) COMPRESSOR

Removal and Installation

1982-83 THUNDERBIRD/XR-7 AND LTD/MARQUIS W/3.3L AND 3.8L ENGINES

1. Discharge the system following the recommended service procedures.
2. Disconnect compressor clutch wires at the field coil connector on compressor.
3. Disconnect the discharge and suction hoses from the compressor manifolds. Cap the refrigerant lines and compressor manifolds to prevent the entrance of dirt and moisture.
4. Remove the screw attaching the bottom compressor brace to the front compressor brace and remove the nut attaching the bottom compressor brace to the intake manifold.
5. Remove the two screws holding the rear support to the bracket.
6. Remove the one screw attaching the compressor tab to the front brace and the two screws attaching the compressor front legs to the bracket.
7. Remove the compressor/clutch assembly and rear support from the vehicle as a whole unit.
8. Remove the two screws attaching the compressor to the rear support and remove the rear support.
9. Installation is the reverse order of the removal procedure.
10. Leak test, evacuate and charge the system, also check the system for proper operation.

SIX CYLINDER (FS-6) COMPRESSOR

Removal and Installation

1982-83 THUNDERBIRD/XR-7 AND LTD/MARQUIS W/4.2L Engine

1. Discharge the system following the recommended service procedures.
2. Disconnect compressor clutch wires at the field coil connector on compressor.
3. Disconnect the discharge and suction hoses from the compressor manifolds. Cap the refrigerant lines and compressor manifolds to prevent the entrance of dirt and moisture.
4. Remove two nuts from rear support bracket. Remove three screws from the front bosses on the compressor.
5. Rotate the compressor outboard (toward left side of engine compartment) until compressor upper boss clears support.
6. Remove compressor and rear support from vehicle as a unit.
7. Remove two screws attaching rear support to compresor and remove rear support.
8. If the compressor is to be replaced, remove the clutch and field coil from compressor.
9. Installation is the reverse order of the removal procedure.
10. Leak test, evacuate and charge the system, also check the system for proper operation.

FOUR CYLINDER (HR-980) COMPRESSOR

Removal and Installation

1982-85 THUNDERBIRD/XR-7, LTD/MARQUIS AND 1984-85 COUGAR W/2.3L AND 3.8L ENGINES

1. Discharge the system following the recommended service procedures. Observe all safety precautions.
2. Disconnect compressor clutch wires at the field coil connector on compressor.
3. Disconnect the discharge and suction hoses from the compressor manifolds. Cap the refrigerant lines and compressor manifolds to prevent the entrance of dirt and moisture.
4. Remove screw and washer assembly from the adjusting bracket.

5. Rotate compressor and remove drive belts.
6. Remove compressor mounting bolt attaching bracket to compressor lower mounting lug.
7. Remove compressor and adjusting bracket intact.
8. Remove clutch field coil and adjusting bracket from the compressor if the compressor is to be replaced.
9. Installation is the reverse order of the removal procedure. Leak test, evacuate and charge the system, also check the system for proper operation.

Six Cylinder (FS-6) Compressor

Removal and Installation

1984-85 Thunderbird/Cougar W/5.0L Engine

1. Discharge the system following the recommended service procedures.
2. Disconnect compressor clutch wires at the field coil connector on compressor.
3. Disconnect the discharge and suction hoses from the compressor manifolds. Cap the refrigerant lines and compressor manifolds to prevent the entrance of dirt and moisture.
4. Remove two screws from rear support bracket. Remove three screws attaching compressor tab and front legs to front support. Remove one screw from front of tubular brace. Remove tubular brace from vehicle.
5. Rotate the compressor outboard (toward left side of engine compartment) until compressor upper boss clears support.
6. Remove compressor assembly and rear support from vehicle as unit.
7. Remove two screws attachiig rear support to compressor and remove rear support.
8. If the compressor is to be replaced, remove the clutch and field coil assembly from compressor.
9. Installation is the reverse order of the removal procedure.
10. Leak test, evacuate and charge the system, also check the system for proper operation.

COMPRESSOR

Removal and Installation

1982-83 CONTINENTAL AND MARK V1

1. Discharge the refrigerant from the system following the recommended service procedures.
2. Loosen the idler pulley to remove the tension from the compressor drive belt, and remove the drive belt from the clutch pulley.
3. Remove the refrigerant lines from the compressor manifolds.
4. Disconnect the clutch wires at the wire connector.
5. Remove one bolt attaching top of the compressor to the compressor front bracket.
6. Remove the locknut and stud from the compressor front lower inboard attachment at the front bracket.
7. Remove three compressor lower attaching bolts, and remove the compressor.
8. Installation is the reverse order of the removal procedure.
9. Leak test, evacuate and charge the system, also check the system for proper operation.

COMPRESSOR

Removal and Installation

1984-85 CONTINENTAL AND MARK VII

1. Discharge the system following the recommended service procedures.
2. Disconnect compressor clutch wires at the field coil connector on compressor.

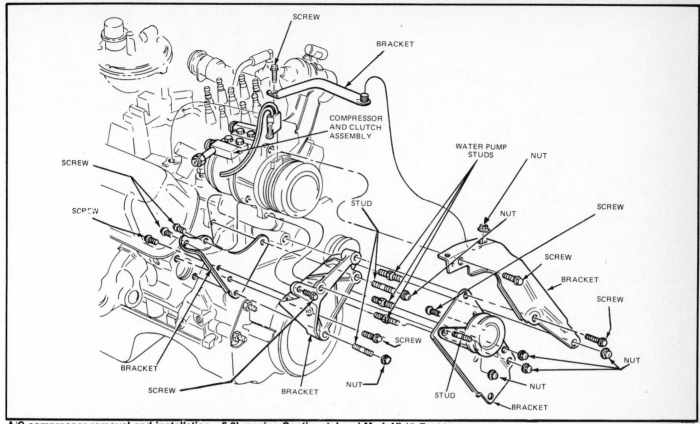

A/C compressor removal and installation—5.0L engine Continental and Mark VI (© Ford Motor Co.)

3. Disconnect the discharge and suction hoses from the compressor manifolds. Cap the refrigerant lines and compressor manifolds to prevent the entrance of dirt and moisture.

4. Remove two nuts from rear support bracket. Remove three screws attaching compressor tab and front legs to front support. Remove one screw from front of tubular brace. Remove tubular brace from vehicle.

5. Rotate the compressor outboard (toward left side of engine compartment) until compressor upper boss clears support.

6. Remove compressor assembly and rear support from vehicle as a unit.

7. Remove two screws attaching rear support to compressor and remove rear support.

8. If the compressor is to be replaced, remove the clutch and field coil assembly from compressor.

9. Installation is the reverse order of the removal procedure.

10. Leak test, evacuate and charge the system, also check the system for proper operation.

Fixed Orifice Tube Refrigerant System

GENERAL INFORMATION

The fixed orifice tube system is being used on all domestic passenger cars and light duty trucks, except the Econoline. The fixed orifice tube system, replaces the therm-expansion valve and the suction throttle valve with an orifice tube and a clutch cycling pressure switch. The fixed orifice tube assembly is the restriction between the high and the low pressure liquid refrigerant and meters the flow of the liquid refrigerant into the evaporator core. The fixed orifice tube is constructed of filter screens, which are located in the inlet and outlet ends of the tube body and two O-rings. The screens act as strainers for the liquid refrigerant flowing through the fixed orifice opening. The two O-rings

on the tube body prevent the high pressure liquid refrigerant from bypassing the orifice tube assembly. The fixed orifice tube is located in the liquid line near the evaporator inlet tube on some models and in the liquid line near the condensor in other models. Adjustments or repairs can not be made to the orifice tube, if the tube is not operating properly it should be replaced.

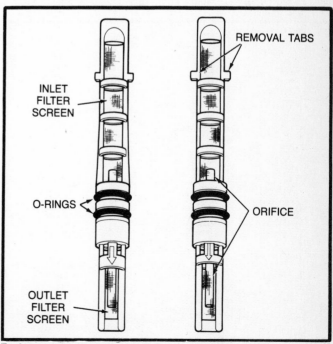

Typical fixed orifice tube assembly (© Ford Motor Co.)

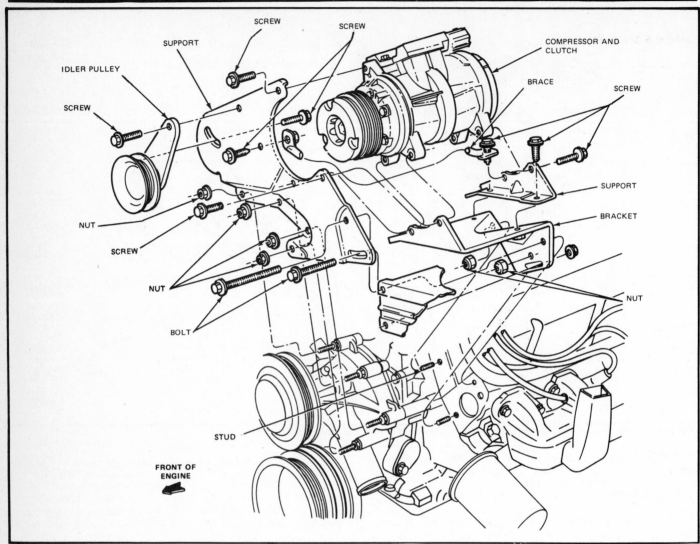

1984-85 A/C compressor installation—Continental and Mark VII (© Ford Motor Co.)

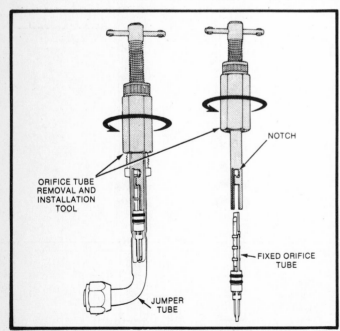

Fixed orifice tube removal—1982-83 Escort/EXP, Lynx/LN7 (© Ford Motor Co.)

FIXED ORIFICE TUBE

Removal and Installation

1982-83 ESCORT/EXP AND LYNX/LN7

1. Discharge the refrigerant from the A/C system following the recommended service procedures. Observe all safety precautions.

2. Raise the vehicle and disconnect the liquid line jumper tube from the evaporator core.

3. Lower the vehicle and pull the jumper tube end of the liquid line up above the top of the engine. Then, disconnect the jumper tube from the end of the liquid line.

4. Pour a small amount of clean refrigerant oil into the jumper tube to lubricate the jumper tube and the orifice tube O-rings during removal of the fixed orifice tube from the liquid line jumper tube.

5. Engage the orifice remover (Tool D80L-19990-A or equivalent with the two tangs on the fixed orifice tube.

NOTE: Do not twist or rotate the fixed orifice tube in the jumper tube as the orifice tube may break.

6. Hold the T-handle of the remover tool to keep it from turning and run the nut on the tool down against the jumper tube until the orifice tube is pulled from the jumper tube.

7. If the fixed orifice tube breaks in the jumper tube, it can be removed from the tube with a orifice tube extractor (#D80L-19990-B or equivalent).

Vehicle & Model Year		Orifice Tube Location		
		Evaporator Inlet Tube	Jumper Tube at Evaporator	Liquid Line Near Condenser
Ford	1980–83	X		
Mercury	1980–83	X		
Lincoln	1980–83	X		
Mark VI	1980–83	X		
Escort	1981–82		X	
	1983			X
Lynx	1981–82		X	
	1983			X
EXP	1982		X	
	1983			X
LN7	1982		X	
	1983			X
Fairmont	1982–83			X①
Zephyr	1982–83			X①
Mustang	1982–83			X①
Capri	1982–83			X①
Granada	1982			X
Cougar	1982			X
Thunderbird	1982–83			X①
XR-7	1982–83			X①
Lincoln Continental	1982–83			X①
LTD	1983			X①
Marquis	1983			X①
F-Series and Bronco	1980–83	X		
Ranger	1982–83	X		

① Some 1983 models have non-removable orifice tubes. On these models, the liquid line must be replaced the orifice tube. This was a running charge during the 1983 model year and does not affect all models.

8. Installaion is the reverse order of the removal procedure.

9. Leak test, evacuate and charge the system. Check the system for proper operation.

FIXED ORIFICE TUBE

Removal

1982–85 ALL MODELS EXCEPT: 1983–85 TEMPO/TOPAZ, 1984–85 ESCORT/EXP AND LYNX, 1984–85 CONTINENTAL/MARK VII, THUNDERBIRD/COUGAR, LTD/MARQUIS AND MUSTANG/CAPRI

1. Discharge the refrigerant from the A/C system following the recommended service procedures.

2. Disconnect or separate the liquid line at the orifice tube location.

3. Pour a small amount of clean refrigerant oil into the inlet tube or liquid line containing the orifice tube. This will lubricate the tube and the orifice tube O-rings during removal.

4. Engage the orifice remover tool (Motorcraft Tool YT-1008 or equivalent) with the two tangs on the fixed orifice tube.

NOTE: Do not twist or rotate the fixed orifice tube in the evaporator core tube as it may break off in the evaporator core tube.

5. Hold the T-handle of the remover Tool YT-1008 or equivalent, to keep it from turning and run the nut on the tool down against the evaporator core tube until the orifice is pulled from the tube.

6. If the fixed orifice tube breaks in the evaporator core tube, it must be removed from the tube with an extractor, Motorcraft Tool YT-1009 or equivalent.

7. To remove a broken orifice tube, insert the screw end of the extractor, Tool YT-1009 or equivalent, into the evaporator core tube and thread the screw end of the tool into the brass tube in the center

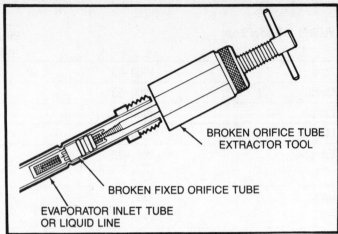

Removing a broken orifice tube (© Ford Motor Co.)

of the fixed orifice tube. Then, pull the fixed orifice tube from the evaporator core tube.

8. If only the brass center tube is removed during Step 7, insert the screw end of Tool YT-1009 or equivalent, into the evaporator core tube and screw the end of the tool into the fixed orifice tube body. Then, pull the fixed orifice tube body from the evaporator core tube.

Installation

1. Lubricate the O-rings on the fixed orifice tube body liberally with clean, specified refrigerant oil.

2. Place the fixed orifice tube in the remover, Tool YT-1008 or equivalent, and insert the fixed orifice tube into the evaporator core tube until the orifice is seated at the stop.

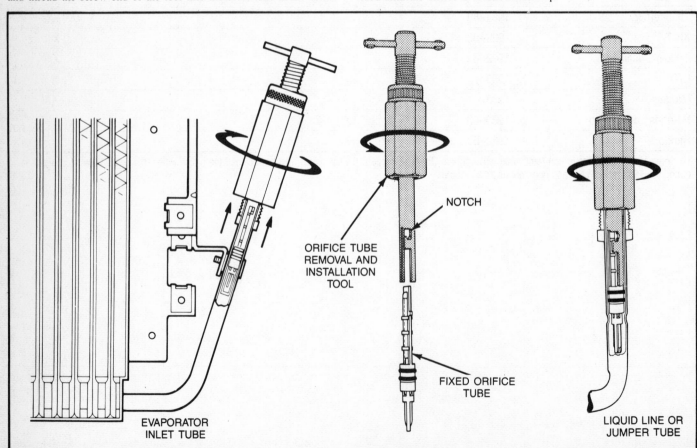

Typical fixed orifice tube removal from all equipped models (© Ford Motor Co.)

3. Remove the remover tool from the fixed orifice tube.

4. Using a new O-ring lubricated with clean refrigerant oil, connect the liquid line to the evaporator core tube. Tighten the fitting to the specific torque using a backup wrench.

5. Leak test, evacuate and charge the system following the recommended service procedures. Observe all safety precautions.

6. Check the system for proper operation.

FIXED ORIFICE TUBE

Removal and Installation

1983–85 TEMPO/TOPAZ, 1984–85 ESCORT/EXP AND LYNX, 1984–85 CONTINENTAL/MARK VII, THUNDERBIRD/COUGAR, LTD/MARQUIS AND MUSTANG/CAPRI

NOTE: The fixed orifice tube is an integral part of the refrigerant line. If the fixed orifice tube has to be replaced, the system has to be evacuated and the liquid line containing the fixed orifice tube has to be removed and replaced. Do not attempt to remove the fixed orifice tube with pliers or to twist or rotate the orifice tube in the liquid line. To do so will only break the fixed orifice tube body in the liquid line.

Refrigerant (Liquid) Lines

Removal and Installation

1. Discharge the refrigerant from the A/C system at the low pressure service access gauge port valve located on the suction line following the recommended service procedures.

2. Disconnect and remove the refrigerant line using a wrench on each side of each fitting or the special tool required for spring-lock couplings at the condenser.

3. Route the new refrigerant line with the protective caps.

4. Connect condenser lines spring-lock couplings.

5. Connect all other refrigerant lines into the system using new O-rings lubricated with clean refrigerant oil. Use two wrenches when tightening the fittings.

6. Leak test, evacuate and charge the system, also check the system for proper operation.

Condenser

CONDENSER COIL

Removal

1982–83 GRANADA/COUGAR, FAIRMONT/FUTURA, ZEPHYR AND 1982–85 MUSTANG/CAPRI

NOTE: The condensor refrigerant lines on all models are connected with spring-lock couplings. These couplings require the use of special tools to remove and install them. The procedures for the removal and installation of the spring-lock couplings are covered in the back of this section.

1. Discharge the refrigerant from the A/C system at the service access gauge port valve located on the suction line.

2. Drain the coolant from the radiator into a clean container and save coolant.

3. Close the radiator draincock.

4. Disconnect the cables from the battery and remove the battery and heat shield.

5. Loosen the refrigerant line fittings (spring-lock couplings) at the right side of the radiator.

6. Remove two fan shroud attaching screws, disengage the fan shroud and position it rearward.

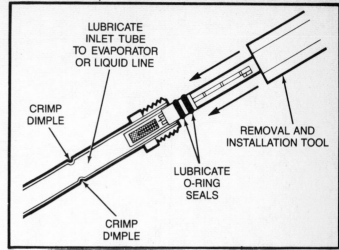

Typical orifice tube installation on all equipped models (© Ford Motor Co.)

7. Disconnect line upper hose from the radiator.

8. Remove the two radiator retaining clamps and tilt the radiator rearward.

9. Remove two screws attaching the top of the condenser to the radiator support.

10. Disconnect the refrigerant lines from the condenser and lift the condenser from the vehicle. Cap the refrigerant lines to prevent entry of dirt and excessive moisture.

Installation

1. If the condenser is to be replaced, transfer the rubber isolators from the bottom of the old condenser to the new condenser. Add one fluid ounce of clean refrigerant oil to the condenser.

2. Position the condenser assembly to the vehicle making sure the lower isolators are properly seated. Then, install the condenser upper two attaching screws.

3. Position the radiator to the radiator support and install the two retaining clamps.

4. Connect the upper hose to the radiator and fill the radiator with the coolant removed from the radiator in Step 2 of Removal. Be sure the radiator draincock is closed.

5. Position the fan shroud to the radiator and install the two attaching screws.

6. Connect the refrigerant lines to the condenser.

7. Install the battery and heat shield in the vehicle. Then, connect the cables to the battery, the positive cable first.

8. Leak test, evacuate and charge the system.

CONDENSER COIL

Removal and Installation

1982–83 ESCORT/EXP AND LYNX/LN7

1. Discharge the refrigerant system to be sure that no charge remains in the system.

2. Drain the engine coolant from the cooling system.

3. Remove the carburetor air intake tube and alternator air tube from the radiator support.

4. Remove two (2) nuts retaining the fan shroud to the radiator and disconnect the A/C discharge line retaining clip from the radiator fan shroud left retaining bolt.

5. Disconnect the fan motor wires and remove the fan shroud.

6. Disconnect the upper hose from the radiator.

7. Disconnect the radiator lower hose from the engine water tube.

8. Disconnect and cap the transmission oil cooler hoses from the oil tubes on the automatic transaxle.

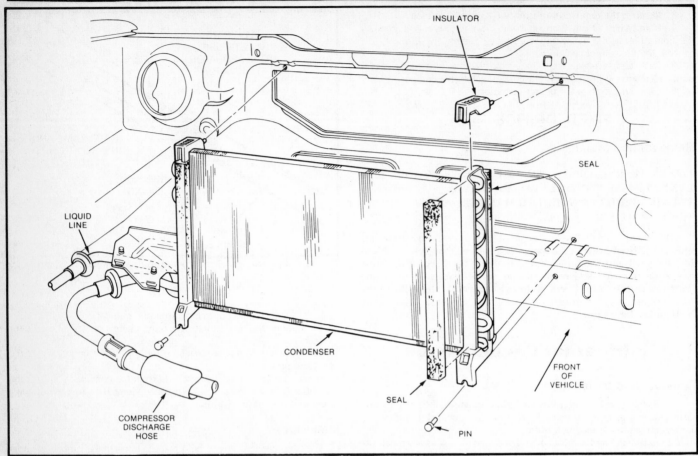

Condensor installation—1984-85 Tempo/Topaz, Escort/EXP and Lynx (© Ford Motor Co.)

9. Remove the two nuts holding the radiator to the radiator support and remove the radiator and lower hose.

10. Disconnect the refrigerant line and compressor discharge line from the condensor, (use tool #T81P-19623-G or equivalent).

11. Hold the upper corners of the condensor and move the top of the condensor toward the engine and remove the condensor from the rubber mounts.

12. Installation is the reverse of the removal procedure. Leak test, evacuate and charge the system.

CONDENSER COIL

Removal and Installation

1983–85 TEMPO/TOPAZ, 1984–85 ESCORT/EXP AND LYNX

1. Discharge the refrigerant system to be sure that no charge remains in the system. Observe all safety precautions.

2. Drain the engine coolant from the cooling system.

3. Remove the ignition coil from the engine.

4. Remove one screw and one nut retaining the fan shroud to the radiator and disconnect the A/C discharge line retaining clip from the radiator fan shroud.

5. Disconnect the fan motor wires and remove the fan shroud.

6. Disconnect the upper hose from the radiator.

7. Disconnect the radiator lower hose from the engine water tube.

8. Disconnect and cap the transmission oil cooler hoses from the oil tubes on the automatic transaxle.

9. Remove two nuts attaching the radiator to the radiator support and remove the radiator and lower hose as assembly.

10. Discount the refrigerant line and the compressor discharge line from the condensor, (use tool #T81P-19623-G or equivalent).

11. Remove the condensor upper bracket attaching screws and remove the condensor.

12. Installation is the reverse order of the removal procedure. Leak test, evacuate and charge the system.

CONDENSER COIL

Removal and Installation

1982–85 FORD/MERCURY, TOWN CAR, CROWN VICTORIA AND GRAND MARQUIS

1. Disconnect battery cables and remove the battery.

2. Loosen the radiator cap and open the radiator draincock allowing the engine coolant to drain from the cooling system into a clean container for re-use.

3. Close the draincock tightly.

4. Disconnect the radiator upper hose at the radiator.

5. Discharge the refrigerant from the A/C system at the service access valve located on the suction accumulator-drier.

6. Disconnect the two refrigerant lines at the fittings near the radiator on the right side of the vehicle. Plug the lines to prevent dirt and excessive moisture from entering.

7. Remove the two retaining screws from the carburetor air intake duct and position it away from the radiator/condenser area.

8. Remove the two retaining screws from the fan shroud and position it rearward away from the radiator/condenser area.

9. Remove the screw from each of the two radiator brackets and tilt the radiator rearward.

10. Remove the two retaining screws from the top back side of the condenser assembly and lift the condenser from the vehicle. Make certain to remove and retain the four corner condenser isomounts.

11. Installation is the reverse order of the removal procedure. Leak test, evacuate and charge the system.

CONDENSER COIL

Removal

1982–85 THUNDERBIRD/XR-7, LTD/MARQUIS AND 1984–85 COUGAR

1. Discharge the refrigerant from the A/C system at the service access gauge port valve located on the suction line.
2. Disconnect and remove the battery from the battery tray.
3. Disconnect the two refrigerant lines at the fittings on the right side of the radiator.
4. Remove four bolts attaching the condenser to the radiator support and remove the condenser from the vehicle.

Installation

1. Position the condenser assembly to the radiator support brackets and install the attaching bolts.
2. Connect the refrigerant lines to the condenser assembly.
3. Install and connect the battery.
4. Leak test, evacuate and charge the refrigerant system.

CONDENSER COIL

Removal and Installation

1982–85 CONTINENTAL, MARK VI AND MARK VII

1. Disconnect battery cables and remove the battery.
2. Loosen the radiator cap and open the radiator draincock allowing the engine coolant to drain from the cooling system into a clean container for re-use.
3. Close the draincock tightly.
4. Disconnect the radiator upper hose at the radiator.
5. Discharge the refrigerant from the A/C system at the service access valve located on the suction accumulator-drier.
6. Disconnect the two refrigerant lines at the fittings near the radiator on the right side of the vehicle. Plug the lines to prevent dirt and excessive moisture from entering.
7. Remove the two retaining screws from the carburetor air intake duct and position it away from the radiator/condenser area.
8. Remove the two retaining screws from the fan shroud and position it rearward away from the radiator/condenser area.
9. Remove the screw from each of the two radiator brackets and tilt the radiator rearward.
10. Remove the two retaining screws from the top back side of the condenser assembly and lift the condenser from the vehicle. Make certain to remove and retain the four corner condenser isomounts.
11. Installation is the reverse order of the removal procedure. Leak test, evacuate and charge the system.

Evaporator

NOTE: In order to remove the evaporator core the evaporator case must be removed first.

EVAPORATOR CASE

Removal and Installation

1982–83 GRANADA/COUGAR, FAIRMONT/FUTURA, ZEPHYR AND 1982–84 MUSTANG/CAPRI

1. Remove the instrument panel and lay it on the front seat.
2. Discharge the refrigerant from the A/C system at the service access gauge port valve located on the suction line.

3. Once the refrigerant is discharged from the system, remove the high and low pressure hoses. Use a backup wrench to prevent component damage. Cap the hose openings to prevent the entrance of dirt and excessive moisture.
4. Disconnect the heater hoses from the heater core tubes and plug the hoses with suitable ⅝-inch and ¾-inch plugs. Cap the heater core tubes to prevent coolant loss from the heater core during removal of the evaporator case.
5. Remove the screw attaching the air inlet duct and blower housing assembly support brace to the cowl top panel.
6. Disconnect the vacuum supply hose (black) from the in-line vacuum check valve in the engine compartment.
7. Disconnect the blower motor wires from the wire harness. Disconnect the wire harness from the blower motor resistor.
8. Working under the hood, remove two nuts retaining the evaporator case to the dash panel.
9. In the passenger compartment, remove two screws attaching the evaporator case support brackets to the cowl top panel.
10. Remove one screw retaining the bracket below the evaporator case to the dash panel.
11. Carefully pull the evaporator case away from the dash panel and remove the evaporator case assembly from the vehicle.
12. Installation is the reverse order of the removal procedure. Leak test, evacuate and charge the system. Use new O-rings lubricated in clean refrigerant oil wherever possible.

EVAPORATOR CORE

Removal

1. Remove the evaporator case from the vehicle. Then, remove the air inlet duct and blower housing assembly from the evaporator case.
2. Remove seven screws and six snap clips retaining the two halves of the evaporator case together, and separate the two halves of the evaporator case.
3. Lift the evaporator core and seal from the lower half of the evaporator case.

NOTE: On the '82 models, remove the heater core access cover and the heater core from the evaporator case. There are also eleven screws instead of seven retaining the two halves of the evaporator case together.

Installation

1. Position the evaporator core in the lower half of the evaporator case fitting the seal over the edge of the case lower half.
2. Position the case upper half on the case lower half making sure the temperature blend door and the heat defrost door are properly positioned.
3. Install the seven screws and six snap clips to retain the two halves of the housing together.
4. Install the air inlet duct and blower housing assembly on the evaporator case.
5. Be sure on the '82 models to install the heater core and the heater core access cover.
6. Install the evaporator case into the vehicle.

EVAPORATOR CASE

Removal and Installation

1985 MUSTANG/CAPRI

1. Remove the instrument panel and lay it on the front seat.
2. Discharge the refrigerant from the A/C system at the service access gauge port valve located on the suction line.
3. Disconnect the liquid line and accumulator/drier inlet tube from the evaporator core at the dash panel. Cap the refrigerant lines and evaporator core tubes to prevent the entrance of dirt and excess moisture.
4. Once the refrigerant is discharged from the system, remove the high and low pressure hoses. Use a backup wrench to prevent com-

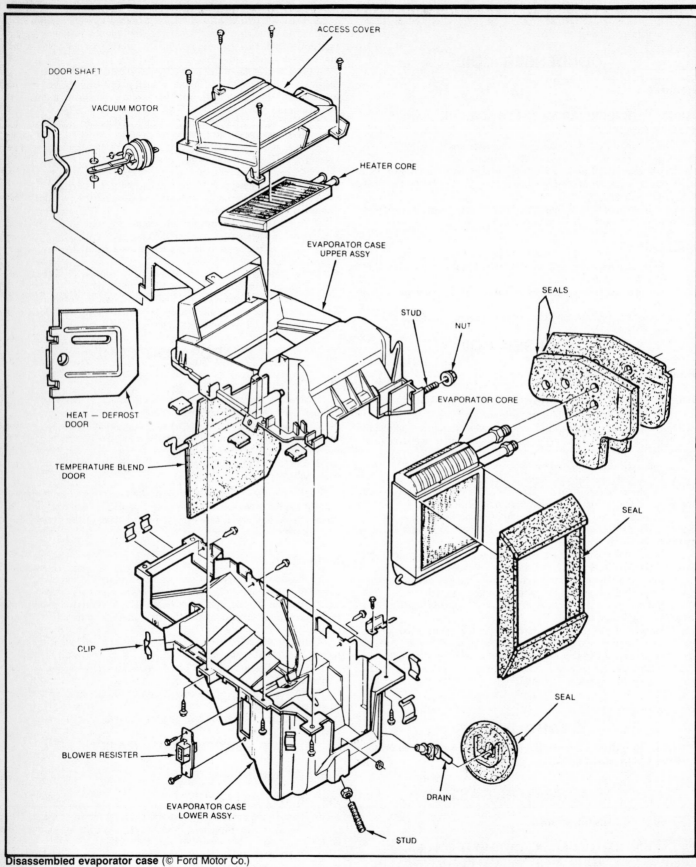

ACCESS COVER

DOOR SHAFT

VACUUM MOTOR

HEATER CORE

EVAPORATOR CASE
UPPER ASSY

SEALS

STUD

NUT

HEAT — DEFROST
DOOR

EVAPORATOR CORE

TEMPERATURE BLEND
DOOR

SEAL

CLIP

SEAL

BLOWER RESISTER

DRAIN

EVAPORATOR CASE
LOWER ASSY.

STUD

Disassembled evaporator case (© Ford Motor Co.)

ponent damage. Cap the hose openings to prevent the entrance of dirt and excessive moisture.

5. Disconnect the heater hoses from the heater core tubes and plug the hoses with suitable ⅝-inch and ¾ inch plugs. Cap the heater core tubes to prevent coolant loss from the heater core during removal of the evaporator case.

6. Remove the screw attaching the air inlet duct and blower housing assembly support brace to the cowl top panel.

7. Disconnect the vacuum supply hose (black) from the in-line vacuum check valve in the engine compartment.

8. Disconnect the blower motor wires from the wire harness. Disconnect the wire harness from the blower motor resistor.

9. Working under the hood, remove two nuts retaining the evaporator case to the dash panel.

10. In the passenger compartment, remove two screws attaching the evaporator case support brackets to the cowl top panel.

11. Remove one screw retaining the bracket below the evaporator case to the dash panel.

12. Carefully pull the evaporator case away from the dash panel and remove the evaporator case assembly from the vehicle.

13. Installation is the reverse order of the removal procedure. Leak test, evacuate and charge the system and install new O-rings lubricated in refrigerant oil wherever possible.

EVAPORATOR CORE

Removal

1. Remove the evaporator case as outlined.
2. Remove the air inlet duct from the evaporator case.
3. Remove the foam seal from the evaporator core tubes.
4. Drill a ³⁄₁₆ inch hole in both upright tabs on top of the evaporator case and two holes in the front.

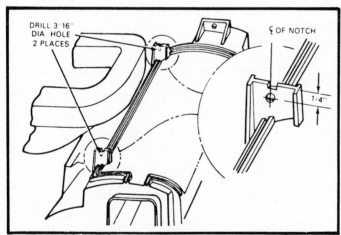

³⁄₁₆ drill hole locations (© Ford Motor Co.)

5. Using a small saw blade, cut the top of the evaporator case between the raised outlines.

6. Remove the blower motor resistor from the evaporator case.

7. Fold the cut-out flap from the opening and lift the evaporator core from the case.

Installation

1. Transfer the two foam core seals to the new evaporator core.
2. Position the evaporator core in the case and close the cut out cover.
3. Install a spring nut on each of the two upright tabs and over the two holes drilled in the front flange.

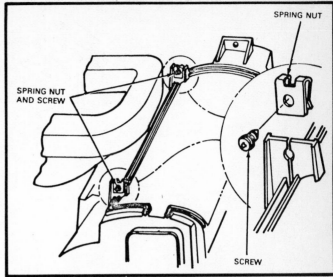

Installing the spring nuts (© Ford Motor Co.)

NOTE: Be sure the hole in the spring nut is aligned with the ³⁄₁₆ inch hole drilled in the tab and flange. Then, install and tighten a screw in each spring nut (through the hole in the tab or flange) to secure the cut-out cover in the closed position.

4. Install caulking cord D9AZ-19560-A or equivalent to seal the evaporator case against leakage along the cut line.

EVAPORATOR CASE

Removal and Installation

1982-83 ESCORT/EXP AND LYNX/LN7

1. Disconnect the ground cable from the battery negative (−) terminal.

2. Drain the coolant from the radiator into a clean container.

3. Discharge the refrigerant from the A/C system.

4. Disconnect the heater hoses from the heater core. Plug the heater core tubes or blow any coolant from the heater core with low pressure air.

5. Disconnect the liquid and suction refrigerant lines from the evaporator core at the dash panel. Cap the refrigerant lines and evaporator core to prevent the entrance of dirt and excess moisture.

6. Remove the steering column opening cover from the instrument panel.

7. Remove the lower half of the shroud from the steering column.

8. Remove four nuts attaching the steering column to the support bracket and allow the steering wheel to rest on the front seat.

9. Remove one screw attaching the instrument panel to the steering column support bracket at the top of the steering column opening.

10. Disconnect the center brace from the lower flange of the instrument panel.

11. Remove the three radio speaker opening covers from the instrument panel.

12. Remove one screw attaching the instrument panel to the top of the dash panel at each radio speaker opening.

13. Disconnect the speedometer cable from the transmission.

14. Disconnect the wire harness connectors from the blower motor and the blower motor resistor.

15. Disconnect the evaporator case vacuum harness at the in-line multiple vacuum connector.

16. Disconnect the wires from the right door courtesy light switch and remove the wires from the A-pillar (if so equipped).

17. Move the A/C temperature selector lever to COOL. Disconnect the temperature cable self-adjusting clip from the temperature door crank arm. Then, disengage the cable end retainer from the cable bracket.

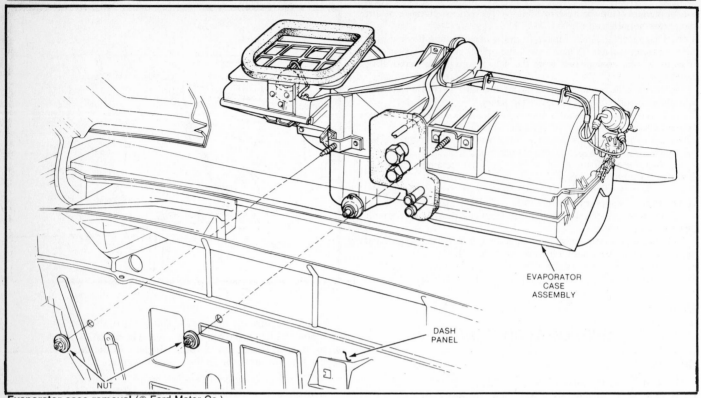

Evaporator case removal (© Ford Motor Co.)

18. Remove one screw attaching the bottom of the evaporator case to the dash panel.

19. Remove one screw attaching each end of the instrument panel to the cowl side panels.

20. Pull the instrument panel rearward to gain access to the evaporator case.

21. Remove the instrument panel center brace from the cowl top panel.

22. Disconnect the vacuum harness supply hose from the check valve in the engine compartment.

23. Remove two washer nuts attaching the evaporator case to the dash panel.

24. Loosen the sound insulation from the cowl top panel in the area around the air inlet opening.

25. Installation is the reverse order of the removal procedure. Leak test, evacuate and charge the system, install new O-rings lubricated in refrigerant oil wherever possible

EVAPORATOR CORE

Removal

1. Remove the evaporator case from the vehicle.

2. Remove the blower motor and mounting plate from the evaporator case.

3. Remove the air inlet duct seal from the duct flange.

4. Disconnect the vacuum hose from the outside-recirc door vacuum motor. Then, disengage the hose retainer and hose from the air inlet duct.

5. Remove the air inlet duct from the evaporator case.

6. Remove the floor duct from the evaporator case.

7. Remove the four heater core cover attaching screws and remove the cover and heater core from the lower half of the evaporator case.

8. Remove twelve screws attaching the two halves of the evaporator case together.

9. Lift the top half of the evaporator case (includes the floor-defrost door) from the lower half of the case.

10. Remove the evaporator core and dash panel seals from the case lower half.

11. Remove the dash panel seals from the evaporator core.

Installation

1. Position the evaporator core and seals in the case lower half.

2. Position the case top half on the lower half making sure the temperature blend door and the heat-defrost door are properly positioned.

3. Install the twelve screws to attach the case halves together. Then, check the temperature blend door and the heat-defrost door for proper operation.

4. Apply rope type sealer around the perimeter of the opening betweeen the air inlet duct and the blower housing.

5. Position the air inlet duct to the evaporator case and install the four attaching screws.

6. Route the outside-recirc door motor vacuum hose to the motor, engaging the retainer in the hole in the air inlet duct. Then, connect the vacuum hose to the motor and press the hose in the recess of the air duct flange.

7. Install the seal on the air inlet duct flange.

8. Install the blower motor and wheel (4 washer screws).

9. Install the heater core and cover.

10. Install the floor duct.

11. Install the dash panel seals (largest first) over the evaporator and heater core tubes and the supply vacuum hose.

12. Check the operation of the system air doors. Then, install the evaporator case in the vehicle.

EVAPORATOR CASE

Removal and Installation

1983-85 TEMPO/TOPAZ, 1984-85 ESCORT/EXP AND LYNX

1. Disconnect the ground cable from the battery negative terminal.

2. Drain the coolant from the radiator into a clean container.

3. Discharge the refrigerant from the A/C system as outlined.

4. Disconnect the heater hoses from the heater core. Plug the heater core tubes or blow any coolant from the heater core with low pressure air.

5. Disconnect the liquid line and the accumulator/drier inlet tube from the evaporator core at the dash panel. Cap the refrigerant lines and evaporator core to prevent the entrance of dirt and exess moisture.

6. Remove the instrument panel.

7. Disconnect the wire harness connector from the blower motor resistor.

8. Remove one screw attaching the bottom of the evaporator case to the dash panel.

9. Remove the instrument panel brace from the cowl top panel.

10. Remove two nuts attaching the evaporator case to the dash panel in the engine compartment.

11. Loosen the sound insulation from the cowl top panel in the area around the air inlet opening.

12. Remove the two screws attaching the support bracket and the brace to the cowl top panels.

13. Insulation is the reverse order of the removal procedure. Leak test, evacuate and charge the system, install new O-rings lubricated in refrigerant oil wherever possible.

EVAPORATOR CORE

Removal

1. Remove the evaporator case as outlined.

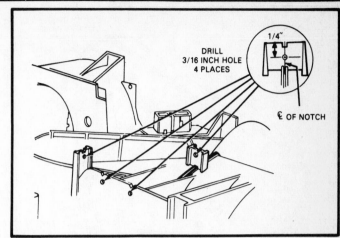

Drilling hole locations (© Ford Motor Co.)

2. Remove the air inlet duct from the evaporator case.

3. Remove the foam seal from the evaporator core tubes.

4. Drill a $\frac{3}{16}$ inch hole in both upright tabs on top of the evaporator case.

5. Using a hot knife or small saw blade, cut the top of the evaporator case between the raised outlines.

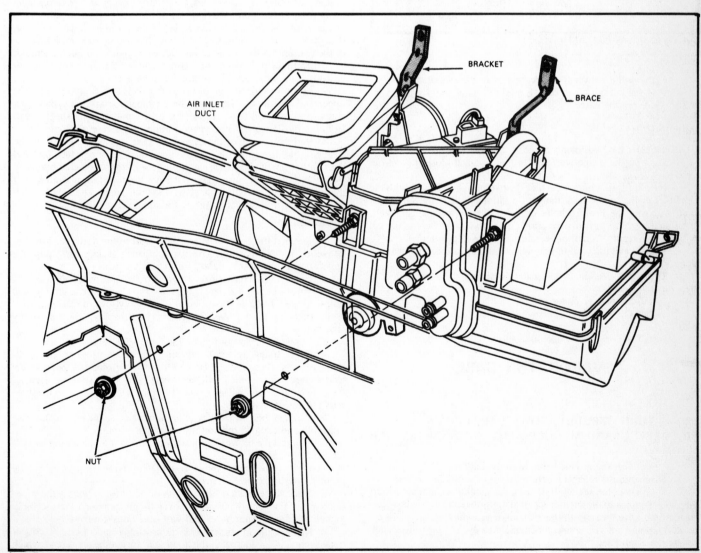

Installation of the evaporator case (© Ford Motor Co.)

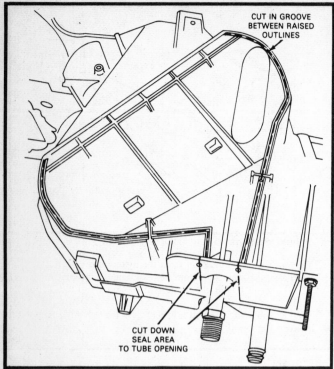

CUT IN GROOVE BETWEEN RAISED OUTLINES

CUT DOWN SEAL AREA TO TUBE OPENING

Cutting locations (© Ford Motor Co.)

6. Remove the blower motor resistor from the evaporator case.

7. Fold the cut-out cover back from the opening and lift the evaporator core from the case.

Installation

1. Transfer the two foam core seals to the new evaporator core.

2. Position the evaporator core in the case and close the cut-out cover.

3. Install a spring nut on each of the two upright tabs and with the two holes drilled in the front flange. Be sure the hole in the spring nut is aligned with the 3/16-inch holes drilled in the tab and flange. Then, install and tighten screw in each spring nut (through the hole in the tab or flange) to secure the cut-out cover in the closed position.

4. Install caulking cord to seal the evaporator case against leakage along the cut line.

5. Using new caulking (rope sealer), assemble the air inlet duct to the evaporator case.

6. Install the blower motor resistor.

7. Install the foam seal over the evaporator core and heater core tubes.

8. Install the evaporator case assembly.

EVAPORATOR CASE

Removal

1982-85 FORD/MERCURY, TOWN CAR, CROWN VICTORIA, GRAND MARQUIS, 1982 CONTINENTAL AND MARK VI

1. Disconnect the ground cable from the battery.

2. Discharge the refrigerant from the air conditioning system.

3. Disconnect the suction hose from the suction accumulator/drier. Plug the openings to the suction accumulator/drier and suction hose and position the hose away from the evaporator assembly.

4. Unplug two-wire connector from clutch cycling pressure switch on suction accumulator/drier.

5. Disconnect the liquid line from the evaporator inlet tube. Plug the openings to the liquid line and evaporator inlet tube and position the liquid line away from the evaporator assembly.

6. Drain radiator coolant into clean container. Save coolant for refilling cooling system.

7. Loosen the heater hose clamps and disconnect the heater hoses from the inlet and outlet heater core tubes.

8. From the passenger compartment, turn the steering wheel to the left to position the right front wheel so that the wheel well splash panel support bracket is accessible.

9. Remove the screw and splash panel support bracket from the back portion of the wheel well. This will allow the splash panel to be depressed slightly for extra clearance when removing and replacing the evaporator assembly.

10. Remove the six screws holding the right side of the hood seal bracket assembly. Remove the copper hood ground clip from underneath the hood seal and remove the hood seal bracket assembly to the right side of the vehicle.

11. Loosen the retaining clamp and disconnect the emission hose that passes over the top of the evaporator case assembly. Position the emission hose and all vacuum hoses and movable wires away from the evaporator case assembly.

12. Disconnect the blower motor ground wire from the body frame and position away from the evaporator assembly.

13. Disconnect the blower motor wiring connector from the wiring harness hard shell connector.

14. Disconnect the two large wire harnesses (which cross the evaporator assembly) at the various connecting points and position them away from the evaporator assembly.

15. From the passenger side of dash panel, fold back the carpeting, if necessary, on the right side of floor. Remove the bottom left screw of the two screws that support the inlet recirculation air duct assembly.

16. From the passenger compartment, disconnect the ambient sensor air tube from the evaporator sensor air tube port.

17. From the engine side of the dash panel, remove three nuts (one upper and two lower) from the three evaporator assembly mounting studs. Also remove two screws (one drill point and one sheet metal) from the blower motor and wheel portion of the case assembly.

18. Pull the bottom of the evaporator case assembly away from the dash panel to disengage the evaporator ambient sensor air tube port and the two bottom studs. Move the top of the evaporator assembly away from the dash panel, disengaging it from the top stud, and maneuver the case up and over the wheel well splash panel. The splash panel may be pushed downward slightly for additional clearance.

Installation

1. Position the evaporator assembly near to the dash panel by maneuvering it down past the wheel splash panel. If necessary, push the splash panel downward slightly for extra clearance.

2. Engage the sensor air tube port into the dash panel port opening and the two bottom dash panel studs into the evaporator assembly stud holes. Move the top of the evaporator assembly toward the dash panel while engaging the top dash panel stud into the evaporator assembly stud hole.

3. Replace but do not tighten the three stud nuts.

4. Replace and tighten to specification the two screws (one drill-point and one sheet metal). Be careful to return the drill-point screw to the correct hole which is located on top of the case to the right of the blower motor and wheel assembly. Tighten to specification the three nuts previously installed.

5. Position the two large wire harnesses across the evaporator case assembly and connect the various connectors.

6. Connect the blower motor wiring connector to the wiring harness hard shell connector.

7. Connect the blower motor ground wire and accompanying engine ground wire to the body frame.

8. Place the emission hose clamp on the hose, connect the hose, tighten the clamp and position it over the evaporator case assembly along with the vacuum hoses and wires previously moved.

9. Replace the hood seal bracket assembly and insert the copper hood ground clip underneath the hood seal. Install the six screws which secure the right side of the hood seal bracket assembly.

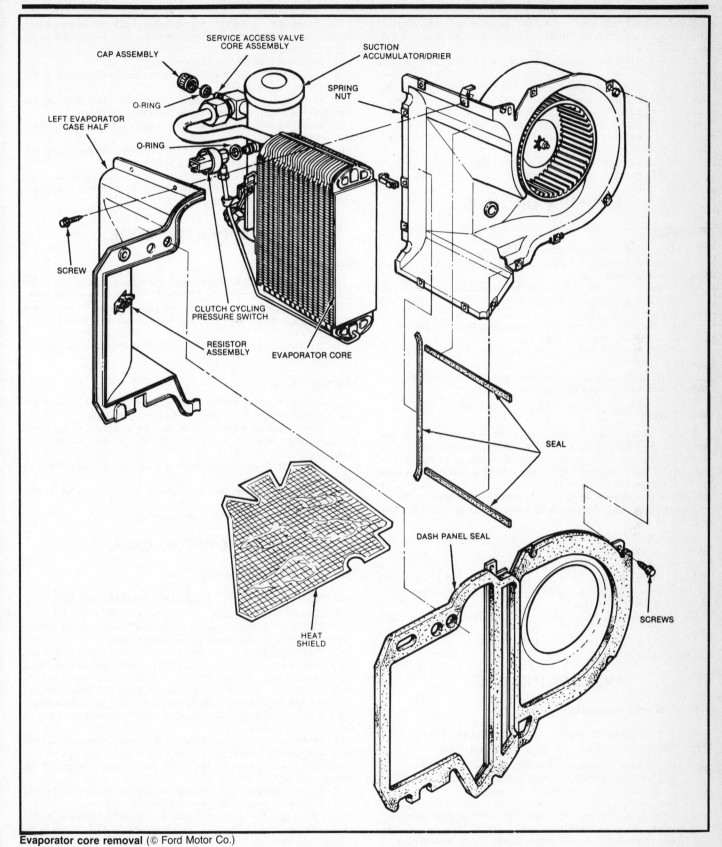

CAP ASSEMBLY

SERVICE ACCESS VALVE
CORE ASSEMBLY

SUCTION
ACCUMULATOR/DRIER

SPRING
NUT

O-RING

LEFT EVAPORATOR
CASE HALF

O-RING

SCREW

CLUTCH CYCLING
PRESSURE SWITCH

RESISTOR
ASSEMBLY

EVAPORATOR CORE

SEAL

DASH PANEL SEAL

SCREWS

HEAT
SHIELD

Evaporator core removal (© Ford Motor Co.)

10. Place heater core hose clamps onto the heater hoses and connect the inlet and outlet hoses to the inlet and outlet heater core tubes. Position the hose clamps and tighten them to specification. Replace coolant.

11. Remove the plugs from the liquid line and the evaporator inlet tube and install new O-rings dipped in clean specified refrigerant oil. Connect the liquid line to the evaporator inlet tube. Tighten to specification.

12. Remove the plugs from the suction accumulator/drier and the

suction hose and install new O-rings dipped in clean specified refrigerant oil. Connect the suction hose to the suction accumulator/drier. Tighten to specification.

13. Connect two-wire electrical connector to clutch cycling pressure switch.

14. Leak test, evacuate and charge the refrigeration system following the recommended procedures and safety precautions.

15. Connect the ground cable to the battery.

16. Install the wheel well splash panel bracket.

17. From the passenger compartment, install the recirculation air duct assembly screw.

18. Connect the ambient air tube to the evaporator air tube port.

19. Check the air conditioning system for proper operation.

EVAPORATOR CORE

Removal

1. Remove the evaporator case from the vehicle

2. Remove six screws attaching the dash panel gasket to the right half of the evaporator case.

3. Remove the heat shield from the bottom of the evaporator case.

4. Remove seven screws attaching the two halves of the evaporator case together.

5. Separate the two halves of the evaporator case and remove the evaporator core and mounting bracket.

6. Disconnect the suction accumulator/drier inlet from the evaporator core outlet tube.

7. Remove the retaining screw from the suction accumulator/drier and evaporator core mounting brackets.

Installation

NOTE: When replacing the evaporator core in a refrigerant system that contains a six cylinder aluminum compressor, a measured quantity of refrigerant oil should be added to the core to assure that the total oil charge in the system is correct before the system is operated. Three fluid ounces of clean 500 viscosity refrigerant oil should be poured directly into the inlet pipe of the replacement core with the pipe held vertically so the oil will drain into the core.

1. Attach the suction accumulator/drier to the evaporator core mounting brackets with a retaining screw.

2. Install a new O-ring lubricated with clean, specified refrigerant oil and connect the accumulator/drier inlet to the outlet tube of the evaporator core. Tighten to specification using a back-up wrench to prevent component damage.

3. Position the evaporator core to the right half of the evaporator case.

4. Apply caulking cord sealer to the case flange and around the evaporator core tubes.

EVAPORATOR CASE

Removal and Installation

1982-84 THUNDERBIRD/XR-7, LTD/MARQUIS, 1983 CONTINENTAL, MARK VI AND 1984 COUGAR

1. Remove the instrument panel and lay it on the front seat.

2. Discharge the refrigerant from the A/C system at the service access gauge port valve located on the suction line.

3. Once refrigerant is discharged from system, remove high and low pressure hoses. Use backup wrench to prevent component damage. Cap the hose openings to prevent entrance of dirt and excessive moisture.

4. Disconnect heater hoses from the heater core tubes and plug the hoses with suitable ⅝-inch and ¾-inch plugs. Cap the heater core tubes to prevent coolant loss from the heater core during removal of the evaporator case.

5. Remove the screw attaching the air inlet duct and blower housing assembly support brace to the cowl top panel.

6. Disconnect the vacuum supply hose (black) from the in-line vacuum check valve and the vacuum hoses from the TBL switch in the engine compartment.

7. Disconnect the blower motor wiring.

8. Working under the hood, remove two nuts retaining the evaporator case to the dash panel.

9. In the passenger compartment, remove the screw attaching the evaporator case support bracket to the cowl top panel.

10. Remove one screw retaining the bracket below the evaporator case to the dash panel.

11. Carefully pull the evaporator case away from the dash panel and remove the evaporator case assembly from the vehicle.

12. Installation is the reverse order of the removal procedure. Leak test, evacuate and charge the system, install new O-rings lubricated with refrigerant oil wherever possible.

EVAPORATOR CORE

Removal

1. Remove the evaporator case from the vehicle. Then, remove the air inlet duct and blower housing assembly from the evaporator case.

2. Remove seven screws and six snap clips retaining the two halves of the evaporator case together, and separate the two halves of the evaporator case.

3. Lift the evaporator core and seal from the lower half of the evaporator case.

Installation

1. Position the evaporator core in the lower half of the evaporator case fitting the seal over the edge of the case lower half.

2. Position the case upper half on the case lower half making sure the temperature blend door and the heat defrost door are properly positioned.

3. Install the seven screws and six snap clips to retain the two halves of the housing together.

4. Install the air inlet duct and blower housing assembly on the evaporator case.

5. Install the evaporator case in the vehicle.

EVAPORATOR CASE

Removal and Installation

1985 THUNDERBIRD/COUGAR AND LTD/MARQUIS

1. Remove the instrument panel and lay it on the front seat.

2. Discharge the refrigerant from the A/C system at the service access gauge port valve located on the suction line.

3. Once refrigerant is discharged from system, remove high and low pressure hoses. Use backup wrench to prevent component damage. Cap the hose openings to prevent entrance of dirt and excessive moisture.

4. Remove the accumulator by disconnecting the liquid line and accumulator/drier inlet tube from the evaporator core at the dash panel. Cap the refrigerant lines and evaporator core to prevent the entry of dirt and excess moisture.

5. Disconnect heater hoses from the heater core tubes and plug the hoses with suitable ⅝-inch and ¾ inch plugs. Cap the heater core tubes to prevent coolant loss from the heater core during removal of the evaporator case.

6. Remove the screw attaching the air inlet duct and blower housing assembly support brace to the cowl top panel.

7. Disconnect the vacuum supply hose (black) from the in-line vacuum check valve and the vacuum hoses from the TBL switch in the engine compartment.

8. Disconnect the blower motor wiring.

9. Working under the hood, remove two nuts retaining the evaporator case to the dash panel.

10. In the passenger compartment, remove the screw attaching the evaporator case support bracket to the cowl top panel.

11. Remove one screw retaining the bracket below the evaporator case to the dash panel.

12. Carefully pull the evaporator case away from the dash panel and remove the evaporator case assembly from the vehicle.

13. Installation is the reverse order of the removal procedure. Leak test, evacuate and charge the system, install new O-rings lubricated with refrigerant oil wherever possible.

EVAPORATOR CORE

Removal

1. Remove the evaporator case.

2. Remove the four retaining screws and remove the air inlet duct from the evaporator case.

3. Remove the foam seal from the evaporator core tubes.

4. Drill a ³⁄₁₆ inch hole in both upright tabs on top of evaporator case.

5. Using a small saw blade, or equivalent, cut the top of the evaporator case between the raised outlines.

6. Remove the two retaining screws and remove the blower motor resistor from the evaporator case.

Installation

1. Transfer the two foam core seals to the new evaporator core.

2. Position the evaporator core in the case and close the cut-out cover.

3. Install a spring nut on each of the two upright tabs. Be sure the hole in the spring nut is aligned with the ³⁄₁₆ inch holes drilled in the tab and flange. Then, install and tighten a screw in each spring nut (through the hole in the tab or flange) to secure the cut-out cover in the closed position.

4. Install Caulking Cord, to seal the evaporator against leakage along the cut line.

5. Using new caulking cord, assemble the air inlet duct to the evaporator and tighten the four retaining screws.

6. Install the blower motor resistor and tighten the two screws.

7. Install the foam seal over the evaporator core and heater core tubes.

8. Install the evaporator case.

EVAPORATOR CASE

Removal and Installation

1984-85 CONTINENTAL AND MARK VII

1. Remove instrument panel and lay it on the front seat.

2. Discharge the refrigerant from the A/C system at the service gauge port valve located on the suction line.

3. Once refrigerant is discharged from system, remove high and low pressure hoses. Use backup wrench to prevent component damage. Cap the hose openings to prevent entrance of dirt and excessive moisture.

4. Drain the engine coolant from the cooling system and remove the hoses from the heater core. Plug the hoses and core.

5. Remove the screw attaching the air inlet duct and blower housing assembly support brace to the cowl top panel.

6. Disconnect the ATC wiring as necessary.

7. Working under the hood, remove two nuts retaining the evaporator case to the dash panel.

8. In the passenger compartment, remove the screw attaching the evaporator case support bracket to the cowl to panel.

9. Remove one screw retaining the bracket below the evaporator case to the dash panel.

10. Carefully pull the evaporator case away from the dash panel and remove the evaporator case assembly from the vehicle.

11. Installation is the reverse order of the removal procedure. Leak test, evacuate and charge the system, install new O-rings lubricated with refrigerant oil wherever possible.

EVAPORATOR CORE

Removal

1. Remove the evaporator case from the vehicle. Then, remove the air inlet duct and blower housing assembly from the evaporator case.

2. Remove seven screws and six snap clips retaining the two halves of the evaporator case together, and separate the two halves of the evaporator case.

3. Lift the evaporator core and seal from the lower half of the evaporator case.

Installation

1. Position the evaporator core in the lower half of the evaporator case fitting the seal over the edge of the case lower half.

2. Position the case upper half on the case lower half making sure the temperature blend door and the heat defrost door are properly positioned.

3. Install the seven screws and six snap clips to retain the two halves of the housing together.

4. Install the air inlet duct and blower housing assembly on the evaporator case.

5. Install the evaporator case in the vehicle.

Air Conditioning Operating Components

CLUTCH CYCLING PRESSURE SWITCH

Removal

1982-85—ALL MODELS

1. Disconnect the wire harness connector from the pressure switch.

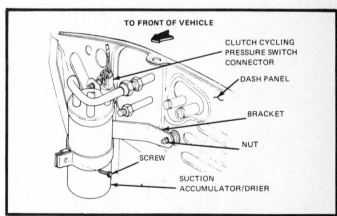

Typical accumulator drier and clutch cycling pressure switch (© Ford Motor Co.)

2. Unscrew the pressure switch from the top of the suction accumulator/drier.

Installation

1. Lubricate the O-ring on the accumulator nipple with clean refrigerant oil.

2. Screw the pressure switch on the accumulator nipple and hand tighten.

3. Connect the wire connector to the pressure switch.

4. Check the pressure switch installation for refrigerant leaks.

5. Check the system for proper operation

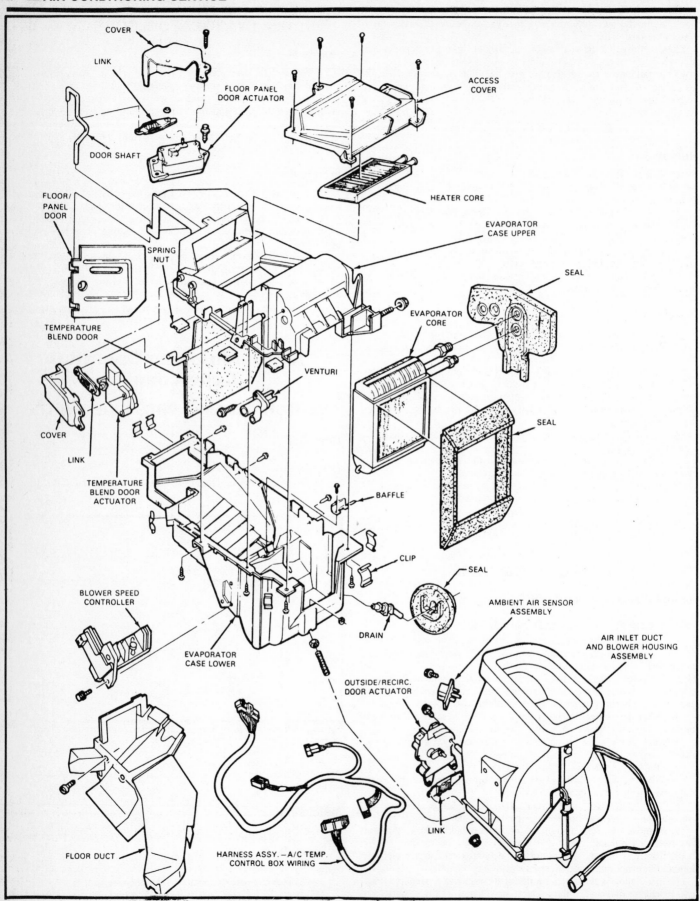

COVER

LINK

FLOOR PANEL
DOOR ACTUATOR

ACCESS
COVER

DOOR SHAFT

HEATER CORE

FLOOR/
PANEL
DOOR

EVAPORATOR
CASE UPPER

SPRING
NUT

SEAL

TEMPERATURE
BLEND DOOR

EVAPORATOR
CORE

VENTURI

SEAL

COVER

LINK

TEMPERATURE
BLEND DOOR
ACTUATOR

BAFFLE

CLIP

SEAL

BLOWER SPEED
CONTROLLER

DRAIN

AMBIENT AIR SENSOR
ASSEMBLY

AIR INLET DUCT
AND BLOWER HOUSING
ASSEMBLY

EVAPORATOR
CASE LOWER

OUTSIDE/RECIRC.
DOOR ACTUATOR

LINK

FLOOR DUCT

HARNESS ASSY.—A/C TEMP.
CONTROL BOX WIRING

1984-85 Continental and Mark VII—disassembled evaporator case (© Ford Motor Co.)

COOLING FAN CONTROLLER

Removal

1982-85 ESCORT/EXP, LYNX/LN7 AND TEMPO/TOPAZ

1. Open the glove compartment and remove any contents from the glove compartment.
2. Push the sides of the glove compartment liner inward and pull the liner from the opening. Allow the glove compartment and door to hang on the hinges.
3. Working through the glove compartment opening, remove one screw attaching the cooling fan controller mounting bracket to the cowl top panel.
4. Disconnect the electrical connector and remove the controller.

Installation

1. Connect the electrical connector to the cooling fan controller.
2. Position the controller to the cowl top panel and engage the mounting tab in the hole. Then, install the attaching screw.
3. Return the glove compartment liner to the opening and restore the contents to the glove compartment.
4. Check the controller for proper operation.

COOLING FAN CONTROLLER

Location

1982-85—ALL MODELS EXCEPT: ESCORT/EXP, LYNX/LN7 AND TEMPO/TOPAZ

Mustang/Capri: Between the steering column and the left side cowl panel under the instrument panel.
Thunderbird/Cougar: Under the instrument panel between the glove box and the center of the instrument panel.
LTD/Marquis; Attached to the right side cowl panel, under the instrument panel.

Removal and Installation

1. Disconnect the negative battery cable and locate the controller.
2. Remove the electrical connector to the cooling fan controller.
3. Remove the mounting screws from the controller and remove the controller.
4. Installation is the reverse order of the removal procedure.

VACUUM SELECTOR SWITCH

Removal

1982-85—ALL MODELS EXCEPT: ESCORT/EXP, LYNX/LN7 AND TEMPO/TOPAZ

1. Remove the control assembly.
2. Move the function selector lever to the Off position.
3. Remove two screws attaching the vacuum switch to the control assembly and remove the vacuum selector switch.

Installation

1. Move the function selector lever to the Off position.
2. Position the vacuum selector switch to the arm of the function selector lever making sure the lever arm engages the sliding carriage in the vacuum selector switch and control assembly bracket pins are inserted into selector assembly holes.
3. Install two screws to attach the vacuum switch to the control assembly.
4. Install the control assembly.

Automatic Temperature Control (ATC)

SENSOR ASSEMBLY

Removal

1982-85 FORD/MERCURY, TOWN CAR, CROWN VICTORIA AND GRAND MARQUIS

1. Remove the instrument panel pad.
2. Remove the two mounting screws from the sensor assembly.
3. Remove the control cable housing-to-sensor attaching screw.
4. Disconnect the cable end loop from the lever arm and remove the cable from the sensor assembly.

NOTE: Secure the control cable with tape or service wire to prevent it from falling from sight behind the instrument panel.

5. Disconnect the vacuum hose plug from the sensor assembly.

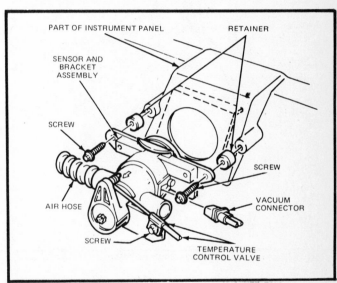

Ford/Mercury ATC sensor removal (© Ford Motor Co.)

6. Remove the ambient air hose from the end of the sensor assembly by rotating the sensor assembly in a clockwise direction.
7. Remove the sensor assembly from the vehicle.

Installation

1. Connect the ambient air hose to the sensor by turning it in a counterclockwise direction.
2. Connect the vacuum harness connector to the sensor vacuum ports and ensure the locking tabs are snapped onto the sensor body.
3. Position the sensor assembly to the screw mounting bosses and install the two mounting screws.

NOTE: Use a mirror to help align the sensor screw holes to the mounting bosses. If necessary, position a trouble lamp on the windshield for additional light. A small amount of body caulk in the end of the rachet socket will help prevent the screws from falling from the socket.

4. Remove the tape or service wire securing the cable and connect the control cable to the lever arm and loosely install the attaching screw.
5. Set the cable calibration following the procedure under adjustments.
6. Check the A/C system for proper operation.

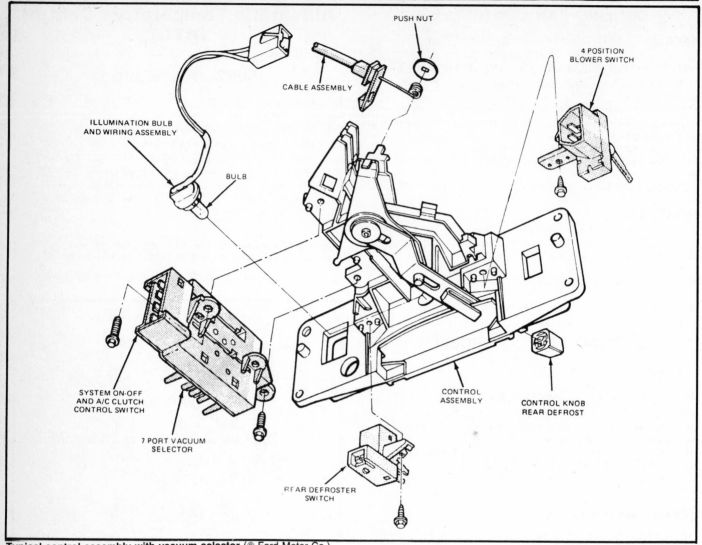

PUSH NUT

CABLE ASSEMBLY

4 POSITION BLOWER SWITCH

ILLUMINATION BULB AND WIRING ASSEMBLY

BULB

SYSTEM ON-OFF AND A/C CLUTCH CONTROL SWITCH

7 PORT VACUUM SELECTOR

REAR DEFROSTER SWITCH

CONTROL ASSEMBLY

CONTROL KNOB REAR DEFROST

Typical control assembly with vacuum selector (© Ford Motor Co.)

SENSOR ASSEMBLY

Removal

1982-85 THUNDERBIRD/XR-7, LTD/MARQUIS AND 1984-85 COUGAR

1. Disconnect the ground cable from the battery negative terminal.
2. Remove the instrument panel pad.
3. Remove the two mounting screws from the sensor assembly.
4. Remove the control cable housing-to-sensor attaching screw.
5. Disconnect the cable end loop from the lever arm and remove the cable from the sensor assembly.

NOTE: Secure control cable with tape or service wire to prevent it from falling from sight behind the instrument panel.

6. Remove the ambient air hoses from each end of the sensor assembly.
7. Disconnect the vacuum hose plug and remove the sensor assembly from the vehicle.

Installation

1. While moving the temperature control lever, rotate the calibration locking pin into the calibration notch of the sensor control lever base.

2. Connect the vacuum harness connector to the sensor vacuum ports and secure the locking tabs.
3. Connect the ambient air hose connector to the sensor.
4. Position the sensor assembly to the screw mounting bosses and install the two mounting screws.

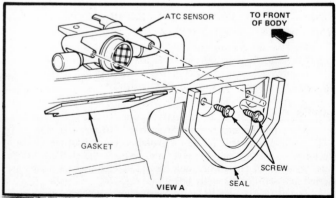

ATC SENSOR

TO FRONT OF BODY

GASKET

SCREW

SEAL

VIEW A

ATC sensor removal for 1982-83 Thunderbird and XR-7 (© Ford Motor Co.)

NOTE: Use a mirror to help align the sensor screw holes to the mounting bosses. If necessary, position a trouble light on the windshield for additional light. A small amount of body caulk in the end of the rachet socket will help prevent the screws from falling from the socket.

5. Remove the tape or service wire securing the cable and connect the control cable to the lever arm and loosely install the attaching screw.
6. Set the cable calibration.
7. Connect battery ground cable to the battery negative terminal.
8. Check the A/C system for proper operation.

SENSOR ASSEMBLY

Removal and Installation

1982-85 CONTINENTAL, MARK VI AND MARK VII

1. Disconnect the negative battery cable and remove the instrument pad.
2. Remove the two mounting screws from the sensor assembly.
3. Remove the control cable housing to sensor attaching screw and disconnect the electrical connector from the sensor assembly.
4. On the '82–'83 models, disconnect the cable end loop from the lever arm and remove the cable from the sensor assembly.

NOTE: Secure the control cable with tape or equivalent to prevent the cable from falling behind the instrument panel.

5. On the '82 models, remove the glove box door retaining straps and light harness with the glove box sight shield.
6. On the '82-'83 models, disconnect the and plug the vacuum hose.
7. Hold the aspirator hose and rotate the sensor assembly clockwise to disconnect the hose from the sensor assembly and remove the sensor.
8. Installation is the reverse order of the removal procedure.

SENSOR ASSEMBLY

Removal and Installation

1984-85 MARK VII

1. Disconnect the negative battery cable and remove the instrument cluster finish panel assembly.
2. Disconnect the aspirator hose from the sensor assembly by slowly disengaging the elbow latch.
3. Disconnect the electric connectors from the warning lamp module and the sensor.
4. Remove the two sensor attaching screws and remove the sensor assembly.
5. Installation is the reverse order of the removal procedure.

SERVO MOTOR

Removal and Installation

1982-85—ALL MODELS EXCEPT: ESCORT/EXP, LYNX/LN7, TEMPO/TOPAZ AND MUSTANG/CAPRI

1. Disconnect the negative battery cable and the glove box door stop.
2. Remove the vacuum hose from the servo motor, and on the later models unplug the electrical harness connectors.
3. Remove the two screws from the servo motor assembly mounting bracket and position the servo motor out of the way to gain access to the vacuum diverter valve.
4. Remove the retaining push nut and vacuum connector clip, unplug the multiple vacuum connector from the vacuum diverter valve.

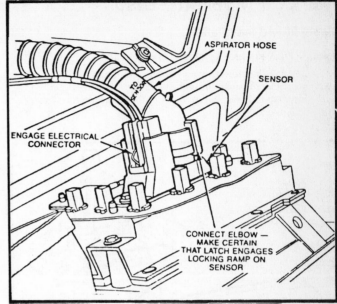

Mark VII ATC sensor installation (© Ford Motor Co.)

5. On the earlier models, remove the servo motor protective cover.
6. Remove the push nut that retains the servo motor over travel spring and arm link to the blend door crank arm and remove the servo assembly from the vehicle.
7. Installation is the reverse order of the removal procedure.

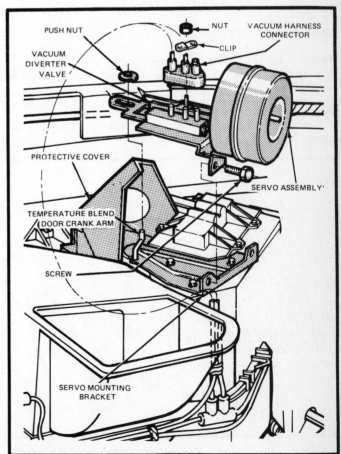

Typical servo assembly removal (© Ford Motor Co.)

AMBIENT SENSOR

Removal and Installation

1984–85 CONTINENTAL AND MARK VII

1. Remove the blower motor housing and the two ambient sensor mounting screws, remove the ambient sensor.
2. Installation is the reverse order of the removal procedure.

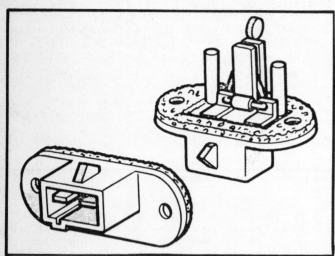

Typical ambient sensor (© Ford Motor Co.)

ASPIRATOR

Removal and Installation

1984–85 CONTINENTAL AND MARK VII

1. Disconnect the glove box door stops and remove the shield behind the glove box.
2. Remove one hex head screw and lift the aspirator up and out to disengage the lower locating tab.
3. Disengage the sensor hose assembly locking tab from the aspirator elbow and remove the aspirator.

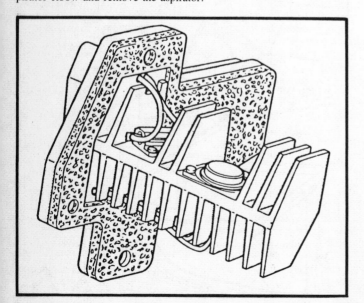

Typical blower motor control (© Ford Motor Co.)

4. Installation is the reverse order of the removal procedure.

BLOWER MOTOR CONTROLLER

Removal

1984–85 CONTINENTAL AND MARK VII

1. Disengage glove compartment door stops and allow the door to hang by the hinge.
2. Remove sight shield behind the glove compartment.
3. Remove screw attaching the lower right end of the instrument panel to the side cowl panel.
4. On Continental, open ashtray door and remove the ash receptacle.
5. On Mark VII:
   a. Loosen floor console and move it rearward.
   b. Remove ATC control assembly.
   c. Remove screws attaching the instrument panel to the floor pan.
6. Working through the glove box opening, disconnect the snap-lock wire connector from the blower controller.
7. Remove the three screws attaching the blower controller to the evaporator case and remove the controller. **Do not touch** the fins of the controller if it is **HOT**.

Installation

1. Position the blower controller to the evaporator case and install the three attaching screws.
2. Connect wire connector to the blower controller.
3. On Mark VII:
   a. Install screws to attach the instrument panel to the floor pan.
   b. Install the ATC control assembly.
   c. Position the floor console forward to the instrument panel and secure in place.
4. On Continental, reinstall the ash receptacle.
5. Install the screw to attach the lower right end of the instrument panel to the side cowl.
   a. Install screws to attach the instrument panel to the floor pan.
   b. Install the ATC control assembly.
   c. Position the floor console forward to the instrument panel and secure in place.
4. On Continental, reinstall the ash receptacle.
5. Install the screw to attach the lower right end of the instrument panel to the side cowl.
6. Install the sight shield behind the glove compartment opening.
7. Close the glove compartment door.
8. Check system for proper operation.

ATC SENSOR CALIBRATION

1982–83 THUNDERBIRD/XR-7

1. Remove the instrument panel pad and visually determine which direction to rotate the sensor calibration locking pin.
2. While moving the temperature control lever, rotate the calibration locking pin into the calibration notch of the sensor control arm.
3. Check the position of the temperature control lever, it should be at 75. If it is not, loosen the cable housing-to-sensor attaching screw and move the temperature control lever to 75 while the sensor control arm is locked in the calibration position.
4. Retighten the cable housing-to-sensor attaching screw, making sure the temperature control stays at 75 and the sensor arm stays locked.

ATC SENSOR CALIBRATION

1982–85 FORD/MERCURY, TOWN CAR, CROWN VICTORIA, GRAND MARQUIS, THUNDERBIRD, LTD/MARQUIS, CONTINENTAL, MARK VI, MARK VII AND 1984–85 COUGAR

1. Remove the instrument panel pad.
2. Move the temperature selector lever to 75°F position.

3. The control arm of the ATC sensor should be aligned with the arrow on the sensor body.

4. If it is not, loosen cable housing-to-sensor attaching screw and align the sensor control arm with the arrow while maintaining the 75°F position of the temperature selector lever.

5. Retighten the cable housing-to-sensor attaching screw, making sure the temperature control stays at 75°F and the sensor arm stays locked.

Re-adjusting ATC Sensor Calibration Point

1982–85—ALL MODELS

1. Establish the customer's preference and the difference between the present and desired comfort level setting.

2. Determine the direction of change.

3. To decrease or increase, adjust the temperature control lever position with the sensor arm locked in the calibration notch. Loosen the cable housing-to-sensor attaching screw, move the temperature control lever the desired amount and retighten the attaching screw.

NOTE: Move the temperature control lever Higher to Decrease and Lower to Increase the controlled temperature at a given setting. Do not attempt to change the internal sensor calibration screw as the sensor can become damaged.

— CAUTION —

If a readjustment of the temperature control lever of more than 2°C (4°F) is required and the cable adjustment is correct per Sensor Calibration procedure, replace the sensor assembly.

NOTE: On a new service part, the sensor is aligned to the calibration arrow and held in position by a calibration pin. Once the sensor control arm is moved, the calibration pin breaks and falls out, thereafter, the sensor control arm must be aligned to the calibration arrow manually.

THERMAL BLOWER LOCKOUT SWITCH

The thermal blower lockout (TBL) switch is a combination vacuum valve and electrical switch powered by a thermal element. It is located in the heater supply hose in the engine compartment and the thermal element is in contact with the engine coolant. With the function lever in the heat position and a cold engine, the blower is locked out and the outside- recirculation door is in the recirculation position (with vacuum applied). When the engine coolant reaches approximately 120

degrees F. (49 C.), the electrical switch contacts close and the vacuum valve closes, permitting the blower motor to operate and the out side—recirculation door to move to the out side air position (with no applied vacuum).

THERMAL BLOWER LOCKOUT SWITCH

Removal and Installation

1982–85 FORD/MERCURY, TOWN CAR, CROWN VICTORIA, GRAND MARQUIS, THUNDERBIRD/XR-7, LTD/MARQUIS, CONTINENTAL, MARK VI, MARK VII AND 1984–85 COUGAR

1. Disconnect the negative battery cable and remove the electrical and vacuum connectors from the thermal blower lockout switch.

2. Loosen the hose clamps at the TBL switch and remove the thermal blower lockout switch from the heater hose.

NOTE: It may be necessary to drain out some of the coolant before removing the TBL switch.

3. Installation is the reverse order of the removal procedure.

HEATER CORE

Removal and Installation

1982–83 GRANADA/COUGAR, THUNDERBIRD/XR-7, CONTINENTAL AND FAIRMONT/ZEPHYR

NOTE: The instrument panel must be removed for access to the heater core. The A/C system must be evacuated in order to remove the dash panel and gain access to the heater core. It is advisable to remove and replace the A/C receiver drier when the system has been evacuated.

1. Disconnect the negative battery cable.

2. Remove the instrument panel pad:

  a. Remove the screws attaching the instrument cluster trim panel to the pad.

  b. Remove the screw attaching the pad to the panel at each defroster opening.

  c. Remove the screws attaching the edge of the pad to the panel.

3. Remove the steering column opening cover.

4. Remove the nuts and bracket holding the steering column to the instrument panel and lay the column across the seat.

5. Remove the instrument panel to brake pedal support screw at the column opening.

6. Remove the screws attaching the lower brace to the panel below the radio, and below the glove compartment.

7. Disconnect the temperature cable from the door and case bracket.

8. Unplug the seven port vacuum hose connectors at the evaporator case.

9. Disconnect the resistor wire connector and the blower motor feed wire.

10. Remove the screws attaching the top of the panel; to the cowl and support the panel while removing the screws.

11. Remove the one screw at each end attaching the panel to the cowl panels.

12. Move the panel rearward and disconnect the speedometer cable and any wires preventing the panel from laying flat on the seat.

13. Drain the coolant and disconnect the heater hoses from the heater core, plug the heater core tubes.

14. Remove the nuts retaining the evaporator case to the firewall in the engine compartment.

15. Remove the case support bracket screws and air inlet duct support bracket.

16. Remove the nut retaining the bracket to the dash panel at the left side of the evaporator case, and the nut retaining the bracket below the case to dash panel.

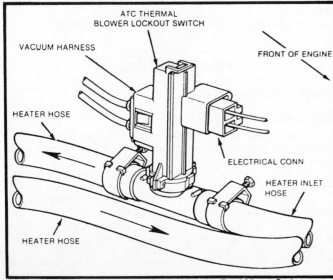

Thermal blower lockout switch location (© Ford Motor Co.)

Labels: ATC THERMAL BLOWER LOCKOUT SWITCH; VACUUM HARNESS; FRONT OF ENGINE; HEATER HOSE; ELECTRICAL CONN.; HEATER INLET HOSE; HEATER HOSE

17. Pull the case assembly away from the panel to get to the screws retaining the heater core cover to the case.

18. Remove the cover screws and cover, lift the heater core and seals out of the case assembly.

19. Installation is the reverse order of the removal procedure.

HEATER CORE

Removal and Installation

1982–85 FORD/MERCURY, TOWN CAR, CROWN VICTORIA AND GRAND MARQUIS

NOTE: It is necessary to remove the plenum assembly to reach the heater core.

1. Drain the coolant and disconnect the negative battery cable.

2. Disconnect the heater hoses from the heater core tubes and plug the tubes to prevent any coolant from spilling out.

3. Remove the one bolt located beneath the wiper motor that attaches the left side of the plenum to the dash. Remove the nut that retains the upper left corner of the heater case.

4. Disconnect the control system vacuum supply hose from the vacuum source and push the grommet and vacuum supply hose into the passenger compartment.

5. Remove the glove compartment, loosen the right still plate and remove the right side cowl trim plate.

6. Remove the attaching bolt on the lower right side of the instrument panel.

7. Remove the instrument panel pad, there are five screws attaching the lower edge, one screw on each outboard end, and two screws near the defroster openings.

8. Disengage the temperature control cable from the top of the plenum. Disconnect the cable from the temperature blend door crank arm.

9. Remove the clip attaching the center register bracket to the plenum and rotate the bracket up to the right.

10. Disconnect the vacuum harness at the multiple connector near the floor duct.

11. Disconnect the white vacuum hose from the vacuum motor.

12. Remove the two screws attaching the passenger side air duct to the plenum. It may be necessary to remove the two screws which attach the lower panel door vacuum motor to the mounting bracket to gain access.

13. Remove the one plastic fastener retaining the floor air distribution duct to the left end of the plenum, and remove the duct.

14. Remove the nuts from the lower flange of the plenum and move the plenum rearward and rotate the top of the plenum downward and out from under the instrument panel.

15. Once the plenum is removed, remove the heater core cover and the heater core.

16. Installation is the reverse order of the removal procedure.

HEATER CORE

Removal and Installation

1982–85 ESCORT/EXP, LYNX/LN7 AND TEMPO/TOPAZ

1. Drain the cooling system and disconnect the heater hose from the heater core tubes, be sure to plug the heater core tubes to prevent any leakage of coolant.

2. Remove the glove compartment door, liner and lower reinforcement and move the temperature control lever to the warm position.

3. Remove the four attaching screws holding the heater core cover to the heater assembly and remove the cover.

4. From the engine compartment loosen the two mounting nuts holding the heater case assembly to the dash panel.

5. Push the heater core tubes toward the passenger compartment to loosen the heater core from the heater case assembly.

6. Pull the heater core from the heater case assembly and remove the heater core the opening in the glove compartment.

7. Installation is the reverse order of the removal procedure.

HEATER CORE

Removal and Installation

1982–85 FORD/MERCURY, TOWN CAR, CROWN VICTORIA, GRAND MARQUIS AND MARK VI

NOTE: It is necessary to remove the plenum assembly to reach the heater core.

1. Drain the coolant and disconnect the negative battery cable.

2. Disconnect the heater hoses from the heater core tubes and plug the tubes to prevent any coolant from spilling out.

3. Remove the one bolt located beneath the wiper motor that attaches the left side of the plenum to the dash. Remove the nut that retains the upper left corner of the heater case.

4. Disconnect the control system vacuum supply hose from the vacuum source and push the grommet and vacuum supply hose into the passenger compartment.

5. Remove the glove compartment, loosen the right still plate and remove the right side cowl trim plate.

6. Remove the attaching bolt on the lower right side of the instrument panel.

7. Remove the instrument panel pad, there are five screws attaching the lower edge, one screw on each outboard end, and two screws near the defroster openings.

8. Disengage the temperature control cable from the top of the plenum. Disconnect the cable from the temperature blend door crank arm.

9. Remove the clip attaching the center register bracket to the plenum and rotate the bracket up to the right.

10. Disconnect the vacuum harness at the multiple connector near the floor duct.

11. Disconnect the white vacuum hose from the vacuum motor.

12. Remove the two screws attaching the passenger side air duct to the plenum. It may be necessary to remove the two screws which attach the lower panel door vacuum motor to the mounting bracket to gain access.

13. Remove the one plastic fastener retaining the floor air distribution duct to the left end of the plenum, and remove the duct.

14. Remove the nuts from the lower flange of the pelnum and move the plenum rearward and rotate the top of the plenum downward and out from under the instrument panel.

15. Once the plenum is removed, remove the heater core cover and the heater core.

16. Installation is the reverse order of the removal procedure.

HEATER CORE

Removal and Installation

1982–85 MUSTANG/CAPRI

1. Drain the coolant and disconnect the heater hoses from the heater core tubes and plug the heater core tubes to prevent any coolant from leaking out.

2. Remove the glove compartment liner and remove the two instrument panel to cowl brace retaining screws and remove the brace.

3. Move the temperature control lever to the warm position and remove the four heater core cover retaining screws.

4. Remove the heater core cover and push the heater core tubes and seal towards the passenger compartment to loosen the heater core from the heater case assembly.

5. Remove the heater core from the heater case through the glove compartment opening.

6. Installation is the reverse order of the removal procedure.

HEATER CORE

Removal

1982–85 CONTINENTAL AND MARK VII

1. Remove the instrument panel and lay it on the front seat.
2. Remove evaporator case asembly from vehicle.
3. Remove five heater core access cover attaching screws, and remove the access cover from the evaporator case.
4. Lift the heater core and seals from the evaporator case.
5. Remove the two seals from the heater core tubes.

Installation

1. Install the heater core tube seals on the heater core tubes, the thin seal first.
2. Install the heater core in the evaporator case with the seals on the outside of the case.
3. Position the heater core access cover on the evaporator case and install the five attaching screws.
4. Install evaporator case assembly into vehicle.

SPRING-LOCK COUPLING SERVICE

1. Fit Ford special tool #T81P-19623-G (or its equivalent) to the coupling so that the tool enters the cage to release the coupling spring.

—————— **CAUTION** ——————

Make sure that the proper size tool end is used, as the sizes of the tubes will differ.

2. Close the special tool around the coupling and push the tool into the cage to release the female fitting from the spring.
3. Push the tool towards the condenser and pull the hose away from the condensor.
4. The coupling is now disconnected and the special tool may be removed.

NOTE: Refer to the Ford heater section for the removal and installation procedures, of the control head and temperature control cables.

ELECTRONIC AUTOMATIC CLIMATE CONTROL

Self-Test

The control head has a self test feature that aids in locating trouble in the EATC system. To get reliable results the following procedure must be followed. Turn On the ignition and set the control head to 90, OFF.

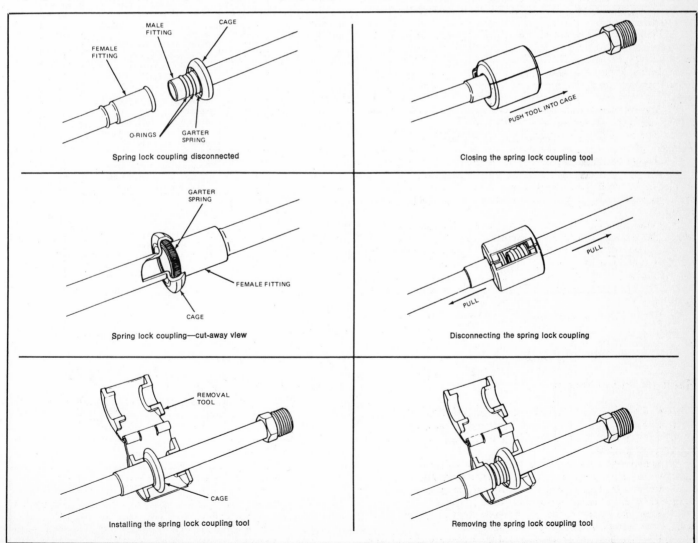

Spring lock coupling disconnected

Closing the spring lock coupling tool

Spring lock coupling—cut-away view

Disconnecting the spring lock coupling

Installing the spring lock coupling tool

Removing the spring lock coupling tool

Spring lock coupling service tool (© Ford Motor Co.)

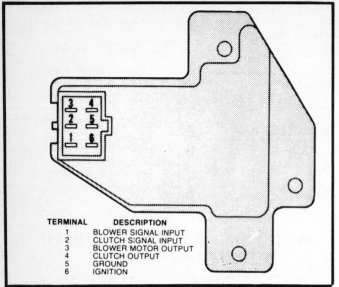

TERMINAL	DESCRIPTION
1	BLOWER SIGNAL INPUT
2	CLUTCH SIGNAL INPUT
3	BLOWER MOTOR OUTPUT
4	CLUTCH OUTPUT
5	GROUND
6	IGNITION

EATC blower and A/C clutch control terminals (© Ford Motor Co.)

Wait 40 seconds. If the vacuum fluorescent display (VFD) begins to flash, then there is a malfunction in the blend actuator wiring, the actuator itself or the control head. If the light emitting diode (LED) begins to flash then there is a malfunction in one or more of the other actuators' wiring, the actuator (mode, PAN/DEF, or FA/REC) or the control assembly. If no flashing occurs, set the control assembly to 60, DEF. Wait 40 seconds, look for a flashing VFD or LED. If no flashing occurs, then no malfunctions in the actuator drive or feedback circuits have been detected. Whether or not flashing has occurred, the self test mode should now be entered for further diagnostic information. To ensure accurate self rest results the above procedure must be followed before entering the self test mode.

To enter the self test mode push the OFF and DEFROST mode buttons simultaneously. Within two seconds, push the AUTO mode button. If an 88 is displayed, no malfunctions have been detected by the control assembly. If a control assembly detectable malfunction has occurred the appropriate error code will be displayed. Refer to Self Test—Error Code. The error code sequence will continue until the cooler button is pushed. When the cooler button is pushed the system will revert to the AUTO mode at a temperature setting one less than the setting before entering the self test mode. Always exit the self test mode by pushing the cooler button before turning Off the ignition. This procedure will ensure the proper resetting of the control assembly when the ignition is turned On.

MODE SELECTOR SWITCH

SWITCH SCHEMATIC	TERMINAL CONNECTIONS						
	OFF	VENT	A/C	HI-LO	HEAT	MIX	DEF
5–6	5-6	5-6	5-6	5-6	NONE	5-6	5-6
CURRENT	NONE	25	25	25	NONE	25	25
1–2 / 3–4	NONE	1-3	1-3 / 2-4	1-3 / 2-4	1-3	1-3 / 2-4	1-3 / 2-4
CURRENT (AMPS)	NONE	25	25/4	25/4	25	25/4	25/4

BLOWER SWITCH

BLOWER SPEED	TERMINAL CONNECTIONS	CURRENT IN CAR AMPS	BLOWER VOLTAGE
AUTO	3 + 1	25	
LO	NONE	6	5
MED	3 + 2	17	10
HIGH	3 + 5	25	12.4

CIRCUIT NO.	WIRE COLOR	WIRE GA.
57 A/B	BLACK	12/14
347	BLACK W/YELLOW HASH	16
753	YELLOW/RED STRIPE	12
755	BROWN W/WHITE STRIPE	14
181	BROWN W/ORANGE STRIPE	10
752	YELLOW W/RED DOT	14
754	LT GREEN W/WHITE HASH	14
37	YELLOW	10
687	GREY W/LT BLUE STRIPE	10
249A	DK BLUE W/LT GREEN STRIPE	12
249B	DK BLUE W/LT GREEN STRIPE	14
250 A/B	ORANGE	12/14
261	ORANGE W/BLACK STRIPE	12
261A	ORANGE W/BLACK STRIPE	14
244	YELLOW W/WHITE HASH	20

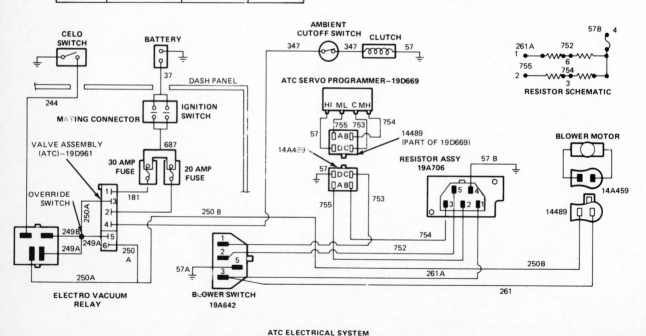

ATC ELECTRICAL SYSTEM

ATC system wiring schematic (© Ford Motor Co.)

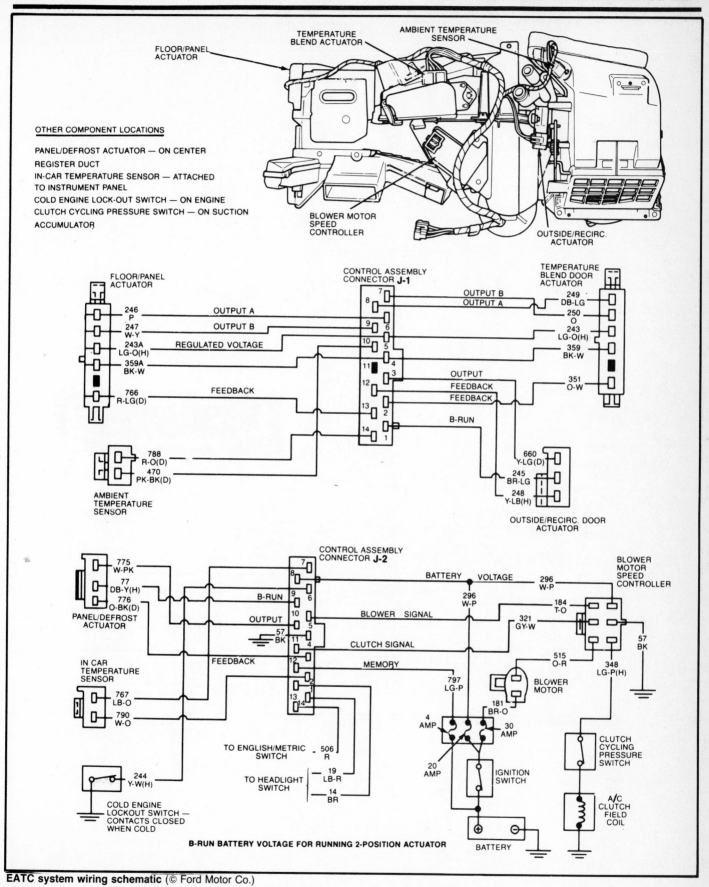

OTHER COMPONENT LOCATIONS

PANEL/DEFROST ACTUATOR — ON CENTER
REGISTER DUCT
IN-CAR TEMPERATURE SENSOR — ATTACHED
TO INSTRUMENT PANEL
COLD ENGINE LOCK-OUT SWITCH — ON ENGINE
CLUTCH CYCLING PRESSURE SWITCH — ON SUCTION
ACCUMULATOR

B-RUN BATTERY VOLTAGE FOR RUNNING 2-POSITION ACTUATOR

EATC system wiring schematic (© Ford Motor Co.)

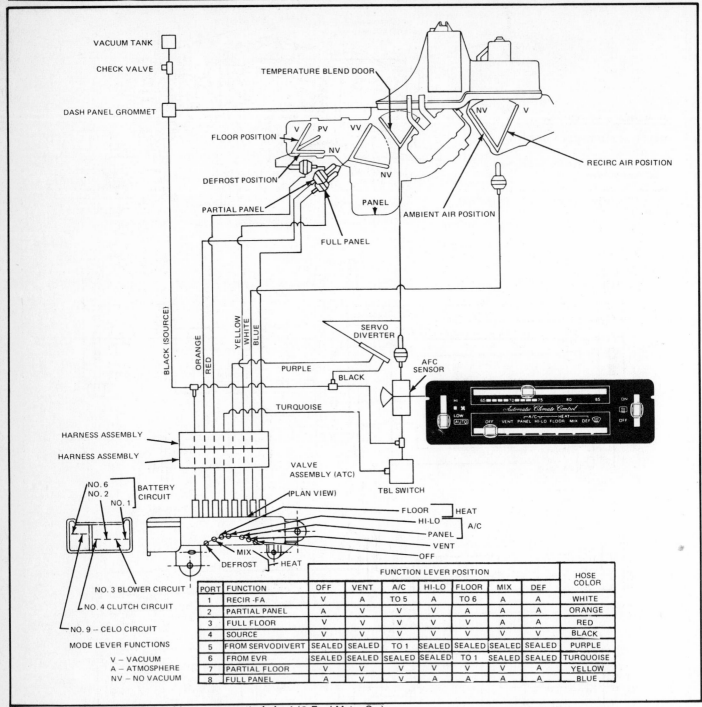

VACUUM TANK

CHECK VALVE

DASH PANEL GROMMET

TEMPERATURE BLEND DOOR

FLOOR POSITION

V PV VV

NV

NV

V

RECIRC AIR POSITION

DEFROST POSITION

PARTIAL PANEL

NV

PANEL

AMBIENT AIR POSITION

FULL PANEL

BLACK (SOURCE)

ORANGE
RED
YELLOW
WHITE
BLUE

PURPLE

BLACK

SERVO DIVERTER

AFC SENSOR

TURQUOISE

HARNESS ASSEMBLY

HARNESS ASSEMBLY

NO. 6
NO. 2
NO. 1

BATTERY CIRCUIT

VALVE ASSEMBLY (ATC)

(PLAN VIEW)

TBL SWITCH

FLOOR
HI-LO
PANEL
VENT
OFF

HEAT

A/C

MIX

DEFROST   HEAT

NO. 3 BLOWER CIRCUIT

NO. 4 CLUTCH CIRCUIT

NO. 9 – CELO CIRCUIT

MODE LEVER FUNCTIONS

V – VACUUM
A – ATMOSPHERE
NV – NO VACUUM

		FUNCTION LEVER POSITION							HOSE COLOR
PORT	FUNCTION	OFF	VENT	A/C	HI-LO	FLOOR	MIX	DEF	
1	RECIR -FA	V	A	TO 5	A	TO 6	A	A	WHITE
2	PARTIAL PANEL	A	V	V	A	A	A	A	ORANGE
3	FULL FLOOR	V	V	V	V	V	A	A	RED
4	SOURCE	V	V	V	V	V	V	V	BLACK
5	FROM SERVODIVERT	SEALED	SEALED	TO 1	SEALED	SEALED	SEALED	SEALED	PURPLE
6	FROM EVR	SEALED	SEALED	SEALED	SEALED	TO 1	SEALED	SEALED	TURQUOISE
7	PARTIAL FLOOR	V	V	V	V	V	V	A	YELLOW
8	FULL PANEL	A	V	V	A	A	A	A	BLUE

ATC system airflow schematic with vacuum control chart (© Ford Motor Co.)

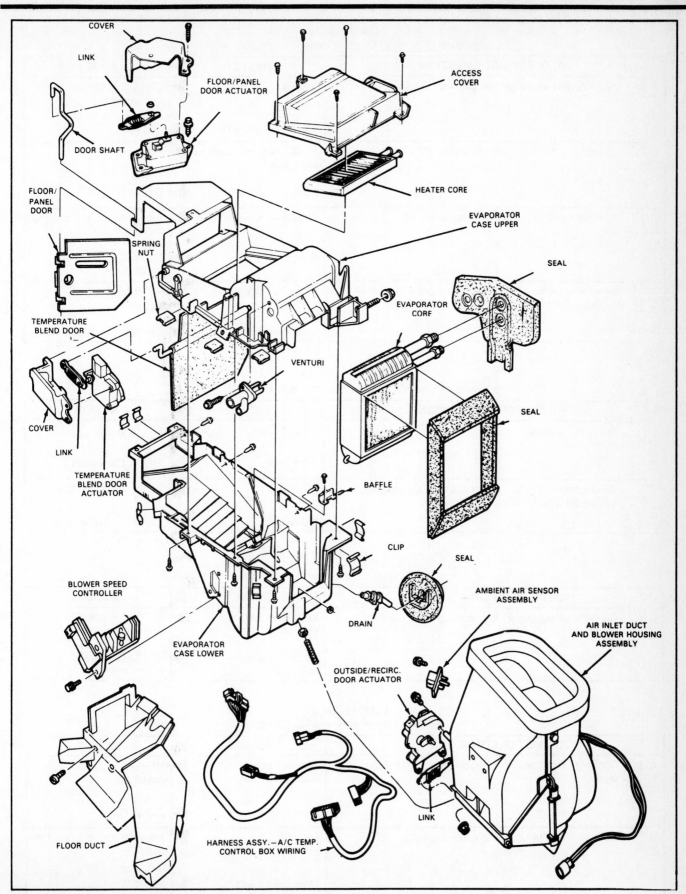

COVER

LINK

FLOOR/PANEL DOOR ACTUATOR

DOOR SHAFT

FLOOR/ PANEL DOOR

SPRING NUT

ACCESS COVER

HEATER CORE

EVAPORATOR CASE UPPER

SEAL

EVAPORATOR CORE

TEMPERATURE BLEND DOOR

VENTURI

SEAL

COVER

LINK

TEMPERATURE BLEND DOOR ACTUATOR

BAFFLE

SEAL

CLIP

SEAL

AMBIENT AIR SENSOR ASSEMBLY

AIR INLET DUCT AND BLOWER HOUSING ASSEMBLY

BLOWER SPEED CONTROLLER

EVAPORATOR CASE LOWER

DRAIN

OUTSIDE/RECIRC. DOOR ACTUATOR

LINK

FLOOR DUCT

HARNESS ASSY.—A/C TEMP. CONTROL BOX WIRING

1984—85 Continental/Mark VII, exploded view of the evaporator case assembly (© Ford Motor Company)

CONDITION #1
No blower — ignition On, Auto Mode, 60 degree setting.

	VOLTMETER CONNECTION	RESULT	▶	ACTION
A	V ignition pin #6 to ground pin #5.	0 volts	▶	CHECK V ignition circuit continuity/fuse.
		More than 10 volts	▶	GO to B.
B	Controller input pin #1 to ground pin #5.	Fluctuating voltage less than 3 volts	▶	GO to C.
		More than 3 volts	▶	GO to D.
C	Controller output pin #3 to ground pin #5.	Less than 1 volt	▶	Faulty motor, B+ feed to motor.
		More than 1 volt	▶	REPLACE blower controller.
D	Driver side control head connector, pin #5 to pin #4, same connector.	More than 3 volts	▶	REPLACE control assembly.
		Less than 3 volts	▶	CHECK circuit continuity.

CONDITION #2
No blower — ignition On, engine warm, Auto Mode, 90° setting.

	VOLTMETER CONNECTION	RESULT	▶	ACTION
A	Go to 60° setting.	Blower On	▶	GO to B.
		No blower	▶	GO to Condition 1.
B	Disconnect cold engine lock out (CELO) switch connector at engine, go to 90° setting.	Blower On	▶	Faulty CELO switch.
		No blower	▶	CELO wire grounded

CONDITION #3
High blower only. No low blower in Lo Mode.

	VOLTMETER CONNECTION	RESULT	▶	ACTION
A	Controller input pin #1 to ground pin #5, Lo Auto Mode.	Less than 7 volts fluctuating	▶	REPLACE control assembly.
		Above 7 volts fluctuating	▶	REPLACE blower controller.

CONDITION #4
No high blower in Hi Auto or Defrost.

	VOLTMETER CONNECTION	RESULT	▶	ACTION
A	Controller input pin #1 to ground pin #5, Hi Auto Mode.	Above 3 volts fluctuating	▶	REPLACE control assembly.
		Less than 3 volts	▶	GO to B.
B	Controller output pin #3 to ground pin #5.	Less than 1	▶	Faulty motor, B+ feed to motor.
		More than 1 volt	▶	REPLACE blower controller

CONDITION #5

Blower speed does not vary in Econ, Auto or Mix Modes.

	VOLTMETER CONNECTION	RESULT	▶	ACTION
A	Controller input pin #1 to ground pin #5, Auto Mode. Change temperature setting from 65°F to 85°F.	Voltage fluctuates below 7 volts, then above 7 Volts, then back below 7 volts	▶	GO to **B**.
		No change in voltage	▶	REPLACE control assembly.
B	Controller output pin #3 to ground pin #5, Auto Mode. Change temperature setting from 60° to 90°	Voltage changes from less than 1 volt to 7 volts, then back to 1 volt	▶	Faulty blower motor, B+ feed to motor
		No change in voltage	▶	REPLACE blower controller.

Self-Testing the blower controller (© Ford Motor Co.)

Do not use test lamp, testing requires volt-ohm meter.

CONDITION #6

No clutch operation — ignition On, Auto Mode, 60° setting, ambient temperature above 50°F.

	VOLTMETER CONNECTION	RESULT	▶	ACTION
A	Across clutch coil.	8-12 volts	▶	Poor ground or faulty clutch.
		0 volts	▶	GO to **B**.
B	Remove pressure switch connector and install a jumper wire.	Clutch engages	▶	Low freon charge or faulty pressure switch.
		Clutch does not engage	▶	GO to **C**.
C	V ignition pin #6 to ground pin #5.	0 volts	▶	CHECK V ignition circuit continuity.
		More than 10 volts	▶	GO to **D**.
D	Clutch input pin #2 to ground pin #5.	8-12 volts	▶	GO to **E**.
		Less than 8 volts	▶	GO to **F**.
E	Driver side control head connector, pin #11 to pin #4, same connector.	8-12 volts	▶	REPLACE control head.
		Less than 8 volts	▶	CHECK circuit continuity.
F	Clutch output pin #4 to ground pin #5.	8-12 volts	▶	CHECK clutch output circuit continuity.
		0 volts	▶	REPLACE blower controller.

Self-Testing the clutch control (© Ford Motor Co.)

CONDITION #7
Clutch does not disengage — ignition Off, Econ Mode.

	VOLTMETER CONNECTION	RESULT	▶	ACTION
A	Across clutch coil.	0 volts	▶	Faulty clutch.
		8-12 volts	▶	GO to **B**.
B	Clutch input pin #2 to ground pin #5.	8-12 volts	▶	REPLACE blower controller.
		Less than 8 volts	▶	GO to **C**.
C	Driver side control head connector, pin #11 to pin #4, same connector.	8-12 volts	▶	CHECK circuit continuity.
		Less than 8 volts	▶	REPLACE control assembly.

HISSING ATC VACUUM SYSTEM OR CONTROL ASSEMBLY SELECTOR VALVE

	TEST STEP	RESULT	▶	ACTION TO TAKE
A0	CHECK CONNECTORS • Check in-line and control assembly multiple connectors for proper installation • Listen for hiss.	Hiss stops Hiss continues	▶ ▶	RECHECK system for proper operation. GO to **A1**.
A1	DETERMINE LEAKING VALVE POSITION(S) • Move function lever to determine what selector valve position(s) are leaking.	All leak Some leak but not all	▶ ▶	REFER to "All Function Selector Valve Positions Leak" diagnostic chart. GO to **A2**.
A2	DETERMINE LEAKING TUBE(S) COLOR • Determine what color tube(s) are used in leaking function selector valve positions (Refer to Air Flow Schematic and Vacuum Control Chart). • Pinch off suspect tube(s), one at a time, near each respective vacuum motor. • Listen for hiss.	Hiss stops Hiss continues	▶ ▶	CHECK tube connection to vacuum motor and REPAIR and/or RE-CONNECT if loose or split. If hiss still continues, REPLACE vacuum motor.* GO to **A3**.
A3	PINCH OFF SUSPECT TUBE(S) • Pinch off suspect tube(s), one at a time, near control assembly and/or in-line connector. • Listen for hiss.	Hiss stops Hiss continues	▶ ▶	CHECK tube for cut or damage. REPAIR if required. REPLACE function vacuum selector valve.

*Never manually operate any vacuum motor or vacuum motor controlled door — this may cause internal damage to the vacuum motor diaphragm.

CODE	SYMPTOM	POSSIBLE SOURCE
1	Blend actuator is out of position. VFD flashes.	• Open circuit in one or more of the actuator leads. • Actuator output arm jammed. • Actuator inoperative. • Control assembly inoperative.
2	Mode actuator is out of position. LED flashes.	• Same as 1.
3	Pan/Def actuator is out of position. LED flashes.	• Same as 1.
4	Fresh air/recirculator actuator is out of position. LED flashes.	• Same as 1.
1, 5	Blend actuator output shorted. VFD flashes.	• Outputs A or B shorted to ground, or to the supply voltage or together. • Actuator inoperative. • Control assembly inoperative.
2, 6	Mode actuator output shorted. LED flashes.	• Same as 1, 5.
3, 7	Pan/Def actuator output shorted. LED flashes.	• The actuator output is shorted to the supply voltage. • Actuator inoperative. • Control assembly inoperative.
4, 8	Fresh air/recirculator actuator output shorted. LED flashes.	• Same as 3, 7.
9	No failures found. See Supplemental Diagnosis.	
10, 11	A/C clutch never on.	• Circuit 321 open. • BSC inoperative. • Control assembly inoperative.
10, 11	A/C clutch always on.	• Circuit 321 shorted to ground. • BSC inoperative. • Control assembly inoperative.
12	System stays in full heat. In-car temperature must be stabilized above 60°F for this test to be valid.	• Circuit 788, 470, 767, or 790 is open. • The ambient or in-car temperature sensor is inoperative.
13	System stays in full A/C.	• Remove control assembly connectors. Measure the resistance between pin 10 of connector #1 and pin 2 of connector #2. • If the resistance is less than 3K ohms, check the wiring and in-car and ambient temperature sensors. • If the resistance is greater than 3K ohms, replace the control assembly.
14	Blower always at maximum speed.	• Turn off ignition. Remove connector #2 from control assembly. Using a small screwdriver remove terminal #5 from the connector. Replace connector, tape terminal end and turn on ignition. • If blower still at maximum speed, then check circuit 184 and the BSC. • If the blower stops then the control assembly is inoperative.
15	Blower never runs.	• Circuit 184 shorted to the power supply. • BSC inoperative. • Control assembly inoperative.

Error code chart for self-test EATC (© Ford Motor Co.)

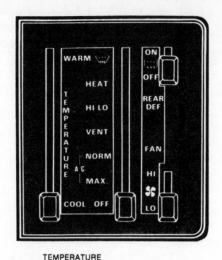

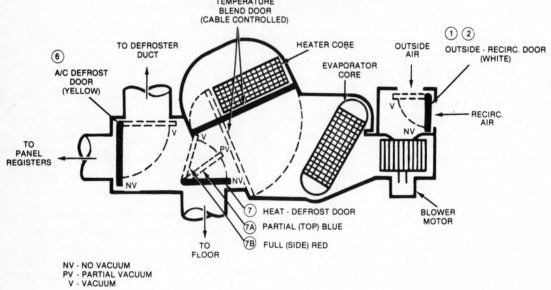

TEMPERATURE
BLEND DOOR
(CABLE CONTROLLED)

TO DEFROSTER
DUCT

HEATER CORE

OUTSIDE
AIR

①②

OUTSIDE - RECIRC. DOOR
(WHITE)

⑥

A/C DEFROST
DOOR
(YELLOW)

EVAPORATOR
CORE

RECIRC.
AIR

TO
PANEL
REGISTERS

V

PV

V

NV

NV

NV

V

TO
FLOOR

⑦ HEAT - DEFROST DOOR

⑦A PARTIAL (TOP) BLUE

⑦B FULL (SIDE) RED

BLOWER
MOTOR

NV - NO VACUUM
PV - PARTIAL VACUUM
V - VACUUM

MANUAL A/C-HEATER SYSTEM VACUUM MOTOR TEST CHART

FUNCTION SELECTOR LEVER POSITION	TEMPERATURE SELECTOR LEVER POSITION	VACUUM MOTORS APPLIED WITH VACUUM			
		OUTSIDE RECIRC. DOOR	HEAT - DEFROST DOOR		A/C - DEFROST DOOR
			PARTIAL	FULL	
OFF	ANY POSITION	1-2	7A	7B	6
A/C ⸢ MAX.	ANY POSITION	1-2	—	—	6
A/C ⸤ NORM.	ANY POSITION	—	—	—	6
VENT	ANY POSITION	—	—	—	6
HI-LO	ANY POSITION	—	7A	—	6
HEAT	ANY POSITION	—	7A	7B	—
DEFROST	ANY POSITION	—	—	—	—
VACUUM HOSE COLOR CODE		White	Blue	Red	Yellow

— No Vacuum (atmosphere).

1982—85 Escort/EXP, Lynx/LN7, Tempo/Topaz, manual A/C system vacuum schematic (© Ford Motor Company)

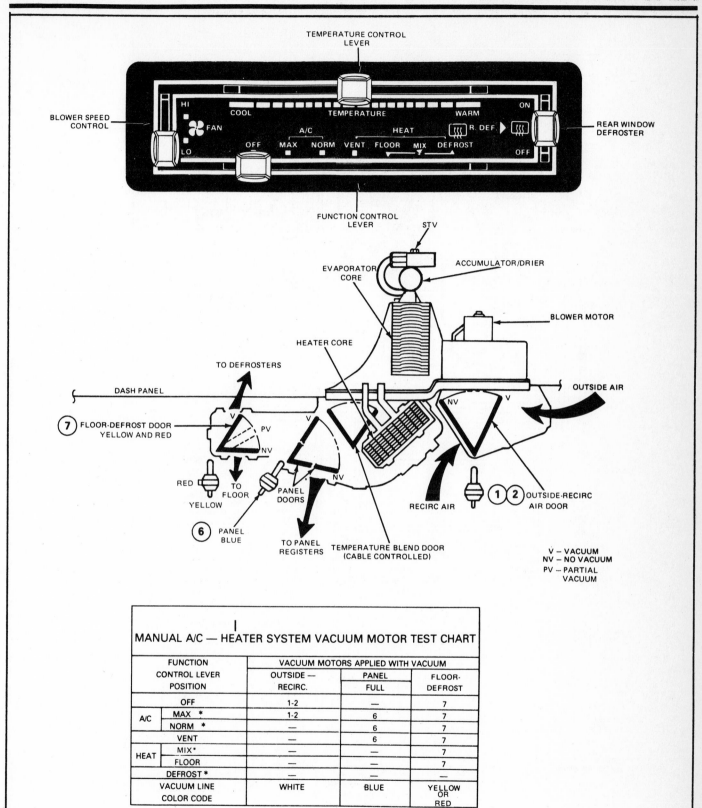

TEMPERATURE CONTROL LEVER

BLOWER SPEED CONTROL

HI

FAN

COOL · TEMPERATURE · WARM

ON

A/C · HEAT

R. DEF.

REAR WINDOW DEFROSTER

OFF · MAX · NORM · VENT · FLOOR · MIX · DEFROST

LO

OFF

FUNCTION CONTROL LEVER

STV

EVAPORATOR CORE

ACCUMULATOR/DRIER

BLOWER MOTOR

HEATER CORE

TO DEFROSTERS

DASH PANEL

OUTSIDE AIR

7 FLOOR-DEFROST DOOR YELLOW AND RED

PV

NV

V

NV

V

RED

YELLOW

TO FLOOR

PANEL DOORS

NV

RECIRC AIR

1 2 OUTSIDE-RECIRC AIR DOOR

6 PANEL BLUE

TO PANEL REGISTERS

TEMPERATURE BLEND DOOR (CABLE CONTROLLED)

V – VACUUM
NV – NO VACUUM
PV – PARTIAL VACUUM

		MANUAL A/C — HEATER SYSTEM VACUUM MOTOR TEST CHART		
FUNCTION CONTROL LEVER POSITION		VACUUM MOTORS APPLIED WITH VACUUM		
		OUTSIDE — RECIRC.	PANEL FULL	FLOOR-DEFROST
	OFF	1-2	—	7
A/C	MAX *	1-2	6	7
	NORM *	—	6	7
	VENT	—	6	7
HEAT	MIX*	—	—	7
	FLOOR	—	—	7
	DEFROST *	—	—	—
VACUUM LINE COLOR CODE		WHITE	BLUE	YELLOW OR RED

— No Vacuum

*Compressor clutch engaged when ambient cut-off switch is closed.

1982—85 Ford/Mercury, manual A/C system vacuum schematic (© Ford Motor Company)

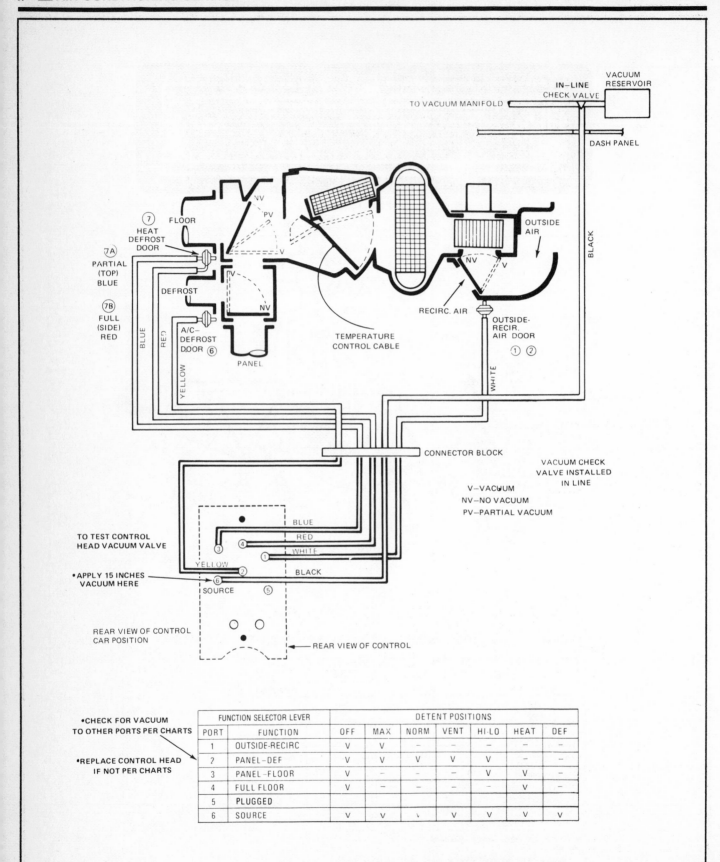

1982—85 Granada/Cougar, Fairmont/Zephyr, Mustang/Capri, manual A/C system vacuum schematic (© Ford Motor Company)

FUNCTION SELECTOR LEVER		DETENT POSITIONS						
PORT	FUNCTION	OFF	MAX	NORM	VENT	HI·LO	HEAT	DEF
1	OUTSIDE-RECIRC	V	V	–	–	–	–	–
2	PANEL-DEF	V	V	V	V	V	–	–
3	PANEL-FLOOR	V	–	–	–	V	V	–
4	FULL FLOOR	V	–	–	–	–	V	–
5	PLUGGED							
6	SOURCE	V	V	V	V	V	V	V

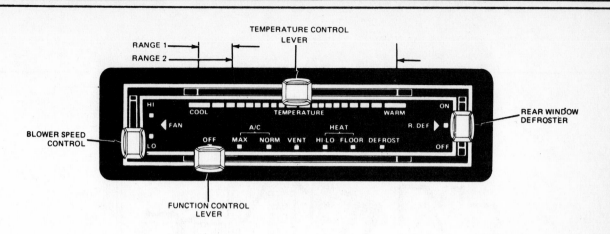

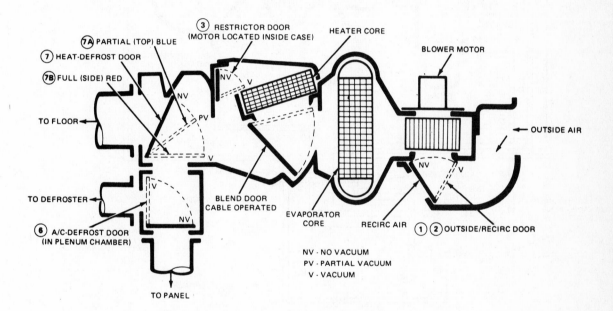

MANUAL A/C-HEATER SYSTEM VACUUM MOTOR TEST CHART

FUNCTION SELECTOR LEVER POSITION		TEMPERATURE SELECTOR LEVER POSITION	VACUUM MOTORS APPLIED WITH VACUUM				
			OUTSIDE RECIRC. DOOR	RESTRICTOR DOOR	HEAT DEFROST DOOR		A/C-DEFROST DOOR
					PARTIAL	FULL	
OFF		ANY POSITION	1-2	—	7A	7B	6
A/C	MAX	RANGE 1	1-2	3	—	—	6
		RANGE 2	1-2	—	—	—	6
	NORM	RANGE 1	—	3	—	—	6
		RANGE 2	—	—	—	—	6
VENT		RANGE 1	—	3	—	—	6
		RANGE 2	—	—	—	—	6
HEAT	HI-LO	ANY POSITION	—	—	7A	—	6
	FLOOR	ANY POSITION	—	—	7A	7B	—
*DEFROST		ANY POSITION	—	—	—	—	—
VACUUM HOSE COLOR CODE			White	Green	Blue	Red	Yellow

*Compressor clutch engaged when ambient cut-off switch is closed.
— No Vacuum (atmosphere).

1982—83 Thunderbird/XR-7, LTD/Marquis, manual A/C system vacuum schematic (© Ford Motor Company)

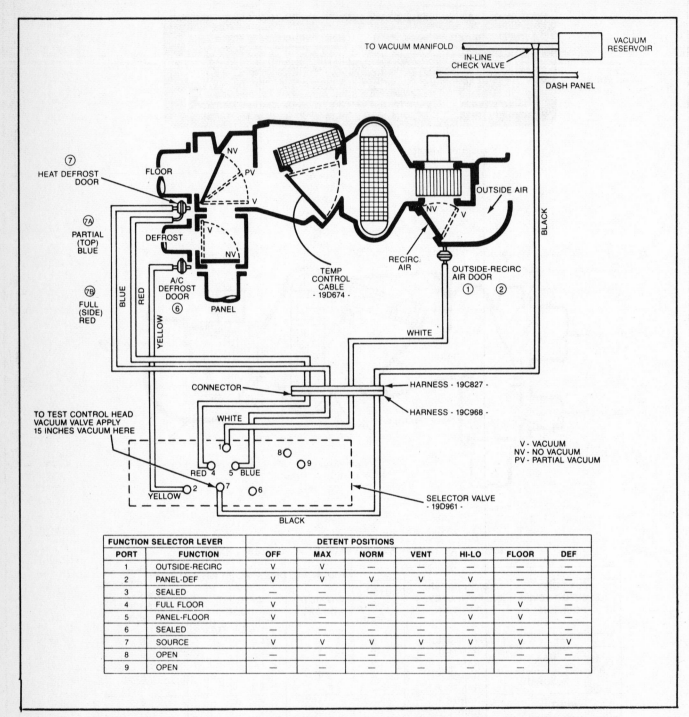

1984—85 Thunderbird/Cougar, LTD/Marquis, manual A/C system vacuum schematics (© Ford Motor Company)

FUNCTION SELECTOR LEVER		DETENT POSITIONS						
PORT	FUNCTION	OFF	MAX	NORM	VENT	HI-LO	FLOOR	DEF
1	OUTSIDE-RECIRC	V	V	—	—	—	—	—
2	PANEL-DEF	V	V	V	V	V	—	—
3	SEALED	—	—	—	—	—	—	—
4	FULL FLOOR	V	—	—	—	—	V	—
5	PANEL-FLOOR	V	—	—	—	V	V	—
6	SEALED	—	—	—	—	—	—	—
7	SOURCE	V	V	V	V	V	V	V
8	OPEN	—	—	—	—	—	—	—
9	OPEN	—	—	—	—	—	—	—

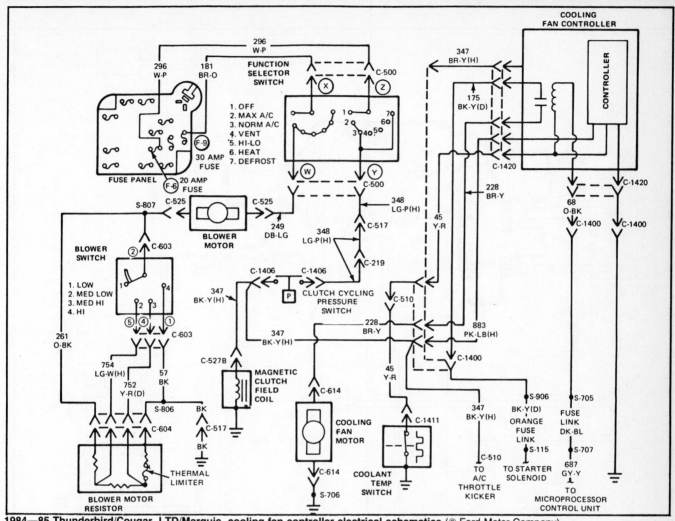

1984—85 Thunderbird/Cougar, LTD/Marquis, cooling fan controller electrical schematics (© Ford Motor Company)

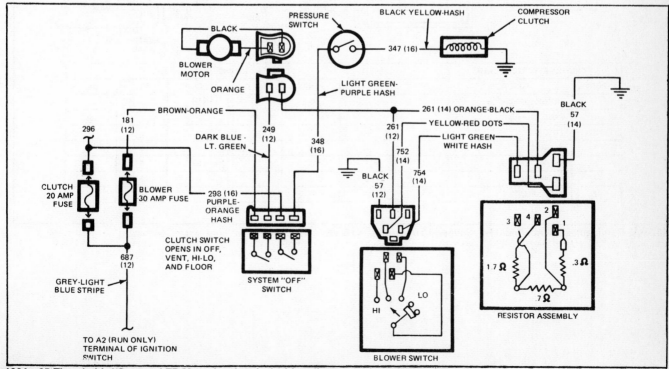

1984—85 Thunderbird/Cougar, LTD/Marquis, electrical wiring diagram and continuity test (© Ford Motor Company)

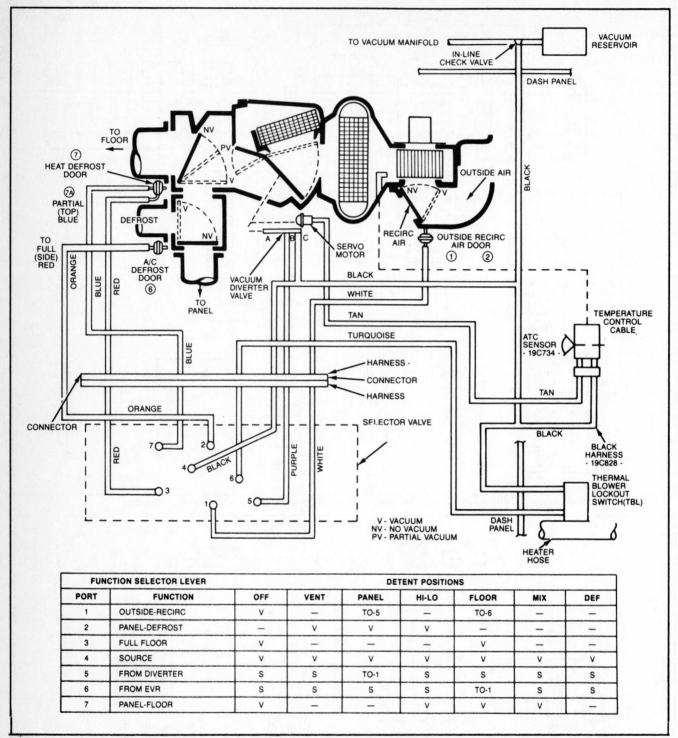

1982—85 Continental, Thunderbird/XR-7/Cougar, LTD/Marquis, ATC vacuum schematic (© Ford Motor Company)

FUNCTION SELECTOR LEVER		DETENT POSITIONS						
PORT	FUNCTION	OFF	VENT	PANEL	HI-LO	FLOOR	MIX	DEF
1	OUTSIDE-RECIRC	V	—	TO-5	—	TO-6	—	—
2	PANEL-DEFROST	—	V	V	V	—	—	—
3	FULL FLOOR	V	—	—	—	V	—	—
4	SOURCE	V	V	V	V	V	V	V
5	FROM DIVERTER	S	S	TO-1	S	S	S	S
6	FROM EVR	S	S	S	S	TO-1	S	S
7	PANEL-FLOOR	V	—	—	V	V	V	—

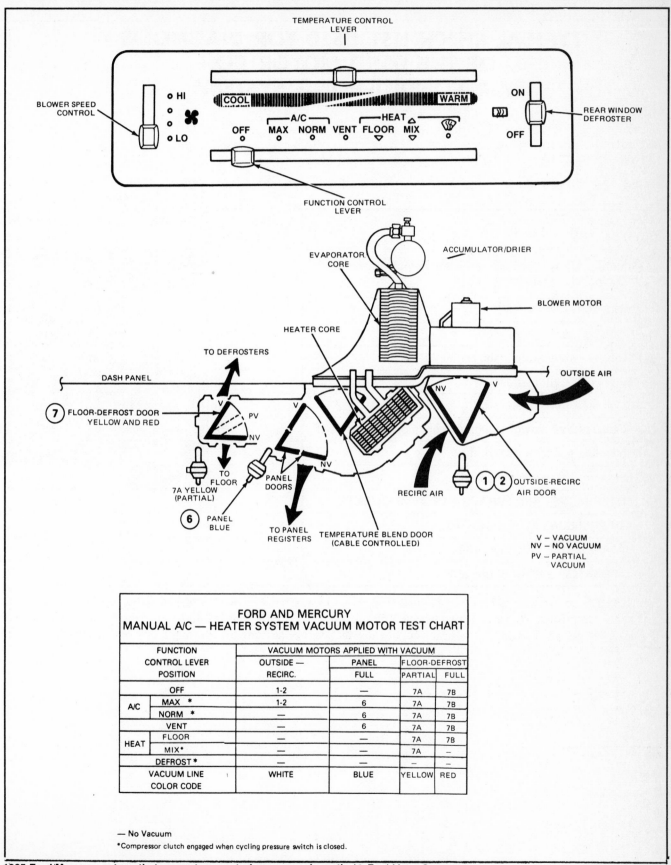

TEMPERATURE CONTROL
LEVER

BLOWER SPEED
CONTROL

HI
LO

COOL | WARM

A/C | HEAT
OFF | MAX | NORM | VENT | FLOOR | MIX

ON
OFF

REAR WINDOW
DEFROSTER

FUNCTION CONTROL
LEVER

EVAPORATOR
CORE

ACCUMULATOR/DRIER

BLOWER MOTOR

HEATER CORE

TO DEFROSTERS

DASH PANEL

OUTSIDE AIR

7 FLOOR-DEFROST DOOR
YELLOW AND RED

NV | V

TO
FLOOR

7A YELLOW
(PARTIAL)

PANEL
DOORS

NV

6 PANEL
BLUE

TO PANEL
REGISTERS

TEMPERATURE BLEND DOOR
(CABLE CONTROLLED)

RECIRC AIR

1 2 OUTSIDE-RECIRC
AIR DOOR

V — VACUUM
NV — NO VACUUM
PV — PARTIAL
VACUUM

FORD AND MERCURY
MANUAL A/C — HEATER SYSTEM VACUUM MOTOR TEST CHART

FUNCTION CONTROL LEVER POSITION		VACUUM MOTORS APPLIED WITH VACUUM			
		OUTSIDE — RECIRC.	PANEL FULL	FLOOR-DEFROST PARTIAL	FLOOR-DEFROST FULL
	OFF	1-2	—	7A	7B
A/C	MAX *	1-2	6	7A	7B
	NORM *	—	6	7A	7B
	VENT	—	6	7A	7B
HEAT	FLOOR	—	—	7A	7B
	MIX*	—	—	7A	—
	DEFROST *	—	—	—	—
VACUUM LINE COLOR CODE		WHITE	BLUE	YELLOW	RED

— No Vacuum

*Compressor clutch engaged when cycling pressure switch is closed.

1985 Ford/Mercury, automatic temperature control vacuum schematic (© Ford Motor Company)

TYPICAL CHECK LIST USED FOR DIAGNOSIS OF THE FORD MOTOR CO. AIR CONDITIONING SYSTEMS

Vehicle Make _____   Model Year _____   System Type   Cycling Clutch ☐   STV ☐   STV/BPO ☐   Refrigerant Capacity _____

CHECK ITEM	READY TO TEST ✔	READING:	BEHAVIOR RATING (normal, high, low)
1. Vehicle properly tuned and adjusted; engine at normal operating temperatures			
2. AMBIENT TEMPERATURE			
3. ALTITUDE (Above Sea Level) *			
4. In-vehicle temperature stabilized at 70° - 80°F			
5. Compressor Clutch engaged			
6. A/C on MAX (recirculating air)			
7. A/C Blower on medium or high (depends on system type)			
8. Engine idle speed at 1500 rpm			
9. Refrigerant pressures stabilized			
10. CENTER REGISTER DISCHARGE AIR TEMPERATURE			
11. HIGH PRESSURE (DISCHARGE PSI)			
12. LOW PRESSURE (SUCTION PSI)			
13. EVAPORATOR GAUGE PRESSURE			

*ALTITUDE for your area may be obtained from your local Chamber of Commerce or by referring to a World Almanac and Book of Facts listing entitled "Latitude, Longtitude and Altitude of United States Cities". If your city is not given, select a city near yours or use the average altitude by selecting a city on each side of you.

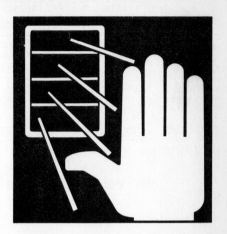

SECTION 5
GENERAL MOTORS
Buick

INDEX

BUICK MOTORS
Rear Wheel Drive Models

1982	1983	1984	1985
Regal	Regal	Regal	Regal
LeSabre	LeSabre	LeSabre	LeSabre
Electra	Electra	Electra	Electra
Electra Estate	Electra Estate	Electra Estate	Electra Estate

Note: The vehicles listed are base models.

Drive Belt Tension

Adjustment

Different methods of air conditioning compressor belt tensioning are used by various vehicle manufacturers. The adjustments involves the movements of one or more of the components within the belt span, such as the A/C compressor, alternator power steering pump or an idler pulley.

Caution must be exercised to avoid missing hidden retaining bolts/nuts before adjusting and to apply tensioning pressure on the component without causing internal damage or misalignment of the pulleys.

——— CAUTION ———
Do not attempt to adjust the belt tension while the engine is running.

COMPRESSOR DRIVE BELT TENSION
Buick

Year	New	Used
1982	80–140 lbs.	50–70 lbs.
1983	80–140 lbs.	50–70 lbs.
1984	80–140 lbs.	50–70 lbs.
1985	80–150 lbs.	50–70 lbs.

BUICK MOTORS
Front Wheel Drive Models

1982	1983	1984	1985
Skylark	Skylark	Skylark	Electra
Skyhawk	Skyhawk	Skyhawk	Park Avenue
Century	Century	Century	Riviera
Riviera	Riviera	Riviera	Somerset Regal
			Skylark
			Skyhawk
			Century

Note: The vehicles listed are base models.

DEFLECTION METHOD

Adjustments

A predetermined location on the belt span or the center of the longest span between pulleys are used in the deflection method adjustment. A straight edge or an imaginary line is used between the two pulleys involved, along the top of the belt surface. Either a predetermined pressure or a moderate thumb pressure is used to depress the belt in the center of the span. The amount of movement is measured and compared to specifications. Corrections are made as required by moving the adjusting component.

TORQUE METHOD

Adjustments

Brackets are supplied on the adjusting component to accept a ½ inch drive torque wrench. With the adjusting component retaining bolts loosened, the torque wrench can be inserted into the bracket hole and a tightening torque can be applied against the component and belt until the specification is reached. Tighten the adjusting component retaining bolts while holding the specified torque with the wrench.

REFRIGERANT CAPACITIES—BUICK
1982–85 Models

Refrigerant given in ounces, Refrigerant oil given in fluid ounces

1982 Models	Recharge Capacities R-12	Oil	1983 Models	Recharge Capacities R-12	Oil	1984 Models	Recharge Capacities R-12	Oil	1985 Models	Recharge Capacities R-12	Oil
Regal	52	6	Regal	52	8①	Regal	52	8①	Regal	52	8①
LeSabre	56	6	LeSabre	56	8①	LeSabre	56	8①	LeSabre	56	8①
Electra	56	6	Electra	56	8①	Electra	56	8①	Electra	56	8①
Electra Estate	56	6	Electra Estate	56	8①	Electra Estate	56	8①	Electra Estate	56	8①
Skylark	44	6	Skylark	44	8①	Skylark	44	8①	Riviera	52	8①
Skyhawk	44	6	Skyhawk	44	8①	Skyhawk	44	8①	Somerset Regal	52	8①
Century	44	6	Century	44	8①	Century	44	8①	Skylark	44	8①
Riviera	52	6	Riviera	52	8①	Riviera	52	8①	Skyhawk	44	8①
									Century	44	8①

①Refrigerant oil capacities are given for vehicles equipped with the DA-6 compressor. Vehicles equipped with the R-4 compressor require 4 fluid ounces of refrigerant oil.

TENSIONING GAUGE METHOD

Adjustments

A tensioning gauge is placed on the A/C belt at its center, between its longest span between the pulleys. The adjusting component retaining bolts are loosened and forced outward against the belt. When the specified belt tension is reached on the gauge dial, the adjusting component retaining bolts are tightened without loss of tension. An alternate name for this method is the strand tension adjustment.

The following precautions should always be observed:

1. Use only the belt which is specifically recommended for the application.

2. Check all mountings and pulleys for cracks, looseness. Check for, and if necessary, correct misalignment.

3. Never pry a belt on. Always loosen the adjustment so that the belt can be installed without force.

4. Applying pressure in a manner that will not damage any of the components, adjust the belt to the factory specifications.

Blower Motor

Removal and Installation

1982–1985 MODELS

1. Disconnect the negative battery cable.

2. Tag and disconnect the electrical connections from the blower motor.

3. If the vehicle is equipped with a plastic splash shield, remove from the right side of the cowl.

4. Remove the blower motor retaining bolts from the blower motor shaft. Remove the blower motor and cage assembly.

5. Installation is the reverse of the removal procedure.

Compressor

Removal and Installation

1982–1985 MODELS

NOTE: For the compressor overhaul procedure, refer to the compressor section.

1. Disconnect the negative battery cable.

2. Tag and disconnect the electrical connections from the compressor.

3. Discharge the air conditioning system as outlined earlier in this section.

4. Remove the refrigerant line at the rear of the compressor.

5. Remove the upper and lower air conditioning bolts.

NOTE: Some vehicles may require the power steering pump, alternator or plug wires to be repositioned or removed. Other components may need to be removed depending on the optional accessories.

6. Remove the air conditioning compressor from the vehicle.

7. When installing the compressor, keep dirt and foreign material from getting into the compressor parts and system. Clean tools and a clean work area are important for proper service. The compressor connections and the outside of the compressor should be cleaned before the compressor is installed. If new components are being installed, note that they are dehydrated and sealed prior to shipping. All sub-assemblies are to remain sealed until use, with the sub-assemblies at room temperature before uncapping. This helps prevent moisture from the air entering the system due to condensation. Use a small amount of refrigerant oil on all tube and hose joints. Always use new ''O'' rings

dipped in refrigerant oil before assembling joints. This oil will aid assembly and help to provide leak-proof joints.

8. Install any accessories that may have been removed to make room for the compressor.

9. Evacuate, charge and leak test the system. Check for the proper operation of the system.

Expansion Tube (Orifice)

Removal and Installation

1. Discharge the air conditioning system.

2. Loosen the nut holding the liquid line to the evaporator inlet pipe. Remove the tube using needle nose pliers.

3. Install the new orifice tube.

NOTE: When installing the orifice tube, make sure that the short screen is facing the condensor.

4. Install the liquid line to the evaporator.

5. Evacuate and charge the air conditioning system. Check the system for proper operation.

The following procedure is recommended for an expansion tube that is broken or difficult to remove.

1. Discharge the air conditioning system.

2. Remove the liquid line to evaporator inlet pipe.

3. Using a heat gun, apply heat approximately one quarter of an inch from the inlet pipe dimples.

NOTE: If a pressure switch is located near the orifice tube, remove it before applying heat so as not to damage the circuit.

4. Using a twisting motion, loosen the orifice tube and remove it from its holder.

NOTE: Commercial tools are available to remove the expansion tube after the system has been discharged.

5. Clean the inside of the evaporator pipe with R-12 or equivalent.

6. Add one ounce of 525 viscosity refrigerant oil to the system. Lubricate the new orifice tube and ''O'' ring with the refrigerant oil.

7. Install the new orifice tube in the inlet pipe.

NOTE: When installing the new orifice tube, make sure that the short screen is facing the condenser.

8. Install the liquid line to the evaporator.

9. Evacuate and charge the system. Check the system for proper operation.

Condenser

Removal and Installation

1982 AND LATER MODELS EXCEPT CENTURY AND SKYLARK

1. Discharge the air conditioning system. Disconnect the negative battery cable.

2. Drain the cooling system.

3. Remove the radiator shields from the radiator assembly. Remove the radiator.

4. Disconnect the condensor lines and cap the line ends.

5. Remove the condensor from the vehicle.

6. Installation is the reverse of the removal procedure. Be sure to add any necessary refrigerant oil the air conditioning system.

7. Evacuate and charge the system. Check for leaks and proper system operation.

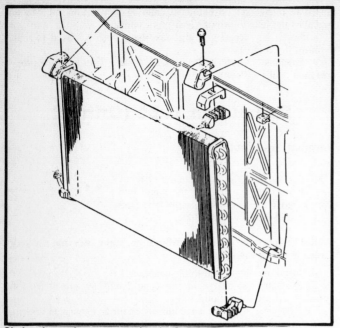

Skyhawk condensor mounting (© General Motors Corporation)

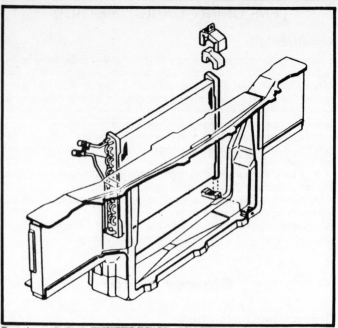

Regal condensor mounting (© General Motors Corporation)

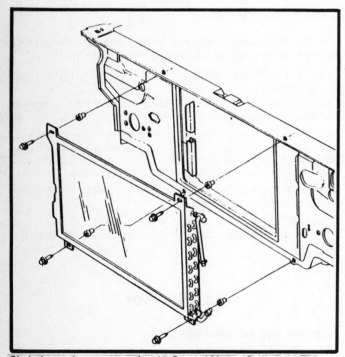

Skylark condensor mounting (© General Motors Corporation)

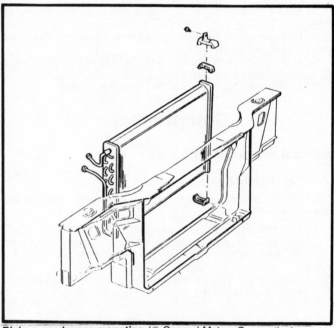

Riviera condensor mounting (© General Motors Corporation)

1982 AND LATER CENTURY AND SKYLARKS

1. Discharge the air conditioning system. Disconnect the negative battery cable.
2. Disconnect the condensor lines.
3. On certain models it may be necessary to remove the center grill support.
4. Remove the condensor from the vehicle.
5. Installation is the reverse of the removal procedure.
6. Evacuate and charge the system. Check for leaks and proper system operation.

Evaporator

Removal and Installation

EXCEPT 1982 AND LATER SKYHAWK

1. Disconnect the negative battery cable. Discharge the air conditioning system. Drain the cooling system.
2. On diesel equipped vehicles, remove the air cleaner in order to gain working clearance.
3. Tag and disconnect the electrical connections from the blower motor, thermostatic switch and blower relay.
4. Remove the vacuum tank.

5. Disconnect the condensor line from the evaporator and the suction line from the accumulator.

6. Remove the blower motor.

NOTE: On certain models it may be necessary to remove obstructing engine support struts in order to gain access to the evaporator assembly.

7. Remove the blower case bolts. Remove the blower motor assembly.

8. Installation is the reverse of the removal procedure.

9. Evacuate and charge the system. Check the system for leaks and proper operation.

1982 AND LATER SKYHAWKS

1. Disconnect the negative battery cable. Drain the cooling system and remove the heater hoses.

2. Discharge the air conditioning system.

3. Disconnect the lines to the evaporator. Disconnect the heater hoses at the heater core.

4. Remove the steering column trim cover, glove box and heater outlet. Remove the right and left instrument panel sound insulators.

5. Remove the heater core cover.

6. Remove the heater core clamps. Remove the heater core.

7. Remove the defroster vacuum actuator from the module case.

8. Remove the evaporator cover. Remove the evaporator assembly.

9. Evacuate and charge the system. Check the system for leaks and proper operation.

Accumulator

Removal and Installation

1982 AND LATER MODELS

1. Disconnect the negative battery cable.

2. Discharge the air conditioning system.

3. Disconnect the accumulator inlet and outlet lines. Cap all open lines.

4. Tag and disconnect the pressure cycling switch connection. Remove the switch.

5. Remove the accumulator bracket bolts. Remove the accumulator assembly.

6. Installation is the reverse of the removal procedure.

7. Evacuate and charge the system. Check for proper operation and leaks.

High/Low Pressure Cooling Fan Switch

Removal and Installation

DIESEL EQUIPPED VEHICLES

1. Disconnect the negative battery cable.

2. Tag and disconnect the electrical connector from the switch to be removed.

NOTE: The switch is located in the Shrader valve fitting and its removal will not discharge the system.

3. Unscrew the switch from the fitting. Remove the switch.

4. Installation is the reverse of the removal procedure.

NON-DIESEL EQUIPPED VEHICLES

1. Disconnect the negative battery cable.

2. Discharge the air conditioning system as outlined earlier.

3. Remove the coupled hose assembly from the rear of the compressor.

4. Tag and disconnect the electrical connection at the switch.

5. Remove the switch from the rear of the compressor.

6. Installation is the reverse of the removal procedure.

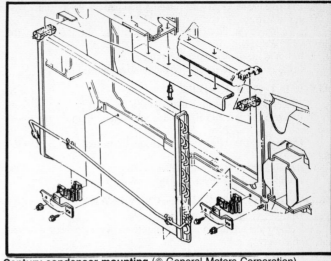

Century condensor mounting (© General Motors Corporation)

Coupled Hose Assembly

Removal and Installation

1982 AND LATER MODELS

1. Disconnect the negative battery cable. Discharge the air conditioning system.

2. On diesel equipped vehicles, remove the low and high pressure cooling fan switches. Mark the switches accordingly so as to avoid reversing the switches when reinstalling.

3. Remove the low pressure line at the accumulator outlet fitting. Disconnect the high pressure line at the condensor fitting.

4. Disconnect the coupled hose from the compressor.

5. Remove the coupled hose clamps. Remove the coupled hose assembly from the vehicle.

6. Installation is the reverse of the removal procedure. Evacuate and charge the system. Check the system for leaks and proper operation.

Temperature Sensors

Vehicles equipped with Electronic Touch Climate Control use two temperature sensors, an in car sensor and an ambient (outside temperature) sensor. The ambient sensor is located under the air inlet screen. The in car sensor is located on the instrument panel carrier. The in car sensor is connected to the aspirator on the heater case by a rubber hose.

IN CAR SENSOR

Removal and Installation

1982 AND LATER LESABRE AND ELECTRA

1. Disconnect the negative battery cable.

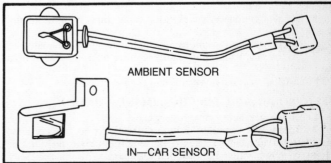

In car sensor and ambient sensor (© General Motors Corporation)

2. Remove the necessary instrument panel pad screws to gain access to the in car sensor.

3. Disconnect the hose from the sensor. Tag and disconnect the wire from the sensor.

4. Remove the sensor from the vehicle.

5. Installation is the reverse of the removal procedure.

1982 AND LATER RIVIERA

1. Disconnect the negative battery cable.

2. Remove the left and right side kick panels. Remove the lower dash panel.

3. Disconnect the wire from the sensor. Remove the hose from the sensor.

4. Remove the sensor from the vehicle.

5. Installation is the reverse of the removal procedure.

1982 AND LATER REGAL AND SKYHAWK

1. Disconnect the negative battery cable.

2. Remove the top instrument panel screws. Remove the instrument panel top cover.

3. Disconnect the electrical connection and the hose from the sensor.

4. Release the locking tabs while removing the sensor from its carrier.

5. Installation is the reverse of the removal procedure making sure the locking tabs snap into place preventing the sensor from working loose.

Ambient Sensor

Removal and Installation

1982 AND LATER MODELS

1. Disconnect the negative battery cable.

2. If the vehicle is equipped with a hood seal, remove from the lip of the air conditioning module.

3. Remove the screw holding the leaf screen closest to the ambient sensor.

4. Tag and disconnect the electrical connector from the sensor.

5. Remove the ambient sensor from the vehicle.

6. Installation is the reverse of the removal procedure.

Heater and A/C Control

Removal and Installation

STANDARD A/C

1. Disconnect the negative battery cable.

2. Remove the necessary instrument panel trim to gain access to the control head retaining screws. On certain models it may first be necessary to remove the right and left dash panels.

3. Remove the screws holding the control head to the dash assembly.

4. Pull the control head out of the dash assembly and remove the bulb and socket. This can be done by twisting and pulling back on the socket.

5. Tag and disconnect the electrical connections from the control head.

6. Disconnect the vacuum harness by removing the push nuts.

7. Remove the temperature cable. Remove the control head from the vehicle.

8. Installation is the reverse of the removal procedure.

ELECTRONIC AND TOUCH CLIMATE CONTROL

1. Disconnect the negative battery cable.

2. Remove the necessary instrument panel trim to gain access to the control head retaining screws. On certain models it may first be necessary to remove the right and left dash panels.

3. Remove the control head to dash assembly retaining screws.

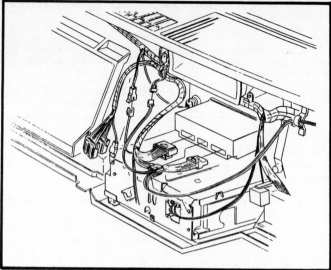

Typical electrical connections at back of control panel (© General Motors Corporation)

4. Pull the control head out of the dash assembly far enough to remove the electrical connectors from the back of the control head.

5. Tag and disconnect the electrical connections from the back of the control head.

6. Remove the control head.

7. Installation is the reverse of the removal procedure.

Control Cables

When replacing the control cable, use equal lengths of cable from a cable service kit. Use the original cable housing if possible. Most of the time only the wire portion of the cable will need replacing.

Diagnosing Automatic Air Conditioning Systems

CONTROL PANEL

Procedure

1. With the ignition switched on, set the air conditioning system to the automatic mode and the temperature setting to 75 degrees.

2. Check to see that the Light Emitting Diodes (LED's) are glowing. If not this indicates that ignition power is not reaching the control head.

3. Check the system for a blown fuse or an electrical short in the control panel feed wire. Repair or replace the wire as necessary.

ACTUATORS

Procedure

NOTE: To test the acturators the engine must be running and at normal operating temperature.

1. With the engine running, set the air conditioning system to the automatic mode and the temperature setting to 65 degrees. The blower should increase to maximum blower speed. If not refer to blower motor diagnosis.

2. Set the temperature setting to 85 degrees. The blower should decrease in speed and then gradually increase to maximum blower speed. If not refer to blower motor diagnosis.

3. Set the temperature setting to 85 degrees. Set the air conditioning system to the defroster setting. Blower speed should remain at maximum

speed and the temperature should become hot. If not refer to blower motor diagnosis.

4. Set the temperature setting to 75 degrees. Set the air conditioning system to the bi-level setting. The blower speed should slow down, if not there is a sensor problem. If there is a malfunction with the actuator door, the bi-level LED will flash.

TEMPERATURE DOOR ACTUATOR

Procedure

NOTE: In order to test the temperature door actuator, it is necessary to have the engine running and at normal operating temperature.

Set the temperature setting to 65 degrees. Wait approximately one minute and readjust the setting to 85 degrees. If no LED flashing is noted, then the component is operating properly. If the LED's are flashing in either temperature setting, the actuator door arm needs adjustment.

To Adjust:
1. Start the engine and allow it to reach normal operating temperature.
2. Disconnect the rod from the actuator arm.
3. Set the temperature setting to 85 degrees.
4. When the motor stops, pull the rod down as far as it will go. Adjust connector so that the rod snaps in place.

BLOWER MOTOR

NOTE: The following troubleshooting is performed with the ignition on and the engine off. The engine must be at normal operating temperature and the LED's must be lit.

Procedure

NO BLOWER AT 85 DEGREE TEMPERATURE SETTING
1. Set the temperature setting to 65 degrees.
2. If the blower comes on, check the electrical connectors at the air conditioning clutch and the blower.
3. If the connections are good, the blower delay timer is bad.
4. Replace the blower delay timer located in the control panel.

NO BLOWER AT 65 DEGREE TEMPERATURE SETTING
1. With the connector attached, measure the voltage between blower control pin "1" and ground "7".
2. If voltage is fluctuating above 3 volts, measure the voltage between pin "6" and "7". If the voltage is 3 volts or more, the blower motor is malfunctioning.

HIGH BLOWER ONLY
1. Connect a voltmeter between ground pin "7" and blower pin "1".
2. If the voltage is greater than 3 volts and less than 7, replace the blower control.
3. If the voltage is above 7 volts and fluctuates, replace the control panel.

NO BLOWER IN DEFROST OR HIGH MODE
1. Measure the voltage between control pin "1" and ground pin "7". If the voltage is greater than 3 volts and less than 7, replace the control panel.
2. If the voltage measured is greater than 7 volts, measure the voltage between feed pin "6" and ground pin "7".
3. If more than 11 volts are present, replace the blower motor.
4. If the voltage is less than 10 volts, replace the blower control panel.

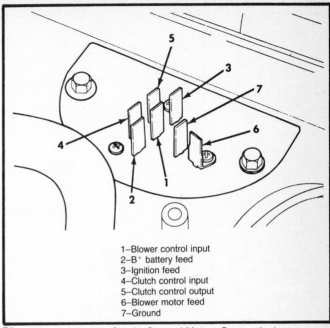

1–Blower control input
2–B⁺ battery feed
3–Ignition feed
4–Clutch control input
5–Clutch control output
6–Blower motor feed
7–Ground

Blower motor power pins (© General Motors Corporation)

BLOWER SPEED DOES NOT VARY IN AUTO, HEAT, BI-LEVEL OR ECONOMY SETTINGS
1. Connect a voltmeter between control pin "1" and ground.
2. Move the temperature setting between 65 and 85 degrees.
3. Voltage should fluctuate above and below 7 volts.
4. If no fluctuation is noted, the control panel is defective. Repair or replace as necessary.
5. If the voltage does vary and the blower is still inoperative, the blower motor is defective. Repair or replace as necessary.

AMBIENT AND IN CAR TEMPERATURE SENSOR

1. Remove the suspected faulty sensor from the vehicle.
2. Do not hold the sensor with the bare hand or apply a meter test for more than 5 seconds since both affect the sensor resistance and measurement of accuracy.
3. The ambient sensor resistance should read between 5000 and 6000 ohms with the room temperature between 60 and 70 degrees.
4. The in car temperature sensor should read between 20,000 and 25,000 ohms with the room temperature approximately 60 degrees.

PROGRAMMER ASSEMBLY

The programmer is connected to the air conditioning module assembly behind the glove box. It contains four vacuum solenoids, electronic switching amplifiers and drivers, and a small 8 volt motor.

The programmer controls certain solenoids through electronic switches. Vacuum is then applied to different vacuum motor actuators which control the air flow in the air conditioning module.

Adjustments to the programmer may be needed for passenger compartment comfort. Adjustments can be made without removing the programmer from the vehicle. These adjustments are accomplished by readjusting the link rod. However, the manufacturer does not recommend any attempt be made to repair the programmer's vacuum solenoids or electronic circuits.

Programmer repair should only consist of disconnecting and removing the faulty assembly and replacing it with a properly working exchange.

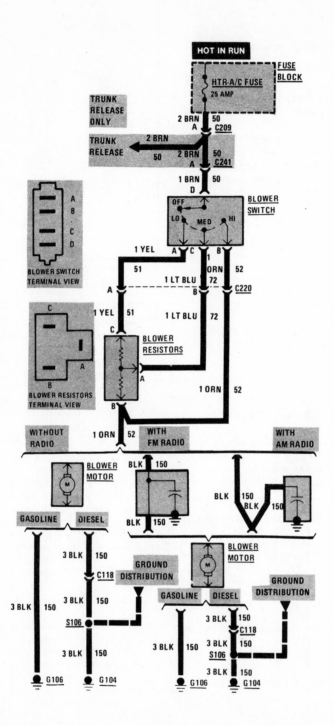

1982 and Later Buick heater schematic—typical (© General Motors Corporation)

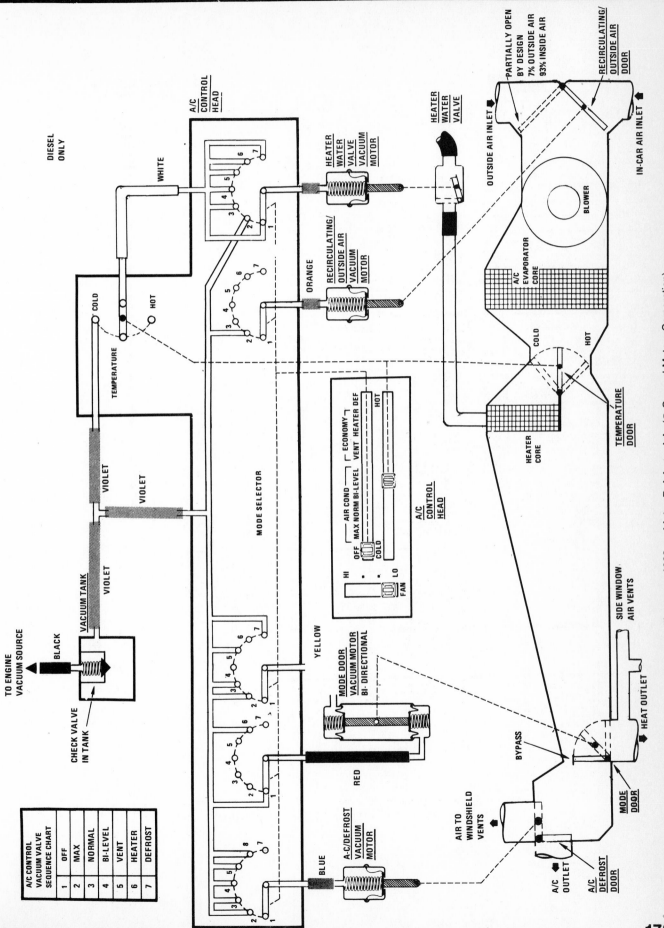

Vacuum diagram—1982 and later Buick models (© General Motors Corporation)

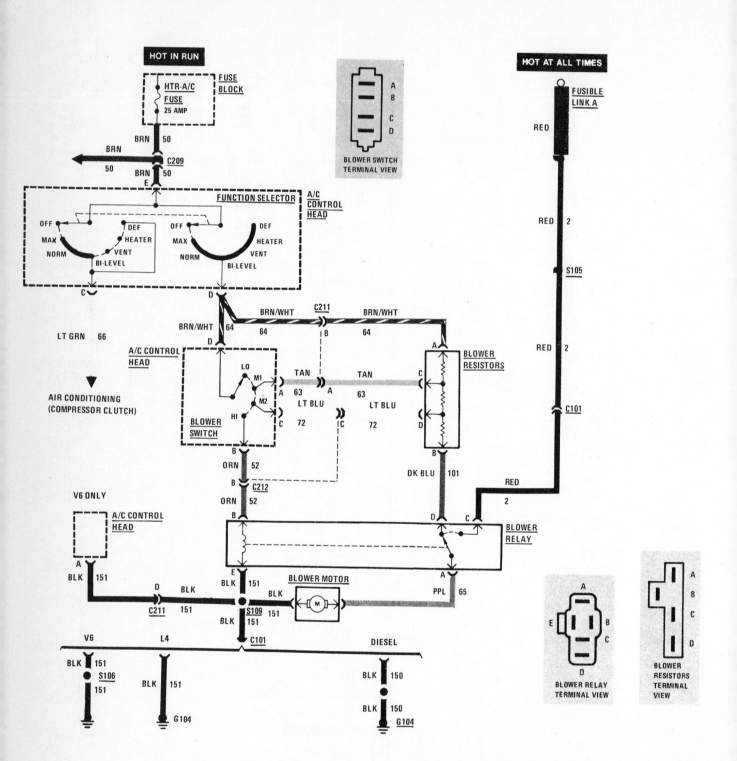

1982 and later Century blower schematic (© General Motors Corporation)

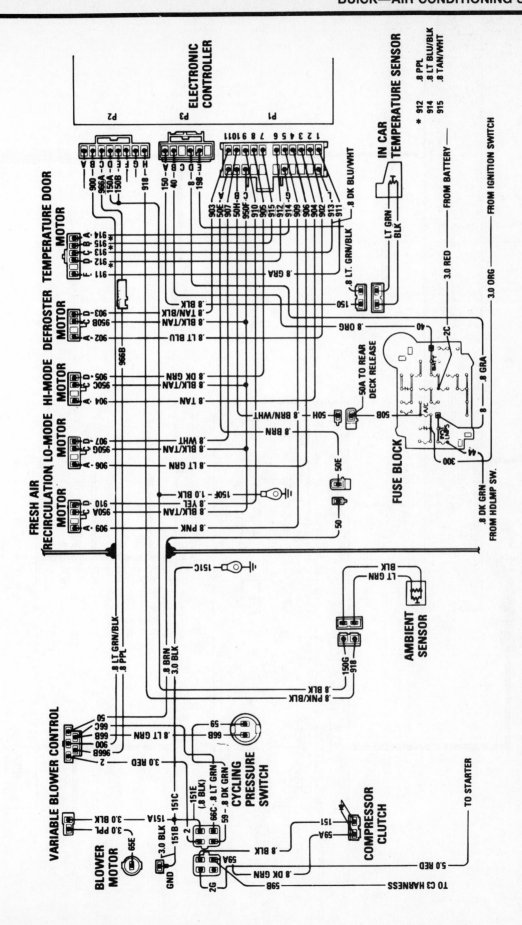

1982—1984 Electronic air conditioning—LeSabre and Electra (© General Motors Corporation)

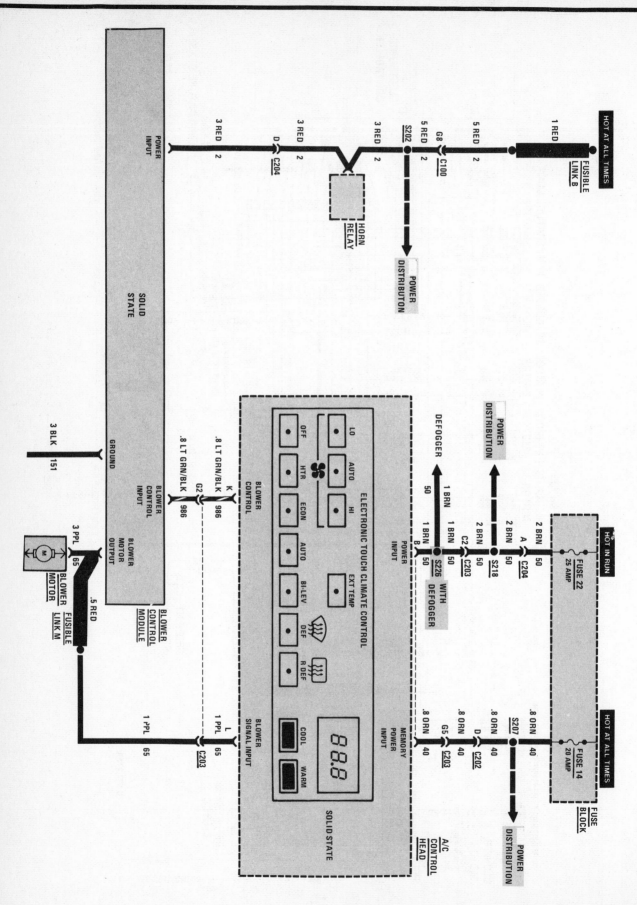

1985—Electra touch control wiring diagram (© General Motors Corporation)

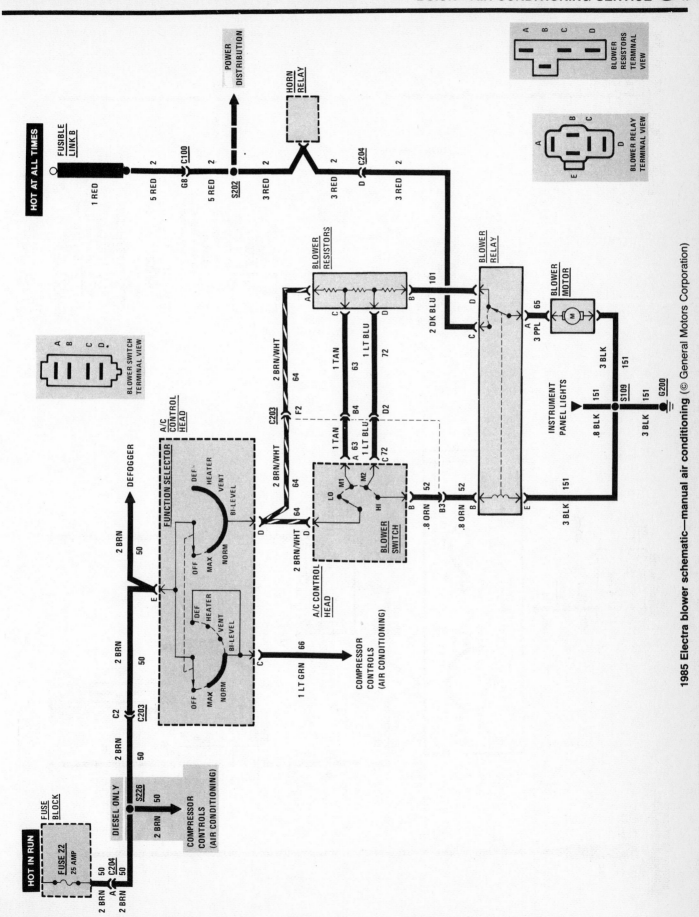

1985 Electra blower schematic—manual air conditioning (© General Motors Corporation)

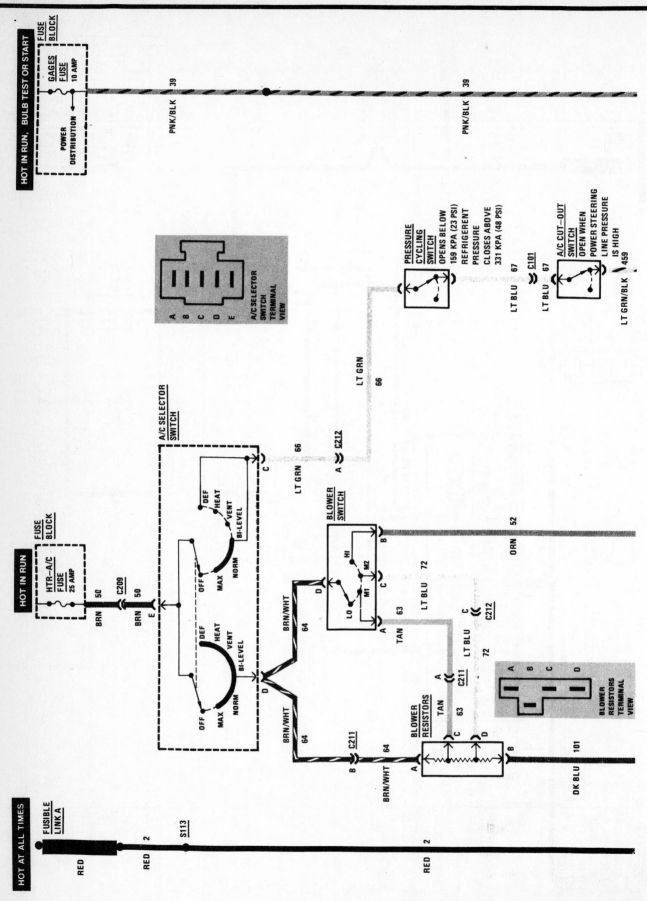

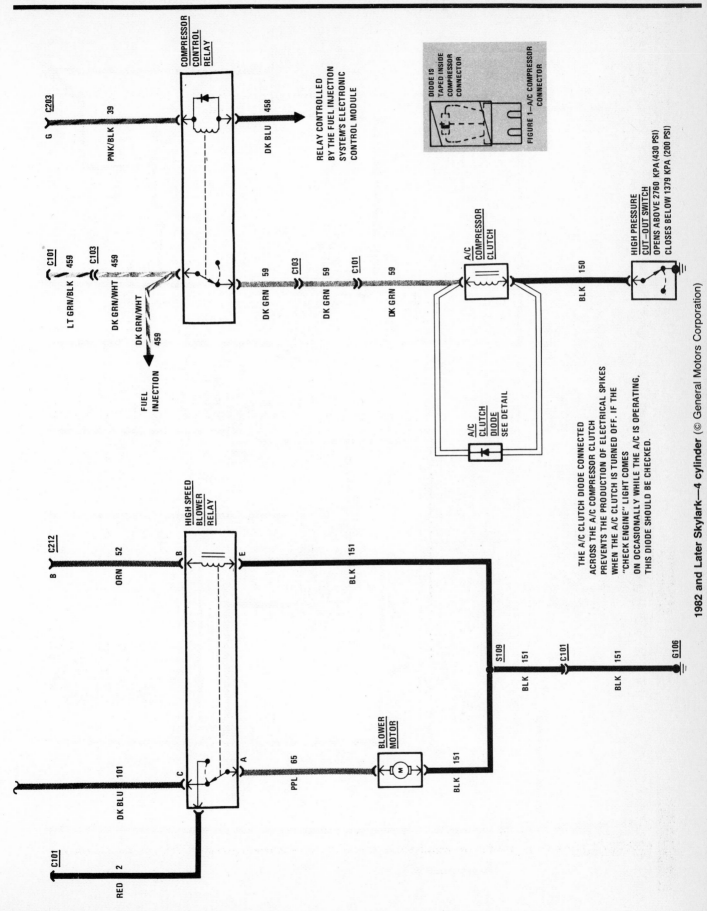

DIODE IS TAPED INSIDE COMPRESSOR CONNECTOR

FIGURE 1—A/C COMPRESSOR CONNECTOR

COMPRESSOR CONTROL RELAY

G C203

PNK/BLK 39

DK BLU 458

RELAY CONTROLLED BY THE FUEL INJECTION SYSTEM'S ELECTRONIC CONTROL MODULE

C101 459 C103 459
LT GRN/BLK
DK GRN/WHT

DK GRN/WHT 459

FUEL INJECTION

DK GRN 59 C103 59 C101 59 DK GRN DK GRN

A/C COMPRESSOR CLUTCH

BLK 150

HIGH PRESSURE CUT-OUT SWITCH
OPENS ABOVE 2760 KPA (430 PSI)
CLOSES BELOW 1379 KPA (200 PSI)

A/C CLUTCH DIODE SEE DETAIL

THE A/C CLUTCH DIODE CONNECTED ACROSS THE A/C COMPRESSOR CLUTCH PREVENTS THE PRODUCTION OF ELECTRICAL SPIKES WHEN THE A/C CLUTCH IS TURNED OFF. IF THE "CHECK ENGINE" LIGHT COMES ON OCCASIONALLY WHILE THE A/C IS OPERATING, THIS DIODE SHOULD BE CHECKED.

HIGH SPEED BLOWER RELAY

B C212
ORN 52
B
E
BLK 151

S109 BLK 151 C101 BLK 151 G106

BLOWER MOTOR

C
A
PPL 65
BLK 151
M

C101 DK BLU 101

C101 RED 2

1982 and Later Skylark—4 cylinder (© General Motors Corporation)

GENERAL MOTORS CORPORATION
BUICK—AIR CONDITIONING SERVICE

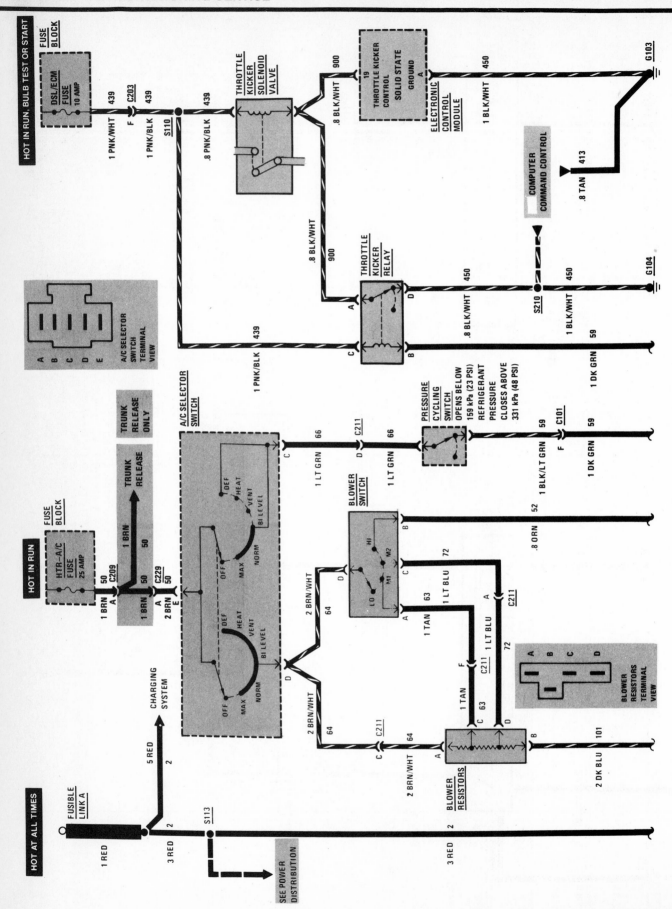

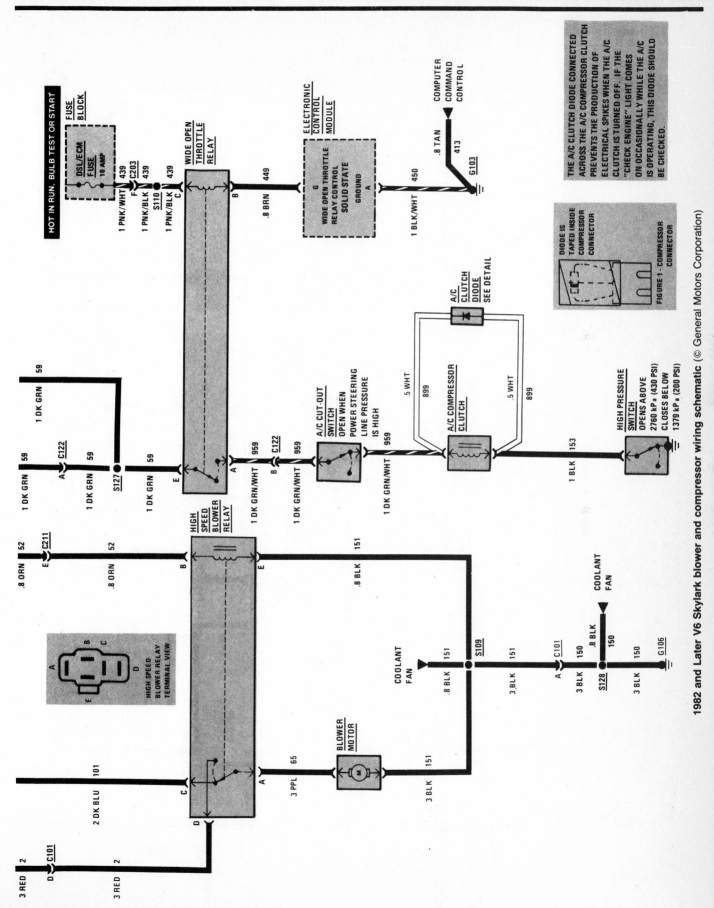

THE A/C CLUTCH DIODE CONNECTED ACROSS THE A/C COMPRESSOR CLUTCH PREVENTS THE PRODUCTION OF ELECTRICAL SPIKES WHEN THE A/C CLUTCH IS TURNED OFF. IF THE "CHECK ENGINE" LIGHT COMES ON OCCASIONALLY WHILE THE A/C IS OPERATING, THIS DIODE SHOULD BE CHECKED.

DIODE IS TAPED INSIDE COMPRESSOR CONNECTOR

FIGURE 1 - COMPRESSOR CONNECTOR

1982 and Later V6 Skylark blower and compressor wiring schematic (© General Motors Corporation)

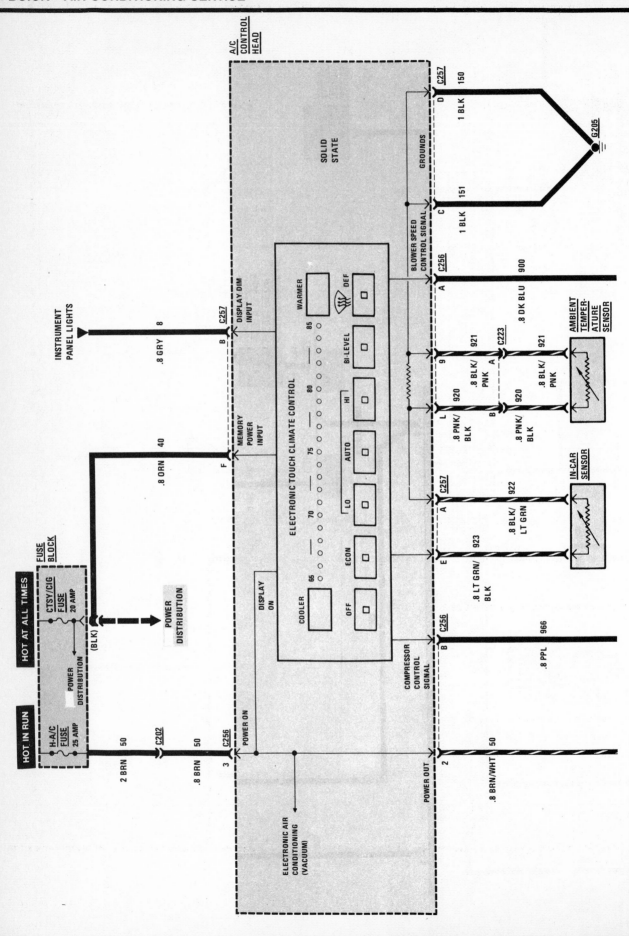

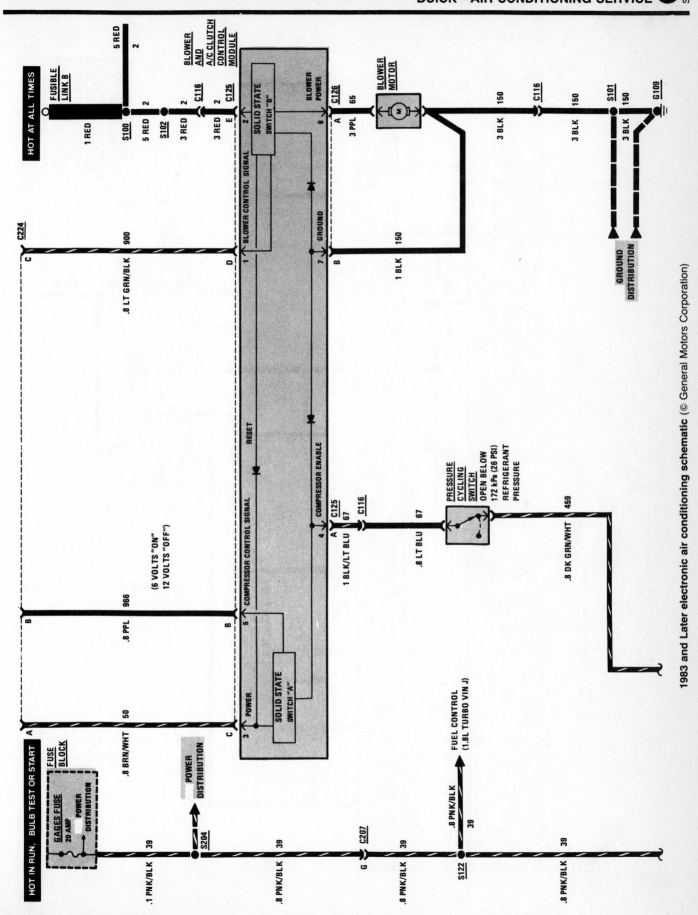

1983 and Later electronic air conditioning schematic (© General Motors Corporation)

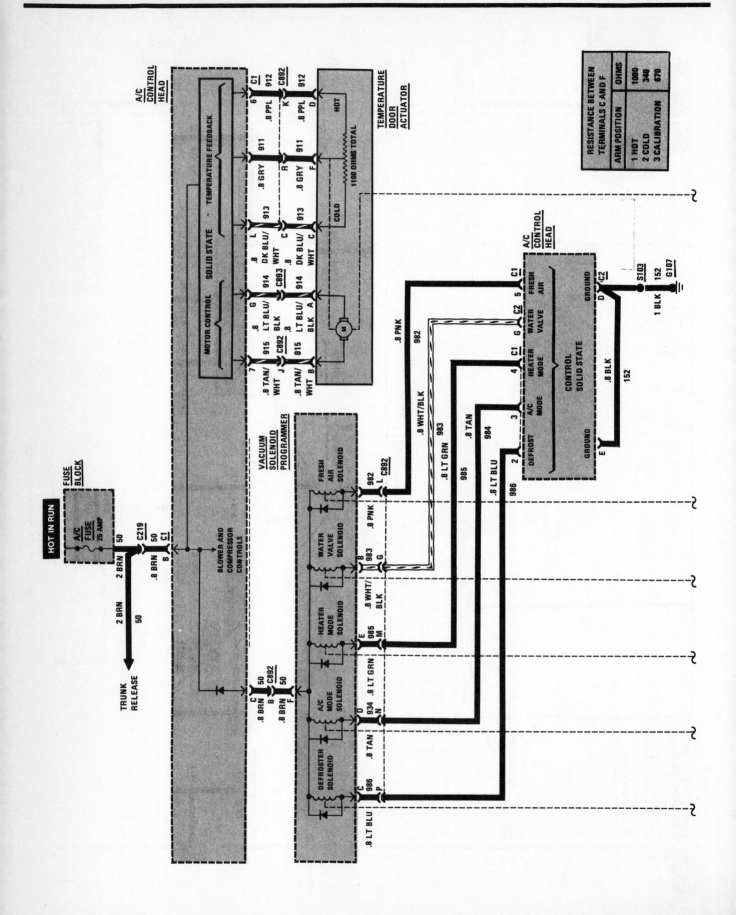

RESISTANCE BETWEEN TERMINALS C AND F	
ARM POSITION	OHMS
1 HOT	1000
2 COLD	340
3 CALIBRATION	670

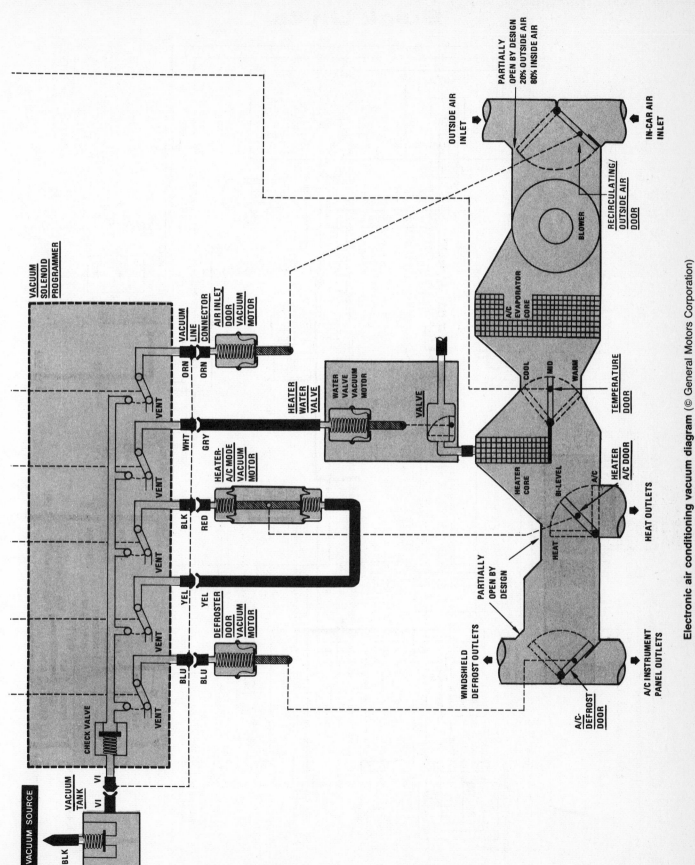

Electronic air conditioning vacuum diagram (© General Motors Corporation)

Buick Units

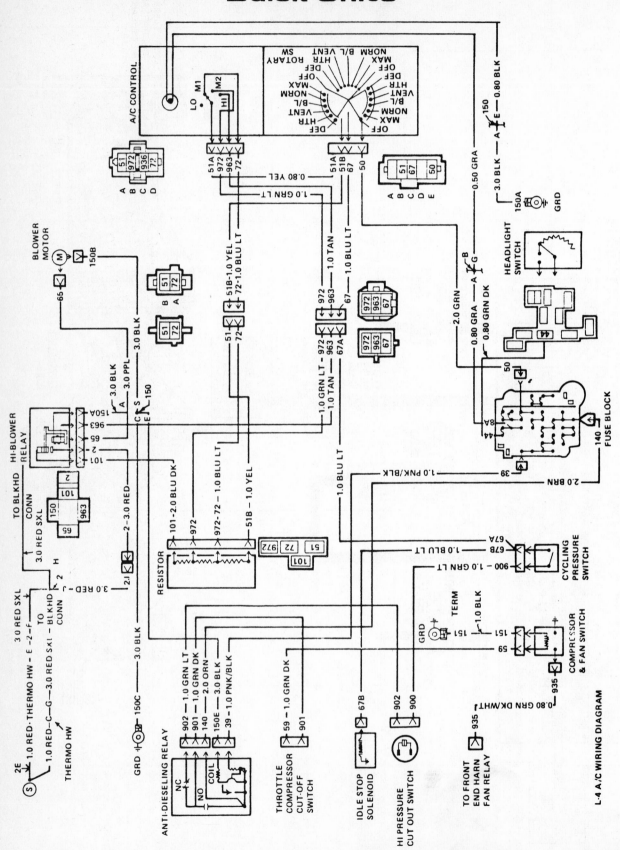

SECTION 5
GENERAL MOTORS
Cadillac

INDEX

CADILLAC
Rear Wheel Drive Models

1982	1983	1984	1985
Fleetwood Brougham	Fleetwood Brougham	Fleetwood Brougham	Fleetwood Brougham
Fleetwood Limousine	Fleetwood Limousine	Fleetwood Limousine	Commercial Chassis
Deville	Deville	Deville	
Commercial Chassis	Commercial Chassis	Commercial Chassis	

Note: The vehicles listed are base models.

CADILLAC
Front Wheel Drive Models

1982	1983	1984	1985
Eldorado	Eldorado	Eldorado	Eldorado
Seville	Seville	Seville	Seville
Cimarron	Cimarron	Cimarron	Cimarron
			Deville
			Fleetwood Limousine

Note: The vehicles listed are base models.

REFRIGERANT CAPACITIES—CADILLAC
1982–85 Models
Refrigerant given in ounces, Refrigerant oil given in fluid ounces

	1982			1983			1984			1985		
	Recharge Capacities			Recharge Capacities			Recharge Capacities			Recharge Capacities	
Models	R-12	Oil	Models	R-12	Oil	Models	R-12	Oil	Models	R-12	Oil
Fleetwood	56	6	Fleetwood	56	6	Fleetwood	56	8①	Fleetwood	56	8①
DeVille	56	6	DeVille	56	6	DeVille	56	8①	DeVille	56	8①
Eldorado	56	6	Eldorado	56	6	Eldorado	56	8①	Eldorado	56	8①
Seville	44	6	Seville	44	6	Seville	44	6	Seville	44	8①
Cimarron	30	6	Cimarron	30	6	Cimarron	30	6	Cimarron	30	6

① Refrigerant oil capacities are given for vehicles equipped with the DA-6 compressor. Depending on the available engine, compressor application may vary. The R-4 compressor uses 4 fluid ounces of refrigerant oil.

COMPRESSOR DRIVE BELT TENSION

Year	New	Used
1982	160–200 lbs.	90–130 lbs.
1983	160–200 lbs.	90–130 lbs.
1984	150–190 lbs. (gas)	100–140 lbs. (gas)
	130–160 lbs. (diesel)	100–130 lbs. (diesel)
1985	80–120 lbs. (serpentine)	80–120 lbs. (serpentine)

Drive Belt Tension

Adjustment

1. Loosen the A/C compressor bolts and adjustment bracket bolt.
2. Move the compressor until the compressor is properly adjusted.
3. Tighten the compressor bolts and adjustment bracket bolt.
4. Check the adjustment using a belt tensioning gauge.

NOTE: Do not attempt to adjust the belt tension while the engine is running.

Blower Motor

Removal and Installation

1982 AND LATER

1. Disconnect the negative battery cable.
2. Tag and disconnect the electrical connections from the back of the blower motor.
3. Disconnect the cooling hose from the case.
4. Remove the right side water shield from Cimarron models located in the right side of the cowl.
5. Remove the blower motor mounting screws. Remove the blower motor from the vehicle.
6. Installation is the reverse of the removal procedure. Use a silicone sealer on the blower motor sealing surfaces.

Compressor

Removal and Installation

1982 AND LATER CIMARRON

1. Disconnect the negative battery cable. Discharge the A/C system.
2. Raise the vehicle and support safely.
3. Remove the right air dam and splash shield.
4. Tag and disconnect the electrical connections at the compressor clutch. Remove the refrigerant line at the rear of the compressor.
5. Remove the compressor attaching bolts. Remove the compressor and the drive belt from the vehicle.
6. Installation is the reverse of the removal procedure. Leak test the compressor connections.

1982 AND LATER DIESEL ENGINES

1. Disconnect the negative battery cables. Discharge the air conditioning system.
2. Remove the air cleaner partially to gain working clearance.
3. Remove the high and low pressure lines from the compressor. Be sure the air conditioning system has been discharged.
4. Tag and disconnect the electrical connections at the low pressure switch and the clutch coil.
5. Remove the bolts securing the compressor to the mounting brackets. Move the mounting brackets out of the way. Remove the drive belt.
6. Remove the compressor from the vehicle.
7. Installation is the reverse of the removal procedure. Leak test the compressor system.

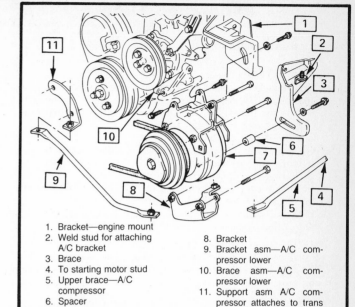

1. Bracket—engine mount
2. Weld stud for attaching A/C bracket
3. Brace
4. To starting motor stud
5. Upper brace—A/C compressor
6. Spacer
7. R4 compressor
8. Bracket
9. Bracket asm—A/C compressor lower
10. Brace asm—A/C compressor lower
11. Support asm A/C compressor attaches to trans support bracket

Cimarron compressor mounting (© General Motors Corporation)

1982 AND LATER GAS ENGINES

1. Disconnect the negative battery cable. Discharge the air conditioning system.
2. Partially remove the air cleaner in order to gain working clearance.
3. Remove the high and low pressure lines from the compressor. Cap the lines to prevent dirt infiltration.
4. Tag and disconnect the electrical connections at the compressor.
5. If necessary, remove the power steering pump and bracket along with the alternator and bracket.
6. Remove the compressor mounting bolts and brackets. Remove the drive belt.
7. Remove the compressor from the vehicle.
8. Installation is the reverse of the removal procedure. Leak test the compressor connections.

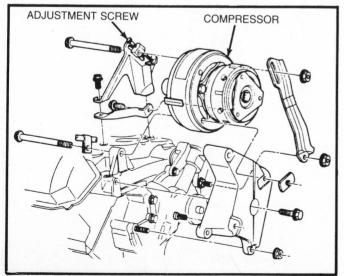

Gasoline engine compressor mounting
(© General Motors Corporation)

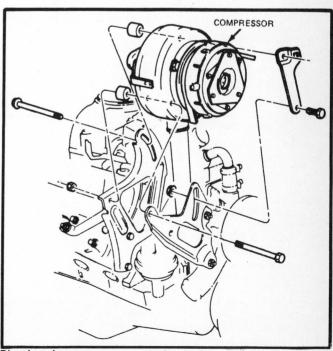

Diesel engine compressor mounting (© General Motors Corporation)

189

Expansion Tube

Removal and Installation

1982 AND LATER

The expansion tube is located in the evaporator inlet pipe at the liquid line connection. It provides a restriction to the high pressure liquid refrigerant in the liquid line, metering the flow of refrigerant to the evaporator as a low pressure liquid.

The expansion tube and orifice are protected from contamination by filter screens on both inlet and outlet sides. No adjustment or repair is possible to the unit and must be replaced as an assembly only.

1. Discharge the air conditioning system.
2. Disconnect the evaporator inlet line. Remove as much of the impacted dirt as possible. Cap all open lines.
3. Using a twisting motion, remove the expansion tube from the line using orifice removal tool J-26549-C or equivalent.

NOTE: If the expansion tube is difficult to remove, apply heat to the surface of the assembly using a heat source such as a hair dryer. Apply the heat approximately ¼ inch from the dimples on the inlet pipe. Do not overheat the pipe.

4. Remove the expansion tube O-ring from the inlet pipe.
5. Reverse the procedure for installation, using a new O-ring lubricated with fresg refrigerant oil.
6. Evacuate, charge and leak test the system.

NOTE: Install the new tube with the shorter screen end in the evaporator inlet pipe (towards evaporator). Use new O rings during this procedure.

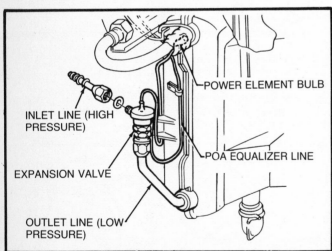

Expansion valve installation—typical (© General Motors Corporation)

Condenser

Removal and Installation

1982 AND LATER CIMARRON

1. Discharge the A/C system.
2. Raise the vehicle and support safely.
3. Remove the front air dams and bolts securing the lower fascia to fender bolts. Disconnect the lower line at the condenser.
4. Lower the vehicle. Remove the core support to fascia filler panels.
5. Remove the headlight housings.
6. Pull the fascia assembly forward and disconnect the upper condenser line.

7. Remove the condenser brackets. Remove the condenser.
8. Installation is the reverse of the removal procedure.

1982 AND LATER—ALL EXCEPT CIMARRON

1. Disconnect the negative battery cable.
2. Drain the cooling system. Remove the radiator as described earlier.
3. Remove the high side pressure fitting to and from the condenser.
4. Remove the condenser brackets and cushions. Remove the condenser from the vehicle.
5. Installation is the reverse of the removal procedure.

Evaporator

Removal and Installation

1982–1984 DEVILLE AND BROUGHAM

1. Disconnect the negative battery cable. Discharge the air conditioning system.
2. Tag and disconnect the electrical connections from the blower motor, power module and radio lead in connection.
3. Remove the electrical connections from the compressor cycling switch. Remove the compressor cycling switch.
4. If necessary to gain working clearance, remove the secondary and primary inlet screens along with the rubber moulding above the plenum.
5. Remove the blower motor.
6. Disconnect the refrigerant lines at the accumulator. Cap open lines to prevent contamination.
7. Remove the evaporator cover.
8. Disconnect the condensor to evaporator connections. Remove the evaporator from the vehicle.
9. Installation is the reverse of the removal procedure.

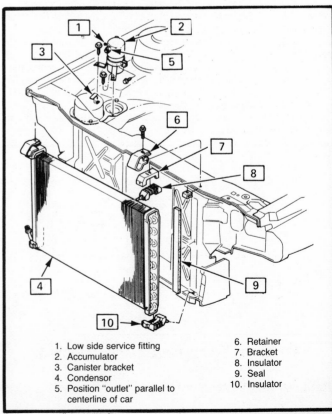

1. Low side service fitting
2. Accumulator
3. Canister bracket
4. Condensor
5. Position "outlet" parallel to centerline of car
6. Retainer
7. Bracket
8. Insulator
9. Seal
10. Insulator

Cimarron accumulator and condensor mounting (© General Motors Corporation)

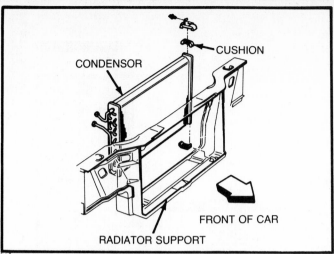

Condensor mounting—Seville and Eldorado (© General Motors Corporation)

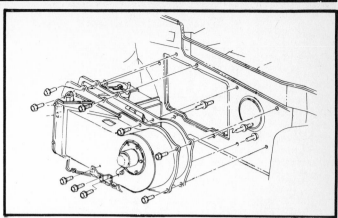

Evaporator assembly—typical (© General Motors Corporation)

1982–1984 ELDORADO AND SEVILLE

1. Disconnect the negative battery cable. Discharge the air conditioning system.
2. Tag and disconnect the electrical connection at the compressor cycling switch. Remove the compressor cycling switch.
3. Remove the accumulator from the vehicle.
4. Remove any insulation preventing access to the condensor to evaporator pipe inlet connection.
5. Remove the evaporator core connections. Remove the evaporator.
6. Installation is the reverse of the removal procedure.

1982 AND LATER CIMARRON

1. Disconnect the negative battery cable. Discharge the air conditioning system.
2. Drain the cooling system.
3. Raise the vehicle and support safely.
4. Disconnect the heater hoses at the heater core. Disconnect the evaporator line from the evaporator.
5. Lower the vehicle.
6. Remove the heater outlet and glove box. Remove the steering column and the hush panels.
7. Remove the heater core cover. Remove the heater core.
8. Remove the evaporator cover. Remove the evaporator core.
9. Installation is the reverse of the removal procedure.

1985 AND LATER MODELS—EXCEPT CIMARRON

1. Disconnect the negative battery cable. Drain the cooling system.
2. Disconnect the heater core hoses.
3. Tag and disconnect the electrical connections at the blower motor. Remove the blower motor.
4. To gain working clearance, remove the power steering pump and reservoir.
5. Remove the lower sound insulator bolts. Remove the module cover retaining bolts. Remove the module cover.
6. Remove the hose assembly from the evaporator.
7. Remove the evaporator case retaining bolts. Remove the evaporator.
8. Installation is the reverse of the removal procedure.

In Car Temperature Sensor

Removal and Installation

1982 AND LATER

1. Disconnect the negative battery cable.

2. Remove the top instrument panel cover screws. Remove the top instrument panel.
3. Tag and disconnect the electrical connection from the sensor. Remove the aspirator hose.
4. Remove the screws securing the sensor to its housing. Remove the sensor.
5. Installation is the reverse of the removal procedure.

Outside Temperature Sensor

1982 AND LATER

1. Disconnect the negative battery cable.
2. Remove the necessary components to gain access to the sensor located behind the grille.
3. Tag and disconnect the sensor connector wire.
4. Remove any temperature sensor retaining screws. Remove the temperature sensor.
5. Installation is the reverses of the removal procedure.

Heater Core

Removal and Installation

1982–1985 MODELS

1. Disconnect the negative battery cable.
2. Drain the coolant. Disconnect the heater hoses at the firewall.
3. Tag and disconnect the electrical connections.
4. If the vehicle is equipped with V6 engine, it may be necessary to remove the lower instrument panel sound absorber.
5. Remove the heater core cover. Remove the heater duct and lower heater outlet.
6. Remove the heater core retaining straps.
7. Remove the heater core from the vehicle.
8. Installation is the reverse of the removal procedure. Refill the cooling system and check for leaks.

Control Head

Removal and Installation

1982 AND LATER

1. Disconnect the negative battery cable.
2. Remove the necessary trim plates in order to gain access to the screws securing the control head to the dash panel.
3. Remove the control head retaining screws. Remove the control head.
4. Tag and disconnect the electrical connections at the back of the head assembly. Remove the vacuum lines.
5. On manual control systems, remove the control cables.
6. The installation is the reverse of the removal procedure.

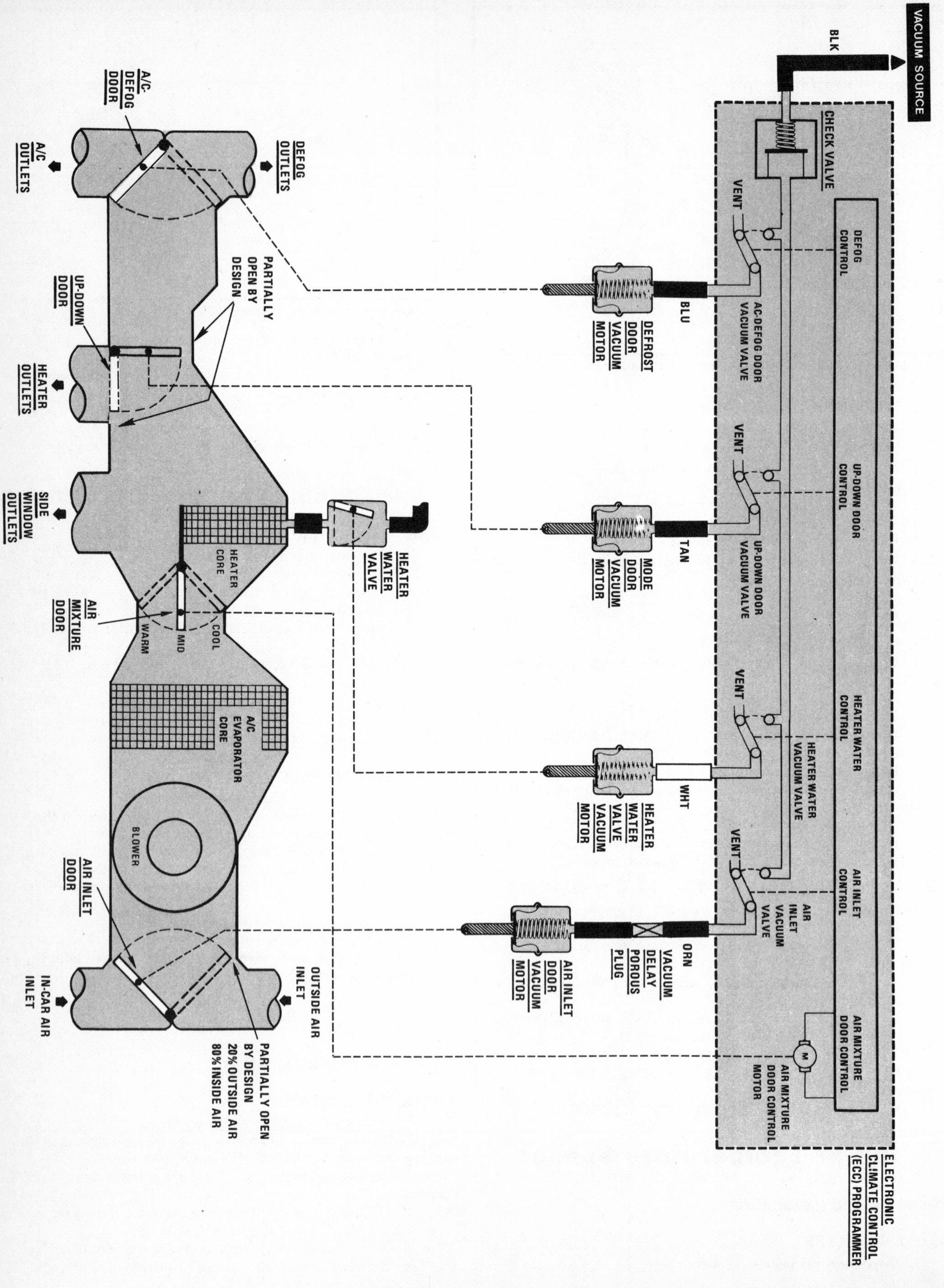

Cadillac vacuum diagram except Cimarron (© General Motors Corporation)

A/C DEFOG DOOR

A/C OUTLETS

DEFOG OUTLETS

PARTIALLY OPEN BY DESIGN

UP-DOWN DOOR

HEATER OUTLETS

SIDE WINDOW OUTLETS

HEATER WATER VALVE

HEATER CORE

AIR MIXTURE DOOR

WARM

MID

COOL

A/C EVAPORATOR CORE

BLOWER

AIR INLET DOOR

IN-CAR AIR INLET

OUTSIDE AIR INLET

PARTIALLY OPEN BY DESIGN 20% OUTSIDE AIR 80% INSIDE AIR

BLK

VACUUM SOURCE

CHECK VALVE

VENT

DEFROST DOOR VACUUM MOTOR

BLU

AC-DEFOG DOOR VACUUM VALVE

DEFOG CONTROL

VENT

MODE DOOR VACUUM MOTOR

TAN

UP-DOWN DOOR VACUUM VALVE

UP-DOWN DOOR CONTROL

VENT

HEATER WATER VALVE VACUUM MOTOR

WHT

HEATER WATER VACUUM VALVE

HEATER WATER CONTROL

VENT

AIR INLET DOOR VACUUM MOTOR

ORN

VACUUM DELAY POROUS PLUG

AIR INLET VACUUM VALVE

AIR INLET CONTROL

AIR MIXTURE DOOR CONTROL

M

AIR MIXTURE DOOR CONTROL MOTOR

ELECTRONIC CLIMATE CONTROL (ECC) PROGRAMMER

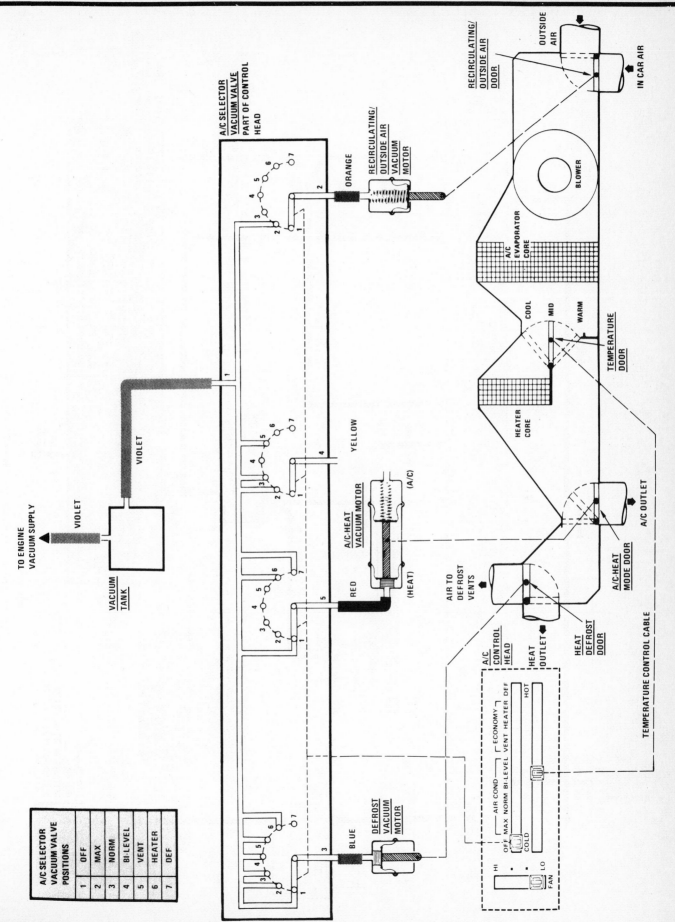

Cimarron vacuum diagram (© General Motors Corporation)

A/C SELECTOR VACUUM VALVE POSITIONS		
1	OFF	
2	MAX	
3	NORM	
4	BI-LEVEL	
5	VENT	
6	HEATER	
7	DEF	

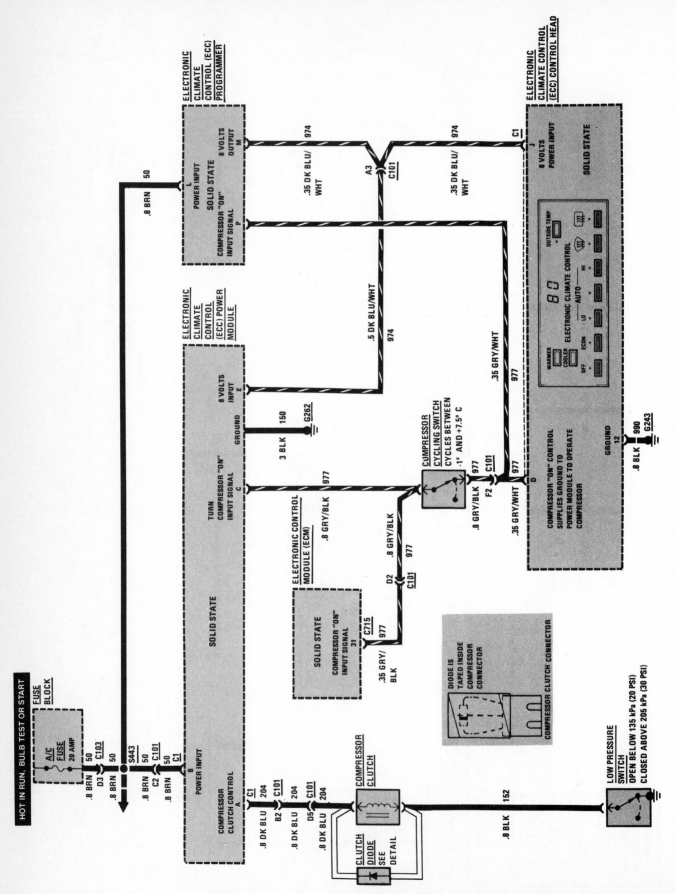

Electronic climate control—gasoline engines (© General Motors Corporation)

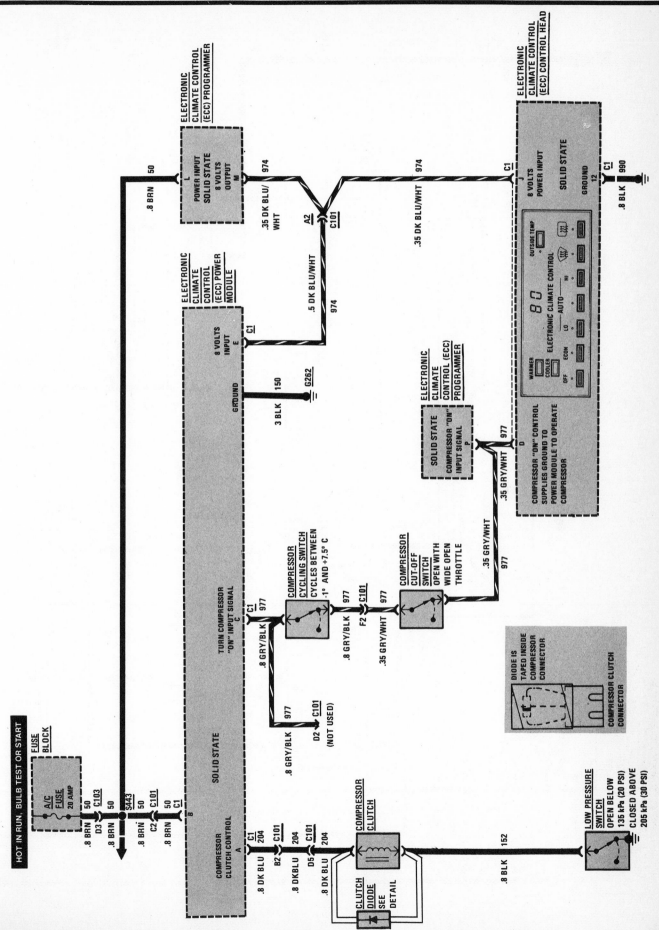

Electronic climate control—diesel engines (© General Motors Corporation)

GENERAL MOTORS CORPORATION
CADILLAC—AIR CONDITIONING SERVICE

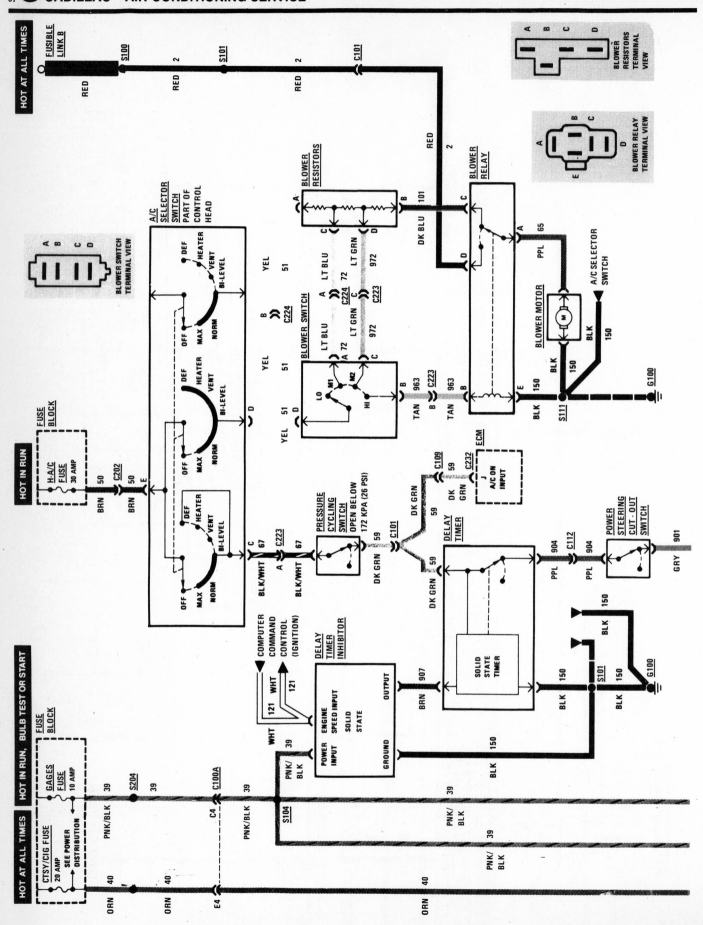

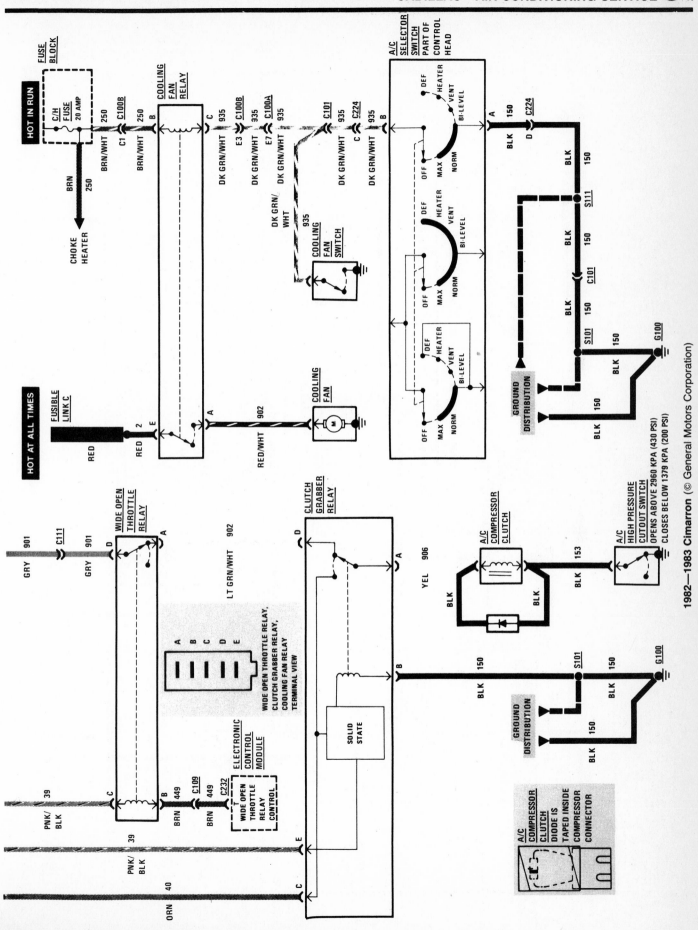

1982—1983 Cimarron (© General Motors Corporation)

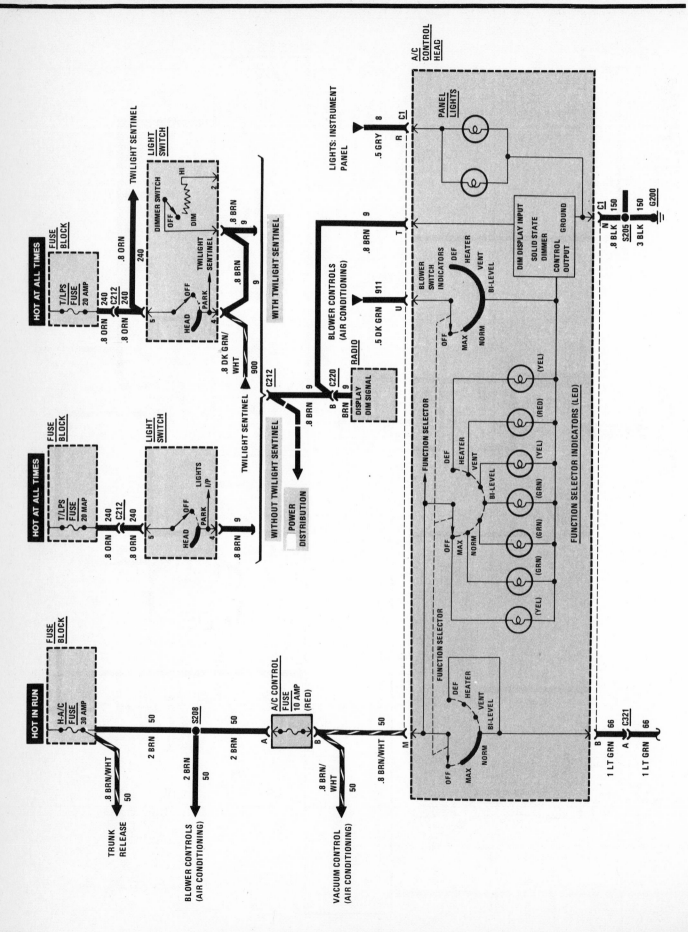

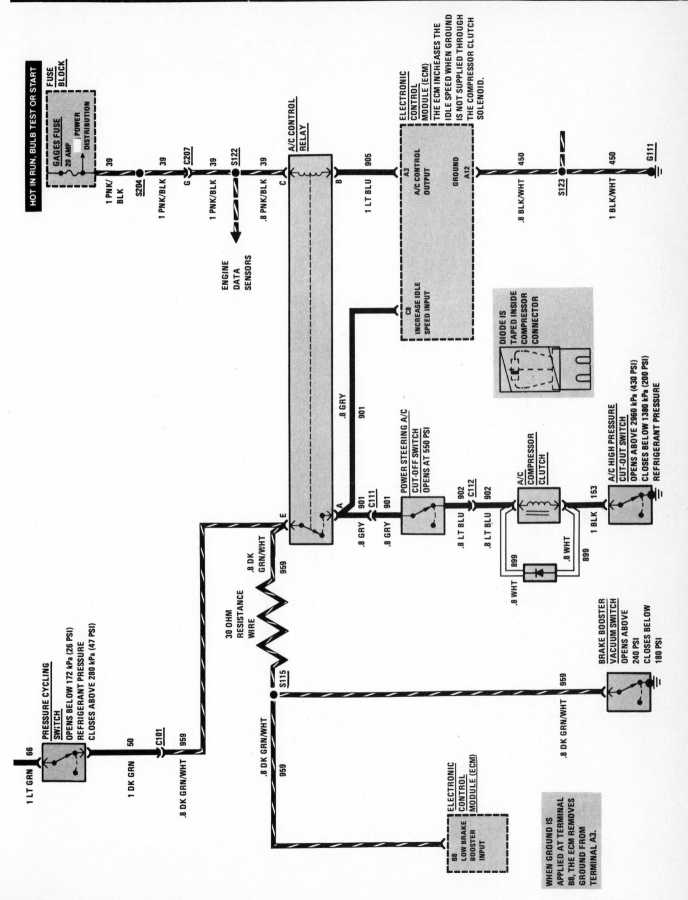

Air conditioning compressor controls—1984 and later Cimarron (© General Motors Corporation)

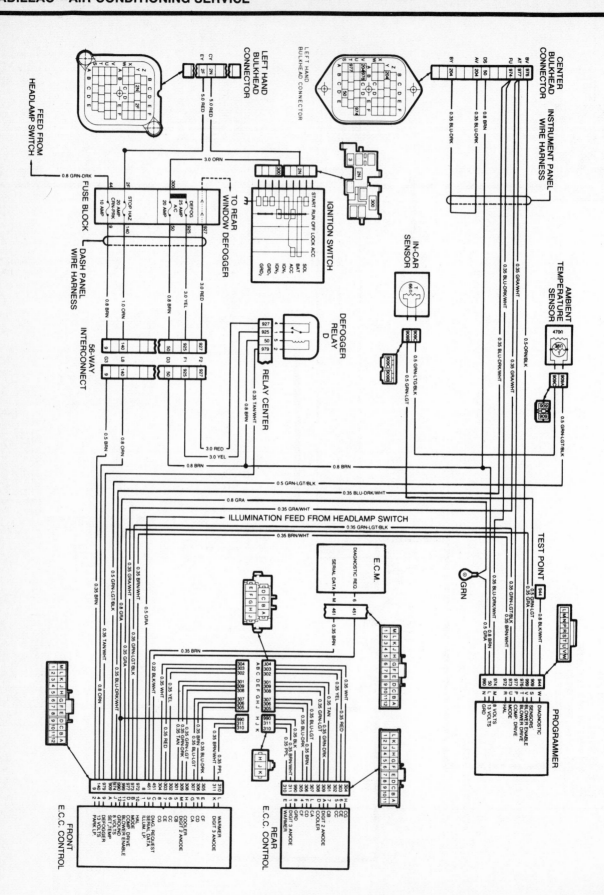

1983 and later limousine wiring diagram (© General Motors Corporation)

SECTION 5
GENERAL MOTORS
Chevrolet

INDEX

CHEVROLET
Front Wheel Drive Models

1982	1983	1984	1985
Celebrity	Celebrity	Celebrity	Celebrity
Citation	Citation	Citation	Citation
Cavalier	Cavalier	Cavalier	Cavalier
			Sprint
			Spectrum

Note: The vehicles listed are base models.

CHEVROLET
Rear Wheel Drive Models

1982	1983	1984	1985
Corvette	Corvette	Corvette	Corvette
Monte Carlo	Monte Carlo	Monte Carlo	Monte Carlo
Camaro	Camaro	Camaro	Camaro
Impala	Impala	Impala	Impala
Caprice	Caprice	Caprice	Caprice
Chevette	Chevette	Chevette	Chevette
Malibu	Malibu		

Note: The vehicles listed are base models.

REFRIGERANT CAPACITIES—CHEVROLET
1982–85 Models

Refrigerant given in ounces, Refrigerant oil given in fluid ounces

1982			1983			1984			1985		
	Recharge Capacities			Recharge Capacities			Recharge Capacities			Recharge Capacities	
Models	R-12	Oil	Models	R-12	Oil	Models	R-12	Oil	Models	R-12	Oil
Corvette	48	8①	Corvette	48	8①	Corvette	48	8①	Corvette	48	8①
Monte Carlo	52	8①	Monte Carlo	52	8①	Monte Carlo	52	8①	Monte Carlo	52	8①
Camaro	48	8①	Camaro	48	8①	Camaro	48	8①	Camaro	48	8①
Impala	56	8①	Impala	56	8①	Impala	56	8①	Impala	56	8①
Caprice	56	8①	Caprice	56	8①	Caprice	56	8①	Caprice	56	8①
Chevette	36	8①	Chevette	36	8①	Chevette	36	8①	Chevette	36	8①
Malibu	44	8①	Malibu	44	8①	Celebrity	44	8①	Celebrity	44	8①
Celebrity	44	8①	Celebrity	44	8①	Citation	44	8①	Citation	44	8①
Citation	44	8①	Citation	44	8①	Cavalier	44	8①	Cavalier	44	8①
Cavalier	44	8①	Cavalier	44	8①				Sprint		
									Spectrum		

① Refrigerant oil capacities are given for vehicles equipped with the DA-6 compressor. Vehicles equipped with the R-4 compressor require 4 fluid ounces of refrigerant oil.

DRIVE BELT TENSION

Air conditioning compressor tension adjustment involves movements of one or more of the components within the belt span. Caution must be exercised to avoid missing hidden bolts and retaining nuts. No attempt should be made to adjust the drive belt tension while the engine is running.

Adjustment

1. Loosen the A/C compressor bolts and any adjustment bracket bolt.
2. Move the compressor against the drive belt until the proper tension is applied to the compressor.
3. Tighten the compressor bolts and the adjustment bracket.
4. Check the adjustment using a belt tensioning gauge.

COMPRESSOR DRIVE BELT TENSION
Chevrolet

Year	New	Used
1982	90–100 lbs.	45–65 lbs.
1983	100–140 lbs.	65–95 lbs.
1984	130–140 lbs.	80–90 lbs.
1985	130–140 lbs.	80–90 lbs.

Blower Motor

Removal and Installation

1982 AND LATER—EXCEPT CORVETTE

1. Disconnect the negative battery cable.

2. Tag and disconnect the electrical connections from the blower motor.

3. Remove the blower motor flange screws. Remove the blower motor assembly from the heater case.

4. Installation is the reverse of the removal procedure.

1982 CORVETTE

1. Disconnect the negative battery cable.

2. Remove the air conditioner compressor bolts and move the compressor aside for access.

3. Remove the front and right side air cleaner inlet ducts and move the air cleaner assembly aside for working clearance.

4. Remove the overflow hose from the coolant recovery bottle. Remove the attaching screws. Remove the coolant recovery bottle.

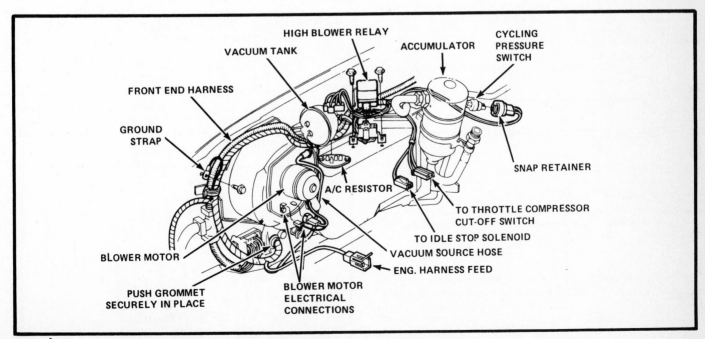

Blower and A/C installation—Citation (© Chevrolet Motor Division)

5. Disconnect the blower wire and the cooling tube.

6. Remove the flange screws and gently pry the assembly from the case.

7. Reverse the procedure for installation.

1984 AND LATER CORVETTE

1. Disconnect the negative battery cable.

2. Remove the front wheel house panel. Move the wheel house seal aside.

3. Remove the heater motor cooling tube. Remove the heater motor relay.

4. Remove the blower motor retaining screws and remove the blower motor assembly from the vehicle.

5. Installation is the reverse of the removal procedure.

Compressor

Removal and Installation

1982 AND LATER

1. Disconnect the negative battery cable.

2. Discharge the air conditioning system as described earlier.

3. Tag and disconnect the electrical leads at the compressor.

4. Remove the refrigerant lines from the compressor.

5. Remove the air conditioning compressor retaining bolts from the brackets.

NOTE: Some vehicles may require the power steering pump, alternator or plug wires to be repositioned or removed. Other components may need to be removed depending on the optional accessories.

6. Remove the air conditioning compressor from the vehicle.

7. When installing the compressor, keep dirt and foreign material from getting into the compressor parts and system. Clean tools and a clean work area are important for proper service. The compressor connections and the outside of the compressor should be cleaned before the compressor is installed. If new components are being installed, note that they are dehydrated and sealed prior to shipping. All sub-assemblies are to remain sealed until use, with the sub-assemblies at room temperature before uncapping. This helps prevent moisture from the air entering the system due to condensation. Use a small amount of refrigerant oil on all tube and hose joints. Always use new rings dipped in refrigerant oil before assembling joints. This oil will aid assembly and help to provide leak-proof joints.

8. Install any accessories that may have been removed to make room for the compressor.

9. Evacuate, charge and leak test the system. Check for the proper operation of the system.

NOTE: For compressor overhaul, refer to the compressor section.

Expansion Tube (Orifice)

Removal and Installation

1982 AND LATER

1. Discharge the air conditioning system.

2. Loosen the nut holding the liquid line to the evaporator inlet pipe. Remove the tube using needle nose pliers.

3. Install the new orifice tube and O-ring. Lubricate with clean refrigeration oil before installing.

NOTE: When installing the orifice tube inside the evaporator inlet pipe, it must be installed with the shorter screen end inserted first.

4. Install the liquid line to the evaporator.

5. Evacuate and charge the air conditioning system. Check the system for proper operation.

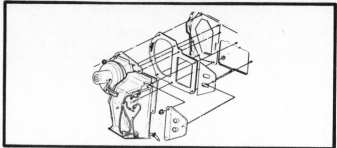

Blower motor—Corvette (typical) (© Chevrolet Motor Division)

The following procedure is recommended for an expansion tube that is broken or difficult to remove.

1. Discharge the air conditioning system.

2. Remove the liquid line to evaporator inlet pipe.

3. Using a heat gun, apply heat approximately one quarter of an inch from the inlet pipe dimples.

NOTE: If a pressure switch is located near the orifice tube, remove it before applying heat so as not to damage the circuit.

4. Using a twisting motion, loosen the orifice tube and remove it from its holder.

NOTE: Commercial tools are available to remove the expansion tube after the system has been discharged.

5. Clean the inside of the evaporator pipe with R-11 or equivalent.

6. Add one ounce of 525 viscosity refrigerant oil to the system. Lubricate the new orifice tube and O-ring with refrigerant oil.

7. Install the new orifice tube in the inlet pipe.

NOTE: When installing the new orifice tube, make sure that the short screen is installed first into the evaporator inlet pipe.

8. Install the liquid line to the evaporator.

9. Evacuate and charge the system. Check the system for proper operation.

Condenser

Removal and Installation

1982 AND LATER—EXCEPT CORVETTE

1. Disconnect the negative battery cable. Discharge the air conditioning system.

2. Remove the upper radiator support brackets. Remove the condenser support brackets. Save the rubber bushings for installation.

3. Disconnect the air conditioning lines at the condenser.

NOTE: Certain vehicles require the removal of various engine compartment components in order to gain access to the condenser. These may include the fan shroud, left and right air dams and certain fascia to fender bolts.

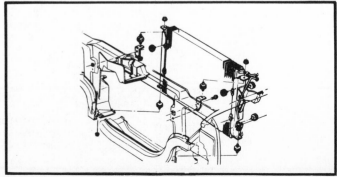

Condensor mounting—typical Chevrolet (© Chevrolet Motor Division)

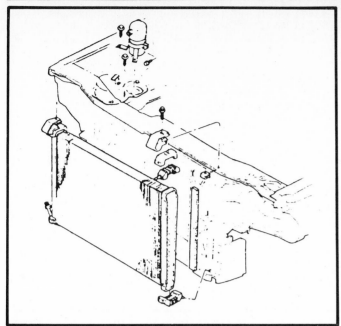

Condensor and accumulator mounting—Cavalier (© Chevrolet Motor Division)

4. Position the radiator rearward and lift out the condenser.

5. Installation is the reverse of the removal procedure. When assembling, use a small amount of refrigerant oil on all tube and hose joints. Always use new O-rings dipped in clean refrigerant oil (where applicable) when assembling the joints. The oil will aid assembly and help to provide leak-proof connections.

6. Evacuate, leak test and charge the system. Check the performance of the system.

NOTE: When there is no sign of excessive leakage, and a new condenser is installed, add 1 fluid ounce of refrigerant oil.

1982 CORVETTE

1. Disconnect the negative battery cable. Discharge the air conditioning system.

2. Using a scribe or similar tool, mark the location of the hood and remove.

3. Disconnect the condenser lines at the condenser. Cap all openings.

4. Remove the support screws and lift out the condenser.

5. Installation is the reverse of the removal procedure. When assembling, use a small amount of refrigerant oil on all tube and hose joints. Always use new C-rings dipped in clean refrigerant oil (where applicable) when assembling the joints.

6. Evacuate, leak test and charge the system. Check for proper operation of the system.

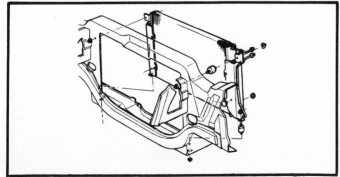

Condensor mounting—Camaro (© Chevrolet Motor Division)

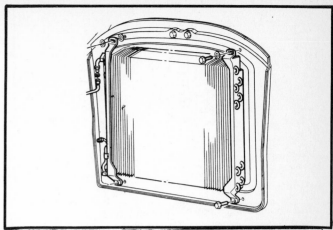

Condensor mounting—1982 Corvette (© Chevrolet Motor Division)

1984 AND LATER CORVETTE

1. Disconnect the negative battery cable. Discharge the air conditioning system.

2. Remove the radiator cap. Remove the accumulator hold down clamp. Remove the accumulator bolts and brackets. Remove the accumulator.

3. Remove the fan shroud attaching screws. Remove the fan shroud.

4. Disconnect the condenser lines at the condenser.

5. Remove the condenser from the vehicle.

6. Installation is the reverse of the removal procedure. When assembling, use a small amount of refrigerant oil on all tube and hose joints. Always use new O-rings dipped in clean refrigerant oil (where applicable) when assembling the joints.

7. Evacuate, leak test and charge the system. Check for proper operation of the system.

NOTE: When a new condenser is being installed, and there is no sign of excessive leakage, add 1 fluid ounce of refrigerant oil.

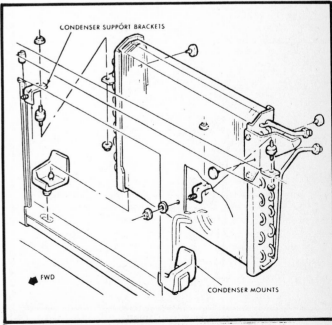

Chevette condensor mounting (© Chevrolet Motor Division)

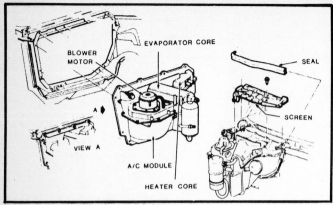

Typical air conditioning module mounting
(© Chevrolet Motor Division)

Evaporator

Removal and Installation

1982 AND LATER MONTE CARLO, IMPALA AND CAPRICE

1. Disconnect the negative battery cable. Discharge the air conditioning system.
2. Remove the module screen.
3. Remove the right hand windshield wiper arm.
4. Remove the diagnostic connection, Hi blower relay and the thermostatic switch mounting.
5. Tag and disconnect the electrical connectors at the module top.
6. Remove the accumulator bracket screws.
7. Disconnect the refrigerant lines at the accumulator and the liquid line.
8. Remove the evaporator core.
9. Installation is the reverse of the removal procedure.

1982 AND LATER CAMARO

1. Disconnect the negative battery cable. Discharge the air conditioning system.

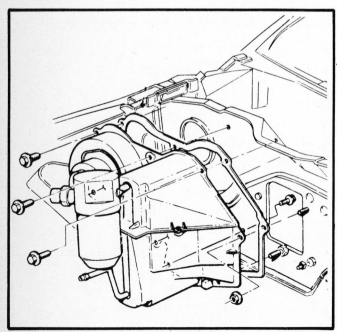

Blower evaporator case assembly—Camaro
(© Chevrolet Motor Division)

2. Tag and disconnect the necessary electrical connections.
3. Disconnect the blower motor cooling tube.
4. Remove the nuts holding the evaporator cover to dash panel and the screws securing the cover to the evaporator.
5. Remove the evaporator cover. Remove the evaporator screws.
6. Remove the evaporator.
7. Installation is the reverse of the removal procedure.

1982 AND LATER CHEVETTE

1. Disconect the negative battery cable. Discharge the system.
2. Remove the heater core case screws. Remove the heater core case.
3. Remove the accumulator and brackets.
4. Remove the insulation and clamp from the thermostatic switch sensiong element.
5. Remove the temperature door cable and the temperature door access cover. Position the control door arm out of the way of the upper evaporator case cover.
6. Remove the blower motor.
7. Remove the sealer around the exposed portion of the outlet tube at the upper surface of the evaporator case.
8. Remove the upper evaporator case. Remove the evaporator core.
9. Installation is the reverse of the removal procedure.

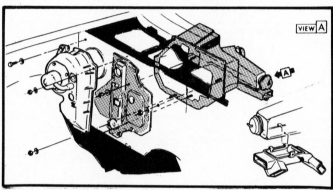

Blower evaporator case assembly—Chevette (© Chevrolet Motor Division)

1982 CORVETTE

1. Disconnect the negative battery cable. Discharge the air conditioning system.
2. Remove the air cleaner. Remove the coolant recovery tank.
3. Disconnect the oil bleed and core inlet and outlet lines at the accumulator assembly.
4. Tag and disconnect all electrical and vacuum connections from the evaporator case.
5. Remove the nuts securing the evaporator cover to the dash panel. Remove the screws securing the cover to the evaporator case.
6. Remove the cover outward and upward.
7. Remove the evaporator core from the case.
8. Installation is the reverse of the removal procedure.

1984 AND LATER CORVETTE

1. Disconnect the negative battery cable. Discharge the air conditioning system.
2. Remove the air cleaner.
3. Remove the front wheel house rear panel and seal.
4. Tag and disconnect the electrical connections from the evaporator housing.
5. Remove the windshield washer hose and the hood release cable and wire off to the side.
6. Remove the evaporator outlet hose bracket located on the inner fender. Disconnect the evaporator outlet hose.
7. Drain the cooling system. Cut the heater hoses from the heater core inlet and outlet. Remove the heater hose bracket.

NOTE: During installation, new heater hoses will have to be used.

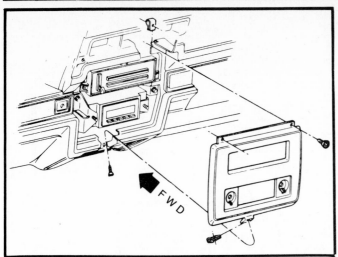

Trim panel removal—Chevrolet (typical) (© Chevrolet Motor Division)

8. Disconnect the evaporator inlet hose. Remove the transmission cooler line rear bracket located near the frame.

9. Remove the evaporator cover bolts. Remove the evaporator core.

10. Installation is the reverse of the removal procedure.

1982 AND LATER CELEBRITY AND CITATION

1. Disconnect the negative battery cable. Discharge the air conditioning system.

2. Remove the vacuum tank. Tag and disconnect the air conditioning electrical connections along the cowl and move the harness to the right side of the vehicle.

3. Disconnect the liquid line at the evaporator inlet and the low pressure line at the accumulator inlet.

4. Remove the outer blower case to cowl screws and remove the blower case assembly.

5. Remove the evaporator.

6. Installation is the reverse of the removal procedure. Use new sealer on the case assembly to avoid possible water leaks.

1982 AND LATER CAVALIER

1. Disconnect the negative battery cable. Discharge the air conditioning system.

2. Drain the cooling system.

3. Remove the heater lines from the heater core.

4. Remove the evaporator lines from the evaporator core. Remove the drain tube.

5. From inside the vehicle remove the steering column trim cover, glove box, heater outlet and the right and left side hush panels.

6. Remove the heater core cover.

7. Remove the heater core clamps. Remove the heater core.

8. Remove the defroster vacuum actuator to module case.

9. Remove the evaporator cover. Remove the evaporator.

10. Installation is the reverse of the removal procedure.

Heater Core
Removal and Installation

NOTE: For Removal and Installation of the heater core assembly, Refer to the Heater section of this manual.

Control Head

Removal and Installation

1982 AND LATER—EXCEPT CORVETTE

The removal and installation of the dash mounted temperature control unit is general in the various vehicles. The outlined steps may not be in the correct order for a specific model. Re-arrange the steps to relate to the vehicle being repaired.

1. Disconnect the negative battery cable.

2. Remove the necessary instrument panel trim to expose the control head retaining screws.

3. Remove the radio and/or knobs, radio speaker, ash tray, cigar lighter and the floor console trim plate if equipped.

4. After exposing the control head retaining screws, remove them and pull the control head away from the dash assembly.

5. Disconnect the bowden cable, electrical and/or vacuum connections. Remove the control unit.

6. Installation is the reverse of the removal procedure.

1982 Corvette

1. Disconnect the negative battery cable.

2. Remove the floor console trim plate screws. Remove the trim plate.

3. Remove the retaining screws from the console side panels. Remove the side panels.

4. Disconnect the cables, vacuum lines and wiring. Disconnect the temperature control cable. Remove the control head assembly.

5. Installation is the reverse of the removal procedure.

1984 and Later Corvette

1. Disconnect the negative battery cable.

2. Remove the cluster bezel. Remove the tilt wheel lever if equipped.

3. Remove the center bezel above the console assembly.

4. Remove the screws attaching the console assembly to its carrier.

5. Rotate the console assembly to gain access to the electrical connectors, temperature control cable and vacuum hoses. Disconnect these items.

6. Remove the control head assembly from the vehicle.

7. Installation is the reverse of the removal procedure.

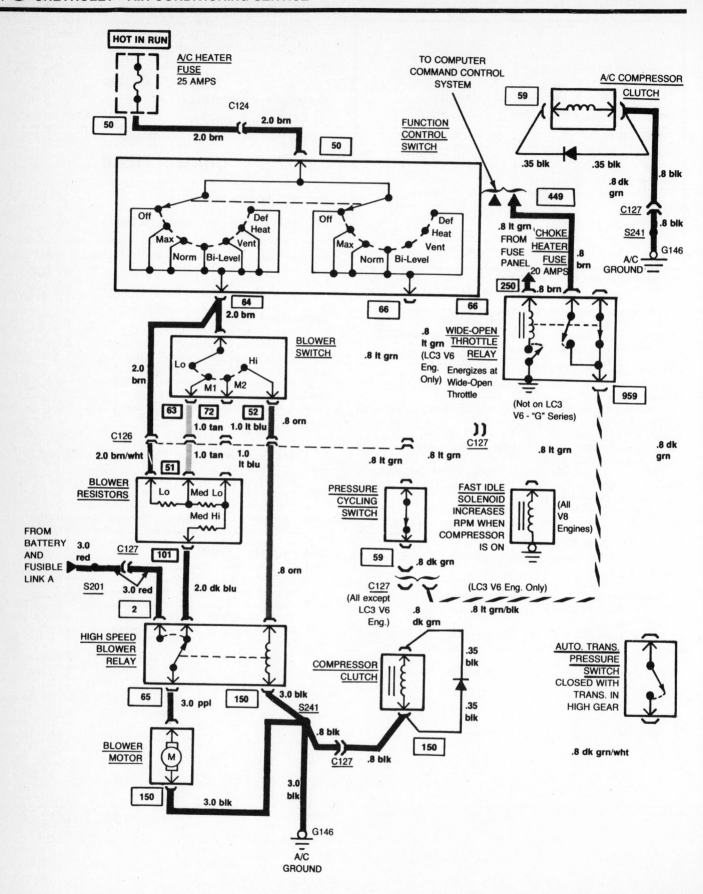

1982 and later Monte Carlo wiring diagram (© General Motors Corporation)

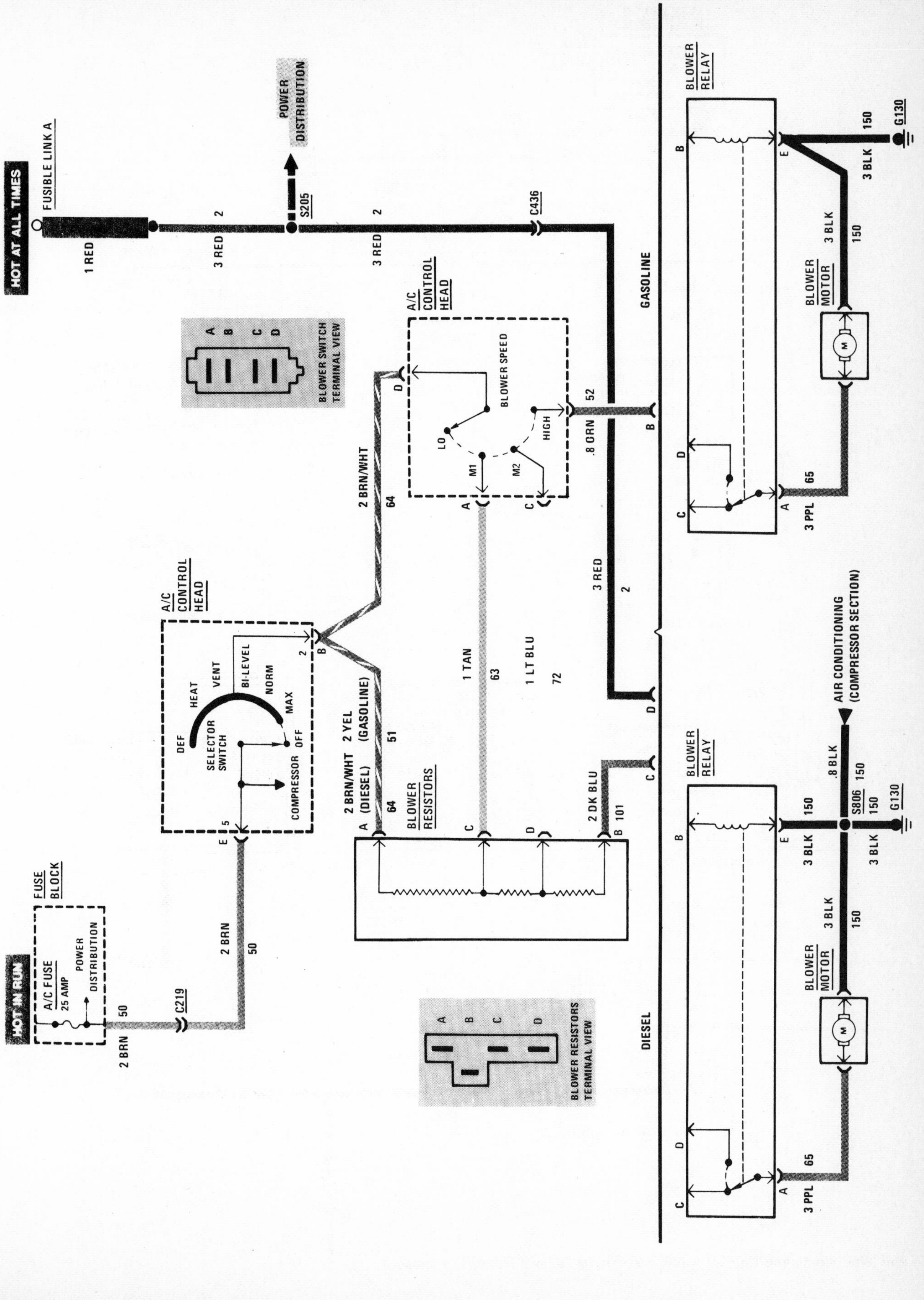

HOT AT ALL TIMES

FUSIBLE LINK A

1 RED

3 RED 2

POWER DISTRIBUTION

S205

3 RED 2

C436

GASOLINE

BLOWER RELAY

B

E

150

G130

3 BLK 150

BLOWER MOTOR

3 BLK 150

BLOWER SWITCH TERMINAL VIEW

A B C D

A/C CONTROL HEAD

BLOWER SPEED

LO

M1 M2

HIGH

D

A

C

.8 ORN 52

B

D

C

3 PPL

65

2 BRN/WHT 64

A/C CONTROL HEAD

DEF HEAT VENT BI-LEVEL NORM MAX OFF

SELECTOR SWITCH

COMPRESSOR

B 2

E 5

3 RED 2

AIR CONDITIONING (COMPRESSOR SECTION)

1 TAN 63

1 LT BLU 72

D

2 BRN/WHT 2 YEL (GASOLINE) 51

2 BRN/WHT (DIESEL) 64

BLOWER RESISTORS

A C D B 101

2 DK BLU

C

BLOWER RELAY

B

E

150

150

S806

150

G130

3 BLK

3 BLK

.8 BLK 150

FUSE BLOCK

HOT IN RUN

A/C FUSE 25 AMP

POWER DISTRIBUTION

2 BRN 50

C219

2 BRN 50

BLOWER MOTOR

3 BLK 150

DIESEL

BLOWER RESISTORS TERMINAL VIEW

A B C D

D

C

A

3 PPL 65

1982 and 1983 Impala and Caprice wiring diagram (© General Motors Corporation)

209

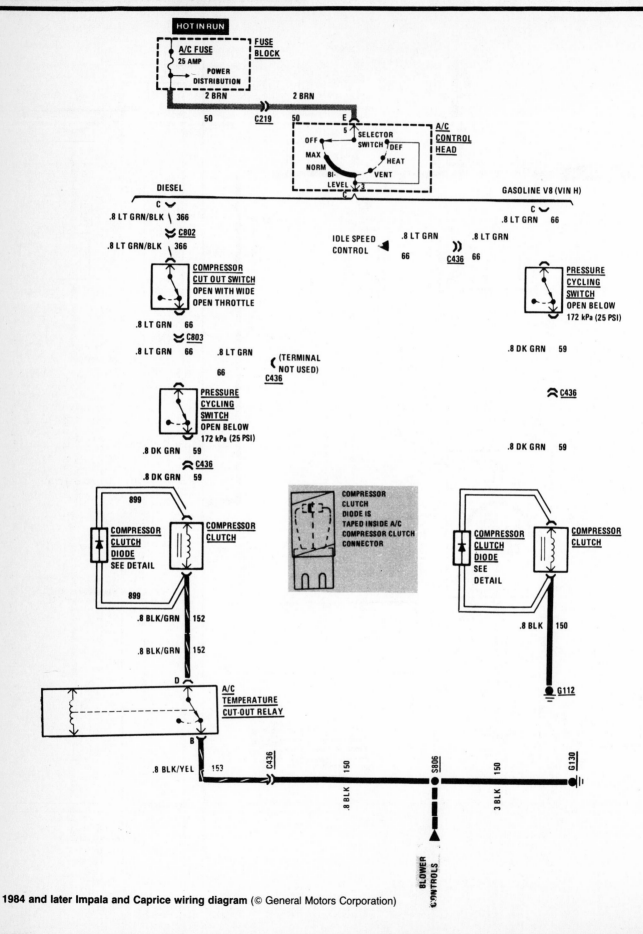

1984 and later Impala and Caprice wiring diagram (© General Motors Corporation)

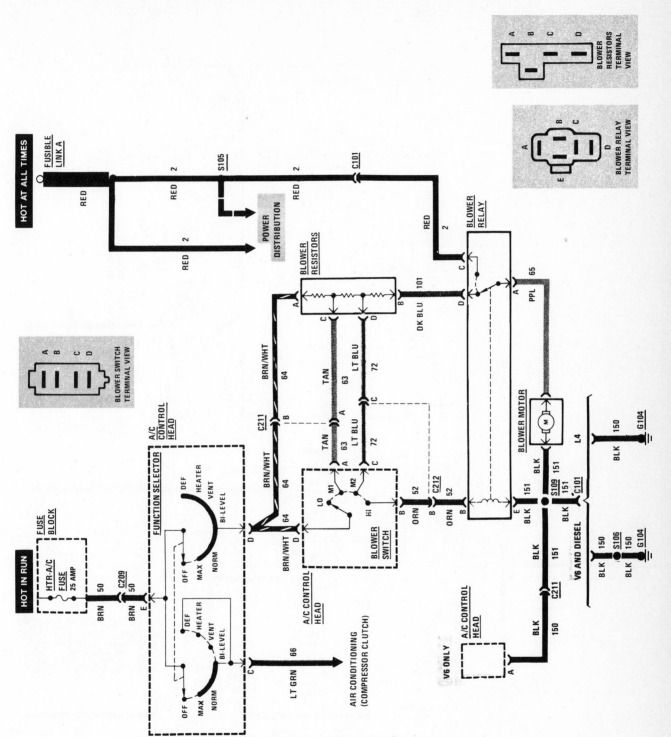

1982 and later Celebrity air conditioning blower wiring diagram (© General Motors Corporation)

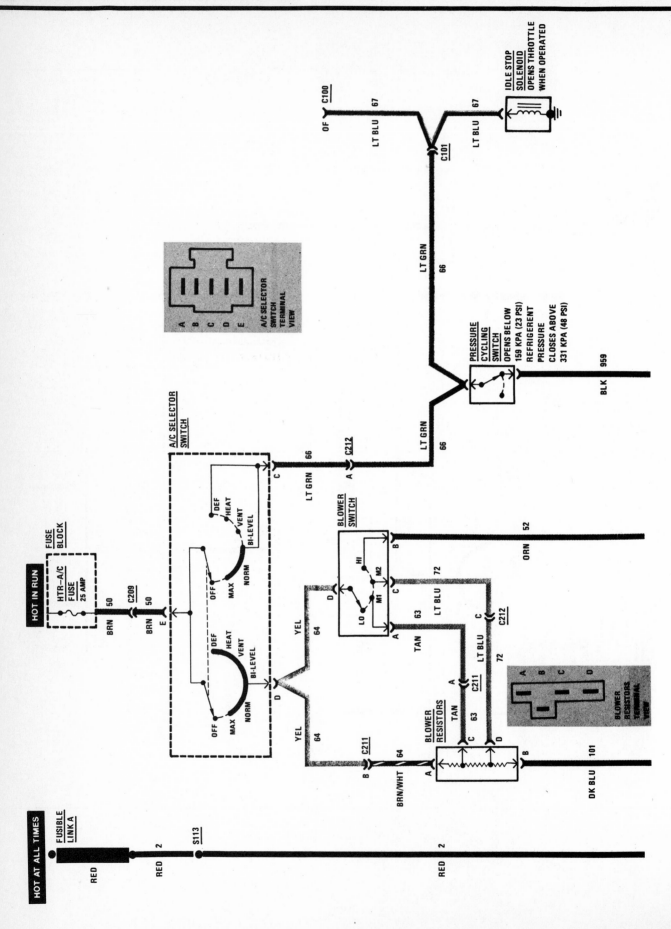

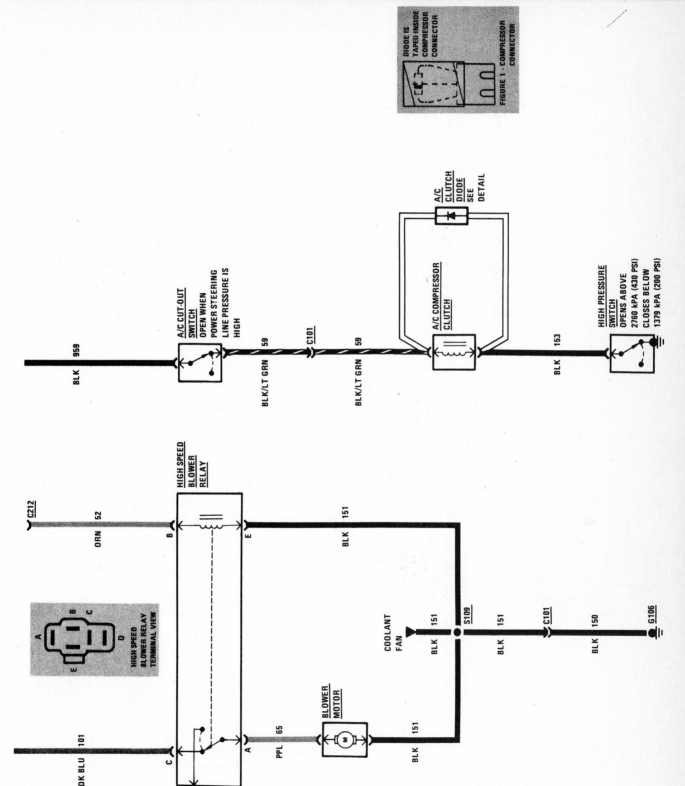

DIODE IS TAPED INSIDE COMPRESSOR CONNECTOR

FIGURE 1 - COMPRESSOR CONNECTOR

A/C CLUTCH DIODE SEE DETAIL

A/C CUT-OUT SWITCH OPEN WHEN POWER STEERING LINE PRESSURE IS HIGH

A/C COMPRESSOR CLUTCH

HIGH PRESSURE SWITCH OPENS ABOVE 2760 kPA (430 PSI) CLOSES BELOW 1379 kPA (200 PSI)

BLK 959

BLK/LT GRN 59

C101

BLK/LT GRN 59

BLK 153

HIGH SPEED BLOWER RELAY

C212

ORN 52

B

E

BLK 151

A

B

C

A

D

E

HIGH SPEED BLOWER RELAY TERMINAL VIEW

COOLANT FAN

BLK 151

S109

BLK 151

C101

BLK 150

G106

DK BLU 101

C

BLOWER MOTOR

PPL 65

A

BLK 151

C101

RED 2

D

1982 and later Citation air conditioning diagram—V6 engine (© General Motors Corporation)

213

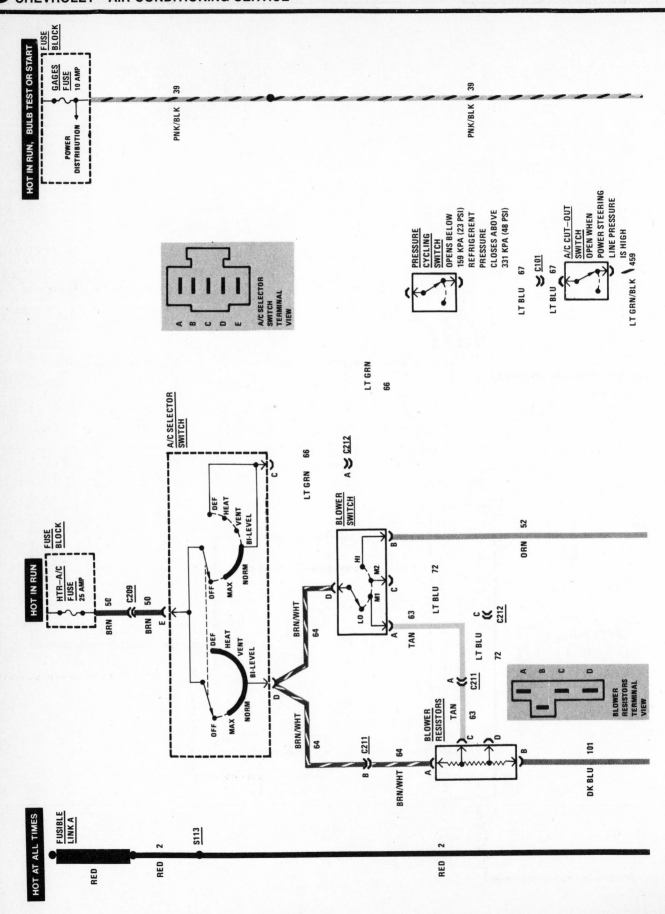

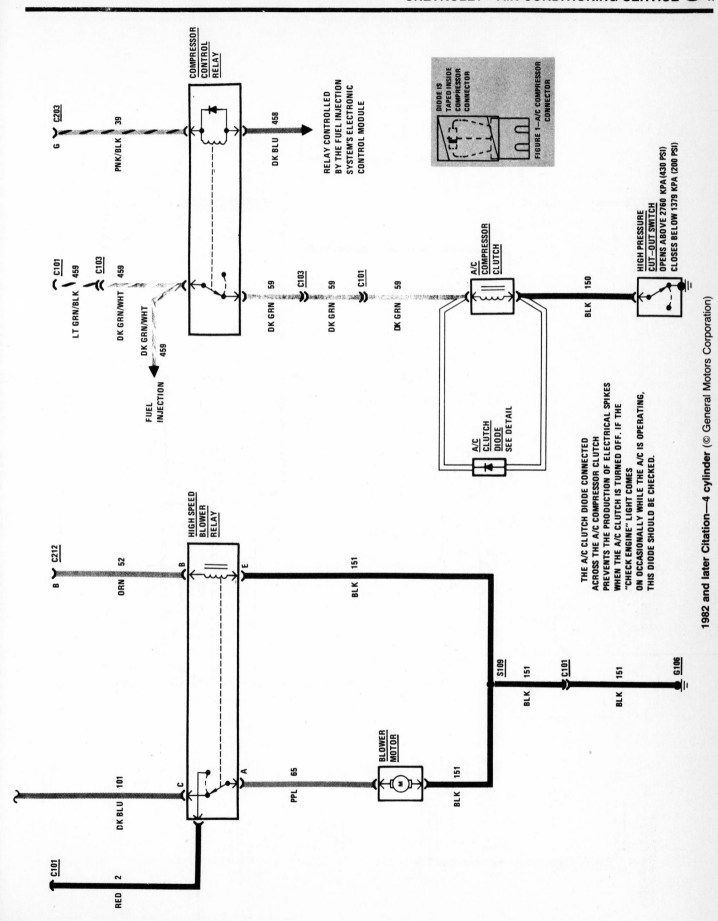

FIGURE 1—A/C COMPRESSOR CONNECTOR

DIODE IS TAPED INSIDE COMPRESSOR CONNECTOR

COMPRESSOR CONTROL RELAY

RELAY CONTROLLED BY THE FUEL INJECTION SYSTEM'S ELECTRONIC CONTROL MODULE

A/C COMPRESSOR CLUTCH

HIGH PRESSURE CUT-OUT SWITCH
OPENS ABOVE 2760 KPA (430 PSI)
CLOSES BELOW 1379 KPA (200 PSI)

A/C CLUTCH DIODE SEE DETAIL

THE A/C CLUTCH DIODE CONNECTED ACROSS THE A/C COMPRESSOR CLUTCH PREVENTS THE PRODUCTION OF ELECTRICAL SPIKES WHEN THE A/C CLUTCH IS TURNED OFF. IF THE "CHECK ENGINE" LIGHT COMES ON OCCASIONALLY WHILE THE A/C IS OPERATING, THIS DIODE SHOULD BE CHECKED.

HIGH SPEED BLOWER RELAY

BLOWER MOTOR

FUEL INJECTION

1982 and later Citation—4 cylinder (© General Motors Corporation)

215

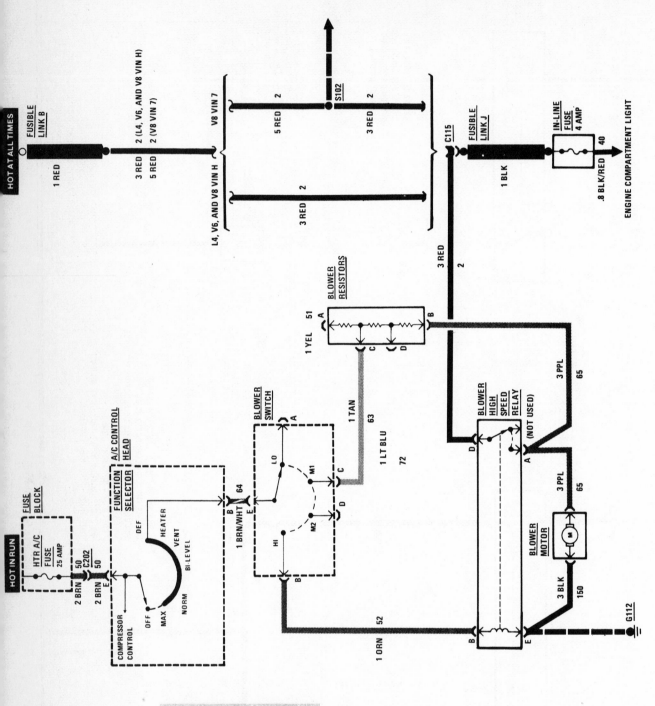

1982 and later blower control—typical Chevrolet except Berlinetta (© General Motors Corporation)

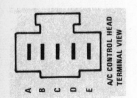

A/C CONTROL HEAD TERMINAL VIEW

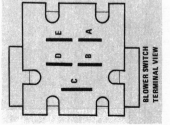

BLOWER SWITCH TERMINAL VIEW

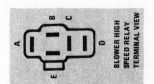

BLOWER HIGH SPEED RELAY TERMINAL VIEW

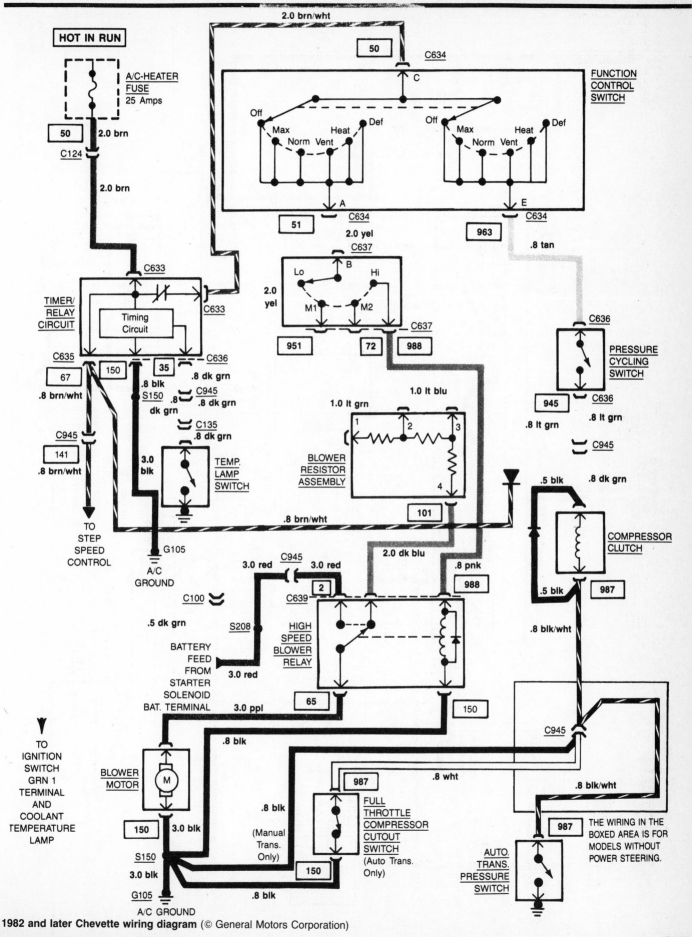

HOT IN RUN

A/C-HEATER FUSE 25 Amps

50

2.0 brn

C124

2.0 brn

2.0 brn/wht

50

C634

C
FUNCTION CONTROL SWITCH

Off   Max   Norm Vent Heat Def
Off   Max   Norm Vent Heat Def

A   C634
E   C634

51   2.0 yel   963   .8 tan

C637
Lo   B   Hi
2.0 yel
M1   M2

C637
951   72   988

C633
TIMER/ RELAY CIRCUIT   Timing Circuit   C633

C635   150   35   C636
67   .8 dk grn
.8 brn/wht
C945
.8 blk   .8 dk grn
S150
C945   dk grn
141   C135
.8 brn/wht   .8 dk grn
3.0 blk   TEMP. LAMP SWITCH

1.0 lt grn   1.0 lt blu
1   2   3
BLOWER RESISTOR ASSEMBLY
4
101

PRESSURE CYCLING SWITCH
C636
945   C636
.8 lt grn   .8 lt grn
C945

.5 blk   .8 dk grn
COMPRESSOR CLUTCH
.5 blk   987
.8 blk/wht

TO STEP SPEED CONTROL

G105
A/C GROUND

.8 brn/wht

2.0 dk blu   .8 pnk
988

C100
.5 dk grn   3.0 red   C945   3.0 red
2
C639
S208   HIGH SPEED BLOWER RELAY
BATTERY FEED FROM STARTER SOLENOID BAT. TERMINAL
3.0 red
65   150

3.0 ppl
▼
TO IGNITION SWITCH GRN 1 TERMINAL AND COOLANT TEMPERATURE LAMP

BLOWER MOTOR   M
.8 blk
987   .8 wht
.8 blk/wht
987

150   3.0 blk
S150
3.0 blk
G105
.8 blk
A/C GROUND

FULL THROTTLE COMPRESSOR CUTOUT SWITCH (Auto Trans. Only)
(Manual Trans. Only)
150

AUTO. TRANS. PRESSURE SWITCH

THE WIRING IN THE BOXED AREA IS FOR MODELS WITHOUT POWER STEERING.

1982 and later Chevette wiring diagram (© General Motors Corporation)

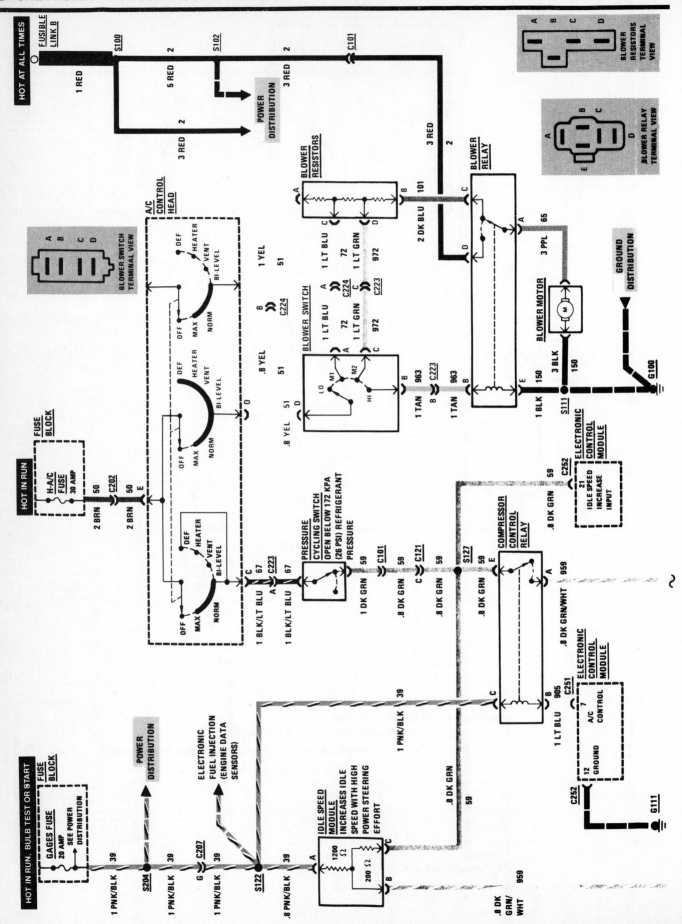

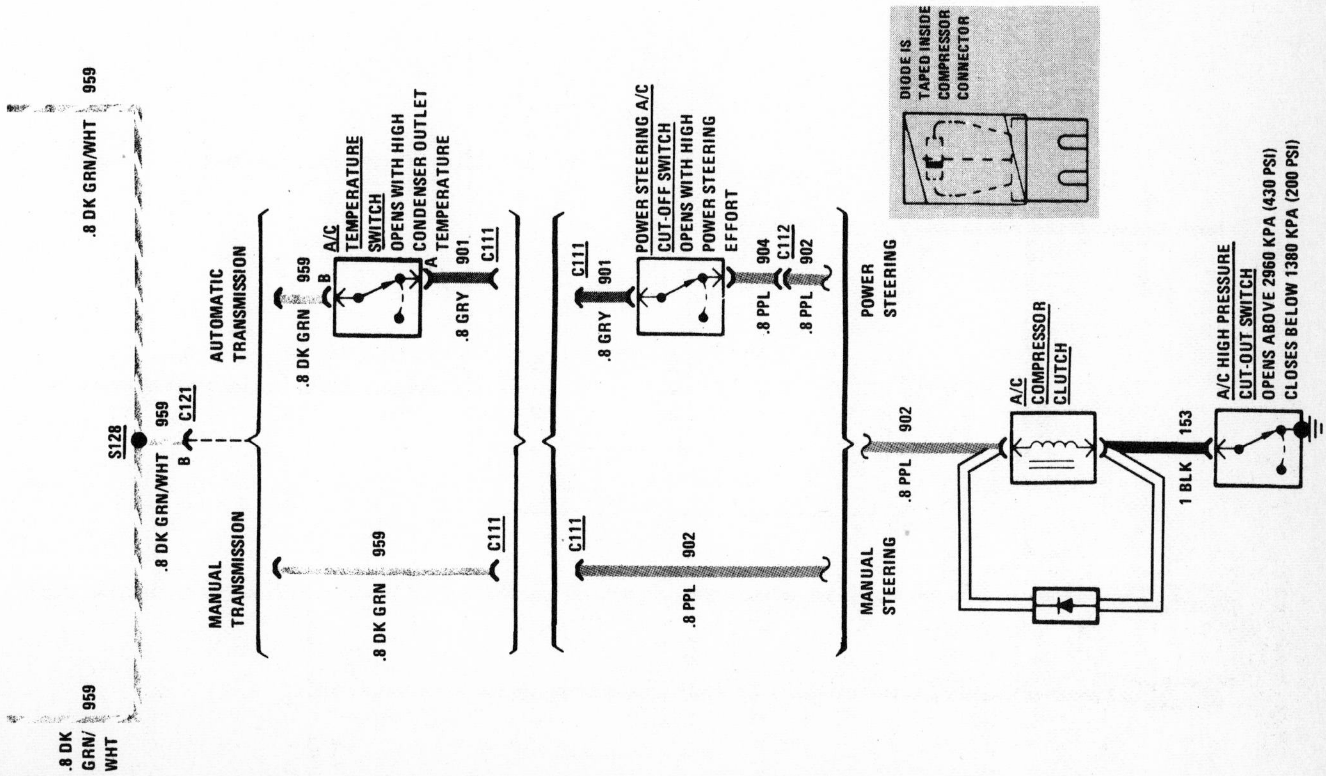

.8 DK GRN/WHT 959

.8 DK GRN/WHT 959

S128

B C121

AUTOMATIC TRANSMISSION

MANUAL TRANSMISSION

.8 DK GRN/WHT

.8 DK GRN 959

.8 DK GRN 959

C111

C111

A/C TEMPERATURE SWITCH
OPENS WITH HIGH CONDENSER OUTLET TEMPERATURE

B

A

901

C111

.8 GRY 959

C111 901

POWER STEERING A/C CUT-OFF SWITCH
OPENS WITH HIGH POWER STEERING EFFORT

904

C112 902

.8 GRY

.8 PPL

.8 PPL

POWER STEERING

C111

902

.8 PPL

MANUAL STEERING

.8 PPL 902

A/C COMPRESSOR CLUTCH

1 BLK 153

A/C HIGH PRESSURE CUT-OUT SWITCH
OPENS ABOVE 2960 KPA (430 PSI)
CLOSES BELOW 1380 KPA (200 PSI)

DIODE IS TAPED INSIDE COMPRESSOR CONNECTOR

1982 and later Cavalier wiring diagram (© General Motors Corporation)

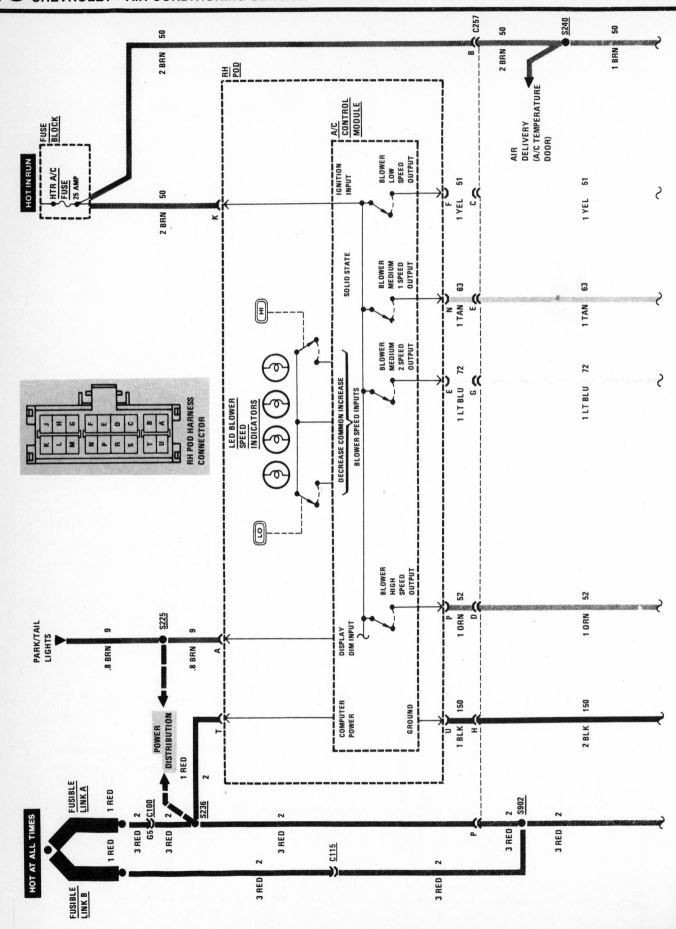

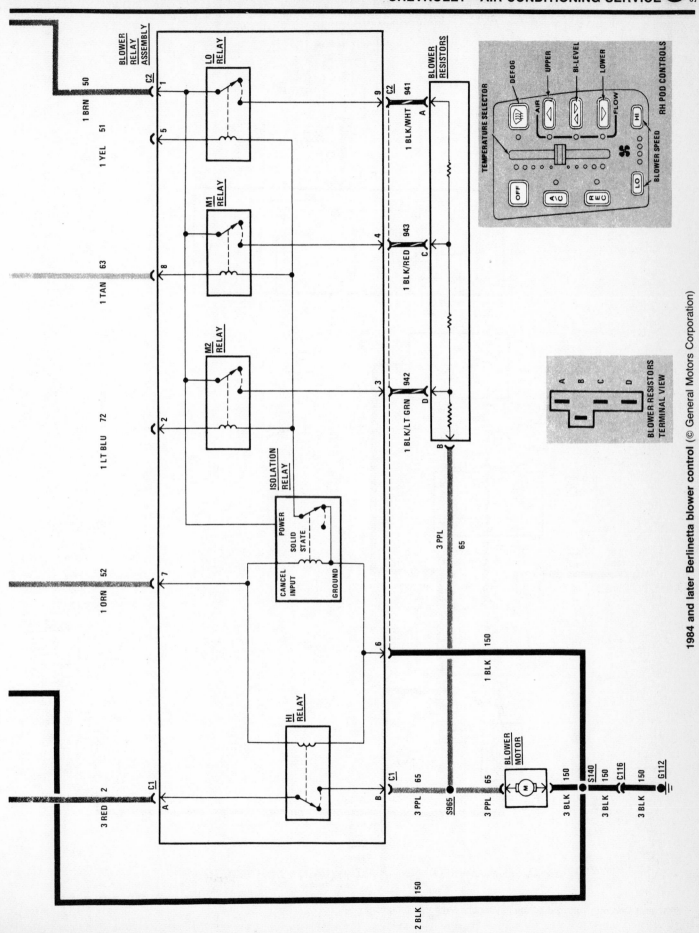

BLOWER RELAY ASSEMBLY

50 1 BRN C2

LO RELAY

51 1 YEL

M1 RELAY

63 1 TAN

M2 RELAY

72 1 LT BLU

ISOLATION RELAY
POWER
SOLID STATE
CANCEL INPUT   GROUND

52 1 ORN

HI RELAY

C1

2 3 RED

BLOWER RESISTORS

9   C2   941   1 BLK/WHT   A

4   943   1 BLK/RED   C

3   942   1 BLK/LT GRN   D

B

65   3 PPL

6   150   1 BLK

C1   65   3 PPL   S965   65   3 PPL   BLOWER MOTOR   150   S140   150   C116   150   G112
A   B

2 BLK   150

TEMPERATURE SELECTOR
DEFOG   UPPER   BI-LEVEL   LOWER
AIR   FLOW   HI
BLOWER SPEED
OFF   A/C   R E C   LO
RH POD CONTROLS

BLOWER RESISTORS
TERMINAL VIEW
A   B   C   D
BLOWER RESISTORS
TERMINAL VIEW (© General Motors Corporation)

1984 and later Berlinetta blower control (© General Motors Corporation)

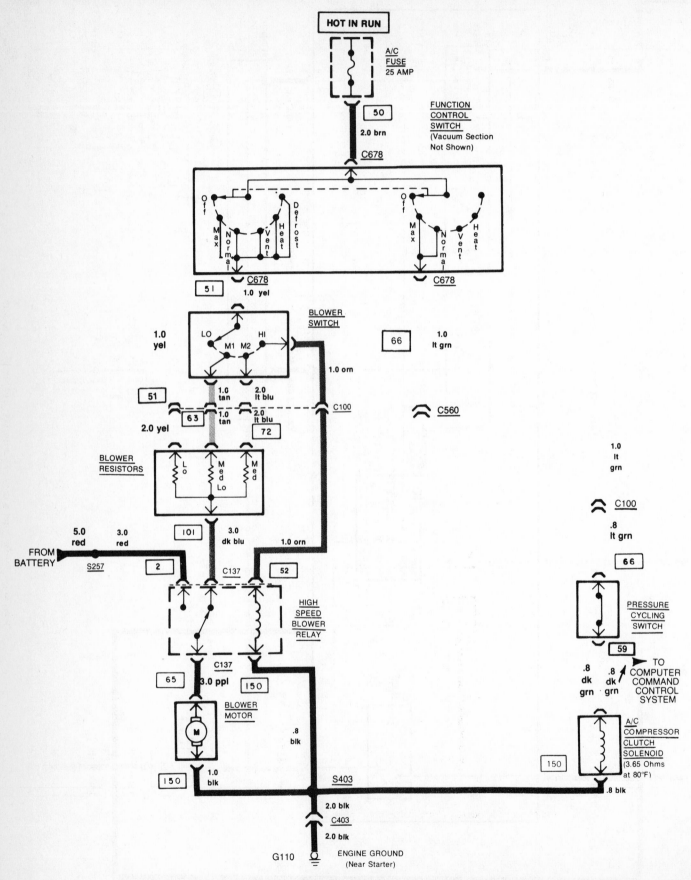

1982 and Corvette wiring diagram (© General Motors Corporation)

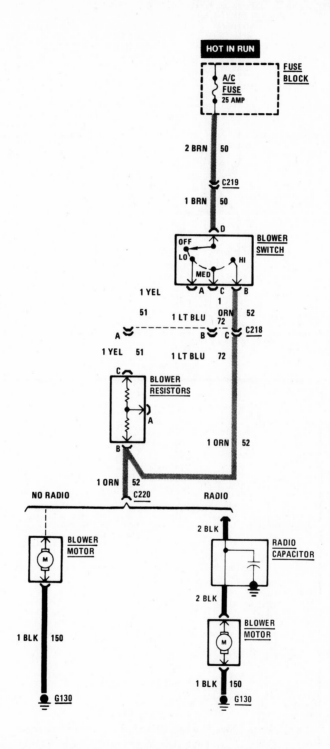

1982 and later heater wiring diagram—typical Chevrolet (© General Motors Corporation)

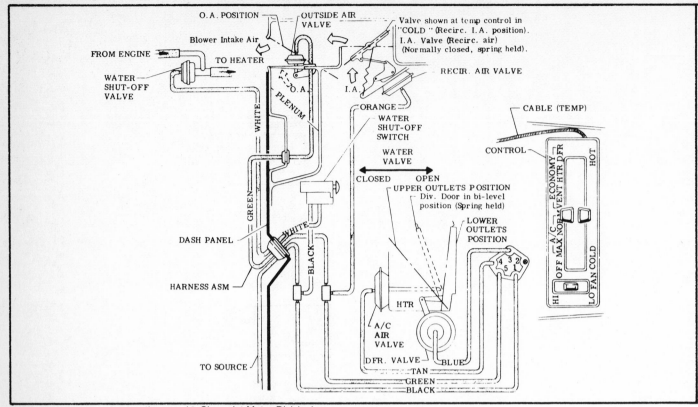

1982–83 Corvette vacuum diagram (© Chevrolet Motor Division)

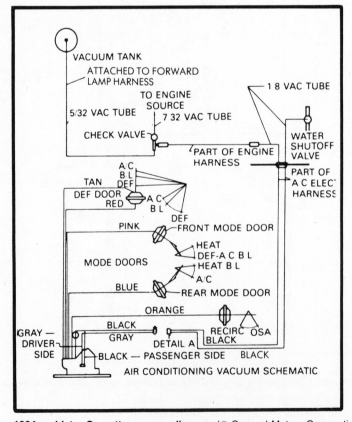

1984 and later Corvette vacuum diagram (© General Motors Corporation)

Oldsmobile

INDEX

SPECIFICATIONS

AIR CONDITIONING SYSTEM

OLDSMOBILE
Front Wheel Drive Models

1982	1983	1984	1985
Firenza	Firenza	Firenza	Firenza
Omega	Omega	Omega	Calais
Cutlass Ciera	Cutlass Ciera	Cutlass Ciera	Ninety-Eight
Toronado	Toronado	Toronado	Cutlass Ciera
			Toronado

Note: The vehicles listed are base models.

OLDSMOBILE
Rear Wheel Drive Models

1982	1983	1984	1985
Cutlass Supreme	Cutlass Supreme	Cutlass Supreme	Cutlass Supreme
Ninety-Eight	Ninety-Eight	Ninety-Eight	Delta 88
Delta 88	Delta 88	Delta 88	

Note: The vehicles listed are base models.

REFRIGERANT CAPACITIES—OLDSMOBILE
1982–85 Models
Refrigerant given in ounces, Refrigerant oil given in fluid ounces

1982			1983			1984			1985		
	Recharge Capacities			Recharge Capacities			Recharge Capacities			Recharge Capacities	
Models	R-12	Oil	Models	R-12	Oil	Models	R-12	Oil	Models	R-12	Oil
Cutlass Supreme	44	6	Cutlass Supreme	44	6	Cutlass Supreme	44	8①	Cutlass Supreme	44	8①
Ninety-Eight	56	6	Ninety-Eight	56	6	Ninety-Eight	56	8①	Ninety-Eight	56	8①
Delta 88	56	6	Delta 88	56	6	Delta 88	56	8①	Delta 88	56	8①
Firenza	40	6	Firenza	40	6	Firenza	40	8①	Firenza	40	8①
Omega	44	6	Omega	44	6	Omega	44	8①	Calais	56	8①
Cutlass Ciera	44	6	Cutlass Ciera	44	6	Cutlass Ciera	44	6	Cutlass Ciera	44	8①
Toronado	52	6	Toronado	52	6	Toronado	52	8①	Toronado	52	8①

① Refrigerant oil capacities are given for vehicles equipped with the DA - 6 compressor. Vehicles equipped with the R - 4 compressor require 4 fluid ounces of refrigerant oil.

COMPRESSOR DRIVE BELT TENSION
Oldsmobile

Year	New	Used
1982	150–170 lbs. ①	90–100 lbs.
1983	120–145 lbs.	70–90 lbs.
1984	120–145 lbs.	70–90 lbs.
1985	120–145 lbs.	70–90 lbs.

① Belt tension on vehicles equipped with serpentine belt should be 80–120 lbs.

DRIVE BELT TENSION

Air conditioning compress tension adjustment involves movement of one or more of the components within the belt span. Caution must be exercised to avoid missing hidden bolts and retaining nuts. No attempt should be made to adjust the drive belt tension while the engine is running.

Adjustment

1. Loosen the A/C compressor bolts and any adjustment bracket bolt.
2. Move the compressor against the drive belt until the proper tension is applied to the compressor.
3. Tighten the compressor bolts and the adjustment bracket.
4. Check the adjustment using a belt tensioning gauge.

Blower Motor

Removal and Installation

1982 AND LATER

1. Disconnect the negative battery cable.
2. Tag and disconnect the electrical connections from the back of the blower motor.
3. Disconnect the cooling hose from the case.
4. Remove the blower motor mounting screws. Remove the blower motor.
5. Installation is the reverse of the removal procedure. Use a silicone sealer on the blower motor sealing surfaces.

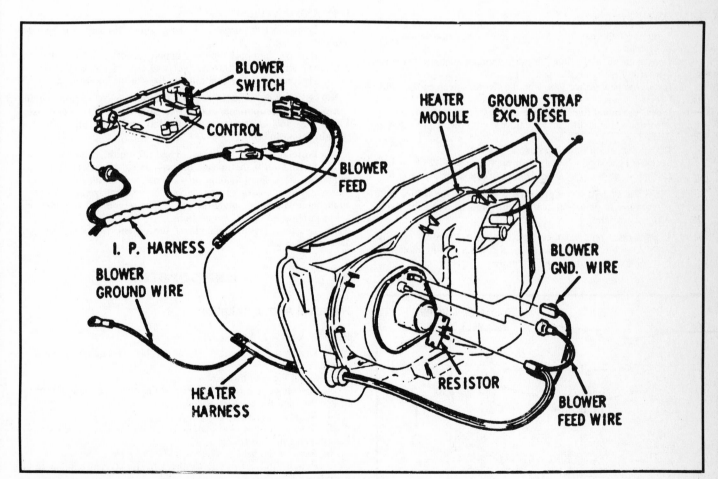

Blower motor wiring connections—typical (© General Motors Corp.)

Compressor

Removal and Installation

1982 AND LATER

1. Disconnect the negative battery cable. Discharge the A/C system.
2. Raise the vehicle and support safely.
3. Remove the right air dam and splash shield if the vehicle is equipped.
4. Tag and disconnect the electrical connections at the compressor clutch. Remove the refrigerant line at the rear of the compressor.
5. Remove the compressor attaching bolts. Remove the compressor and the drive belt from the vehicle.
6. Installation is the reverse of the removal procedure. Leak test the compressor connections.

Expansion Valve

ORIFICE TUBE

Removal and Installation

1982 AND LATER

1. Disconnect the negative battery cable. Discharge the air conditioning system.
2. Loosen the nut at the liquid line to evaporator inlet pipe. Remove the tube carefully using needle nose pliers.
3. Install the new orifice tube with the shorter screen end installed first.
4. Install the liquid line. Evacuate and charge the system.
If the expansion valve is difficult to remove the following procedure is recommended:
1. Remove as much of any residue as possible.
2. Using a heat source, apply heat approximately ¼ of an inch from the dimples on the inlet pipe. Do not overheat the pipe.

NOTE: If the system has a pressure switch near the orifice tube location, remove it prior to heating the pipe in order to avoid damage to the switch.

3. Using orifice removal tube, AC-1002 or J-26549-C, grip the orifice tube assembly. Use a rotating motion and a pulling motion to loosen and remove the orifice tube assembly.

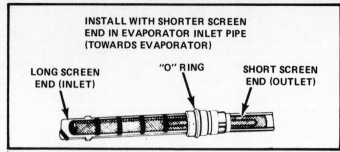

INSTALL WITH SHORTER SCREEN END IN EVAPORATOR INLET PIPE (TOWARDS EVAPORATOR)

LONG SCREEN END (INLET)   "O" RING   SHORT SCREEN END (OUTLET)

Expansion tube (© General Motors Corp.)

4. Lubricate the new orifice tube and O-ring with 525 viscosity refrigerant oil and install into the inlet pipe. Install the smaller screen first.

Condenser

Removal and Installation

1982 AND LATER

1. Disconnect the negative battery cable. Discharge the air conditioning system.
2. Remove the upper radiator support brackets. Remove the condenser support brackets. Save the rubber bushings for installation.
3. Disconnect the air conditioning lines at the condenser.

NOTE: Certain vehicles require the removal of various engine compartment components in order to gain access to the condenser. These may include the fan shroud, left and right air dams and certain fascia to fender bolts.

4. Position the radiator rearward and lift out the condenser.
5. Installation is the reverse of the removal procedure. When assembling, use a small amount of refrigerant oil on all tube and hose joints. Always use new O-rings dipped in clean refrigerant oil (where applicable) when assembling the joints. The oil will aid assembly and hel to provide leak-proof connections.
6. Evacuate, leak test and charge the system. Check the performance of the system.

Evaporator

Removal and Installation

FIRENZA—1982 AND LATER

1. Disconnect the negative battery cable. Discharge the air conditioning system.
2. Drain the cooling system.
3. Disconnect the heater hoses and the evaporator lines from the heater core and the evaporator core.
4. Remove the drain tube.
5. Remove the sound insulators from both sides. Remove the steering column trim cover.
6. Remove the heater core cover. Remove the heater core.
7. Remove the screws holding the defroster vacuum actuator to the module case.
8. Remove the evaporator cover. Remove the evaporator core.
9. Installation is the reverse of the removal procedure.

88 AND 98—1982 AND LATER

1. Disconnect the negative battery cable. Discharge the system.
2. Tag and disconnect the electrical connections from the blower motor, resister, thermostatic switch and Hi blower relay.
3. Remove the thermostatic switch and diagnostic connector attaching screws.

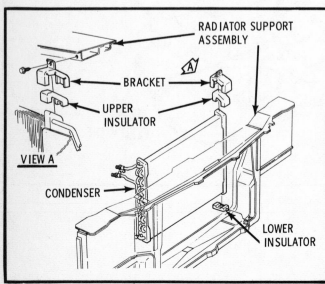

RADIATOR SUPPORT ASSEMBLY

BRACKET

UPPER INSULATOR

VIEW A

CONDENSER

LOWER INSULATOR

Condenser mounting (© General Motors Corp.)

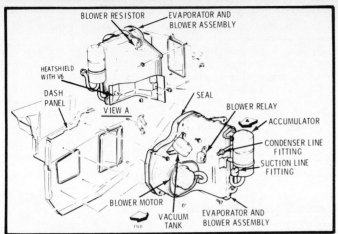

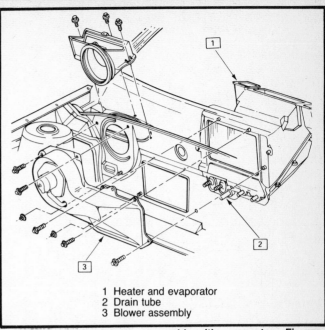

Exploded view of the evaporator assembly—Toronado, 1982 and later (© General Motors Corp.)

4. Disconnect the liquid line refrigerant line from evaporator inlet pipe.

5. Disconnect the compressor suction line at the accumulator outlet pipe.

6. Remove the right end of the hood seal and remove the inlet screen attaching screws and screen.

7. Remove the case to dash bolts along the inside of the air intake plenum.

8. Remove the upper case by lifting straight up and off.

9. Remove the two accumulator pipe bracket to case screws.

10. Remove the evaporator core.

11. Installation is the reverse of the removal procedure.

TORONADO—1982 AND LATER

1. Disconnect the negative battery cable. Discharge the system.

2. Tag and disconnect the wires from the evaporator.

3. Remove the VIR.

4. Remove the right front wheel. Remove the wheel housing bolts.

5. Remove the right wheel housing filler.

6. Remove the fender to dash brace.

7. Remove the brace securing the fender to joint line.

8. Remove the evaporator assembly attaching bolts.

1 Heater and evaporator
2 Drain tube
3 Blower assembly

Exploded view of the heater assembly with evaporator—Firenza 1982 and later (© General Motors Corp.)

9. Disconnect the evaporator vacuum hose. Remove the evaporator.

10. Installation is the reverse of the removal procedure.

OMEGA AND CIERRA—1982 AND LATER

1. Disconnect the negative battery cable. Discharge the air conditioning system.

2. Remove the air cleaner and the vacuum tank.

3. Tag and disconnect the electrical connections along the cowl and position the harness to the right side of the vehicle.

4. Disconnect the liquid line at the evaporator inlet and low pressure line at the accumulator inlet.

5. Remove the outer blower case to cowl screws and remove the blower case assembly.

6. Remove the evaporator assembly.

7. Installation is the reverse of the removal procedure.

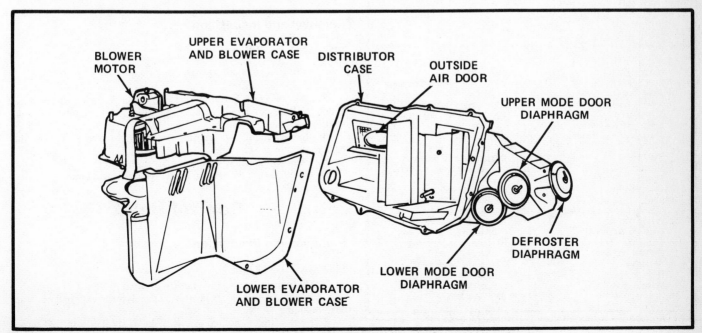

Exploded view of the evaporator assembly—Oldsmobile 88 & 89—1982 and later (© General Motors Corp.)

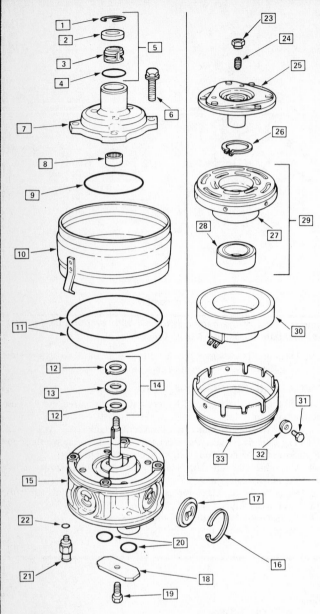

1 Retainer Ring
2 Seal Seat
3 Shaft Seal
4 O-Ring, Seal Seat
5 Shaft Seal Kit
6 Screw and Washer Assembly Front Head Mounting
7 Front Head
8 Main Bearing
9 Ring Seal, Front Head to Cylinder
10 Shell
11 O-Ring, Cylinder to Shell
12 Thrust Washer
13 Belleville Washer
14 Thrust Washer Kit
15 Cylinder and Shaft Assembly
16 Retainer Ring
17 Valve Plate
18 Shipping Plate
19 Screw
20 O-Ring, Suction-Discharge Ports
21 Pressure Relief Valve
22 O-Ring Pressure Relief Valve
23 Shaft Nut
24 Clutch Hub Key
25 Clutch Drive Assembly
26 Retainer Ring
27 Rotor
28 Rotor Bearing
29 Rotor and Bearing Assembly
30 Coil and Housing Assembly
31 Pulley Rim Mounting Screw
32 Special Washer-Pulley Rim Mounting Screw Locking
33 Pulley Rim

R-4 compressor—exploded view (© General Motors Corp.)

CUTLASS—1982 AND LATER

1. Disconnect the negative battery cable. Discharge the air conditioning system.
2. Remove the module seal and screen.
3. Remove the right hand wiper arm.
4. Tag and disconnect all electrical connections at the module.
5. Remove the module top cover.
6. Disconnect the bracket screws, refrigerant lines and the liquid line at the accumulator.
7. Remove the evaporator core.
8. Installation is the reverse of the removal procedure.

Programmer

Removal and Installation

TORONADO—1982 AND LATER

1. Disconnect the negative battery cable.
2. Disconnect the instrument panel sound absorber.
3. Disconnect the temperature door rod (link) from the crank arm.
4. Disconnect the aspirator and vacuum hoses. Remove the temperature cable from the programmer.
5. Remove the programmer retaining screws and remove the programmer from the heater case.
6. Installation is the reverse of the removal procedure.
7. After assembling the programmer to the vehicle, adjust the temperature door and check the system operation.

OLDSMOBILE 88, 98 AND CUTLASS—1982 AND LATER

1. Disconnect the negative battery cable.
2. Remove the glove box.
3. Disconnect the temperature control cable at the programmer.
4. Disconnect the vacuum harness connector at the programmer.
5. Disconnect the in-car air source hose at the programmer.
6. Disconnect the temperature door link threaded rod at the programmer.
7. Remove the retaining screws and remove the programmer.
8. Installation is the reverse of the removal procedure. Check the system operation.

Heater Core

Removal and Installation

1982 AND LATER

1. Disconnect the negative battery cable.
2. Drain the radiator.
3. Disconnect the heater hoses at the heater core tube connections. When the hoses are removed, install plugs into the core tubes to avoid spilling coolant.
4. Remove the screws securing the heater core cover. Remove the heater core cover.
5. Remove the heater core assembly.
6. Installation is the reverse of the removal procedure.

Control Head

Removal and Installation

1982 AND LATER

1. Disconnect the negative battery cable.
2. Remove the necessary instrument panel trim to expose the control head retaining screws.
3. Remove the radio and/or knobs, radio speaker, ash tray, cigar lighter and the floor console trim plate if equipped.

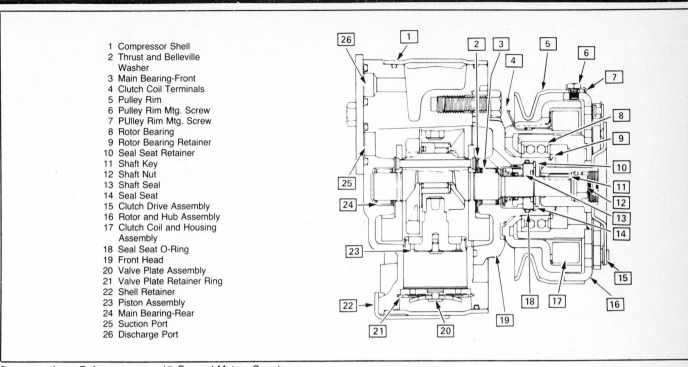

1 Compressor Shell
2 Thrust and Belleville Washer
3 Main Bearing-Front
4 Clutch Coil Terminals
5 Pulley Rim
6 Pulley Rim Mtg. Screw
7 PUlley Rim Mtg. Screw
8 Rotor Bearing
9 Rotor Bearing Retainer
10 Seal Seat Retainer
11 Shaft Key
12 Shaft Nut
13 Shaft Seal
14 Seal Seat
15 Clutch Drive Assembly
16 Rotor and Hub Assembly
17 Clutch Coil and Housing Assembly
18 Seal Seat O-Ring
19 Front Head
20 Valve Plate Assembly
21 Valve Plate Retainer Ring
22 Shell Retainer
23 Piston Assembly
24 Main Bearing-Rear
25 Suction Port
26 Discharge Port

Cross section—R-4 compressor (© General Motors Corp.)

4. After exposing the control head retaining screws, remove them and pull the control head away from the dash assembly.

5. Disconnect the bowden cable, electrical and/or vacuum connections. Remove the control unit.

6. Installation is the reverse of the removal procedure.

A/C FUNCTIONAL TEST

STEP	CONTROL SETTINGS				SYSTEM RESPONSE			
	MODE CONTROL	TEMPERATURE CONTROL	FAN SWITCH	BLOWER SPEED	HEATER OUTLETS	A/C OUTLETS	WINDSHIELD DEFROST OUTLETS	SIDE WINDOW DEFROST OUTLETS
1	OFF	COLD	LO	OFF	NO AIR FLOW	NO AIR FLOW	NO AIR FLOW	NO AIR FLOW
2	MAX	COLD	LO	LOW	NO AIR FLOW	AIR FLOW	NO AIR FLOW	NO AIR FLOW
3	MAX	COLD	LO TO HI	LO TO HI	NO AIR FLOW	AIR FLOW	NO AIR FLOW	NO AIR FLOW
4	NORM	COLD	HI	HIGH	NO AIR FLOW	AIR FLOW	NO AIR FLOW	NO AIR FLOW
5	BI-LEVEL	COLD	HI	HIGH	AIR FLOW	AIR FLOW	NO AIR FLOW	NO AIR FLOW
6	VENT	COLD	HI	HIGH	NO AIR FLOW	AIR FLOW	NO AIR FLOW	NO AIR FLOW
7	HEATER	HOT	HI	HIGH	AIR FLOW	NO AIR FLOW	MINIMUM AIR FLOW	MINIMUM AIR FLOW
8	DEF.	HOT	HI	HIGH	MINIMUM AIR FLOW	NO AIR FLOW	AIR FLOW	AIR FLOW

HI · AIR COND · ECONOMY
OFF MAX NORM BI-LEVEL VENT HEATER
COLD · HOT
LO

A/C Control Operation

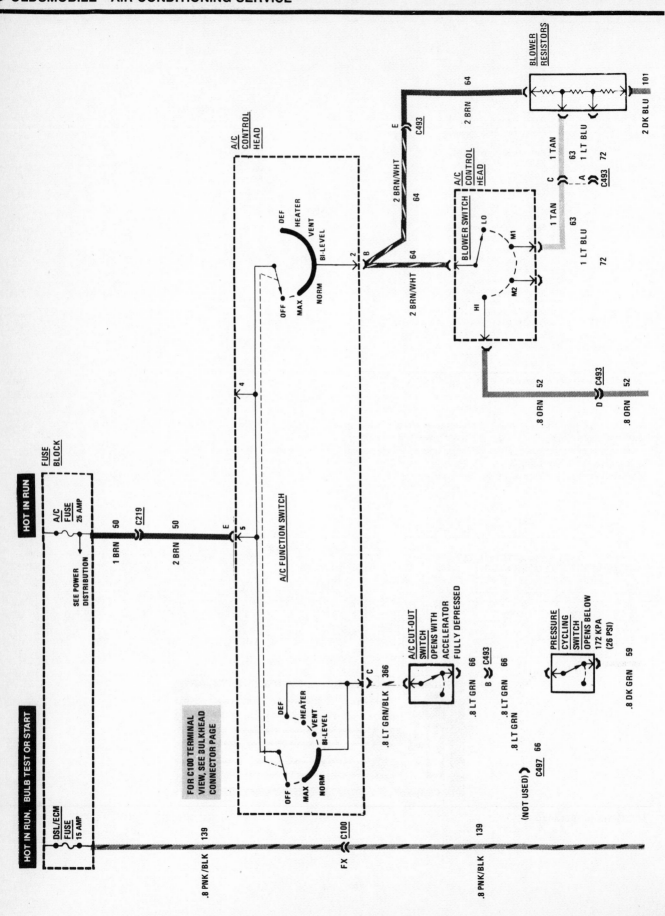

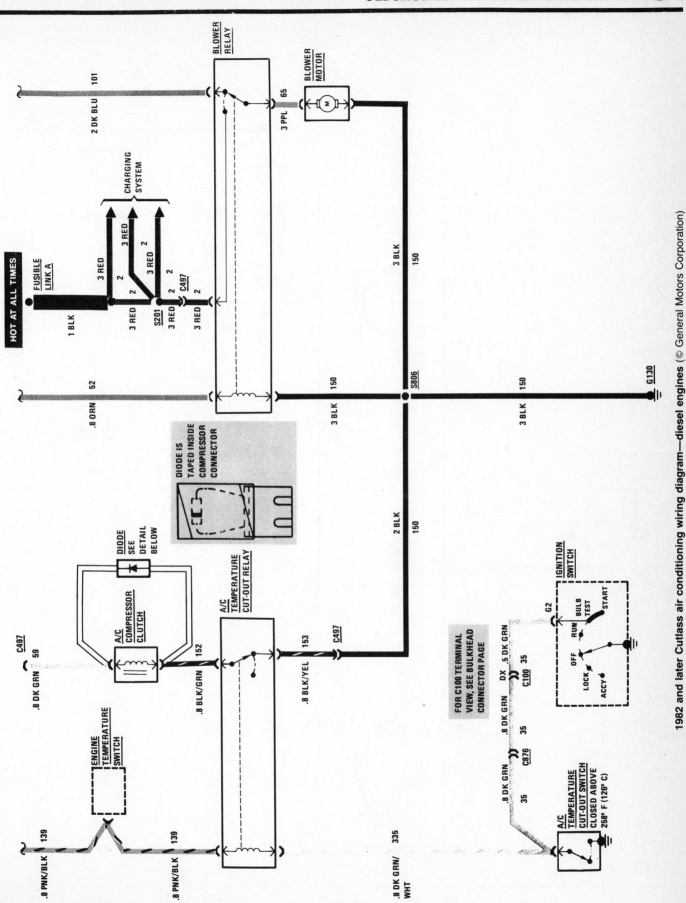

1982 and later Cutlass air conditioning wiring diagram—diesel engines (© General Motors Corporation)

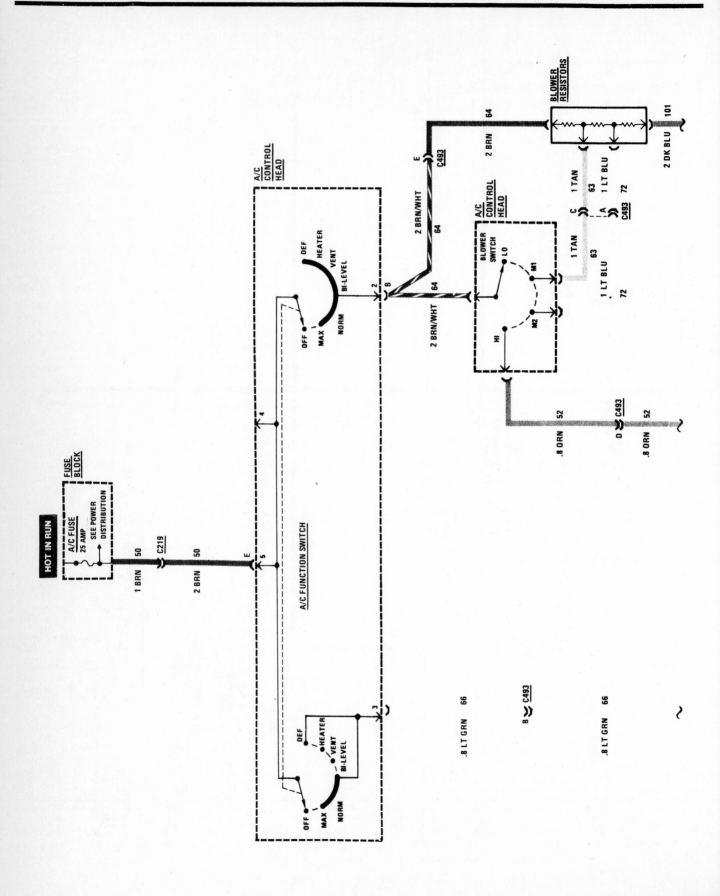

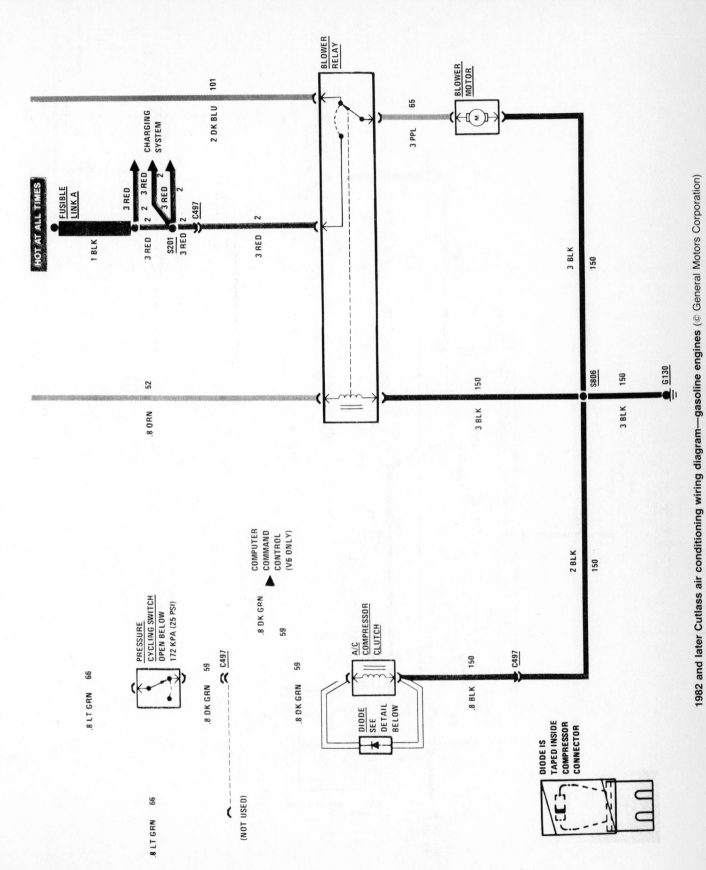

1982 and later Cutlass air conditioning wiring diagram—gasoline engines (© General Motors Corporation)

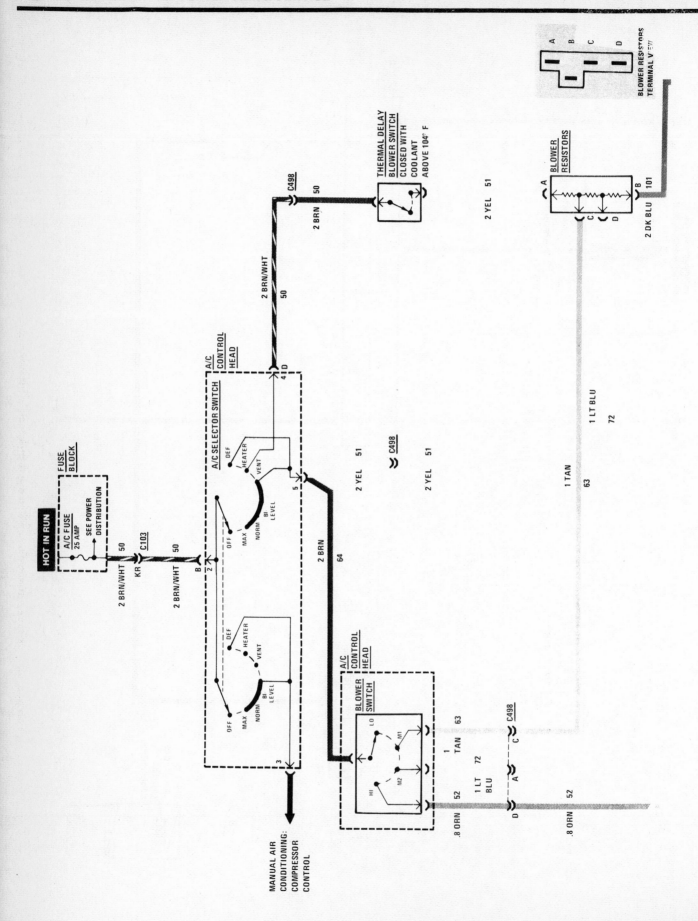

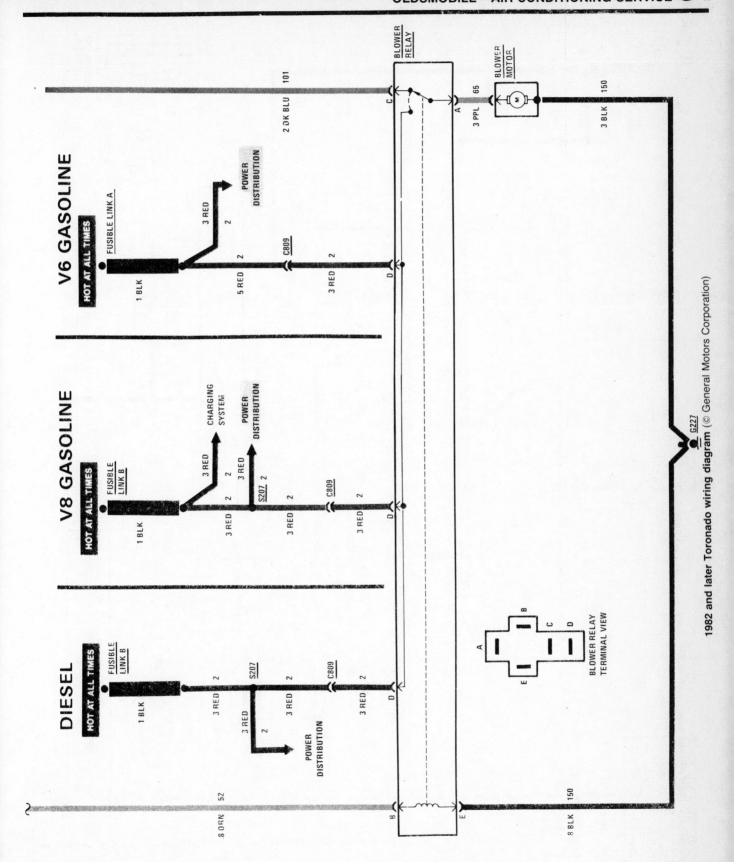

1982 and later Toronado wiring diagram (© General Motors Corporation)

237

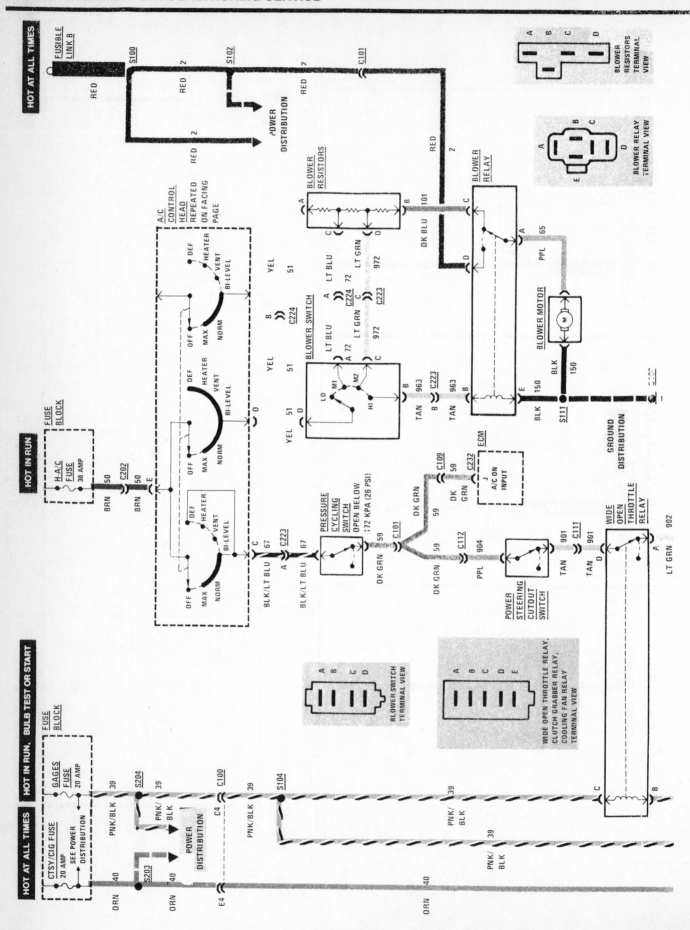

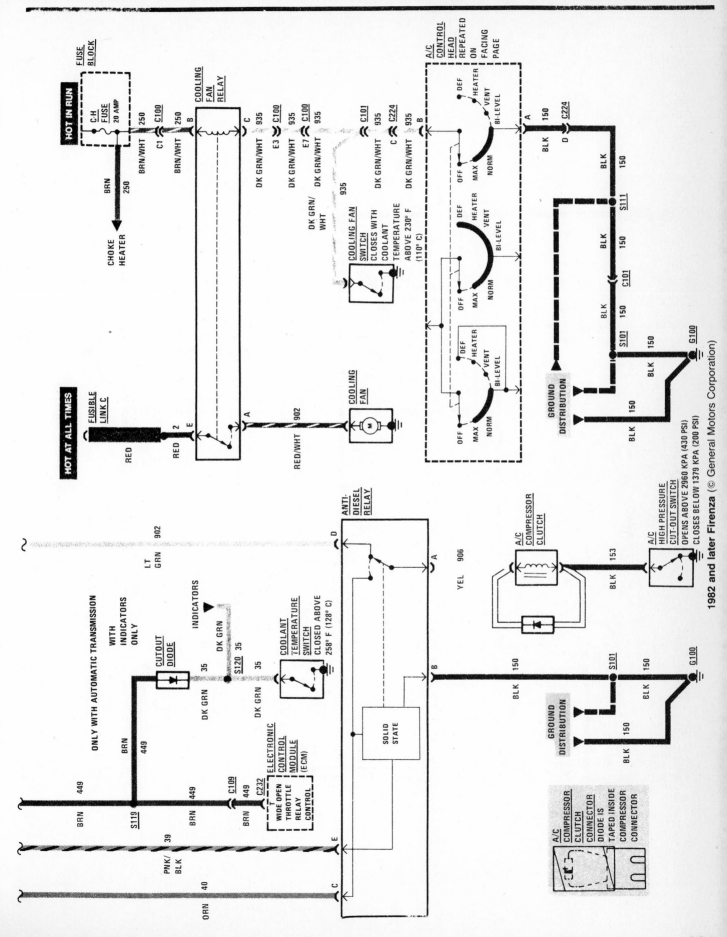

1982 and later Firenza (© General Motors Corporation)

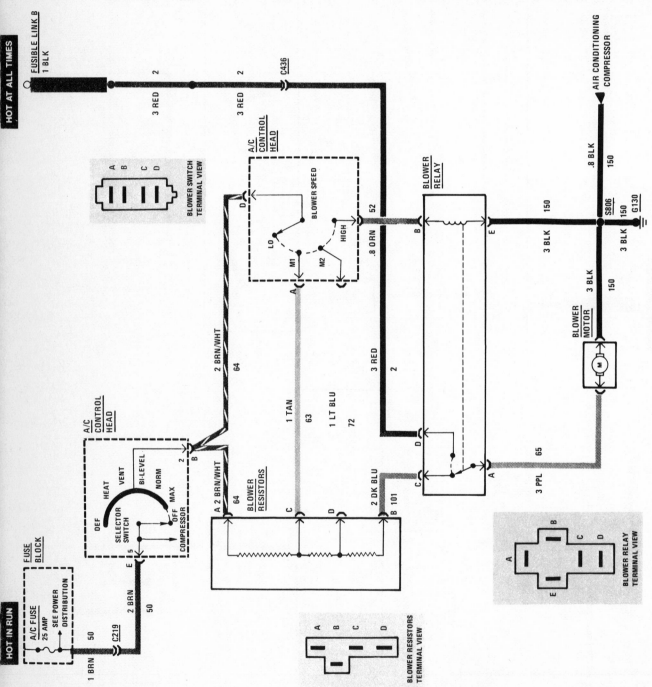

1982 and later Delta 88 and 98 blower schematic (© General Motors Corporation)

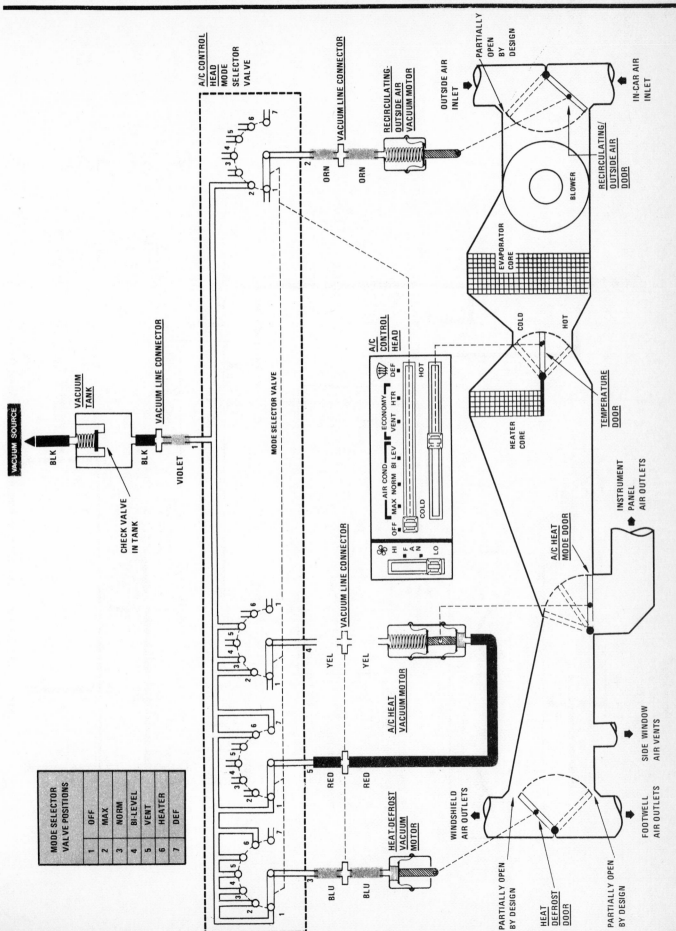

1982 and later vacuum diagram—typical (© General Motors Corporation)

MODE SELECTOR VALVE POSITIONS	
1	OFF
2	MAX
3	NORM
4	BI-LEVEL
5	VENT
6	HEATER
7	DEF

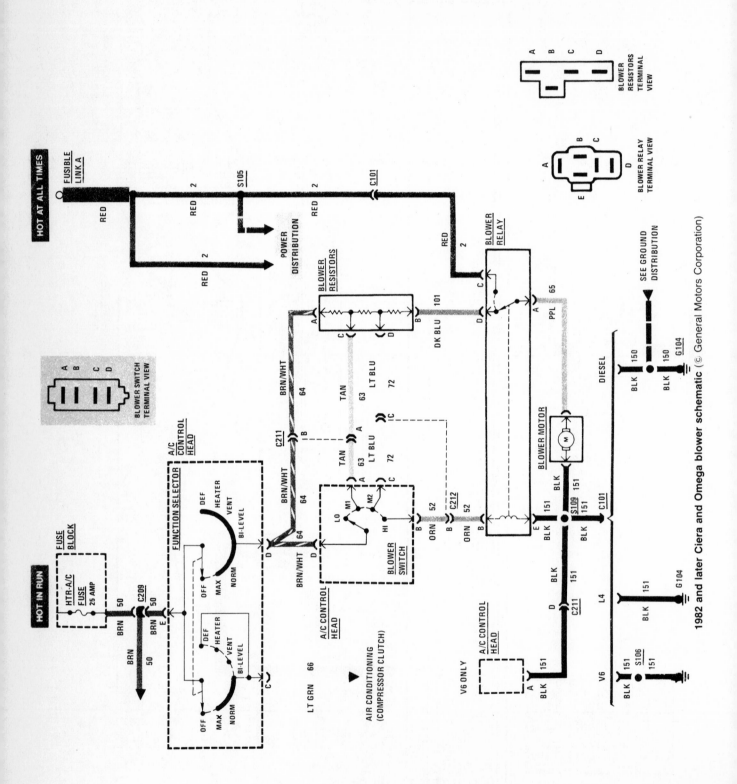

1982 and later Ciera and Omega blower schematic (© General Motors Corporation)

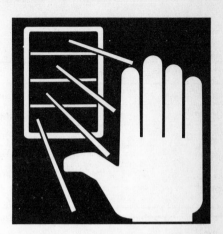

SECTION 5
GENERAL MOTORS
Pontiac

INDEX

SPECIFICATIONS
PONTIAC
Rear Wheel Drive Models

1982	1983	1984	1985
Grand Prix	Parisienne	Parisienne	Parisienne
Bonneville	Grand Prix	Grand Prix	Grand Prix
Firebird	Bonneville	Bonneville	Bonneville
T-1000	Firebird	Fiero	Fiero
	T-1000	Firebird	Firebird
		T-1000	T-1000

NOTE: The vehicles listed are base models.

PONTIAC
Front Wheel Drive Models

1982	1983	1984	1985
6000	6000	6000	Grand Am
Phoenix	Phoenix	Phoenix	6000
J-2000	J-2000	2000-Sunbird	Phoenix

NOTE: The vehicles listed are base models.

REFRIGERANT CAPACITIES—PONTIAC
1982–85 Models
Refrigerant given in ounces, Refrigerant oil given in fluid ounces

1982			1983			1984			1985		
	Recharge Capacities			Recharge Capacities			Recharge Capacities			Recharge Capacities	
Models	R-12	Oil	Models	R-12	Oil	Models	R-12	Oil	Models	R-12	Oil
Grand Prix	53	6	Parisienne	53	6	Parisienne	53	6	Parisienne	53	6
Bonneville	53	6	Grand Prix	53	6	Grand Prix	53	6	Grand Prix	53	6
Firebird	48	6	Bonneville	53	6	Bonneville	53	6	Bonneville	53	6
T-1000	36	6	Firebird	48	6	Fiero	40	8	Fiero	40	8
6000	44	6	T-1000	36	6	Firebird	48	6	Firebird	48	6
Phoenix	44	6	6000	44	6	T-1000	36	6	T-1000	36	6
J-2000	40	6	Phoenix	44	6	6000	44	6	Grand Am	56	6
			J-2000	40	6	Phoenix	44	6	6000	44	6
						2000 Sunbird	40	6	Phoenix	44	6

DRIVE BELT TENSION

Air conditioning compressor tension adjustment involves movement of one or more of the components within the belt span. Caution must be exercised to avoid missing hidden bolts and retaining nuts. No attempt should be made to adjust the drive belt tension while the engine is running.

Adjustment

1. Loosen the A/C compressor bolts and any adjustment bracket bolt.
2. Move the compressor against the drive belt until the proper tension is applied to the compressor.
3. Tighten the compressor bolts and the adjustment bracket.
4. Check the adjustment using a belt tensioning gauge.

COMPRESSOR DRIVE BELT TENSION
Pontiac

Year	New	Used
1982	80–100 lbs.	50–70 lbs.
1983	145–165 lbs.	70–90 lbs.
1984	145–165 lbs.	70–90 lbs.
1985	145–165 lbs.	70–90 lbs.

Blower Motor

Removal and Installation

1982 AND LATER

1. Disconnect the negative battery cable.

2. Tag and disconnect the electrical connections from the back of the blower motor.

3. Remove all necessary components in order to gain access to the blower to case attaching screws.

4. Remove the blower to case attaching screws. Remove the blower motor assembly.

5. Installation is the reverse of the removal procedure.

Compressor

Removal and Installation

1982 AND LATER

1. Disconnect the negative battery cable.
2. Discharge the air conditioning system as described earlier.
3. Tag and disconnect the electrical leads at the compressor.
4. Remove the refrigerant lines from the compressor.
5. Remove the air conditioner compressor retaining bolts from the brackets.

NOTE: Some vehicles may require the power steering pump, alternator or plug wires to be repositioned or removed. Other components may need to be removed depending on the optional accessories.

6. Remove the air conditioning compressor from the vehicle.

7. When installing the compressor, keep dirt and foreign material from getting into the compressor parts and system. Clean tools and a clean work area are important for proper service. The compressor connections and the outside of the compressor should be cleaned before the compressor is installed. If new components are being installed, note that they are dehydrated and sealed prior to shipping. All sub-assemblies are to remain sealed until use, with the sub-assemblies at room temperature before uncapping. This helps prevent moisture from the air entering the system due to condensation. Use a small amount of refrigerant oil on all tube and hose joints. Always use new O-rings dipped in refrigerant oil before assembling joints. This oil will aid assembly and help to provide leak-proof joints.

8. Install any accessories that may have been removed to make room for the compressor.

9. Evacuate, charge and leak test the system. Check for the proper operation of the system.

NOTE: For compressor overhaul, refer to the compressor section.

Expansion Tube (Orifice)

Removal and Installation

1982 AND LATER

1. Discharge the air conditioning system.

2. Loosen the nut holding the liquid line to the evaporator inlet pipe. Remove the tube using needle nose pliers.

3. Install the new orifice tube.

NOTE: When installing the orifice tube inside the evaporator inlet pipe, it must be installed with the shorter screen end inserted first.

4. Install the liquid line to the evaporator.

5. Evacuate and charge the air conditioning system. Check the system for proper operation.

The following procedure is recommended for an expansion tube that is broken or difficult to remove:

1. Discharge the air conditioning system.

2. Remove the liquid line to evaporator inlet pipe.

3. Using a heat gun, apply heat approximately one quarter of an inch from the inlet pipe dimples.

NOTE: If a pressure switch is located near the orifice tube, remove it before applying heat so as not to damage the circuit.

4. Using a twisting motion, loosen the orifice tube and remove it from its holder.

NOTE: Commercial tools are available to remove the expansion tube after the system has been discharged.

5. Clean the inside of the evaporator pipe with R-11 or equivalent.

6. Add one ounce of 525 viscosity refrigerant oil to the system. Lubricate the new orifice tube and O-ring with refrigerant oil.

7. Install the new orifice tube in the inlet pipe.

NOTE: When installing the new orifice tube, make sure that the short screen is facing the condenser.

8. Install the liquid line to the evaporator.

9. Evacuate and charge the system. Check the system for proper operation.

Condenser

Removal and Installation

1982 AND LATER

1. Disconnect the negative battery cable. Discharge the air conditioning system.

2. Remove the upper radiator support brackets. Remove the condenser support brackets. Save the rubber bushings for installation.

3. Disconnect the air conditioning lines at the condenser.

NOTE: Certain vehicles require the removal of various engine compartment components in order to gain access to the condenser. These may include the fan shroud, left and right air dams and certain fascia to fender bolts.

4. Position the radiator rearward and lift out the condenser.

5. Installation is the reverse of the removal procedure. When assembling, use a small amount of refrigerant oil on all tube and hose joints. Always use new O-rings dipped in clean refrigerant oil (where applicable) when assembling the joints. The oil will aid assembly and help to provide leak-proof connections.

6. Evacuate, leak test and charge the system. Check the performance of the system.

Evaporator

Removal and Installation

6000—1982 AND LATER

1. Disconnect the negative battery cable. Discharge the air conditioning system. If necessary remove the air cleaner in order to gain working clearance.

2. Tag and disconnect the air conditioning electrical connections from the vehicle and position them out of the way. Remove the vacuum tank.

3. Disconnect the liquid line at the evaporator inlet. Disconnect the low pressure line at the accumulator inlet.

4. Remove the outer blower case to cowl screws and remove the blower and case assembly. Remove the evaporator.

5. Installation is the reverse of the removal procedure. Evacuate and charge the air conditioning system and check for proper operation.

PARISIENNE, BONNEVILLE AND GRAND PRIX—1984 AND LATER

1. Disconnect the negative battery cable. Discharge the air conditioning system.

2. Remove the module screen and the rubber screen.

3. Remove the right side windshield wiper arm from the vehicle.

4. Tag and disconnect the electrical connections from the diagnostic connection, thermostatic switch and the hi-blower relay.

5. Disconnect the electrical connections from the module.

6. Remove the module top cover. Remove the accumulator bracket screws.

7. Disconnect the refrigerant lines at the accumulator and the liquid line.

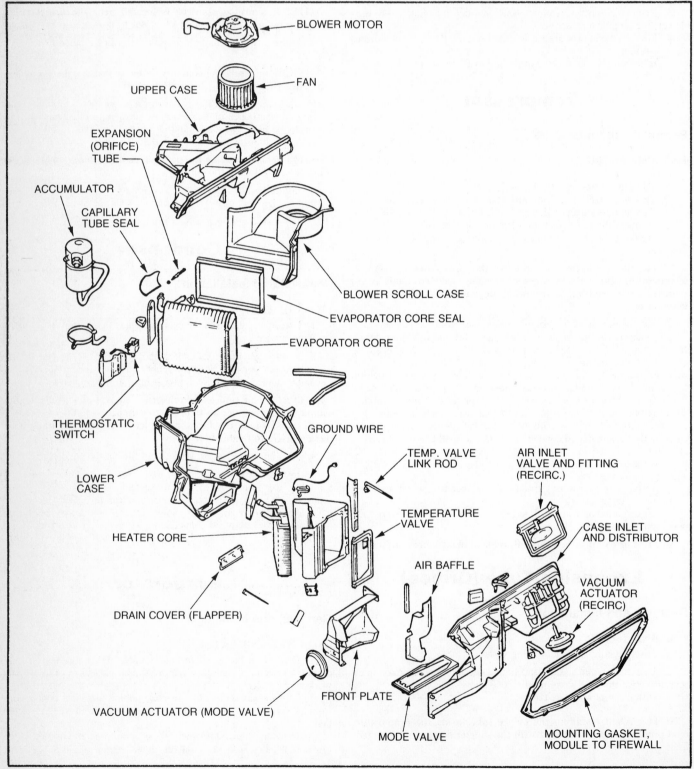

Air conditioning assembly—exploded view (© General Motors Corp.)

8. Remove the evaporator.

9. Installation is the reverse of the removal procedure. Check the system after charging for proper operation.

FIREBIRD—1982 AND LATER

1. Disconnect the negative battery cable. Discharge the air conditioning system.

2. Remove the accumulator from the vehicle.

3. Tag and disconnect the electrical connections from the hi-blower relay. Remove the hi-blower relay.

4. Remove the upper case screws.

5. Disconnect the liquid line fitting.

6. Remove the upper evaporator case. Remove the evaporator core.

7. Installation is the reverse of the removal procedure. Charge the air conditioning system and check for proper operation.

2000/SUNBIRD—1982 AND LATER

1. Disconnect the negative battery cable. Discharge the A/C system. Drain the cooling system.

2. Disconnect the heater hoses at the heater core. Disconnect the evaporator lines at the evaporator. Remove the drain tube.

3. Remove the right and left hand hush panel. Remove the steering column trim cover. Remove the heater cover.

4. Remove the glove box.

5. Remove the heater core cover.

6. Remove the heater core clamps. Remove the heater core.

7. Remove the screws holding the defroster actuator to the module case.

8. Remove the evaporator cover. Remove the evaporator from the vehicle.

9. Installation is the reverse of the removal procedure.

FIERO—1984 AND LATER

1. Disconnect the negative battery cable. Discharge the air conditioning system.

2. Tag and disconnect the electrical connections at the module.

3. Remove the evaporator core tube at the accumulator.

4. Disconnect the heater hoses from the heater core.

5. Remove the windshield washer reservoir from the vehicle.

6. Remove the blower housing assembly.

7. Remove the evaporator to condenser tube. Remove the evaporator core.

8. Installation is the reverse of the removal procedure. Charge the air conditioning system. Check for proper operation.

T1000—1982 AND LATER

1. Disconnect the negative battery cable. Discharge the system.

2. Remove the heater core case screws. Remove the heater core case.

3. Remove the accumulator and brackets.

4. Remove the insulation and clamp from the thermostatic switch sensing element.

5. Remove the temperature door cable and the temperature door access cover. Position the control door arm out of the way of the upper evaporator case cover.

6. Remove the blower motor.

7. Remove the sealer around the exposed portion of the outlet tube at the upper surface of the evaporator case.

8. Remove the upper evaporator case. Remove the evaporator core.

9. Installation is the reverse of the removal procedure.

Heater Core

Removal and Installation

For Removal and Installation Procedures of the heater core assembly, Refer to the Heater section.

Air Conditioning Control Head

Removal and Installation

1982 AND LATER MODELS

1. Disconnect the negative battery cable.

2. Remove the necessary instrument trim panels in order to gain access to the control head retaining screws.

3. Remove the control head retaining screws.

4. Slip the control head out from the dash being careful not to damage the electrical connectors, cables or vacuum hoses.

5. Disconnect the electrical connectors and the vacuum hoses.

6. Disconnect the control cables from the control head. Remove the control head from the vehicle.

7. Installation is the reverse of the removal procedure.

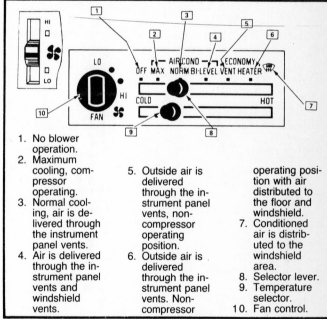

1. No blower operation.
2. Maximum cooling, compressor operating.
3. Normal cooling, air is delivered through the instrument panel vents.
4. Air is delivered through the instrument panel vents and windshield vents.
5. Outside air is delivered through the instrument panel vents, non-compressor operating position.
6. Outside air is delivered through the instrument panel vents. Non-compressor operating position with air distributed to the floor and windshield.
7. Conditioned air is distributed to the windshield area.
8. Selector lever.
9. Temperature selector.
10. Fan control.

A/C control head—typical (© General Motors Corp.)

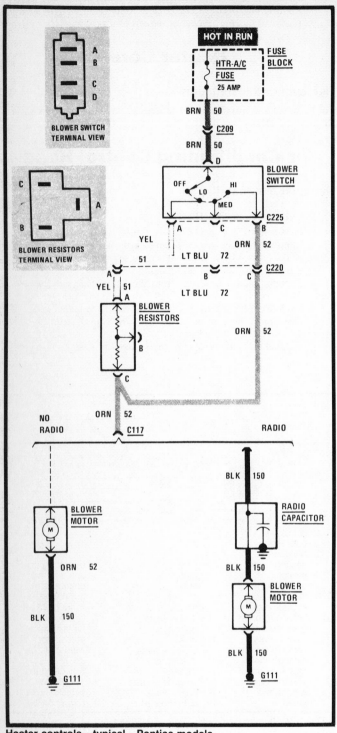

Heater controls—typical—Pontiac models
(© General Motors Corporation)

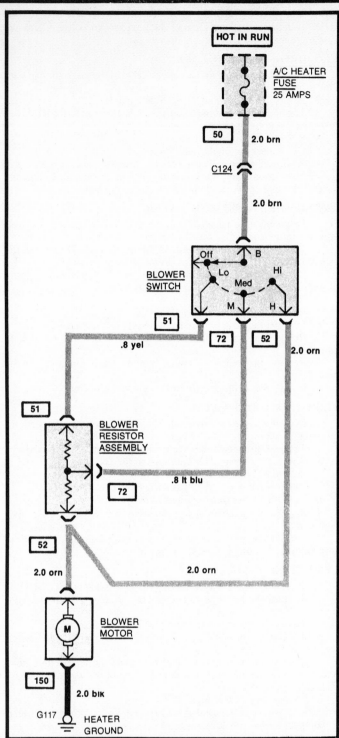

Heater schematics—T1000 models (© General Motors Corporation)

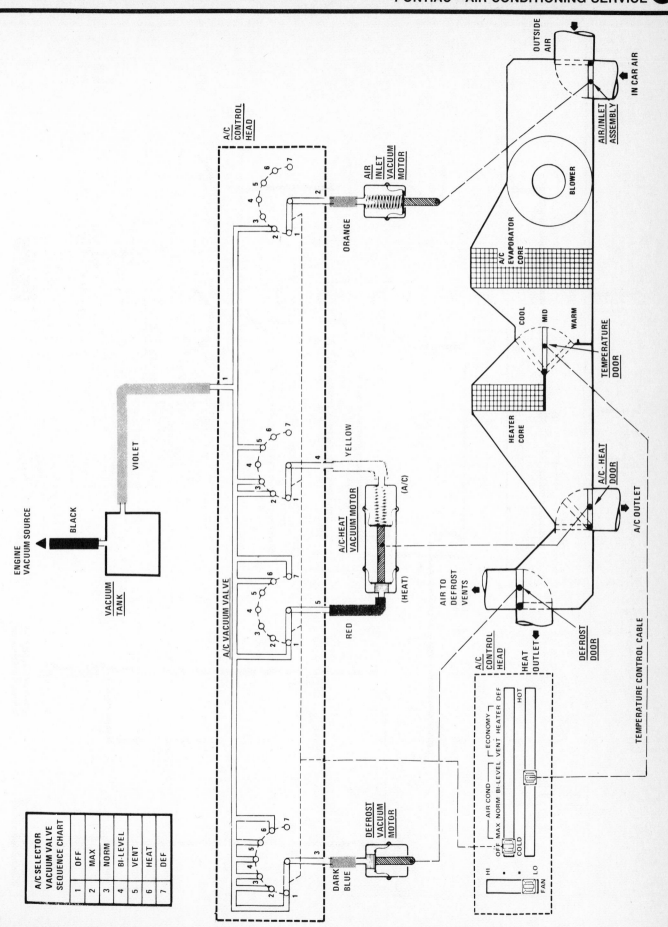

Air conditioning vacuum diagram—6000 models (© General Motors Corporation)

A/C SELECTOR VACUUM VALVE SEQUENCE CHART		
1	OFF	
2	MAX	
3	NORM	
4	BI-LEVEL	
5	VENT	
6	HEAT	
7	DEF	

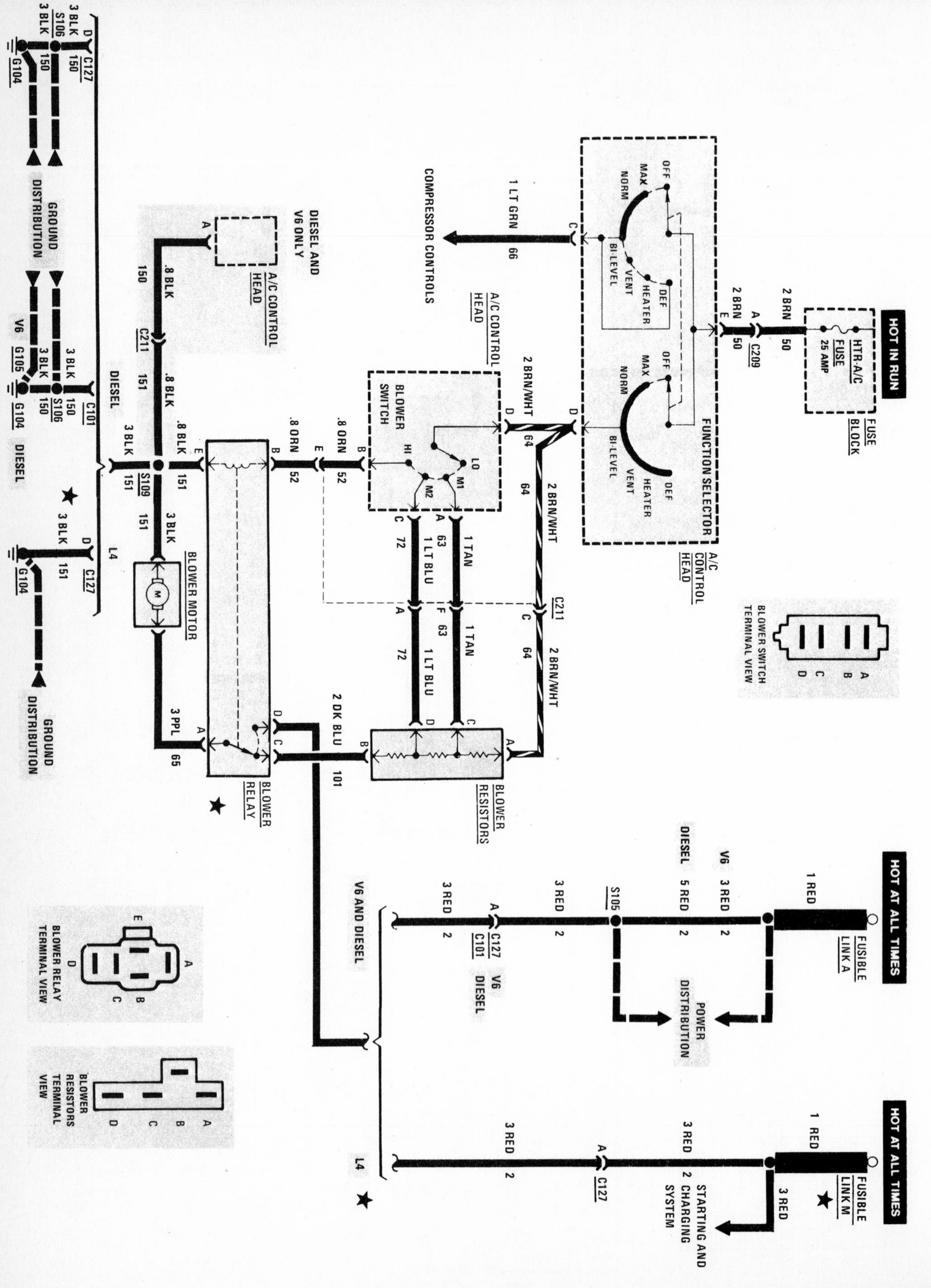

D C127
3 BLK S106
3 BLK 150
G104 150

GROUND DISTRIBUTION

V6
G105 3 BLK
150
3 BLK S106
150
C101 150
DIESEL

3 BLK
S109
151
151
3 BLK
D C127
G104 151

Blower controls—6000 models (© General Motors Corporation)

DIESEL AND V6 ONLY
A/C CONTROL HEAD

A
.8 BLK
150
C211
.8 BLK
151
.8 BLK

3 BLK
151

.8 BLK
E
.8 ORN
52
BLOWER SWITCH
.8 ORN
E 52 B
HI LO
M2 M1
C A
72 63
1 LT BLU 1 TAN

BLOWER MOTOR
M

3 PPL
A
65
BLOWER RELAY

COMPRESSOR CONTROLS
1 LT GRN
66

A/C CONTROL HEAD
2 BRN/WHT
D
64

OFF
MAX NORM
BI-LEVEL VENT DEF HEATER
C

2 BRN
50
E
A C209
50
2 BRN
50
HTR-A/C FUSE 25 AMP
FUSE BLOCK

HOT IN RUN

FUNCTION SELECTOR
A/C CONTROL HEAD

OFF
MAX NORM
BI-LEVEL VENT DEF HEATER
D
64
2 BRN/WHT
C
64
2 BRN/WHT

A 63
F 63
1 TAN
C211

A
72
1 LT BLU

D C
BLOWER RESISTORS
B A
2 DK BLU
101

D C
C

BLOWER SWITCH TERMINAL VIEW
A B
C D

BLOWER RELAY TERMINAL VIEW
E
A
C B

BLOWER RESISTORS TERMINAL VIEW
A B C D

GROUND DISTRIBUTION

V6 AND DIESEL

DIESEL
V6
3 RED
2
A C127
C101
2
3 RED
2
S105
V6 DIESEL
5 RED
2
3 RED
2
1 RED
2
FUSIBLE LINK A

HOT AT ALL TIMES

POWER DISTRIBUTION

L4
3 RED
2
A C127
2
3 RED
2
STARTING AND CHARGING SYSTEM
1 RED
3 RED
FUSIBLE LINK M

HOT AT ALL TIMES

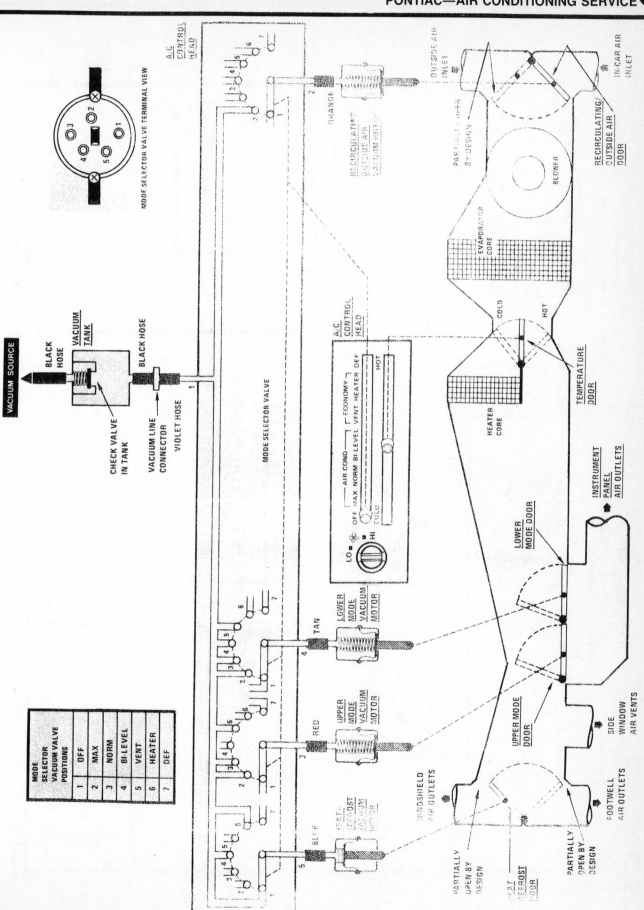

1982 and later Firebird vacuum diagram (© General Motors Corporation)

MODE SELECTOR VACUUM VALVE POSITIONS		
1	OFF	
2	MAX	
3	NORM	
4	BI-LEVEL	
5	VENT	
6	HEATER	
7	DEF	

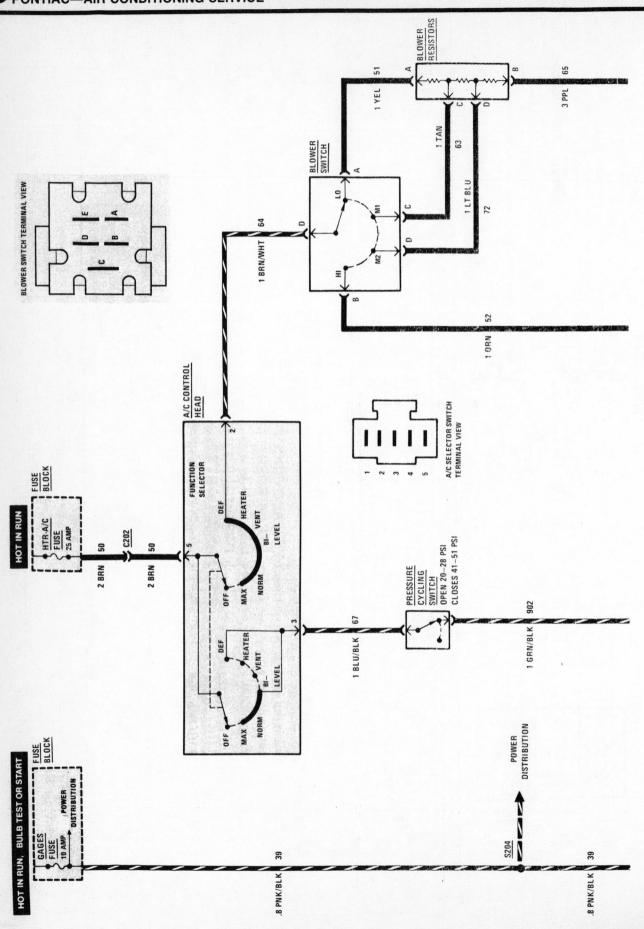

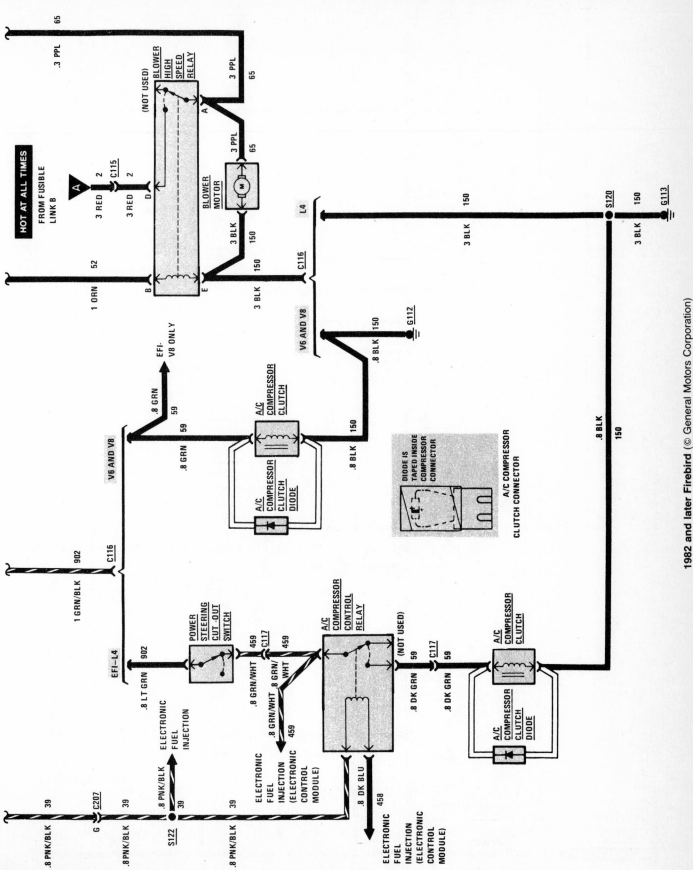

1982 and later Firebird (© General Motors Corporation)

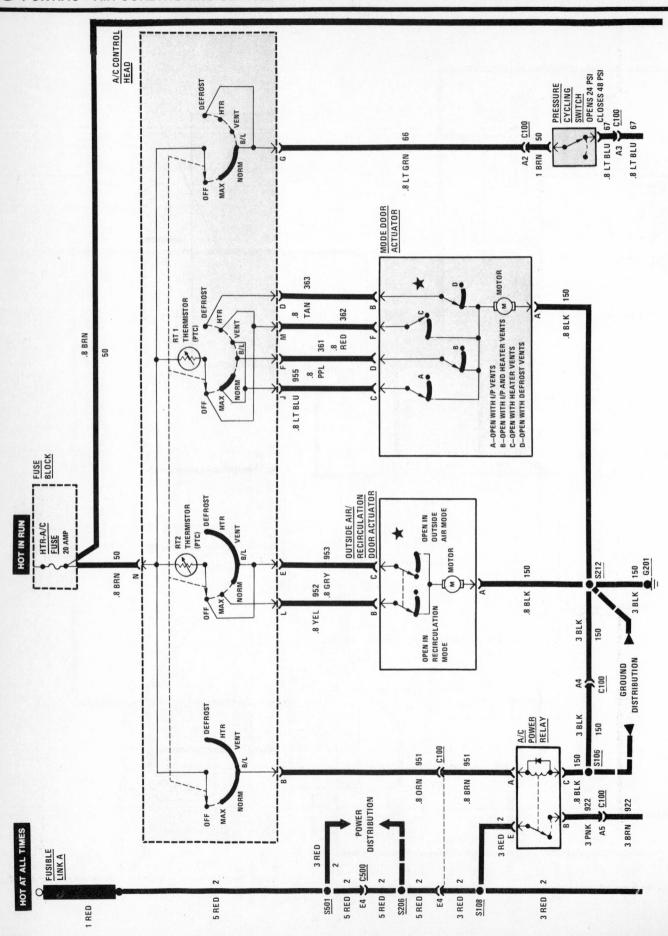

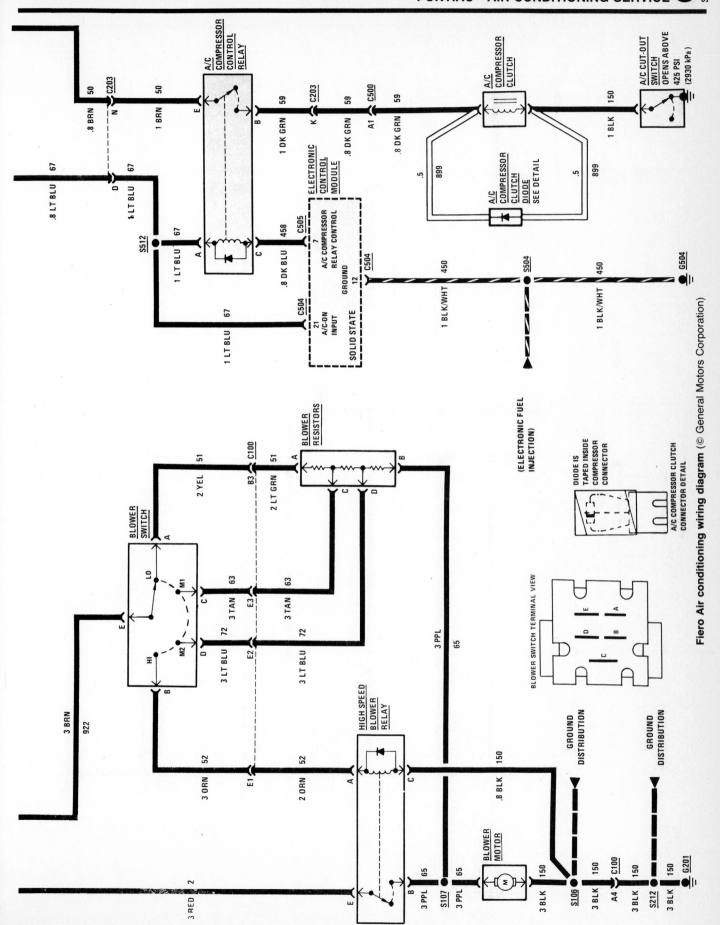

Fiero Air conditioning wiring diagram (© General Motors Corporation)

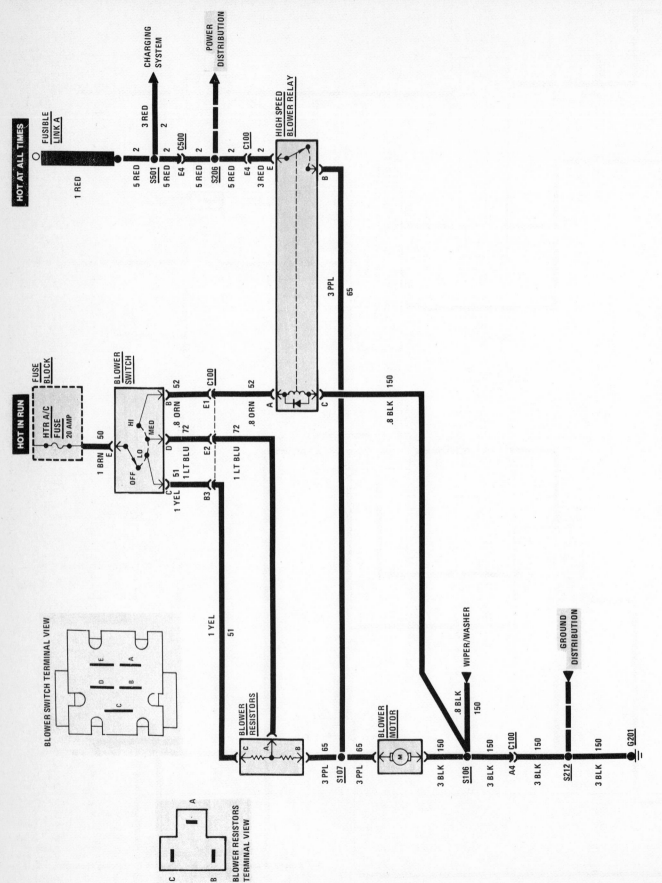

Fiero heater schematic (© General Motors Corporation)

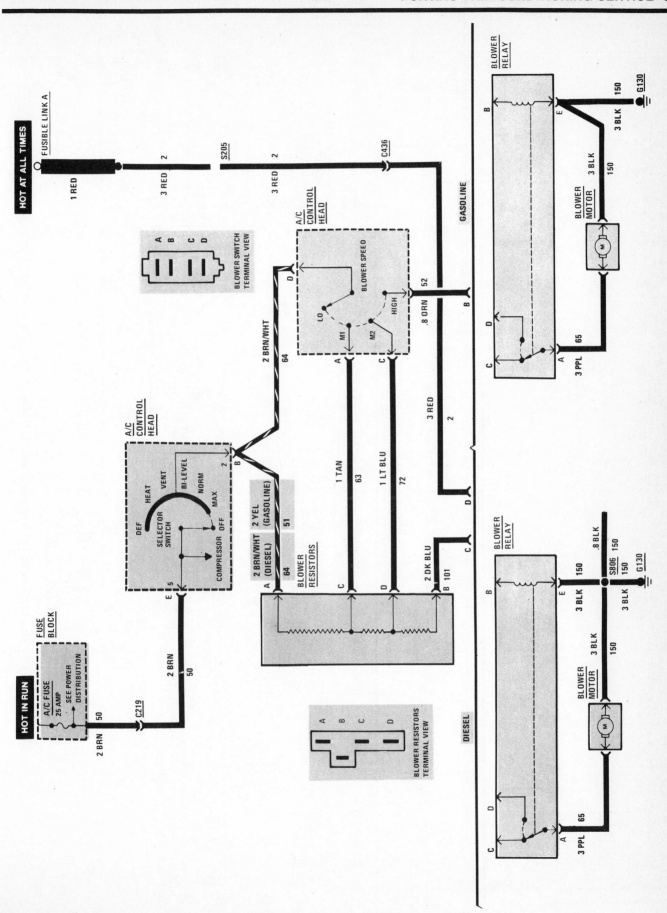

Air conditioner blower schematic—Parisienne—typical (© General Motors Corporation)

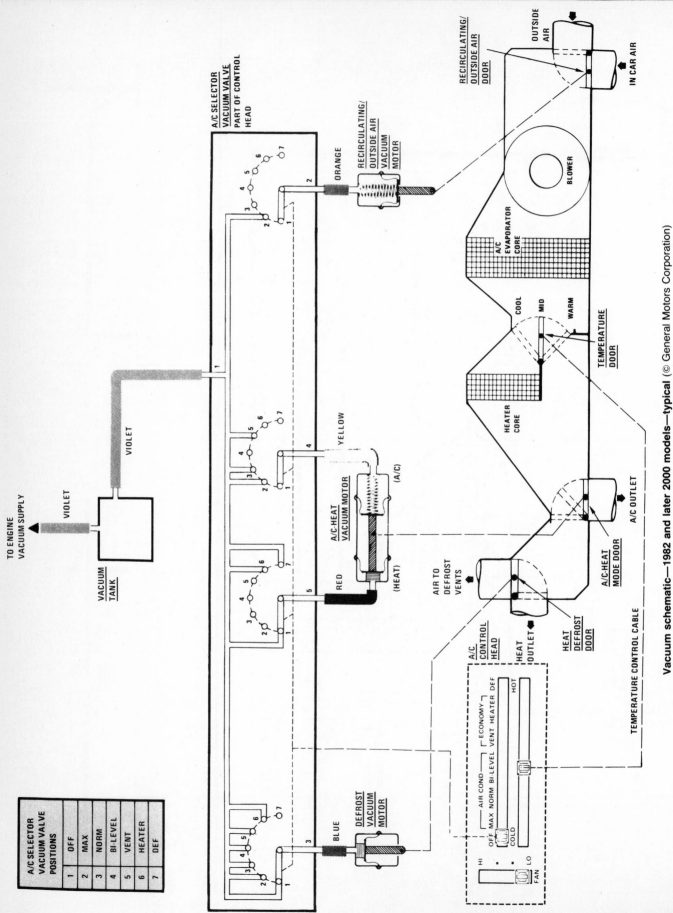

Vacuum schematic—1982 and later 2000 models—typical (© General Motors Corporation)

A/C SELECTOR VACUUM VALVE POSITIONS	
OFF	1
MAX	2
NORM	3
BI-LEVEL	4
VENT	5
HEATER	6
DEF	7

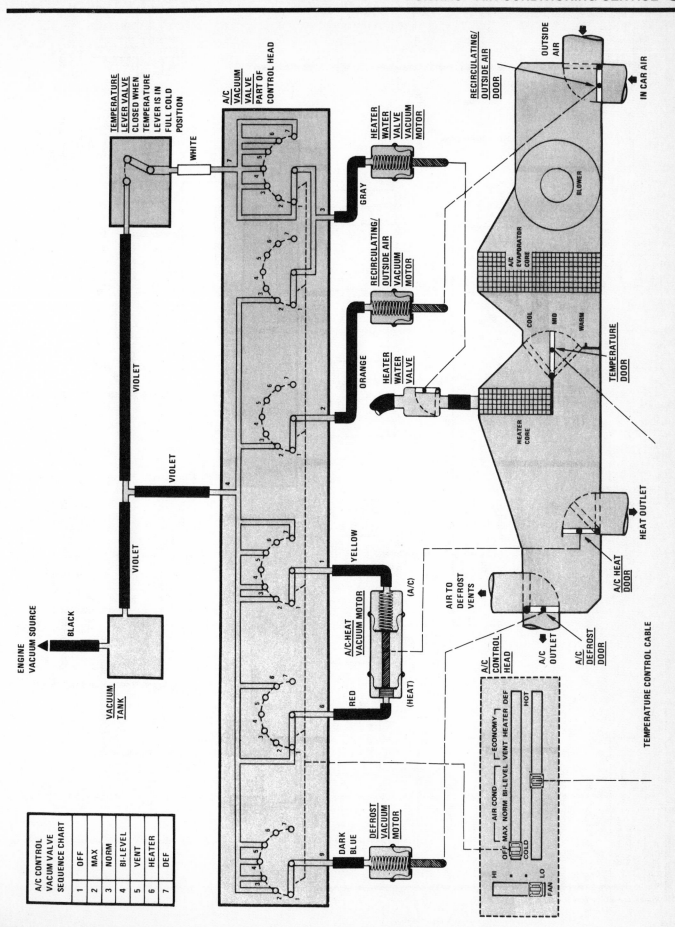

Vacuum diagram—1982 and later Bonneville and Grand Prix (© General Motors Corporation)

TEMPERATURE LEVER VALVE CLOSED WHEN TEMPERATURE LEVER IS IN FULL COLD POSITION

A/C VACUUM VALVE PART OF CONTROL HEAD

WHITE

HEATER WATER VALVE VACUUM MOTOR

RECIRCULATING/OUTSIDE AIR DOOR

OUTSIDE AIR

IN CAR AIR

BLOWER

GRAY

RECIRCULATING/OUTSIDE AIR VACUUM MOTOR

A/C EVAPORATOR CORE

ORANGE

HEATER WATER VALVE

COOL   MID   WARM

TEMPERATURE DOOR

HEATER CORE

VIOLET

VIOLET

VIOLET

HEAT OUTLET

A/C HEAT DOOR

VIOLET

YELLOW

AIR TO DEFROST VENTS

A/C CONTROL HEAD

BLACK

ENGINE VACUUM SOURCE

VACUUM TANK

A/C-HEAT VACUUM MOTOR

(A/C)

(HEAT)

RED

A/C OUTLET

A/C DEFROST DOOR

TEMPERATURE CONTROL CABLE

ECONOMY

AIR COND

OFF MAX NORM BI-LEVEL VENT HEATER DEF

HOT

DARK BLUE

DEFROST VACUUM MOTOR

COLD

HI   LO

FAN

A/C CONTROL VACUUM VALVE SEQUENCE CHART	
1	OFF
2	MAX
3	NORM
4	BI-LEVEL
5	VENT
6	HEATER
7	DEF

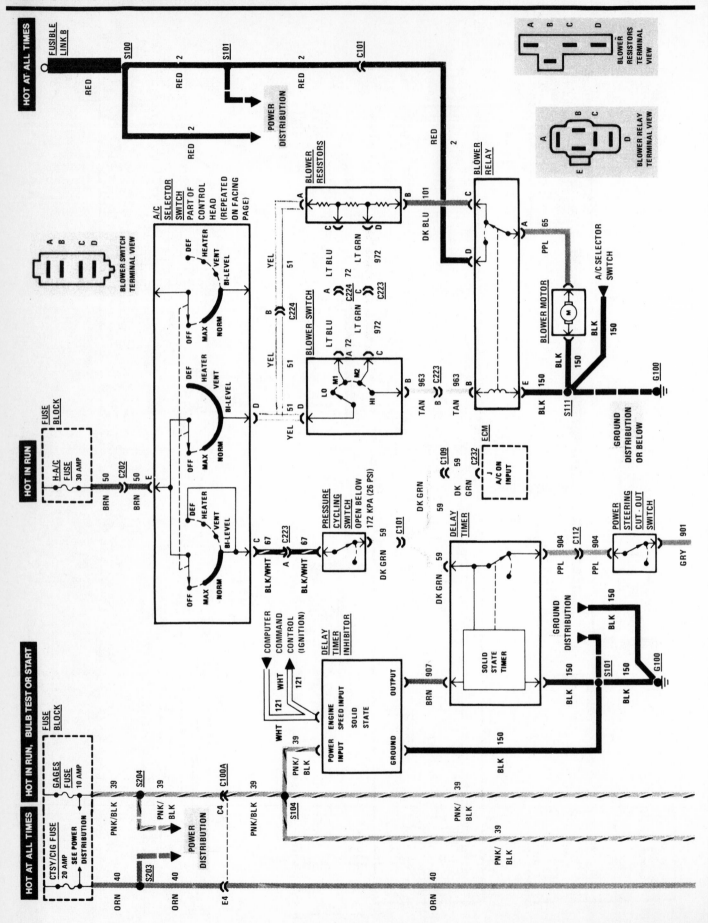

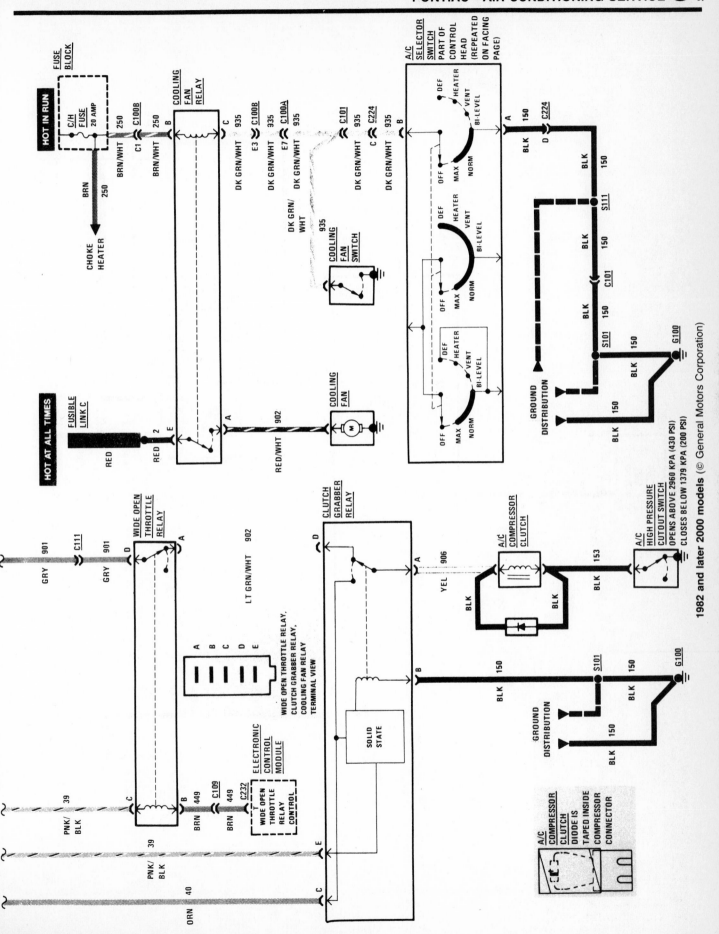

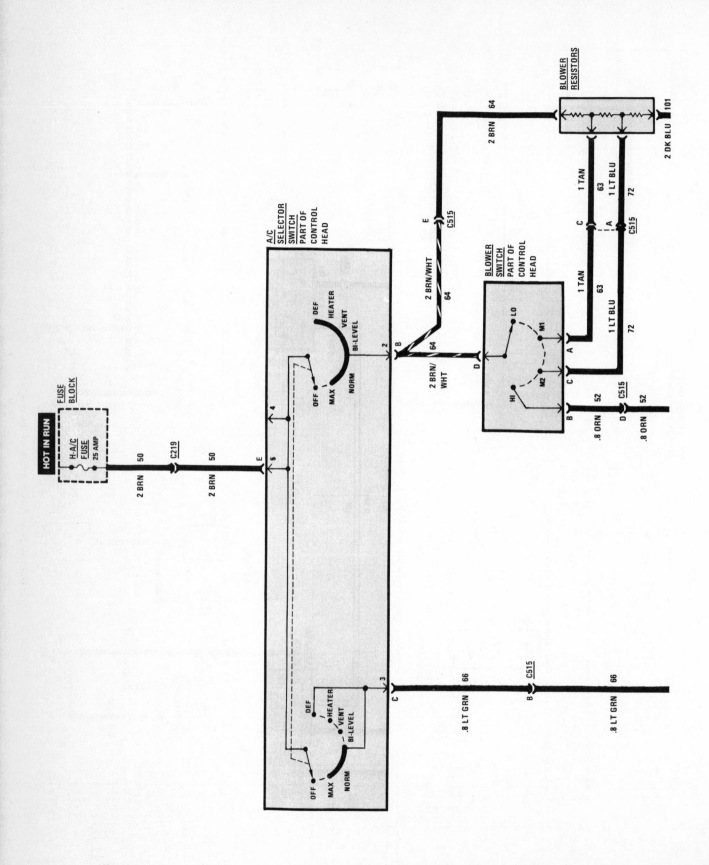

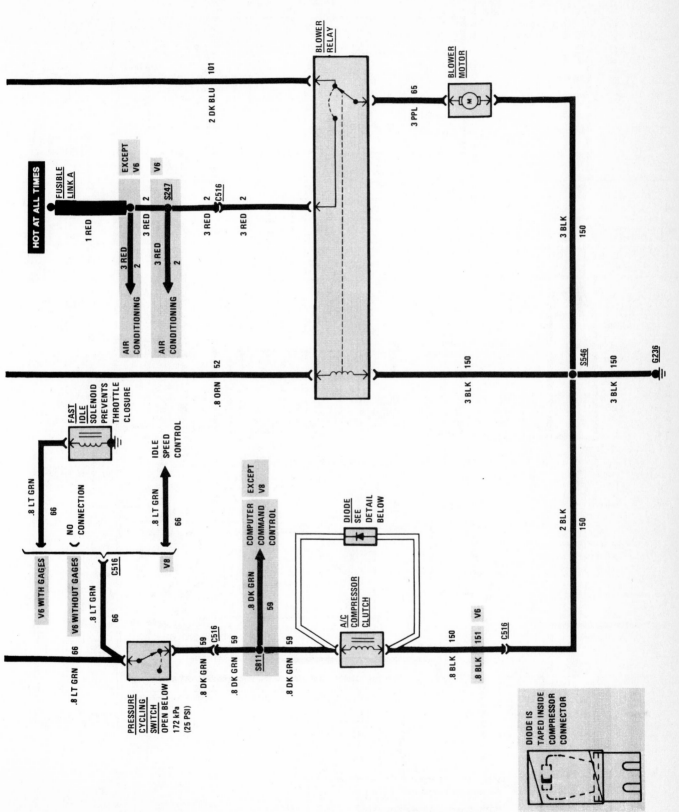

1982 and later Bonneville and Grand Prix wiring diagram (© General Motors Corporation)

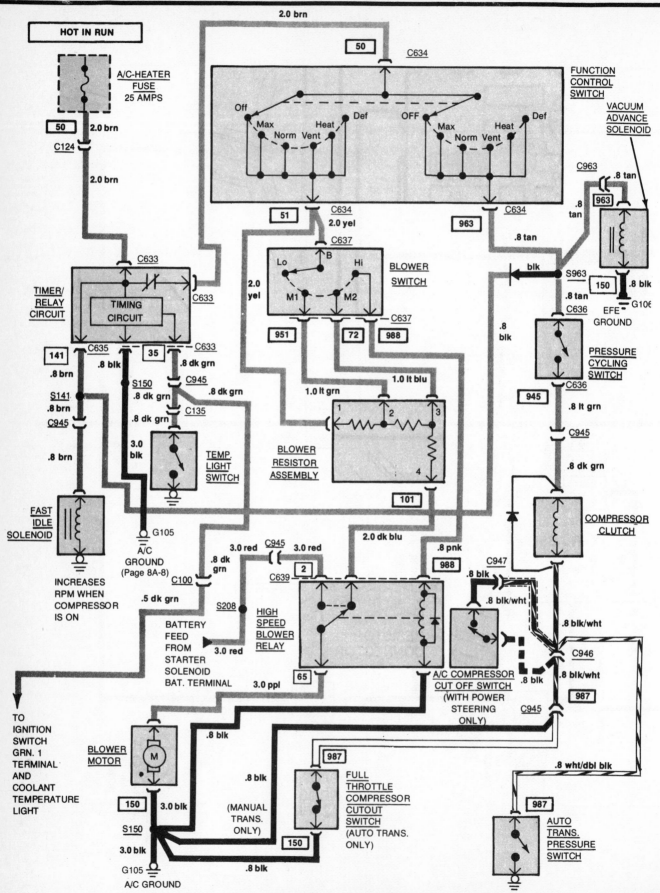

Air conditioner electrical schematic—1982 and later T1000 models (© General Motors Corporation)

C.C.O.T. AIR CONDITIONING SYSTEM DIAGNOSIS

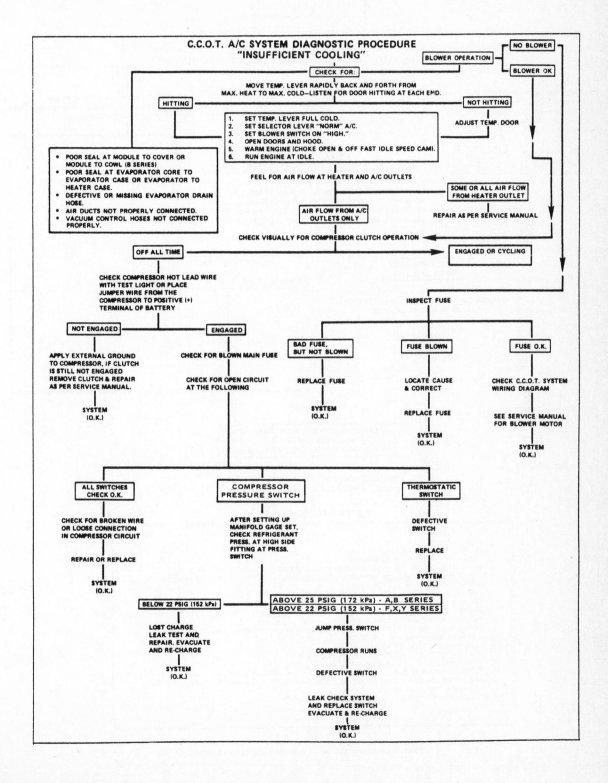

C.C.O.T. A/C SYSTEM DIAGNOSTIC PROCEDURE
"INSUFFICIENT COOLING"

BLOWER OPERATION → NO BLOWER / BLOWER OK

CHECK FOR:

MOVE TEMP. LEVER RAPIDLY BACK AND FORTH FROM
MAX. HEAT TO MAX. COLD—LISTEN FOR DOOR HITTING AT EACH END.

HITTING — NOT HITTING — ADJUST TEMP. DOOR

1. SET TEMP. LEVER FULL COLD.
2. SET SELECTOR LEVER "NORM" A/C.
3. SET BLOWER SWITCH ON "HIGH."
4. OPEN DOORS AND HOOD.
5. WARM ENGINE (CHOKE OPEN & OFF FAST IDLE SPEED CAM).
6. RUN ENGINE AT IDLE.

• POOR SEAL AT MODULE TO COVER OR MODULE TO COWL (B SERIES)
• POOR SEAL AT EVAPORATOR CORE TO EVAPORATOR CASE OR EVAPORATOR TO HEATER CASE.
• DEFECTIVE OR MISSING EVAPORATOR DRAIN HOSE.
• AIR DUCTS NOT PROPERLY CONNECTED.
• VACUUM CONTROL HOSES NOT CONNECTED PROPERLY.

FEEL FOR AIR FLOW AT HEATER AND A/C OUTLETS

SOME OR ALL AIR FLOW FROM HEATER OUTLET

AIR FLOW FROM A/C OUTLETS ONLY

REPAIR AS PER SERVICE MANUAL

CHECK VISUALLY FOR COMPRESSOR CLUTCH OPERATION

OFF ALL TIME → ENGAGED OR CYCLING

CHECK COMPRESSOR HOT LEAD WIRE WITH TEST LIGHT OR PLACE JUMPER WIRE FROM THE COMPRESSOR TO POSITIVE (+) TERMINAL OF BATTERY

INSPECT FUSE

NOT ENGAGED — ENGAGED

APPLY EXTERNAL GROUND TO COMPRESSOR, IF CLUTCH IS STILL NOT ENGAGED REMOVE CLUTCH & REPAIR AS PER SERVICE MANUAL.

SYSTEM (O.K.)

CHECK FOR BLOWN MAIN FUSE

CHECK FOR OPEN CIRCUIT AT THE FOLLOWING

BAD FUSE, BUT NOT BLOWN

REPLACE FUSE

SYSTEM (O.K.)

FUSE BLOWN

LOCATE CAUSE & CORRECT

REPLACE FUSE

SYSTEM (O.K.)

FUSE O.K.

CHECK C.C.O.T. SYSTEM WIRING DIAGRAM

SEE SERVICE MANUAL FOR BLOWER MOTOR

SYSTEM (O.K.)

ALL SWITCHES CHECK O.K.

CHECK FOR BROKEN WIRE OR LOOSE CONNECTION IN COMPRESSOR CIRCUIT

REPAIR OR REPLACE

SYSTEM (O.K.)

COMPRESSOR PRESSURE SWITCH

AFTER SETTING UP MANIFOLD GAGE SET, CHECK REFRIGERANT PRESS. AT HIGH SIDE FITTING AT PRESS. SWITCH

THERMOSTATIC SWITCH

DEFECTIVE SWITCH

REPLACE

SYSTEM (O.K.)

BELOW 22 PSIG (152 kPa)

ABOVE 25 PSIG (172 kPa) - A,B SERIES
ABOVE 22 PSIG (152 kPa) - F,X,Y SERIES

LOST CHARGE LEAK TEST AND REPAIR. EVACUATE AND RE-CHARGE

SYSTEM (O.K.)

JUMP PRESS. SWITCH

COMPRESSOR RUNS

DEFECTIVE SWITCH

LEAK CHECK SYSTEM AND REPLACE SWITCH EVACUATE & RE-CHARGE

SYSTEM (O.K.)

C.C.O.T. AIR CONDITIONING SYSTEM DIAGNOSIS (Cont.)

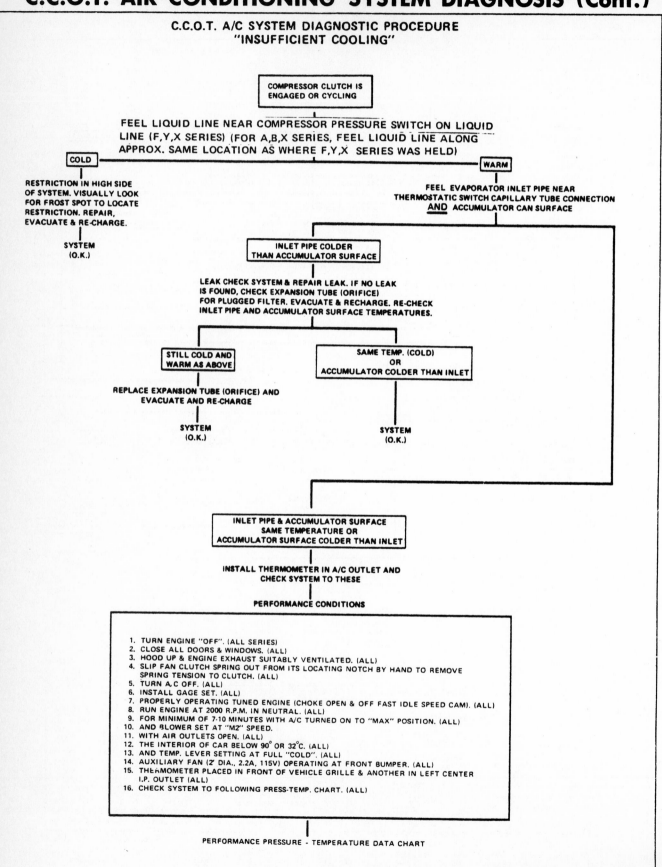

C.C.O.T. A/C SYSTEM DIAGNOSTIC PROCEDURE
"INSUFFICIENT COOLING"

COMPRESSOR CLUTCH IS
ENGAGED OR CYCLING

FEEL LIQUID LINE NEAR COMPRESSOR PRESSURE SWITCH ON LIQUID
LINE (F,Y,X SERIES) (FOR A,B,X SERIES, FEEL LIQUID LINE ALONG
APPROX. SAME LOCATION AS WHERE F,Y,X SERIES WAS HELD)

COLD

WARM

RESTRICTION IN HIGH SIDE
OF SYSTEM. VISUALLY LOOK
FOR FROST SPOT TO LOCATE
RESTRICTION. REPAIR,
EVACUATE & RE-CHARGE.

FEEL EVAPORATOR INLET PIPE NEAR
THERMOSTATIC SWITCH CAPILLARY TUBE CONNECTION
AND ACCUMULATOR CAN SURFACE

SYSTEM
(O.K.)

INLET PIPE COLDER
THAN ACCUMULATOR SURFACE

LEAK CHECK SYSTEM & REPAIR LEAK. IF NO LEAK
IS FOUND, CHECK EXPANSION TUBE (ORIFICE)
FOR PLUGGED FILTER. EVACUATE & RECHARGE. RE-CHECK
INLET PIPE AND ACCUMULATOR SURFACE TEMPERATURES.

STILL COLD AND
WARM AS ABOVE

SAME TEMP. (COLD)
OR
ACCUMULATOR COLDER THAN INLET

REPLACE EXPANSION TUBE (ORIFICE) AND
EVACUATE AND RE-CHARGE

SYSTEM
(O.K.)

SYSTEM
(O.K.)

INLET PIPE & ACCUMULATOR SURFACE
SAME TEMPERATURE OR
ACCUMULATOR SURFACE COLDER THAN INLET

INSTALL THERMOMETER IN A/C OUTLET AND
CHECK SYSTEM TO THESE

PERFORMANCE CONDITIONS

1. TURN ENGINE "OFF". (ALL SERIES)
2. CLOSE ALL DOORS & WINDOWS. (ALL)
3. HOOD UP & ENGINE EXHAUST SUITABLY VENTILATED. (ALL)
4. SLIP FAN CLUTCH SPRING OUT FROM ITS LOCATING NOTCH BY HAND TO REMOVE
   SPRING TENSION TO CLUTCH. (ALL)
5. TURN A.C OFF. (ALL)
6. INSTALL GAGE SET. (ALL)
7. PROPERLY OPERATING TUNED ENGINE (CHOKE OPEN & OFF FAST IDLE SPEED CAM). (ALL)
8. RUN ENGINE AT 2000 R.P.M. IN NEUTRAL. (ALL)
9. FOR MINIMUM OF 7-10 MINUTES WITH A/C TURNED ON TO "MAX" POSITION. (ALL)
10. AND BLOWER SET AT "M2" SPEED.
11. WITH AIR OUTLETS OPEN. (ALL)
12. THE INTERIOR OF CAR BELOW 90° OR 32°C. (ALL)
13. AND TEMP. LEVER SETTING AT FULL "COLD". (ALL)
14. AUXILIARY FAN (2' DIA., 2.2A, 115V) OPERATING AT FRONT BUMPER. (ALL)
15. THERMOMETER PLACED IN FRONT OF VEHICLE GRILLE & ANOTHER IN LEFT CENTER
    I.P. OUTLET (ALL)
16. CHECK SYSTEM TO FOLLOWING PRESS-TEMP. CHART. (ALL)

PERFORMANCE PRESSURE - TEMPERATURE DATA CHART

C.C.O.T. AIR CONDITIONING SYSTEM DIAGNOSIS (Cont.)

C.C.O.T. A/C SYSTEM DIAGNOSTIC PROCEDURE
"INSUFFICIENT COOLING"

PERFORMANCE PRESSURE—TEMPERATURE CHART

|
REFRIGERANT CHARGE
|

TEMPERATURE OF AIR ENTERING CONDENSER			70°F (21°C)	80°F (27°C)	90°F (32°C)	100°F (38°C)	110°F (43°C)
*COMPRESSOR OUT PRESSURE (BEFORE EXPANSION ORIFICE)	A SERIES		125-175 psi 862-1207 kPa	145-195 psi 1000-1345 kPa	170-220 psi 1172-1517 kPa	195-245 psi 1345-1689 kPa	226-275 psi 1551-1896 kPa
	B SERIES		140-180 psi 965-1241 kPa	170-210 psi 1172-1448 kPa	200-240 psi 1379-1655 kPa	235-275 psi 1620-1896 kPa	265-305 psi 1827-2103 kPa
	F SERIES			195-235 psi 1345-1620 kPa		225-265 psi 1551-1827 kPa	
	X SERIES			160-200 psi 1103-1379 kPa		215-255 psi 1482-1758 kPa	
*EVAPORATOR PRESSURE (AT ACCUMULATOR)**	A SERIES		25-32 psi 172-221 kPa	25-32 psi 172-221 kPa	25-32 psi 172-221 kPa	25-32 psi 172-221 kPa	25-32 psi 172-221 kPa
	B SERIES		24-27 psi 165-186 kPa	24-27 psi 165-186 kPa	24-27 psi 165-186 kPa	24-27 psi 165-186 kPa	24-27 psi 165-186 kPa
	F SERIES			24-27 psi 165-186 kPa		24-27 psi 165-186 kPa	
	X SERIES			24-27 psi 165-186 kPa		24-27 psi 165-186 kPa	
*DISCHARGE AIR TEMPERATURE— LEFT CENTER OUTLET	A SERIES		39-44°F 283-303°C	40-45°F 276-310°C	41-46°F 283-317°C	43-48°F 296-331°C	45-50°F 310-345°C
	B SERIES		41-43°F 283-296°C	42-44°F 290-303°C	42-44°F 290-303°C	43-45°F 296-310°C	43-45°F 296-310°C
	F SERIES			38-45°F 262-310°C		38-45°F 262-310°C	
	X SERIES			38-45°F 262-310°C		38-45°F 262-310°C	

*Just before compressor disengages   **At sea level

OUTLET TEMP. O.K. OR TOO COLD AS PER CHART

CHANGE BLOWER SPEED TO LOW, AND OBSERVE ACCUMULATOR AND EVAPORATOR PIPES FOR FROST

NO FROST → SYSTEM (O.K.)

FROST → DEFECTIVE THERMOSTATIC SWITCH → REPLACE → SYSTEM (O.K.)

OUTLET TEMP. HIGH AS PER CHART

CHECK ACCUMULATOR PRESS. (AS PER CHART)

LOW

PLUGGED EXPANSION TUBE (ORIFICE) REPAIR OR REPLACE, REPLACE ACCUMULATOR ASM. AND EVACUATE & RE-CHARGE SYSTEM

SYSTEM (O.K.)

HIGH TO NORMAL

CHECK COMPRESSOR CYCLING

ON CONTINUOUSLY

CHECK FOR MISSING EXPANSION TUBE (ORIFICE)

MISSING → INSTALL EXPANSION TUBE (ORIFICE) EVACUATE & RE-CHARGE → SYSTEM (O.K.)

IN PLACE → CHECK COMPRESSOR INLET SCREEN

PLUGGED → REPAIR OR REPLACE SCREEN, REPLACE ACCUMULATOR ASM. EVACUATE & RE-CHARGE → SYSTEM (O.K.)

CLEAN → SYSTEM OVER-CHARGED EVACUATE & RE-CHARGE → SYSTEM (O.K.)

CYCLES ON AND OFF

DEFECTIVE THERMOSTATIC SWITCH

REPLACE

SYSTEM (O.K.)

AIR CONDITIONING FUNCTIONAL TEST

	CONTROL SETTINGS			SYSTEM RESPONSE					
STEP	MODE CONTROL	TEMPERATURE CONTROL	FAN SWITCH	BLOWER SPEED	COMPRESSOR	AIR VALVE	HEATER OUTLETS	A/C OUTLETS	DEFROSTER OUTLETS
1	OFF	COLD	LO	OFF	OFF	O/S AIR	RAM AIR FLOW	NO AIR FLOW	RAM AIR FLOW
2	MAX	COLD	LO	LO	ON	I/S AIR	NO AIR FLOW	COLD AIR FLOW	NO AIR FLOW
3	MAX	COLD	LO TO HI	LO TO HI	ON	I/S AIR	NO AIR FLOW	COLD AIR FLOW	NO AIR FLOW
4	NORM	COLD	HI	HI	ON	O/S AIR	NO AIR FLOW	COLD AIR FLOW	NO AIR FLOW
5	BI-LEVEL	COLD	HI	HI	ON	O/S AIR	COLD AIR FLOW	COLD AIR FLOW	MINIMUM AIR FLOW
6	VENT	COLD	HI	HI	OFF	O/S AIR	NO AIR FLOW	AMBIENT AIR	NO AIR FLOW
7	HEATER	HOT	HI	HI	OFF	O/S AIR	HOT AIR FLOW	NO AIR FLOW	MINIMUM AIR FLOW
8	DEF	HOT	HI	HI	ON	O/S AIR	MINIMUM AIR FLOW	NO AIR FLOW	MAXIMUM AIR FLOW

Table title: A/C FUNCTIONAL TEST

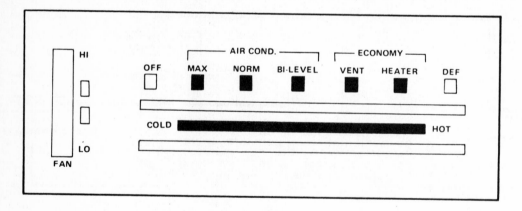

INSUFFICIENT COOLING DIAGNOSIS

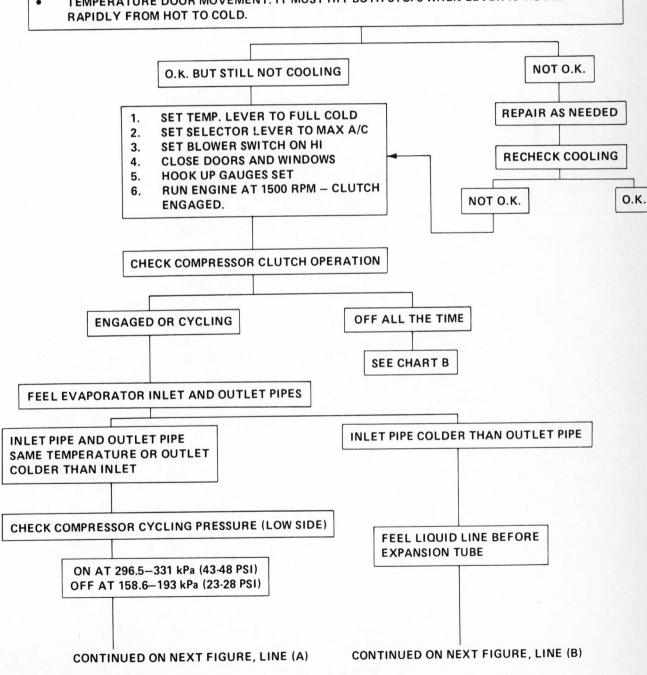

CHECK FOR:

- LOOSE, MISSING OR DAMAGED DRIVE BELT.
- LOOSE OR DISCONNECTED A/C WIRE CONNECTORS UNDER HOOD. INCLUDING: COMPRESSOR, WIDE OPEN THROTTLE SWITCH, HIGH PRESSURE CUT-OFF SWITCH, AND PRESSURE CYCLING SWITCH.
- BLOWN A/C FUSE.
- TEMPERATURE DOOR MOVEMENT. IT MUST HIT BOTH STOPS WHEN LEVER IS MOVED RAPIDLY FROM HOT TO COLD.

O.K. BUT STILL NOT COOLING

NOT O.K.

REPAIR AS NEEDED

RECHECK COOLING

1. SET TEMP. LEVER TO FULL COLD
2. SET SELECTOR LEVER TO MAX A/C
3. SET BLOWER SWITCH ON HI
4. CLOSE DOORS AND WINDOWS
5. HOOK UP GAUGES SET
6. RUN ENGINE AT 1500 RPM — CLUTCH ENGAGED.

NOT O.K.

O.K.

CHECK COMPRESSOR CLUTCH OPERATION

ENGAGED OR CYCLING

OFF ALL THE TIME

SEE CHART B

FEEL EVAPORATOR INLET AND OUTLET PIPES

INLET PIPE AND OUTLET PIPE SAME TEMPERATURE OR OUTLET COLDER THAN INLET

INLET PIPE COLDER THAN OUTLET PIPE

CHECK COMPRESSOR CYCLING PRESSURE (LOW SIDE)

FEEL LIQUID LINE BEFORE EXPANSION TUBE

ON AT 296.5—331 kPa (43-48 PSI)
OFF AT 158.6—193 kPa (23-28 PSI)

CONTINUED ON NEXT FIGURE, LINE (A)

CONTINUED ON NEXT FIGURE, LINE (B)

INSUFFICIENT COOLING DIAGNOSIS (Cont.)

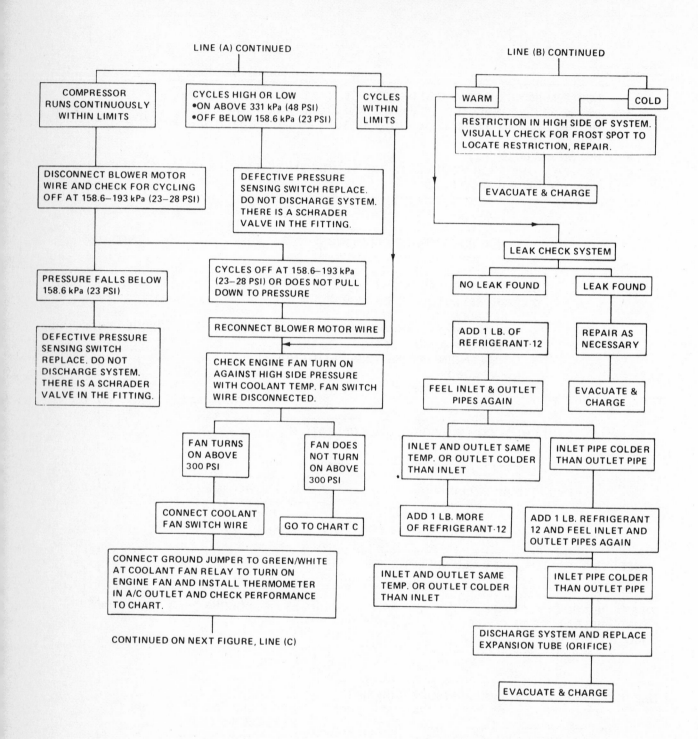

LINE (A) CONTINUED

COMPRESSOR RUNS CONTINUOUSLY WITHIN LIMITS

CYCLES HIGH OR LOW
• ON ABOVE 331 kPa (48 PSI)
• OFF BELOW 158.6 kPa (23 PSI)

CYCLES WITHIN LIMITS

DISCONNECT BLOWER MOTOR WIRE AND CHECK FOR CYCLING OFF AT 158.6–193 kPa (23–28 PSI)

DEFECTIVE PRESSURE SENSING SWITCH REPLACE. DO NOT DISCHARGE SYSTEM. THERE IS A SCHRADER VALVE IN THE FITTING.

PRESSURE FALLS BELOW 158.6 kPa (23 PSI)

CYCLES OFF AT 158.6–193 kPa (23–28 PSI) OR DOES NOT PULL DOWN TO PRESSURE

DEFECTIVE PRESSURE SENSING SWITCH REPLACE. DO NOT DISCHARGE SYSTEM. THERE IS A SCHRADER VALVE IN THE FITTING.

RECONNECT BLOWER MOTOR WIRE

CHECK ENGINE FAN TURN ON AGAINST HIGH SIDE PRESSURE WITH COOLANT TEMP. FAN SWITCH WIRE DISCONNECTED.

FAN TURNS ON ABOVE 300 PSI

FAN DOES NOT TURN ON ABOVE 300 PSI

CONNECT COOLANT FAN SWITCH WIRE

GO TO CHART C

CONNECT GROUND JUMPER TO GREEN/WHITE AT COOLANT FAN RELAY TO TURN ON ENGINE FAN AND INSTALL THERMOMETER IN A/C OUTLET AND CHECK PERFORMANCE TO CHART.

CONTINUED ON NEXT FIGURE, LINE (C)

LINE (B) CONTINUED

WARM   **COLD**

RESTRICTION IN HIGH SIDE OF SYSTEM. VISUALLY CHECK FOR FROST SPOT TO LOCATE RESTRICTION, REPAIR.

EVACUATE & CHARGE

LEAK CHECK SYSTEM

NO LEAK FOUND   **LEAK FOUND**

ADD 1 LB. OF REFRIGERANT-12

REPAIR AS NECESSARY

FEEL INLET & OUTLET PIPES AGAIN

EVACUATE & CHARGE

INLET AND OUTLET SAME TEMP. OR OUTLET COLDER THAN INLET

INLET PIPE COLDER THAN OUTLET PIPE

ADD 1 LB. MORE OF REFRIGERANT-12

ADD 1 LB. REFRIGERANT 12 AND FEEL INLET AND OUTLET PIPES AGAIN

INLET AND OUTLET SAME TEMP. OR OUTLET COLDER THAN INLET

INLET PIPE COLDER THAN OUTLET PIPE

DISCHARGE SYSTEM AND REPLACE EXPANSION TUBE (ORIFICE)

EVACUATE & CHARGE

INSUFFICIENT COOLING DIAGNOSIS (Cont.)

LINE (C) CONTINUED

TEMP. OF AIR ENTERING THE CONDENSER	70°F.	80°F.	90°F.	100°F.	110°F.
*COMPRESSOR OUT PRESSURE	135-170 psi 930-1170 kPa	170-205 psi 1170-1410 kPa	205-245 psi 1410-1690 kPa	245-285 psi 1690-1960 kPa	285-320 psi 1960-2100 kPa
*ACCUMULATOR PRESSURE	23-28 psi 158-193 kPa	23-29 psi 158-200 kPa	26-35 psi 185-240 kPa	31-40 psi 215-275 kPa	35-44 psi 185-305 kPa
DISCHARGE AIR TEMP.—LEFT CENTER OUTLET	36-43°F. 1-6°C.	36-43°F. 1-6°C.	36-43°F. 1-6°C.	42-48°F. 5-9°C.	48-53°F. 9-11°C.

*JUST BEFORE COMPRESSOR ENGAGES, IF CYCLING.

OUTLET TEMPERATURE WITHIN LIMITS

OUTLET TEMPERATURE HIGH

COMPARE COMPRESSOR OUT PRESSURE (HIGH SIDE) TO CHART

CHECK FOR OVERCHARGE BY DISCHARGING REFRIGERANT 30 SECONDS AT A TIME UP TO 4 TIMES CHECK OUTLET TEMPERATURE AFTER EACH DISCHARGE.

WITHIN LIMITS

NOT IN LIMITS

TEMPERATURE O.K.

TEMPERATURE NOT O.K.

DISCONNECT JUMPER FROM FAN RELAY

DISCONNECT JUMPER FROM FAN RELAY

SYSTEM OK

SYSTEM OVERCHARGED

DISCHARGE AND REPLACE EXPANSION TUBE (ORIFICE)

DISCHARGE REFRIGERANT UNTIL CLUTCH CYCLES

EVACUATE AND RECHARGE

DISCONNECT JUMPER FROM FAN RELAY

DISCONNECT JUMPER FROM FAN RELAY

COMPRESSOR CLUTCH OPERATION

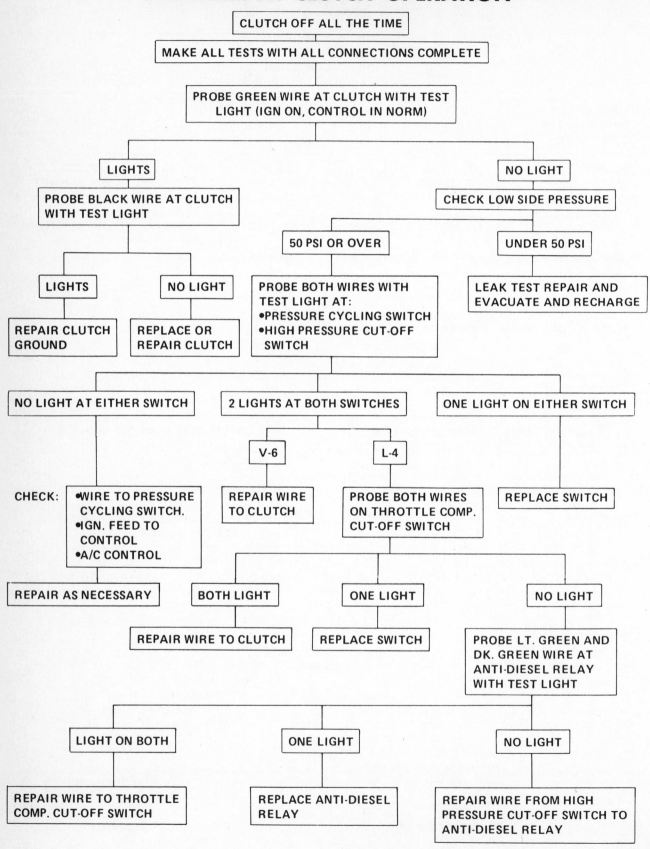

CLUTCH OFF ALL THE TIME

MAKE ALL TESTS WITH ALL CONNECTIONS COMPLETE

PROBE GREEN WIRE AT CLUTCH WITH TEST LIGHT (IGN ON, CONTROL IN NORM)

LIGHTS

PROBE BLACK WIRE AT CLUTCH WITH TEST LIGHT

LIGHTS → REPAIR CLUTCH GROUND

NO LIGHT → REPLACE OR REPAIR CLUTCH

NO LIGHT

CHECK LOW SIDE PRESSURE

50 PSI OR OVER

PROBE BOTH WIRES WITH TEST LIGHT AT:
•PRESSURE CYCLING SWITCH
•HIGH PRESSURE CUT-OFF SWITCH

UNDER 50 PSI

LEAK TEST REPAIR AND EVACUATE AND RECHARGE

NO LIGHT AT EITHER SWITCH

CHECK: •WIRE TO PRESSURE CYCLING SWITCH.
•IGN. FEED TO CONTROL
•A/C CONTROL

REPAIR AS NECESSARY

2 LIGHTS AT BOTH SWITCHES

V-6 → REPAIR WIRE TO CLUTCH

L-4 → PROBE BOTH WIRES ON THROTTLE COMP. CUT-OFF SWITCH

ONE LIGHT ON EITHER SWITCH → REPLACE SWITCH

BOTH LIGHT → REPAIR WIRE TO CLUTCH

ONE LIGHT → REPLACE SWITCH

NO LIGHT → PROBE LT. GREEN AND DK. GREEN WIRE AT ANTI-DIESEL RELAY WITH TEST LIGHT

LIGHT ON BOTH → REPAIR WIRE TO THROTTLE COMP. CUT-OFF SWITCH

ONE LIGHT → REPLACE ANTI-DIESEL RELAY

NO LIGHT → REPAIR WIRE FROM HIGH PRESSURE CUT-OFF SWITCH TO ANTI-DIESEL RELAY

ENGINE COOLING FAN OPERATION

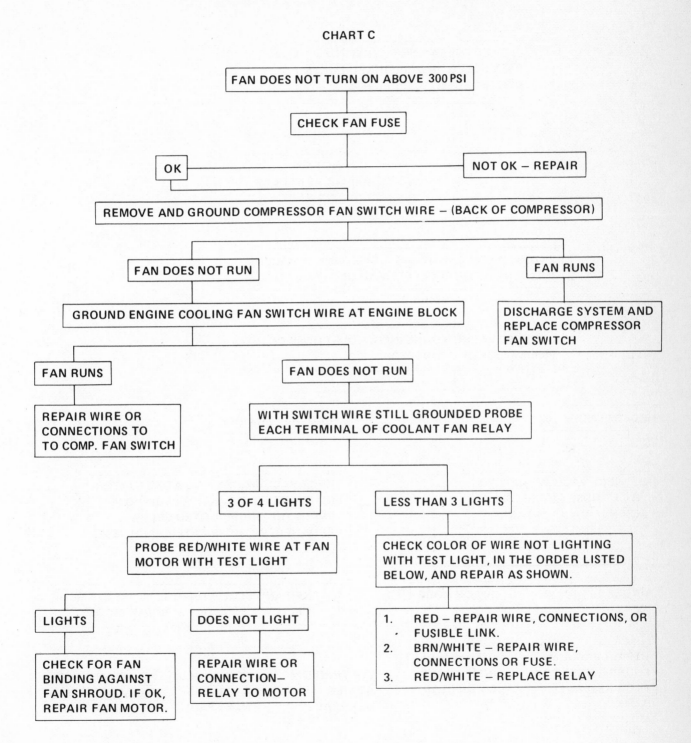

CHART C

FAN DOES NOT TURN ON ABOVE 300 PSI

CHECK FAN FUSE

OK

NOT OK – REPAIR

REMOVE AND GROUND COMPRESSOR FAN SWITCH WIRE – (BACK OF COMPRESSOR)

FAN DOES NOT RUN

FAN RUNS

DISCHARGE SYSTEM AND REPLACE COMPRESSOR FAN SWITCH

GROUND ENGINE COOLING FAN SWITCH WIRE AT ENGINE BLOCK

FAN RUNS

REPAIR WIRE OR CONNECTIONS TO TO COMP. FAN SWITCH

FAN DOES NOT RUN

WITH SWITCH WIRE STILL GROUNDED PROBE EACH TERMINAL OF COOLANT FAN RELAY

3 OF 4 LIGHTS

LESS THAN 3 LIGHTS

PROBE RED/WHITE WIRE AT FAN MOTOR WITH TEST LIGHT

CHECK COLOR OF WIRE NOT LIGHTING WITH TEST LIGHT, IN THE ORDER LISTED BELOW, AND REPAIR AS SHOWN.

LIGHTS

DOES NOT LIGHT

CHECK FOR FAN BINDING AGAINST FAN SHROUD. IF OK, REPAIR FAN MOTOR.

REPAIR WIRE OR CONNECTION– RELAY TO MOTOR

1. RED – REPAIR WIRE, CONNECTIONS, OR FUSIBLE LINK.
2. BRN/WHITE – REPAIR WIRE, CONNECTIONS OR FUSE.
3. RED/WHITE – REPLACE RELAY

AIR FLOW FROM INCORRECT OUTLET

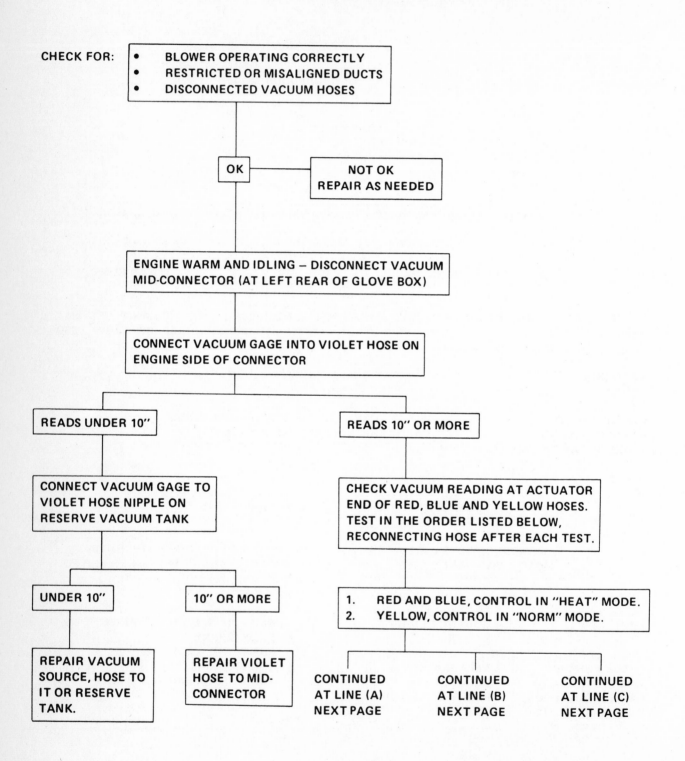

CHECK FOR:
- BLOWER OPERATING CORRECTLY
- RESTRICTED OR MISALIGNED DUCTS
- DISCONNECTED VACUUM HOSES

OK — NOT OK
REPAIR AS NEEDED

ENGINE WARM AND IDLING — DISCONNECT VACUUM MID-CONNECTOR (AT LEFT REAR OF GLOVE BOX)

CONNECT VACUUM GAGE INTO VIOLET HOSE ON ENGINE SIDE OF CONNECTOR

READS UNDER 10''

READS 10'' OR MORE

CONNECT VACUUM GAGE TO VIOLET HOSE NIPPLE ON RESERVE VACUUM TANK

CHECK VACUUM READING AT ACTUATOR END OF RED, BLUE AND YELLOW HOSES. TEST IN THE ORDER LISTED BELOW, RECONNECTING HOSE AFTER EACH TEST.

UNDER 10''

10'' OR MORE

1. RED AND BLUE, CONTROL IN "HEAT" MODE.
2. YELLOW, CONTROL IN "NORM" MODE.

REPAIR VACUUM SOURCE, HOSE TO IT OR RESERVE TANK.

REPAIR VIOLET HOSE TO MID-CONNECTOR

CONTINUED AT LINE (A) NEXT PAGE

CONTINUED AT LINE (B) NEXT PAGE

CONTINUED AT LINE (C) NEXT PAGE

AIR FLOW FROM INCORRECT OUTLET (Cont.)

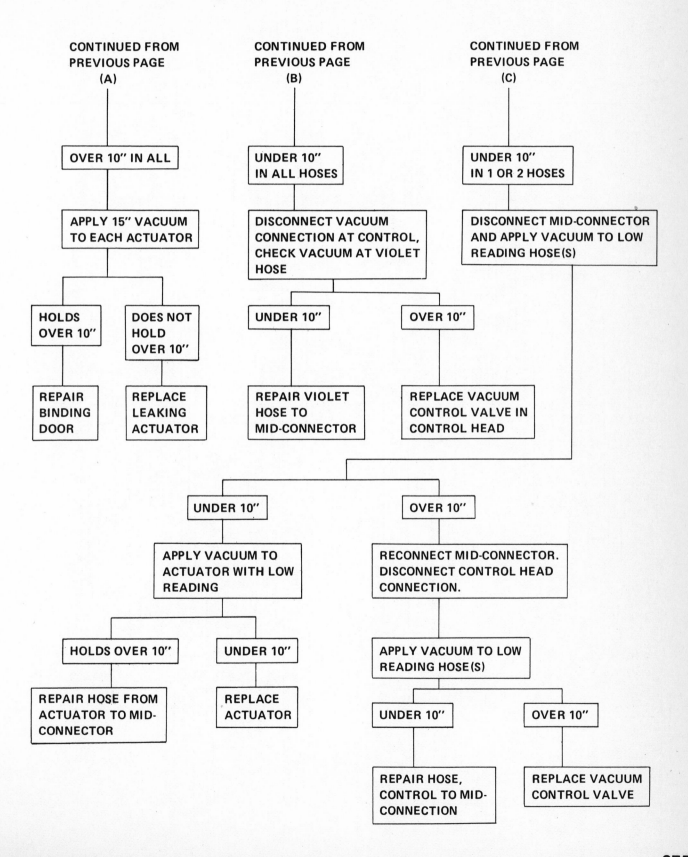

CONTINUED FROM PREVIOUS PAGE (A)

OVER 10" IN ALL

APPLY 15" VACUUM TO EACH ACTUATOR

HOLDS OVER 10"

DOES NOT HOLD OVER 10"

REPAIR BINDING DOOR

REPLACE LEAKING ACTUATOR

CONTINUED FROM PREVIOUS PAGE (B)

UNDER 10" IN ALL HOSES

DISCONNECT VACUUM CONNECTION AT CONTROL, CHECK VACUUM AT VIOLET HOSE

UNDER 10"

OVER 10"

REPAIR VIOLET HOSE TO MID-CONNECTOR

REPLACE VACUUM CONTROL VALVE IN CONTROL HEAD

CONTINUED FROM PREVIOUS PAGE (C)

UNDER 10" IN 1 OR 2 HOSES

DISCONNECT MID-CONNECTOR AND APPLY VACUUM TO LOW READING HOSE(S)

UNDER 10"

APPLY VACUUM TO ACTUATOR WITH LOW READING

HOLDS OVER 10"

UNDER 10"

REPAIR HOSE FROM ACTUATOR TO MID-CONNECTOR

REPLACE ACTUATOR

OVER 10"

RECONNECT MID-CONNECTOR. DISCONNECT CONTROL HEAD CONNECTION.

APPLY VACUUM TO LOW READING HOSE(S)

UNDER 10"

OVER 10"

REPAIR HOSE, CONTROL TO MID-CONNECTION

REPLACE VACUUM CONTROL VALVE

INSUFFICIENT COOLING DIAGNOSIS

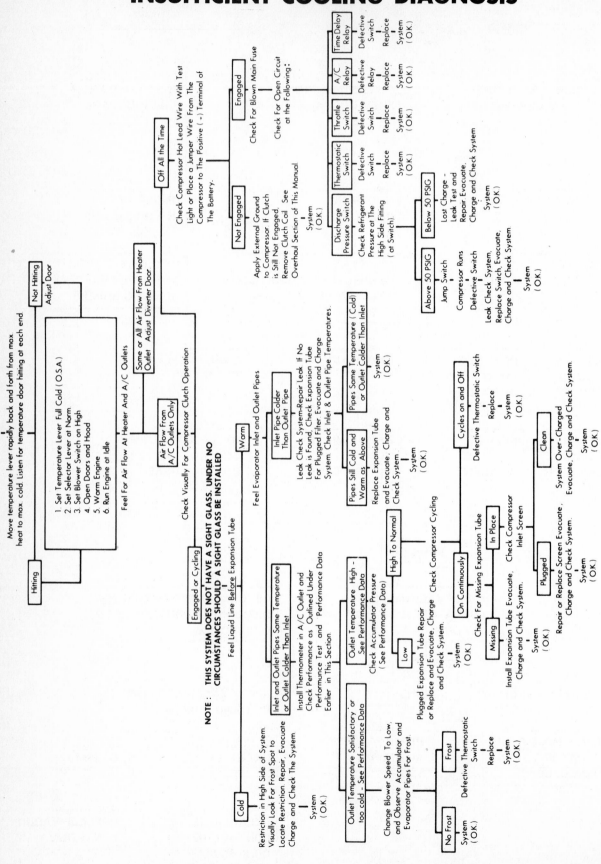

MANUAL AIR CONDITIONING FUNCTIONAL TEST

C60   A/C FUNCTIONAL TEST

Prior to test initiation, the engine should idle off fast idle speed cam, with the temperature lever set to maximum COLD, for about 20 minutes or until the engine thermostat is open (195°F. or 91°C.). Ambient temperature should be about 75°F. (24°C.) but not lower than 45°F. (7°C.) or above 90°F. (32°C.). Control lever efforts must also be checked. These efforts should not be too low (below 2 lb. using pull-scale) or too high (above 6.5 lb.) or repair/adjustment then be made.

1. Slide mode lever to OFF. Set blower switch to HI and leave the temperature lever in the maximum COLD position.

   - Blower air, the same temperature as air outside the vehicle, will be discharged from the heater outlet. The blower will run on LO speed only. The compressor is not running.

2. Slide the mode lever to NORM. Note the detent at each mode position and insure the lever efforts are within requirements above.
   - Blower air increases to HI speed and exits from the A/C outlets. The compressor comes "on" and may cycle off-and-on. Air temperature should be about 45°F. (7°C.) at the A/C outlets.

3. Slide the mode lever to BI LEVEL.
   - Air exits from the A/C outlets and the heater outlet. The air speed from the A/C outlets decreases some from Step 2, the compressor comes "on" and may cycle off-and-on. Air temperature should be about 45°F. (7°C.) from both the heater and A/C outlets.

4. Slide the mode lever to VENT.
   - Air exits from the A/C outlets only. The air speed should be HI (comparable to Step 2). The compressor is not running. Air temperature should be equivalent to air outside the vehicle.

5. Slide the mode lever to HEATER.
   - Air exits mainly from the heater outlet with some air from the defroster nozzle. The compressor is not running. Air temperature should be equivalent to air outside the vehicle. Blower speed should still be HI.

6. Slide the temperature lever from maximum COLD to maximum HOT (far left to far right). Note the lever effort requirements above.
   - The air temperature from the heater outlet should rise rapidly from outside ambient temperature to about 140°F. (60°C.) Blower speed should still be HI.

7. Slide the mode lever to DEFROST.
   - Air exits mainly from the defroster nozzle with some air from the heater outlet. The compressor comes "on" and may cycle off-and-on. Air temperature should be about 140°F. (60°C.). Blower speed should still be HI.

8. Move the blower switch to LO, pausing at each of the two intermediate positions.
   - Blower speed and air flow should decrease accordingly at each position.

9. Slide the temperature lever to maximum COLD (far left) and the mode selector to MAX.
   - Blower comes on HI speed. Air exits from the A/C outlets only. Air noise is heard from the right front corner of the passenger compartment as the system goes on "inside" air. The compressor comes "on" and may cycle off-and-on. Air temperature should be about 45°F. (7°C.) at the A/C outlets.

Troubleshooting

Isolating The Problem

To diagnose an air conditioner problem in the shortest time and with the least effort, it is essential to follow a logical service procedure. Time spent in conducting a system functional performance test and analyzing the malfunction in order to isolate it to a specific control function area will be repaid in reduced repair time. A recommended diagnosis procedure follows:

1. Get an accurate, detailed description of the complaint.
2. To confirm the system malfunction, make a brief check of system operation by sitting in the car and operating the controls, with the engine warmed up and running at 1000 RPM or higher, in the following sequence:

During the above tests, be sure to note the following:

a. Check to assure that air delivery is *not* coming from both the A/C and heater outlets when only one mode is indicated. A split air delivery is indicative of a vacuum leak.

b. Note whether program events (air delivery mode change, recirc air, etc.) occur without change in discharge air temperature. This would indicate the programmer is operating without moving the temperature air door. Check the air mix door link to programmer connection.

c. If neither the program events nor the discharge air temperature change, an incorrect vacuum or electrical signal to the programmer or a programmer malfunction is indicated.

d. Malfunction of a specific vacuum operated door function could indicate a vacuum disconnect of the vacuum diaphragm at that door.

3. Perform the easiest checks first! A simple, visual inspection of the easily accessible underhood and instrument panel electrical and vacuum connections will, in many instances, reveal the problem on the spot.

4. Based on information gained during the functional test performed in step 2, try to elate the problem to one of the following areas:

1. Temperature Control Problems
2. Blower Control Problems
3. Auxiliary Vacuum Problems
4. Refrigeration System Problems

5. After the problem has been properly diagnosed and the repair made, it is important to run through the brief check listed in Step 2 in order to assure that the system is now performing correctly.

Temperature Control Diagnosis

The primary function of the temperature control circuit is to determine the correct temperature of the air to be discharged into the passenger compartment and to set the air mix door position to accomplish that function. The signal used for this purpose (vacuum to position the programmer vacuum motor) is also used in the blower speed control circuit, and the auxiliary vacuum function circuit. Those uses may be disregarded when dealing with problems which relate only to the temperature control circuit.

Examples of temperature control problems are:

"System operates at maximum air conditioning (no heat) or only at maximum heating (no air conditioning)," "Temperature dial does not provide comfort," or "poor heating" or "poor cooling." Blower cycling and mode cycling are also caused by a malfunction in the temperature control circuit.

It is important to separate temperature control circuit problems from refrigeration or heater circuit problems. If the complaint is "poor" or "no" heating or cooling and the programmer moves to both extremes of travel with the air mix door and program functions known to follow, the problem probably lies in the refrigerant or heater water circuits.

Many temperature control problems result from poor electrical or vacuum line connections. The following relationships may aid diagnosis:

- *A disconnected sensor or temperature dial* interrupts the electrical signal and drives the programmer to maximum heating.
- *A poor sensor connection* adds resistance to the sensor string driving the system hotter.
- *An open amplifier power feed* eliminates the output signal and drives the programmer to maximum A/C.

Automatic Temperature Control Functional Test

Control Setting	System Should Operate As Follows
"DEF" DIAL @ 85°	Air should be delivered out of defroster outlets at a fixed high blower speed. Some floor bleed out heater.
"BI-LEVEL" DIAL @ 85°	Air should be delivered from *both* the A/C and heater outlets. Only a small portion of air will come out the defroster outlet.
"HI" DIAL @ 85°	Air should be delivered out the A/C outlets at a fixed high blower speed and cool to cold temperature. The recirculating air door should open (blower noise increases). Door movement will be slow because of vacuum delay porous plug.
"AUTO" DIAL @ 85°	Blower speeds should drop. Recirc air door should close (noise level will drop). Discharge air temperature should increase. Depending on the temperature in the work area, the air delivery mode should change from the A/C outlets to the heater outlets.
"LO" DIAL @ 85°	Air should be delivered at a fixed low blower speed.
"ECONOMY" DIAL @ 65°	Blower speeds should increase. Depending on the temperature in the work area, the air delivery mode should change from the heater outlets to both heater and A/C outlets or the A/C outlets only. The A/C compressor should not operate.
"OFF" DIAL @ 65°	Air should be discharged out the heater outlet at a fixed low blower speed. No A/C compressor operation.

• *A disconnected vacuum hose* supplying the vacuum checking relay actuating nipple will lock the relay in an intermediate position.

• *A disconnected vacuum hose* in the transducer-programmer vacuum motor line will drive the system to maximum cooling.

• *A leak* in the auxiliary vacuum circuit may reduce the transducer vacuum supply level below control requirements, causing an ''off-calibration'' or ''poor heating'' type complaint.

• *A loss* of supply vacuum usually results in cold air flow on the floor.

The following diagnosis causes and corrections should be considered.

System Operates Only At Maximum Air Conditioning

This can be a vacuum or electrical problem. The problem can be separated into problems of erroneous signal external to the programmer or internal programmer malfunctions. To isolate this problem, install test harness J-23678-77 with single connector open and 8 pin connectors fastened together, between amplifier connector and amplifier terminals. With the system operating, observe the vacuum motor position through the slot at the bottom of the programmer cover. If the programmer remains in the maximum air conditioner position, remove the vacuum harness and check for vacuum. If no (or low) vacuum supply, check for leaks or disconnects in vacuum hose assembly. If vacuum supply is okay, programmer is malfunctioning. Remove programmer cover and inspect for obvious disconnects. If no programmer problem is obvious, use Tester J-23678, Adapter Harness J-23678-77 and Instructions J-23678-51 to analyze and correct problem.

If the programmer moved to the maximum heater position with the test harness installed, the problem is *external* to the programmer. Check the following items:

1. Shorted in-car sensor.
2. Shorted or miscalibrated temperature dial.
3. A short in the sensor circuit of the wiring harness.
4. Disconnect or open in ground circuit (black wire) between control head and programmer.
5. No electrical power to programmer.

Use Tester, J-23678, Adapter Harness J-23678-77 and Instructions J-23678-51 to analyze and correct the above problems.

System Operates Only At Maximum Heating

This is usually an electrical problem. The problem can be separated into problems of erroneous signal external to the programmer or internal programmer malfunctions by disconnecting the three-wire amplifier connector from the programmer. With the system operating, observe the programmer movement through the slot at the bottom of the programmer cover. If the programmer remains in the maximum heater position, remove the multiple vacuum connector and check for supply vacuum at the black hose. If no (or low) vacuum supply, check for leaks or disconnects in vacuum hose assembly. If vacuum supply is okay, programmer is malfunctioning. Remove programmer cover and inspect for obvious disconnects. If no programmer problem is obvious, use Tester J-23678, Adapter Harness J-23678-77 and Instructions J-23678-51 to analyze and correct problem.

If the programmer moved to the maximum A/C position when the amplifier connector was removed, the problem is *external* to the programmer. Check the following items:

1. Disconnected or malfunctioning in-car sensor.
2. Disconnected or malfunctioning ambient sensor.
3. Open circuit or backed-out terminal in the wiring harness sensor string circuit.
4. Disconnected or malfunctioning temperature dial.

Use Tester, J-23678, Adapter Harness J-23678-77 and Instructions J-23678-51 to analyze and correct problem.

System Fluctuates Blower Speeds and/or Mode Shifts During Acceleration

1. Malfunctioning vacuum checking relay (inside programmer).
2. Leaking programmer vacuum motor.

It is possible to distinguish between the two above items. With the system operating and the programmer cover removed, reinstall the vacuum and electrical connectors, and perform the following steps:

a. Install Test Harness J-23678-77 with single connector open and 8 pin connectors fastened together, between amplifier connector and amplifier terminals to force the programmer to maximum heating (full vacuum).

b. Remove the vacuum hose assembly connector. The programmer should remain in the maximum heat position. If it does not, repeat Step a, and then pinch the programmer vacuum motor supply hose with a pair of needle-nose pliers. If the programmer still moves, the vacuum motor is leaking. If the programmer does not move, the checking relay is malfunctioning.

c. If the original complaint was mode shifts without blower change, the check valve portion of the checking relay is probably malfunctioning.

Dial Setting Does Not Provide Comfort

The best approach to solving problems of the ''off calibration'' variety, is to use Tester, J-23678, Adapter Harness J-23678-77 and Instructions J-23678-51 to check and reset calibration on *all* of the following parts:

1. The temperature dial.
2. The feedback potentiometer in the programmer.
3. The temperature door link adjustment.

NOTE: Check to assure that in-car sensor aspirator hose is attached at both the in-car sensor and the aspirator and not kinked in routing.

Refer to the instruction sheet included with the Tester or the section on System Adjustments for procedures on checking and calibrating the above items.

Blower Cycling and Mode Cycling

Erratic system performance may be caused by poor electrical connections, ''cold'' solder joints, or a malfunctioning sensor or amplifier. The problem may be intermittent and occur from the shock of going over road bumps. Such a problem may be accompanied by a clicking or buzzing of the transducer. To isolate the problem area, ''rap'' the areas around the sensors, control head, and programmer, and shake the wire attached to those areas. Listen for buzzing or clicking of the transducer. If the problem cannot be pinpointed by transducer buzzing, remove the programmer cover, (reinstall the vacuum and electrical connectors) and attach a *good* voltmeter to the transducer output terminal (gray wire). Repeat the rapping and wire shaking, and observe the voltmeter for violent, erratic voltage fluctuations. Replacement of parts or resoldering of terminals may be necessary. The sensors may be individually checked to the sensor resistance curve.

NOTE: Some system cycling may also occur and is normal if the temperature dial is moved in large increments. Instruct owner of this, and explain system operation.

Insufficient Heating or Cooling

This problem may be caused by a control system malfunction or by the refrigerant or heater systems. Determine first which area to pursue:

1. Check for compressor clutch actuation (no cooling).
2. Check temperature of heater hoses by feel with engine hot to see if hot water is entering the heater core (no heating).
3. Check for proper air flow at the ''Auto'' and ''HI'' lever settings. (Improper air flow may be a blower relay problem, a blocked air passage, or a disconnected air hose.)

If the problem appears to be caused by the temperature control system, locate problem area using Tester, J-23678, Adapter Harness J-23678-77 and Instructions J-23678-51.

Blower Speeds and Mode Shift Occurs Without Temperature Change

Check connection of air mix door link to programmer shift.

ELECTRONIC CLIMATE CONTROL SYSTEM PERFORMANCE DIAGNOSIS
(Engine Warm and Idling)

Control Settings	Temp.	System Should Operate as Follows
FRT DEF	90°	Warm air should be delivered from defroster outlets at a fixed high blower speed. Some floor bleed from heater outlet.
HI	90°	Warm air should be delivered from the heater outlet with only a small amount from the defroster outlets. The blower should stay at high speed.
AUTO	75°	After a short delay, the blower speed should gradually decrease. Discharged air should become cooler. Depending on the temperature in the work area, the air delivery mode should change to A/C outlets from the heater outlets.
AUTO	60°	Blower speed should increase to a fixed high value. Discharged air should become maximum cold. The recirculating air door should slowly open (signalled by blower noise increase).
LO	60°	After a short delay, the blower speed should gradually decrease to a very low value. The discharged air should remain cold and come from the A/C outlets. The recirc. door should slowly close.
ECON	60°	The A/C compressor should be off. Blower speed should gradually increase to a fixed high value. Discharged air should continue to come from A/C outlets and should be warmer than the temperature in the work area.
OFF	60°	After a short delay, the blower speed should gradually decrease to a very low value. The discharged air should be delivered from the heater outlet and should be somewhat warmer than the temperature in the work area. The A/C compressor should be off.
RR DEF	NONE	LED above button should light up. Heat should be applied to rear window.

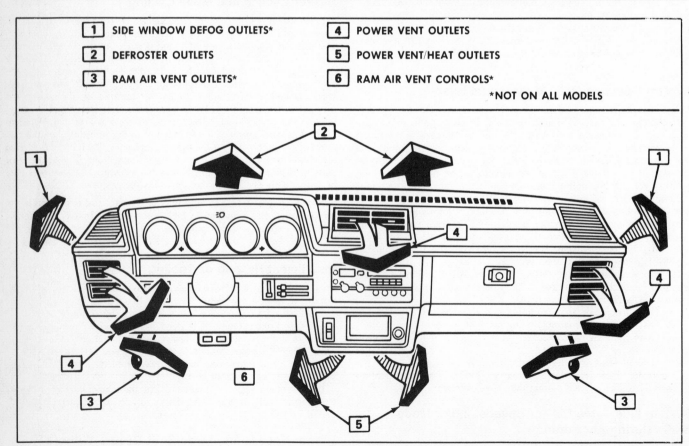

1 SIDE WINDOW DEFOG OUTLETS*	**4** POWER VENT OUTLETS
2 DEFROSTER OUTLETS	**5** POWER VENT/HEAT OUTLETS
3 RAM AIR VENT OUTLETS*	**6** RAM AIR VENT CONTROLS*

*NOT ON ALL MODELS

ELECTRONIC CLIMATE CONTROL SYSTEM RESPONSE

CONTROL LEVER SETTINGS	BLOWER SPEED	AIR INLET DOOR POSITION	TEMPERATURE DOOR POSITION	MODE DOORS POSITION	DEFROSTER DOOR POSITION	COMPRESSOR	HTR-WATER SHUT-OFF VALVE	IS BLOWER DELAYED FOR ENGINE WATER WARMUP?
OFF	FIXED LOW			FORCED TO HEATER		DOESN'T OPERATE		
ECON.	VARIABLE BLOWER PROGRAM	OUTSIDE AIR		EITHER HEATER OR A/C MODE DEPENDING ON PROGRAMMER POSITION	DOOR WILL ASSUME "BLEED" POSITION AFTER 45 SECOND DELAY AND WILL DELIVER BLEED AIR TO W/S IF IN HEATER MODE		USUALLY OPEN EXC. CLOSED AT MAX. A/C POSITION OF PROGRAMMER	YES EXCEPT IN A/C MODE IN WHICH CASE THE CONTROL HEAD TURNS ON THE BLOWER IMMEDIATELY EVEN IF ENGINE IS COLD
LO	FIXED LOW		VARIES RESPONSIVE TO SENSORS					
AUTO	VARIABLE BLOWER PROGRAM	RECIRCULATE AIR WHEN PROGRAMMER IS AT MAX. A/C OTHERWISE OUTSIDE				CYCLES ON AND OFF TO MAINTAIN EVAPORATOR BETWEEN MINUS 1°C AND 71/2°C (31°F TO 34° F)		
HI	FIXED HI							
DEF	FIXED HI	OUTSIDE AIR		FORCED TO HEATER	FULL OPEN TO W/S		OPEN	NO DELAY

System Operates Only At Low Blower

1. Back-out terminal or disconnect at control head. Trace blower circuit using electrical wiring diagram.
2. Open in blower circuit wiring.

No Blower Operation in Any Lever Setting

1. Electrical disconnect at blower motor.
2. Disconnect at blower relay or malfunction of blower relay.
3. Blown or open 15 amp. A/C-heater fuse.
4. Stalled blower motor.
5. Open circuit in wiring harness to blower motor.

No Blower In "Off" Or "Lo" Settings

1. Open resistor on blower resistor board.
2. Open in blower circuit wiring. Refer to wiring diagram.

Operates at Low Blower Only Except in "HI" and "DEF"

1. Problem in programmer wiper contacts or board.
2. Backed-out terminal or disconnect at programmer electrical connector.
3. Back-out terminal at blower resistor connector or open resistor in blower resistor assembly.
4. Backed-out terminal at control head programmer feed terminal.
5. Open in blower circuit wiring.

Blower Operation Only in "HI" or "DEF"

1. Electrical disconnect at blower resistor assembly.
2. Open in circuit wiring between resistor assembly and blower motor.

Blower Operates at Low Speed in "HI" and "DEF"

1. Malfunction in control head wipers or circuit board.
2. Open in by-pass circuit in wiring harness.

Blower Operates With Ignition Off

1. Malfunctioning blower relay (closed contacts).

Blower Speeds Skipped in "Economy," "Auto" or "Bi-Level" Setting

Open resistor in blower resistor circuit board.

No Heater Turn-On In Cold Weather Except In "DEF"

1. Electrical disconnect at heater turn-on switch (loaded at front of R.H. cylinder head).
2. Heater turn-on switch inoperative (will not close). Check by grounding switch feed wire.
3. If problem persists, refer to electrical circuit diagrams for wiring discontinuity.

NOTE: If problem does not occur in shop, it is probable that the system is turned on by the in-car switch. Disconnect control head electrical connector to disarm the in-car switch. If the blower turns off (with the engine warmed up), ground the heater turn-on switch feed wire. If the blower now turns on (in low blower speed), the heater switch is probably malfunctioning.

Immediate Heater Turn-On In Cold Weather

1. Normal condition in "Def" lever setting.
2. Malfunctioning (closed) heater turn-on switch (remove and check cold).
3. Malfunctioning (closed) in-car switch.
4. If problem persists, refer to electrical circuit diagram.

A/C Delayed in Hot Weather Until Engine Warms Up

1. Malfunctioning (open) in-car switch.
2. Open in control head wiring harness (in-car switch circuit).
3. If problem persists, check wiring continuity in the in-car switch circuit.

How to "Enter" Diagnostic Mode

To enter diagnostic mode, proceed as follows:
1. Turn the ignition "ON".
2. Depress the "OFF" and "WARMER" buttons on the ECC panel simultaneously and hold until ".." appears. "−1.8.8" will then be displayed which indicates the beginning of the diagnostic readout.
3. Trouble codes will be displayed on the ECC control head beginning with the lowest numbered code.

How to "Clear" Trouble Codes

Trouble codes stored in the ECM's memory may be cleared by entering the diagnostic mode and then depressing the "OFF" and "HI" buttons simultaneously. Hold until ".0.0" appears. After ".0.0" is displayed, the ECM will display ".7.0".

How to "Exit" Diagnostic Mode

To get out of the diagnostic mode, depress any of the ECC "Function" keys (Auto, Econ, etc.) except Lo or Outside Temperature or turn ignition switch off for 10 seconds. Trouble codes are not erased when this is done. The temperature setting will reappear in the display panel.

Climate Control in Diagnostic Mode

Upon entering the diagnostic mode, the ECC will automatically operate in the "Lo" mode. Air temperature will be controlled to whatever value was displayed on the ECC control head just prior to entering diagnostics.

Compressor Clutch operation can be controlled using the "outside temp" button on the ECC control head. When diagnostics is first entered, the light next to the "outside temp" button will be on. This light indicates whether the clutch is enabled or disabled. By depressing the "outside temp" button, the clutch can either be enabled (status light on) or disabled (status light off).

Status Light Display

While in the diagnostic mode, the lights next to the ECC control head buttons are used to indicate the status of certain system operating modes. The different modes of operation are indicated by the status light either being turned on or turned off. A brief summary of each status light is provided below:
1. The "Off" button status light is turned on whenever the ECM is operating in "closed-loop" fuel control. This light should come on after the coolant and oxygen sensors have reached normal operating temperatures.
2. The "Econ" button status light is turned on whenever the oxygen sensor signal indicates a "rich" exhaust condition.
3. The "Lo" button status light is turned on whenever the throttle switch is closed. This light should be off whenever the throttle is applied.
4. The "Auto" button status light is turned on whenever the ECM is commanding the TCC to engage. This light only indicates whether the TCC is enabled or disabled by the ECM. Actual operation depends on the integrity of the TCC system.
5. The "Hi" button status light is turned on whenever the 4th gear pressure switch is open. This light should only be on while in 4th gear operation.
6. The "Outside Temp" button status light indicates whether the ECC compressor clutch is enabled or disabled. When diagnostics is first entered, the ECC will be in the "Lo" mode and the status light will be turned on. If compressor operation is not desired, the "Outside Temp" button can be depressed which will disable the clutch and turn the status light off. By depressing the button again, the light will turn on and compressor operation should resume. This light only indicates

whether the compressor clutch is enabled or disabled. Actual compressor operation depends on the compressor cycling switch and system integrety.

Diagnosis Procedure

When the check engine light turns on, it indicates that a malfunction has occurred for which a trouble code has been stored. The trouble code can be displayed on the ECC control head. The malfunction may or may not result in abnormal engine operation.

To determine which system(s) has malfunctioned, proceed as follows:
1. Turn the ignition switch "ON" for 5 seconds.
2. Depress the "OFF" and "WARMER" buttons on the ECC control head simultaneously and hold until ".." appears.
3. The numerals " – 1.8.8" should then appear. The purpose of the " – 1.8.8" display is to check that all segments of the display are working. Diagnosis should not be attempted unless the entire " – 1.8.8" appears as this could lead to misdiagnosis. If any of the segments are inoperative, the ECC control head will need to be replaced.
4. If trouble codes other than Code 51 are present, they will be displayed on the ECC control panel as follows:
   a. The lowest numbered code will be displayed for approximately two seconds.
   b. Progressively higher numbered codes, if present, will be displayed consecutively for two second intervals until the highest code present has been displayed.
   c. " – 1.8.8" is again displayed.
   d. Parts A, B, and C above will be repeated during the second pass.
   e. On the third pass, only "hard" trouble codes will be displayed. These are the codes which indicate a currently present malfunction and are keeping the check engine light on. Codes which are displayed during the first and second pass but not during the third are "intermittent" codes.
   f. " – 1.8.8" is displayed again.
   g. When the trouble codes have been displayed, code .7.0 will then be displayed. Code .7.0 indicates that the ECM is ready for the next diagnostic feature to be selected.
5. If a Code 51 is present, it will be displayed continuously until the diagnostic mode is exited. During this display of Code 51, none of the other diagnostic features will be possible.
6. Begin the diagnosis with the lowest code number which is displayed unless a Code 16 is present. If present, Code 16 should be diagnosed first since this malfunction can affect the setting of other codes.
7. If the vehicle exhibits performance problems and has no codes set, refer to the performance diagnosis charts. A component which is checked by the trouble codes will rarely cause a performance problem when no trouble codes are set.
8. If no trouble codes are present, " – 1.8.8" will be displayed for two seconds, and then the ECM will display Code .7.0. Code .7.0 indicates that the ECM is ready for the next diagnostic feature to be selected.

Code .7.0

Code .7.0 is a decision point. When Code .7.0 is displayed, the technician should select the diagnostic feature that he wants to display. The following choices are available:
   A. Switch tests
   B. Engine data display
   C. Output cycling tests
   D. Fixed spark mode
   E. Exit diagnostics or clear codes and exit diagnostics

Switch Tests Procedure

Code .7.0 must be displayed on the ECC control head before the switch tests can begin. To start the switch tests sequence depress and release

the brake pedal; the switch tests begin as the display switches from Code .7.0 to Code .7.1. (If the display doesn't advance to Code .7.1, refer to the diagnosis chart, Code .7.1, because the ECM is not processing the brake signal.)

As each code is displayed, the associated switch must be cycled within 10 seconds or the code will be recorded in the ECM's memory as a failure. After the ECM recognizes a test as passing or after the 10 second time-out elapses without the proper cycling being recognized, the display automatically advances to the next switch test code. The switch tests sequence is performed as follows:
   1. With Code .7.1 displayed, **depress and release the brake pedal again** to test the Cruise Control brake circuit.
   2. With Code .7.2 displayed, **depress the throttle from the idle position to an open throttle position and then release the throttle.** While this action is being performed, the ECM checks the throttle switch for proper operation.
   3. With Code .7.3 displayed, **shift the transmission lever into drive and then neutral.** This action checks the operation of the drive switch.
   4. With Code .7.4 displayed, **shift the transmission lever to reverse and then into park.** This action checks the operation of the reverse switch.

On cars **without** Cruise Control, codes .7.5, .7.6 and .7.7 will be displayed but cannot be performed during the switch tests. When these codes are displayed during the switch tests, allow the code to reach it's 10 second time out. After this time out has elapsed, the display will advance to the next code. Allow codes .7.5, .7.6 and .7.7 to time out (30 seconds). Since these codes will be recorded as failures in the switch tests sequence, a display of .0.0 will never be observed at the completion of the tests (see Step #12). To confirm proper operation of the remaining switches, codes .7.8, .7.9 and .8.0 must be observed as having advanced within their 10 second time out. If the code cannot be advanced within its time out, it should be considered a failed test.
   5. With Code .7.5 displayed, **switch the Cruise Control instrument panel switch from off to on and back to off** to check the operation of this switch.
   6. With Code .7.6 displayed and **with the cruise instrument panel switch in the on position, depress and release the set/coast button** to check the operation of this switch.
   7. With Code .7.7 displayed and **with the cruise instrument panel switch in the on position, depress and release the resume/acceleration switch** to check the operation of this switch.
   8. With Code .7.8 displayed, **depress and release the "instant/average" button** on the Fuel Data panel to test the operation of this switch.
   9. With Code .7.9 displayed, **depress and release the "reset" button** on the Fuel Data panel to test the operation of this switch.
   10. With Code .8.0 displayed, **depress and release the "outside temperature" button TWICE.** When diagnostics are first entered, compressor clutch engagement is commanded as indicated by the "outside temperature" status light being on. When the "outside temperature" button is pushed the status light will go out and the clutch should disengage. When the button is pushed the second time the status light will come back on and the clutch should reengage. This action checks the ECM's ability to recognize and process the air conditioning clutch signal. However, the compressor cycling switch in series with the compressor drive circuit must be closed in order to energize the A/C compressor clutch. Sometimes, the engine may need to be running and the ECC may need to be operating in auto and 60°F to close the contacts of the compressor cycling switch.
   11. When the switch tests are completed, the ECM will now go back and display the switch codes which did not test properly. Each code which did not pass will be displayed beginning with the lowest number. The codes will not disappear until the affected switch circuit has been repaired and retested. Refer to the appropriate diagnosis chart for each trouble code.
   12. After the switch tests are completed and all circuits pass, the ECC panel displays ".0.0" and then returns to Code .7.0. ".0.0" indicates that all of the switch circuits are operating properly.

1982 DIAGNOSTIC CODES

Code	Circuit Affected
12	No distributor (tach) signal
13	O$_2$ sensor not ready
14	Shorted coolant sensor circuit
15	Open coolant sensor circuit
16	Generator voltage out of range
18	Open crank signal circuit
19	Shorted fuel pump circuit
20	Open fuel pump circuit
21	Shorted throttle position sensor circuit
22	Open throttle position sensor circuit
23	EST circuit problem in run mode
24	Speed sensor circuit problem
25	EST circuit problem in bypass mode
26	Shorted throttle switch circuit
27	Open throttle switch circuit
28	Open fourth gear circuit
29	Shorted fourth gear circuit
30	ISC circuit problem
31	Shorted map sensor circuit
32	Open map sensor circuit
33	Map/baro sensor correlation
34	Map signal too high
35	Shorted baro sensor circuit
36	Open baro sensor circuit
37	Shorted mat sensor circuit
38	Open mat sensor circuit
39	TCC engagement problem
44	Lean exhaust signal
45	Rich exhaust signal
51	Prom error indicator
52	ECM memory reset indicator
60	Transmission not in drive
63	Car and set speed tolerance exceeded
64	Car acceleration exceeds max. limit
65	Coolant temperature exceeds maximum limit
66	Engine rpm exceeds maximum limit
67	Shorted set or resume circuit
.7.0	System ready for further tests
.7.1	Cruise control brake circuit test
.7.2	Throttle switch circuit test
.7.3	Drive (adl) circuit test
.7.4	Reverse circuit test
.7.5	Cruise on/off circuit test
.7.6	"Set/coast" circuit test
.7.7	"Resume/acceleration" circuit test
.7.8	"Instant/average" circuit test
.7.9	"Reset" circuit test
.8.0	A/C clutch circuit test
−1.8.8	Display check
.9.0	System ready to display engine data
.9.5	System ready for output cycling or in fixed spark mode
.9.6	Output cycling
.0.0	All diagnostics complete

Note: Cruise is disengaged with any "service now" light or with codes 60–67.

1983 AND LATER DIAGNOSTIC CODES

Code	Circuit Affected
■■ 12	No distributor (tach) signal
☐ 13	O$_2$ sensor not ready
☐ 14	Shorted coolant sensor circuit
☐ 15	Open coolant sensor circuit
■■ 16	Generator voltage out of range
☐ 18	Open crank signal circuit
☐ 19	Shorted fuel pump circuit
■■ 20	Open fuel pump circuit
☐ 21	Shorted throttle position sensor circuit
☐ 22	Open throttle position sensor circuit
☐ 23	Est/bypass circuit problem
☐ 24	Speed sensor circuit problem
☐ 26	Shorted throttle switch circuit
☐ 27	Open throttle switch circuit
☐ 28	Open fourth gear circuit
☐ 29	Shorted fourth gear circuit
☐ 30	ISC circuit problem
■■ 31	Shorted map sensor circuit
■■ 32	Open map sensor circuit
■■ 33	Map/baro sensor correlation
☐ 34	Map signal too high
☐ 35	Shorted baro sensor circuit
☐ 36	Open baro sensor circuit
☐ 37	Shorted mat sensor circuit
☐ 38	Open mat sensor circuit
☐ 39	TCC engagement problem
■■ 44	Lean exhaust signal
■■ 45	Rich exhaust signal
■■ 51	Prom error indicator
▼ 52	ECM memory reset indicator
▼ 53	Distributor signal interrupt
▼ 60	Transmission not in drive
▼ 63	Car and set speed tolerance exceeded
▼ 64	Car acceleration exceeds max. limit
▼ 65	Coolant temperature exceeds max. limit
▼ 66	Engine rpm exceeds maximum limit
▼ 67	Shorted set or resume circuit
.7.0	System ready for further tests
.7.1	Cruise control brake circuit test
.7.2	Throttle switch circuit test
.7.3	Drive (adl) circuit test
.7.4	Reverse circuit test
.7.5	Cruise on/off circuit test
.7.6	"Set/coast" circuit test
.7.7	"Resume/acceleration" circuit test
.7.8	"Instant/average" circuit test
.7.9	"Reset" circuit test
.8.0	A/C clutch circuit test
−1.8.8	Display check
.9.0	System ready to display engine data
.9.5	System ready for output cycling or in fixed spark mode
.9.6	Output cycling
.0.0	All dianostics complete

■■	Turns on "service now" light
☐	Turns on "service soon" light
▼	Does not turn on any telltale light

LOW PRESSURE SWITCH DIAGNOSIS

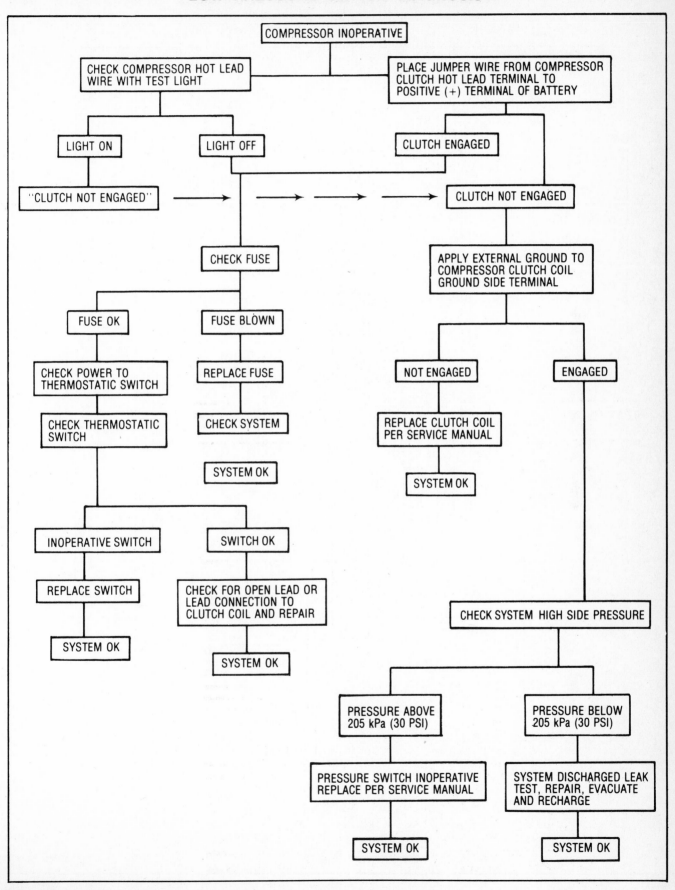

INSUFFICIENT REFRIGERANT DIAGNOSIS

INSUFFICIENT REFRIGERATION

Compressor operates properly but discharge temperature varies over 8°C (15°F) or greater range or is too warm.

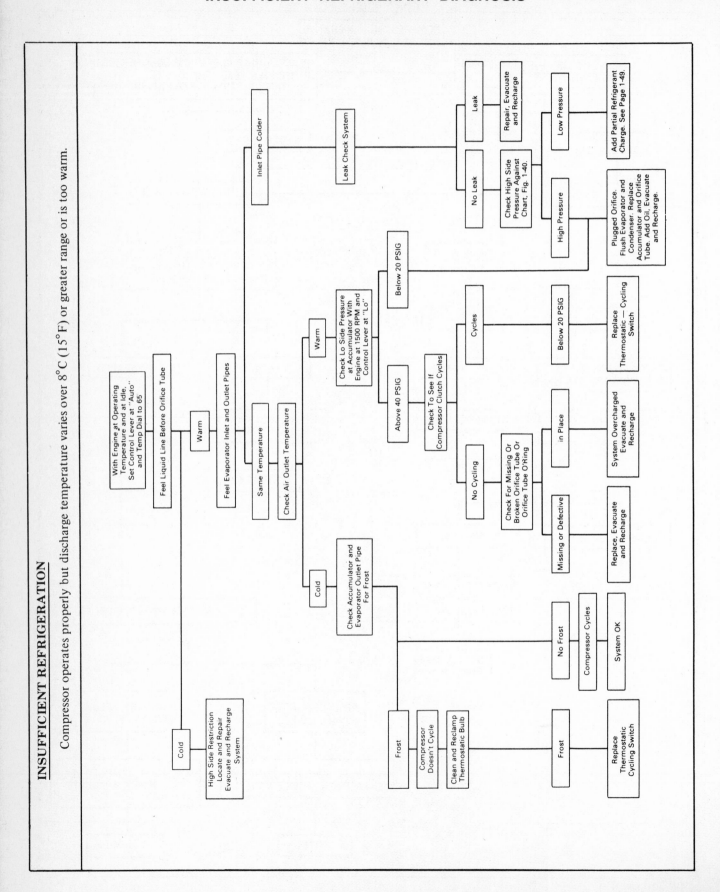

ELECTRONIC CLIMATE CONTROL SYSTEM TROUBLESHOOTING
Low Blower Only

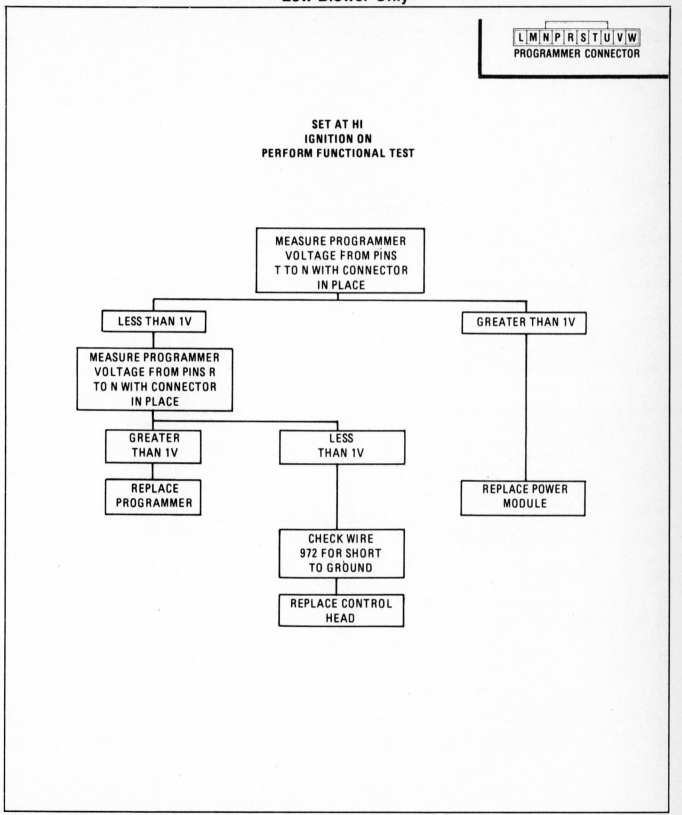

L M N P R S T U V W
PROGRAMMER CONNECTOR

SET AT HI
IGNITION ON
PERFORM FUNCTIONAL TEST

MEASURE PROGRAMMER
VOLTAGE FROM PINS
T TO N WITH CONNECTOR
IN PLACE

LESS THAN 1V

GREATER THAN 1V

MEASURE PROGRAMMER
VOLTAGE FROM PINS R
TO N WITH CONNECTOR
IN PLACE

GREATER
THAN 1V

LESS
THAN 1V

REPLACE
PROGRAMMER

REPLACE POWER
MODULE

CHECK WIRE
972 FOR SHORT
TO GROUND

REPLACE CONTROL
HEAD

ELECTRONIC CLIMATE CONTROL SYSTEM TROUBLESHOOTING
Hi-Blower Only

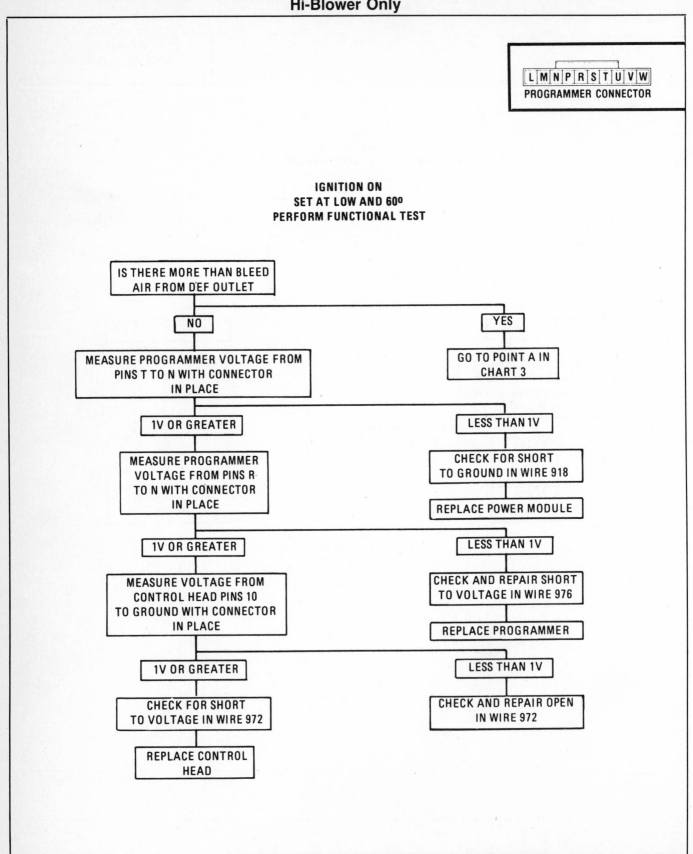

LMNPRSTUVW
PROGRAMMER CONNECTOR

IGNITION ON
SET AT LOW AND 60°
PERFORM FUNCTIONAL TEST

IS THERE MORE THAN BLEED
AIR FROM DEF OUTLET

NO — MEASURE PROGRAMMER VOLTAGE FROM PINS T TO N WITH CONNECTOR IN PLACE

YES — GO TO POINT A IN CHART 3

1V OR GREATER — MEASURE PROGRAMMER VOLTAGE FROM PINS R TO N WITH CONNECTOR IN PLACE

LESS THAN 1V — CHECK FOR SHORT TO GROUND IN WIRE 918 — REPLACE POWER MODULE

1V OR GREATER — MEASURE VOLTAGE FROM CONTROL HEAD PINS 10 TO GROUND WITH CONNECTOR IN PLACE

LESS THAN 1V — CHECK AND REPAIR SHORT TO VOLTAGE IN WIRE 976 — REPLACE PROGRAMMER

1V OR GREATER — CHECK FOR SHORT TO VOLTAGE IN WIRE 972 — REPLACE CONTROL HEAD

LESS THAN 1V — CHECK AND REPAIR OPEN IN WIRE 972

ELECTRONIC CLIMATE CONTROL SYSTEM TROUBLESHOOTING
No Blower Operation

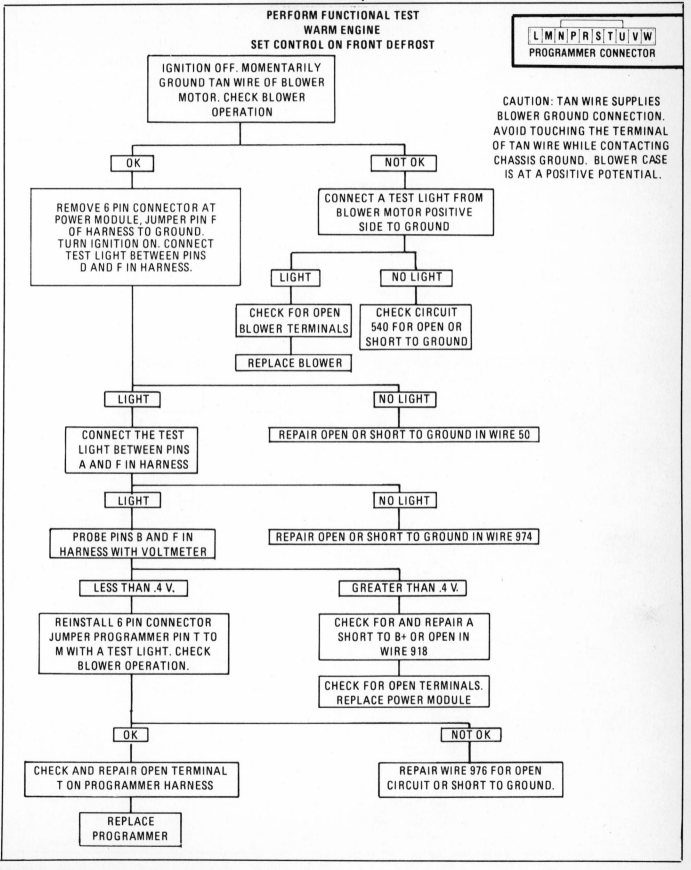

PERFORM FUNCTIONAL TEST
WARM ENGINE
SET CONTROL ON FRONT DEFROST

| L | M | N | P | R | S | T | U | V | W |
PROGRAMMER CONNECTOR

CAUTION: TAN WIRE SUPPLIES
BLOWER GROUND CONNECTION.
AVOID TOUCHING THE TERMINAL
OF TAN WIRE WHILE CONTACTING
CHASSIS GROUND. BLOWER CASE
IS AT A POSITIVE POTENTIAL.

IGNITION OFF. MOMENTARILY GROUND TAN WIRE OF BLOWER MOTOR. CHECK BLOWER OPERATION

OK → REMOVE 6 PIN CONNECTOR AT POWER MODULE, JUMPER PIN F OF HARNESS TO GROUND. TURN IGNITION ON. CONNECT TEST LIGHT BETWEEN PINS D AND F IN HARNESS.

NOT OK → CONNECT A TEST LIGHT FROM BLOWER MOTOR POSITIVE SIDE TO GROUND

LIGHT → CHECK FOR OPEN BLOWER TERMINALS → REPLACE BLOWER

NO LIGHT → CHECK CIRCUIT 540 FOR OPEN OR SHORT TO GROUND

LIGHT → CONNECT THE TEST LIGHT BETWEEN PINS A AND F IN HARNESS

NO LIGHT → REPAIR OPEN OR SHORT TO GROUND IN WIRE 50

LIGHT → PROBE PINS B AND F IN HARNESS WITH VOLTMETER

NO LIGHT → REPAIR OPEN OR SHORT TO GROUND IN WIRE 974

LESS THAN .4 V. → REINSTALL 6 PIN CONNECTOR JUMPER PROGRAMMER PIN T TO M WITH A TEST LIGHT. CHECK BLOWER OPERATION.

GREATER THAN .4 V. → CHECK FOR AND REPAIR A SHORT TO B+ OR OPEN IN WIRE 918 → CHECK FOR OPEN TERMINALS. REPLACE POWER MODULE

OK → CHECK AND REPAIR OPEN TERMINAL T ON PROGRAMMER HARNESS → REPLACE PROGRAMMER

NOT OK → REPAIR WIRE 976 FOR OPEN CIRCUIT OR SHORT TO GROUND.

ELECTRONIC CLIMATE CONTROL SYSTEM TROUBLESHOOTING
SENSOR STRING PROBLEM

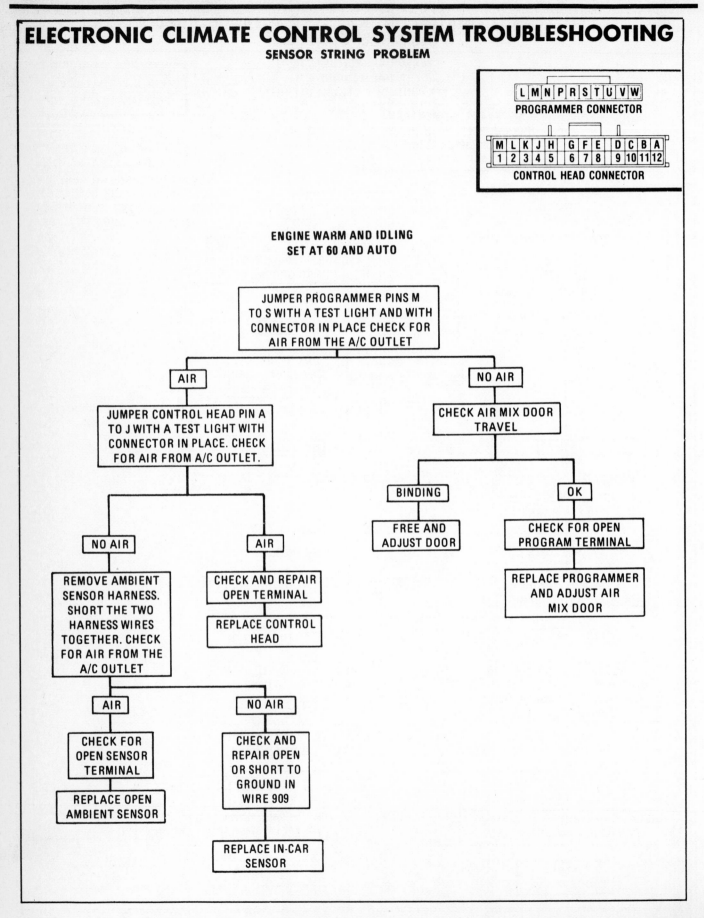

PROGRAMMER CONNECTOR

| L | M | N | P | R | S | T | U | V | W |

CONTROL HEAD CONNECTOR

| M | L | K | J | H | G | F | E | D | C | B | A |
| 1 | 2 | 3 | 4 | 5 | 6 | 7 | 8 | 9 | 10 | 11 | 12 |

ENGINE WARM AND IDLING
SET AT 60 AND AUTO

JUMPER PROGRAMMER PINS M TO S WITH A TEST LIGHT AND WITH CONNECTOR IN PLACE CHECK FOR AIR FROM THE A/C OUTLET

AIR

JUMPER CONTROL HEAD PIN A TO J WITH A TEST LIGHT WITH CONNECTOR IN PLACE. CHECK FOR AIR FROM A/C OUTLET.

NO AIR

REMOVE AMBIENT SENSOR HARNESS. SHORT THE TWO HARNESS WIRES TOGETHER. CHECK FOR AIR FROM THE A/C OUTLET

AIR

CHECK FOR OPEN SENSOR TERMINAL

REPLACE OPEN AMBIENT SENSOR

NO AIR

CHECK AND REPAIR OPEN OR SHORT TO GROUND IN WIRE 909

REPLACE IN-CAR SENSOR

AIR

CHECK AND REPAIR OPEN TERMINAL

REPLACE CONTROL HEAD

NO AIR

CHECK AIR MIX DOOR TRAVEL

BINDING

FREE AND ADJUST DOOR

OK

CHECK FOR OPEN PROGRAM TERMINAL

REPLACE PROGRAMMER AND ADJUST AIR MIX DOOR

LOW PRESSURE SWITCH DIAGNOSIS

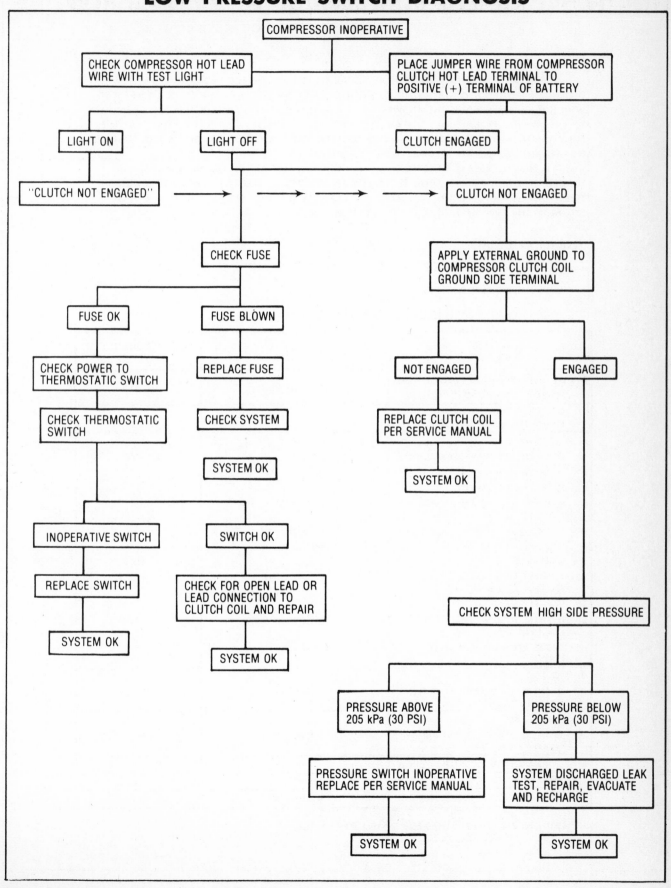

ELECTRONIC CLIMATE CONTROL FUNCTIONAL TEST

A LOGICAL SERVICE PROCEDURE IS AVAILABLE TO ISOLATE AN ECC PROBLEM. ALL SYSTEM DIAGNOSIS SHOULD BEGIN BY CONDUCTING THE FUNCTIONAL TEST IN THE EXACT ORDER IN WHICH IT IS PRESENTED. IF THE ANSWER TO ANY FUNCTIONAL TEST QUESTION IS NO, THEN TURN TO THE SPECIFIC TROUBLE TREE FOR ANALYSIS OF THE MALFUNCTION. IT IS ESSENTIAL THAT THE FUNCTIONAL TEST BE PERFORMED WITHOUT OMITTING STEPS BECAUSE OMISSIONS MAY RESULT IN THE INABILITY TO ISOLATE SPECIFIC MALFUNCTIONS.

IT IS NOT NECESSARY TO PERFORM THE FUNCTIONAL TEST AT THE BEGINNING OF EACH TROUBLE TREE IF THE FUNCTIONAL TEST HAS BEEN UTILIZED TO SELECT THE PROPER TROUBLE TREE. WHEN A MALFUNCTION HAS BEEN ISOLATED AND REPAIRED, THE TECHNICIAN SHOULD EXIT FROM THE TROUBLE TREE AT THE POINT OF REPAIR.

PROCEDE AS FOLLOWS:

1. CHECK FUSES (CHECK STOP HAZARD OPERATION TO VERIFY STOP HAZARD FUSE)

2. WARM ENGINE BEFORE TESTS

3. CHECK LED ABOVE EACH BUTTON AS TEST IS PERFORMED.

SYSTEM CHECKS	CONTROL SETTING	TROUBLE TREES
1. DO THE MPG AND CONTROL HEAD DISPLAY? (MPG IS OPTIONAL)	ALL	1
2. DO COOLER AND WARMER PUSHBUTTONS OPERATE?	ALL	1
3. SET AT 60°		
A. DOES THE BLOWER OPERATE?	LO, AUTO, HI	2A
B. IS THERE LO BLOWER?	LO	2B
C. IS THERE HI BLOWER?	HI	2C
D. IS THERE AIR FROM A/C OUTLETS?	ECON, LO, AUTO, HI	3
E. DOES COMP CLUTCH ENGAGE?	LO, AUTO, HI	4
F. DOES COMP CLUTCH DISENGAGE?	OFF, ECON	5
G. IS THERE COLD AIR FROM A/C OUTLETS? IF NOT:	LO, AUTO, HI	6
1) IS THERE HEAT ONLY?		
2) IS THERE INSUFFICIENT COOLING		7
H. *DOES RECIRC DOOR OPEN FULLY?	AUTO, HI	8
4. *SET AT 90°		
A. IS THERE SUFFICIENT HEAT FROM HEATER OUTLETS?	AUTO	9
5. *SET AT 85°		
A. IS THERE WARM OR HOT AIR AT HEATER OUTLET?	LO, AUTO	10
6. DOES FRONT DEFROSTER OPERATE?	FRT DEF	11
7. DOES REAR DEFROSTER OPERATE?	RR DEF	12
8. DOES REAR DEFROSTER TURN OFF?	RR DEF OFF	13

*WAIT ONE OR TWO MINUTES FOR SYSTEM TO CHANGE.

ELECTRONIC CLIMATE CONTROL SYSTEM TROUBLESHOOTING
NO DISPLAY

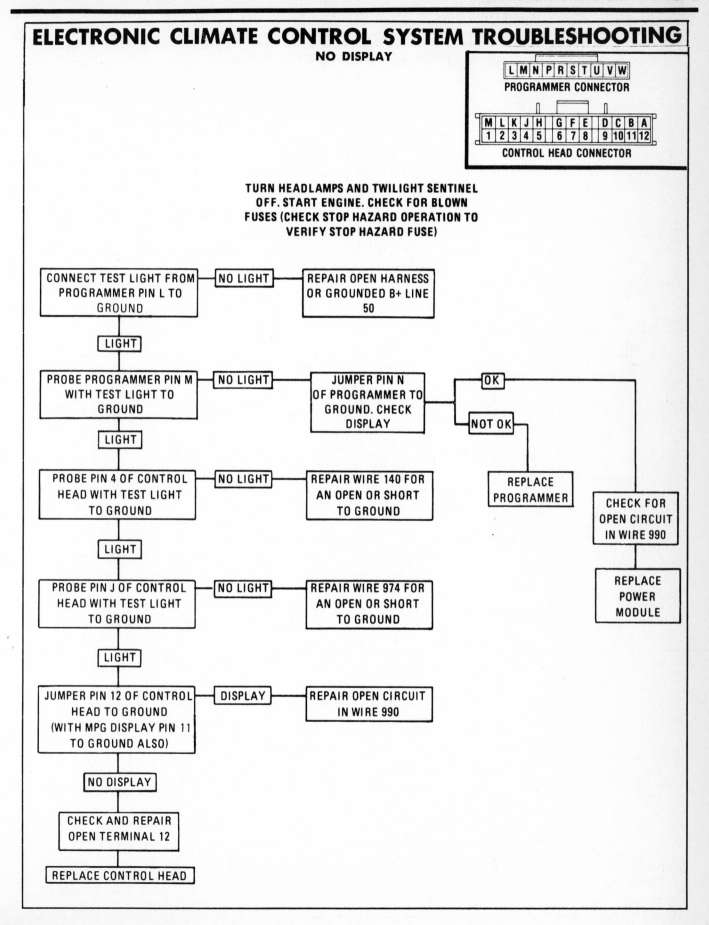

PROGRAMMER CONNECTOR

| L | M | N | P | R | S | T | U | V | W |

CONTROL HEAD CONNECTOR

| M | L | K | J | H | G | F | E | D | C | B | A |
| 1 | 2 | 3 | 4 | 5 | 6 | 7 | 8 | 9 | 10 | 11 | 12 |

TURN HEADLAMPS AND TWILIGHT SENTINEL
OFF. START ENGINE. CHECK FOR BLOWN
FUSES (CHECK STOP HAZARD OPERATION TO
VERIFY STOP HAZARD FUSE)

CONNECT TEST LIGHT FROM PROGRAMMER PIN L TO GROUND
— NO LIGHT — REPAIR OPEN HARNESS OR GROUNDED B+ LINE 50

LIGHT

PROBE PROGRAMMER PIN M WITH TEST LIGHT TO GROUND
— NO LIGHT — JUMPER PIN N OF PROGRAMMER TO GROUND. CHECK DISPLAY
— OK
— NOT OK — REPLACE PROGRAMMER

LIGHT

PROBE PIN 4 OF CONTROL HEAD WITH TEST LIGHT TO GROUND
— NO LIGHT — REPAIR WIRE 140 FOR AN OPEN OR SHORT TO GROUND

CHECK FOR OPEN CIRCUIT IN WIRE 990

REPLACE POWER MODULE

LIGHT

PROBE PIN J OF CONTROL HEAD WITH TEST LIGHT TO GROUND
— NO LIGHT — REPAIR WIRE 974 FOR AN OPEN OR SHORT TO GROUND

LIGHT

JUMPER PIN 12 OF CONTROL HEAD TO GROUND (WITH MPG DISPLAY PIN 11 TO GROUND ALSO)
— DISPLAY — REPAIR OPEN CIRCUIT IN WIRE 990

NO DISPLAY

CHECK AND REPAIR OPEN TERMINAL 12

REPLACE CONTROL HEAD

ELECTRONIC CLIMATE CONTROL SYSTEM TROUBLESHOOTING
NO AIR FROM A/C OUTLET IN THE A/C MODE

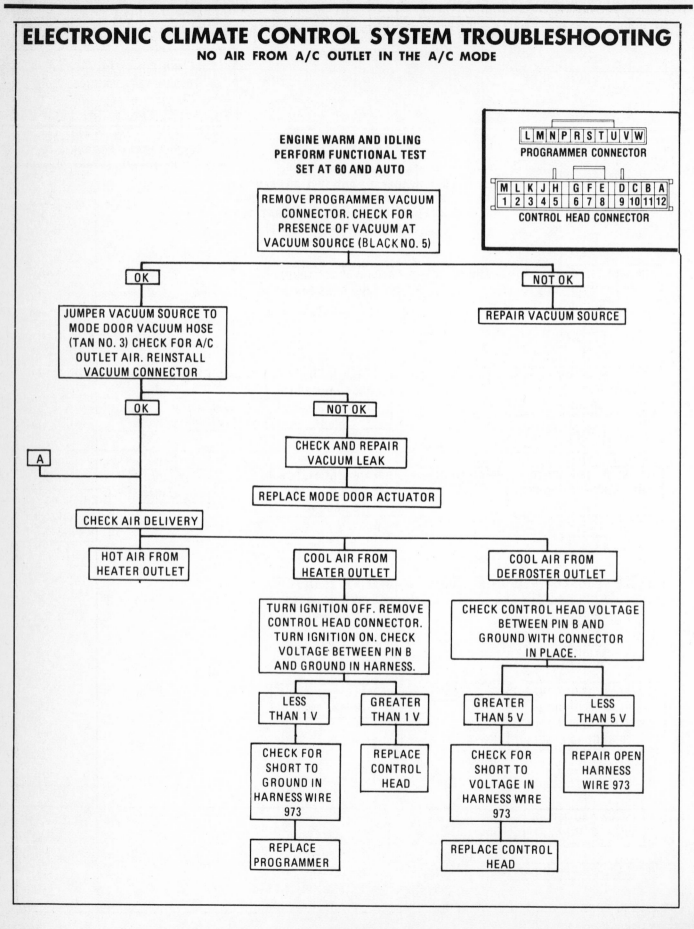

ENGINE WARM AND IDLING
PERFORM FUNCTIONAL TEST
SET AT 60 AND AUTO

REMOVE PROGRAMMER VACUUM CONNECTOR. CHECK FOR PRESENCE OF VACUUM AT VACUUM SOURCE (BLACK NO. 5)

L M N P R S T U V W
PROGRAMMER CONNECTOR

M L K J H | G F E | D C B A
1 2 3 4 5 | 6 7 8 | 9 10 11 12
CONTROL HEAD CONNECTOR

OK

NOT OK

JUMPER VACUUM SOURCE TO MODE DOOR VACUUM HOSE (TAN NO. 3) CHECK FOR A/C OUTLET AIR. REINSTALL VACUUM CONNECTOR

REPAIR VACUUM SOURCE

OK

NOT OK

A

CHECK AND REPAIR VACUUM LEAK

REPLACE MODE DOOR ACTUATOR

CHECK AIR DELIVERY

HOT AIR FROM HEATER OUTLET

COOL AIR FROM HEATER OUTLET

COOL AIR FROM DEFROSTER OUTLET

TURN IGNITION OFF. REMOVE CONTROL HEAD CONNECTOR. TURN IGNITION ON. CHECK VOLTAGE BETWEEN PIN B AND GROUND IN HARNESS.

CHECK CONTROL HEAD VOLTAGE BETWEEN PIN B AND GROUND WITH CONNECTOR IN PLACE.

LESS THAN 1 V

GREATER THAN 1 V

GREATER THAN 5 V

LESS THAN 5 V

CHECK FOR SHORT TO GROUND IN HARNESS WIRE 973

REPLACE CONTROL HEAD

CHECK FOR SHORT TO VOLTAGE IN HARNESS WIRE 973

REPAIR OPEN HARNESS WIRE 973

REPLACE PROGRAMMER

REPLACE CONTROL HEAD

ELECTRONIC CLIMATE CONTROL SYSTEM TROUBLESHOOTING
ECONOMY DOES NOT OPERATE

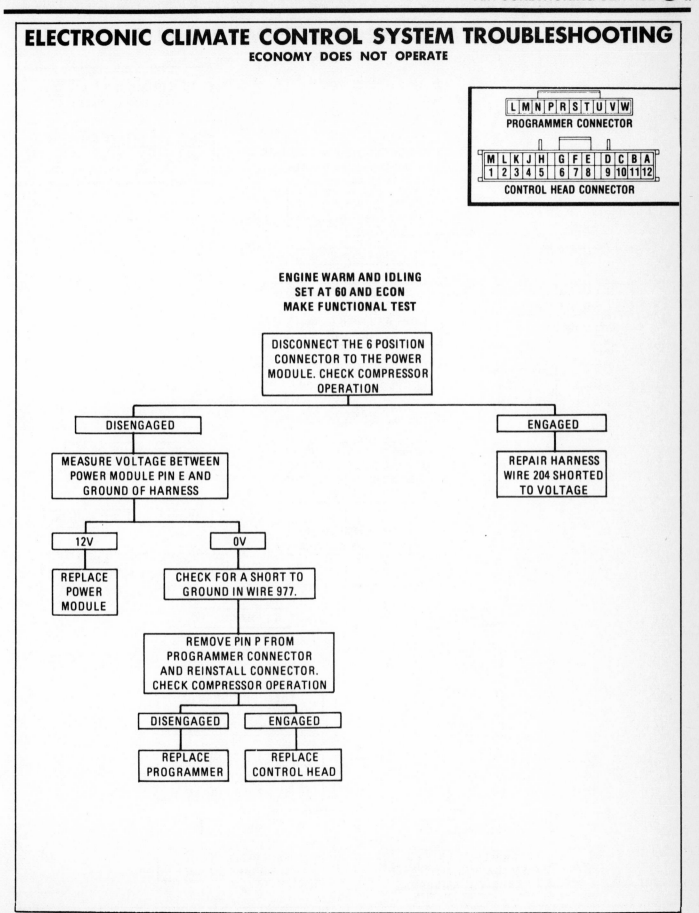

PROGRAMMER CONNECTOR

L M N P R S T U V W

M L K J H | G F E | D C B A
1 2 3 4 5 | 6 7 8 | 9 10 11 12

CONTROL HEAD CONNECTOR

ENGINE WARM AND IDLING
SET AT 60 AND ECON
MAKE FUNCTIONAL TEST

DISCONNECT THE 6 POSITION
CONNECTOR TO THE POWER
MODULE. CHECK COMPRESSOR
OPERATION

DISENGAGED

ENGAGED

MEASURE VOLTAGE BETWEEN
POWER MODULE PIN E AND
GROUND OF HARNESS

REPAIR HARNESS
WIRE 204 SHORTED
TO VOLTAGE

12V

0V

REPLACE
POWER
MODULE

CHECK FOR A SHORT TO
GROUND IN WIRE 977.

REMOVE PIN P FROM
PROGRAMMER CONNECTOR
AND REINSTALL CONNECTOR.
CHECK COMPRESSOR OPERATION

DISENGAGED

ENGAGED

REPLACE
PROGRAMMER

REPLACE
CONTROL HEAD

ELECTRONIC CLIMATE CONTROL SYSTEM TROUBLESHOOTING
INSUFFICIENT COOLING

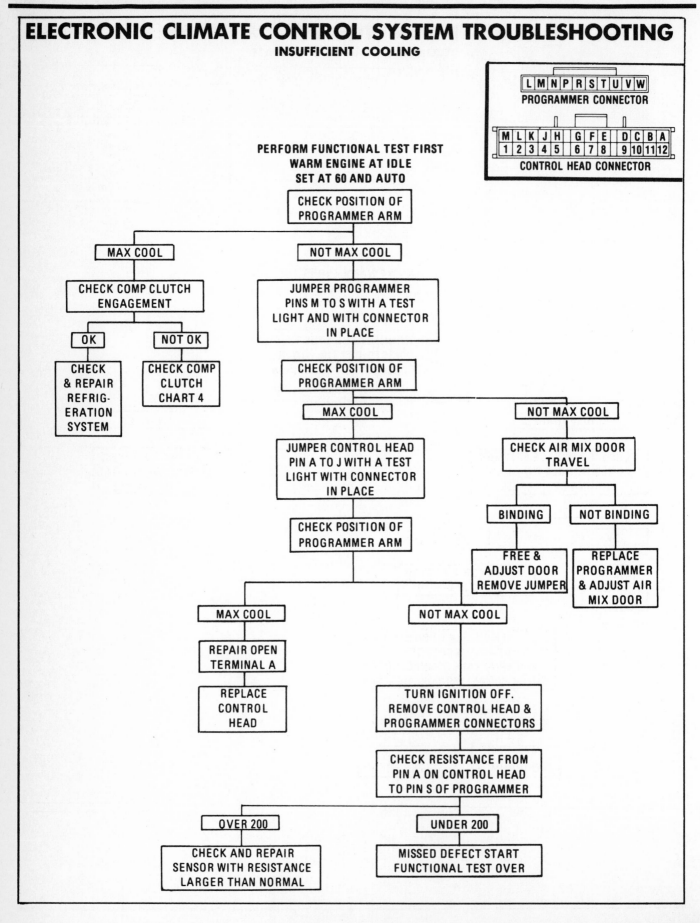

PERFORM FUNCTIONAL TEST FIRST
WARM ENGINE AT IDLE
SET AT 60 AND AUTO

PROGRAMMER CONNECTOR
L M N P R S T U V W

CONTROL HEAD CONNECTOR
M L K J H G F E D C B A
1 2 3 4 5 6 7 8 9 10 11 12

CHECK POSITION OF PROGRAMMER ARM

MAX COOL — CHECK COMP CLUTCH ENGAGEMENT
- OK → CHECK & REPAIR REFRIGERATION SYSTEM
- NOT OK → CHECK COMP CLUTCH CHART 4

NOT MAX COOL → JUMPER PROGRAMMER PINS M TO S WITH A TEST LIGHT AND WITH CONNECTOR IN PLACE → CHECK POSITION OF PROGRAMMER ARM

MAX COOL → JUMPER CONTROL HEAD PIN A TO J WITH A TEST LIGHT WITH CONNECTOR IN PLACE → CHECK POSITION OF PROGRAMMER ARM
- MAX COOL → REPAIR OPEN TERMINAL A → REPLACE CONTROL HEAD
- NOT MAX COOL → TURN IGNITION OFF. REMOVE CONTROL HEAD & PROGRAMMER CONNECTORS → CHECK RESISTANCE FROM PIN A ON CONTROL HEAD TO PIN S OF PROGRAMMER
  - OVER 200 → CHECK AND REPAIR SENSOR WITH RESISTANCE LARGER THAN NORMAL
  - UNDER 200 → MISSED DEFECT START FUNCTIONAL TEST OVER

NOT MAX COOL → CHECK AIR MIX DOOR TRAVEL
- BINDING → FREE & ADJUST DOOR REMOVE JUMPER
- NOT BINDING → REPLACE PROGRAMMER & ADJUST AIR MIX DOOR

ELECTRONIC CLIMATE CONTROL SYSTEM TROUBLESHOOTING
NO RECIRCULATE ONLY

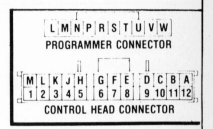

```
L M N P R S T U V W
PROGRAMMER CONNECTOR

M L K J H | G F E | D C B A
1 2 3 4 5 | 6 7 8 | 9 10 11 12
CONTROL HEAD CONNECTOR
```

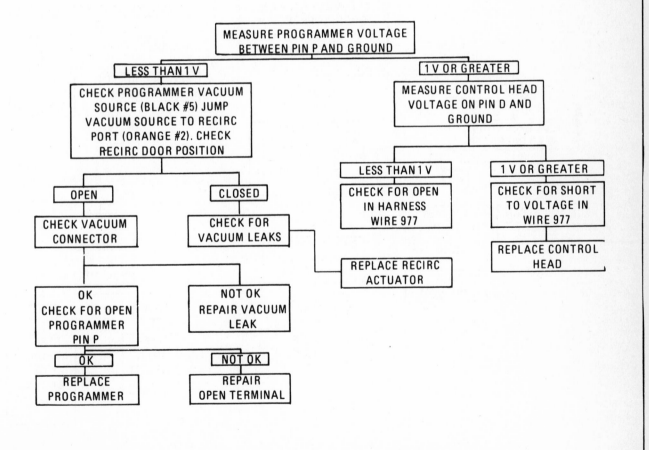

MAKE FUNCTIONAL CHECK
ENGINE WARM AND IDLING
SET AT 60 AND AUTO

MEASURE PROGRAMMER VOLTAGE
BETWEEN PIN P AND GROUND

LESS THAN 1 V

CHECK PROGRAMMER VACUUM
SOURCE (BLACK #5) JUMP
VACUUM SOURCE TO RECIRC
PORT (ORANGE #2). CHECK
RECIRC DOOR POSITION

1 V OR GREATER

MEASURE CONTROL HEAD
VOLTAGE ON PIN D AND
GROUND

OPEN

CHECK VACUUM
CONNECTOR

CLOSED

CHECK FOR
VACUUM LEAKS

LESS THAN 1 V

CHECK FOR OPEN
IN HARNESS
WIRE 977

1 V OR GREATER

CHECK FOR SHORT
TO VOLTAGE IN
WIRE 977

REPLACE CONTROL
HEAD

OK
CHECK FOR OPEN
PROGRAMMER
PIN P

NOT OK
REPAIR VACUUM
LEAK

REPLACE RECIRC
ACTUATOR

OK

REPLACE
PROGRAMMER

NOT OK

REPAIR
OPEN TERMINAL

ELECTRONIC CLIMATE CONTROL SYSTEM TROUBLESHOOTING
REAR DEFROSTER INOPERATIVE

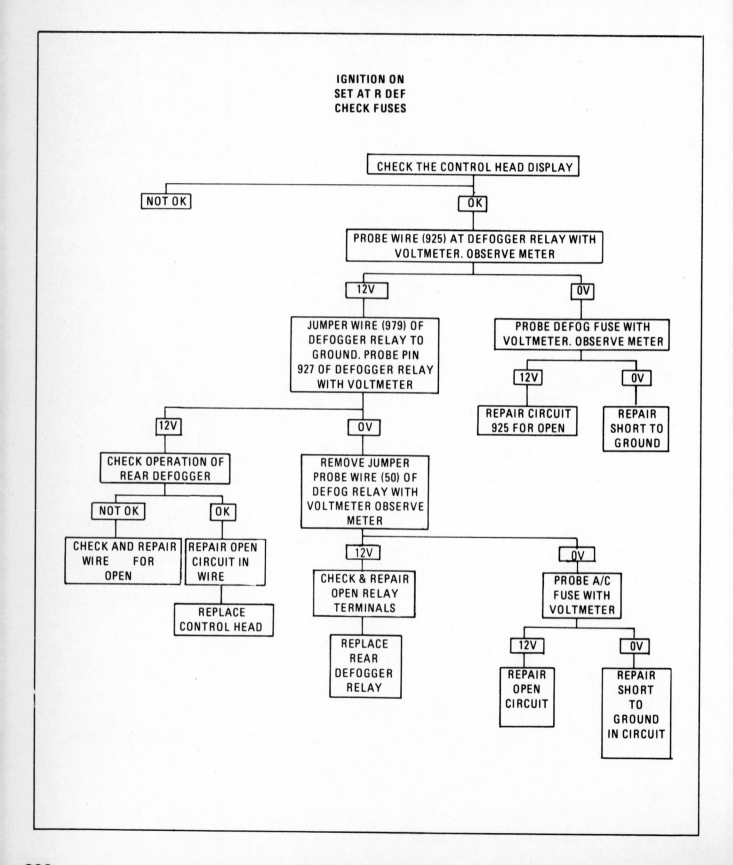

IGNITION ON
SET AT R DEF
CHECK FUSES

CHECK THE CONTROL HEAD DISPLAY

NOT OK

OK

PROBE WIRE (925) AT DEFOGGER RELAY WITH
VOLTMETER. OBSERVE METER

12V

0V

JUMPER WIRE (979) OF
DEFOGGER RELAY TO
GROUND. PROBE PIN
927 OF DEFOGGER RELAY
WITH VOLTMETER

PROBE DEFOG FUSE WITH
VOLTMETER. OBSERVE METER

12V

0V

REPAIR CIRCUIT
925 FOR OPEN

REPAIR
SHORT TO
GROUND

12V

0V

CHECK OPERATION OF
REAR DEFOGGER

REMOVE JUMPER
PROBE WIRE (50) OF
DEFOG RELAY WITH
VOLTMETER OBSERVE
METER

NOT OK

OK

CHECK AND REPAIR
WIRE   FOR
OPEN

REPAIR OPEN
CIRCUIT IN
WIRE

12V

0V

CHECK & REPAIR
OPEN RELAY
TERMINALS

PROBE A/C
FUSE WITH
VOLTMETER

REPLACE
CONTROL HEAD

REPLACE
REAR
DEFOGGER
RELAY

12V

0V

REPAIR
OPEN
CIRCUIT

REPAIR
SHORT
TO
GROUND
IN CIRCUIT

ELECTRONIC CLIMATE CONTROL SYSTEM TROUBLESHOOTING
FRONT DEFROSTER INOPERATIVE

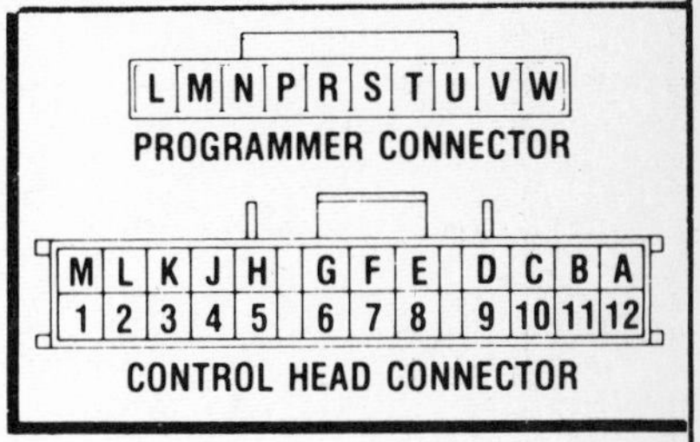

```
L M N P R S T U V W
PROGRAMMER CONNECTOR

M L K J H   G F E   D C B A
1 2 3 4 5   6 7 8   9 10 11 12
CONTROL HEAD CONNECTOR
```

PERFORM FUNCTIONAL TEST
ENGINE WARM AT IDLE
SET CONTROL TO FRONT DEFROST

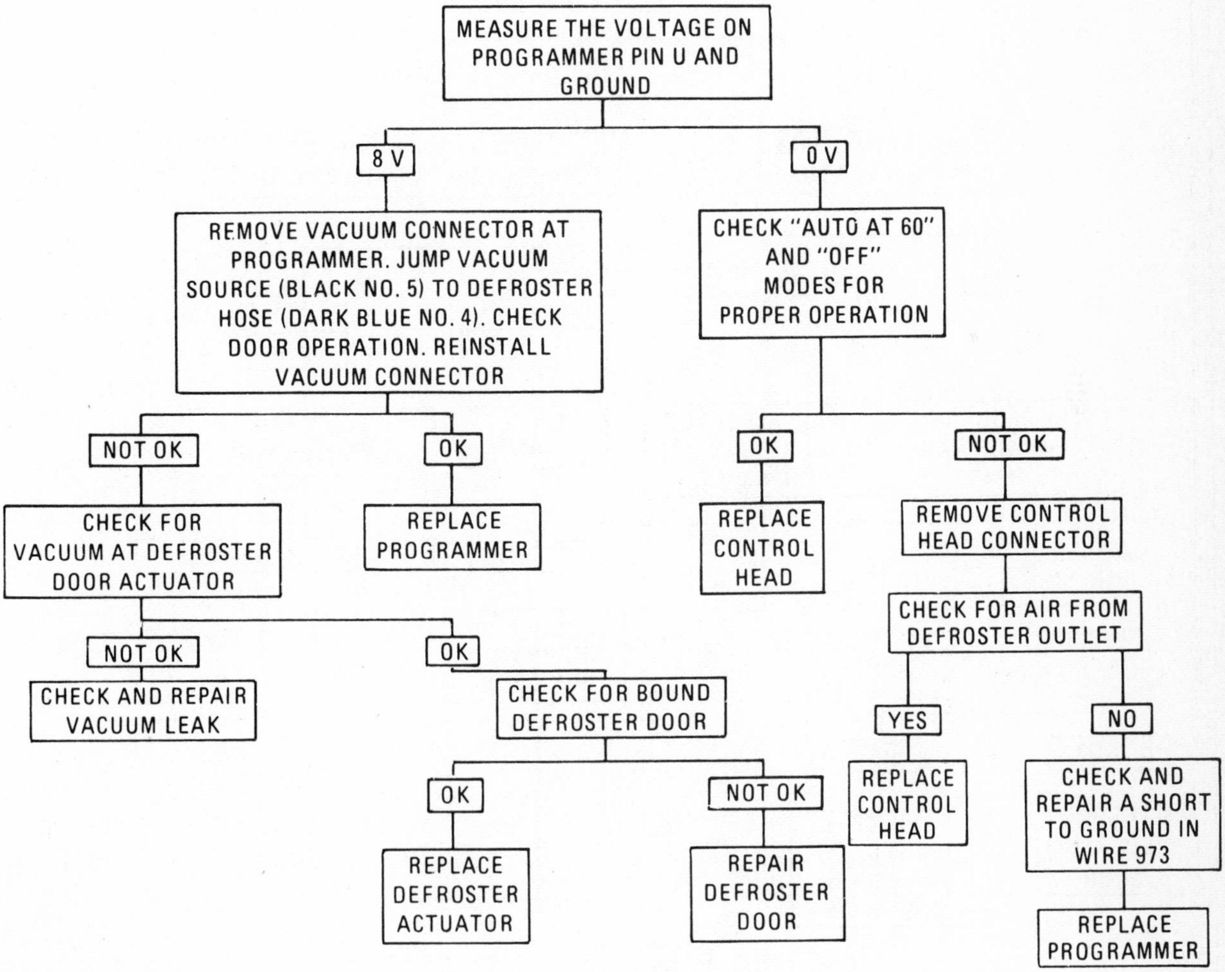

MEASURE THE VOLTAGE ON PROGRAMMER PIN U AND GROUND

8 V

REMOVE VACUUM CONNECTOR AT PROGRAMMER. JUMP VACUUM SOURCE (BLACK NO. 5) TO DEFROSTER HOSE (DARK BLUE NO. 4). CHECK DOOR OPERATION. REINSTALL VACUUM CONNECTOR

NOT OK

CHECK FOR VACUUM AT DEFROSTER DOOR ACTUATOR

NOT OK

CHECK AND REPAIR VACUUM LEAK

OK

REPLACE PROGRAMMER

OK

CHECK FOR BOUND DEFROSTER DOOR

OK

REPLACE DEFROSTER ACTUATOR

NOT OK

REPAIR DEFROSTER DOOR

0 V

CHECK "AUTO AT 60" AND "OFF" MODES FOR PROPER OPERATION

OK

REPLACE CONTROL HEAD

NOT OK

REMOVE CONTROL HEAD CONNECTOR

CHECK FOR AIR FROM DEFROSTER OUTLET

YES

REPLACE CONTROL HEAD

NO

CHECK AND REPAIR A SHORT TO GROUND IN WIRE 973

REPLACE PROGRAMMER

ELECTRONIC CLIMATE CONTROL SYSTEM TROUBLESHOOTING
INSUFFICIENT HEAT

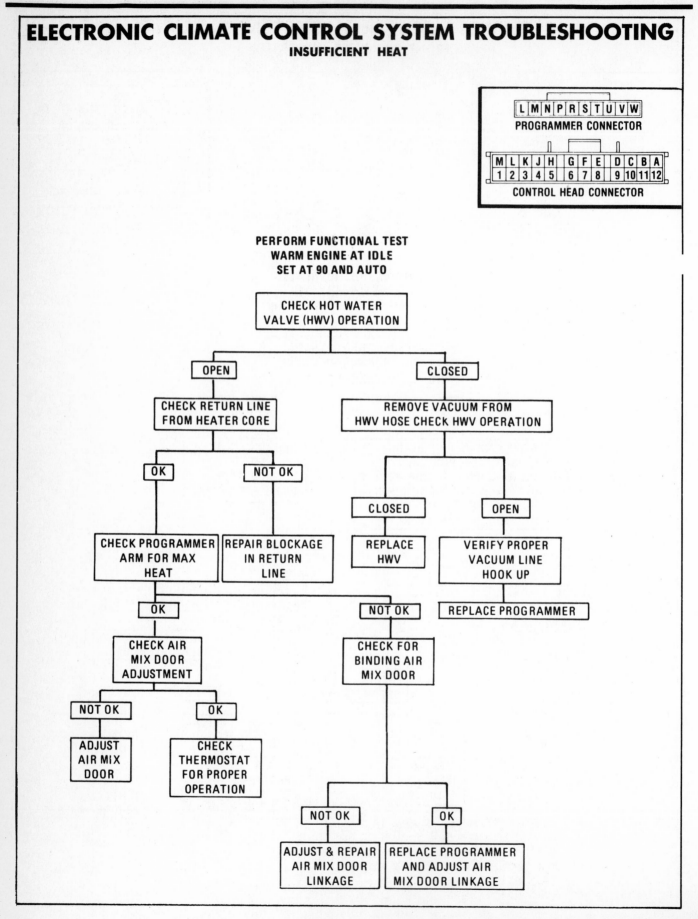

PROGRAMMER CONNECTOR

| L | M | N | P | R | S | T | U | V | W |

CONTROL HEAD CONNECTOR

| M | L | K | J | H | | G | F | E | | D | C | B | A |
| 1 | 2 | 3 | 4 | 5 | | 6 | 7 | 8 | | 9 | 10 | 11 | 12 |

PERFORM FUNCTIONAL TEST
WARM ENGINE AT IDLE
SET AT 90 AND AUTO

CHECK HOT WATER VALVE (HWV) OPERATION

OPEN

CHECK RETURN LINE FROM HEATER CORE

OK → CHECK PROGRAMMER ARM FOR MAX HEAT

NOT OK → REPAIR BLOCKAGE IN RETURN LINE

OK → CHECK AIR MIX DOOR ADJUSTMENT

NOT OK → ADJUST AIR MIX DOOR

OK → CHECK THERMOSTAT FOR PROPER OPERATION

CLOSED

REMOVE VACUUM FROM HWV HOSE CHECK HWV OPERATION

CLOSED → REPLACE HWV

OPEN → VERIFY PROPER VACUUM LINE HOOK UP → REPLACE PROGRAMMER

NOT OK → CHECK FOR BINDING AIR MIX DOOR

NOT OK → ADJUST & REPAIR AIR MIX DOOR LINKAGE

OK → REPLACE PROGRAMMER AND ADJUST AIR MIX DOOR LINKAGE

INDEX

CHEVROLET/GMC LIGHT TRUCKS SERIES S-10, S-15 PICK-UP, MULTI-PURPOSE VEHICLE (SMALL BLAZER)

Specifications

REFRIGERANT AND OIL CAPACITY

ALL MODELS

Refrigerant 12	37 ounces
Refrigerant Oil	10 fluid ounces

BELT TENSION

Engine	New (lbs)	Used (lbs)
LQ-7 (2.2L, Diesel L-4, Vin Code S)	135	79
LR-1 (1.9L, L-4, Vin Code A)	157	90
LR-2 (2.8L, V-6, Vin Code B)	146	67
LQ-2 (2.0L, L-4, Vin Code Y)	169	90

NOTE: Check belt tension with tool number BT-7825 or its equivalent.

Blower Motor

Removal and Installation

1. Disconnect the battery ground cable.
2. Remove the vacuum tank assembly.
3. Remove the blower motor flange attaching screws.
4. Remove the blower motor.
5. The installation is the reverse of the removal procedure.

Blower Resistor

Removal and Installation

NOTE: The blower resistor is located on the blower side of the blower-evaporator case.

1. Disconnect the negative battery cable.
2. Disconnect the wiring harness connector at the resistor.
3. Remove the resistor mounting screws and remove the resistor.
4. The installation is the reverse of the removal procedure.

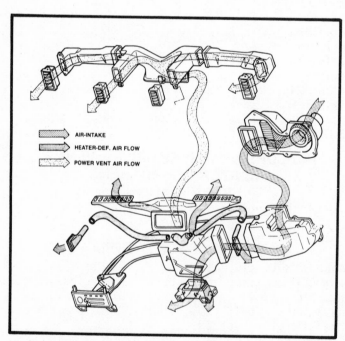

AIR-INTAKE

HEATER-DEF. AIR FLOW

POWER VENT AIR FLOW

Air conditioning system air flow (© General Motors Corporation)

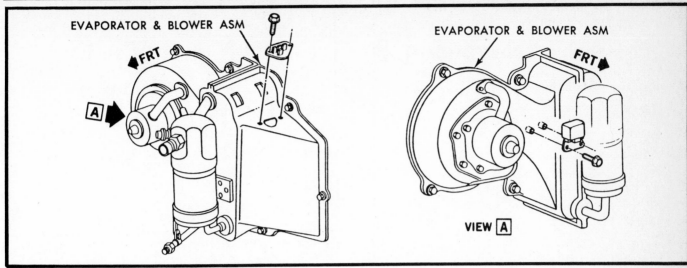

A/C relay and resistor locations (© General Motors Corporation)

Blower Motor Relay

Removal and Installation

1. Disconnect the battery ground cable, the relay electrical connections and mounting screws. Remove the relay.
2. The installation is the reverse of the removal procedure.

Fuses

A fuse located in the junction block, protects the entire air conditioning system except the blower when operating at high speeds. A second fuse, located in the electrical wiring between the junction terminal and the air conditioning relay, protects the blower high speed circuit.

Compressor

Removal

L-4 ENGINE

1. Discharge the air conditioning system as previously outlined.
2. Disconnect the negative battery terminal. Disconnect the electrical connection at the compressor.
3. Remove the brace between the power steering pump bracket and engine.
4. Remove the air cleaner attaching bolts and lay aside for access to the compressor.
5. Remove the brace from the A/C bracket to the engine.
6. Remove the compressor mounting bolts.
7. Remove the drive belt and the manifold at the rear of the compressor.
8. Remove the compressor from the engine.

Installation

1. Position the compressor on the engine.
2. Install the drive belt and the manifold at the rear of the compressor.
3. Install the compressor mounting bolts. Install the brace between the A/C bracket and the engine.
4. Reposition the air cleaner and secure.

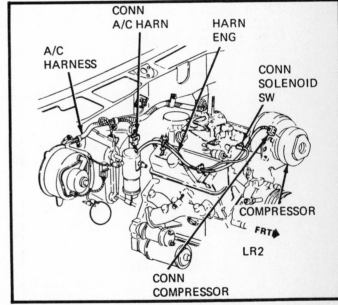

Typical compressor and wiring harness routing (© General Motors Corporation)

5. Install the brace between the power steering bracket and the engine.
6. Connect the electrical connector at the compressor and the negative battery cable.
7. Evacuate and charge the system as previously outlined. Install proper amount of refrigerant oil to system.

Removal

V-6 ENGINE

1. Discharge the A/C system and disconnect the negative battery cable.
2. Remove the manifold at the rear of the compressor.
3. Remove the compressor mounting bolts and remove the compressor.

Installation

1. Position the compressor to the engine and install the mounting bolts.
2. Install the manifold at the rear of the compressor.

3. Install the negative battery cable, evacuate and recharge the A/C system as previously outlined.

Expansion Tube (Orifice)

Removal and Installation

1. Discharge the A/C system.
2. Disconnect the liquid line at the evaporator inlet pipe. Cap the liquid line.
3. Using needle nose pliers, remove the expansion tube from the evaporator inlet tube.

NOTE: Commercial tools are available to remove and install the expansion tube in either a whole or broken state.

4. Remove the expansion tube ''O'' ring from the evaporator inlet tube.

Installation

1. Install the expansion tube using a new ''O'' ring coated with refrigerant oil. Insert the short screen end of the tube into the evaporator inlet tube first.
2. Evacuate and recharge the A/C system.

Condenser

Removal and Installation

1. Discharge the A/C system and disconnect the negative battery cable.
2. Remove the upper fan shroud assembly.
3. Drain the cooling system and remove the radiator.
4. Remove the shields on either side of the radiator support.
5. Remove the condenser mounts and disconnect the condenser lines. Cap the line ends as soon as possible.
6. Remove the condenser from the vehicle.
7. The installation is the reverse of the removal procedure.
8. Add the necessary refrigerant oil to the condenser.
9. Fill the cooling system, connect the negative battery cable, evacuate and recharge the A/C system.

Evaporator

Removal and Installation

1. Discharge the A/C system and disconnect the negative battery cable.
2. Remove the resistor from the case without removing the wiring.
3. Remove the air cleaner and lay aside for access to the evaporator assembly. Disconnect the A/C lines to the Evaporator.

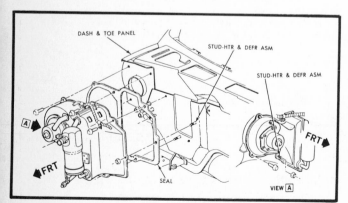

Evaporator/accumulator assembly (© General Motors Corporation)

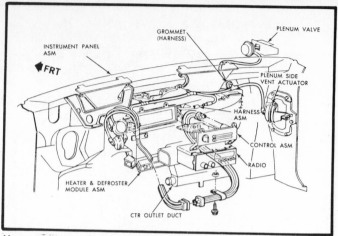

Vacuum line routing, S series (© General Motors Corporation)

4. Remove the five retaining screws and the two nuts at the case side.
5. Disconnect the connect at the A/C harness. Remove the evaporator case assembly.
6. Separate the case halves and remove the core cover.
7. Disconnect the liquid line and evaporator to accumulator line.
8. Remove the screw at the evaporator line bracket to accumulator bracket.
9. Remove the evaporator core, including the expansion tube.
10. To install the evaporator core, reverse the removal procedure.
11. Connect the negative battery cable, evacuate and recharge the system.

Accumulator

Removal and Installation

1. Discharge the A/C system and disconnect the negative battery cable.
2. Disconnect the accumulator inlet and outlet connections. Cap or plug the lines immediately.
3. Remove the accumulator retaining screws and remove the accumulator.
4. Measure the amount of refrigerant oil in the accumulator and install this amount, plus two ounces, into the new accumulator assembly.
5. Install the accumulator, using new ''O'' rings coated with fresh refrigerant oil.
6. Install the retaining screws. Connect the negative battery cable, evacuate and recharge the A/C system.

Air Conditioning Control Head And Blower Switch

Removal

1. Disconnect the negative battery cable.
2. Remove the instrument panel center bezel by removing the retaining screws and carefully pulling the bezel away from the instrument panel.
3. Remove the control attaching screws. Pull unit away from dash and remove the bulb socket, vacuum and electrical connections.
4. Remove the control head from the instrument panel. The blower switch can be replaced or serviced with the control head out.

Installation

1. Position the control head on the instrument panel, install the vacuum and electrical connections to the control head. Install the bulb socket.
2. Install the control head retaining screws.
3. To adjust the temperature cable, disengage the temperature cable

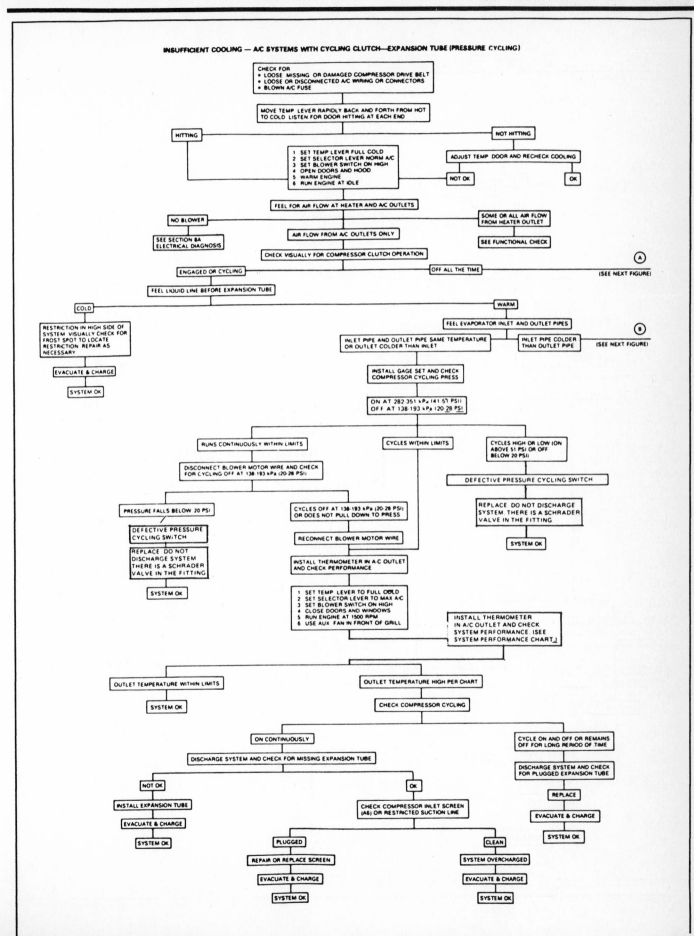

INSUFFICIENT COOLING — A/C SYSTEMS WITH CYCLING CLUTCH—EXPANSION TUBE (PRESSURE CYCLING)

CHECK FOR
- LOOSE, MISSING OR DAMAGED COMPRESSOR DRIVE BELT
- LOOSE OR DISCONNECTED A/C WIRING OR CONNECTORS
- BLOWN A/C FUSE

MOVE TEMP LEVER RAPIDLY BACK AND FORTH FROM HOT TO COLD LISTEN FOR DOOR HITTING AT EACH END

HITTING / NOT HITTING

1 SET TEMP LEVER FULL COLD
2 SET SELECTOR LEVER NORM A/C
3 SET BLOWER SWITCH ON HIGH
4 OPEN DOORS AND HOOD
5 WARM ENGINE
6 RUN ENGINE AT IDLE

ADJUST TEMP DOOR AND RECHECK COOLING
NOT OK / OK

FEEL FOR AIR FLOW AT HEATER AND A/C OUTLETS

NO BLOWER / AIR FLOW FROM A/C OUTLETS ONLY / SOME OR ALL AIR FLOW FROM HEATER OUTLET

SEE SECTION 8A ELECTRICAL DIAGNOSIS / SEE FUNCTIONAL CHECK

CHECK VISUALLY FOR COMPRESSOR CLUTCH OPERATION

ENGAGED OR CYCLING / OFF ALL THE TIME (SEE NEXT FIGURE) Ⓐ

FEEL LIQUID LINE BEFORE EXPANSION TUBE

COLD / WARM

RESTRICTION IN HIGH SIDE OF SYSTEM VISUALLY CHECK FOR FROST SPOT TO LOCATE RESTRICTION REPAIR AS NECESSARY

FEEL EVAPORATOR INLET AND OUTLET PIPES

INLET PIPE AND OUTLET PIPE SAME TEMPERATURE OR OUTLET COLDER THAN INLET / INLET PIPE COLDER THAN OUTLET PIPE (SEE NEXT FIGURE) Ⓑ

EVACUATE & CHARGE

INSTALL GAGE SET AND CHECK COMPRESSOR CYCLING PRESS

SYSTEM OK

ON AT 282-351 kPa (41-51 PSI)
OFF AT 138-193 kPa (20-28 PSI)

RUNS CONTINUOUSLY WITHIN LIMITS / CYCLES WITHIN LIMITS / CYCLES HIGH OR LOW (ON ABOVE 51 PSI OR OFF BELOW 20 PSI)

DISCONNECT BLOWER MOTOR WIRE AND CHECK FOR CYCLING OFF AT 138-193 kPa (20-28 PSI)

DEFECTIVE PRESSURE CYCLING SWITCH

PRESSURE FALLS BELOW 20 PSI / CYCLES OFF AT 138-193 kPa (20-28 PSI) OR DOES NOT PULL DOWN TO PRESS

REPLACE DO NOT DISCHARGE SYSTEM THERE IS A SCHRADER VALVE IN THE FITTING

DEFECTIVE PRESSURE CYCLING SWITCH / RECONNECT BLOWER MOTOR WIRE

REPLACE DO NOT DISCHARGE SYSTEM THERE IS A SCHRADER VALVE IN THE FITTING / INSTALL THERMOMETER IN A/C OUTLET AND CHECK PERFORMANCE

SYSTEM OK

SYSTEM OK

1 SET TEMP LEVER TO FULL COLD
2 SET SELECTOR LEVER TO MAX A/C
3 SET BLOWER SWITCH ON HIGH
4 CLOSE DOORS AND WINDOWS
5 RUN ENGINE AT 1500 RPM
6 USE AUX FAN IN FRONT OF GRILL

INSTALL THERMOMETER IN A/C OUTLET AND CHECK SYSTEM PERFORMANCE. (SEE SYSTEM PERFORMANCE CHART.)

OUTLET TEMPERATURE WITHIN LIMITS / OUTLET TEMPERATURE HIGH PER CHART

SYSTEM OK / CHECK COMPRESSOR CYCLING

ON CONTINUOUSLY / CYCLE ON AND OFF OR REMAINS OFF FOR LONG PERIOD OF TIME

DISCHARGE SYSTEM AND CHECK FOR MISSING EXPANSION TUBE / DISCHARGE SYSTEM AND CHECK FOR PLUGGED EXPANSION TUBE

NOT OK / OK / REPLACE

INSTALL EXPANSION TUBE / CHECK COMPRESSOR INLET SCREEN (A6) OR RESTRICTED SUCTION LINE / EVACUATE & CHARGE

EVACUATE & CHARGE / SYSTEM OK

SYSTEM OK / PLUGGED / CLEAN

REPAIR OR REPLACE SCREEN / SYSTEM OVERCHARGED

EVACUATE & CHARGE / EVACUATE & CHARGE

SYSTEM OK / SYSTEM OK

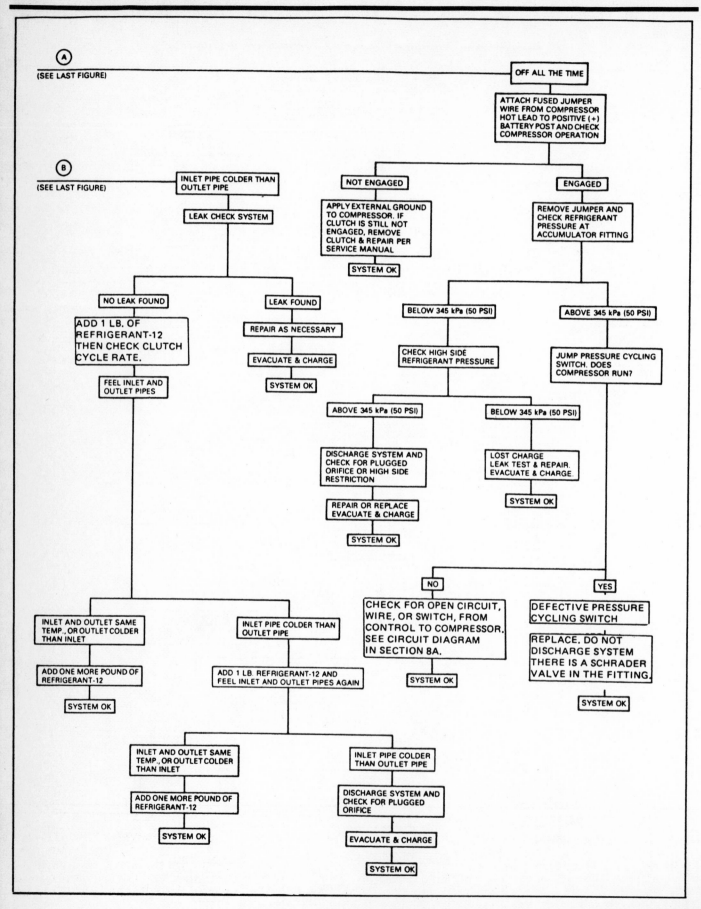

(A) (SEE LAST FIGURE)

OFF ALL THE TIME

ATTACH FUSED JUMPER WIRE FROM COMPRESSOR HOT LEAD TO POSITIVE (+) BATTERY POST AND CHECK COMPRESSOR OPERATION

(B) (SEE LAST FIGURE)

INLET PIPE COLDER THAN OUTLET PIPE

LEAK CHECK SYSTEM

NOT ENGAGED

APPLY EXTERNAL GROUND TO COMPRESSOR. IF CLUTCH IS STILL NOT ENGAGED, REMOVE CLUTCH & REPAIR PER SERVICE MANUAL

SYSTEM OK

ENGAGED

REMOVE JUMPER AND CHECK REFRIGERANT PRESSURE AT ACCUMULATOR FITTING

NO LEAK FOUND

ADD 1 LB. OF REFRIGERANT-12 THEN CHECK CLUTCH CYCLE RATE.

FEEL INLET AND OUTLET PIPES

LEAK FOUND

REPAIR AS NECESSARY

EVACUATE & CHARGE

SYSTEM OK

BELOW 345 kPa (50 PSI)

CHECK HIGH SIDE REFRIGERANT PRESSURE

ABOVE 345 kPa (50 PSI)

JUMP PRESSURE CYCLING SWITCH. DOES COMPRESSOR RUN?

ABOVE 345 kPa (50 PSI)

DISCHARGE SYSTEM AND CHECK FOR PLUGGED ORIFICE OR HIGH SIDE RESTRICTION

REPAIR OR REPLACE EVACUATE & CHARGE

SYSTEM OK

BELOW 345 kPa (50 PSI)

LOST CHARGE LEAK TEST & REPAIR. EVACUATE & CHARGE.

SYSTEM OK

NO

CHECK FOR OPEN CIRCUIT, WIRE, OR SWITCH, FROM CONTROL TO COMPRESSOR. SEE CIRCUIT DIAGRAM IN SECTION 8A.

SYSTEM OK

YES

DEFECTIVE PRESSURE CYCLING SWITCH

REPLACE. DO NOT DISCHARGE SYSTEM THERE IS A SCHRADER VALVE IN THE FITTING.

SYSTEM OK

INLET AND OUTLET SAME TEMP., OR OUTLET COLDER THAN INLET

ADD ONE MORE POUND OF REFRIGERANT-12

SYSTEM OK

INLET PIPE COLDER THAN OUTLET PIPE

ADD 1 LB. REFRIGERANT-12 AND FEEL INLET AND OUTLET PIPES AGAIN

INLET AND OUTLET SAME TEMP., OR OUTLET COLDER THAN INLET

ADD ONE MORE POUND OF REFRIGERANT-12

SYSTEM OK

INLET PIPE COLDER THAN OUTLET PIPE

DISCHARGE SYSTEM AND CHECK FOR PLUGGED ORIFICE

EVACUATE & CHARGE

SYSTEM OK

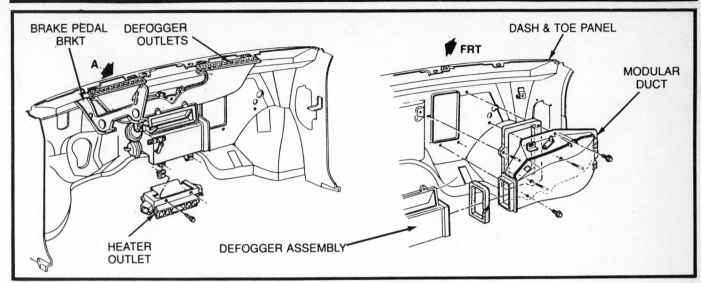

Heater defroster assembly (© General Motors Corporation)

retaining clip from the bellcrank post. Move the temperature control lever to its full travel in both directions. The cable will automatically adjust its self.

4. Reconnect the temperature cable retaining clip.

5. Install the center bezel on the instrument panel and connect the negative battery cables.

Heater Core

Removal and Installation

1. Disconnect the negative battery cable.

2. Drain the coolant from the cooling system.

3. Remove the heater hose from the core tubes and plug the core tubes to prevent coolant leakage during core removal.

4. Remove the heater core cover attaching screws and remove the cover.

5. Remove the four screw retainers at the ends of the heater core.

6. Remove the core from under the dash assembly.

7. To install the heater core, reverse the removal procedure as required.

8. Fill the coolant system, connect the negative battery cable and verify that repairs are correct.

CHEVROLET/GMC LIGHT TRUCKS PICK-UPS, 4 WHEEL DRIVE, VANS, BLAZER, SUBURBAN

Specifications

REFRIGERANT CAPACITY

PICK-UPS, FRONT WHEEL DRIVE, SUBURBANS, BLAZER
C-60 System (CCOT)
3 lbs. 12 oz.
Overhead System (C-69)
5 lbs. 4 oz.

VAN MODELS
C-60 System (CCOT)
3 lbs.
Overhead System (C-69)
5 lbs.

REFRIGERANT OIL CAPACITY

NOTE: When replacing accumulator, the removed oil must be measured and the same amount plus two ounces must be installed into the system. When replacing compressors and the vehicle is equipped with the A-6 Compressor, Measure the removed oil. If less than six ounces, add six ounces to the system, if more than six ounces, add the same amount of new oil as was removed and measured. When equipped with the R-4 compressor, remove the oil, measure and replace with the same amount plus one ounce.

1982–85 MODELS

Models	Conventional System	Overhead System
Pick-ups, Four Wheel Vehicles, Suburbans, Vans, Blazer		
With A-6 Compressor	16 ounces	19 ounces
With R-4 Compressor	12 ounces	—

BELT TENSION

Engine	New (lbs.)	Used (lbs.)
All L6 and V8 Gasoline engines	145	65–100
6.2 Diesel Engine	175	55–100

NOTE: A used belt is one that has been rotated at least one complete turn of the engine belt pulleys. This procedure begins the seating of the new belt and it should never be reset to new belt specifications.

REFRIGERANT — 12 PRESSURE — TEMPERATURE RELATIONSHIP	(°F)(°C)		(PSIG)(kPa)		(°F)(°C)		(PSIG)(kPa)	
	−21.7	−29.8C	0(ATMOSPHERIC PRESSURE)	0(kPa)	55	12.7C	52.0	358.5
	−20	−28.8C	2.4	16.5	60	15.5C	57.7	397.8
	−10	−23.3C	4.5	31.0	65	18.3C	63.7	439.2
	−5	−20.5C	6.8	46.9	70	21.1C	70.1	482.7
The table below indicates the pressure of Refrigerant — 12 at various temperatures. For instance, a drum of Refrigerant at a temperature	0	−17.7C	9.2	63.4	75	23.8C	76.9	530.2
	5	−15.0C	11.8	81.4	80	26.6C	84.1	579.9
	10	−12.2C	14.7	101.4	85	29.4C	91.7	632.3
of 80°F (26.6°C) will have a pressure of 84.1 PSI	15	−9.4C	17.7	122.0	90	32.2C	99.6	686.7
(579.9 kPa). If it is heated to 125°F (51.6°C), the	20	−6.6C	21.1	145.5	95	35.0C	108.1	745.3
pressure will increase to 167.5 PSI (1154.9	25	−3.8C	24.6	169.6	100	37.7C	116.9	806.0
kPa). It also can be used conversely to deter-	30	−1.1C	28.5	196.5	105	40.5C	126.2	870.2
mine the temperature at which Refrigerant —	32	0C	30.1	207.5	110	43.3C	136.0	937.7
12 boils under various pressures. For example,	35	1.6C	32.6	224.8	115	46.1C	146.5	1010.1
at a pressure of 30.1 PSI (207.5 kPa), Refriger-	40	4.4C	37.0	255.1	120	48.8C	157.1	1083.2
ant — 12 boils at 32°F (0°C).	45	7.2C	41.7	287.5	125	51.6C	167.5	1154.9
	50	10.0C	46.7	322.0	130	54.4C	179.0	1234.2
					140	60.0C	204.5	1410.0

Pressure-temperature relationship of Refrigerant R-12 (© General Motors Corporation)

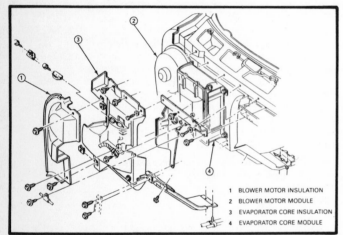

1 BLOWER MOTOR INSULATION
2 BLOWER MOTOR MODULE
3 EVAPORATOR CORE INSULATION
4 EVAPORATOR CORE MODULE

Extra insulation used on vans equipped with the 6.2 L diesel engine

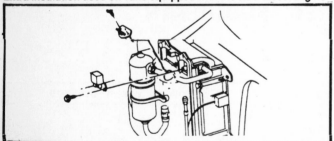

Location of blower motor resistor and relay components (© General Motors Corporation)

Blower Motor

Removal and Installation

PICK-UP TRUCKS, FOUR WHEEL DRIVE, BLAZER AND SUBURBANS

1. Disconnect the negative battery cable.
2. Disconnect the blower motor electrical feed wire and the ground wire.
3. Disconnect the blower motor cooling tube.
4. Remove the blower to case retaining screws and remove the blower motor assembly.
5. The nut can be removed from the motor shaft and the blower wheel removed.
6. To install, replace the sealer on the motor flange as required and reverse the removal procedure.

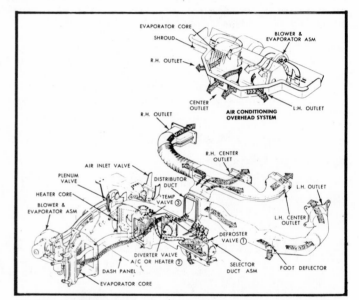

Air flow through A/C-Heater system and rear overhead system, typical of all except van models (© General Motors Corporation)

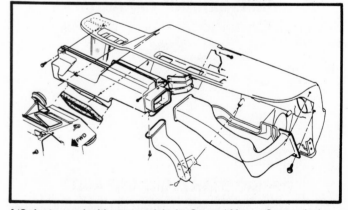

A/C ducts used with van models (© General Motors Corporation)

VAN MODELS

1. Disconnect the negative battery cable.
2. Remove the coolant recovery tank and the power antenna, if equipped.

3. Disconnect the blower motor lead wire connector.

4. Remove the retaining screws from the blower motor to housing and remove the blower motor.

5. If required, remove the nut from the motor shaft and remove the blower fan.

6. To install, replace the sealer on the motor flange as required and reverse the removal procedure.

NOTE: The Van models equipped with the 6.2 liter diesel engine have extra insulation around the blower motor and evaporator core. The parking lamp must be removed, along with the radiator overflow tank. Remove the retaining screws and remove the insulation through the hood opening. Proceed with the normal blower motor removal and installation procedure.

Compressor

Removal

PICK-UP TRUCKS, FOUR WHEEL DRIVE, BLAZER AND SUBURBANS

1. Discharge the air conditioning system safely.

2. Remove the connector attaching bolt and connector. Cap or plug all open connections at once.

3. Disconnect the electrical leads to the compressor clutch unit.

4. Loosen the brace and pivot bolts. Remove the drive belt.

5. Remove the nuts and bolts holding the compressor brackets to the mounting brackets. Remove the compressor from the engine.

6. Before servicing the compressor, drain and measure the oil in the compressor. Check for evidence of contamination to determine if the remainder of the system requires service.

Installation

1. If the oil that was drained from the compressor shows no signs of contamination, replace the same amount of fresh refrigerant oil into the compressor before installation. If other components were removed, serviced or replaced, and the correct amount of refrigerant oil to the system.

2. Position the compressor to the mounting bracket and install all nuts and bolts.

3. Install the connector assembly to the rear of the compressor head, using new "O" rings coated with clean refrigerant oil.

4. Connect the electrical lead to the coil and install and adjust the compressor belt.

5. Evacuate, charge and check the system for proper operation.

Removal

VAN MODELS

1. Disconnect the negative battery cable.

2. Disconnect the compressor clutch electrical connector.

3. Discharge the system safely.

4. Release the belt tension at the idler pulley and remove the drive belt from the compressor pulley.

NOTE: It may be necessary to remove the crankshaft pulley on some vehicles to remove the compressor drive belt.

5. Remove the engine cover from inside the vehicle.

6. Remove the air cleaner to aid in clearance for compressor removal.

7. Remove the fitting and the muffler assembly. Cap or plug all openings.

8. Remove the nuts and bolts attaching the compressor to the bracket.

9. Remove the engine oil tube support bracket bolt and nut from the compressor and the compressor clutch ground lead.

10. Remove the compressor from the engine. Before compressor service, drain and measure the oil in the compressor. Check for evidence of contamination to determine if other components require service.

Installation

1. If the oil drained from the compressor showed no signs of contamination, replace the same amount of fresh refrigerant oil into the compressor, plus the correct amount for any other component that may have been replaced, also.

2. Position the compressor on its brackets and install the nuts and bolts.

3. Install the connector assembly to the compressor rear head, using a new "O" ring coated with fresh refrigerant oil.

4. Connect the electrical lead to the clutch coil and install and adjust the compressor drive belt, using the idler pulley.

5. Complete the assembly (air cleaner and engine cover).

6. Evacuate, charge and check the system for proper operation.

NOTE: On some Van models, it may be necessary to increase the idler slack adjustment. This may be accomplished by removing and discarding the idler adjustment bolt. Remove the idler backing plate and elongate all three adjusting slots approximately one-half inch, either inboard or outboard, as required. Reinstall the idler assembly and adjust the belt tension using a lever to move the pulley outboard until the proper belt tension is reached. If the belt is being replaced, it may be necessary to remove and replace the throttle cable during the belt replacement procedure. If so, check the throttle cable adjustment when done. It may also be necessary to remove the crankshaft pulley on some models to replace the compressor drive belt.

Fixed Orifice (Expansion) Tube

Removal and Installation

ALL MODELS

1. Discharge the air conditioning system safely.

2. Disconnect the condenser to evaporator line at the evaporator inlet. Cap or plug the lines immediately.

3. Using needle nose pliers or a special removing tool, pull the expansion tube from the inlet tube.

4. To install the expansion tube, coat the new "O" ring with fresh refrigerant oil and insert the short screen end of the tube into the evaporator inlet tube.

5. Remove the caps or plugs from the lines and connect.

6. Evacuate, charge and check the system for proper operation.

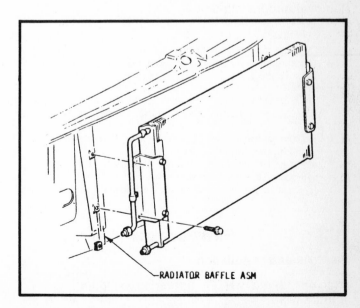

RADIATOR BAFFLE ASM

Condensor attachment, van models (© General Motors Corporation)

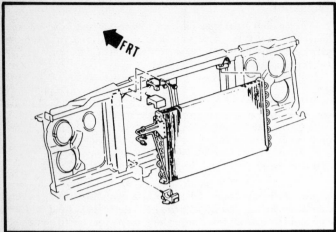

Condensor attachments, all except van models (© General Motors Corporation)

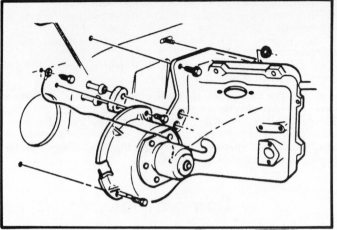

Evaporator-blower motor housing attachment, all except van models (© General Motors Corporation)

Condenser

Removal and Installation

PICK-UP TRUCKS, FOUR WHEEL DRIVE, BLAZER AND SUBURBANS

1. Disconnect the negative battery cable.
2. Discharge the air conditioning system safely.
3. Remove the grille assembly and the radiator center grille support.
4. Remove the left grille support to upper fender support screws.
5. Disconnect the condenser inlet and outlet lines. Disconnect the outlet tube line at the right side of the condenser. Cap or plug all lines immediately.
6. Remove the condenser to radiator support screws.
7. Bend the left grille support outboard to gain clearance for the condenser removal.
8. Remove the condenser by pulling it forward and then lowering it from the vehicle.
9. To install the condenser, add one fluid ounce of fresh refrigerant oil to the condenser and install it in the reverse of the removal procedure.
10. Evacuate, charge and check the air conditioning system for proper operation.

Removal and Installation

VAN MODELS

1. Disconnect the negative battery cable.
2. Discharge the air conditioning system safely.
3. Remove the grille, hood lock and center hood lock support as an assembly.
4. Disconnect the condenser inlet and outlet lines at the condenser.
5. Remove the condenser bracket attaching screws on the left and right sides.
6. Remove the condenser from the vehicle. If necessary, remove the left hand bracket from the condenser.
7. To install the condenser, add one fluid ounce of refrigerant oil to the unit and reverse the removal procedure.
8. Evacuate, charge and check the air conditioning system for proper operation.

Evaporator

Removal and Installation

PICK-UPS, FOUR WHEEL DRIVE, BLAZER AND SUBURBANS

1. Disconnect the negative battery cable.

2. Discharge the air conditioning system safely.
3. Remove the nuts from the selector duct studs projecting through the dash panel.
4. Remove the cover to dash and cover to case crews. Remove the evaporator case cover.
5. Disconnect the evaporator core inlet and outlet lines. Cap or plug all open connections immediately.
6. Remove the expansion tube as outlined previously. Remove the evaporator core assembly.
7. To install the evaporator, add three fluid ounces of fresh refrigerant oil to the evaporator, coat the "O" rings with fresh refrigerant oil and install the orifice tube by inserting the short screen end of the tube into the evaporator inlet line. Reverse the removal procedure to complete the installation.
8. Evacuate, charge and check the system for proper operation.

Removal and Installation

VAN MODELS
WITH 6.2 L DIESEL ENGINE

1. Disconnect the negative battery cable. Remove the cold air intake.
2. Disconnect the hood latch assembly and cable retainer. Move the assembly out of the way and secure.
3. Remove the windshield solvent reservoir.
4. Discharge the air conditioning system safely.
5. Disconnect the low pressure vapor line and move it out of working area. Cap or plug the line connections immediately.
6. Remove the accumulator. Cap or plug the openings immediately.
7. Disconnect, cap or plug the openings and remove the high pressure line inlet to the evaporator and remove the connecting bracket.
8. Remove the wiring harness going to the blower motor relay and resistors. Remove the relay and resistors.
9. Remove the upper half of the fan shroud.
10. Drain the cooling system and remove the radiator.
11. Disconnect the heater valve assembly bracket and move it out of the way.
12. Remove the upper screws from the lower bracket and push it down and out of the way.
13. Remove the insulation retaining screws and remove the insulation through the hood opening.
14. Refer to the following outline for Evaporator removal and installation from Van models without the diesel engine and continue the removal procedure. During the installation, reverse these removal procedures to complete the installation of the evaporator in the diesel engine equipped van models.

Removal and Installation

VAN MODELS WITHOUT 6.2 L DIESEL ENGINE

NOTE: If any of the following steps have been done during the

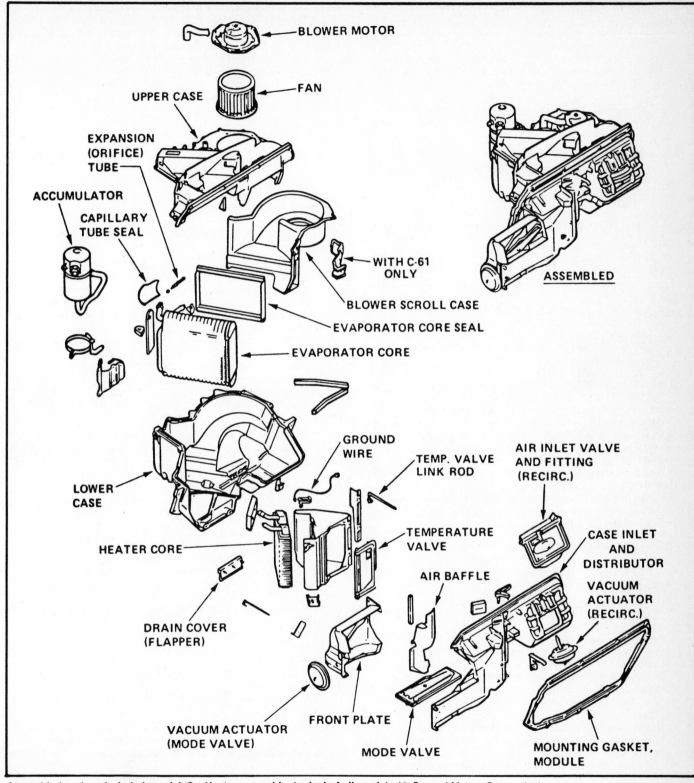

BLOWER MOTOR

FAN

UPPER CASE

EXPANSION (ORIFICE) TUBE

ACCUMULATOR

CAPILLARY TUBE SEAL

WITH C-61 ONLY

BLOWER SCROLL CASE

EVAPORATOR CORE SEAL

EVAPORATOR CORE

ASSEMBLED

GROUND WIRE

TEMP. VALVE LINK ROD

AIR INLET VALVE AND FITTING (RECIRC.)

LOWER CASE

TEMPERATURE VALVE

CASE INLET AND DISTRIBUTOR

HEATER CORE

AIR BAFFLE

VACUUM ACTUATOR (RECIRC.)

DRAIN COVER (FLAPPER)

VACUUM ACTUATOR (MODE VALVE)

FRONT PLATE

MODE VALVE

MOUNTING GASKET, MODULE

Assembled and exploded view of A/C—Heater assembly, typical of all models (© General Motors Corporation)

removal procedure of Van Models equipped with the diesel engine, proceed to the next appropriate step. Reverse the procedure to install the evaporator assembly.

1. Disconnect the negative battery cable.
2. Discharge the air conditioning system safely.
3. Remove the coolant recovery reservoir and bracket.
4. Disconnect all electrical connections from the case assembly.

5. Remove the bracket at the evaporator case.
6. Remove the right hand marker lamp for access.
7. Disconnect the accumulator inlet and outlet lines and the two brackets attaching the accumulator to the evaporator case. Cap or plug the open lines immediately.
8. Disconnect the evaporator inlet line, cap or plug the line immediately.

9. Remove the three retaining nuts and the one screw attaching the evaporator module to the dash panel.

10. Remove the evaporator core case from the vehicle. Remove the retaining screws and separate the case sections.

11. Remove the evaporator core and complete the required repairs.

12. Add three fluid ounces of refrigerant oil to the evaporator upon installation. Reverse the removal procedure to install the evaporator assembly.

13. Fill the cooling system and verify correct level of coolant.

14. Evacuate, charge and check the air conditioning system for proper operation.

Heater Core

Removal and Installation

PICK-UP TRUCKS, FOUR WHEEL DRIVE, BLAZER AND SUBURBANS

1. Disconnect the negative battery cable.

2. Drain the cooling system and remove the heater hoses from the core tubes. Plug the core tubes and the hose ends to prevent coolant leakage.

3. Remove the glove box and door as an assembly.

4. Remove the center duct to selector duct and instrument panel screws. Remove the center lower and center upper ducts.

5. Disconnect the bowden cable at the temperature door.

6. Remove the retaining nuts from the three selector duct studs projecting through the dash panel.

7. Remove the selector duct to dash panel screws from inside the vehicle.

8. Pull the selector duct assembly rearward until the core tubes clear the dash panel. Lower the selector assembly far enough to gain access to all vacuum and electrical harnesses.

9. Disconnect the vacuum and electrical harness and remove the selector duct assembly.

10. Remove the core mounting strap screws and remove the core assembly.

11. To install the heater core assembly, reverse the removal procedure.

12. Fill the cooling system, operate the engine and verify the coolant level is correct and the heater assembly operates correctly.

Removal and Installation

VAN MODELS

1. Disconnect the negative battery cable.

2. Remove the engine cover from inside the vehicle.

3. Remove the steering column to instrument panel attaching bolts and lower the steering column.

4. Remove the upper and lower instrument panel attaching screws and the radio support bracket attaching screw.

5. Raise and support the right side of the instrument panel.

6. Remove the right lower instrument panel support bracket.

7. Remove the recirculating air door vacuum actuator and plate.

8. Disconnect the temperature cable and vacuum hoses at the distributor case.

9. Remove the heater distributor duct and retaining screws.

10. Remove the two defroster duct to dash panel attaching screws, located below the windshield.

11. From the engine compartment, remove the heater hoses and plug the heater hoses and core tubes to prevent coolant spillage during removal.

12. Remove the three retaining nuts holding the heater core case to the dash panel and the one screw at the lower right corner on the inside.

13. Remove the distributor housing from the vehicle.

14. Remove the gasket, exposing the case half retaining screws. Remove the screws, separate the case and remove the heater core.

15. To install the heater core, reverse the removal procedure.

16. Install the coolant into the system, start the vehicle and verify the operation of the heating system and correct coolant level.

Control Assembly and Blower Switch

Removal and Installation

PICK-UPS, FOUR WHEEL DRIVE, BLAZER AND SUBURBANS

1. Disconnect the negative battery cable.

2. Remove the radio from the instrument panel.

3. Remove the instrument panel bezel.

4. Remove the control head retaining screws and drop the control head enough to gain access to the control head cable retaining points without bending the bowden cable.

5. Disconnect the bowden cable, the vacuum harness and electrical connections.

6. Remove the control head from the instrument panel.

7. The master blower switch can be removed, serviced or replaced, as required.

8. The installation of the control head is the reverse of the removal procedure.

NOTE: If just the master blower switch is to be replaced, the control head assembly or radio does not have to be completely removed.

Removal and Installation

VAN MODELS

1. Disconnect the negative battery cable.

2. Remove the headlamp switch control knob.

3. Remove the instrument panel bezel.

4. Remove the control to instrument panel attaching screws.

5. Remove the temperature cable eyelet clip and mounting tab screw.

6. Pull the control head through the instrument panel opening by first pulling the lower right mounting tab through the opening, then the upper tab and finally the lower right tab.

7. Disconnect the vacuum and electrical connections and remove the control head assembly.

8. The master blower switch can be removed from the control head if repairs require it.

9. The installation of the control head is the reverse of the removal procedure.

NOTE: If just the master blower switch has to be replaced, remove the left foot cooler outlet assembly at the instrument panel, the electrical harness and the switch mounting screws. Remove the switch.

REAR OVERHEAD AIR CONDITIONING SYSTEM

The rear overhead air conditioning system is used in conjunction with the C-60 system (CCOT) components and is known as the C-69 system. A three speed blower motor switch is located on the instrument panel, to the left of the ash receiver. The Four Season portion of this system is protected by a 25 amp fuse in the junction block, while the rear blower high speed circuit is protected by a 20 amp in-line fuse, located between the junction block and the rear blower motor switch. The blower motor resistor is located on the cover side of the blower-evaporator assembly. This system incorporates an expansion valve which does not utilize an external equalizer line.

Rear Overhead Duct

Removal and Installation

ALL MODELS

1. Disconnect the negative battery cable.
2. Disconnect the condensation drain tube from the rear duct.
3. Remove the screws securing the duct to the roof panel and remove the rear header bracket.
4. Remove the duct assembly.
5. To install the duct assembly, reverse the removal procedure.

Rear Overhead Blower Motor Assembly

Removal and Installation

ALL MODELS

1. Disconnect the negative battery cable.
2. Remove the rear duct assembly.
3. Disconnect the blower motor lead wire and the motor ground strap.
4. Remove the lower to upper blower-evaporator case screws and lower the lower case and motor asembly.

NOTE: Before removing the case assembly screws, support the case to prevent damage to the motor or case.

5. Remove the motor retaining strap and remove the motor and wheels. The wheels can be removed from the motor shaft.
6. The installation is the reverse of the removal procedure. Be sure the blower wheels rotate freely and no binding exists.

Rear Overhead Expansion Valve

Removal and Installation
ALL MODELS

1. Disconnect the negative battery cable.
2. Discharge the air conditioning system safely.
3. Remove the rear duct assembly.
4. Disconnect the blower motor lead and ground wires.
5. Remove the lower to upper blower-evaporator case screws and lower the case and motor assembly.

NOTE: Before removing the case screws, support the case assembly to avoid damage to the motor-evaporator case assembly.

6. Remove the expansion valve sensing bulb clamps.
7. Disconnect the valve inlet and outlet lines. Remove the expansion valve assembly. Cap or plug the openings immediately.
8. To install the expansion valve, remove the caps or plugs, install new "O" rings, lubricated with fresh refrigerant oil as required during the expansion valve assembly.

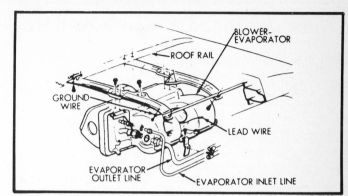

Typical rear overhead A/C system (© General Motors Corporation)

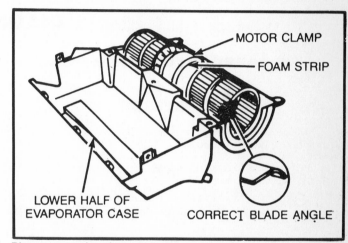

Blower motor location within the rear overhead unit (© General Motors Corporation)

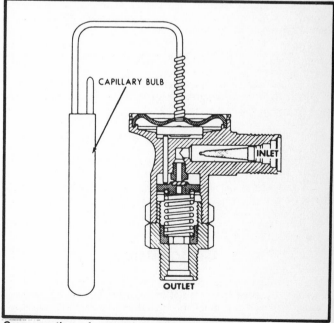

Cross section of expansion valve assembly (© General Motors Corporation)

9. Install the sensing bulb to make good contact with the core outlet line.

10. Complete the installation, reversing the removal procedure.

11. Refer to the specifications for the correct refrigerant charge. Evacuate, charge and check the system for proper operation.

Rear Overhead Evaporator Core

Removal and Installation

ALL MODELS

1. Disconnect the negative battery cable.

2. Discharge the air conditioning system safely.

3. Remove the rear duct. Disconnect the power lead and the ground lead to the blower motor.

4. Disconnect the refrigerant lines at the rear of the blower-evaporator assembly. Cap or plug the openings immediately.

5. Support the blower-evaporator assembly and remove the retaining screws between the case and the roof rail. Lower the blower-evaporator assembly and place it on a work area away from the vehicle.

6. Remove the lower to upper case screws and remove the lower case assembly. Remove the support to upper case screws and remove the upper case from the evaporator core.

7. Remove the expansion valve inlet and outlet lines, capping or plugging the openings immediately. Remove the expansion valve capillary tube from the evaporator outlet line and remove the valve.

8. Remove the plastic pins holding the screen to the core and remove the screen.

9. The installation of the evaporator core is the reverse of the removal procedure. New "O" rings must be used and lubricated with fresh refrigerant oil. Install the sensing bulb to the evaporator outlet tube, making sure the tube is in proper contact with the line.

10. Add three fluid ounces of refrigerant oil to the evaporator. Refer to the specifications for the correct refrigerant charge.

11. Evacuate, charge and check the system for proper operation.

DIAGNOSIS

Component Troubleshooting

COMPRESSOR

A compressor defect will appear in one of four ways, noise, seizure, leakage or low discharge pressure.

NOISE

Irregular rattles or noises may indicate broken internal parts or excessive clearances due to wear. However, resonant compressor noises are not causes for alarm.

SEIZURE

To check seizure, De-energize the magnetic clutch and check to see if the drive plate can be rotated. If rotation is not possible, the compressor is seized internally.

LEAKAGE

Leakage may occur from line attachment connections or internal malfunctions. Refer to the compressor overhaul section for procedure to test for internal leakage.

LOW DISCHARGE PRESSURE

Low discharge pressure may be due to a faulty internal seal of the compressor or a restriction in the compressor. Insufficient refrigerant charge or a restriction elsewhere in the system can also cause low discharge pressure. These possibilities must be checked prior to servicing the compressor.

Condenser

A condenser may be defective in two ways, either restricted or leaking. A restricted condenser will result in excessive compressor discharge pressure. If a partial restriction is present, ice or frost will sometimes form immediately after the restriction as the refrigerant expands after passing through the restriction. If the air flow through the condenser or radiator is blocked, high discharge pressure will result. During normal condenser operation, the outlet tube will be slightly cooler than the inlet pipe.

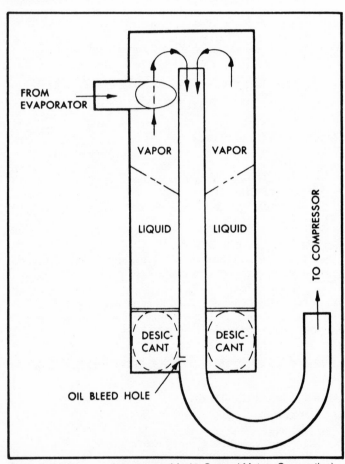

Operation of accumulator assembly (© General Motors Corporation)

Evaporator

A defective evaporator will show up as an inadequate supply of cool air in the vehicle. A partially plugged core due to dirt, a cracked case or a leaking seal will generally be the cause.

Refrigerant Line Restrictions

Restrictions in the refrigerant lines will be indicated as follows:

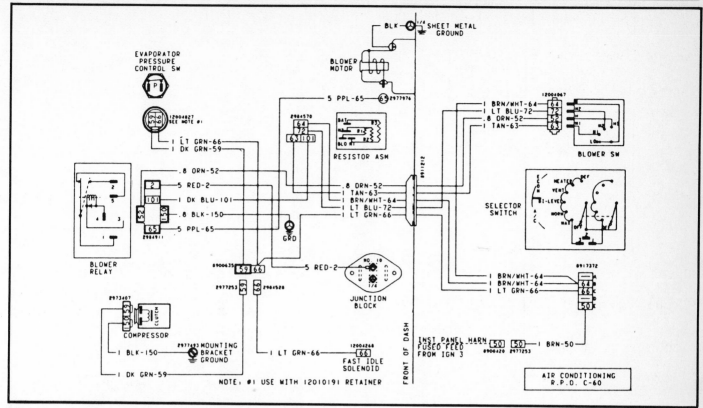

Electrical schematic, all except van models (© General Motors Corporation)

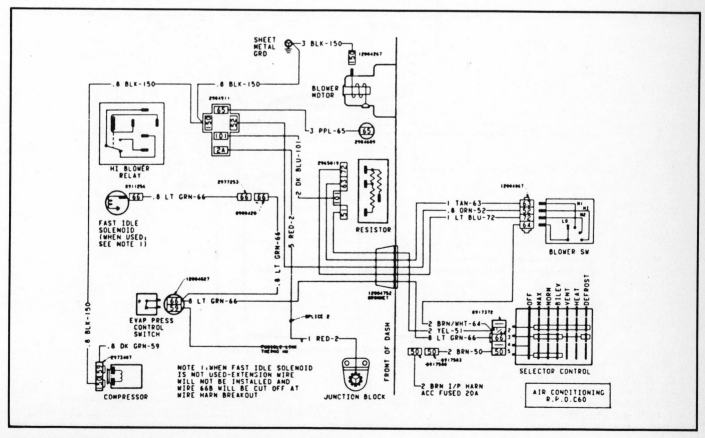

Electrical schematic, van models (© General Motors Corporation)

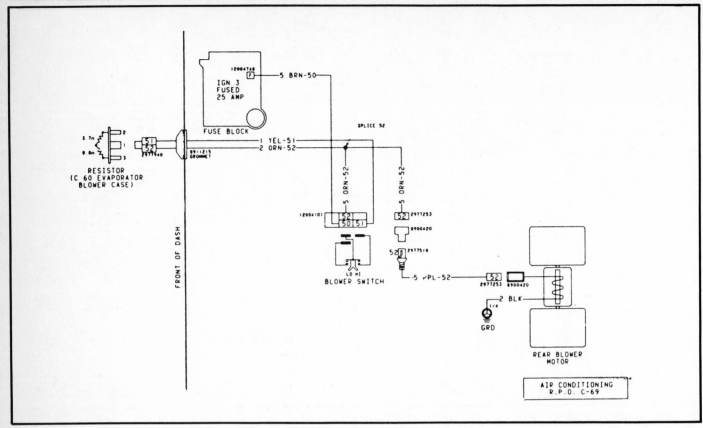

Electrical schematic, rear overhead A/C unit, typical of all models (© General Motors Corporation)

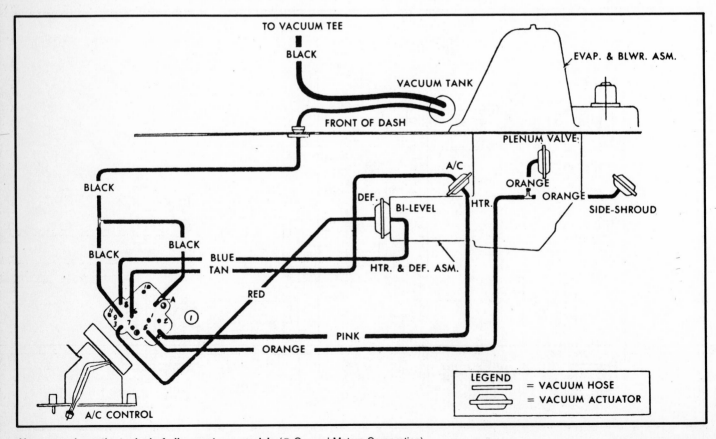

Vacuum schematic, typical of all except van models (© General Motors Corporation)

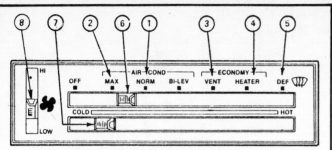

1 CONDITIONED AIR IS DIRECTED THROUGH W/SHLD. I.P. & FLOOR DISTRIBUTOR OUTLETS.

CONDITIONED AIR IS DIRECTED THROUGH I.P. OUTLETS.

2 IN THIS MODE LEVER POSITION, MAXIMUM COOLING IS OFFERED WITH THE CONDITIONED AIR DISTRIBUTED THROUGH I.P. OUTLETS AT ANY BLOWER SPEED.

3 A NON-COMPRESSOR OPERATING POSITION, WITH OUTSIDE AIR DELIVERED THROUGH I.P. OUTLETS.

4 A NON-COMPRESSOR OPERATING POSITION, WITH OUTSIDE AIR DISTRIBUTED ABOUT 80% TO FLOOR & 20% TO W/SHLD.

5 CONDITIONED AIR DISTRIBUTED ABOUT 80% TO W/SHLD. & 20% TO FLOOR.

6 VACUUM OPERATED SYSTEM SELECTOR (MODE) LEVER.

7 TEMPERATURE LEVER POSITION REGULATES TEMPERATURE OF THE AIR ENTERING THE PASSENGER COMPARTMENT BY CABLE OPERATION OF THE HEATER CORE TEMPERATURE DOOR.

8 4-SPEED FAN CONTROL LEVER.

Control head operation, typical of all models (© General Motors Corporation)

1. A suction line restriction will cause low suction pressure at the compressor, low discharge pressure and little or no cooling.

2. A discharge line restriction will generally cause the pressure relief valve to open.

3. A liquid line restriction will be evidenced by low discharge and suction pressure, causing insufficient cooling.

Orifice Tube

An orifice tube restriction can cause frosting on the evaporator inlet pipe, can cause low high and low side pressures.

Refrigerant Quick Check Procedure

1. The engine must be up to normal operating temperature.

2. Have the hood and body doors open, the selector lever set at the NORM position, the temperature lever set on COLD and the blower motor on HIGH.

3. Have the engine at normal idle.

4. Feel the temperature of the evaporator inlet and outlet pipes with the compressor engaged.

5. Both pipes should be of the same temperature and slightly cooler than the ambient temperature.

6. If the inlet pipe is cooler, (or frosted) than the outlet pipe, low freon charge is indicated.

7. Add a slight amount of refrigerant until both pipes are of the same temperature to the touch.

8. Then add two fourteen ounce cans of refrigerant to the system.

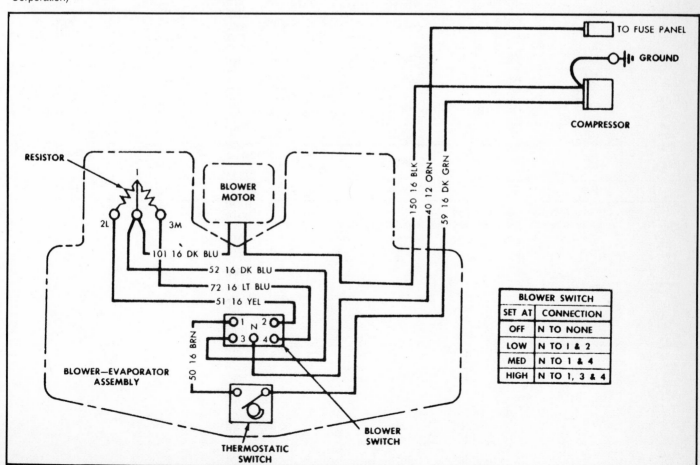

BLOWER SWITCH	
SET AT	CONNECTION
OFF	N TO NONE
LOW	N TO 1 & 2
MED	N TO 1 & 4
HIGH	N TO 1, 3 & 4

19--C60 Motor Home Chassis Wiring Diagram

SYSTEM OPERATION
All Except Van Models

Selector Lever Position	Compressor	Blower Speeds Avail	Air Source	Air Enters Vehicle	Heater A/C Door-Open To:	Heater Defroster Door-Open To:
Off	Off	Low	Outside	Floor Outlets	Heater	Heater
Max A/C	On	Hi	Inside	Dash Outlets	A/C	Heater
Norm A/C	On	All	Outside	Dash Outlets	A/C	Heater
Bi-Level	On	All	Outside	Floor and Dash Outlets	A/C & Heater	Heater
Vent	Off	All	Outside	Dash Outlets	A/C	Heater
Htr	Off	All	Outside	Floor Outlets	Heater	Heater
Def	On	All	Outside	Defrost Outlets	Heater	Defrost

Note: 100% Inside air is not available, some bleed through of outside air is allowed.

SYSTEM OPERATION
Van Models

Compressor		Blower Speeds Avail	Air Source	Air Enters Vehicle	Heater Defroster Door	Heater A/C Door
Off	Off	None	Outside	Floor Outlets	Open To Heater	Open To Heater-Def
Max	On	All	Inside	Dash Outlets	Heater	A/C
Norm	On	All	Outside	Dash Outlets	Heater	A/C
Bi Lev	On	All	Outside	Dash Outlets Floor Outlets	Heater	A/C & Heater
Vent	Off	All	Outside	Dash Outlets	Heater	A/C
Heater	Off	All	Outside	Bleed To Defrost & Floor Outlets	Heater	Heater
Defr	On*	All	Outside	Defrost Outlets	Defrost	Heater

*Provided compressor pressure switch closed.
Note: 100% Inside air is not available, some bleed through of outside air is allowed.

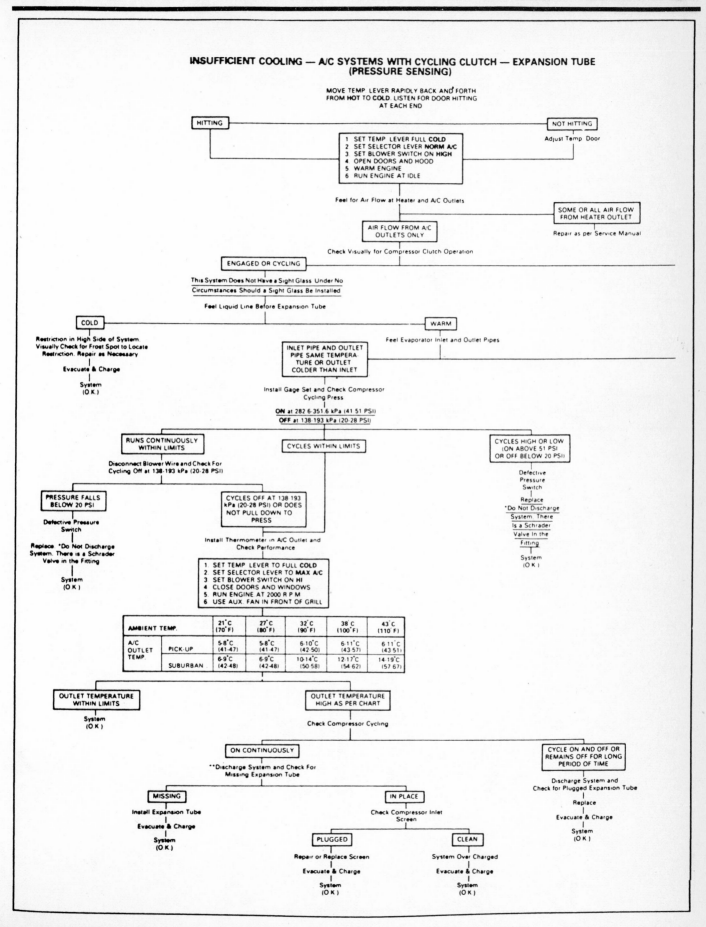

INSUFFICIENT COOLING — A/C SYSTEMS WITH CYCLING CLUTCH — EXPANSION TUBE (PRESSURE SENSING)

MOVE TEMP LEVER RAPIDLY BACK AND FORTH
FROM HOT TO COLD. LISTEN FOR DOOR HITTING
AT EACH END

HITTING — NOT HITTING
Adjust Temp Door

1 SET TEMP LEVER FULL COLD
2 SET SELECTOR LEVER NORM A/C
3 SET BLOWER SWITCH ON HIGH
4 OPEN DOORS AND HOOD
5 WARM ENGINE
6 RUN ENGINE AT IDLE

Feel for Air Flow at Heater and A/C Outlets

SOME OR ALL AIR FLOW FROM HEATER OUTLET
Repair as per Service Manual

AIR FLOW FROM A/C OUTLETS ONLY

Check Visually for Compressor Clutch Operation

ENGAGED OR CYCLING

This System Does Not Have a Sight Glass Under No Circumstances Should a Sight Glass Be Installed

Feel Liquid Line Before Expansion Tube

COLD — WARM

Restriction in High Side of System. Visually Check for Frost Spot to Locate Restriction. Repair as Necessary

Evacuate & Charge

System (O.K.)

Feel Evaporator Inlet and Outlet Pipes

INLET PIPE AND OUTLET PIPE SAME TEMPERATURE OR OUTLET COLDER THAN INLET

Install Gage Set and Check Compressor Cycling Press

ON at 282 6-351.6 kPa (41 51 PSI)
OFF at 138-193 kPa (20-28 PSI)

RUNS CONTINUOUSLY WITHIN LIMITS

CYCLES WITHIN LIMITS

CYCLES HIGH OR LOW (ON ABOVE 51 PSI OR OFF BELOW 20 PSI)

Defective Pressure Switch

Replace *Do Not Discharge System. There Is a Schrader Valve In the Fitting

System (O K)

Disconnect Blower Wire and Check For Cycling Off at 138-193 kPa (20-28 PSI)

PRESSURE FALLS BELOW 20 PSI

Defective Pressure Switch

Replace *Do Not Discharge System. There is a Schrader Valve in the Fitting

System (O K)

CYCLES OFF AT 138 193 kPa (20-28 PSI) OR DOES NOT PULL DOWN TO PRESS

Install Thermometer in A/C Outlet and Check Performance

1 SET TEMP LEVER TO FULL COLD
2 SET SELECTOR LEVER TO MAX A/C
3 SET BLOWER SWITCH ON HI
4 CLOSE DOORS AND WINDOWS
5 RUN ENGINE AT 2000 R P M
6 USE AUX. FAN IN FRONT OF GRILL

AMBIENT TEMP.		21°C (70°F)	27°C (80°F)	32°C (90°F)	38 C (100°F)	43°C (110°F)
A/C OUTLET TEMP.	PICK-UP	5-8°C (41-47)	5-8°C (41-47)	6-10°C (42-50)	6-11°C (43-57)	6-11°C (43-51)
	SUBURBAN	6-9°C (42-48)	6-9°C (42-48)	10-14°C (50-58)	12-17°C (54-62)	14-19°C (57-67)

OUTLET TEMPERATURE WITHIN LIMITS

System (O K)

OUTLET TEMPERATURE HIGH AS PER CHART

Check Compressor Cycling

ON CONTINUOUSLY

**Discharge System and Check For Missing Expansion Tube

CYCLE ON AND OFF OR REMAINS OFF FOR LONG PERIOD OF TIME

Discharge System and Check for Plugged Expansion Tube

Replace

Evacuate & Charge

System (O K)

MISSING

Install Expansion Tube

Evacuate & Charge

System (O.K.)

IN PLACE

Check Compressor Inlet Screen

PLUGGED

Repair or Replace Screen

Evacuate & Charge

System (O K)

CLEAN

System Over Charged

Evacuate & Charge

System (O K)

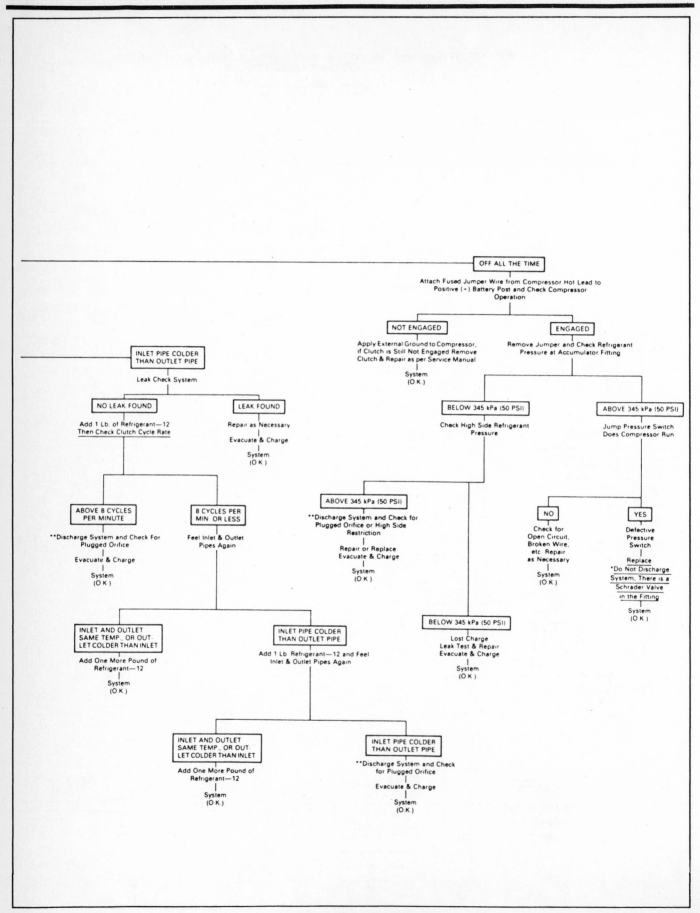

INSUFFICIENT COOLING DIAGNOSIS CHART
DASH MOUNTED UNIT (MOTOR HOME CHASSIS UNITS)

The following procedures should be applied before performance testing an A/C System.

1. Check for proper belt installation and tension with J-23600.
2. Check for proper clutch coil terminal connector installation.
3. Check for clutch air Gap (.022 - .057).
4. Check for broken, burst, or cut hoses. Also check for loose fittings on all components.
5. Check for condenser air blockage due to foreign material.
6. Check for proper air ducting hose connections.
7. Check heater temperature door adjustment, adjust if incorrect.
8. Check evaporator sealing for air leak, repair if leaking.
9. Install pressure gages and thermometer and make performance test.

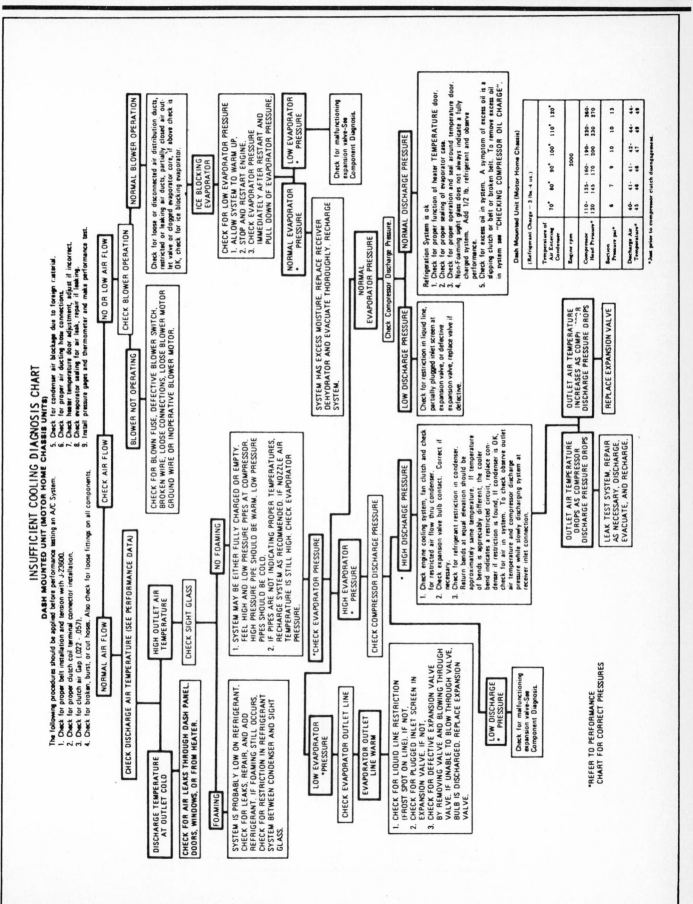

Dash Mounted Unit (Motor Home Chassis) (Refrigerant Charge — 3 lbs.-4 oz.)

Temperature of Air Entering Condenser	70°	80°	90°	100°	110°	120°
Engine rpm			2000			
Compressor Head Pressure*	110-120	135-145	160-170	190-200	220-230	260-270
Suction Pressure psi*	6	7	9	10	13	
Discharge Air Temperature*	40-45	41-46	41-47	42-48	44-49	44-49

*Just prior to compressor clutch disengagement.

*REFER TO PERFORMANCE CHART FOR CORRECT PRESSURES

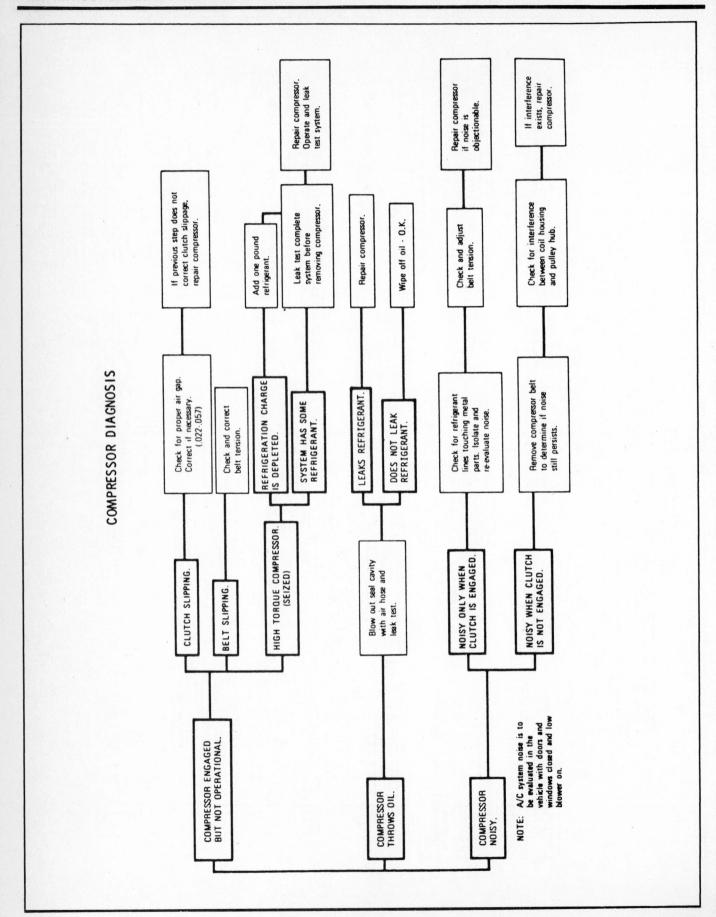

COMPRESSOR DIAGNOSIS

CLUTCH SLIPPING. — Check for proper air gap. Correct if necessary. (.022-.057) — If previous step does not correct clutch slippage, repair compressor.

BELT SLIPPING. — Check and correct belt tension.

HIGH TORQUE COMPRESSOR. (SEIZED) — REFRIGERATION CHARGE IS DEPLETED. — Add one pound refrigerant. / Leak test complete system before removing compressor. — Repair compressor. Operate and leak test system.

SYSTEM HAS SOME REFRIGERANT.

COMPRESSOR ENGAGED BUT NOT OPERATIONAL.

Blow out seal cavity with air hose and leak test. — LEAKS REFRIGERANT. — Repair compressor.

DOES NOT LEAK REFRIGERANT. — Wipe off oil - O.K.

COMPRESSOR THROWS OIL.

NOISY ONLY WHEN CLUTCH IS ENGAGED. — Check for refrigerant lines touching metal parts. Isolate and re-evaluate noise. — Check and adjust belt tension. — Repair compressor if noise is objectionable.

NOISY WHEN CLUTCH IS NOT ENGAGED. — Remove compressor belt to determine if noise still persists. — Check for interference between coil housing and pulley hub. — If interference exists, repair compressor.

COMPRESSOR NOISY.

NOTE: A/C system noise is to be evaluated in the vehicle with doors and windows closed and low blower on.

ELECTRICAL SYSTEM DIAGNOSTIC CHART

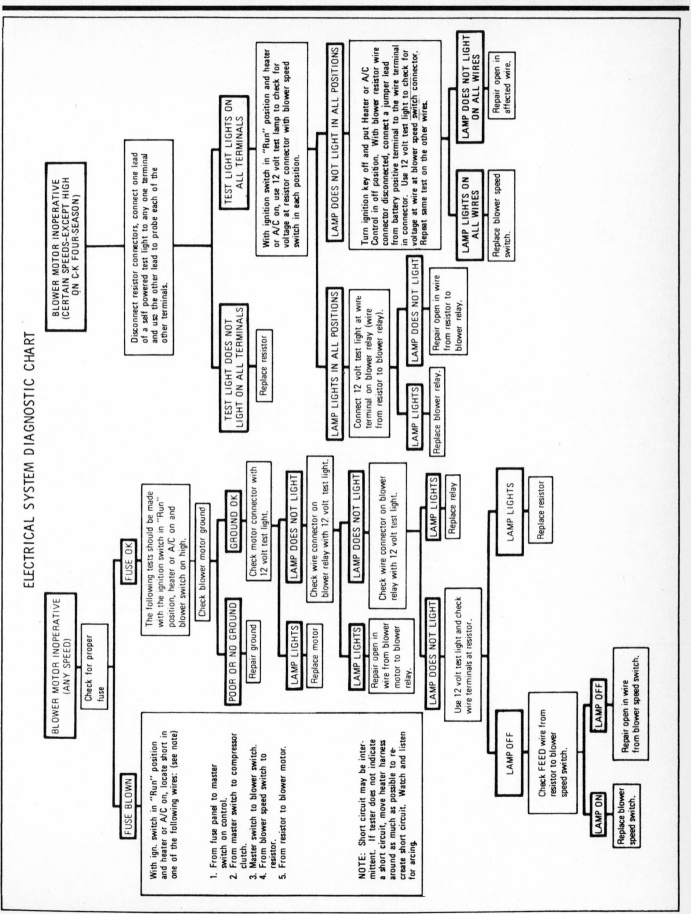

BLOWER MOTOR INOPERATIVE
(CERTAIN SPEEDS-EXCEPT HIGH ON C-K FOUR-SEASON)

Disconnect resistor connectors, connect one lead of a self powered test light to any one terminal and use the other lead to probe each of the other terminals.

TEST LIGHT LIGHTS ON ALL TERMINALS

With ignition switch in "Run" position and heater or A/C on, use 12 volt test lamp to check for voltage at resistor connector with blower speed switch in each position.

LAMP DOES NOT LIGHT IN ALL POSITIONS

Turn ignition key off and put Heater or A/C Control in off position. With blower resistor wire connector disconnected, connect a jumper lead from battery positive terminal to the wire terminal in connector. Use 12 volt test light to check for voltage at wire at blower speed switch connector. Repeat same test on the other wires.

LAMP DOES NOT LIGHT ON ALL WIRES

Repair open in affected wire.

LAMP LIGHTS ON ALL WIRES

Replace blower speed switch.

TEST LIGHT DOES NOT LIGHT ON ALL TERMINALS

Replace resistor

LAMP LIGHTS IN ALL POSITIONS

Connect 12 volt test light at wire terminal on blower relay (wire from resistor to blower relay).

LAMP DOES NOT LIGHT

Repair open in wire from resistor to blower relay.

LAMP LIGHTS

Replace blower relay.

BLOWER MOTOR INOPERATIVE
(ANY SPEED)

Check for proper fuse

FUSE OK

The following tests should be made with the ignition switch in "Run" position, heater or A/C on and blower switch on high.

Check blower motor ground

POOR OR NO GROUND

Repair ground

GROUND OK

Check motor connector with 12 volt test light.

LAMP DOES NOT LIGHT

Check wire connector on blower relay with 12 volt test light.

LAMP DOES NOT LIGHT

Check wire connector on blower relay with 12 volt test light.

LAMP LIGHTS

Replace relay

LAMP LIGHTS

Replace resistor

LAMP LIGHTS

Replace motor

LAMP LIGHTS

Repair open in wire from blower motor to blower relay.

LAMP DOES NOT LIGHT

Use 12 volt test light and check wire terminals at resistor.

LAMP OFF

Check FEED wire from resistor to blower speed switch.

LAMP OFF

Repair open in wire from blower speed switch.

LAMP ON

Replace blower speed switch.

FUSE BLOWN

With ign. switch in "Run" position and heater or A/C on, locate short in one of the following wires: (see note)

1. From fuse panel to master switch on control.
2. From master switch to compressor clutch.
3. Master switch to blower switch.
4. From blower speed switch to resistor.
5. From resistor to blower motor.

NOTE: Short circuit may be intermittent. If tester does not indicate a short circuit, move heater harness around as much as possible to re-create short circuit. Watch and listen for arcing.

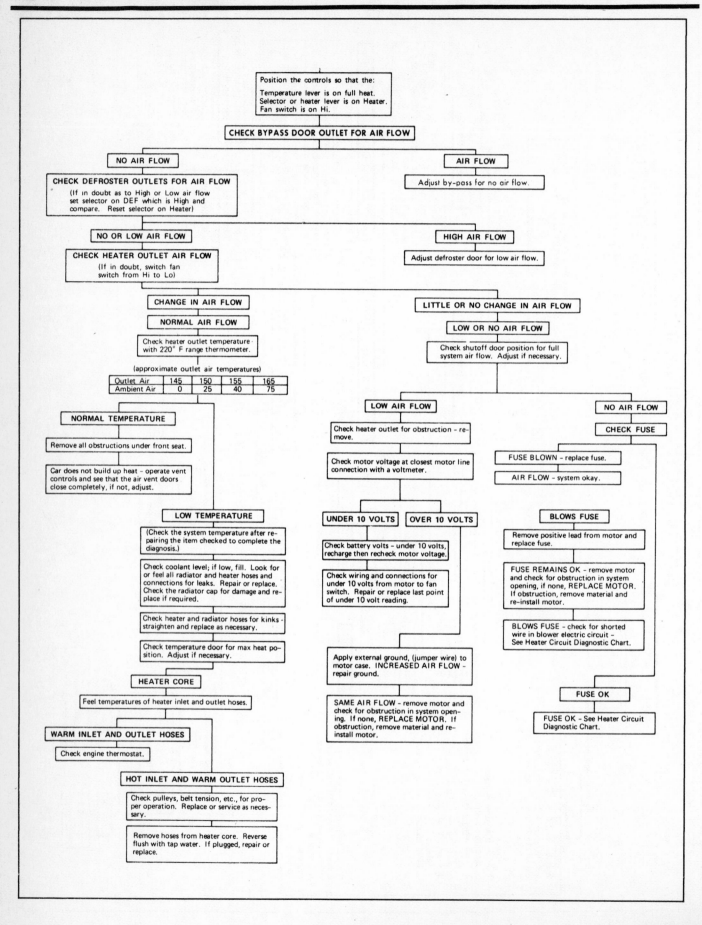

Position the controls so that the:

Temperature lever is on full heat.
Selector or heater lever is on Heater.
Fan switch is on Hi.

CHECK BYPASS DOOR OUTLET FOR AIR FLOW

NO AIR FLOW

AIR FLOW

Adjust by-pass for no air flow.

CHECK DEFROSTER OUTLETS FOR AIR FLOW

(If in doubt as to High or Low air flow set selector on DEF which is High and compare. Reset selector on Heater)

NO OR LOW AIR FLOW

HIGH AIR FLOW

Adjust defroster door for low air flow.

CHECK HEATER OUTLET AIR FLOW

(If in doubt, switch fan switch from Hi to Lo)

CHANGE IN AIR FLOW

NORMAL AIR FLOW

Check heater outlet temperature with 220° F range thermometer.

(approximate outlet air temperatures)

Outlet Air	145	150	155	165
Ambient Air	0	25	40	75

LITTLE OR NO CHANGE IN AIR FLOW

LOW OR NO AIR FLOW

Check shutoff door position for full system air flow. Adjust if necessary.

NORMAL TEMPERATURE

Remove all obstructions under front seat.

Car does not build up heat – operate vent controls and see that the air vent doors close completely, if not, adjust.

LOW AIR FLOW

Check heater outlet for obstruction – remove.

Check motor voltage at closest motor line connection with a voltmeter.

NO AIR FLOW

CHECK FUSE

FUSE BLOWN – replace fuse.

AIR FLOW – system okay.

LOW TEMPERATURE

(Check the system temperature after repairing the item checked to complete the diagnosis.)

Check coolant level; if low, fill. Look for or feel all radiator and heater hoses and connections for leaks. Repair or replace. Check the radiator cap for damage and replace if required.

Check heater and radiator hoses for kinks - straighten and replace as necessary.

Check temperature door for max heat position. Adjust if necessary.

UNDER 10 VOLTS | **OVER 10 VOLTS**

Check battery volts – under 10 volts, recharge then recheck motor voltage.

Check wiring and connections for under 10 volts from motor to fan switch. Repair or replace last point of under 10 volt reading.

BLOWS FUSE

Remove positive lead from motor and replace fuse.

FUSE REMAINS OK – remove motor and check for obstruction in system opening, if none, REPLACE MOTOR. If obstruction, remove material and re-install motor.

BLOWS FUSE – check for shorted wire in blower electric circuit – See Heater Circuit Diagnostic Chart.

HEATER CORE

Feel temperatures of heater inlet and outlet hoses.

WARM INLET AND OUTLET HOSES

Check engine thermostat.

Apply external ground, (jumper wire) to motor case. INCREASED AIR FLOW – repair ground.

SAME AIR FLOW – remove motor and check for obstruction in system opening. If none, REPLACE MOTOR. If obstruction, remove material and re-install motor.

FUSE OK

FUSE OK – See Heater Circuit Diagnostic Chart.

HOT INLET AND WARM OUTLET HOSES

Check pulleys, belt tension, etc., for proper operation. Replace or service as necessary.

Remove hoses from heater core. Reverse flush with tap water. If plugged, repair or replace.

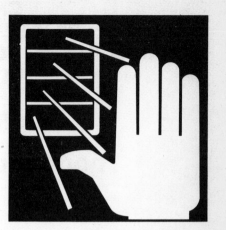

SECTION 6
LIGHT TRUCKS
Dodge/Plymouth

INDEX

CHRYSLER CORPORATION
1982—85 DODGE/PLYMOUTH DOMESTIC TRUCKS
MINI-VANS (VOYAGER, CARAVAN, MINI RAM VAN)
PICK-UPS (RAM D 100—350)
VANS (PB,B 150—350)
SPORT UTILITY (RAMCHARGER)

DODGE/PLYMOUTH PICK-UPS AND VANS

SPECIFICATIONS

R-12 Freon Capacity

Mini-Vans	38 ounces
Pick-ups, Sport Utility	42 ounces
Vans	
Front	48 ounces (Plus or minus 1 ounce)
Front and rear	64 ounces (Plus or minus 1 ounce)

Refrigerant Oil Capacity

Type of refrigerant oil recommended—500 SUS Viscosity, wax free oil

MINI VANS, VOYAGER, CARAVAN

Compressor (C-171)	7–7.25 fluid ounces

PICK-UPS, SPORT UTILITY, VAN MODELS

Compressor (C-171)	9–10 fluid ounces

ALL MODELS

Evaporator	2 fluid ounces
Condenser	1 fluid ounce
Filter/drier	1 fluid ounce

NOTE: If a replacement compressor is installed, completely drain the new compressor of its 9 to 10 or 7 to 7.25 fluid ounces of refrigerant oil and add back only 5 fluid ounces in Pick-ups, Sport Utility and Vans or 3 fluid ounces in the Mini Vans, Voyager and Caravan models, to avoid having excessive oil in the system. This adjustment is not necessary if the system has been flushed, causing the removal of the retained oil.

Drive Belt Tension

MINI-VANS, VOYAGER, CARAVAN MODELS W/2.2 LITER ENGINE

DEFLECTION METHOD

New Belt	5/16 in. deflection
Used Belt	7/16 in. deflection

TORQUE METHOD

New Belt	40 ft. lbs.
Used Belt	30 ft. lbs.

GAUGE METHOD

New Belt	105 lbs.
Used Belt	80 lbs.

WITH 2.6 LITER ENGINE

DEFLECTION METHOD

New Belt	1/4 in. deflection
Used Belt	5/16 in. deflection

NOTE: Measured midway between pulleys with a ten pound push or pull.

BORROUGH'S GAUGE METHOD

New Belt	115 lbs.
Used Belt	80 lbs.

NOTE: Checked midway between two pulleys. The A/C belt is considered to be used after one-half hour of operation.

PICK-UPS, VANS, SPORT UTILITY

BELT DEFLECTION METHOD

New Belt	1/4–1/2 inch deflection
Used Belt	1/4–5/16 inch deflection

NOTE: Measured midway between pulleys with a ten pound push or pull.

BORROUGH'S GAUGE METHOD

New Belt	120 ft. lbs.
Used Belt	65 ft. lbs.

NOTE: Checked midway between two pulleys. A belt is considered to be used after fifteen (15) minutes of running time.

Blower Motor

Removal and Installation

MINI VAN, VOYAGER, CARAVAN

1. Disconnect the negative battery cable.
2. Disconnect the blower motor feed wire connector and ground wire.
3. Remove the five retaining screws from the blower motor helmet to the fan scroll housing.
4. Remove the blower motor assembly. Remove the blower motor wheel from the motor shaft as required.
5. The installation is the reverse of the removal procedure.

PICK-UP TRUCKS, SPORT UTILITY

1. Disconnect the negative battery cable.
2. Disconnect the blower motor feed wire connector and ground wire.
3. Remove the retaining screws to separate the blower motor plate from the housing.
4. Remove the blower motor assembly and separate the fan from the motor shaft.
5. The blower motor can be removed from the plate after the fan wheel is removed.
6. The installation is the reverse of the removal procedure. Be sure the gasket or sealer has no breaks for proper adhesion.

VAN MODELS

1. Disconnect the negative battery cable.
2. Remove the top half of the shroud and move out of the way.

NOTE: Top right screw on the shroud of a six cylinder engine, is hidden behind the discharge line muffler.

3. Disconnect the electrical connection to the blower motor.
4. Remove the motor cooling tube and the three retaining bolts holding the blower motor to the blower housing.
5. Pull the A/C suction and discharge lines inboard and upward while pulling the blower motor assembly from the housing.
6. The blower motor can then be repaired or replaced, as required.
7. Rubber adhesive should be applied to the blower mounting plate gasket seal during the installation. The installation is the reverse of the removal procedure.

Compressor

Removal

MINI VANS, VOYAGER, CARAVAN WITH 2.2 LITER ENGINE

1. Discharge the air conditioning system.
2. Cover the alternator assembly to prevent refrigerant oil from dripping on the assembly.
3. Disconnect the suction and the discharge lines from the compressor ports. Cap the lines and the openings on the compressor.
4. Disconnect the clutch coil electrical wire connector.
5. Remove the compressor to bracket attaching bolts and nuts.
6. Remove the compressor from the brackets.
7. Measure the amount of refrigerant oil drained from the compressor. Record the amount.
8. Remove the clutch coil assembly from the compressor before service work is done.

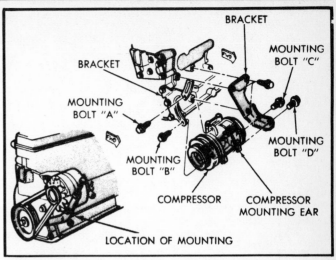

Compressor mounting on 2.6 Liter engine—others similar
(© Chrysler Corp.)

Installation

1. Adjust the compressor oil level through the compressor suction port to 5 fluid ounces, if necessary. Refer to the amount of refrigerant oil drained from the assembly when removed.
2. Install the compressor on the vehicle and install the retaining bolts. Torque the compressor mounting bolts to 40 ft. lbs. (plus or minus 10 ft. lbs.).
3. Connect the clutch electrical connector.
4. Remove the caps from the compressor and the lines. Connect the lines to the compressor ports.
5. Install the drive belt and adjust as specified from the belt adjusting chart.
6. Evacuate and recharge the system as previously outlined.

NOTE: The clutch should be cycled off and on with the engine at fast idle, 15 to 20 times to ensure the clutch parts reseat with each other before the clutch engages with high head pressure at the compressor.

Removal

MINI VANS, VOYAGER, CARAVAN WITH 2.6 LITER ENGINE

1. Raise the front of the vehicle and support safely.
2. Remove the negative battery cable and discharge the system.
3. Disconnect the suction line from the suction port of the compressor. Cap the line immediately.
4. Release the belt tension and remove the drive belts.
5. Disconnect the clutch electrical lead connector, the clevis and the clamping screw.
6. Remove the right front wheel assembly. Remove the shipping tie-down, if still in place.
7. Remove the three screws from the dust shield.
8. Remove the mounting front support bracket to engine.
9. Remove the compressor and bracket mounting bolts.

10. Raise the compressor slightly and hook the rear mounting ears over the rear mounting bracket.

11. Tip the nose of the compressor down and remove the mounting bolt and the front bracket.

12. Disconnect the discharge line from the compressor discharge port.

13. Cap the line immediately to prevent dirt and moisture from entering.

14. Remove the compressor from the vehicle.

15. To service the compressor, it is necessary to remove the compressor clutch assembly.

Installation

1. The installation of the compressor is the reverse of the removal procedure.

2. Fill or check to verify the correct level of refrigerant oil is installed in the compressor.

3. Adjust the drive belts to the specified limits as outlined in the Belt Tension Chart.

4. Evacuate and recharge the system as previously outlined. Check the system for proper operation.

Removal

PICK-UP TRUCKS, SPORT UTILITY

1. Discharge the system.

2. Disconnect the suction and the discharge lines from the compressor. Cap the lines and ports immediately to prevent dirt and moisture from entering the system.

3. Remove the electric clutch wire connector.

4. Remove the compressor to bracket attaching bolts, remove the belts and remove the compressor.

5. Drain the refrigerant oil and record the amount. The clutch assembly must be removed before the compressor can be disassembled.

Installation

1. The installation of the compressor is the reverse of the removal procedure.

2. Verify the correct level of refrigerant oil is installed in the system.

3. Correct the belt tension as specified in the Belt Tension Chart.

4. Evacuate and recharge the system. Verify the system operates properly.

Removal

VAN MODELS

1. Discharge the system of refrigerant.

2. Disconnect the suction and discharge lines from the compressor and cap each to prevent dirt and moisture from entering the system.

3. Disconnect the electrical clutch wire connector.

4. Remove the compressor to bracket mounting bolts and remove the compressor.

NOTE: It may be necessary to loosen the bracket to engine attaching bolts.

5. Drain and measure the refrigerant oil. Record the amount.

6. The clutch assembly must be removed before the compressor can be disassembled.

Assembly

1. The installation of the compressor is the reverse of its removal procedure.

2. Adjust the belt tension to the specifications as listed in the Belt Tension Chart.

3. Verify the correct level of refrigerant oil is in the system.

4. Evacuate and recharge the system. Verify the system operates properly.

Oil Level

A new compressor, installed at the factory, contains 9–10 fluid ounces on the Pick-up trucks, Sport Utility and Van Models. The Mini Vans, Voyager and Caravan model compressors contains 7–7.25 fluid ounces. Since the oil is carried through out the system and retained in various parts, the amount of oil left in the compressor will always be less than the original amount. Although replacement compressors are charged with the same amount of oil as factory units, the compressors must be drained and only the same amount of oil as drained from the original compressor put back in, but no more than 5 fluid ounces, so the amount of refrigerant oil in the system will not be excessive. This adjustment is not needed, however, if the system has been flushed, removing the oil retained by the components.

"H" Expansion Valve Assembly

Removal

ALL MODELS

1. Discharge the system safely as previously outlined.

2. Disconnect the wire connector from the low pressure switch.

3. Remove the bolt from the center of the plumbing seal plate.

4. Carefully pull the refrigerant line assembly towards the front of the vehicle.

— CAUTION —
Do not scratch the valve sealing surface with the tube pilots.

5. Remove the two torx headed bolts while holding valve assembly. Remove the valve assembly from the vehicle.

Installation

1. Replace the two aluminum gaskets, one on the "H" valve and one on the plumbing plate.

2. Remove the sealing cap from the "H" valve control head side sealing surface only and carefully hold it against the evaporator sealing plate. Install the two torx headed bolts and torque to 200 inch pounds (plus or minus 30 inch pounds).

3. Connect the wire connector to the low pressure switch.

4. Evacuate and recharge the system. Operate the system and verify its performance.

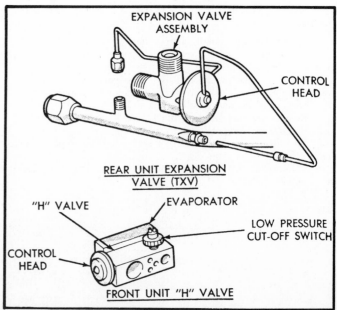

Front and rear expansion valve (© Chrysler Corp.)

Rear Unit Expansion Valve

VAN MODELS

The expansion valve is located in the auxiliary air conditioning evaporator housing. The housing must be removed to gain access to the expansion valve. The removal and installation of the valve assembly is accomplished after the system has been discharged, by its removal from the plumbing and the evaporator core. Do not break the capillary tube during the removal and installation procedure.

Condenser

Removal and Installation

MINI VAN, VOYAGER, CARAVAN

No removal and installation procedure has been released by the manufacturer. However, the grille must be removed before the condenser can be removed. Discharge the system and cap all openings immediately to prevent moisture and dirt from entering the system.

PICK-UP TRUCKS, SPORT UTILITY

No removal and installation procedure has been released by the manufacturer. The condenser can be removed from the top front of radiator yoke after the system has been discharged. Cap all openings immediately to prevent moisture and dirt from entering the system.

VAN MODELS

No removal and installation procedure has been released by the manufacturer. The condenser can be removed from the bottom after the system has been discharged. Cap all openings immediately to prevent moisture and dirt from entering the system.

Evaporator/Heater Core

Removal

MINI VAN, VOYAGER, CARAVAN

NOTE: The evaporator and heater core must be removed and installed as an assembly.

1. Position the vehicle and set brakes.
2. Disconnect the negative battery cable.
3. Discharge the air conditioning system safely. Drain the cooling system and retain the coolant, if it is to be used again.
4. From inside the vehicle, perform the following from the lower instrument panel area:
   a. Remove the steering column cover which is secured to the lower portion of the instrument panel with seven screws.
   b. Remove the lower reinforcement under the steering column.
   c. Remove the right side cowl and sill trim.

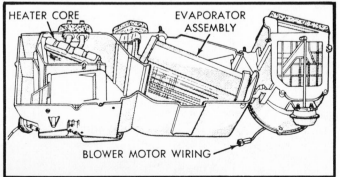

Evaporator/heater assembly (© Chrysler Corp.)

d. Remove the bolt holding the right side instrument panel to the right cowl.
   e. Loosen the two brackets supporting the lower edge to the A/C and heater housing.
   f. Remove the instrument panel trim moulding covering mid-reinforcement.
   g. Remove the retaining screws from the right side to center of the steering column.
5. From the engine side, perform the following procedures:
   a. Complete the refrigerant discharge.
   b. Disconnect the source vacuum line at the brake booster and the vacuum line at the water valve.
   c. Clamp off the heater hoses before the core and remove the hoses from the core tubes. Plug the hose ends and the core tubes to prevent spillage of coolant.
   d. Disconnect the "H" valve connections at the "H" valve.
   e. Remove the four retaining nuts from the package mounting studs.
6. Disconnect the blower motor wiring, resistor wiring and the temperature control cable.
7. Disconnect the hanger strap from the package and bend rearward.
8. Pull the right side of the instrument panel rearward until it reaches the passengers seat.
9. Pull the evaporator/heater core assembly rearward from the dash panel and remove it from the vehicle.
10. To disassemble the evaporator/heater core assembly, remove the retaining screws from the cover. Remove the cover and the temperature control door.
11. Remove the retaining screw from the heater core and remove the core from the housing assembly. Remove the evaporator core.
12. The mode doors, the blower motor and wheel assembly can then be removed from the housing.

Installation

1. The installation of the evaporator coil and the heater coil are in the reverse of the removal procedure.
2. Install the cover and the temperature control door to the housing assembly.
3. Reverse the removal procedure to install the evaporator/heater core housing into the vehicle.
4. After the installation, connect the heater hoses to the core tubes and the air conditioning tubes to the evaporator core assembly.
5. Fill the cooling system, start the engine and recharge the air conditioning system in the prescribed manner.
6. Verify the cooling and the air conditioning systems are functioning properly.

PICK-UP TRUCK, SPORT UTILITY

1. Disconnect the negative battery cable.
2. Discharge the air conditioning system safely. Drain the cooling system and retain the coolant, if to be used again.
3. Disconnect the heater hoses and the refrigerant lines from the evaporator and the heater core. Cap and plug all openings in both the A/C and heater core tubes.
4. Remove the condensate tube from the housing.
5. Move the transfer case and/or gear shift levers away from the instrument panel.
6. If equipped, remove the right side cowl trim panel.
7. Remove the glove box and swing out from the bottom to avoid catches and stops.
8. Remove the structural brace from through the glove box opening.
9. Remove the ash receiver assembly.
10. Remove the right lower half of the reinforcement by removing the retaining screws holding it to the instrument panel and to the cowl side trim panel.
11. Disconnect the radio ground strap, if equipped.
12. Remove the center distribution duct by removing the following:
   a. Remove the instrument panel cluster.
   b. Disconnect the shift indicator cable.
   c. Lower the steering column.

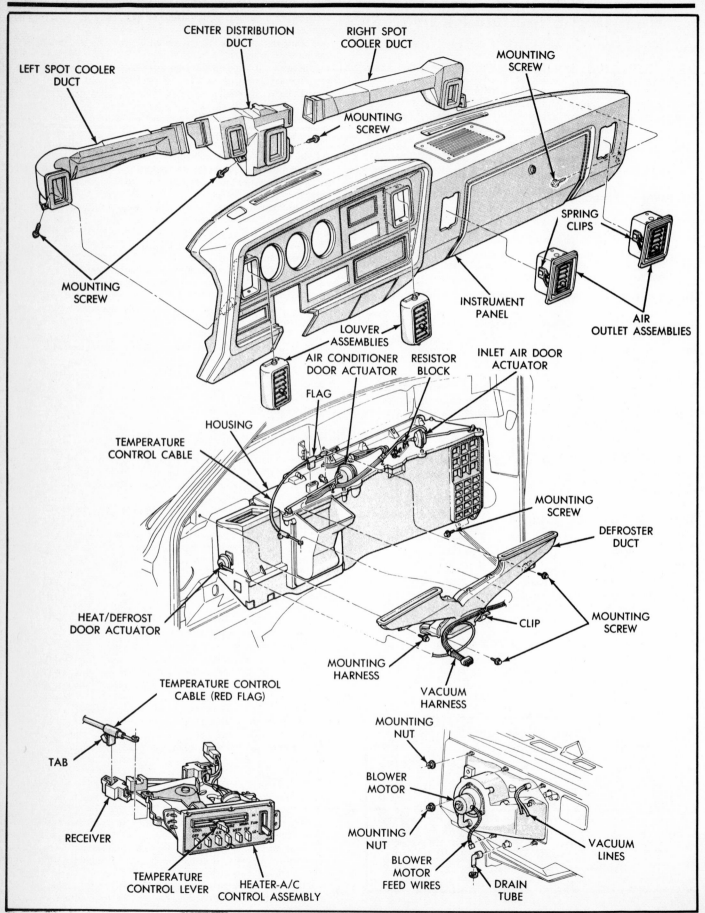

CENTER DISTRIBUTION DUCT

RIGHT SPOT COOLER DUCT

MOUNTING SCREW

LEFT SPOT COOLER DUCT

MOUNTING SCREW

MOUNTING SCREW

SPRING CLIPS

INSTRUMENT PANEL

AIR OUTLET ASSEMBLIES

LOUVER ASSEMBLIES

AIR CONDITIONER DOOR ACTUATOR

RESISTOR BLOCK

INLET AIR DOOR ACTUATOR

FLAG

HOUSING

TEMPERATURE CONTROL CABLE

MOUNTING SCREW

DEFROSTER DUCT

HEAT/DEFROST DOOR ACTUATOR

CLIP

MOUNTING SCREW

MOUNTING HARNESS

VACUUM HARNESS

TEMPERATURE CONTROL CABLE (RED FLAG)

MOUNTING NUT

BLOWER MOTOR

TAB

MOUNTING NUT

RECEIVER

BLOWER MOTOR FEED WIRES

VACUUM LINES

DRAIN TUBE

TEMPERATURE CONTROL LEVER

HEATER-A/C CONTROL ASSEMBLY

Air conditioning/heater assembly—Pick-up trucks and Sport Utility (© Chrysler Corp.)

d. Remove the steering column studs.

e. Remove the radio, if equipped.

f. Remove the two mounting screws and remove the scoop connecting the heater unit to the center distribution duct.

g. Remove the two mounting screws and remove the center distribution duct by pulling outward on the bottom of the instrument panel and dropping the duct out.

13. Remove the floor distribution duct.

14. Disconnect the temperature control cable from the unit through the glove box and tape it out of the way.

15. Disconnect the vacuum lines from the extension on the control unit and unclip the vacuum lines from the defroster duct.

16. Remove the wiring connector from the resistor block and the blower motor.

17. Disconnect the vacuum lines from the engine side to the evaporator/heater housing.

18. Remove the seven retaining screws from the engine side.

19. Remove the screw that retains the housing to the cowl side sheetmetal.

20. Remove the evaporator/heater assembly from the vehicle.

NOTE: The instrument panel may have to be flexed outward.

21. To remove the evaporator and heater cores, remove the three door arms and the seven screws retaining the cover to the housing.

22. Remove the cover from the housing and slide the evaporator core out of the housing.

23. Remove the mounting screw and slide the heater core from the housing assembly.

24. Remove the retaining screws and remove the blower from the housing.

Installation

1. Assemble the evaporator/heater housing using the necessary new or repaired parts by reversing the disassembly procedure.

2. To install the evaporator/heater assembly into the vehicle, reverse the removal procedure as outlined in the removal section.

3. Fill the cooling system, evacuate and recharge the air conditioning system.

4. Check the operation of the controls and performance of the air conditioning system. Verify the cooling system is at its correct level.

VAN MODELS

1. Discharge the air conditioning system. Drain the cooling system, both in a safe manner.

2. Disconnect the negative battery cable.

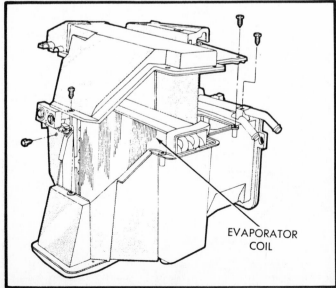

Removal of the evaporator coil—Van models (© Chrysler Corp.)

3. Remove the heater hoses from the core tubes and cap or plug both the hoses and the tubes.

4. Disconnect the refrigerant plumbing from the "H" Valve. Remove the two screws from the filter drier bracket and swing the plumbing out of the way towards the center of the vehicle.

5. Cap or plug the air conditioning openings immediately to avoid dirt and moisture from entering the system.

6. Remove the temperature control cable from the evaporator/heater housing.

7. Working from inside the vehicle, remove the glove box, spot cooler bezel and the appearance shield.

8. Working through the glove box opening and under the instrument panel, remove the screws and nuts attaching the evaporator/heater core housing to the dash panel.

9. Remove the two screws from the flange connection to the blower housing. Separate the evaporator/heater core housing from the blower housing.

10. Carefully remove the evaporator/heater core housing from the vehicle.

11. Remove the cover from the housing and remove the screw retaining the strap to heater core. Remove the heater core.

12. Remove one screw from under the plumbing and remove the evaporator coil from the housing.

Installation

1. Examine all air seal for leakage and replace or repair any damaged seals.

2. Install the evaporator and heater cores in the reverse of their removal.

3. Install the cover onto the housing and retain with the attaching screws.

4. Install the evaporator/Heater core housing assembly into the vehicle in the reverse of the removal procedure.

5. Refill the cooling system, evacuate and recharge the air conditioning system.

6. Verify the cables operate properly, the air conditioning performs properly and the cooling system level is correct.

Auxiliary Air Conditioning Evaporator Coil

Removal and Installation

VAN MODELS

1. Completely discharge the air conditioning system. Cap or plug the air conditioning openings immediately.

2. Remove the auxiliary unit lower cover.

3. Remove the line seal and cover plate.

4. Remove the evaporator coil.

5. To install the evaporator coil, reverse the removal procedure.

6. Evacuate and recharge the air conditioning system and check its performance.

Air Conditioning Controls

Removal and Installation

MINI VANS, VOYAGER, CARAVAN

1. Remove the radio/heater/Air conditioning bezel from the instrument panel.

2. Remove the two screws retaining the control base to the instrument panel.

3. Withdraw the control from the front face of the panel until the cable, electrical and vacuum connections are exposed and accessible.

4. Disconnect the control cable from the heater control.

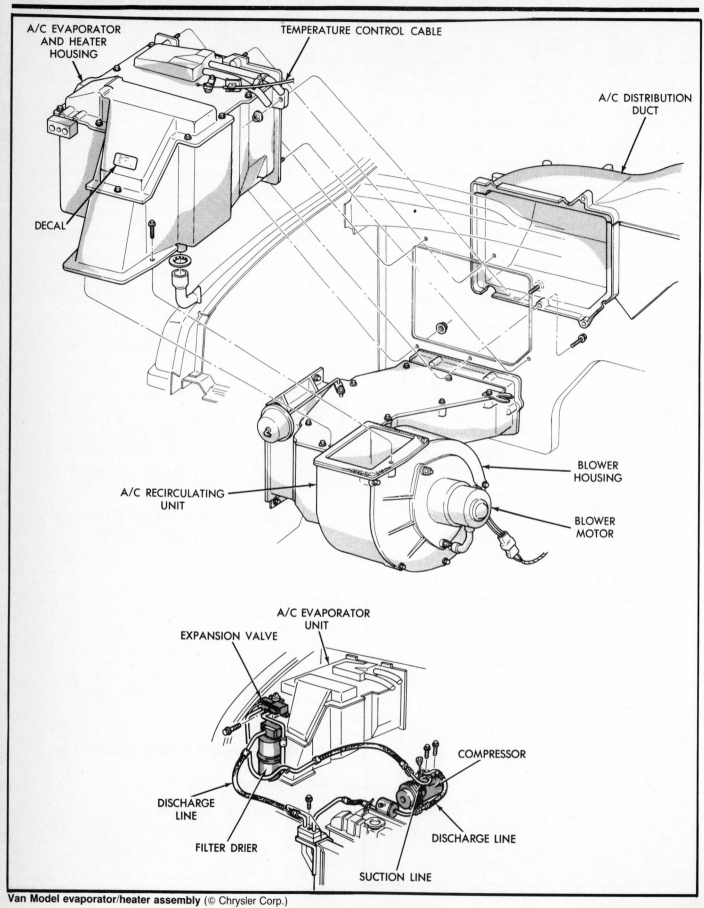

A/C EVAPORATOR AND HEATER HOUSING

TEMPERATURE CONTROL CABLE

A/C DISTRIBUTION DUCT

DECAL

A/C RECIRCULATING UNIT

BLOWER HOUSING

BLOWER MOTOR

A/C EVAPORATOR UNIT

EXPANSION VALVE

COMPRESSOR

DISCHARGE LINE

DISCHARGE LINE

FILTER DRIER

SUCTION LINE

Van Model evaporator/heater assembly (© Chrysler Corp.)

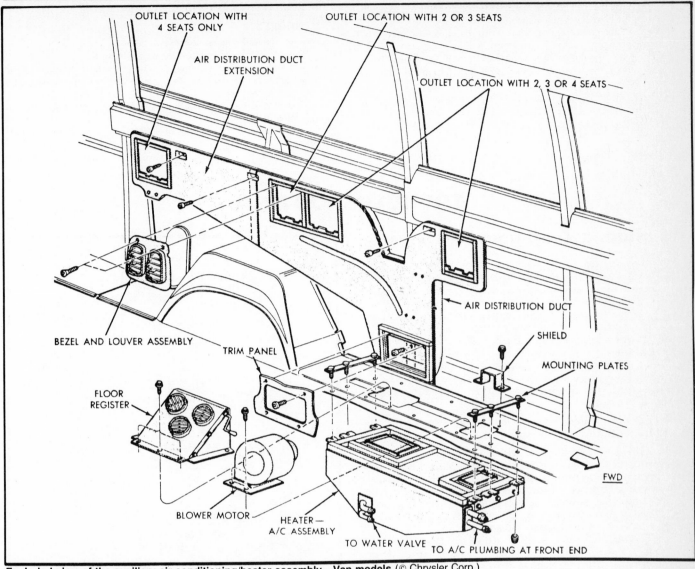

Exploded view of the auxiliary air conditioning/heater assembly—Van models (© Chrysler Corp.)

Labels in figure: OUTLET LOCATION WITH 4 SEATS ONLY; OUTLET LOCATION WITH 2 OR 3 SEATS; AIR DISTRIBUTION DUCT EXTENSION; OUTLET LOCATION WITH 2, 3 OR 4 SEATS; AIR DISTRIBUTION DUCT; SHIELD; MOUNTING PLATES; BEZEL AND LOUVER ASSEMBLY; TRIM PANEL; FLOOR REGISTER; BLOWER MOTOR; HEATER—A/C ASSEMBLY; TO WATER VALVE; TO A/C PLUMBING AT FRONT END; FWD

5. Remove the vacuum lines from the base of the push button switch and air conditioning control.

6. Remove the electrical connectors and remove the control from the dash.

7. The blower switch can be removed or repaired with the control out of its dash seat.

8. To install the control head assembly, reverse the removal procedure.

9. Verify the operation of the control unit when reassembled.

NOTE: The temperature control cable is attached to the heater/air conditioning control by means of a snap-in flag which fits into a moulded receiver. A vertical rib is located on one side of the flag which engages with a corresponding slot in the receiver in order to ensure correct alignment of the flag and cable. To remove the cable, depress the tab on the flag and pull the cable from its receiver. To install, push the flag into the receiver until an audible click is heard. The flag is color coded red for identification purposes.

PICK-UP, SPORT UTILITY

1. Remove the map lamp and the retaining screws holding the face plate to the base panel.

2. Pull the column shift lever into the "1" position.

3. Remove the faceplate by pulling the top edge rearward to clear the brow, disengaging the attaching clips around the bottom of the faceplate and remove.

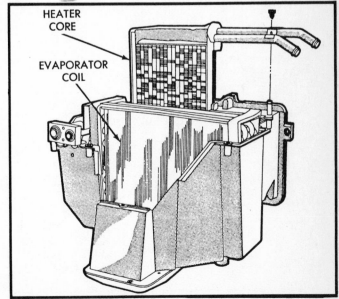

Removal of the heater core—Van models (© Chrysler Corp.)

Labels in figure: HEATER CORE; EVAPORATOR COIL

4. Disconnect the wire to the four wheel drive indicator if so equipped.

5. Open the glove box past its stops.

6. Remove the control unit from the instrument panel by removal of the retaining screws.

7. To remove the temperature control cable with the control head out, remove the cable from the control lever pin and remove the flag from the receiver.

8. Detach the cable from the unit by removing the self-adjusting clip from the crank arm and flag from its receiver.

9. The cable can be removed and replaced through the glove box opening.

10. To install the control head assembly, reverse the removal procedure.

VAN MODELS

1. Disconnect the negative battery cable.

2. Remove the heater/air conditioning control bezel.

3. Remove the screws retaining the control to the instrument panel.

4. Disconnect the temperature control cable, electrical leads and remove the control unit.

5. The blower motor switch can be replaced or repaired with the control out of the dash.

6. The installation of the control unit is the reverse of the removal procedure.

TROUBLESHOOTING

Handling Tubing and Fittings

Kinks in the refrigerant tubing or sharp bends in the refrigerant hose lines will greatly reduce the capacity of the entire system. High pressures are produced in the system when it is operating. Extreme care must be exercised to make sure that all connections are pressure tight. Dirt and moisture can enter the system when it is opened for repair or replacement of lines or components. The following precautions must be observed.

The system must be completely discharged before opening any fitting or connection in the refrigeration system. Open fittings with caution even after the system has been discharged. If any pressure is noticed as a fitting is loosened, allow trapped pressure to bleed off very slowly. Use a suitable tube bender when bending the refrigerant lines to avoid kinking.

NOTE: Never attempt to rebend formed lines to fit. Use the correct line for the installation you are servicing.

A good rule for the flexible hose lines is to keep the radius of all bends at least 10 times the diameter of the hose. Sharper bends will reduce the flow of refrigerant. The flexible hose lines should be routed so they are at least 3 inches from the exhaust manifold. It is a good practice to inspect all flexible hose lines at least once a year to make sure they are in good condition and properly routed.

There are two types of refrigerant fittings

1. Tube fittings with "O" rings (including the unified plumbing plates with "O" rings) which need to be coated with refrigerant oil before installation . Failure to do so may result in a leak.

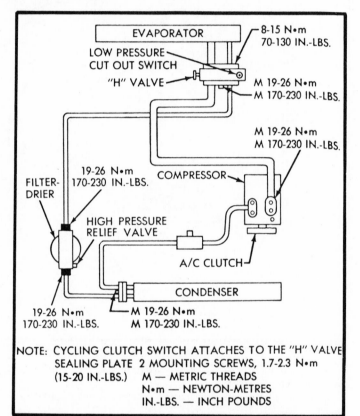

Typical torque of air conditioning components—all models (© Chrysler Corp.)

2. Unified plumbing connections with aluminum N-gaskets which cannot be serviced with "O" rings. These gaskets are not reusable and do not require lubrication before installing.

The use of proper wrenches when making connections is very important. Improper wrenches or improper use of wrenches can damage the fittings. Always use two wrenches when loosening or tightening tube fittings. Use one wrench to hold the stationary part of the fitting to prevent distorting or kinking while loosening or torquing with the other wrench.

The internal parts of the refrigeration system will remain in a state of chemical stability as long as pure-moisture-free Refrigerant 12 and refrigerant oil are used. Abnormal amounts of dirt, moisture or air can upset the chemical stability and cause operational troubles or even serious damage if present in more than minute quantities.

When it is necessary to open the refrigeration system, have everything you will need to service the system ready so the system will not be left open any longer than necessary. Cap or plug all lines and fittings as soon as they are open to prevent the entrance of dirt and moisture. All

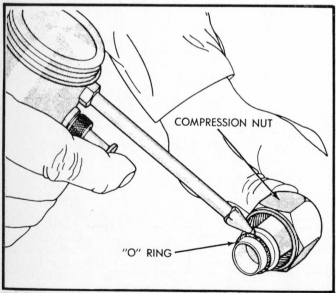

Lubrication of the 'O' rings used on the air conditioning tubing with refrigerant oil (© Chrysler Corp.)

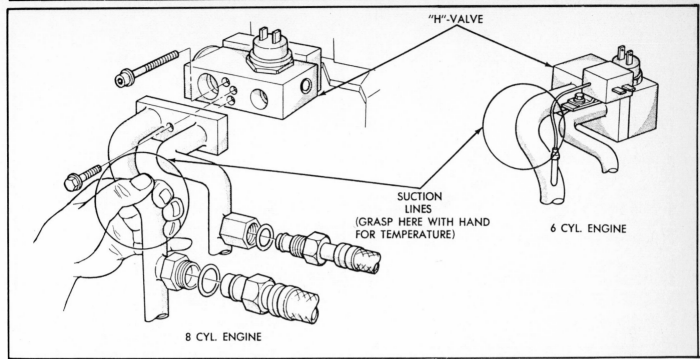

"H"-VALVE

SUCTION LINES
(GRASP HERE WITH HAND FOR TEMPERATURE)

6 CYL. ENGINE

8 CYL. ENGINE

Removal of the suction line from the 'H' valve, six and eight cylinder engine applications illustrated (© Chrysler Corp.)

lines and components in parts stock should be capped or sealed until they are ready to be used.

All tools, including the refrigerant dispensing manifold, the manifold gauge set and test hoses should be kept clean and dry.

The special refrigeration oil supplied for the system is as clean and dry as it is possible to make it. **Only refrigeration oil** should be used in the system or on the fittings and lines. The oil container should be kept tightly capped until it is ready for use, and then tightly capped after use to prevent entrance of dirt and moisture. Refrigerant oil will quickly absorb any moisture it comes in contact with.

Vacuum Control System

Adjustments and Tests

The test of the push-button operation determines whether or not the vacuum and electrical circuits are properly connected and the controls are functioning properly. However, it is possible that a vacuum control system that operates perfectly during high vacuum produced at engine idle may not function properly at high engine speeds. Before starting this test, stop engine and make certain the vacuum source hose at engine intake manifold is tight on its connector.

Start vacuum pump and connect to the vacuum test set. Adjust bleed valve on test set to obtain vacuum of exactly 8″ of mercury with a finger blocking the prod on end of test hose.

It is essential that the bleed valve be adjusted so the vacuum gauge pointer will return to exactly 8 inches when the prod is covered by a finger. Otherwise a false reading will be obtained when the control circuit is tested.

Alternately release and reblock the hose prod several times. Make sure the bleed valve is adjusted so the vacuum gauge pointer returns to exactly 8 inches of vacuum when the prod is covered with a finger.

Disconnect engine vacuum source hose at engine intake manifold and insert vacuum tester hose prod into source hose leading to push-button switch. Place vacuum gauge on the cowl so it can be observed from the driver's position as push buttons are operated.

Start the test by pushing the "HEAT" button. Vacuum tester gauge needle will drop until the actuator has operated, and should then return to 7¼–8 inches depending on vacuum leakage. Continue to push buttons: OFF, A/C MAX, A/C, DEFROST and HEAT allowing time for

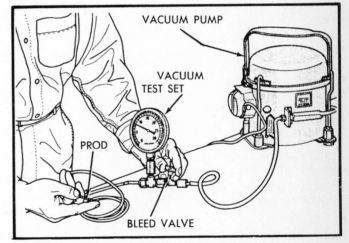

VACUUM PUMP

VACUUM TEST SET

PROD

BLEED VALVE

Adjusting the vacuum test bleed valve (© Chrysler Corp.)

actuators to operate after each button is pushed, and for the vacuum to stabilize. Note the vacuum drop below 8 inches after each operation. The maximum allowable vacuum drops below 8 inches after each operation is ¾ inch.

If the vacuum drop is more than ¾ inch, first recheck the tester for a reading of exactly 8 inches. If correct, inspect the fit of the 7-hole switch connector plug on the pushbutton switch. This plug must be positioned all the way onto the 7 ports on the pushbutton switch.

--- **CAUTION** ---

Do not use lubricant on the switch ports or in the holes in the plug, as lubricant will ruin the vacuum valves in the switch. If it is difficult to properly position the connector plug all the way on the switch ports, put a drop or two of clean water in the holes of the connector plug. This will allow the plug to slide completely on the switch ports.

If vacuum drop is now within limits, proceed with the over-all performance test. If vacuum drop is still in excess of ¾ inch, remove connector plug from the switch. Insert the vacuum test prod alternately

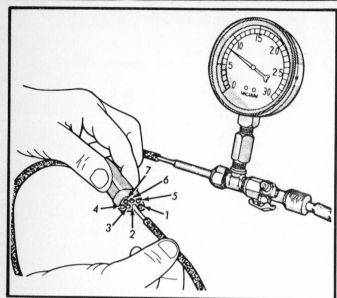

Testing vacuum tube assembly with vacuum (© Chrysler Corp.)

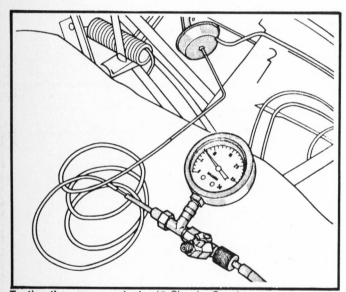

Testing the vacuum actuator (© Chrysler Corp.)

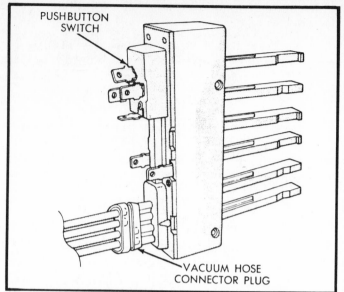

Testing the pushbutton control for vacuum leakage (© Chrysler Corp.)

OVER-ALL PERFORMANCE TEST

Humidity (the amount of moisture in the air) has an important bearing on the temperature of the air delivered to the vehicle's interior. This is true of all air-conditioning systems whether in the home, office or vehicle. It is important to understand the effect humidity has on the performance of the system. When humidity is high, the evaporator has to perform a double duty. It must lower the air temperature and the temperature of the moisture carried in the air. Condensing the moisture in the air transfers a great deal of heat energy into the evaporator fins and tubing. This reduces the amount of heat the evaporator can absorb from the air. In other words, high humidity greatly reduces the evaporator's ability to lower the temperature of the air delivered to the vehicle interior.

Evaporator capacity used to reduce the amount of moisture in the air is not wasted. Wringing some of the moisture out of the air entering the vehicle adds to the comfort of the passengers. However, an owner may expect too much from their air-conditioning system on humid days. A performance test is the best way to determine whether or not the system is performing up to standard. This test also provides valuable clues to the possible cause of trouble.

FRONT UNIT/REAR UNIT PERFORMANCE TEST

VAN MODELS

Air temperature in test room must be 70°F (21°C) minimum for this test.

1. Connect a Tachometer and manifold gauge set.
2. Set A/C controls to Max A/C, temperature lever on full cool, and blower on high.

NOTE: Vans with dual A/C must be run separately for this test. The front unit is disabled by disconnecting the feed wire to the front unit blower motor.

3. Start engine and adjust R.P.M. to 1000 with A/C clutch engaged.
4. Engine should be warmed up with doors, windows, and hood closed.
5. Insert a thermometer in the left center A/C outlet for the front unit test and for rear unit test use center panel outlet. Operate the engine for 5 minutes. The A/C clutch may cycle depending on ambient temperatures.
6. After 5 minutes note the discharge air temperature. If the clutch cycles, take the reading before the clutch disengages.

in each of the connector ports when checking source hose cover connector port with a finger.

Note amount of vacuum drop **below** 8 inches after each actuator has operated. If vacuum test gauge comes back to 8 inches at each of the 6 ports, the hoses and actuators are not leaking. The pushbutton switch is faulty and must be replaced. If excessive vacuum drop shows up at one or more ports in connector block, isolate faulty hose or actuator.

Inspect hose connections to the actuator involved. Then test whether actuator or hose is at fault; use the test hose on the actuator involved.

A leak in a hose may be detected with vacuum test set by running the fingers along the hose and watching vacuum gauge reading. The tube can be repaired by cutting out the "leak" and inserting the tube "ends" into a ⅛ inch inside diameter rubber tube. Wet the tube with water to aid assembly.

A vacuum drop in excess of ¾ inch below the 8 inches needed in this test will not interfere with engine operation, other than perhaps to cause a rough idle. It can, however, interfere with the proper operation of the air conditioning and heating controls at high speeds and during acceleration.

7. Open the hood and disconnect the gray vacuum line going to the heater water control valve. Observe the valve arm for movement as the line is disconnected. If it does not move refer to the heater valve control section of this group. Plug the vacuum line to prevent leakage.

8. Operate the A/C for 2 more minutes and take the discharge air temperature reading again. If the temperature increased by more than 5°F check the blend air door cable for correct operation. If the temperature does not increase more than 5°F compare the discharge air temperature, suction, and discharge pressures with the valves in the performance charts corresponding with the garage ambient temperature. Reconnect the gray vacuum line.

9. If the discharge air temperature fails to meet the specifications in the performance temperature charts, refer to the diagnostic analysis charts for further test information.

"H" VALVE TEST WITH C-171 COMPRESSOR

IN VEHICLE SINGLE FRONT UNIT ONLY

Procedure

Test must be made at ambient temperature of 70° to 85°F.

After performing all previously mentioned tests, conduct the "H" valve test as follows:

1. A/C system—Close the windows and operate the engine at 800 RPM. Set air conditioning controls for Max. A/C, high blower, temperature control lever in warm position, cycling clutch switch and low pressure cut out switch electrically by-passed. Disconnect and plug the water valve vacuum hose in the engine compartment. Ambient 70°–85°F.

2. Operate the system for at least five (5) minutes in order to obtain partial stabilization and sufficient reheat to load the system. Pressure at the discharge service port should reach 140–240 psig. If head pressure of 140–240 psig cannot be obtained, check system charge level.

3. Spray the "H" valve control head with liquid freon (refrigerant)

for 10 to 15 seconds. The evaporator suction pressure must drop to below 15″ of vacuum. If the condition is not met, the "H" valve is stuck open and should be replaced. Discontinue spraying with freon and watch the evaporator suction pressure; it should increase to a minimum of 38 psig and then stabilize to a pressure of 25 to 35 psig. Any "H" valve that does not produce this response is stuck closed and should be replaced.

ALTERNATE METHOD—Put crushed dry ice on control head (completely cover head) for a minimum of 30 seconds.

NOTE: Extreme care must be used when handling dry ice as skin injury can occur if protective gloves are not worn.

Evaporator suction pressure must drop to below 15″ of vacuum. If the condition is not met the "H" valve is stuck open and should be replaced. Remove dry ice and watch evaporator suction pressure; it should increase to a minimum of 38 psig and then stabilize to a pressure of 25 to 35 psig. Any "H" valve which does not produce this response is stuck open and should be replaced.

4. Reconnect A/C water valve vacuum hose (gray) and set temperature control in cool position.

5. Set engine speed at 800 RPM and blower on HI. The evaporator suction pressure should be in the range of 20–30 psig. If compressor discharge is higher than 240 psig, check for restricted discharge line, radiator overheating, air in system or faulty viscous fan drive. If discharge pressure is less than 140 psig check compressor gaskets and discharge reeds.

6. Reconnect the electrical wires to the cycling clutch switch and low pressure cut out switch.

Expansion Valve Tests (Dual Unit)

1. Close vehicle doors and windows. Operate the engine at 800 RPM. Set air-conditioning controls at MAX. A/C, high blower (front and rear units), and temperature control lever in full heat (extreme right). Disconnect and plug water valve vacuum hose in the engine compartment. Attach the gauge set.

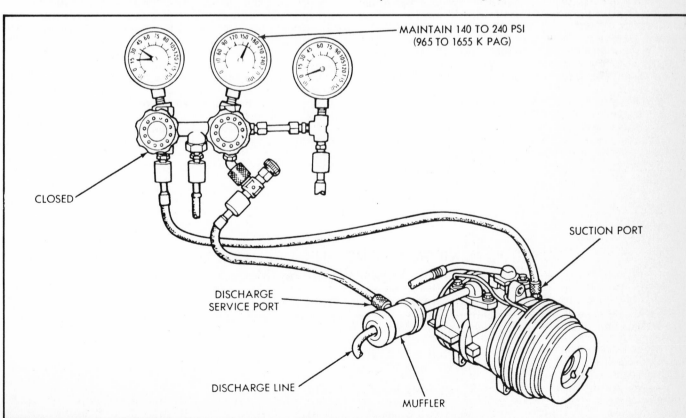

MAINTAIN 140 TO 240 PSI
(965 TO 1655 K PAG)

CLOSED

SUCTION PORT

DISCHARGE SERVICE PORT

DISCHARGE LINE

MUFFLER

Testing the 'H' valve and/or rear expansion valve—Van models (© Chrysler Corp.)

2. Operate the A/C system for at least five minutes to obtain partial stabilization and sufficient reheat to load front and rear evaporators. Pressure at the compressor discharge service port should reach 140 psig to 240 psig. If this compressor discharge pressure cannot be obtained, check the system charge level.

3. EXPANSION VALVE TEST—The "H" valve (front unit) and the TXV (Rear unit) are both checked for correct operation using a "hands on" test technique. The control head of the expansion valve is sprayed with liquid refrigerant (R12) for ten to fifteen seconds. Extreme care must be taken in handling refrigerant. Remove the cover to the rear unit and spray rear expansion valve head. Grasp the suction line (large line) off the evaporator with the bare hand and hold for at least two minutes. Use the same procedure with the front unit "H" valve. Grasp the suction line below the "H" valve (before the rear suction line tee in) with the bare hands and hold for at least two minutes. When testing front "H" valve, place rear blower motor in OFF position.

With a correct operating expansion valve, the suction line will be warm with the closing of the valve (Refrigerant Spray) and then cool sharply within two minutes as the valve opens. If this temperature change does not occur, the valve is plugged or failed shut, and should be replaced.

4. Unplug and replace vacuum line on water valve.

LEAK TESTS

The Chrysler Leak Detector Torch Tool, C-3569-A, is a butane gas-burning torch used to locate a leak in any part of the rfrigeration system. Refrigerant gas drawn into the sampling or "sniffer" hose will cause the flame to change color in proportion to the size of the leak. A very small leak will produce a flame varying from yellowish-green to bright green. A large leak will produce a brilliant blue flame.

CAUTION

Do not use the lighted detector in any place where explosive gases, dust or vapors are present. Do not breathe the fumes that are produced by the burning of refrigerant gas. Large concentrations of refrigerant in the presence of a live flame become dangerously toxic.

If the flame remains bright yellow when the tester is removed from possible leak point, insufficient air is being drawn in through the sampling tube, or the copper reaction wire is dirty.

1. Assemble leak detector. Be sure detector is seated tightly over torch gasket.

2. Holding torch upright screw-in butane charger (clockwise) until punctured. (Do not use force).

3. Screw-out butane charger (counterclockwise) about ¼ turn.

4. Point torch away from body—then light escaping gas with match. Always keep torch in upright position.

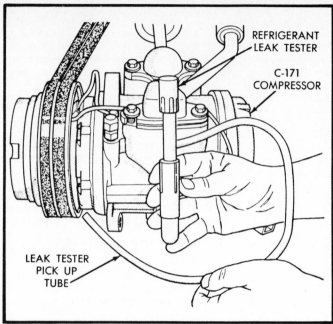

Testing with special refrigerant leak tester (© Chrysler Corp.)

5. Adjust flame by turning cartridge in or out as required.

6. Allow 30 seconds to heat copper reaction wire.

CAUTION

Never remove butane charger while torch is lighted or in presence of any open flame.

---

7. Examine all tube connectors and other possible leak points by moving the end of the sampling hose from point to point. Always keep torch in an upright position. Since Refrigerant 12 is heavier than air, it is a good practice to place the open end of the sampling hose directly below the point being tested. Be careful not to pinch the sampling tube since this will shut off the air supply to the flame and cause a color change.

8. Watch for a change in the color of the flame. Small leaks will produce a green color and large leaks a bright blue color. If leaks are observed at tube fittings, tighten the connection, using the correct wrenches, and retest.

9. To extinguish tester, close off torch by turning butane charger clockwise (screw-in) without using force. Escaping gas will stop in a few seconds.

CONTROL HEAD POSITIONS AND OPERATING MODES
Mini Vans, Voyager, Caravan Models

CONTROL CHART						
Control Position	**Off**	**Max**	**Norm***	**Bi-Level***	**Heat**	**Defrost**
Inlet Air Door (Open To)	Inside	Inside	Outside	Outside	Outside	Outside
Mode Door (Open To)	A/C	A/C	A/C	Bi-Level	Heat/Def.	Heat/Def.
Heat Defrost (Open To)	Heat	Heat	Heat	Heat	Heat	Defrost
Compressor Clutch	Off	On	On*	On*	Off	On
Blower Motor	Off	On	On	On	On	On
Water Valve	Closed	Closed	Open	Open	Open	Open

*Push button is pulled out to disengage compressor and allow Normal Vent and Bi-Level Vent modes.

COMPRESSOR OIL LEVEL ADJUSTMENT
All Models

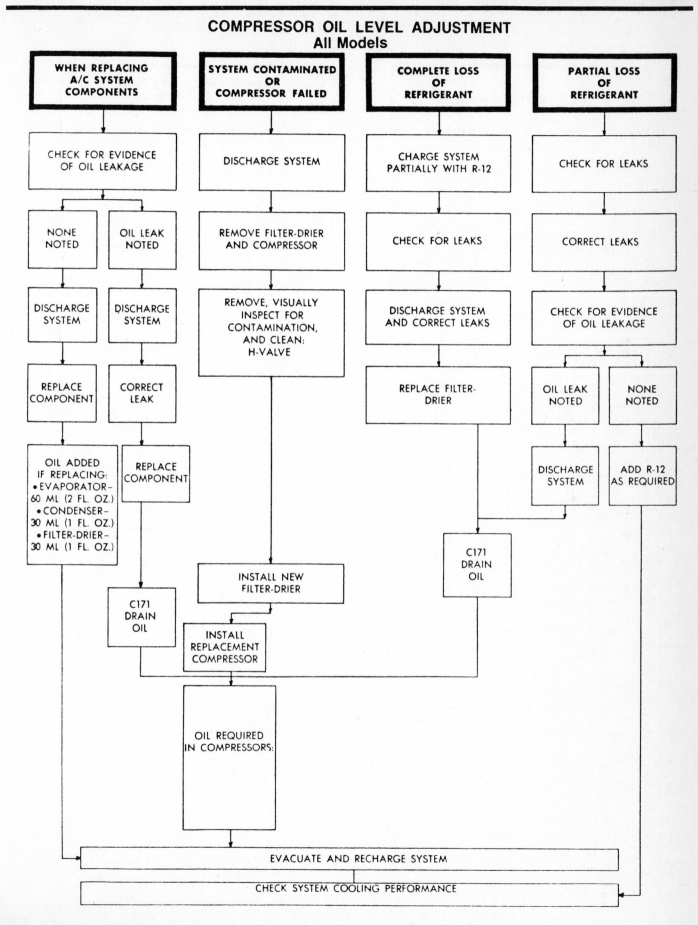

COMPRESSOR AND CLUTCH DIAGNOSIS
All Models

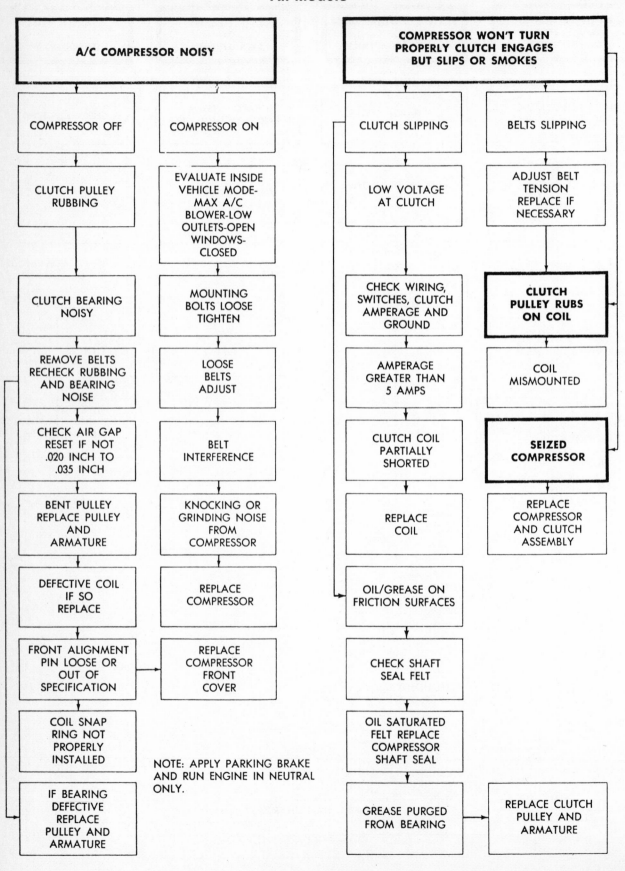

A/C COMPRESSOR NOISY

COMPRESSOR OFF

CLUTCH PULLEY RUBBING

CLUTCH BEARING NOISY

REMOVE BELTS RECHECK RUBBING AND BEARING NOISE

CHECK AIR GAP RESET IF NOT .020 INCH TO .035 INCH

BENT PULLEY REPLACE PULLEY AND ARMATURE

DEFECTIVE COIL IF SO REPLACE

FRONT ALIGNMENT PIN LOOSE OR OUT OF SPECIFICATION

COIL SNAP RING NOT PROPERLY INSTALLED

IF BEARING DEFECTIVE REPLACE PULLEY AND ARMATURE

COMPRESSOR ON

EVALUATE INSIDE VEHICLE MODE- MAX A/C BLOWER-LOW OUTLETS-OPEN WINDOWS- CLOSED

MOUNTING BOLTS LOOSE TIGHTEN

LOOSE BELTS ADJUST

BELT INTERFERENCE

KNOCKING OR GRINDING NOISE FROM COMPRESSOR

REPLACE COMPRESSOR

REPLACE COMPRESSOR FRONT COVER

NOTE: APPLY PARKING BRAKE AND RUN ENGINE IN NEUTRAL ONLY.

COMPRESSOR WON'T TURN PROPERLY CLUTCH ENGAGES BUT SLIPS OR SMOKES

CLUTCH SLIPPING

LOW VOLTAGE AT CLUTCH

CHECK WIRING, SWITCHES, CLUTCH AMPERAGE AND GROUND

AMPERAGE GREATER THAN 5 AMPS

CLUTCH COIL PARTIALLY SHORTED

REPLACE COIL

OIL/GREASE ON FRICTION SURFACES

CHECK SHAFT SEAL FELT

OIL SATURATED FELT REPLACE COMPRESSOR SHAFT SEAL

GREASE PURGED FROM BEARING

BELTS SLIPPING

ADJUST BELT TENSION REPLACE IF NECESSARY

CLUTCH PULLEY RUBS ON COIL

COIL MISMOUNTED

SEIZED COMPRESSOR

REPLACE COMPRESSOR AND CLUTCH ASSEMBLY

REPLACE CLUTCH PULLEY AND ARMATURE

COMPRESSOR AND CLUTCH DIAGNOSIS
All Models

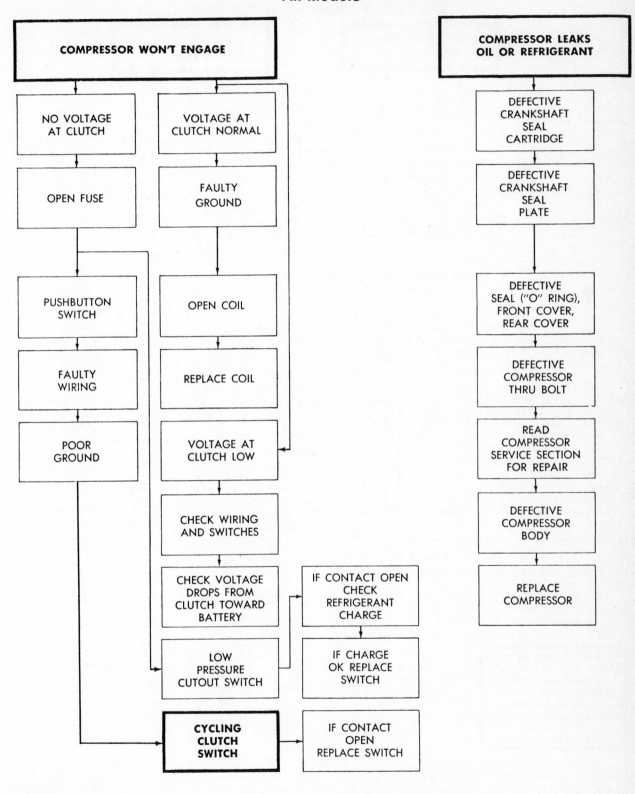

NOTE: APPLY PARKING BRAKE
AND RUN ENGINE IN NEUTRAL
ONLY.

AIR CONDITIONING BLOWER MOTOR AND CONTROL SYSTEM ELECTRICAL DIAGNOSIS
Mini Vans, Voyager, Caravan Models

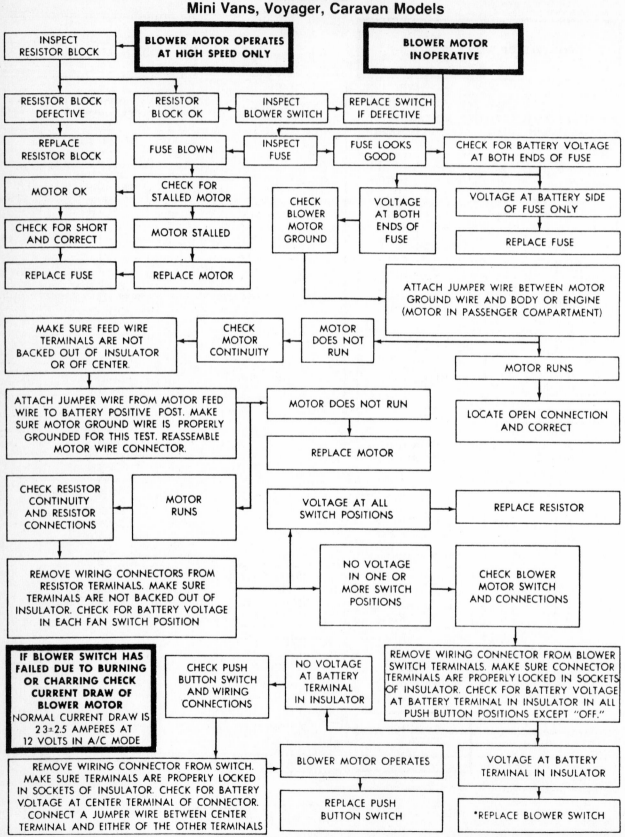

REFRIGERANT SYSTEM DIAGNOSIS
Mini Vans, Voyager, Caravan Models

EVAPORATOR SUCTION GAUGE KPAG (PSIG) 1	CHECK REFRIGERANT LEVEL	TEST CONDITIONS AMBIENT: 21° TO 29°C (70° TO 85°F); MODE – MAX A/C WINDOWS – CLOSED; SET VEHICLE IN NEUTRAL; APPLY PARKING BRAKE
COMPRESSOR DISCHARGE GAUGE KPAG (PSIG) 2	INSTALL GAUGE SET	
	PROCEED WITH OVERALL PERFORMANCE TEST	USING GAUGE SET FOLLOW DIAGNOSIS SEQUENCE AS INDICATED

DISCONNECT AND PLUG WATER VALVE VACUUM HOSE; BYPASS CYCLING CLUTCH AND LOW PRESSURE CUT-OUT SWITCHES ; SET TEMPERATURE CONTROL IN FULL HEAT

H-VALVE TEST

ENGINE RPM	BLOWER MOTOR SPEED	EVAPORATOR SUCTION GAUGE KPAG (PSIG) 1	COMPRESSOR DISCHARGE GAUGE KPAG (PSIG) 2	DIAGNOSIS
1000	HI	138 TO 240 KPAG (20 TO 35 PSIG)	965 TO 1655 K PAG 140-240 PSIG	NORMAL

| SPRAY "H" VALVE HEAD WITH LIQUID REFRIGERANT FOR 10 SECONDS | -50 K PAG 15 INCHES OF VACUUM | "H" VALVE STUCK OPEN IF CONDITION CANNOT BE MET |
| DISCONTINUE SPRAY | STABILIZES AT 20-35 PSIG (138 TO 240 K PAG) | "H" VALVE STUCK CLOSED IF CONDITIONS CANNOT BE MET |

HIGH SIDE TEST

| 1100 | HI | 138 TO 240 K PAG (20-35 PSIG) | OVER 1655 K PAG (240 PSIG) | RESTRICTED CONDENSER RESTRICTED DISCHARGE LINE – RADIATOR OVERHEATING – AIR IN SYSTEM – OVERCHARGED SYSTEM – FAULTY FAN MOTOR |

RECONNECT WATER VACUUM HOSE

RECONNECT CYCLING CLUTCH SWITCH AND LOW PRESSURE CUT-OUT SWITCH . SEE CYCLING CLUTCH SWITCH TEST TO CHECK FOR PROPER OPERATION

NOTE: APPLY PARKING BRAKE AND RUN ENGINE IN NEUTRAL ONLY

AIR CONDITIONING BLOWER MOTOR AND CONTROL SYSTEM MECHANICAL DIAGNOSIS
All Models

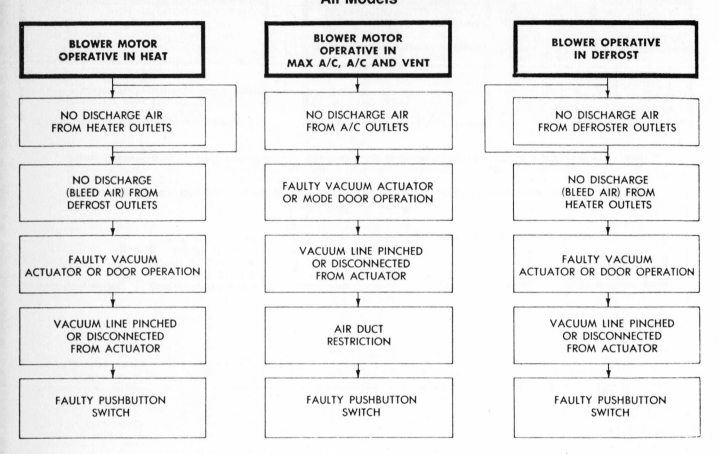

BLOWER MOTOR OPERATIVE IN HEAT	BLOWER MOTOR OPERATIVE IN MAX A/C, A/C AND VENT	BLOWER OPERATIVE IN DEFROST
NO DISCHARGE AIR FROM HEATER OUTLETS	NO DISCHARGE AIR FROM A/C OUTLETS	NO DISCHARGE AIR FROM DEFROSTER OUTLETS
NO DISCHARGE (BLEED AIR) FROM DEFROST OUTLETS	FAULTY VACUUM ACTUATOR OR MODE DOOR OPERATION	NO DISCHARGE (BLEED AIR) FROM HEATER OUTLETS
FAULTY VACUUM ACTUATOR OR DOOR OPERATION	VACUUM LINE PINCHED OR DISCONNECTED FROM ACTUATOR	FAULTY VACUUM ACTUATOR OR DOOR OPERATION
VACUUM LINE PINCHED OR DISCONNECTED FROM ACTUATOR	AIR DUCT RESTRICTION	VACUUM LINE PINCHED OR DISCONNECTED FROM ACTUATOR
FAULTY PUSHBUTTON SWITCH	FAULTY PUSHBUTTON SWITCH	FAULTY PUSHBUTTON SWITCH

TEMPERATURE PERFORMANCE CHART
Pick-Up Trucks, Sport Utility

Garage Ambient Temperature	70°F (21°C)	80°F (26.5°C)	90°F (32°C)	100°F (37.5°C)	110°F (43°C)
Discharge Air Temperature	38-50°F (3-10°C)	42-54°F (6-12°C)	46-58°F (8-14°C)	50-62°F (10-17°C)	54-66°F (12-19°C)
Compressor Discharge Pressure	120 / 195 psig	160 / 235 psig	200 / 270 psig	240 / 305 psig	280 / 340 psig
Evaporator Suction Pressure	18 / 30 psig	20 / 35 psig	22 / 39 psig	25 / 43 psig	26 / 47 psig

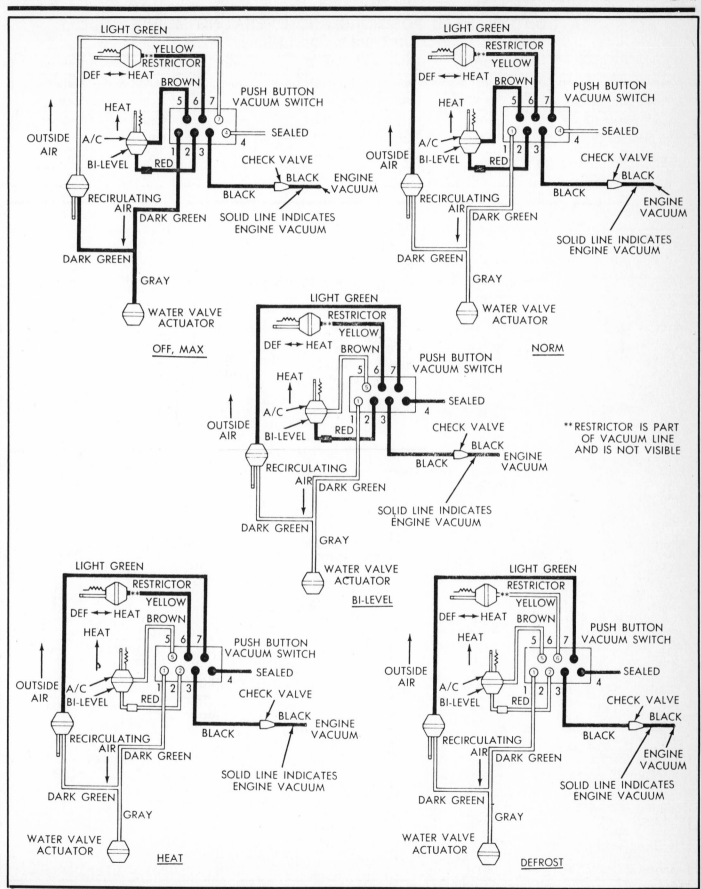

Vacuum circuits in the varied control modes—Mini Vans, Voyager and Caravan (© Chrysler Corp.)

CONTROL HEAD POSITIONS AND OPERATING MODES
Pick-Up Trucks, Sport Utility

Control Position	Off	Max. A/C	A/C	Vent	Heat	Defrost
Inlet Air Door (Open To)	Inside	Inside	Outside	Outside	Outside	Outside
Mode Door (Open To)	A/C	A/C	A/C	A/C	Heat	Heat
Heat Defrost (Open To)	Heat	Heat	Heat	Heat	Heat	Defrost
Compressor Clutch	Off	On	On	Off	Off	On
Blower Motor	Off	On	On	On	On	On
Water Valve	Off	Off	On	On	On	On

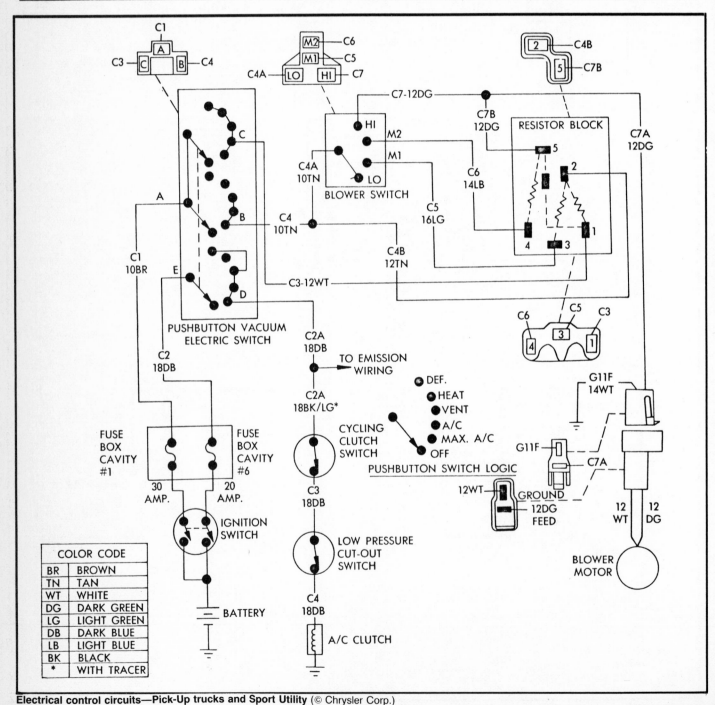

Electrical control circuits—Pick-Up trucks and Sport Utility (© Chrysler Corp.)

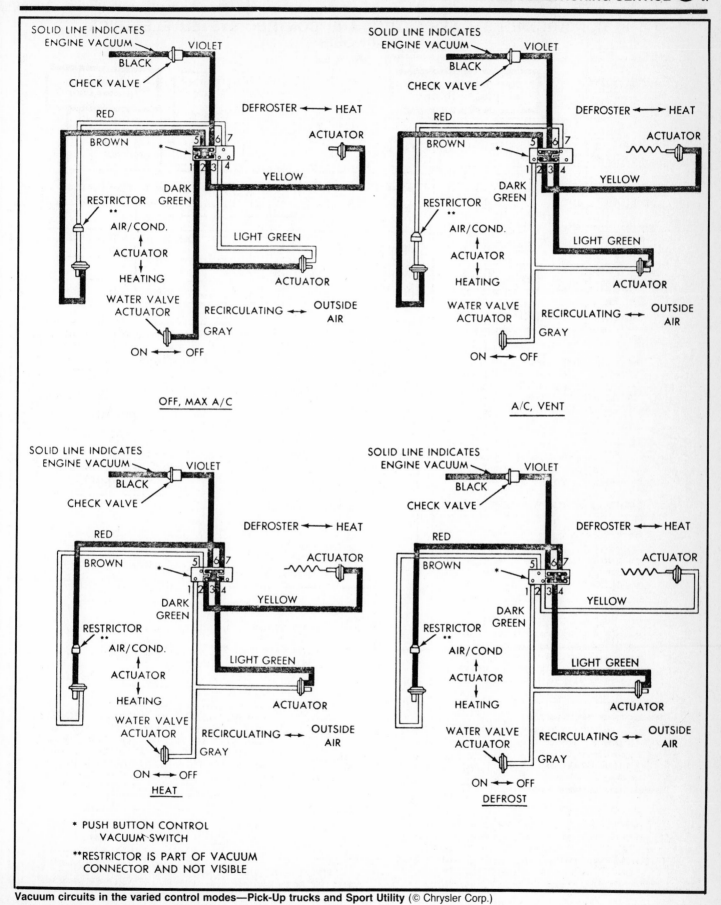

OFF, MAX A/C

A/C, VENT

HEAT

DEFROST

* PUSH BUTTON CONTROL
  VACUUM SWITCH

**RESTRICTOR IS PART OF VACUUM
  CONNECTOR AND NOT VISIBLE

Vacuum circuits in the varied control modes—Pick-Up trucks and Sport Utility (© Chrysler Corp.)

AIR CONDITIONING BLOWER MOTOR AND CONTROL SYSTEM ELECTRICAL DIAGNOSIS
Van Models

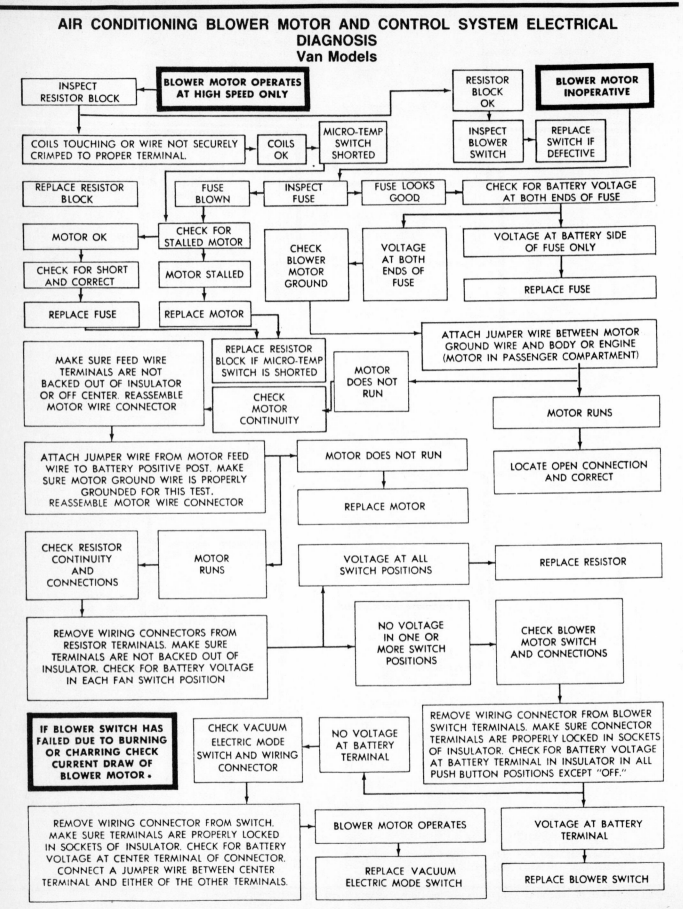

COMPRESSOR DIAGNOSIS
Van Models with C-171 Compressor

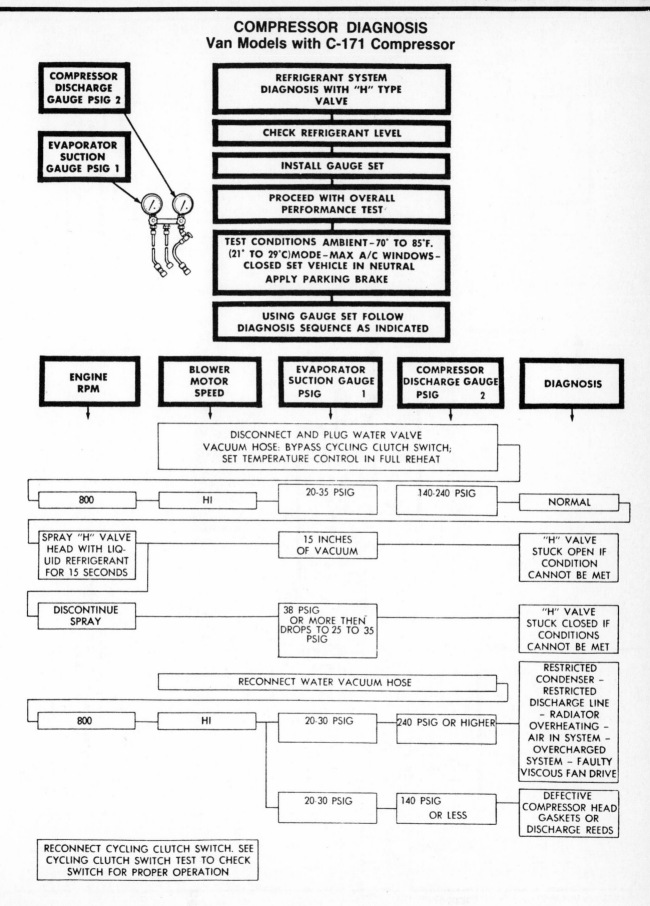

COMPRESSOR DISCHARGE GAUGE PSIG 2

EVAPORATOR SUCTION GAUGE PSIG 1

REFRIGERANT SYSTEM DIAGNOSIS WITH "H" TYPE VALVE

CHECK REFRIGERANT LEVEL

INSTALL GAUGE SET

PROCEED WITH OVERALL PERFORMANCE TEST

TEST CONDITIONS AMBIENT – 70° TO 85°F. (21° TO 29°C) MODE – MAX A/C WINDOWS – CLOSED SET VEHICLE IN NEUTRAL APPLY PARKING BRAKE

USING GAUGE SET FOLLOW DIAGNOSIS SEQUENCE AS INDICATED

ENGINE RPM	BLOWER MOTOR SPEED	EVAPORATOR SUCTION GAUGE PSIG 1	COMPRESSOR DISCHARGE GAUGE PSIG 2	DIAGNOSIS
DISCONNECT AND PLUG WATER VALVE VACUUM HOSE: BYPASS CYCLING CLUTCH SWITCH; SET TEMPERATURE CONTROL IN FULL REHEAT				
800	HI	20-35 PSIG	140-240 PSIG	NORMAL
SPRAY "H" VALVE HEAD WITH LIQUID REFRIGERANT FOR 15 SECONDS		15 INCHES OF VACUUM		"H" VALVE STUCK OPEN IF CONDITION CANNOT BE MET
DISCONTINUE SPRAY		38 PSIG OR MORE THEN DROPS TO 25 TO 35 PSIG		"H" VALVE STUCK CLOSED IF CONDITIONS CANNOT BE MET
RECONNECT WATER VACUUM HOSE				RESTRICTED CONDENSER – RESTRICTED DISCHARGE LINE – RADIATOR OVERHEATING – AIR IN SYSTEM – OVERCHARGED SYSTEM – FAULTY VISCOUS FAN DRIVE
800	HI	20-30 PSIG	240 PSIG OR HIGHER	
		20-30 PSIG	140 PSIG OR LESS	DEFECTIVE COMPRESSOR HEAD GASKETS OR DISCHARGE REEDS
RECONNECT CYCLING CLUTCH SWITCH. SEE CYCLING CLUTCH SWITCH TEST TO CHECK SWITCH FOR PROPER OPERATION				

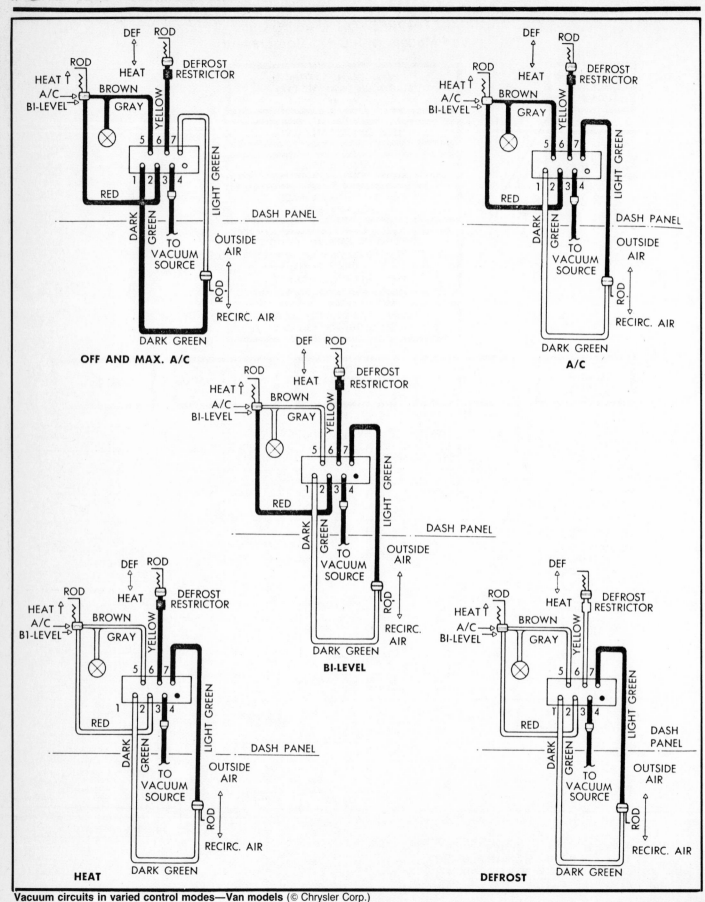

Vacuum circuits in varied control modes—Van models (© Chrysler Corp.)

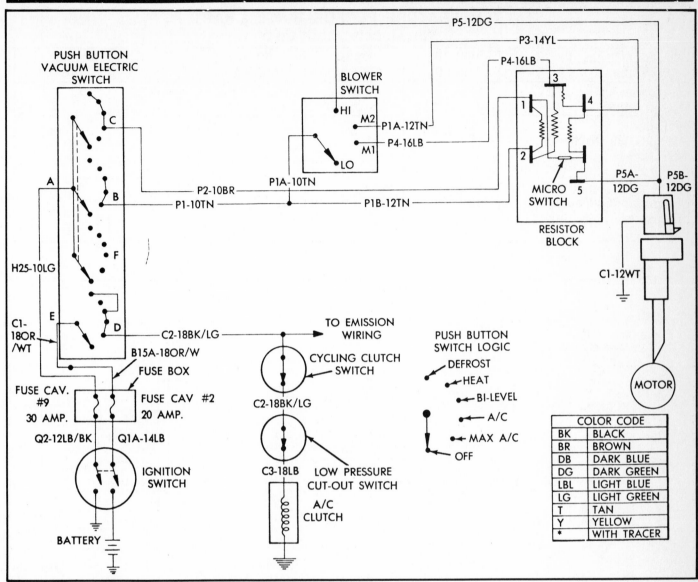

Air conditioning electrical control circuits—Van models (© Chrysler Corp.)

CONTROL HEAD POSITIONS AND OPERATING MODES
Van Models

Push Button	Off	Max. A/C	A/C	Bi-Level	Heat	Defrost
Inlet Air Door (Open To)	Inside	Inside	Outside	Outside	Outside	Outside
Bi-Level Door (Open To)	A/C	A/C	A/C	Bi-Level	Heat	Heat
Heat Defrost Door (Open To)	Heat	Heat	Heat	Heat	Heat	Defrost
Compressor Clutch	Off	On	On*	On*	Off	On**
Blower Motor	Off	On	On	On	On	On
Water Valve	Off	Off	Off	On	On	On

* Pull out A/C or Bi-Level Button Achieves Vent or Bi-Level mode with compressor clutch off.
** Pulling out **Defrost** button achieves defrost mode with compressore clutch off.

TEMPERATURE PERFORMANCE CHART
Van Models, Front Units

Garage Ambient Temperature	70°F (21°C)	80°F (26.5°C)	90°F (32°C)	100°F (37.5°C)	110°F (43°C)
Discharge Air Temperature	40-56°F (4-13°C)	42-60°F (6-16°C)	40-63°F (4-17°C)	48-67°F (9-19°C)	53-71°F (12-22°C)
Compressor Discharge Pressure	120 195 psig	160 235 psig	200 270 psig	240 305 psig	280 340 psig
Evaporator Suction Pressure	18 30 psig	20 35 psig	22 39 psig	25 43 psig	26 47 psig

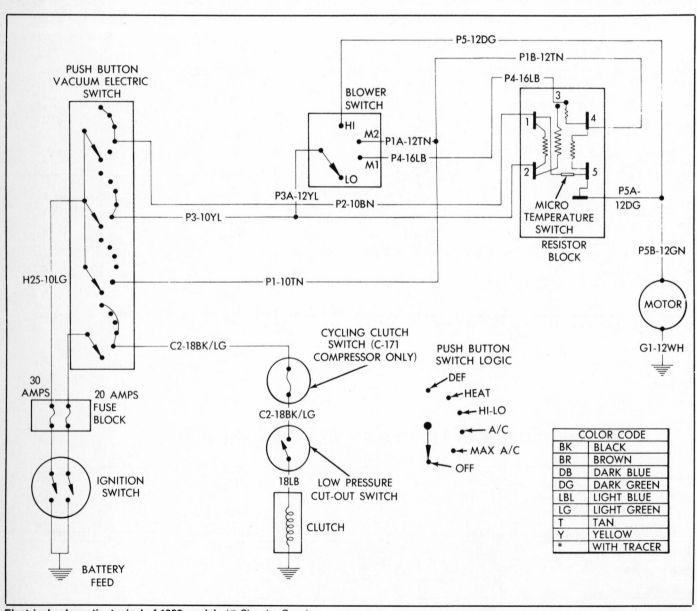

Electrical schematic, typical of 1982 models (© Chrysler Corp.)

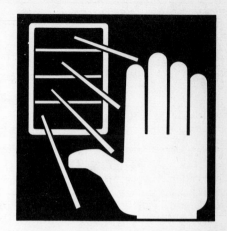

Ford Motor Company

INDEX

VEHICLE IDENTIFICATION CHART

1982	1983	1984	1985
Bronco	Bronco	Bronco	Bronco
Econoline	Econoline	Econoline	Econoline
Pick Up	Pick Up	Pick Up	Pick Up
	Bronco II	Bronco. II	Bronco II
	Ranger	Ranger	Ranger
			Aerostar

FREON CAPACITIES OUNCES

Year	Bronco	Pick Up	Econoline	Ranger	Bronco II	Aerostar
1982	52	52	56①	—	—	—
1983	52	52	56①	40	40	—
1984	52	52	56①	40	40	—
1985	52	52	56①	40	40	N/A

① 68 ounces with auxilary air.

REFRIGERANT OIL CAPACITIES FLUID OUNCES

Year	Model	Capacity	Compressor Type
1982	Bronco	10	York 3
	Pick Up	10	York 3
	Econoline	11	Tecumseh
1983	Bronco	10	FS6
	Pick Up	10	FS6
	Econoline	10	FS6
	Bronco II	10	FS6
	Ranger	10	FS6
1984	Bronco	10	FS6
	Pick Up	10	FS6
	Econoline	10	FS6
	Bronco II	10	FS6
	Ranger	10	FS6
1985	Bronco	10	FS6
	Pick Up	10	FS6
	Econoline	10	FS6
	Bronco II	10	FS6
	Ranger	10	FS6
	Aerostar	N/A	N/A

Blower Motor

Removal and Installation

1982 AND LATER—ALL VEHICLES EXCEPT ECONOLINE

For blower motor removal and installation procedures refer to the heating section.

1982 AND LATER—ECONOLINE

1. Disconnect the resistor electrical leads on the front of the blower cover inside the truck.
2. Remove the blower cover.

3. Push the wiring grommet forward out of the housing hole.
4. Remove the blower motor mounting plate. Remove the blower motor.
5. Reverse the procedure for installation.

Compressor

Removal and Installation

1982 AND LATER—ALL VEHICLES

1. Disconnect the negative battery cable.
2. Remove all the necessary equipment in order to gain access to the compressor mounting bolts.
3. Remove the compressor drive belt.
4. Discharge the system.
5. Disconnect and plug the refrigerant lines.
6. Disconnect all electrical connections from the unit.
7. Remove the compressor mounting bolts. Remove the compressor from the vehicle.
8. Installation is the reverse of the removal procedure. Evacuate and charge the system as required.

NOTE: For compressor overhaul information refer to the compressor overhaul section of this manual.

Fixed Orifice Tube Refrigerant System

GENERAL INFORMATION

The fixed orifice tube system is being used on all, except the Econoline. The fixed orifice tube system, replaces the therm-expansion valve and the suction throttle valve with an orifice tube and a clutch cycling pressure switch. The fixed orifice tube assembly is the restriction between the high and the low pressure liquid refrigerant and meters the flow of the liquid refrigerant into the evaporator core. The fixed orifice tube is constructed of filter screens, which are located in the inlet and outlet ends of the tube body and two O-rings. The screens act as strainers for the liquid refrigerant flowing through the fixed orifice opening. The two O-rings on the tube body prevent the high pressure liquid refrigerant from by-passing the orifice tube assembly. The fixed orifice tube is located in the liquid line near the evaporator inlet tube on some models and in the liquid line near the condensor in other models. Adjustment or repairs can not be made to the orifice tube, if the tube is not operating properly it should be replaced.

FIXED ORIFICE TUBE

Removal and Installation

1982 AND LATER

1. Discharge the refrigerant from the A/C system following the recommended service procedures.
2. Disconnect or separate the liquid line at the orifice tube location.
3. Pour a small amount of clean refrigerant oil into the inlet tube or liquid line containing the orifice tube. This will lubricate the tube and the orifice tube O-rings during removal.
4. Engage the orifice remover tool (Motorcraft Tool YT-1008 or equivalent) with the two tangs on the fixed orifice tube.

NOTE: Do not twist or rotate the fixed orifice tube in the evaporator core tube as it may break off in the evaporator core tube. ·

5. Hold the T-handle of the remover Tool YT-1008 or equivalent, to keep it from turning and run the nut on the tool down against the evaporator core tube until the orifice is pulled from the tube.

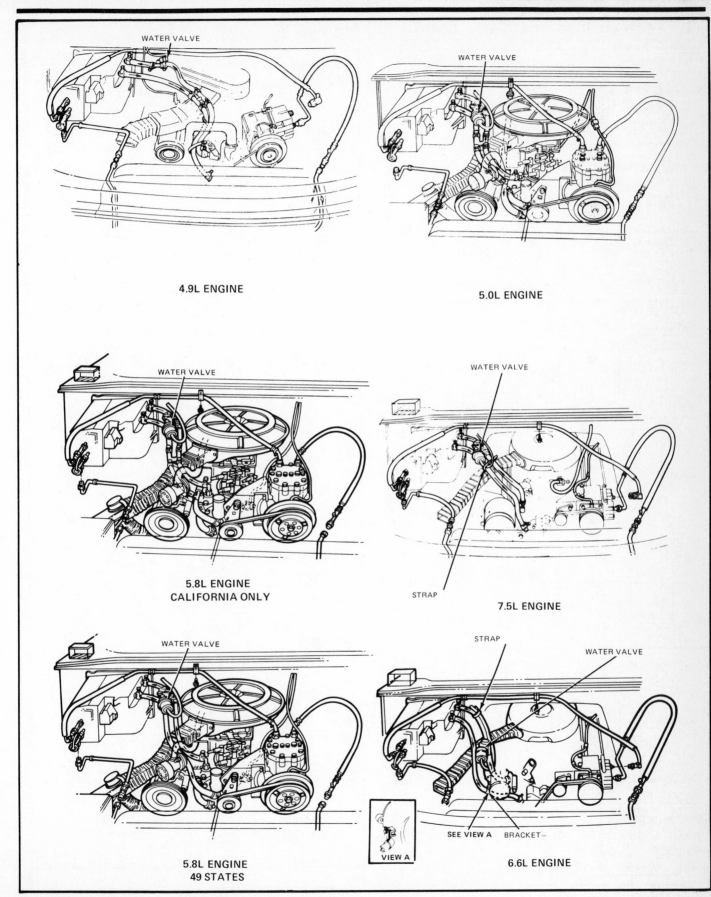

WATER VALVE

4.9L ENGINE

WATER VALVE

5.0L ENGINE

WATER VALVE

**5.8L ENGINE
CALIFORNIA ONLY**

WATER VALVE

STRAP

7.5L ENGINE

WATER VALVE

**5.8L ENGINE
49 STATES**

STRAP

WATER VALVE

VIEW A

SEE VIEW A   BRACKET—

6.6L ENGINE

1982-83 typical compressor and refrigerant line routing—Econoline (© Ford Motor Company)

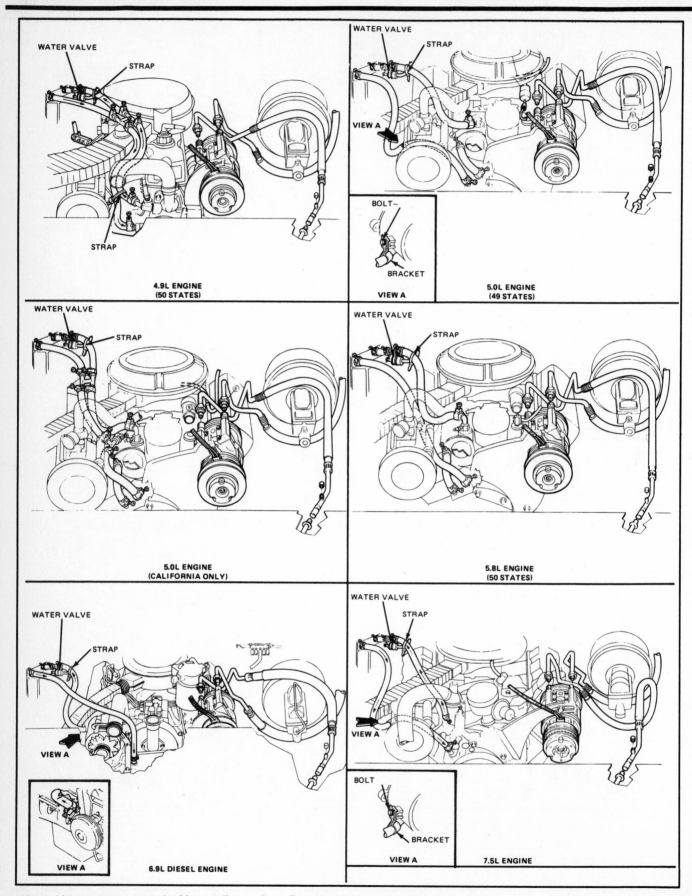

WATER VALVE

STRAP

STRAP

**4.9L ENGINE
(50 STATES)**

WATER VALVE

STRAP

VIEW A

BOLT

BRACKET

VIEW A

**5.0L ENGINE
(49 STATES)**

WATER VALVE

STRAP

**5.0L ENGINE
(CALIFORNIA ONLY)**

WATER VALVE

STRAP

**5.8L ENGINE
(50 STATES)**

WATER VALVE

STRAP

VIEW A

VIEW A

6.9L DIESEL ENGINE

WATER VALVE

STRAP

VIEW A

BOLT

BRACKET

VIEW A

7.5L ENGINE

1984 and later compressor and refrigerant line routing—Econoline (© Ford Motor Company)

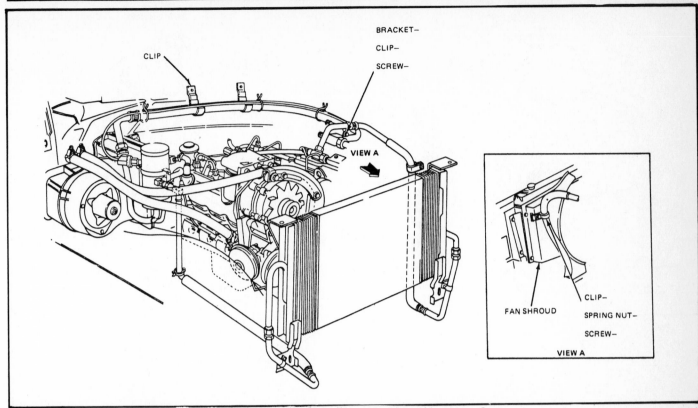

Compressor and refrigerant line routing—Bronco and Pick-Up (with diesel engine) (© Ford Motor Company)

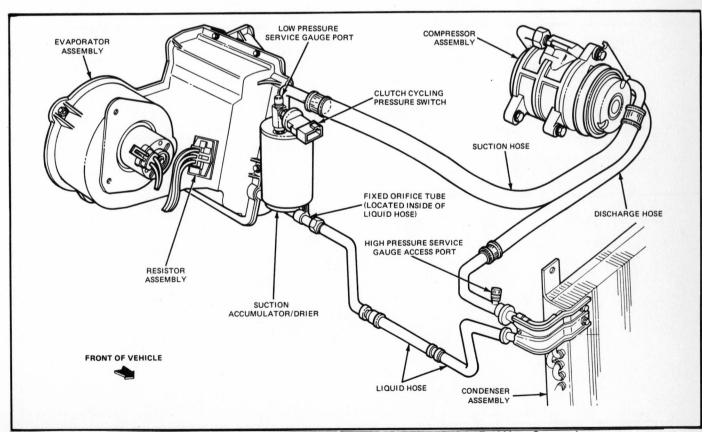

1983 and later compressor and refrigerant line routing—Bronco II and Ranger (V-6 engine) (© Ford Motor Company)

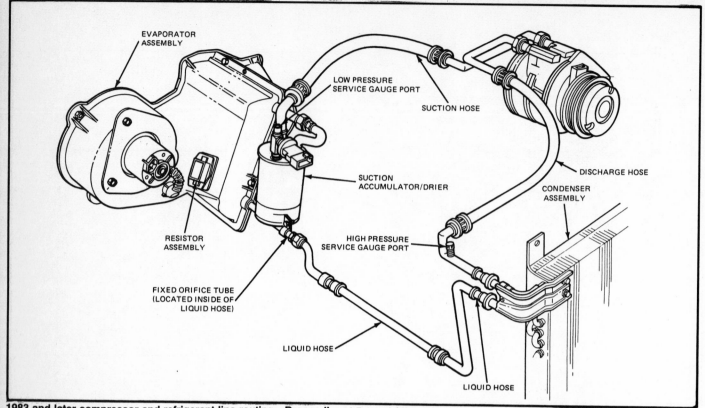

1983 and later compressor and refrigerant line routing—Bronco II and Ranger (diesel engine) (© Ford Motor Company)

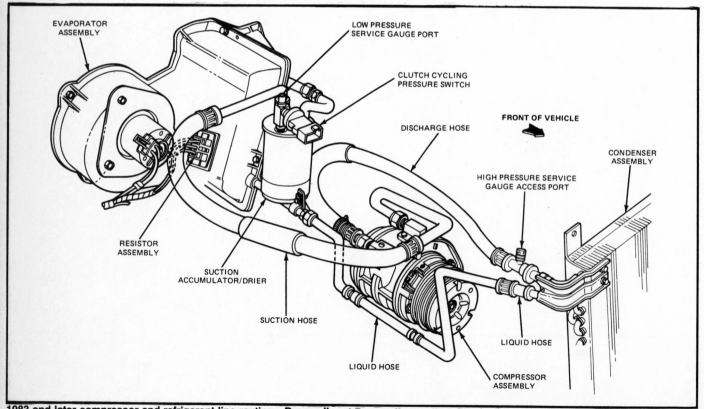

1983 and later compressor and refrigerant line routing—Bronco II and Ranger (four cylinder engine) (© Ford Motor Company)

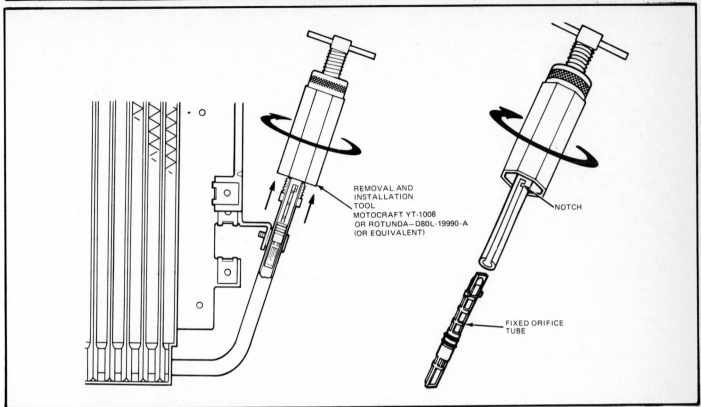

REMOVAL AND INSTALLATION TOOL MOTORCRAFT YT-1008 OR ROTUNDA—D80L-19990-A (OR EQUIVALENT)

NOTCH

FIXED ORIFICE TUBE

Fixed orifice tube location—except Bronco II and Ranger (© Ford Motor Company)

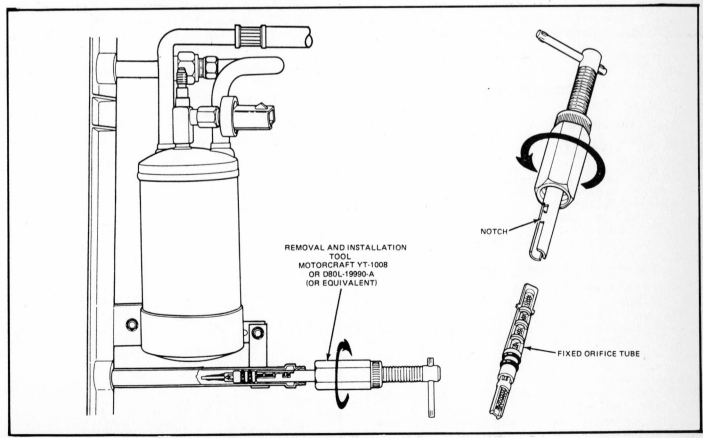

REMOVAL AND INSTALLATION TOOL MOTORCRAFT YT-1008 OR D80L-19990-A (OR EQUIVALENT)

NOTCH

FIXED ORIFICE TUBE

Fixed orifice tube location—Bronco II and Ranger (© Ford Motor Company)

6. If the fixed orifice tube breaks in the evaporator core tube, it must be removed from the tube with an extractor, Motorcraft Tool YT-1009 or equivalent.

7. To remove a broken orifice tube, insert the screw end of the extractor, Tool YT-1009 or equivalent, into the evaporator core tube and thread the screw end of the tool into the brass tube in the center of the fixed orifice tube. Then, pull the fixed orifice tube from the evaporator core tube.

8. If only the brass center tube is removed during Step 7, insert the screw end of Tool YT-1009 or equivalent, into the evaporator core tube and screw the end of the tool into the fixed orifice tube body. Then, pull the fixed orifice tube body from the evaporator core tube.

9. Lubricate the O-rings on the fixed orifice tube body liberally with clean, specified refrigerant oil.

10. Place the fixed orifice tube in the remover, Tool YT-1008 or equivalent, and insert the fixed orifice tube into the evaporator core tube until the orifice is seated at the stop.

11. Remove the remover tool from the fixed orifice tube.

12. Using a new O-ring lubricated with clean refrigerant oil, connect the liquid line to the evaporator core tube. Tighten the fitting to the specified torque using a backup wrench.

13. Leak test, evacuate and charge the system following the recommended service procedures. Observe all safety precautions.

14. Check the system for proper operation.

EXPANSION VALVE

Removal and Installation

1982 AND LATER

1. Disconnect battery cables and remove battery from the vehicle.
2. Discharge the refrigerant from the system.
3. Disconnect liquid inlet hose from expansion valve.
4. Remove bulb insulation from the suction (outlet) line.
5. Remove capillary tube bulb clamp from the suction outlet line.
6. Remove the expansion valve from the evaporator liquid inlet line.
7. Installation is the reverse of the removal procedure.

Condenser

Removal and Installation

1982 AND LATER—ALL VEHICLES EXCEPT ECONOLINE

1. Disconnect the negative battery cable.
2. Remove all the necessary components in order to gain access to the condenser retaining bolts.
3. Discharge the system. Remove the condenser refrigeratnt lines. Be sure to plug them.
4. Remove the condenser retaining bolts and remove the condenser from the vehicle.
5. Installation is the reverse of the removal procedure.

1982 AND LATER—ECONOLINE

1. Discharge the refrigerant from the system.
2. Using a back-up wrench disconnect the compressor discharge line and the liquid line from the condenser. Cap the refrigerant lines to prevent the entry of excessive moisture and dirt. If equipped with 6.9L diesel engine, disconnect the spring lock coupling.
3. Remove two screws attaching the hood latch to the radiator support and position the hood latch out of the way.
4. Remove the nine screws attaching the to edge of the radiator grille to the radiator support.
5. Remove the one screw attaching the center area of the grille to the grille center support.
6. Remove the one screw attaching the grille center support to the radiator support.

7. Working under the vehicle, reposition the splash shields and remove the two condenser lower retaining nuts.
8. Remove the two bolts attaching the top of the condenser to the radiator upper support.
9. Remove the four bolts attaching each end of the radiator upper support to the radiator side supports.
10. Carefully pull the top edge of the grille forward and remove the radiator upper support.
11. Lift the condenser from the vehicle.
12. Installation is the reverse of the removal procedure.

Evaporator

Removal and Installation

1982 AND LATER—BRONCO AND PICK-UP

1. Discharge the refrigerant system.
2. Disconnect the electrical connector from the pressure switch on the side of the suction accumulator.
3. Remove the pressure switch from the accumulator.
4. Disconnect the suction hose from the suction accumulator. Use a back-up wrench to loosen the fitting. Cap the suction hose to prevent the entry of dirt and excess moisture.
5. Disconnect the liquid line from the evaporator core. Use two wrenches. Cap the liquid line to prevent the entry of dirt and excess moisture.
6. Working in the passenger compartment, remove one screw attaching the bottom of the plenum to the dash panel.
7. Working under the hood, remove one nut retaining the upper left corner of the evaporator case to the dash panel.
8. Remove six screws attaching the left evaporator housing to the evaporator case.
9. Remove spring clip holding the left side of the housing cover plate and the left evaporator housing together at the dash panel.
10. Remove the left evaporator housing from the evaporator case.
11. Remove the evaporator core and suction accumulator from the evaporator case.
12. Installation is the reverse of the removal procedure.

1982 AND LATER—ECONOLINE

1. Disconnect electrical leads from resistor on front face of A/C blower scroll cover.
2. Disconnect vacuum line from the outside recirculated door vacuum motor.
3. Remove A/C blower cover (five screws plus two screws attaching the blower scroll cover to plenum assembly).

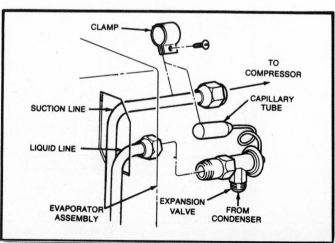

Expansion valve location—Econoline (© Ford Motor Company)

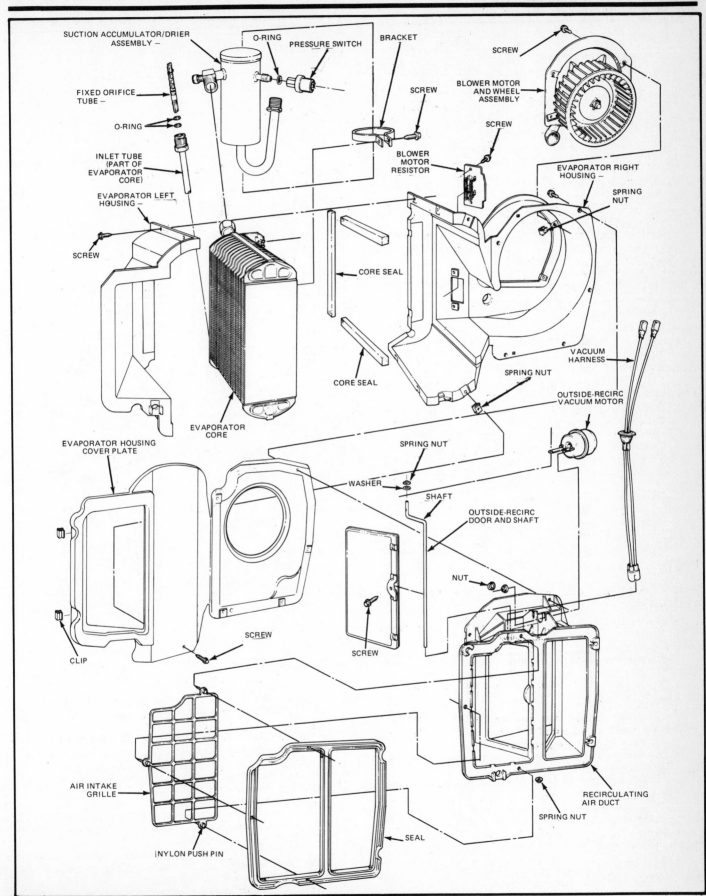

SUCTION ACCUMULATOR/DRIER ASSEMBLY —

O-RING

PRESSURE SWITCH

BRACKET

SCREW

FIXED ORIFICE TUBE —

O-RING

SCREW

BLOWER MOTOR AND WHEEL ASSEMBLY

INLET TUBE (PART OF EVAPORATOR CORE)

BLOWER MOTOR RESISTOR

SCREW

EVAPORATOR RIGHT HOUSING —

SPRING NUT

EVAPORATOR LEFT HOUSING —

SCREW

CORE SEAL

CORE SEAL

VACUUM HARNESS

OUTSIDE-RECIRC VACUUM MOTOR

SPRING NUT

EVAPORATOR HOUSING COVER PLATE

EVAPORATOR CORE

SPRING NUT

WASHER

SHAFT

OUTSIDE-RECIRC DOOR AND SHAFT

NUT

CLIP

SCREW

SCREW

AIR INTAKE GRILLE

RECIRCULATING AIR DUCT

SPRING NUT

SEAL

NYLON PUSH PIN

Evaporator and related components—Bronco and Pick-Up (© Ford Motor Company)

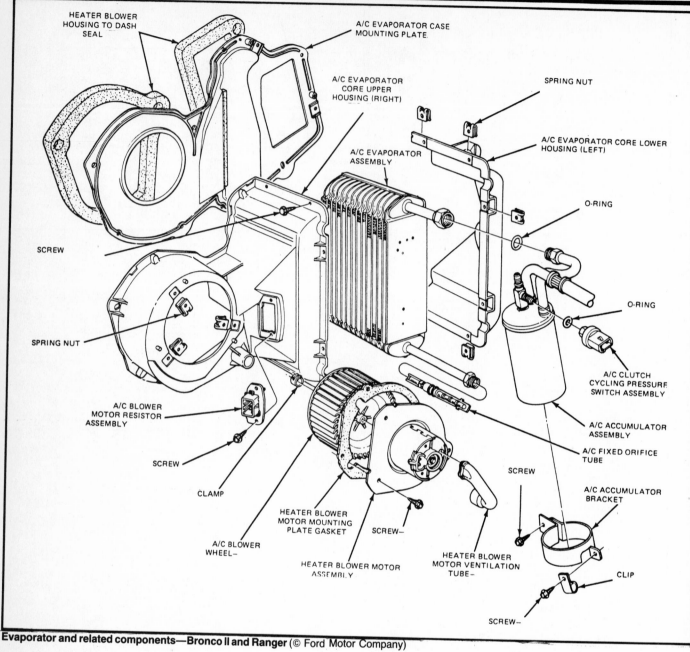

Evaporator and related components—Bronco II and Ranger (© Ford Motor Company)

4. Remove push nut and washer from the outside recirculated door shaft.

5. Remove control cable from bracket and slide it over bracket. Remove cable wire loop from blend door shaft.

6. Remove A/C blower housing.

7. Remove the heater hoses from the heater core (two clamps), and plug the hoses.

8. Discharge the refrigerant from the system observing all safety precautions.

9. Disconnect battery cables and remove the battery.

10. Disconnect suction line and liquid line from the evaporator core assembly.

11. Remove the drain tube from the bottom of the evaporator case assembly.

12. Remove evaporator assembly from dash.

13. Remove blend door and housing.

14. Remove cork insulation tape from expansion valve bulb.

15. Remove evaporator tube retainer and seal.

16. Remove evaporator core and seal assembly.

17. Installation is the reverse of the removal procedure.

1983 AND LATER—BRONCO II AND RANGER

1. Disconnect the cable from the battery negative terminal.

2. Discharge the refrigerant from the A/C system.

3. Disconnect the electrical connector from the pressure switch located on top of the accumulator/drier.

4. Remove the pressure switch from the accumulator/drier.

5. Disconnect the suction hose from the accumulator/drier and cap the openings to prevent dirt and/or moisture from entering. Use a back-up wrench to loosen the fitting.

6. Disconnect the liquid line from the evaporator core inlet tube using a back-up wrench to loosen the fitting. Cap the openings to prevent dirt and/or moisture from entering.

7. Remove the nine screws holding the evaporator case service cover (inboard, nearest center of engine compartment) to the evaporator case assembly.

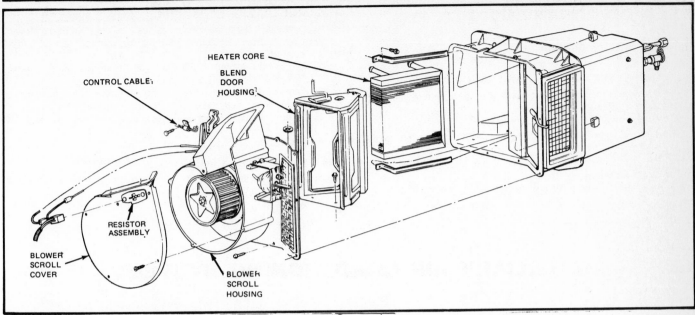

Evaporator and related components—Econoline (© Ford Motor Company)

8. Remove mounting nut from the bottom of the service cover mounting stud of the evaporator case assembly.

9. From the passenger compartment, remove one nut from the stud located near the heater core cover attaching the evaporator case service cover to the dash panel.

10. From the engine compartment, remove the evaporator case service cover from the evaporator case assembly.

11. Remove the evaporator core and suction accumulator/drier assembly from the vehicle.

12. Installation is the reverse of the removal procedure.

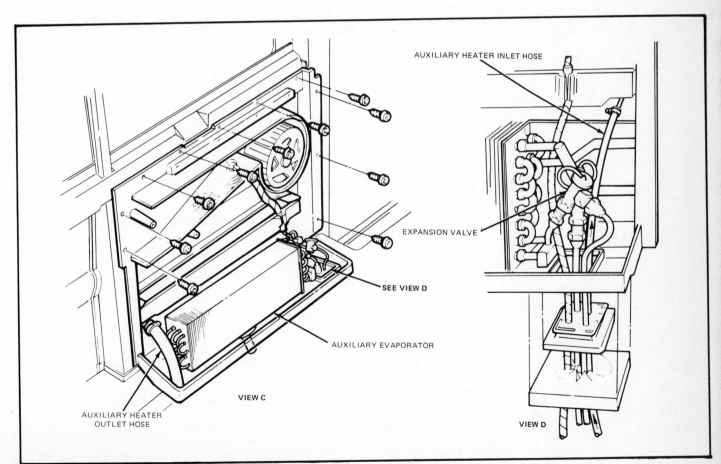

Auxiliary air condition assembly (© Ford Motor Company)

Heater Core

Removal and Installation

1982 AND LATER—BRONCO AND PICK-UP

1. Disconnect the heater hoses from the heater core tubes and plug the hoses with suitable ⅝ inch plugs.

2. Remove the glove compartment liner.

3. Remove eight screws attaching the heater core cover to the plenum and remove the cover.

4. Remove the heater core from the plenum taking care not to spill coolant from the core.

5. Installation is the reverse of the removal procedure.

1982 AND LATER—ECONOLINE

1. Disconnect the resistor electrical leads on the front of the blower cover inside the truck. Detach the vacuum line from the vacuum motor. Remove the blower cover.

2. Remove the nut and push washer from the air door shaft. Remove the control cable from the bracket and the air door shaft.

3. Remove the blower motor housing and the air door housing.

4. Drain the coolant and detach the heater hoses.

5. Remove the heater core retaining brackets. Remove the core and seal assembly.

6. Reverse the procedure for installation.

1983 AND LATER—BRONCO II AND RANGER

For heater core removal and installation procedures, refer to the heater core section in this manual.

AUXILIARY AIR CONDITIONING SYSTEM

Heater Core and Seal Assembly

Removal and Installation

1982 AND LATER—ECONOLINE

1. Remove the first bench seat, if so equipped.

2. Remove the auxiliary heater and/or air conditioner cover attaching screws, and remove the cover.

3. Remove the strap retaining the heater core in the auxiliary system case.

4. Remove the heater hoses from the auxiliary heater core, and plug the hoses with suitable ⅝ inch plugs.

5. Disengage the wire assembly from the heater core seal.

6. Slide the heater core and seal assembly out of the housing slot.

7. Installation is the reverse of the removal procedure.

Heater and Air Conditioning Assembly

Removal and Installation

1982 AND LATER—ECONOLINE

1. Discharge the refrigerant from the A/C system if an auxiliary A/C is installed.

2. Remove the first bench seat (if so equipped).

3. Remove the auxiliary heater and/or air conditioner cover attaching screws, and remove the cover.

4. Disconnect the heater hoses from the heater core tubes and plug the hoses with suitable ⅝ inch plugs (if equipped with an auxiliary heater)

5. Using a back-up wrench to prevent component damage, disconnect the liquid line from the expansion valve and the suction line from the evaporator core (if equipped with auxiliary A/C). Cap the lines and fittings to prevent the entrance of dirt and excessive moisture into the refrigerant system.

6. Working under the vehicle, disconnect the blower motor wires at the connectors and disengage the wire harness from the retaining strap.

7. Remove the case assembly retaining screws. Then, lift the case assembly, disengage the wire harness grommet from the floor seal and remove the case assembly from the vehicle.

8. Installation is the reverse of the removal procedure.

Evaporator Core Assembly

Removal and Installation

1982 AND LATER—ECONOLINE

1. Remove the first bench seat (if so equipped).

2. Remove the auxiliary heater and/or air conditioner cover assembly attaching screws and remove the cover assembly.

3. Discharge the refrigerant system.

4. Using back-up wrenches to prevent component damage, disconnect the suction line from the evaporator core and the liquid line from the expansion valve. Cap all open refrigerant line connections to prevent the entrance of dirt and excessive moisture.

5. Disconnect the heater hoses (if equipped with an auxiliary heater) from the auxiliary heater core and plug the hoses with suitable ⅝ inch plugs.

6. Remove four screws attaching the evaporator core and mounting bracket to the auxiliary case assembly.

7. Remove the evaporator core, expansion valve and core mounting plate from the case assembly.

8. If the evaporator core is to be replaced, remove the expansion valve and mounting plate from the evaporator core.

9. Installation is the reverse of the removal procedure.

Expansion Valve

Removal and Installation

1982 AND LATER—ECONOLINE

1. Remove the first bench seat (if so equipped).

2. Remove the auxiliary heater and/or air conditioner cover assembly.

3. Discharge the refrigerant system.

4. Disconnect the liquid line from the expansion valve. Use a back-

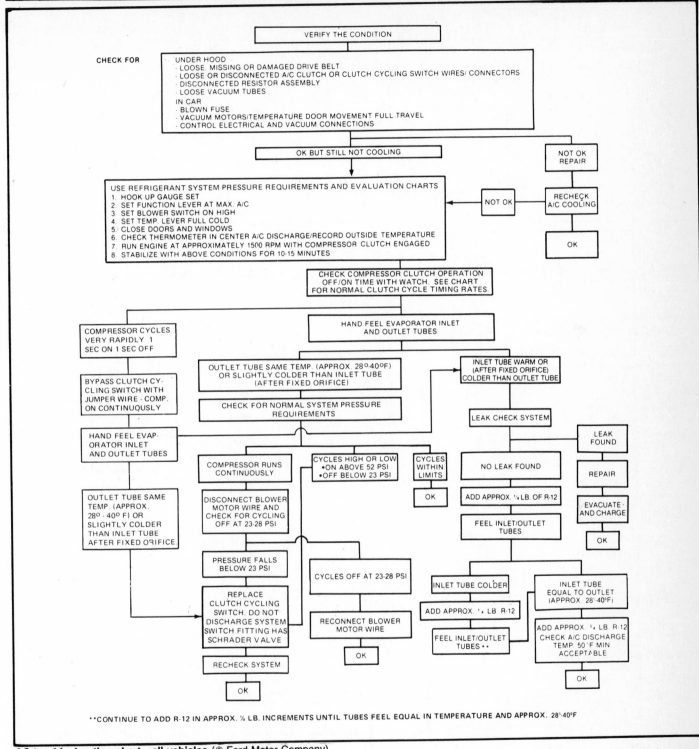

AC troubleshooting chart—all vehicles (© Ford Motor Company)

up wrench to prevent component damage. Cap the liquid line to prevent the entrance of dirt and excessive moisture.

5. Remove the insulating tape from the evaporator core outlet tube. The, remove the clamp and expansion valve capillary bulb from the outlet tube of the evaporator core.

6. Using a back-up wrench, remove the expansion valve from the evaporator core inlet tube.

7. Installation is the reverse of the removal procedure.

Control Head

Removal and Installation

1982 AND LATER—ALL VEHICLES

For removal and installation procedures on the control head, refer to the heating section of this manual.

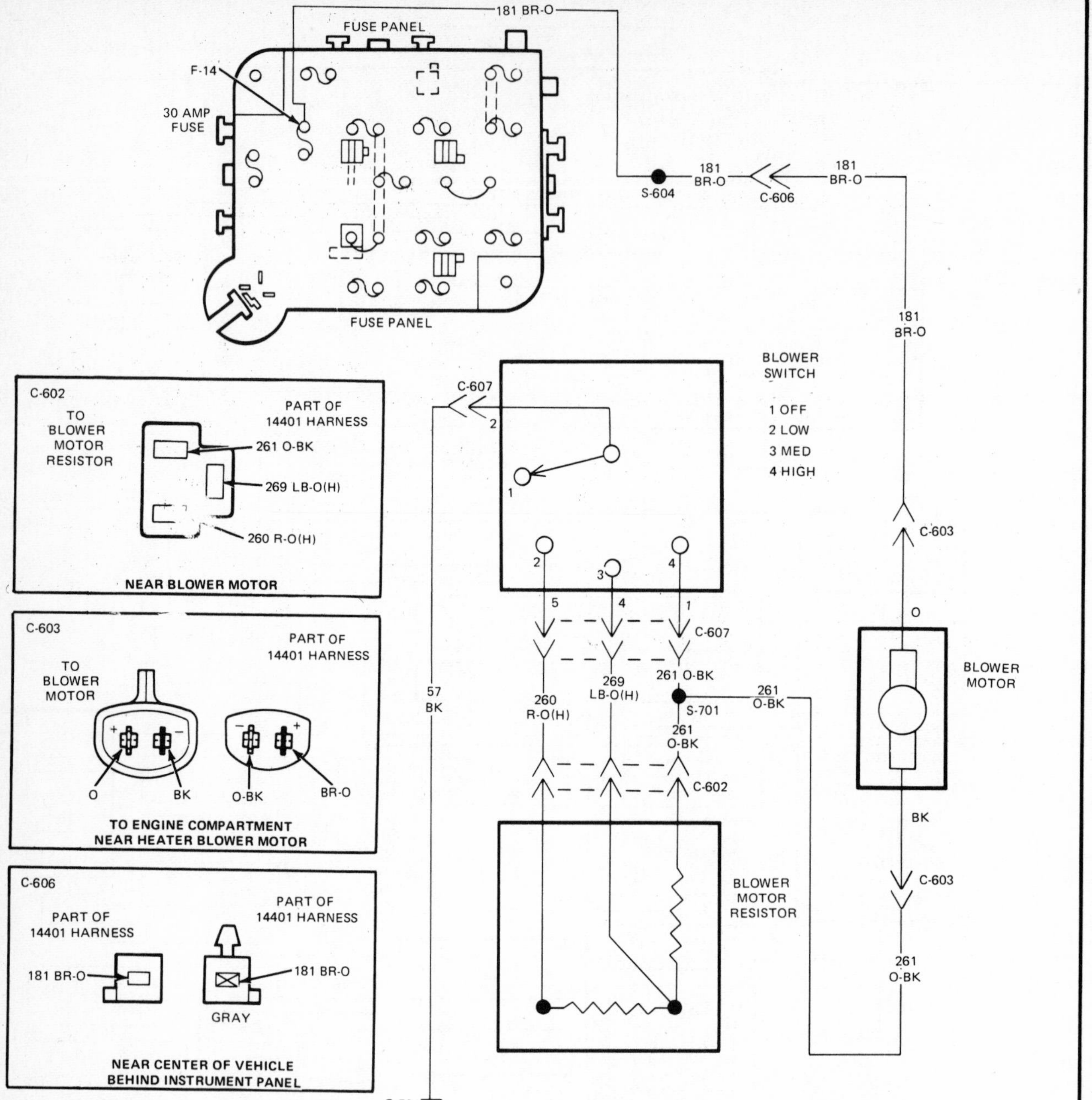
181 BR-O
FUSE PANEL
F-14
30 AMP FUSE
FUSE PANEL
S-604
181 BR-O
C-606
181 BR-O
181 BR-O
BLOWER SWITCH
1 OFF
2 LOW
3 MED
4 HIGH
C-607
C-603
O
BLOWER MOTOR
C-607
261 O-BK
S-701
261 O-BK
57 BK
260 R-O(H)
269 LB-O(H)
261 O-BK
C-602
BLOWER MOTOR RESISTOR
BK
C-603
261 O-BK
G-701
C-602
TO BLOWER MOTOR RESISTOR
PART OF 14401 HARNESS
261 O-BK
269 LB-O(H)
260 R-O(H)
NEAR BLOWER MOTOR
C-603
TO BLOWER MOTOR
PART OF 14401 HARNESS
O
BK
O-BK
BR-O
TO ENGINE COMPARTMENT NEAR HEATER BLOWER MOTOR
C-606
PART OF 14401 HARNESS
PART OF 14401 HARNESS
181 BR-O
181 BR-O
GRAY
NEAR CENTER OF VEHICLE BEHIND INSTRUMENT PANEL

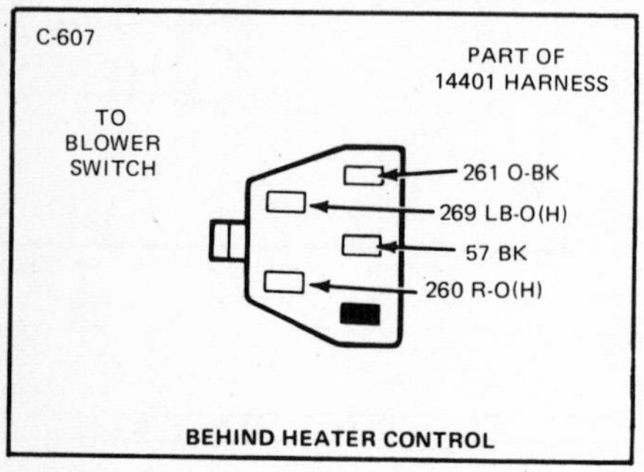
C-607
PART OF 14401 HARNESS
TO BLOWER SWITCH
261 O-BK
269 LB-O(H)
57 BK
260 R-O(H)
BEHIND HEATER CONTROL

BLOWER SWITCH –			
BLOWER SPEED	TERMINAL CONNECTIONS	AMPS	VOLTS
OFF		0	0
LOW	2-5	5	5
MED	2-4	7	6
HIGH	2-1	11	9

GROUND CODE
G-701 IN 14401 HARNESS ATTACHED TO y–BRACE NEAR RADIO SPEAKER

SPLICE CODE
S-701 IN 14401 HARNESS NEAR TAKE OUT TO BLOWER MOTOR RESISTOR

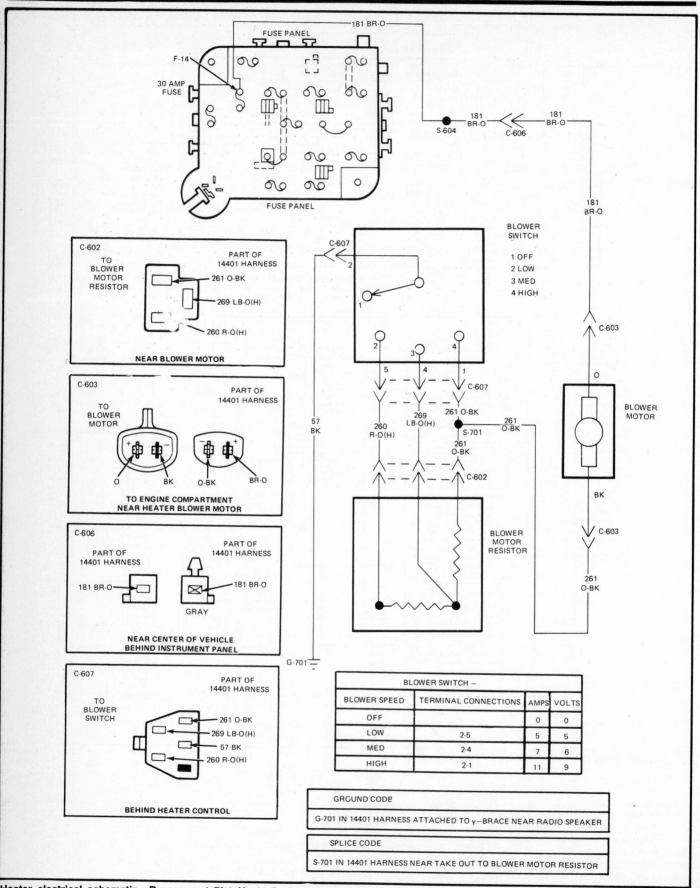

Heater electrical schematic—Bronco and Pick-Up (© Ford Motor Company)

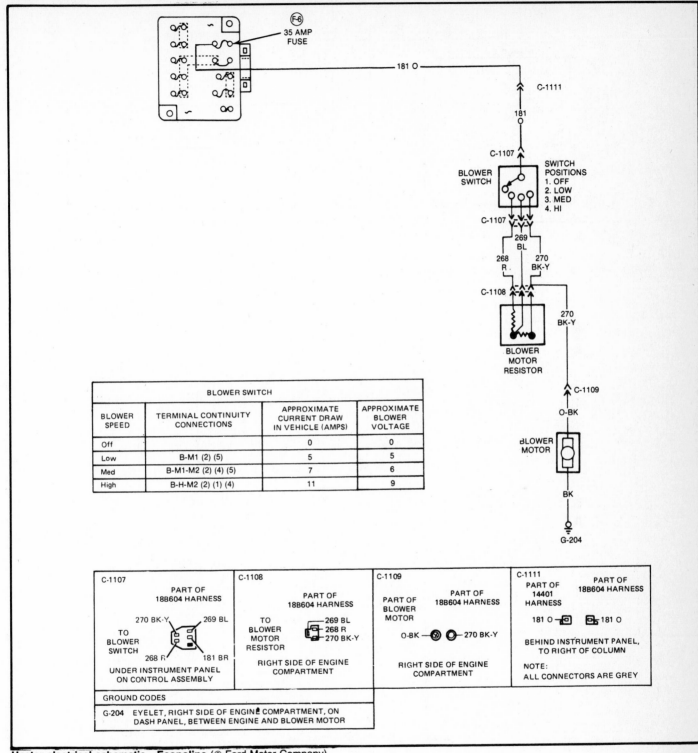

BLOWER SWITCH			
BLOWER SPEED	TERMINAL CONTINUITY CONNECTIONS	APPROXIMATE CURRENT DRAW IN VEHICLE (AMPS)	APPROXIMATE BLOWER VOLTAGE
Off		0	0
Low	B-M1 (2) (5)	5	5
Med	B-M1-M2 (2) (4) (5)	7	6
High	B-H-M2 (2) (1) (4)	11	9

Heater electrical schematic—Econoline (© Ford Motor Company)

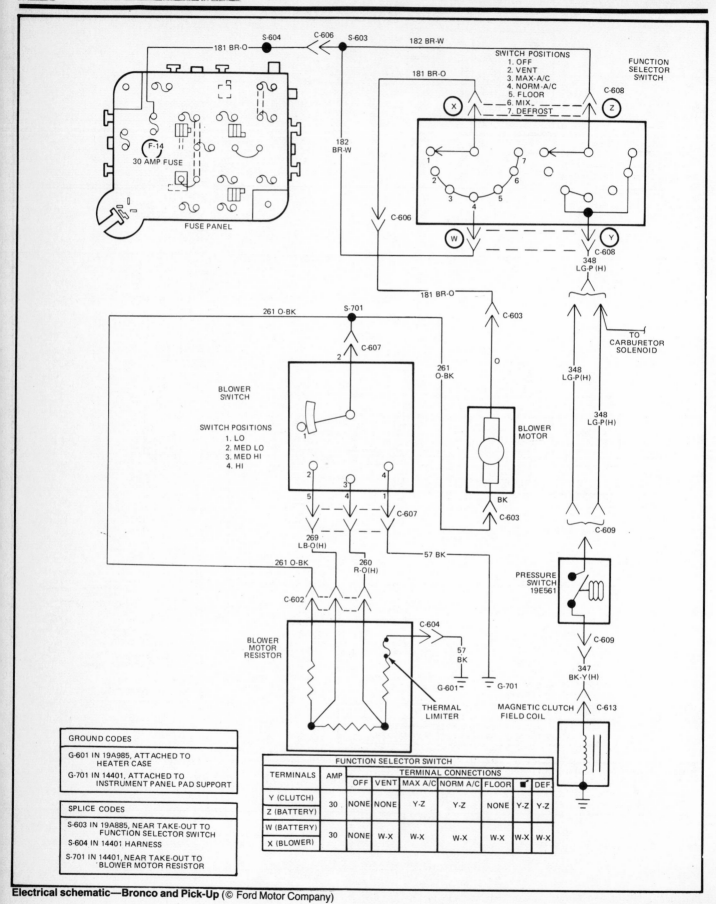

Electrical schematic—Bronco and Pick-Up (© Ford Motor Company)

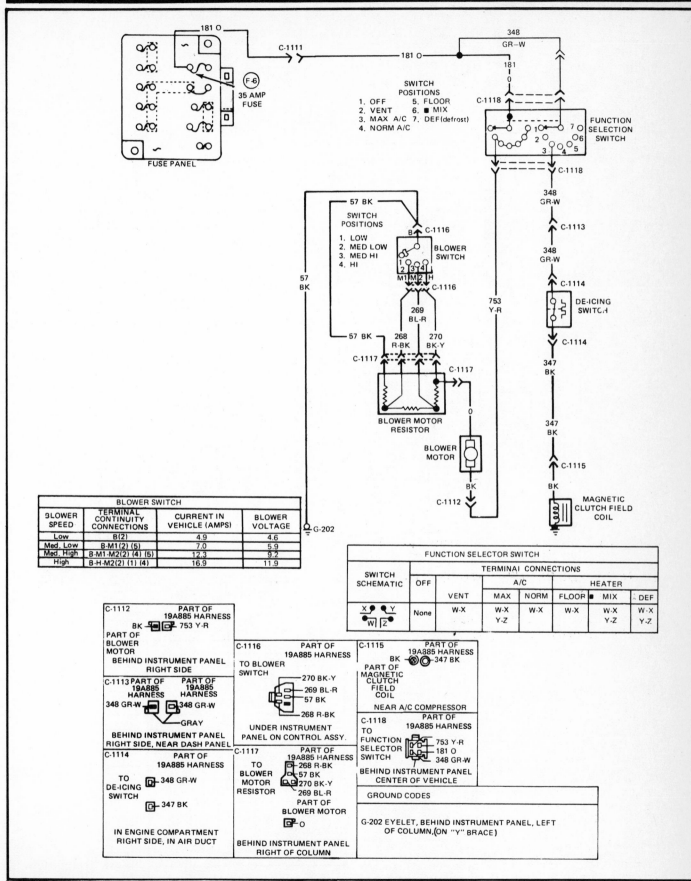

BLOWER SWITCH			
BLOWER SPEED	TERMINAL CONTINUITY CONNECTIONS	CURRENT IN VEHICLE (AMPS)	BLOWER VOLTAGE
Low	B(2)	4.9	4.6
Med. Low	B-M1(2) (5)	7.0	5.9
Med. High	B-M1-M2(2) (4) (5)	12.3	9.2
High	B-H-M2(2) (1) (4)	16.9	11.9

SWITCH POSITIONS
1. OFF   5. FLOOR
2. VENT   6. ■ MIX
3. MAX A/C   7. DEF (defrost)
4. NORM A/C

SWITCH POSITIONS
1. LOW
2. MED LOW
3. MED HI
4. HI

FUNCTION SELECTOR SWITCH							
SWITCH SCHEMATIC	TERMINAL CONNECTIONS						
	OFF	VENT	A/C		HEATER		
			MAX	NORM	FLOOR	■ MIX	DEF
X ○ ○ Y / W ○ ○ Z	None	W-X	W-X Y-Z	W-X	W-X	W-X Y-Z	W-X Y-Z

C-1112   PART OF 19A885 HARNESS
BK ▭ ▭ 753 Y-R
PART OF BLOWER MOTOR
BEHIND INSTRUMENT PANEL RIGHT SIDE

C-1113 PART OF 19A885 HARNESS   PART OF 19A885 HARNESS
348 GR-W ▭ ▭ 348 GR-W
GRAY
BEHIND INSTRUMENT PANEL RIGHT SIDE, NEAR DASH PANEL

C-1114   PART OF 19A885 HARNESS
TO DE-ICING SWITCH ▭ 348 GR-W
▭ 347 BK
IN ENGINE COMPARTMENT RIGHT SIDE, IN AIR DUCT

C-1116   PART OF 19A885 HARNESS
TO BLOWER SWITCH
270 BK-Y
269 BL-R
57 BK
268 R-BK
UNDER INSTRUMENT PANEL ON CONTROL ASSY.

C-1117   PART OF 19A885 HARNESS
TO BLOWER MOTOR RESISTOR
268 R-BK
57 BK
270 BK-Y
269 BL-R
PART OF BLOWER MOTOR
▭ O
BEHIND INSTRUMENT PANEL RIGHT OF COLUMN

C-1115   PART OF 19A885 HARNESS
BK ▭ ▭ 347 BK
PART OF MAGNETIC CLUTCH FIELD COIL
NEAR A/C COMPRESSOR

C-1118   PART OF 19A885 HARNESS
TO FUNCTION SELECTOR SWITCH
753 Y-R
181 O
348 GR-W
BEHIND INSTRUMENT PANEL CENTER OF VEHICLE

GROUND CODES
G-202 EYELET, BEHIND INSTRUMENT PANEL, LEFT OF COLUMN, (ON "Y" BRACE)

Electrical schematic—Econoline except with auxiliary air condition (© Ford Motor Company)

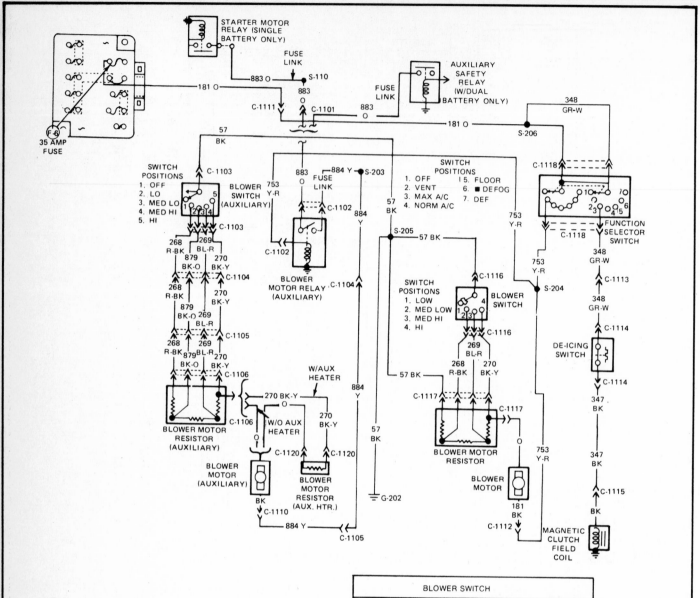

Electrical schematic—Econoline with auxiliary air condition (© Ford Motor Company)

BLOWER SWITCH			
BLOWER SPEED	TERMINAL CONNECTIONS	APPROXIMATE CURRENT DRAW IN VEHICLE (AMPS)	APPROX. BLOWER VOLTAGE
LOW	B(2)	5	5
MED LOW	B-M1(2) (5)	7	6
MED HI	B-M1-M2(2) (4) (5)	11	8
HI	B-H-M2(2) (1) (4)	15	11

AUXILIARY HEATER BLOWER SWITCH			
OFF	—	0	0
LOW	B(2)	4	4
MED LOW	B-M1(2) (5)	6	5
MED HI	B-M1-M2(2) (1) (5)	8	7
HI	B-H-M2(2) (3) (4)	12	8

AUXILIARY A/C BLOWER SWITCH			
OFF	—	0	0
LOW	B-L	5	5
MED. LOW	B-M1-L	7	6
MED. HI	B-M2-M1	11	6
HI	B-H-M2	16	10

FUNCTION SELECTOR SWITCH							
	TERMINAL CONNECTIONS (CONTINUITY)						
SWITCH SCHEMATIC	OFF	VENT	A/C		HEATER		DEF.
			MAX	NORM	FLOOR	(DEFOG)	
	NONE	W-X	W-X	W-X	W-X	W-X	W-X
			Y-Z			Y-Z	Y-Z

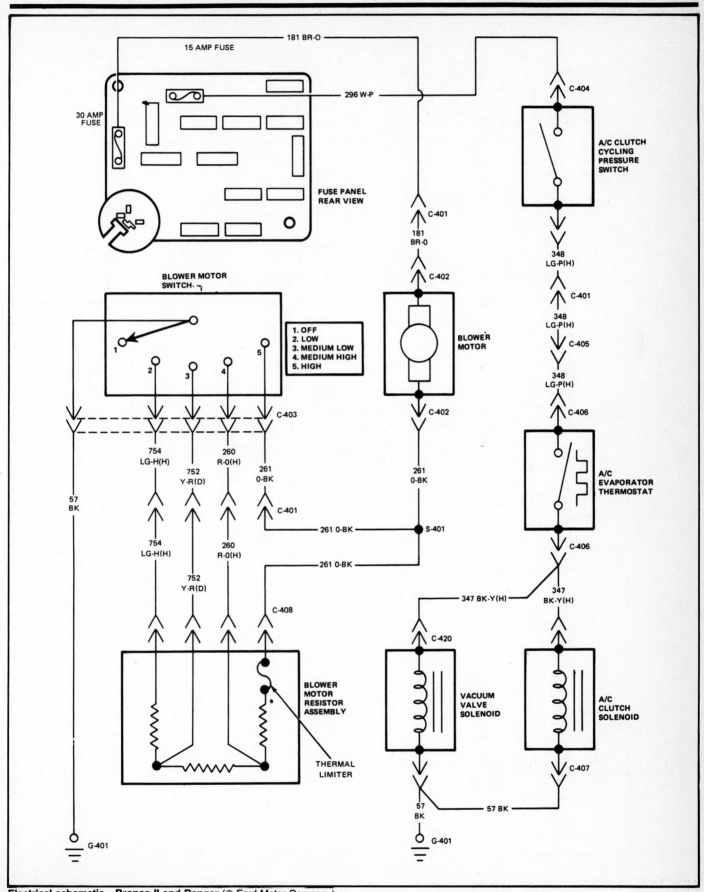

Electrical schematic—Bronco II and Ranger (© Ford Motor Company)

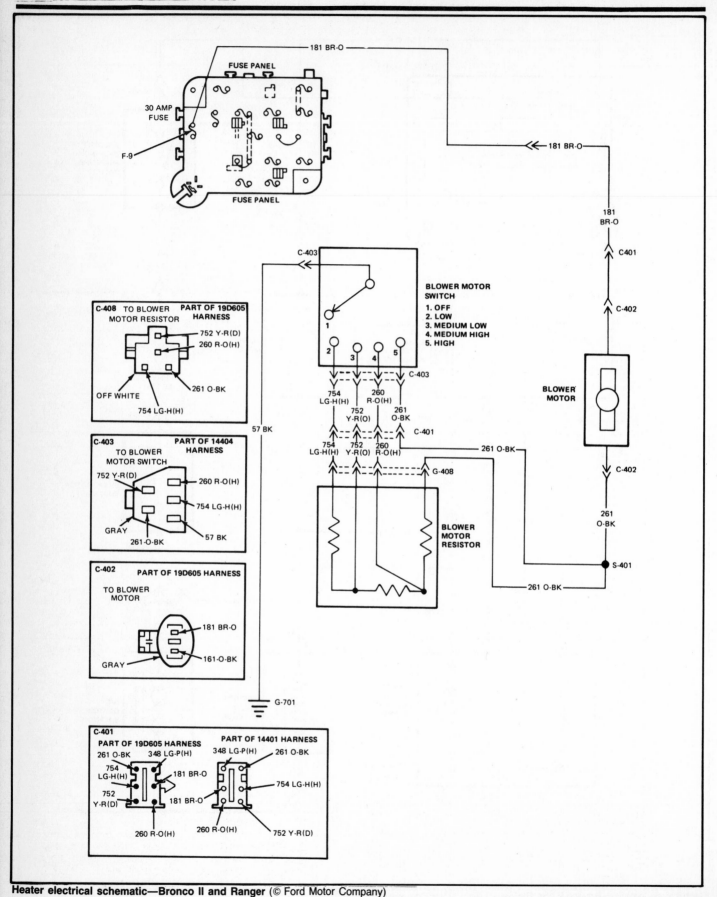

Heater electrical schematic—Bronco II and Ranger (© Ford Motor Company)

VACUUM CONTROL DIAGNOSIS

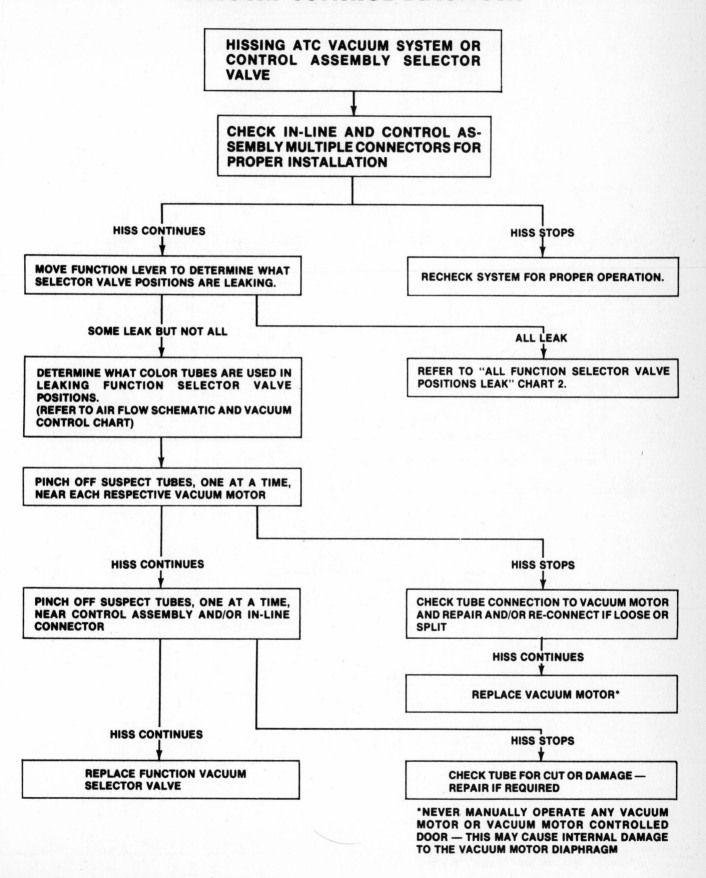

HISSING ATC VACUUM SYSTEM OR CONTROL ASSEMBLY SELECTOR VALVE

↓

CHECK IN-LINE AND CONTROL ASSEMBLY MULTIPLE CONNECTORS FOR PROPER INSTALLATION

HISS CONTINUES

MOVE FUNCTION LEVER TO DETERMINE WHAT SELECTOR VALVE POSITIONS ARE LEAKING.

HISS STOPS

RECHECK SYSTEM FOR PROPER OPERATION.

SOME LEAK BUT NOT ALL

DETERMINE WHAT COLOR TUBES ARE USED IN LEAKING FUNCTION SELECTOR VALVE POSITIONS.
(REFER TO AIR FLOW SCHEMATIC AND VACUUM CONTROL CHART)

ALL LEAK

REFER TO "ALL FUNCTION SELECTOR VALVE POSITIONS LEAK" CHART 2.

PINCH OFF SUSPECT TUBES, ONE AT A TIME, NEAR EACH RESPECTIVE VACUUM MOTOR

HISS CONTINUES

PINCH OFF SUSPECT TUBES, ONE AT A TIME, NEAR CONTROL ASSEMBLY AND/OR IN-LINE CONNECTOR

HISS STOPS

CHECK TUBE CONNECTION TO VACUUM MOTOR AND REPAIR AND/OR RE-CONNECT IF LOOSE OR SPLIT

HISS CONTINUES

REPLACE VACUUM MOTOR*

HISS CONTINUES

REPLACE FUNCTION VACUUM SELECTOR VALVE

HISS STOPS

CHECK TUBE FOR CUT OR DAMAGE — REPAIR IF REQUIRED

*NEVER MANUALLY OPERATE ANY VACUUM MOTOR OR VACUUM MOTOR CONTROLLED DOOR — THIS MAY CAUSE INTERNAL DAMAGE TO THE VACUUM MOTOR DIAPHRAGM

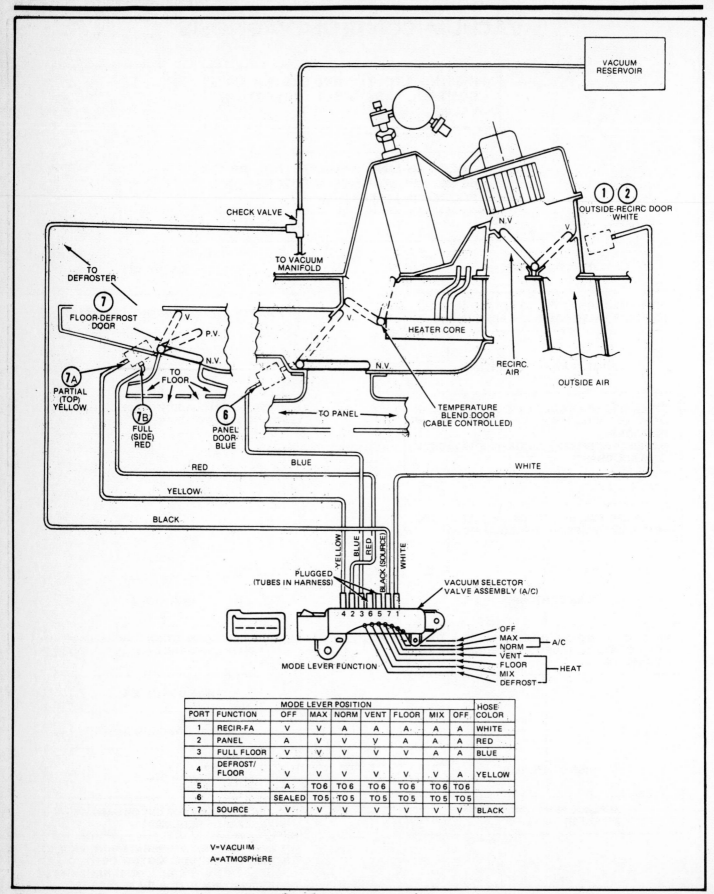

VACUUM RESERVOIR

CHECK VALVE

TO VACUUM MANIFOLD

TO DEFROSTER

⑦ FLOOR-DEFROST DOOR

V.

P.V.

N.V.

⑦A PARTIAL (TOP) YELLOW

⑦B FULL (SIDE) RED

TO FLOOR

⑥ PANEL DOOR-BLUE

① ② OUTSIDE-RECIRC DOOR WHITE

N.V.

V

HEATER CORE

RECIRC. AIR

OUTSIDE AIR

N.V.

TO PANEL

TEMPERATURE BLEND DOOR (CABLE CONTROLLED)

RED

BLUE

WHITE

YELLOW

BLACK

YELLOW

BLUE

RED

BLACK (SOURCE)

WHITE

PLUGGED (TUBES IN HARNESS)

VACUUM SELECTOR VALVE ASSEMBLY (A/C)

4 2 3 6 5 7 1

MODE LEVER FUNCTION

OFF
MAX } A/C
NORM
VENT
FLOOR } HEAT
MIX
DEFROST

| PORT | FUNCTION | MODE LEVER POSITION | | | | | | | HOSE COLOR |
		OFF	MAX	NORM	VENT	FLOOR	MIX	OFF	
1	RECIR-FA	V	V	A	A	A	A	A	WHITE
2	PANEL	A	V	V	V	A	A	A	RED
3	FULL FLOOR	V	V	V	V	V	A	A	BLUE
4	DEFROST/FLOOR	V	V	V	V	V	V	A	YELLOW
5		A	TO 6	TO 6	TO 6	TO 6	TO 6	TO 6	
6		SEALED	TO 5	TO 5	TO 5	TO 5	TO 5		
7	SOURCE	V	V	V	V	V	V	V	BLACK

V=VACUUM

A=ATMOSPHERE

vacuum schematic—1984 and later Bronco and Pick-Up (© Ford Motor Company)

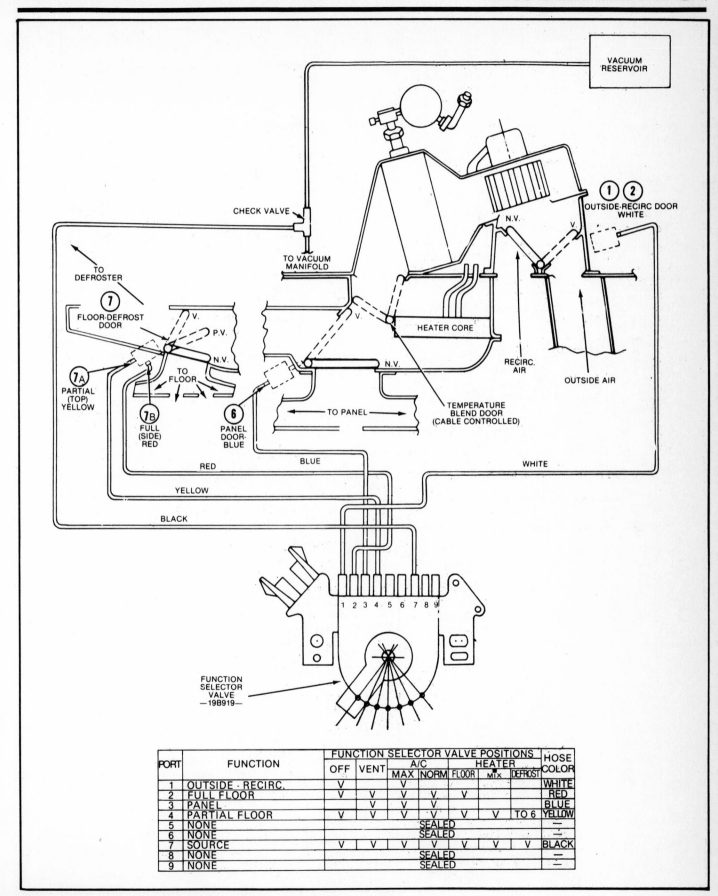

Vacuum schematic—1983 Bronco and Pick-Up (© Ford Motor Company)

PORT	FUNCTION	FUNCTION SELECTOR VALVE POSITIONS							HOSE COLOR
		OFF	VENT	A/C		HEATER			
				MAX	NORM	FLOOR	MIX	DEFROST	
1	OUTSIDE - RECIRC.	V		V					WHITE
2	FULL FLOOR	V	V	V	V	V			RED
3	PANEL		V	V	V				BLUE
4	PARTIAL FLOOR	V	V	V	V	V	V	TO 6	YELLOW
5	NONE				SEALED				—
6	NONE				SEALED				—
7	SOURCE	V	V	V	V	V	V	V	BLACK
8	NONE				SEALED				—
9	NONE				SEALED				—

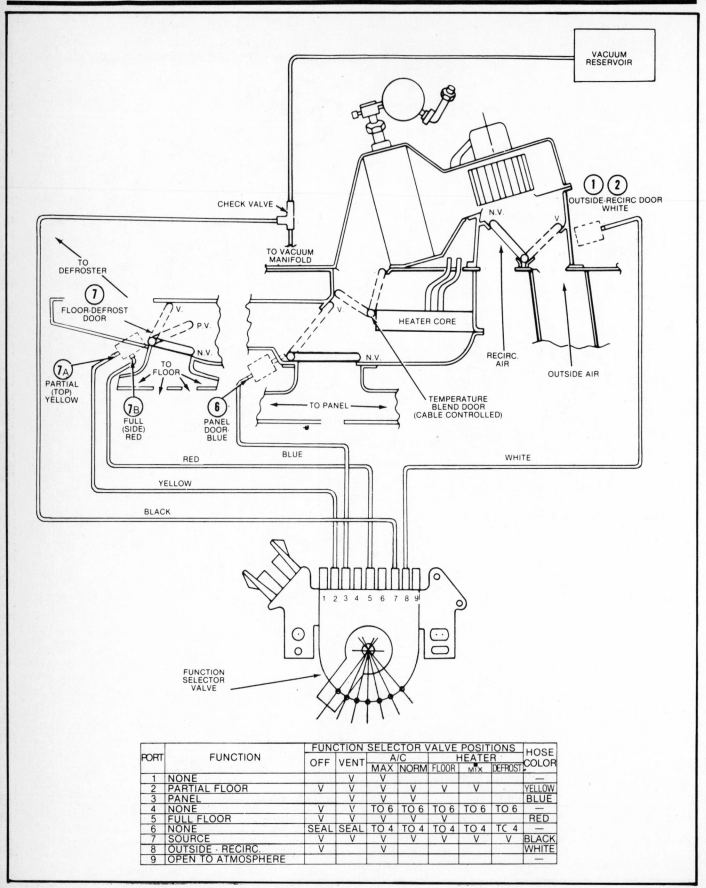

VACUUM RESERVOIR

CHECK VALVE

TO VACUUM MANIFOLD

TO DEFROSTER

FLOOR-DEFROST DOOR

7

7A PARTIAL (TOP) YELLOW

7B FULL (SIDE) RED

TO FLOOR

6 PANEL DOOR-BLUE

TO PANEL

1 2 OUTSIDE-RECIRC DOOR WHITE

N.V.

V

HEATER CORE

RECIRC. AIR

OUTSIDE AIR

TEMPERATURE BLEND DOOR (CABLE CONTROLLED)

RED

BLUE

WHITE

YELLOW

BLACK

FUNCTION SELECTOR VALVE

PORT	FUNCTION	FUNCTION SELECTOR VALVE POSITIONS							HOSE COLOR
		OFF	VENT	A/C		HEATER			
				MAX	NORM	FLOOR	MIX	DEFROST	
1	NONE		V	V					—
2	PARTIAL FLOOR	V	V	V	V	V	V		YELLOW
3	PANEL		V	V					BLUE
4	NONE	V	V	TO 6	TO 6	TO 6	TO 6	TO 6	—
5	FULL FLOOR	V	V	V	V	V			RED
6	NONE	SEAL	SEAL	TO 4	TO 4	TO 4	TO 4	TC 4	—
7	SOURCE	V	V	V	V	V	V	V	BLACK
8	OUTSIDE · RECIRC.	V		V					WHITE
9	OPEN TO ATMOSPHERE	V							—

Vacuum schematic—1982 Bronco an Pick-Up (© Ford Motor Company)

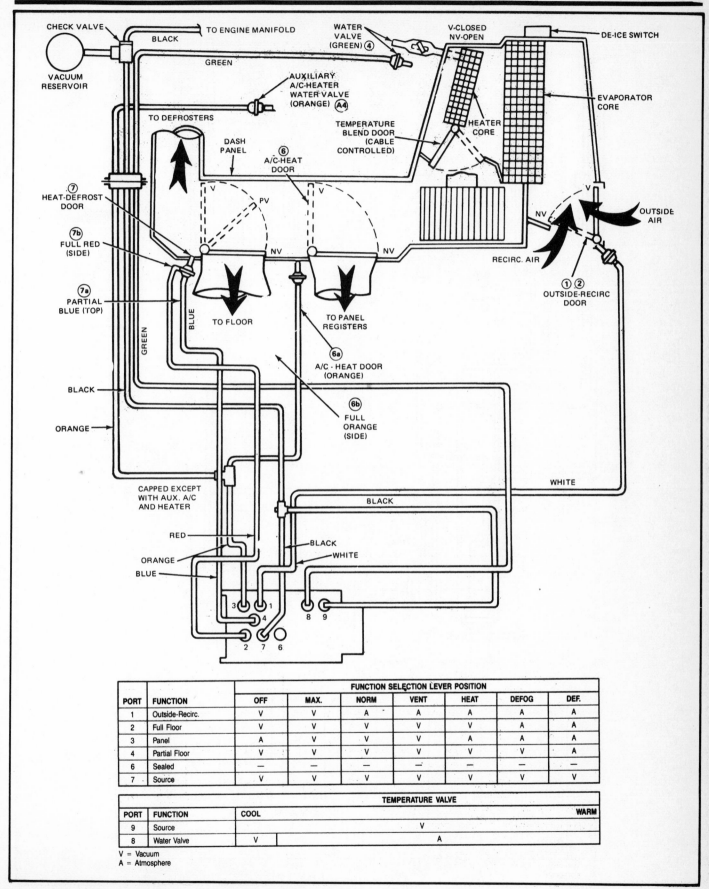

CHECK VALVE
TO ENGINE MANIFOLD
BLACK
VACUUM RESERVOIR
GREEN

WATER VALVE (GREEN) ④
V-CLOSED NV-OPEN
DE-ICE SWITCH

AUXILIARY A/C-HEATER WATER VALVE (ORANGE) A4

EVAPORATOR CORE

TO DEFROSTERS
DASH PANEL
⑥ A/C-HEAT DOOR
TEMPERATURE BLEND DOOR (CABLE CONTROLLED)
HEATER CORE

⑦ HEAT-DEFROST DOOR
PV
V
V
V

⑦b FULL RED (SIDE)
NV
⑦a PARTIAL BLUE (TOP)
NV
NV
OUTSIDE AIR
RECIRC. AIR

GREEN
BLUE
TO FLOOR
TO PANEL REGISTERS
① ② OUTSIDE-RECIRC DOOR

BLACK
ORANGE
⑥a A/C - HEAT DOOR (ORANGE)

⑥b FULL ORANGE (SIDE)

WHITE

CAPPED EXCEPT WITH AUX. A/C AND HEATER
BLACK

RED
BLACK
ORANGE
WHITE
BLUE

3   1
4
8   9
2   7   6

PORT	FUNCTION	\multicolumn{7}{c}{FUNCTION SELECTION LEVER POSITION}
		OFF	MAX.	NORM	VENT	HEAT	DEFOG	DEF.
1	Outside-Recirc.	V	V	A	A	A	A	A
2	Full Floor	V	V	V	V	V	A	A
3	Panel	A	V	V	V	A	A	A
4	Partial Floor	V	V	V	V	V	V	A
6	Sealed	—	—	—	—	—	—	—
7	Source	V	V	V	V	V	V	V

PORT	FUNCTION	\multicolumn{2}{c}{TEMPERATURE VALVE}
		COOL	WARM
9	Source		V
8	Water Valve	V	A

V = Vacuum
A = Atmosphere

Vacuum schematic—1984 Econoline (© Ford Motor Company)

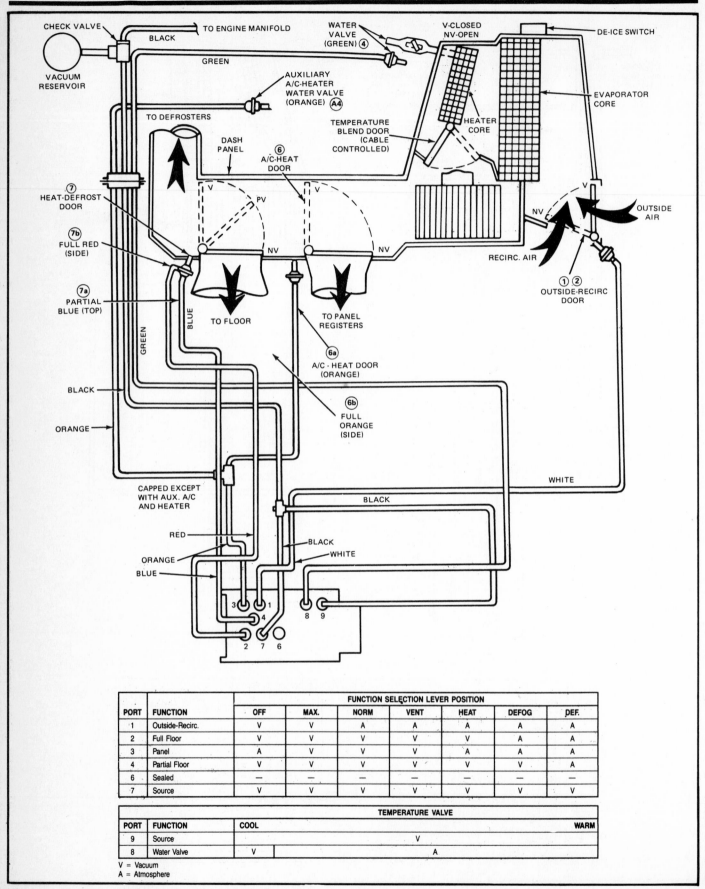

Vacuum schematic—1983 Econoline (© Ford Motor Company)

PORT	FUNCTION	FUNCTION SELECTION LEVER POSITION						
		OFF	MAX.	NORM	VENT	HEAT	DEFOG	DEF.
1	Outside-Recirc.	V	V	A	A	A	A	A
2	Full Floor	V	V	V	V	V	A	A
3	Panel	A	V	V	V	A	A	A
4	Partial Floor	V	V	V	V	V	V	A
6	Sealed	—	—	—	—	—	—	—
7	Source	V	V	V	V	V	V	V

PORT	FUNCTION	TEMPERATURE VALVE		
		COOL		WARM
9	Source		V	
8	Water Valve	V	A	

V = Vacuum
A = Atmosphere

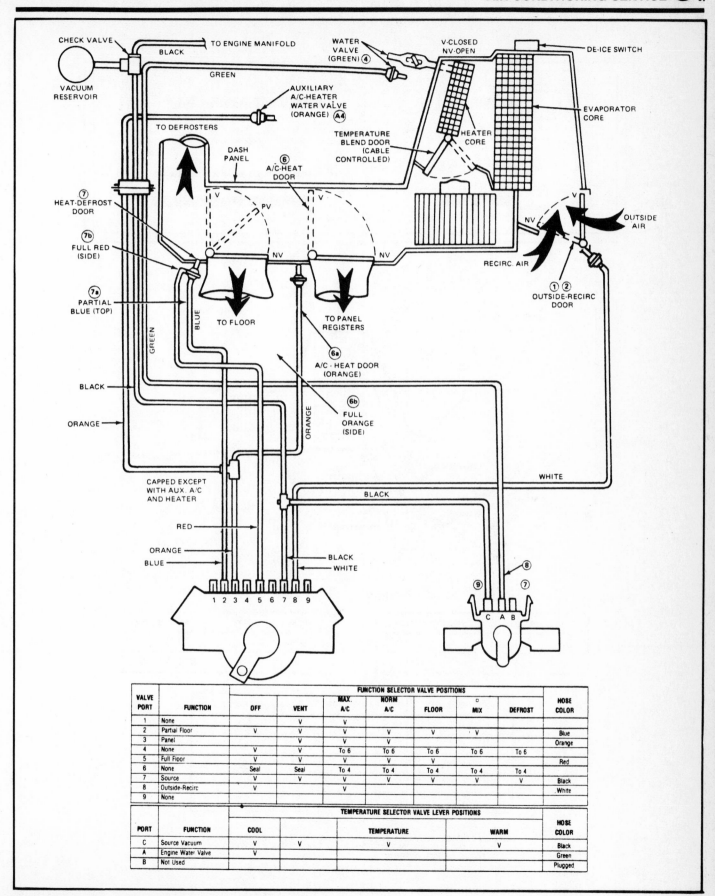

CHECK VALVE — BLACK — **TO ENGINE MANIFOLD**

VACUUM RESERVOIR

GREEN

AUXILIARY A/C-HEATER WATER VALVE (ORANGE) (A4)

WATER VALVE (GREEN) (4)

V-CLOSED NV-OPEN

DE-ICE SWITCH

EVAPORATOR CORE

TO DEFROSTERS

DASH PANEL

(6) **A/C-HEAT DOOR**

TEMPERATURE BLEND DOOR (CABLE CONTROLLED)

HEATER CORE

(7) **HEAT-DEFROST DOOR**

V   PV

V   NV

(7b) **FULL RED (SIDE)**

V   NV   **OUTSIDE AIR**

RECIRC. AIR

(7a) **PARTIAL BLUE (TOP)**

NV

(1)(2) **OUTSIDE-RECIRC DOOR**

BLUE   **TO FLOOR**   **TO PANEL REGISTERS**

GREEN

BLACK

ORANGE

(6a) **A/C - HEAT DOOR (ORANGE)**

(6b) **FULL ORANGE (SIDE)**

WHITE

CAPPED EXCEPT WITH AUX. A/C AND HEATER

BLACK

RED

ORANGE

BLUE

BLACK

WHITE

(8)

(9)   (7)

1 2 3 4 5 6 7 8 9

C A B

VALVE PORT	FUNCTION	FUNCTION SELECTOR VALVE POSITIONS							HOSE COLOR
		OFF	VENT	MAX. A/C	NORM A/C	FLOOR	MIX	DEFROST	
1	None		V	V					
2	Partial Floor	V	V	V	V	V	V		Blue
3	Panel		V	V	V				Orange
4	None	V	V	To 6	To 6	To 6	To 6	To 6	
5	Full Floor	V	V	V	V	V			Red
6	None	Seal	Seal	To 4	To 4	To 4	To 4	To 4	
7	Source	V	V	V	V	V	V	V	Black
8	Outside-Recirc	V			V				White
9	None								

PORT	FUNCTION	TEMPERATURE SELECTOR VALVE LEVER POSITIONS				HOSE COLOR
		COOL		TEMPERATURE	WARM	
C	Source Vacuum	V	V	V	V	Black
A	Engine Water Valve	V				Green
B	Not Used					Plugged

Vacuum schematic—1982 Econoline (© Ford Motor Company)

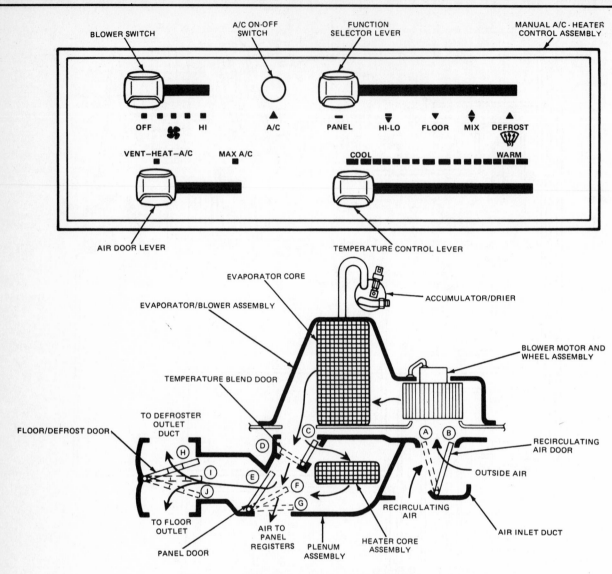

LEVER POSITION VS. DOOR POSITION

AIR DOOR LEVER	RECIRC AIR DOOR
VENT — HEAT — A/C	Ⓐ
MAX A/C	Ⓑ

TEMPERATURE LEVER	TEMPERATURE DOOR
COOL	Ⓒ
WARM	Ⓓ

FUNCTION LEVER	PANEL DOOR	FLOOR – DEFROST DOOR
PANEL	Ⓔ	Ⓗ
HI-LO	Ⓕ	Ⓗ
FLOOR	Ⓖ	Ⓗ
MIX	Ⓖ	Ⓘ
DEFROST	Ⓖ	Ⓙ

NOTE: ALL DOORS ARE CABLE ACTUATED. ADDITIONALLY, THE PANEL DOOR
AND THE FLOOR — DEFROST DOOR ARE CONNECTED BY A CAM AND
ACTUATOR ROD ASSEMBLY.

Vacuum schematic—1983 and later Bronco II and Ranger (© Ford Motor Company)

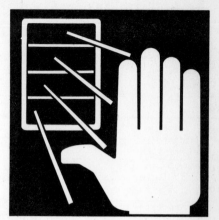

SECTION **6**
LIGHT TRUCKS
Jeep Vehicles

INDEX

JEEP SPECIFICATIONS

FREON CAPACITIES

Measured in lbs.

Year	CJ	Scrambler	Grand Wagoneer	Pick-Up	Cherokee	Wagoneer
1982	2	2	2	2	2	2
1983	2	2	2	2	2	2
1984	2	2	2	2	2	2
1985	2	2	2	2	2	2

VEHICLE IDENTIFICATION CHART

1982	1983	1984	1985
CJ	CJ	CJ	CJ
Scrambler	Scrambler	Scrambler	Scrambler
Grand Wagoneer	Grand Wagoneer	Grand Wagoneer	Grand Wagoneer
Pick-Up	Pick-Up	Pick-Up	Pick-Up
	Cherokee	Cherokee	Cherokee
	Wagoneer	Wagoneer	Wagoneer

REFRIGERANT OIL CAPACITY

Measured in Increments

Year	Model	Capacity	Compressor Type
1982	CJ	4-6	Sankyo
	Scrambler	4-6	Sankyo
	Grand Wagoneer	4-6	Sankyo
	Pick-Up	4-6	Sankyo
1983	CJ	4-6	Sankyo
	Scrambler	4-6	Sankyo
	Grand Wagoneer	4-6	Sankyo
	Pick-Up	4-6	Sankyo
	Cherokee	4-6	Sankyo
	Wagoneer	4-6	Sankyo
1984	CJ	4-6	Sankyo
	Scrambler	4-6	Sankyo
	Grand Wagoneer	4-6	Sankyo
	Pick-Up	4-6	Sankyo
	Cherokee	4-6	Sankyo
	Wagoneer	4-6	Sankyo
1985	CJ	4-6	Sankyo
	Scrambler	4-6	Sankyo

REFRIGERANT OIL CAPACITY

Measured in Increments

Year	Model	Capacity	Compressor Type
1985	Grand Wagoneer	4-6	Sankyo
	Pick-Up	4-6	Sankyo
	Cherokee	4-6	Sankyo
	Wagoneer	4-6	Sankyo

① The oil checking stick used to check the compressor oil level is calibrated in increments. When refiling the compressor use the markings on the stick to determine the number of increments of oil to be added to the compressor.

DRIVE BELT TENSION ADJUSTMENT CHART

Measured in lbs.

Year	Regular Belt	Serpentine Belt
1982	New 125-155 Old 90-115	New 180-200 Old 140-160
1983	New 125-155 Old 90-115	New 180-200 Old 140-160
1984	New 120-160 Old 90-115	New 180-200 Old 140-160
1985	New 120-160 Old 90-115	New 180-200 Old 140-160

Blower Motor

Removal and Installation

1982 AND LATER—ALL VEHICLES

For blower motor removal and installation procedures, refer to the heating section.

Compressor

Removal and Installation

1982 AND LATER—ALL VEHICLES

1. Disconnect the negative battery cable.
2. Remove all the necessary equipment in order to gain access to the compressor mounting bolts.
3. Remove the compressor drive belt.
4. Discharge the system.
5. Disconnect the plug and refrigerant lines.
6. Disconnect all electrical connections from the unit.
7. Remove the compressor mounting bolts. Remove the compressor from the vehicle.
8. Installation is the reverse of the removal procedure. Evacuate and charge the system as required.

Expansion Valve

Removal and Installation

1982 AND LATER—ALL EXCEPT CHEROKEE AND WAGONEER

1. Disconnect the negative battery cable. Discharge the system.
2. Remove the evaporator housing assembly.
3. Remove the insulation wrapped around the suction line and expansion valve. Mark the capillary tube location on the suction line.
4. Disconnect the inlet and outlet connections, capillary tube clamp and equalizer tube.
5. Remove the expansion valve.
6. Installation is the reverse of the removal procedure.

1983 AND LATER CHEROKEE AND WAGONEER

1. Disconnect the negative battery cable. Discharge the system.
2. Disconnect the hoses from the expansion valve.
3. Disconnect the valve from the evaporator core inlet and outlet tubes. Remove the expansion valve.
4. Installation is the reverse of the removal procedure.

Condenser

Removal and Installation

1982 AND LATER—ALL VEHICLES

1. Disconnect the negative battery cable. Discharge the system.
2. On some vehicles it may be necessary to drain the radiator and remove it from the vehicle, along with the fan shroud.
3. Remove all the necessary components in order to gain access to the condenser mounting molts.
4. Remove the condenser mounting bolts. Remove the condenser from the vehicle.
5. Installation is the reverse of the removal procedure. Evacuate and charge the system as required.

Evaporator

Removal and Installation

1982 AND LATER CJ

1. Disconnect the negative battery cable. Discharge the system.
2. Disconnect the inlet (suction) hose fitting from the compressor.
3. Disconnect the receiver/drier-to-evaporator hose fitting.
4. Remove the hose clamps and dash grommet retaining screws.
5. Remove the evapoator housing to instrument panel attaching screws and the evaporator housing to mounting bracket screw.
6. Lower the evaportor housing and pull the hoses and grommet through the opening.
7. Separate the evaporator housing and remove the evaporator core.
8. Installation is the reverse of the removal procedure.

1982 AND LATER GRAND WAGONEER AND PICK-UP

1. Disconnect the negative battery cable. Discharge the system.

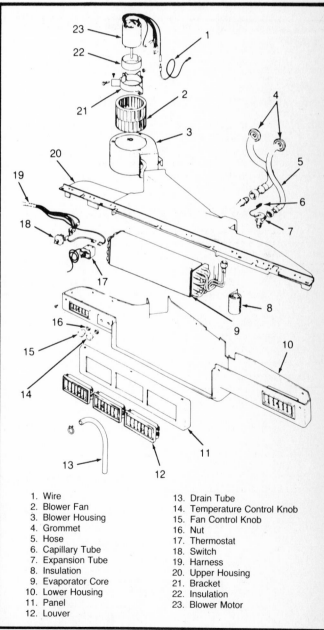

1. Wire	13. Drain Tube
2. Blower Fan	14. Temperature Control Knob
3. Blower Housing	15. Fan Control Knob
4. Grommet	16. Nut
5. Hose	17. Thermostat
6. Capillary Tube	18. Switch
7. Expansion Tube	19. Harness
8. Insulation	20. Upper Housing
9. Evaporator Core	21. Bracket
10. Lower Housing	22. Insulation
11. Panel	23. Blower Motor
12. Louver	

Heating system with A/C—CJ

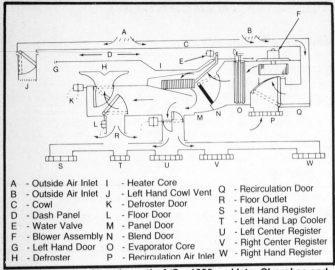

A - Outside Air Inlet	I - Heater Core	Q - Recirculation Door
B - Outside Air Inlet	J - Left Hand Cowl Vent	R - Floor Outlet
C - Cowl	K - Defroster Door	S - Left Hand Register
D - Dash Panel	L - Floor Door	T - Left Hand Lap Cooler
E - Water Valve	M - Panel Door	U - Left Center Register
F - Blower Assembly	N - Blend Door	V - Right Center Register
G - Left Hand Door	O - Evaporator Core	W - Right Hand Register
H - Defroster	P - Recirculation Air Inlet	

Heating system with schematic A/C—1983 and later Cherokee and Wagoneer

2. Disconnect the inlet (suction) line at the compressor.

3. Disconnect the receiver/dryer to evaporator hose at the quick-disconnect coupling.

4. Remove the hose clamps and dash grommet retaining screws.

5. Remove the evaporator housing to instrument panel attaching screws and the evaporator housing to mounting bracket screw.

6. Lower the evaporator housing and pull the hoses and grommet through the opening.

7. Separate the evaporator housing and remove the evaporator.

8. Installation is the reverse of the removal procedure.

1982 AND LATER CHEROKEE AND WAGONEER

1. Disconnect the negative battery cable. Discharge the system.

2. Disconnect the blower motor wires and the vent tube.

3. Remove the console, if equipped.

4. Remove the lower instrument panel.

5. Disconnect the electrical connections at the A/C relay, blower motor resistors and the A/C thermostat. Disconnect the vacuum hose at the vacuum motor.

6. Cut the plastic retaining strap that retains the evaporator/blower housing to the heater core housing.

7. Disconnect and remove the heater control cable.

8. Remove the clip at the rear of the blower housing flange and remove the retaining screws.

9. Remove the housing attaching nuts from the studs on the engine compartment side of the dash panel. Remove the evaporator drain tube.

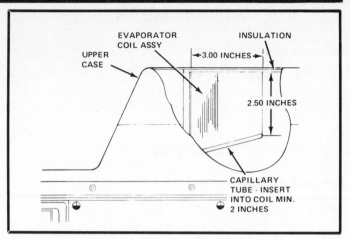

Thermostat Capillary Tube Position—Jeep

10. Remove the right kick panel and then remove the instrument panel support bolt.

11. Gently pull out on the right side of the dash and rotate the housing downward and toward the rear of the vehicle to disengage the housing studs from the dash panel. Then remove the evaporator/blower housing.

12. Remove the top housing retainings screws and remove the top of the evaporator housing.

13. Remove the two evaporator retaining screws and lift the evaporator out of the housing.

14. Remove the expansion valve from the evaporator.

15. Installation is the reverse of the removal procedure.

Heater Core

Removal and Installation

1982 AND LATER—ALL VEHICLES

For removal and installation procedures refer to the heater core section in this book.

Control Head and Fan Switch Assembly

Removal and Installation

1982 AND LATER—ALL VEHICLES

For control head removal and installation procedures refer the heating section.

PERFORMANCE DIAGNOSIS—ALL MODELS

Condition	Possible Cause	Correction
Compressor Noise	a) Broken valves.	a) Replace valve plate.
	b) Overcharged.	b) Discharge, evacuate, and install correct charge.
	c) Incorrect oil level.	c) Isolate compressor and check oil level. Correct as necessary.
	d) Piston slap.	d) Replace compressor.
	e) Broken rings.	e) Replace compressor.

PERFORMANCE DIAGNOSIS—ALL MODELS

Condition	Possible Cause	Correction
Excessive vibration	a) Incorrect belt tention.	a) Set belt tension. Refer to Compressor Belt Tension
	b) Clutch loose.	b) Tighten clutch.
	c) Overcharged.	c) Discharge, evacuate, and install correct charge.
	d) Pulley misaligned.	d) Align pulley.
Condensation dripping in passenger compartment	a) Drain hose plugged or improperly positioned.	a) Clean drain hose and check for proper installation.
	b) Insulation removed or improperly installed.	b) Replace insulation on expansion valve and hoses.
Frozen evaporator coil	a) Faulty thermostat.	a) Replace thermostat.
	b) Thermostat capillary tube improperly installed.	b) Install capillary tube correctly.
Low side low-high side low	a) System refrigerant low.	a) Evacuate, leak test, and charge system.
Low side high-high side low	a) Internal leak in compressor—worn.	a) Remove compressor cylinder head and inspect compressor. Replace valve plate assembly if necessary. If compressor pistons, rings, or cylinders are excessively worn or scored, replace compressor.
	b) Head gasket leaking.	b) Install new cylinder head gasket.
	c) Expansion valve.	c) Replace expansion valve.
	d) Drive belt slipping	d) Set belt tension.
Low side high-high side high	a) Clogged condenser fins.	a) Clean out condenser fins.
	b) Air in system.	b) Evacuate, leak test, and charge system.
	c) Expansion valve.	c) Replace expansion valve.
	d) Loose or worn fan belts	d) Adjust or replace belts as necessary.
Low side low—High side high	a) Expansion valve.	a) Replace expansion valve.
	b) Restriction in liquid line.	b) Check line for kinks—replace if necessary.
	c) Restriction in receiver.	c) Replace receiver.
	d) Restriction in condenser.	d) Replace condenser.
Low side and high side normal inadequate cooling	a) Air in system.	a) Evacuate, leak test, and charge system.
	b) Moisture in system.	b) Evacuate, leak test, and charge system.

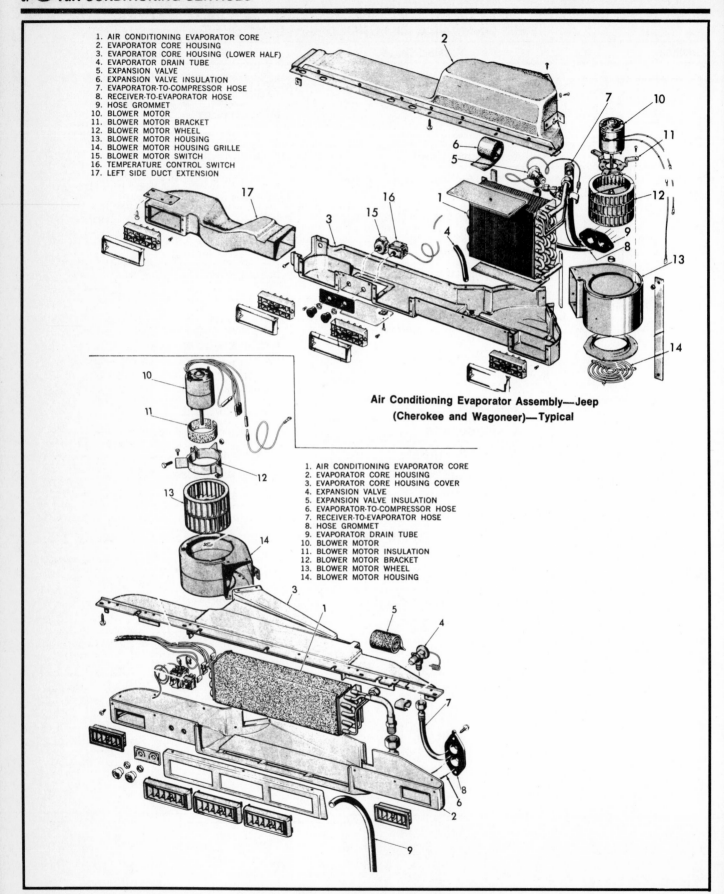

1. AIR CONDITIONING EVAPORATOR CORE
2. EVAPORATOR CORE HOUSING
3. EVAPORATOR CORE HOUSING (LOWER HALF)
4. EVAPORATOR DRAIN TUBE
5. EXPANSION VALVE
6. EXPANSION VALVE INSULATION
7. EVAPORATOR-TO-COMPRESSOR HOSE
8. RECEIVER-TO-EVAPORATOR HOSE
9. HOSE GROMMET
10. BLOWER MOTOR
11. BLOWER MOTOR BRACKET
12. BLOWER MOTOR WHEEL
13. BLOWER MOTOR HOUSING
14. BLOWER MOTOR HOUSING GRILLE
15. BLOWER MOTOR SWITCH
16. TEMPERATURE CONTROL SWITCH
17. LEFT SIDE DUCT EXTENSION

Air Conditioning Evaporator Assembly—Jeep (Cherokee and Wagoneer)—Typical

1. AIR CONDITIONING EVAPORATOR CORE
2. EVAPORATOR CORE HOUSING
3. EVAPORATOR CORE HOUSING COVER
4. EXPANSION VALVE
5. EXPANSION VALVE INSULATION
6. EVAPORATOR-TO-COMPRESSOR HOSE
7. RECEIVER-TO-EVAPORATOR HOSE
8. HOSE GROMMET
9. EVAPORATOR DRAIN TUBE
10. BLOWER MOTOR
11. BLOWER MOTOR INSULATION
12. BLOWER MOTOR BRACKET
13. BLOWER MOTOR WHEEL
14. BLOWER MOTOR HOUSING

Air Conditioning Evaporator Assembly— Jeep (All except Cherokee and Wagoneer)—Typical

Magnetic Clutch Troubleshooting

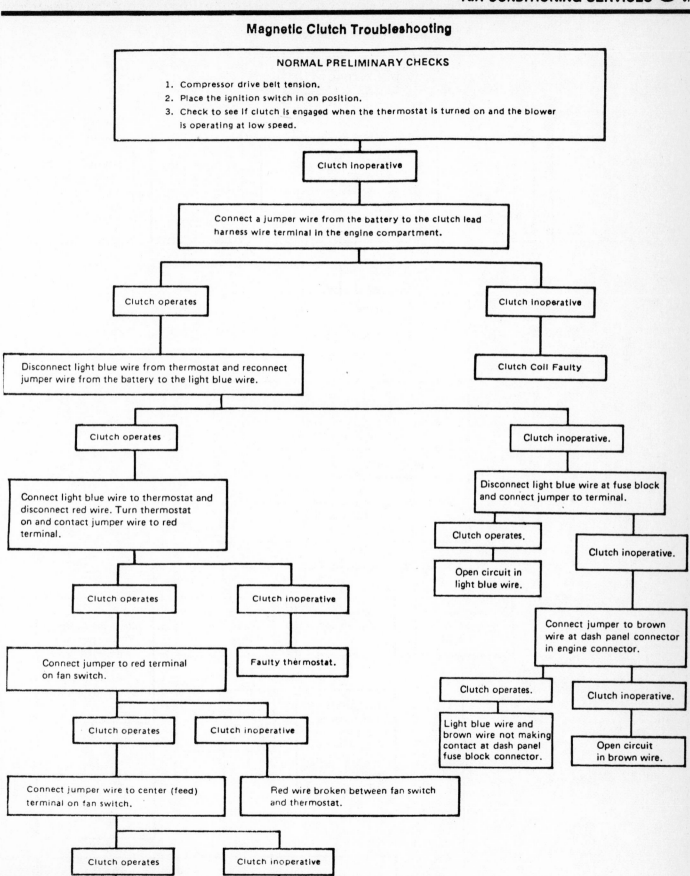

NORMAL PRELIMINARY CHECKS

1. Compressor drive belt tension.
2. Place the ignition switch in on position.
3. Check to see if clutch is engaged when the thermostat is turned on and the blower is operating at low speed.

Clutch inoperative

Connect a jumper wire from the battery to the clutch lead harness wire terminal in the engine compartment.

Clutch operates

Clutch inoperative

Clutch Coil Faulty

Disconnect light blue wire from thermostat and reconnect jumper wire from the battery to the light blue wire.

Clutch operates

Clutch inoperative.

Connect light blue wire to thermostat and disconnect red wire. Turn thermostat on and contact jumper wire to red terminal.

Disconnect light blue wire at fuse block and connect jumper to terminal.

Clutch operates.

Open circuit in light blue wire.

Clutch inoperative.

Clutch operates

Clutch inoperative

Faulty thermostat.

Connect jumper to red terminal on fan switch.

Connect jumper to brown wire at dash panel connector in engine connector.

Clutch operates.

Clutch inoperative.

Light blue wire and brown wire not making contact at dash panel fuse block connector.

Open circuit in brown wire.

Clutch operates

Clutch inoperative

Connect jumper wire to center (feed) terminal on fan switch.

Red wire broken between fan switch and thermostat.

Clutch operates

Clutch inoperative

Wire to switch faulty

Switch defective

System Troubleshooting

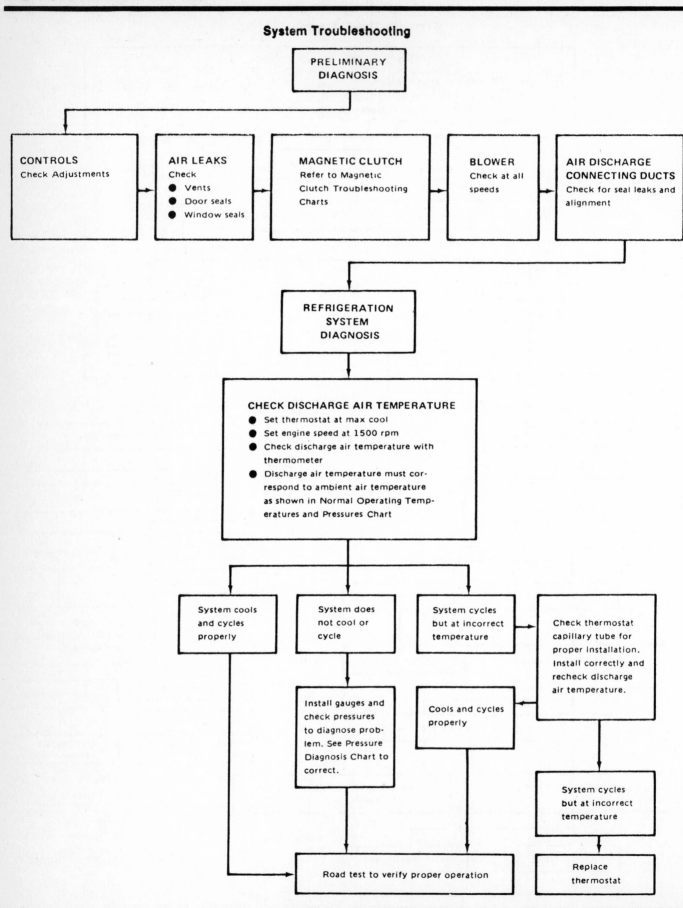

PRELIMINARY
DIAGNOSIS

CONTROLS
Check Adjustments

AIR LEAKS
Check
● Vents
● Door seals
● Window seals

MAGNETIC CLUTCH
Refer to Magnetic
Clutch Troubleshooting
Charts

BLOWER
Check at all
speeds

**AIR DISCHARGE
CONNECTING DUCTS**
Check for seal leaks and
alignment

**REFRIGERATION
SYSTEM
DIAGNOSIS**

CHECK DISCHARGE AIR TEMPERATURE
● Set thermostat at max cool
● Set engine speed at 1500 rpm
● Check discharge air temperature with
thermometer
● Discharge air temperature must correspond to ambient air temperature
as shown in Normal Operating Temperatures and Pressures Chart

System cools
and cycles
properly

System does
not cool or
cycle

System cycles
but at incorrect
temperature

Check thermostat
capillary tube for
proper installation.
Install correctly and
recheck discharge
air temperature.

Install gauges and
check pressures
to diagnose prob-
lem. See Pressure
Diagnosis Chart to
correct.

Cools and cycles
properly

System cycles
but at incorrect
temperature

Road test to verify proper operation

Replace
thermostat

Pressure Diagnosis—All Models

Condition	Possible Cause	Correction
LOW SIDE LOW— HIGH SIDE LOW	(1) System refrigerant low.	(1) Evacuate, leak test, and charge.
	(2) Expansion valve clogged.	(2) Replace expansion valve.
LOW SIDE HIGH— HIGH SIDE LOW	(1) Internal leak in compressor—worn.	(1) Remove compressor cylinder head and inspect compressor. Replace valve plate assembly if necessary. If compressor pistons, rings, or cylinders are excessively worn or scored replace compressor.
	(2) Head gasket leaking.	(2) Install new cylinder head gasket.
	(3) Expansion valve.	(3) Replace expansion valve.
	(4) Drive belt slipping.	(4) Set belt tension.
LOW SIDE HIGH— HIGH SIDE HIGH	(1) Clogged condenser fins.	(1) Clean out condenser fins.
	(2) Air in system.	(2) Evacuate, leak test, and charge system.
	(3) Expansion valve.	(3) Replace expansion valve.
	(4) Loose or worn fan belts.	(4) Adjust or replace belts as necessary.
LOW SIDE LOW— HIGH SIDE HIGH	(1) Expansion valve.	(1) Replace expansion valve.
	(2) Restriction in liquid line.	(2) Check line for kinks—replace if necessary.
	(3) Restriction in receiver.	(3) Replace receiver.
	(4) Restriction in condenser.	(4) Replace condenser.
LOW SIDE AND HIGH SIDE NORMAL (INADEQUATE COOLING)	(1) Air in system.	(1) Evacuate, leak test, and charge system.
	(2) Moisture in system.	(2) Evacuate, leak test, and charge system.

Performance Diagnosis—All Models

Condition	Possible Cause	Correction
COMPRESSOR NOISE	(1) Broken valves.	(1) Replace valve plate.
	(2) Overcharged.	(2) Discharge, evacuate, and install correct charge.
	(3) Incorrect oil level.	(3) Isolate compressor and check oil level. Correct as necessary.
	(4) Piston slap.	(4) Replace compressor.
	(5) Broken rings.	(5) Replace compressor.
	(6) Accessory drive pulley bolts loose.	(6) Tighten to torque specifications.
EXCESSIVE VIBRATION	(1) Incorrect belt tension.	(1) Set belt tension. Refer to Compressor Belt Tension.
	(2) Clutch loose.	(2) Tighten clutch.
	(3) Overcharged.	(3) Discharge, evacuate, and install correct charge.
	(4) Pulley misaligned.	(4) Align pulley.
CONDENSATION DRIPPING IN PASSENGER COMPARTMENT	(1) Drain hose plugged or improperly positioned.	(1) Clean drain hose and check for proper installation.
	(2) Insulation removed or improperly installed.	(2) Replace insulation on expansion valve and hoses.
AC AIRFLOW STOPS ON ACCELERATION	(1) Defective vacuum storage tank.	(1) Check tank. Replace if necessary.
	(2) Vacuum line separated or defective.	(2) Check vacuum lines. Replace as required.
	(3) Vacuum switch defective.	(3) Replace switch.
	(4) Vacuum leak.	(4) Check vacuum motors and lines.
FROZEN EVAPORATOR COIL	(1) Faulty thermostat.	(1) Replace thermostat.
	(2) Thermostat capillary tube improperly installed.	(2) Install capillary tube correctly.
	(3) Thermostat not adjusted properly.	(3) Adjust thermostat.

INDEX

DATSUN/NISSAN SPECIFICATIONS

VEHICLE IDENTIFICATION CHART

1982	1983	1984	1985
210	—	—	—
310	—	—	—
Sentra	Sentra	Sentra	Sentra
Stanza	Stanza	Stanza	Stanza
200SX	200SX	200SX	200SX
Maxima	Maxima	Maxima	Maxima
280ZX	280ZX	—	—
—	Pulsar	Pulsar	Pulsar
—	—	300ZX	300ZX

Blower Motor

Removal and Installation

1982 AND LATER—ALL VEHICLES

For blower motor removal and installation procedures refer to the heating section.

Compressor

Removal and Installation

1982 AND LATER—ALL VEHICLES

1. Disconnect the negative battery cable.
2. Remove all the necessary equipment in order to gain access to the compressor mounting bolts.
3. Remove the compressor drive belt.
4. Discharge the system.
5. Disconnect and plug the refrigerant lines.
6. Disconnect all electrical connections from the unit.
7. Remove the compressor mounting bolts. Remove the compressor from the vehicle.
8. Installation is the reverse of the removal procedure. Evacuate and charge the system as required.

Condenser

Removal and Installation

1982 AND LATER—ALL VEHICLES

1. Disconnect the negative battery cable. Remove the compressor drive belt.

REFRIGERANT OIL CAPACITIES

Refrigerant oil given in fluid ounces

Year	Model	Capacity	Compressor Type
1982	210	5.1	SC–206
	310	5.1	MJS–170
	Sentra	5.1	MJS–170
	Stanza	5.1	MJS–170
	200SX	5.1	MJS–170
	280ZX	5.1	MJ–167
	Maxima	5.1	MJS–170
1983	Sentra	5.1	MJS–170
	Stanza	5.1	MJS–170
	200SX	5.1	MJS–170
	280ZX	5.1	MJ–167
	Maxima	5.1	MJS–170
	Pulsar	5.1	MJS–170
1984	Sentra	5.1	NUR–140
	Stanza	5.1	MJS–170
	200SX	5.1	A–5000
	300SX	5.1	MJS–170
	Maxima	5.1	SWP–167
	Pulsar	5.1	MJS–170
1985	Sentra	5.1	NUR–140
	Stanza	5.1	MJS–170
	200SX	5.1	A–5000
	300ZX	5.1	MJS–170
	Maxima	5.1	SWP–167
	Pulsar	5.1	MJS–170

2. Remove the necessary components in order to gain access to the condenser retaining bolts. If equipped, remove the condenser fan motor, as necessary.

3. Discharge the system. Remove the condenser refrigerant lines and plug them.

4. Remove the condenser retaining bolts. Remove the condenser from the vehicle.

REFRIGERANT CAPACITIES

Refrigerant given in pounds

Year	210	310	Sentra	Stanza	200SX	280ZX	Maxima	Pulsar	300ZX
1982	1.8–2.2	2.2–2.6	1.8–2.2	1.8–2.2	2.0–2.4	1.8–2.2	2.0–2.4	—	—
1983	—	—	1.8–2.2	1.8–2.2	2.0–2.4	1.8–2.2	2.0–2.4	1.8–2.2	—
1984	—	—	1.8–2.2	1.8–2.2	2.0–2.4	1.8–2.2	2.0–2.4	1.8–2.2	2.0–2.4
1985	—	—	1.8–2.2	1.8–2.2	2.0–2.4	1.8–2.2	2.0–2.4	1.8–2.2	2.0–2.4

5. Installation is the reverse of the removal procedure. Charge the system.

Expansion Valve

Removal and Installation

1982 AND LATER—ALL VEHICLES

1. Disconnect the negative battery cable. Discharge the air conditioning system.
2. Remove the evaporator.
3. Remove the heat insulator covering the expansion valve assembly.
4. Remove the clamp attaching the sensing bulb.
5. Loosen the flare nuts and remove the expansion valve from the evaporator and inlet pipe.

————— CAUTION —————
Plug all openings to prevent entrance of dirt and moisture.

6. Installation is in the reverse order of the removal procedure.

Evaporator

Removal and Installation

1982 210

1. Disconnect the negative battery cable. Discharge the system.
2. Loosen the inlet and outlet connections of the evaporator assembly.
3. Plug the openings to prevent air and dirt from entering the system.
4. Remove instrument under cover.
5. Remove glove box.
6. Disconnect wiring harness connectors from compressor relay and thermostat.
7. Remove upper and lower attaching bolts and remove cooling unit.
8. Separate the cooling unit and remove the evaporator.
9. Installation is the reverse of the removal procedure.

1982 310

1. Disconnect the negative battery cable.
2. Discharge the air conditioning system.
3. Remove air cleaner, altitude compensator with bracket, and carburetor cooling fan with bracket.
4. Disconnect refrigerant lines from evaporator. Remove piping grommet and cover.
5. Remove right side dash face finisher.
6. Remove instrument panel.
7. Disconnect A/C harness from cooling unit.
8. Remove clip and disconnect control cable from air intake door shaft.
9. Loosen band seal at joint of cooling unit and heating unit.
10. Remove mounting bolts and then remove cooling unit.
11. Remove clips fixing upper case to lower case.
12. Separate upper case from lower case by pulling it upward.
13. Withdraw evaporator assembly out of lower case.
14. Installation is the reverse of the removal procedure.

1982 AND LATER SENTRA

1. Disconnect the negative battery cable.
2. Discharge the air conditioning system.
3. Disconnect the refrigerant lines from the evaporator assembly.
4. Remove the instrument panel.
5. Remove the cooling unit from the vehicle.
6. Separate the cooling unit and remove the evaporator assembly.
7. Installation is the reverse of the removal procedure.

1983 AND LATER PULSAR

1. Disconnect the negative battery cable.

2. Discharge refrigerant from system.
3. Disconnect refrigerant lines from evaporator. Remove piping grommet and cover.
4. Remove passenger side instrument lower cover and glove box. Remove attachment plate from instrument panel.

NOTE: For vehicles with factory installed air conditioner, cut instrument panel with hacksaw blade on cut-lines. Before cutting, cover blower motor vent holes with tape. After cutting, brush the shavings away from the area around blower motor and remove tape.

5. Remove blower motor unit.
6. Remove cooling unit.
7. Separate the cooling unit and remove the evaporator assembly.
8. Installation is the reverse of the removal procedure.
9. After installing the cooling unit, install the attachment plate to the instrument panel.

1982 AND LATER STANZA

1. Disconnect the negative battery cable.
2. Discharge refrigerant from system.
3. Remove air cleaner.
4. Disconnect vacuum check valve retaining bolt.
5. Disconnect evaporator upper case retaining bolts.
6. Remove evaporator upper case while scraping off sealer.
7. Loosen flare nuts at each connection of inlet and outlet pipes of evaporator.
8. Remove evaporator from evaporator lower case.
9. Installation is in the reverse order of the removal procedure.

1982 AND LATER—MAXIMA AND 200SX

1. Disconnect the negative battery cable.
2. Remove instrument lower cover and cluster lid.
3. Disconnect refrigerant lines and harness from cooling unit.
4. Remove cooling unit with drain tube.
5. Separate the cooling unit and remove the evaporator core.
6. Installation is the reverse of the removal procedure.

1982 AND LATER 280ZX AND 300ZX

1. Disconnect the negative battery cable.
2. Discharge refrigerant from system.
3. Loosen flare nuts at each connection of inlet and outlet pipes of evaporator.
4. Remove heater unit.
5. Remove defroster duct on passenger's side.
6. Remove mounting bolt and then remove cooling unit from dash panel.
7. Remove clips fixing upper case to lower case.
8. Using a knife, cut packings at upper and lower case fit-in portion.
9. Withdraw evaporator assembly out of lower case.
10. Installation is the reverse of the removal procedure.
11. Be sure to join mating surface of packings at upper and lower case fit-in portion.

Refrigerant Leak Warning System

DESCRIPTION

Some vehicles are equipped with a refrigerant leak warning system, which is used in conjunction with the low pressure switch. This system protects the cooler cycle from damage due to continued operation of the air conditioning system when there is a shortage of refrigerant. It also indicates when to replenish the refrigerant.

When the refrigerant in the cooler cycle is insufficient, it vaporizes quickly inside the evaporator. As a result, the super heat of the refrigerant at the outlet of the evaporator increases. If it exceeds the specified level, approximately 104°F, the super heat switch turns on, allowing the current to flow through the timer. If current continues to flow through the timer for the specified length of time, the timer activates to close the contacts which turn on the warning lamp.

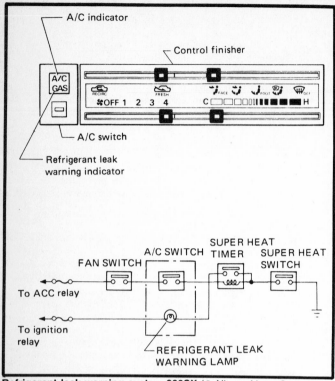

Refrigerant leak warning system-200SX (© Nissan Motor Co.)

Leak Warning Lamp Check

Conduct a continuity test in the leak warning lamp circuit.

1. Turn ignition switch ''ON'' (with engine off) to make sure warning lamp illuminates.

2. Start engine. Warning lamp should go out if the amount of refrigerant is sufficient.

SUPER HEAT SWITCH

The super heat switch, placed, in the refrigerant line at the outlet of the evaporator, consists of a diaphragm, temperature sensor, moving contact and fixed contact. The diaphragm detects the refrigerant line pressure and the temperature sensor senses the refrigerant line temperature.

When the temperature in the refrigerant line increases, the gas charged inside the temperature sensor expands. This causes a force to move the diaphragm upward against the refrigerant line pressure. When the difference between the saturated temperature and the detected temperature in relation to the detected pressure reaches a specified condition, the diaphragm pushes the moving contact point up, thereby turning the switch on.

SUPER HEAT TIMER

During rapid acceleration, the super heat increases momentarily and returns to its original level quickly even when the amount of the refrigerant is normal. Because of this, a timer, used in the warning system, detects an increase in super heat only when the amount of refrigerant is low, thereby preventing erroneous alarms.

Fast Idle Control Device

Adjustment

1982 210

1. Run engine until it reaches operating temperature.
2. With air conditioner in OFF (when compressor is not operated),

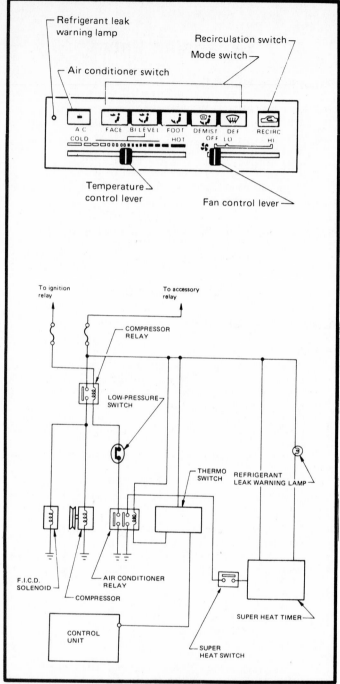

Refrigerant leak warning system-300ZX (© Nissan Motor Co.)

make sure that clearance ''C'' between levers ''A'' and ''B'' is more than 0.12 in. If clearance ''C'' is less than 0.12 in, loosen cable lock screws and push down on lever ''A'' so that clearance ''C'' is more than 0.12 in.

3. Make sure that engine is at correct idle speed.

4. With air conditioner in ON (when F.I.C.D. is actuated), set engine speed to 800 rpm.

a. Turn adjusting screw until engine speed is 800 rpm.

On cars equipped with automatic transmission, make this adjustment with shift control lever in ''N'' position.

b. If engine speed cannot be adjusted properly with adjusting screw, check and adjust clearance ''C'' again.

c. Depress and release accelerator pedal several times, and make

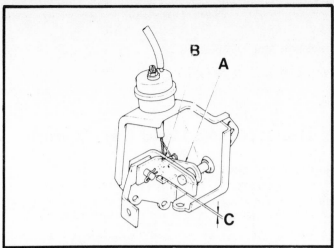

Fast idle control device adjustment (© Nissan Motor Co.)

sure that engine speed reduces to 800 rpm as pedal is released.

If correct adjustment is not made, repeat Steps a–c above until engine speed is 800 rpm at idling.

Removal and Installation

1. Remove vacuum hose from actuator.
2. Remove air cleaner assembly.
3. Remove cotter pin and pin, and disconnect actuator from the fast idle control device lever connected to throttle shaft.
4. Remove actuator attaching nuts, then remove actuator.
5. Install actuator in the reverse order of the removal procedure.

Adjustment

1982 310

1. Run engine until it reaches operating temperature.
2. With air conditioning system OFF (when compressor is not operated), make sure that engine is at correct idle speed.
3. With air conditioning system ON ("A/C-HEATER" selector lever at "A/C", "FAN" control lever at "HI"), make sure that compressor, F.I.C.D. actuator and solenoid valve are functioning properly.
4. If units in step 3 check out okay, set engine idle speed to 800 rpm as follows:
   a. Loosen lock nut, turn adjusting bolt, and then set the idle speed at 800 rpm. Tighten lock nut temporarily.
   b. Depress and release accelerator pedal several times, and make sure that engine speed goes down to 800 rpm as pedal is released.
   c. If correct adjustment is made, tighten lock nut to specified torque. If it is not made, repeat Steps (a) and (b) until engine speed is 800 rpm at idling.

Removal and Installation

1. Disconnect the negative battery cable.
2. Remove the vacuum hose from the fast idle control device.
3. Remove the retaining screws from the component. Remove the component.
4. Installation is the reverse of the removal procedure.

Adjustment

1982 AND LATER SENTRA AND 1983 AND LATER PULSAR

1. Run engine until it reaches operating temperature.
2. With air conditioning system off (when compressor is not operated), make sure that engine is at correct idle speed.
3. With air conditioning system on (Air conditioner switch at "A/C" position, fan control lever at "4" ("3"-1982 vehicles position), make

sure that compressor, F.I.C.D. actuator and solenoid valve are functioning properly.
4. Set idle speed at the specified value.
Gasoline engine model:
M/T—750–850 rpm
A/T—580–660 rpm
  (Shift lever should be in "D" position.)
Diesel engine model:
M/T—800–850 rpm
A/T—900–950 rpm
  (Shift lever should be in "N" position.)

Adjustment

1982 AND LATER STANZA

NOTE: The following procedure is for vehicles equipped with a carburetor.

1. Warm up engine.
2. Make sure engine is at correct idling speed with air conditioner in off position.
3. Set engine speed with air conditioner in ON position (when actuator is actuated).
4. If the vehicle is equipped with automatic transmission set the specification to 600–650 rpm. If the vehicle is equipped with manual transmission set the specification to 800–900 rpm.
   To adjust:
Loosen lock nut and then rotate adjusting screw.
1. Engine speed increases by turning adjusting screw counterclockwise.
2. With automatic transaxle model, adjust in "D" position.
3. Depress and release accelerator pedal several times, and make sure that engine speed meets specifications with air conditioner in "on" and "off" position.

Adjustment

1982 AND LATER 200SX

1. Run engine until it reaches operating temperature.
2. With air conditioning system off (when compressor is not operated), make sure that engine is at correct idle speed.
3. With air conditioning system on (Intake lever at "RECIRC" position, fan control lever at "4" position), make sure that compressor, F.I.C.D. actuator and solenoid valve are functioning properly.
4. Set idle speed at the specified value.

Transmission			Non-turbocharged model	Turbocharged model
A/C is OFF	M/T	rpm	650–850	700–800
	A/T	rpm	600–800 at "D" range	650–750 at "D" range
A/C is ON	M/T	rpm	1,000–1,050	
	A/T	rpm	1,050–1,100 at "N" range	

Adjustment

1984 AND LATER 300ZX

1. Run engine until it reaches operating temperature.
2. With air conditioning system off (when compressor is not operating), make sure that engine is at correct idle speed.
3. With air conditioning system on (Recirculation switch at "RECIRC" position, fan control lever at "HI" position), make sure that compressor and F.I.C.D. solenoid valve are functioning properly.

4. For non-turbocharged model, set idle speed at the specified value. For turbocharged model, make sure that idle speed is at the specified value, as it is non adjustable.

Transmission			Non-turbocharged model	Turbocharged model
A/C is OFF	M/T	rpm	650–750	650–750
	A/T	rpm	650–750 at "D" range	600–700 at "D" range
A/C is ON	M/T	rpm	750–850	750–850
	A/T	rpm	750–850 at "D" range	750–850 at "D" range

Heater Core

Removal and Installation

1982 AND LATER—ALL VEHICLES
For removal and installation procedures refer to the heater core removal and installation procedure in this section,

Control Head and Fan Switch

Removal and Installation
1982 AND LATER—ALL VEHICLES
For removal and installation procedures refer to the control head and fan switch removal and installation procedure in this section,

AUTOMATIC AIR CONDITIONER

NOTE: The information given below is for automatic air condition systems installed in the 280ZX and the 300ZX. At the time of publication, material was not available to indicate that automatic air condition is being used on any other Datsun/Nissan vehicles.

DESCRIPTION—280ZX

The automatic temperature control system consists of a system starting control, compressor switching control, automatic outlet air temperature control, automatic blower speed control, automatic air distribution control and recirculation control.

Each system is activated by an electrical circuit and/or a vacuum mechanism in order to set the positions of the control levers control switch and air mix door.

Each of the above systems contains various sub systems which are described as follows.

System Starting Control

COOLANT TEMPERATURE SWITCH

This switch keeps the blower off until coolant temperature rise over 122°F so that interior air can be warmed up quickly, e.g., during the winter season.

IN-CAR SWITCH

This switch quickly activates the starting control system when the car's interior temperature is extremely high, e.g., during the summer season even if the coolant temperature switch is not activated.

Compressor Switching Control

AMBIENT SWITCH

This switch is used to turn off the compressor when the ambient air temperature is low.

Automatic Outlet Air Temperature Control

IN-CAR SENSOR (THERMISTOR)

This switch is located in the instrument panel and registers a resistance

value which varies with the car's interior temperature and the quantity of heat resulting from sunlight.

AMBIENT SENSOR (THERMISTOR)

This sensor is located behind the front bumper and registers a resistance value which varies with the surrounding temperature.

TEMPERATURE CONTROL RHEOSTAT (VARIABLE RESISTOR)

This rheostat resisters a resistance value which varies with the temperature control lever position.

FEEDBACK RHEOSTAT (VARIABLE RESISTOR)

This rheostat automatically changes its resistance value depending on the air mix door's position, in order to stabilize the power servo's operation.

TEMPERATURE CONTROL AMPLIFIER

This amplifier registers the total resistance value of the in-car sensor, ambient sensor, trimmer, temperature control rheostat and feedback rheostat, which are all connected in series, and then transmits a signal that corresponds to the total resistance value to the transducer.

TRANSDUCER

The transducer sends vacuum that is proportional to the current received from the temperature control amplifier to the power servo.

POWER SERVO (ACTUATOR)

The power servo activates in order to move the air mix door's position in proportion to the vacuum received from the transducer.

BY-PASS VACUUM SELECTOR

By setting temperature lever at the hottest position, the vacuum does not pass through the transducer but is sent directly to the power servo. When it is set at the coldest position, the vacuum line will be blocked.

VACUUM LOCK VALVE

This valve serves to block the vacuum line when the source vacuum momentarily drops.

Automatic Blower Speed

BLOWER CONTROL RHEOSTAT (VARIABLE RESISTOR)

This rheostat is activated in conjunction with the air mix door and registers a resistance value which varies with the air mix door's position.

BLOWER AMPLIFIER

This amplifier sends a voltage to the blower motor which is proportional to the blower control rheostat's resistance value.

Automatic Air Distribution Control

VACUUM SELECTOR

This selector selects the vacuum lines needed to open or close outlets in accordance with mode lever position.

VACUUM PROGRAM SWITCH

This selector also selects the vacuum lines needed to open or close outlets in accordance with air mix door position.

AIR VALVE AND VACUUM SWITCH

The V_1' point of vacuum program switch and the V_1' point of vacuum selector are connected via air valve and vacuum switch for obtaining positive operation of the floor door.

Recirculation Control

RECIRCULATION TIMER

This timer is used to recirculate interior air. When its switch is depressed, the interior air will be recirculated for approximately 10 minutes. Depressing the switch again will stop the process.

AIR VALVE (INTAKE DOOR)

This air valve is controlled by the recirculation timer switch. When the switch is depressed, current stops flowing through the air valve and it closes. This causes the intake door actuator's vacuum line to be blocked and sets the intake door in the recirculation position.

DESCRIPTION—300ZX

The automatic temperature control air conditioning unit for the 300ZX has been redesigned and is somewhat different from the unit used in the 280ZX. The basic air conditioning components have remained the same, but the following new automatic air conditioning innovations have been incorporated into the system.

The vehicle sensors are installed at head level and foot level, in order to maintain the temperatures of both positions at the optimum levels.

When starting the engine in cold season, the system immediately operates in the defroster mode until the coolant temperature rises, thereby preventing fogging on the windshield.

As the coolant temperature rises high enough to use the heater, the outlet door is automatically switched to the foot level for starting the heating operation. The system begins to control the air flow automatically as the outlet air temperature reaches the optimum level.

When the DEF switch is on, the air flow is automatically set to the "HI" position. However, the air flow can also be switched to "LO" by setting the manual switch to "LO" position. The objective temperature fine control switch (Set temp. adjuster) has been adopted. This switch permits adjustment of the upper objective temperature and the lower objective temperature within the range of $\pm 3.6°F$.

The manual DEF switch has been adopted so that the system can be fixed in the available mode for driving (DEF mode) even when trouble occurs in the control function.

The control unit display section (digital display and air flow indicator) is utilized for self-diagnosing each sensor and actuator.

The proportional integral control system newly adopted in the temperature control system provides quick and accurate response without generation of steady-state error during stabilized operation.

System Operation

AIR MIX DOOR CONTROL

The air mix door control system consists of the automatic amplifier with a micro computer, temperature setting switch, two in vehicle sensors, ambient temperature sensor, three duct temperature sensors, sunload sensor, two power servos, two potentio balance resistors (PBR1 and PBR2), and two double solenoid vacuum valves (DSVV1 and DSVV2).

AUTOMATIC AMPLIFIER

This amplifier has a built-in microcomputer enabling it to deal with data and to provide precise control, which is necessary for driving the auto air conditioner system. In addition to the auto air conditioner mode, this microcomputer has the self-diagnosis mode program.

TEMPERATURE SETTING SWITCH

This switch is used for setting the in-vehicle temperature. Temperature set by temperature setting switch is electrically memorized by the microcomputer in automatic amplifier.

IN-VEHICLE SENSOR (HEAD, FOOT)

The in-vehicle sensor converts the temperature value of the inside air which is drawn through (by low pressure) the aspirator fan into resistance value, which is then input into the auto amplifier.

The sensor placed at head level detects the typical temperature at the upper half body level. The sensor placed at foot level detects the foot level temperature.

AMBIENT TEMPERATURE SENSOR

This sensor transforms the value of ambient temperature into a resistance value, which is put into automatic amplifier.

DEFROSTER DUCT TEMP. SENSOR, VENTILATOR DUCT TEMP. SENSOR, FLOOR DUCT TEMP. SENSOR

Each sensor transforms the value of outlet air temperature from each duct into a resistance value, which is put into automatic amplifier.

SUNLOAD SENSOR (PHOTO DIODE)

This sensor transforms sunload into current value, which is put into the automatic amplifier. This sensor is located in defroster grille.

D.S.V.V. (DOUBLE SOLENOID VACUUM VALVE)

D.S.V.V. can drive the power servo, because it transforms the electric signal from automatic amplifier into vacuum pressure or atmospheric pressure.

The objective air mix door opening calculated in the auto amplifier and the actual door opening input from P.B.R. are compared in the auto amplifier. A signal, is then sent to D.S.V.V.

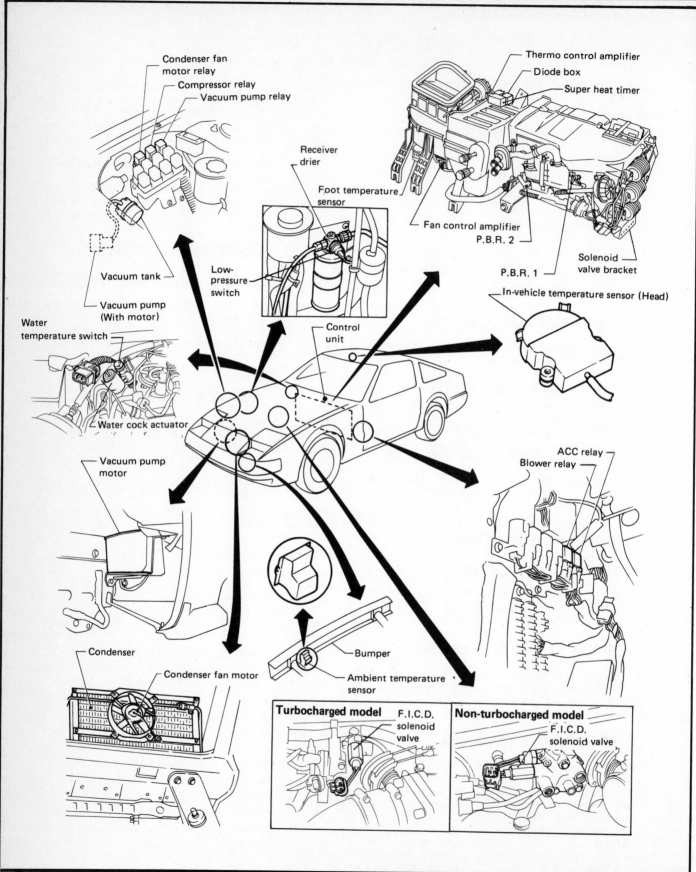

Condenser fan motor relay
Compressor relay
Vacuum pump relay

Thermo control amplifier
Diode box
Super heat timer

Receiver drier

Foot temperature sensor

Fan control amplifier
P.B.R. 2

P.B.R. 1

Solenoid valve bracket

In-vehicle temperature sensor (Head)

Vacuum tank

Low-pressure switch

Vacuum pump (With motor)

Water temperature switch

Control unit

Water cock actuator

Vacuum pump motor

ACC relay
Blower relay

Condenser

Condenser fan motor

Bumper

Ambient temperature sensor

Turbocharged model F.I.C.D. solenoid valve

Non-turbocharged model F.I.C.D. solenoid valve

Automatic temperature control air condition-component location 300ZX (© Nissan Motor Co.)

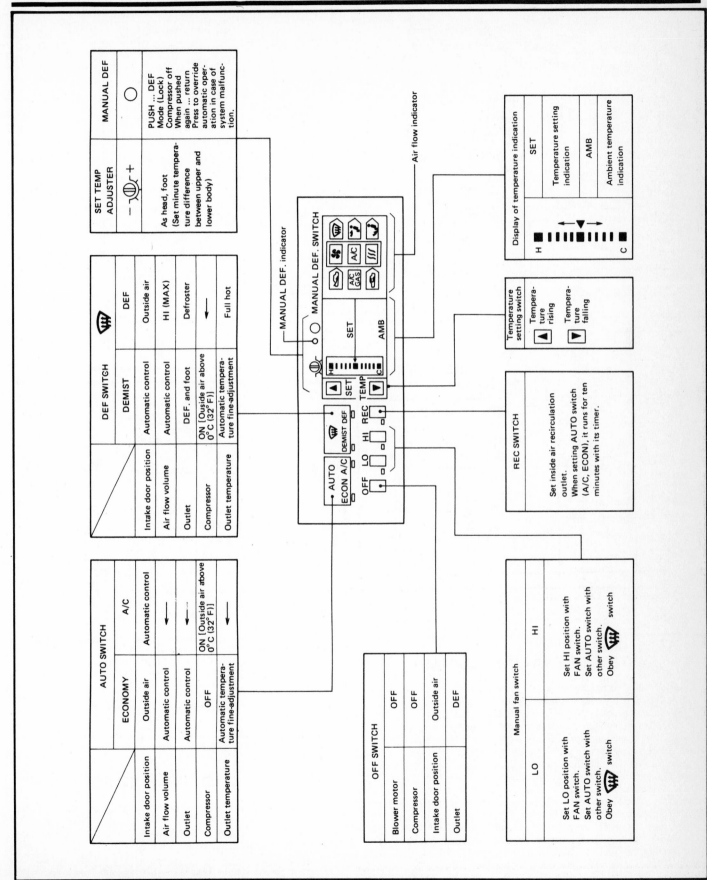

Control head functions–automatic temperature control 300ZX (© Nissan Motor Co.)

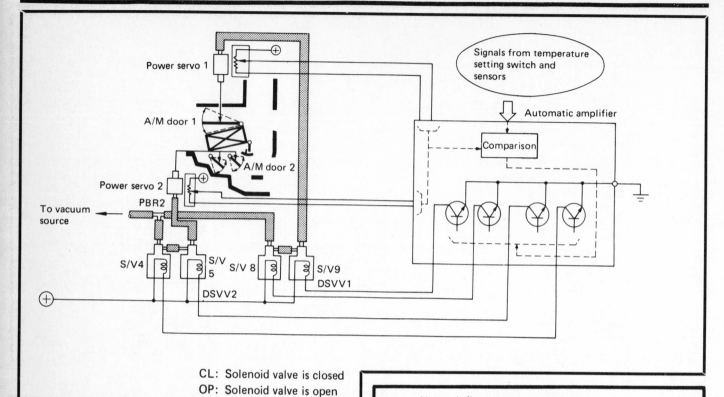

CL: Solenoid valve is closed
OP: Solenoid valve is open

AIR MIX DOOR CONTROL

			HOT side	HOLD	COLD side
Air mix door 1	Operation of solenoid valve	S/V8	CL	CL	OP
		S/V9	OP	CL	OP
Air mix door 2		S/V4	CL	CL	OP
		S/V5	OP	CL	OP

DSVV operation-300SX (© Nissan Motor Co.)

SYSTEM OPERATION SUMMARY

The temperature setting switch in this control system inputs the setting temperature signal to the auto amplifier.

The in-vehicle sensor, sunload sensor, ambient air temperature sensor, and duct temperature sensor also input the resistance value signals respectively to the auto amplifier corresponding to their conditions.

Receiving these input signals, the auto amplifier calculates the desirable air mix door position and causes the air mix door to move to the calculated position from its actual position detected by P.B.R. 1.

This movement of the air mix door is done by the power servo activated by the signal sent from the auto amplifier to the atmosphere side or vacuum side of the D.S.V.V.

The position of the air mix door is confirmed by the P.B.R. when converting the stroke of the power servo into voltage signal, and then by inputting the signal to the auto amplifier. The D.S.V.V. then continues operation until the air mix door position detected in this way coincides with the position determined by the control unit. The D.S.V.V. and the power servo stops operation once coincidence is attained.

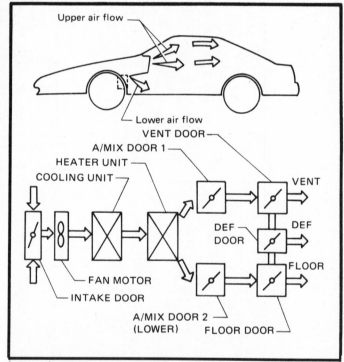

Automatic temperature control air condition system-300ZX
(© Nissan Motor Co.)

INTAKE DOOR CONTROL

The intake door is switched in order to introduce the inside air, partial outside air, or outside air at the positions already memorized in the auto amplifier corresponding to the angle (opening) of the air mix door which is automatically temperature controlled.

OUTLET DOOR CONTROL

The outlet door control consists of a defroster door actuator, ventilator

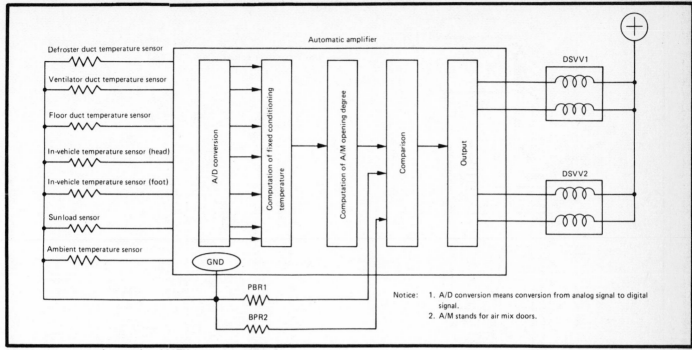

Air mix door control operation-300ZX (© Nissan Motor Co.)

Notice: 1. A/D conversion means conversion from analog signal to digital signal.
2. A/M stands for air mix doors.

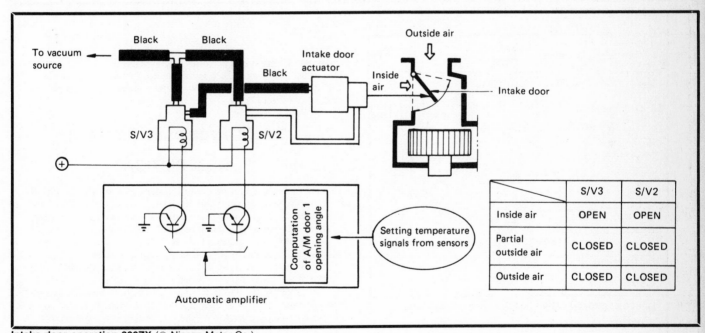

	S/V3	S/V2
Inside air	OPEN	OPEN
Partial outside air	CLOSED	CLOSED
Outside air	CLOSED	CLOSED

Intake door operation-300ZX (© Nissan Motor Co.)

door actuator, defroster and floor door actuator, two solenoid valves, sunload sensor, ambient temperature sensor and an automatic amplifier.

The outlet door is switched to HEAT, B/L, or VENT at the positions already memorized in the auto amplifier, corresponding to the ambient air temperature and sunload.

AIR FLOW VOLUME CONTROL

This device consists of a power transistor which varies the blower speed automatically according to the signal from the automatic amplifier.

The auto amplifier computes signals from the setting temperature switch and sensors that compose the air mix door control, and sends the control signal voltage (V_{IN}: 0.6 to 4 V) to the power transistor.

The power transistor amplifies this control signal voltage to change the voltage (V_M) fed to the motor terminals. Accordingly, the air flow is controlled automatically. With the manual fan switch, the voltage is fixed at 5.5V for LO, and at 12V for HI position.

WITH THE SELECTOR LEVER IN THE VENT POSITION:

The air flow volume control voltage is determined according to the difference between the objective temperature at head level and the actual room temperature at head level. This voltage varies within the range of 5.5V to 12V.

401

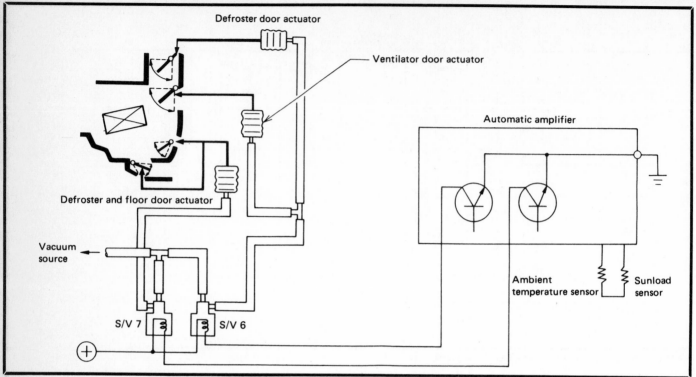

Outlet door control operation-300ZX (© Nissan Motor Co.)

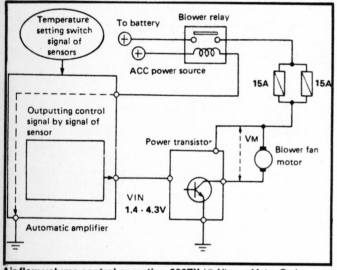

Air flow volume control operation-300ZX (© Nissan Motor Co.)

The V_M max is determined according to the difference between the ambient temperature and objective temperature, and this voltage varies within the range of from 9V to 12V.

WITH THE SELECTOR LEVER IN THE B/L, HEAT POSITION:

The air flow volume control voltage is determined according to the difference between the average room temperature and the objective temperature. This voltage varies within the range of 6V to 12V. The V_M max varies within the range of 9V to 12V. When the DEMIST switch on the DEF switch is ON, the V_M min voltage is fixed at 8V. Accordingly, the control voltage varies within the range of 8V to 12V.

In order to compensate for a change in room temperature depending on whether or not the sunload exists, the air flow volume is corrected accordingly.

In VENT .... V_M min: 5.5 to 7 V
Except VENT .... V_M min: 6 to 7 V
(In both cases, the upper limit of compensation is 7V.)
V_M max is the same as when no sunload exists.

If the DEMIST switch is ON, compensation of air flow volume by sunload does not occur.

Self Diagnosis System

DESCRIPTION

The automatic temperature control system used in the Datsun 300ZX is equipped with an on-board diagnosis program, which is used in solving problems that may arise within the air conditioning system.

The self diagnosis program is used to locate trouble within the system. This program is divided into two steps. They are the inspection of the input system and the inspection of the output system.

To change the system to the diagnosis mode, short the check terminal located at the lower portion of the cooling unit.

The number of the part being checked and the value detected by that part (whether that part is disconnected or shorted) is displayed on the temperature display section by the setting temperature switch.

Whether the parts of the output system are operating normally according to the predetermined pattern can be checked by applying a hand to the outlet door, observing the air flow indicator, listening to the operating noise, or by measuring the applied voltage.

Once the output program starts the air mix door, outlet doors, intake door, water cock, compressor magnet clutch and the blower motor begin their operation.

INPUT SIGNAL

Checking Procedure

1. For Input Test I-0 through I-9, plug the female into the male test connector. Do not connect the wire leads (A and B) at this time.

2. Turn the ignition to "ACC" position and press the "ECON/AC" button once.

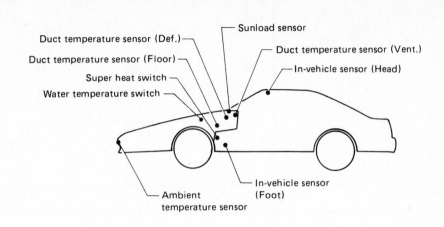

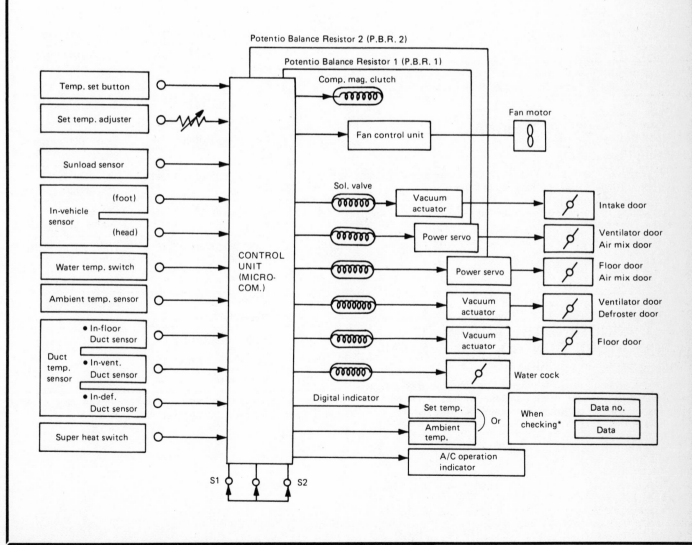

Sensor and switch location-automatic temperature control 300ZX (© Nissan Motor Co.)

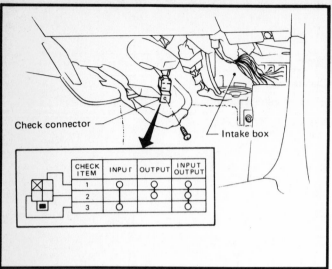

Check terminal location-300ZX automatic temperature control A/C (© Nissan Motor Co.)

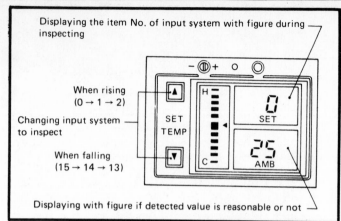

Display function of the control head assembly-300ZX with automatic temperature control A/C (© Nissan Motor Co.)

3. Set data number by tuning set temp. button. Read figures indicated on "AMB" indicator.

4. Analyze figures according to the display input analyzation information.

OUTPUT SIGNAL

Checking Procedure

1. For Input/Output System Test O-1 to O-6 Connect leads A and B, and plug the female lead into the male test connector.

2. Start the engine and press the "ECON/AC" button.

3. Check that output parts operate smoothly using the display output analyzation information.

DIAGNOSING THE AUTOMATIC TEMPERATURE CONTROL A/C SYSTEM— 300ZX

NOTE: In order to properly diagnose trouble with this system, the information from the display function system of the control head must be used in conjunction with the following data.

CONTROL HEAD DISPLAY DIAGNOSIS CHART

Display No.	Item of input signal	Parts name
0	Temperature of inside air temperature sensor (foot)	In-vehicle sensor (foot)
1	Temperature of in-vehicle sensor (head)	In-vehicle sensor (head)
2	Temperature of floor outlet	Floor duct temperature sensor
3	Temperature of ventilator outlet	Ventilator duct temperature sensor
4	Temperature of defroster outlet	Defroster duct temperature sensor
5	Water temperature SW, display ON-OFF	Water temperature SW.
6	Sunload	Sunload sensor
7	Width of objective temperature	Set temp. adjuster
8	Position of A/M door 2	P.B.R. 2
9	Position of A/M door 1	P.B.R. 1
10~ 15	No meaning	No meaning

Note: This chart is used in conjunction with the readings that are obtained from the display function within the control head assembly.

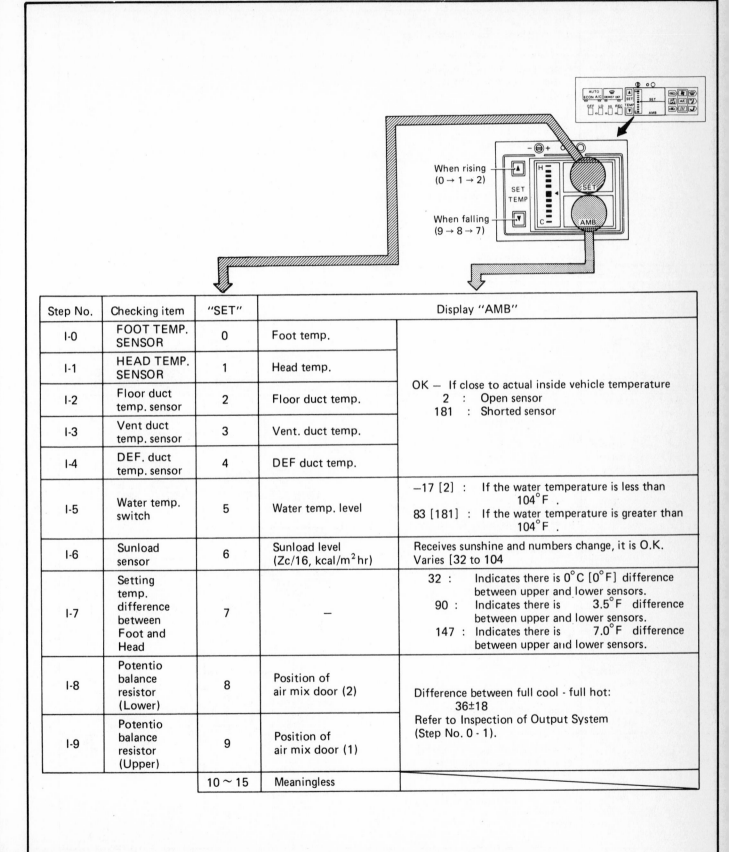

Step No.	Checking item	"SET"	Display "AMB"	

I-0	FOOT TEMP. SENSOR	0	Foot temp.	OK — If close to actual inside vehicle temperature
				    2 : Open sensor
				    181 : Shorted sensor

I-1	HEAD TEMP. SENSOR	1	Head temp.	
I-2	Floor duct temp. sensor	2	Floor duct temp.	
I-3	Vent duct temp. sensor	3	Vent. duct temp.	
I-4	DEF. duct temp. sensor	4	DEF duct temp.	
I-5	Water temp. switch	5	Water temp. level	−17 [2] : If the water temperature is less than 104°F. 83 [181] : If the water temperature is greater than 104°F.
I-6	Sunload sensor	6	Sunload level ($Zc/16$, kcal/m^{2}hr)	Receives sunshine and numbers change, it is O.K. Varies [32 to 104
I-7	Setting temp. difference between Foot and Head	7	—	32 : Indicates there is 0°C [0°F] difference between upper and lower sensors. 90 : Indicates there is 3.5°F difference between upper and lower sensors. 147 : Indicates there is 7.0°F difference between upper and lower sensors.
I-8	Potentio balance resistor (Lower)	8	Position of air mix door (2)	Difference between full cool - full hot: 36±18 Refer to Inspection of Output System (Step No. 0 - 1).
I-9	Potentio balance resistor (Upper)	9	Position of air mix door (1)	
		10 ~ 15	Meaningless	

Display Imput analyzation information-300ZX with automatic temperature control A/C (© Nissan Motor Co.)

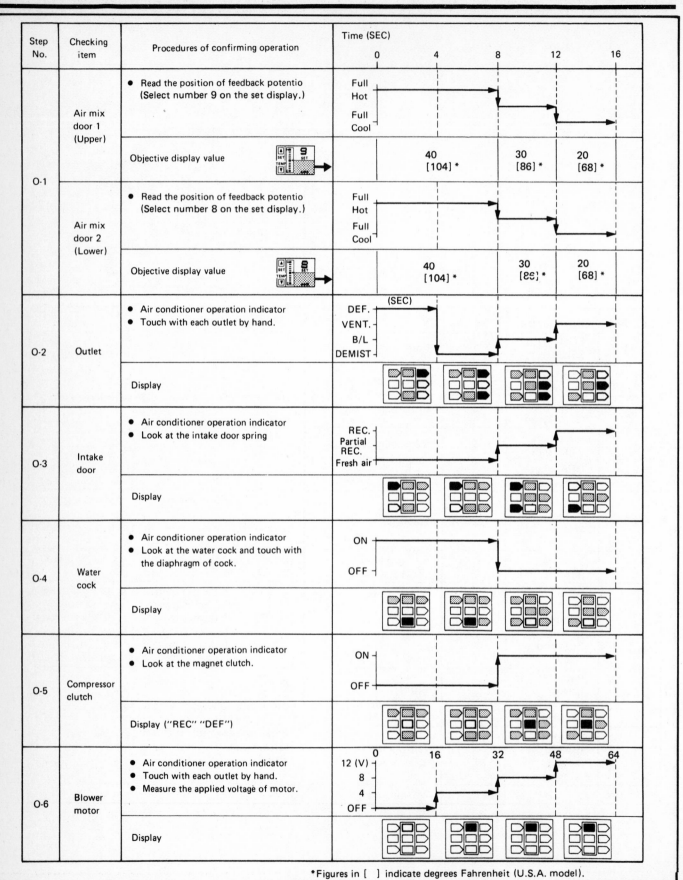

*Figures in [ ] indicate degrees Fahrenheit (U.S.A. model).

Display output analyzation information-300ZX with automatic temperature control A/C (© Nissan Motor Co.)

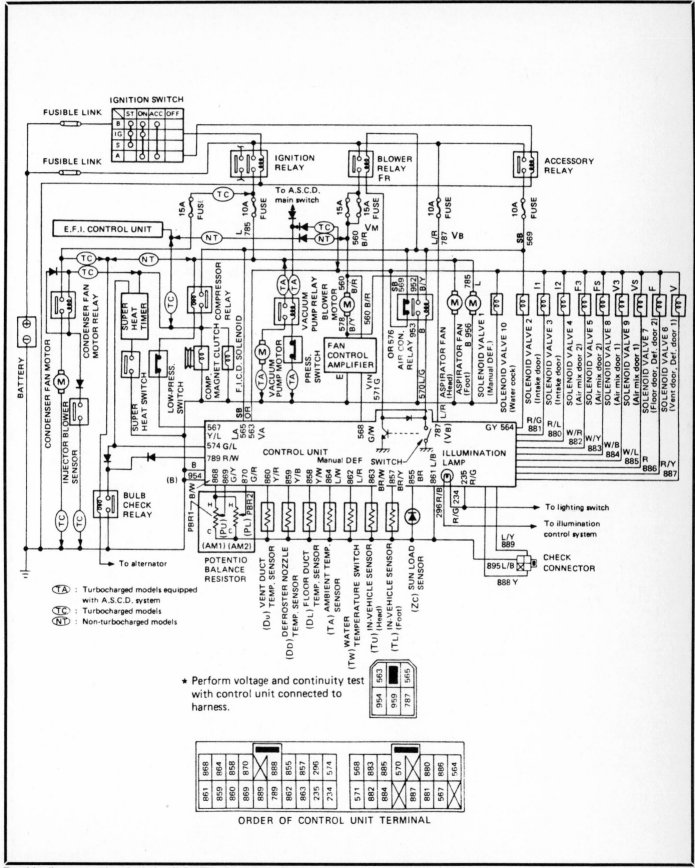

★ Perform voltage and continuity test with control unit connected to harness.

(TA) : Turbocharged models equipped with A.S.C.D. system
(TC) : Turbocharged models
(NT) : Non-turbocharged models

ORDER OF CONTROL UNIT TERMINAL

Trouble diagnoses electrical circuit-300ZX with automatic temperature control (© Nissan Motor Co.)

407

AUTO A/C SYSTEM DIAGNOSIS

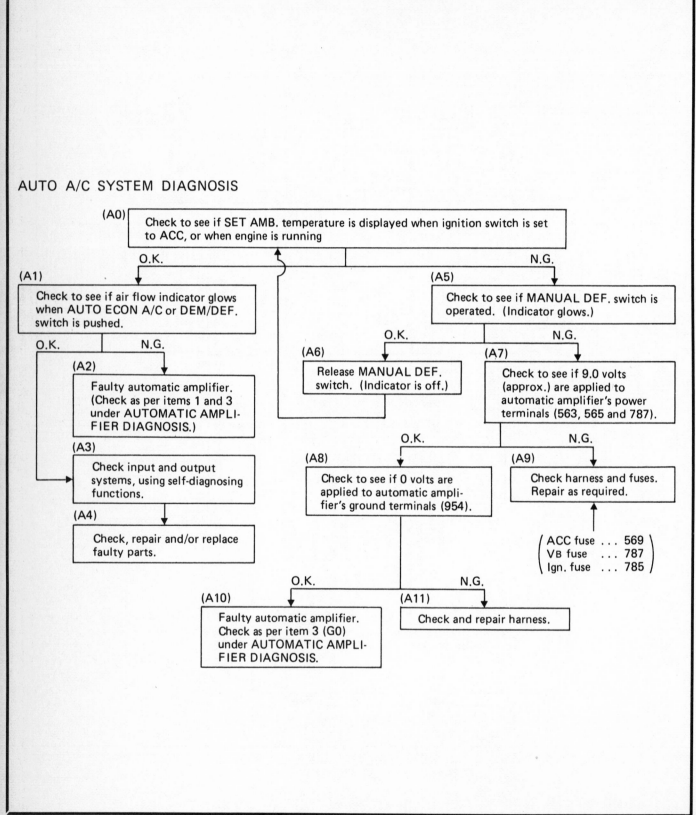

Trouble Shooting the A.T.C. System (© Nissan Motor Co.)

INPUT SYSTEM DIAGNOSIS

Number: Canada model [U.S.A. model]

★Numbers displayed on indicators.
When the indicator at I-0 thru I-4
shows only −17 [1], check line
861 (sensor ground = 0 V).

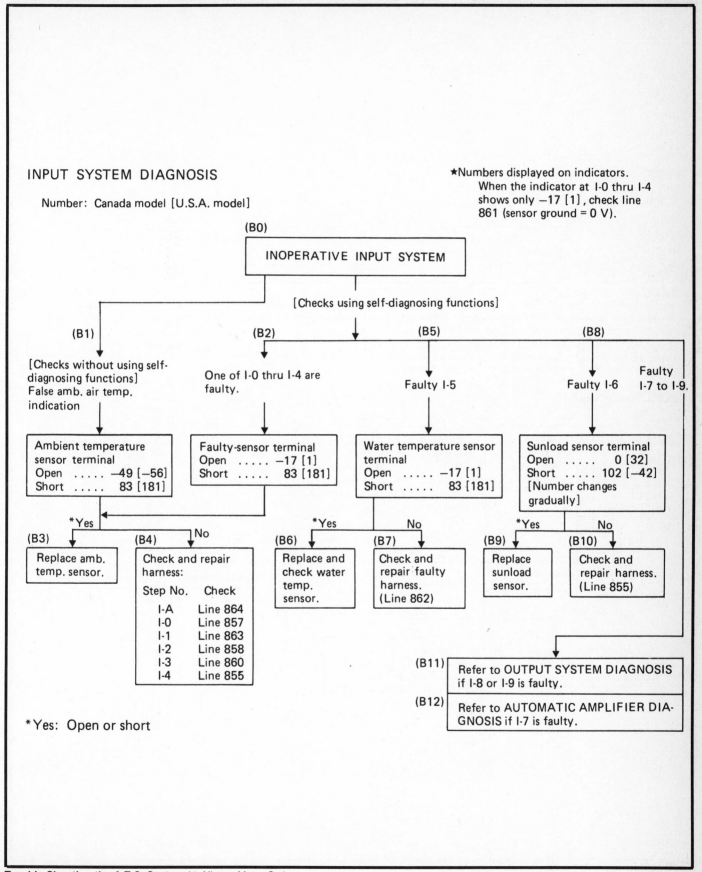

(B0)

INOPERATIVE INPUT SYSTEM

[Checks using self-diagnosing functions]

(B1)

[Checks without using self-diagnosing functions]
False amb. air temp. indication

(B2)
One of I-0 thru I-4 are faulty.

(B5)
Faulty I-5

(B8)
Faulty I-7 to I-9.

Faulty I-6

Ambient temperature sensor terminal
Open ..... −49 [−56]
Short ..... 83 [181]

Faulty-sensor terminal
Open ..... −17 [1]
Short ..... 83 [181]

Water temperature sensor terminal
Open ..... −17 [1]
Short ..... 83 [181]

Sunload sensor terminal
Open ..... 0 [32]
Short ..... 102 [−42]
[Number changes gradually]

*Yes

(B3)
Replace amb. temp. sensor.

(B4)
Check and repair harness:

Step No.	Check
I-A	Line 864
I-0	Line 857
I-1	Line 863
I-2	Line 858
I-3	Line 860
I-4	Line 855

No

*Yes

(B6)
Replace and check water temp. sensor.

No

(B7)
Check and repair faulty harness. (Line 862)

*Yes

(B9)
Replace sunload sensor.

No

(B10)
Check and repair harness. (Line 855)

(B11)
Refer to OUTPUT SYSTEM DIAGNOSIS if I-8 or I-9 is faulty.

(B12)
Refer to AUTOMATIC AMPLIFIER DIAGNOSIS if I-7 is faulty.

*Yes: Open or short

Trouble Shooting the A.T.C. System (© Nissan Motor Co.)

OUTPUT SYSTEM DIAGNOSIS

1) Inoperative air mix door

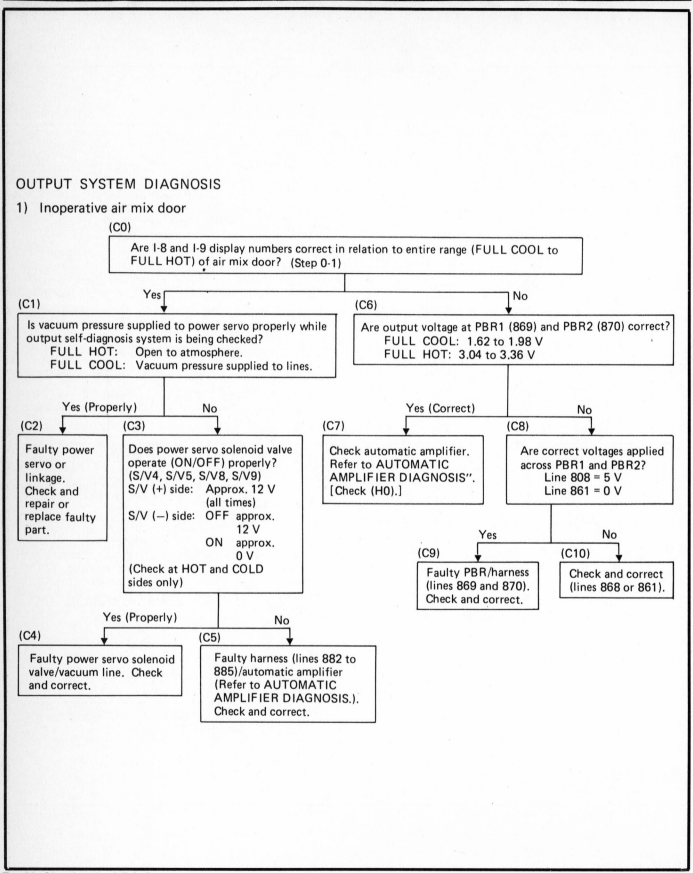

(C0) Are I-8 and I-9 display numbers correct in relation to entire range (FULL COOL to FULL HOT) of air mix door? (Step 0-1)

Yes →

(C1) Is vacuum pressure supplied to power servo properly while output self-diagnosis system is being checked?
FULL HOT: Open to atmosphere.
FULL COOL: Vacuum pressure supplied to lines.

No →

(C6) Are output voltage at PBR1 (869) and PBR2 (870) correct?
FULL COOL: 1.62 to 1.98 V
FULL HOT: 3.04 to 3.36 V

Yes (Properly) →

(C2) Faulty power servo or linkage. Check and repair or replace faulty part.

No →

(C3) Does power servo solenoid valve operate (ON/OFF) properly? (S/V4, S/V5, S/V8, S/V9)
S/V (+) side: Approx. 12 V (all times)
S/V (−) side: OFF approx. 12 V
ON approx. 0 V
(Check at HOT and COLD sides only)

Yes (Correct) →

(C7) Check automatic amplifier. Refer to AUTOMATIC AMPLIFIER DIAGNOSIS". [Check (H0).]

No →

(C8) Are correct voltages applied across PBR1 and PBR2?
Line 808 = 5 V
Line 861 = 0 V

Yes →

(C9) Faulty PBR/harness (lines 869 and 870). Check and correct.

No →

(C10) Check and correct (lines 868 or 861).

Yes (Properly) →

(C4) Faulty power servo solenoid valve/vacuum line. Check and correct.

No →

(C5) Faulty harness (lines 882 to 885)/automatic amplifier (Refer to AUTOMATIC AMPLIFIER DIAGNOSIS.). Check and correct.

Trouble Shooting the A.T.C. System (© Nissan Motor Co.)

2) Doors, water cock and compressor diagnosis

While checking output system, check solenoid valves, relays, vacuum pressure, etc., using the following tables as a guide.

Normal solenoid valve and relay operation
   Positive (+) side: Approx. 12 V (Constant)
   Negative (−) side: OFF (approx. 12 V)
                        ON   (0 volts)

(K1)

Outlet	S/V6 (887)	S/V7 (886)	Actuator		
			DEF. door (Ad)	VENT. door (Av)	Floor door and DEF. door 2 (Af)
DEF.	OFF	OFF	Atmosphere	←	←
VENT.	ON	OFF	Vacuum pressure	←	Atmosphere
B/L	ON	ON	Vacuum pressure	←	Vacuum pressure
HEAT	OFF	ON	Atmosphere	←	Vacuum pressure

(K2)

Inlet	S/V3 (880)	S/V2 (881)	Double action actuator (AI)
Inside air	ON	ON	Vacuum pressure (at both 1st and 2nd position)
Inside-outside air	ON	OFF	Vacuum pressure (only at 1st position)
Outside air	OFF	OFF	Atmosphere

(K3)

	S/V10 (564)	W/C (AW) actuator
Hot water closed	OFF	Atmosphere
Hot water opened	ON	Vacuum pressure

(K4)

	Compressor relay (567)
Compressor ON	ON
Compressor OFF	OFF

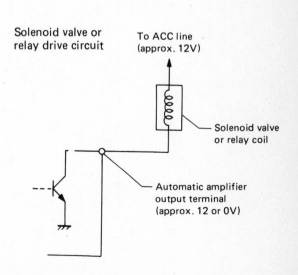

Solenoid valve or relay drive circuit

To ACC line (approx. 12V)

Solenoid valve or relay coil

Automatic amplifier output terminal (approx. 12 or 0V)

Trouble Shooting the A.T.C. System (© Nissan Motor Co.)

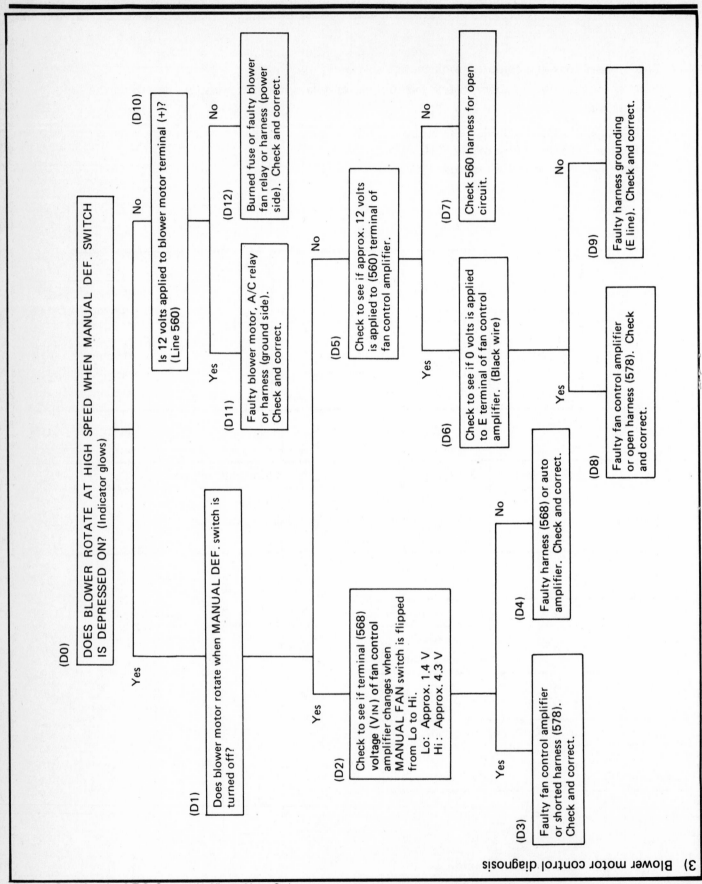

(D0)

DOES BLOWER ROTATE AT HIGH SPEED WHEN MANUAL DEF. SWITCH IS DEPRESSED ON? (Indicator glows)

Yes

(D1) Does blower motor rotate when MANUAL DEF. switch is turned off?

No

(D10) Is 12 volts applied to blower motor terminal (+)? (Line 560)

No

(D12) Burned fuse or faulty blower fan relay or harness (power side). Check and correct.

Yes

(D11) Faulty blower motor, A/C relay or harness (ground side). Check and correct.

Yes

(D2) Check to see if terminal (568) voltage (V_{IN}) of fan control amplifier changes when MANUAL FAN switch is flipped from Lo to Hi.
Lo: Approx. 1.4 V
Hi: Approx. 4.3 V

Yes

(D3) Faulty fan control amplifier or shorted harness (578). Check and correct.

No

(D4) Faulty harness (568) or auto amplifier. Check and correct.

(D5) Check to see if approx. 12 volts is applied to (560) terminal of fan control amplifier.

No

(D7) Check 560 harness for open circuit.

Yes

(D6) Check to see if 0 volts is applied to E terminal of fan control amplifier. (Black wire)

Yes

(D8) Faulty fan control amplifier or open harness (578). Check and correct.

No

(D9) Faulty harness grounding (E line). Check and correct.

3) Blower motor control diagnosis

Trouble Shooting the A.T.C. System (© Nissan Motor Co.)

AUTOMATIC AMPLIFIER DIAGNOSIS

1) LCD (Liquid Crystal Display) or LED (Light Emitting Diode) does not glow.

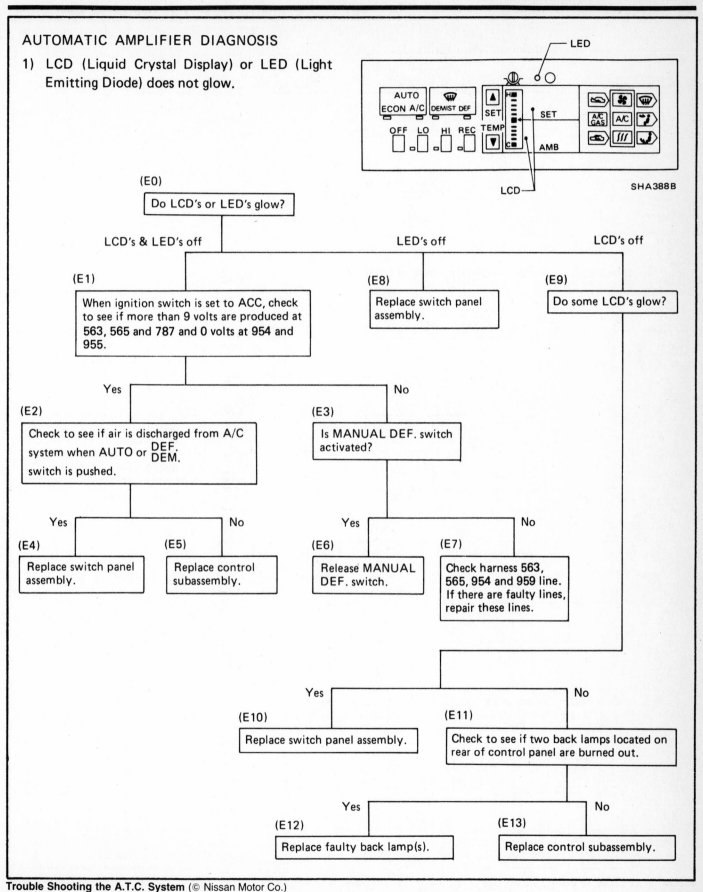

SHA388B

(E0) Do LCD's or LED's glow?

LCD's & LED's off

(E1) When ignition switch is set to ACC, check to see if more than 9 volts are produced at 563, 565 and 787 and 0 volts at 954 and 955.

Yes → **(E2)** Check to see if air is discharged from A/C system when AUTO or DEF./DEM. switch is pushed.

Yes → **(E4)** Replace switch panel assembly.

No → **(E5)** Replace control subassembly.

No → **(E3)** Is MANUAL DEF. switch activated?

Yes → **(E6)** Release MANUAL DEF. switch.

No → **(E7)** Check harness 563, 565, 954 and 959 line. If there are faulty lines, repair these lines.

LED's off → **(E8)** Replace switch panel assembly.

LCD's off → **(E9)** Do some LCD's glow?

Yes → **(E10)** Replace switch panel assembly.

No → **(E11)** Check to see if two back lamps located on rear of control panel are burned out.

Yes → **(E12)** Replace faulty back lamp(s).

No → **(E13)** Replace control subassembly.

Trouble Shooting the A.T.C. System (© Nissan Motor Co.)

2) Operating (Buzzing) Sound is not Emitted.

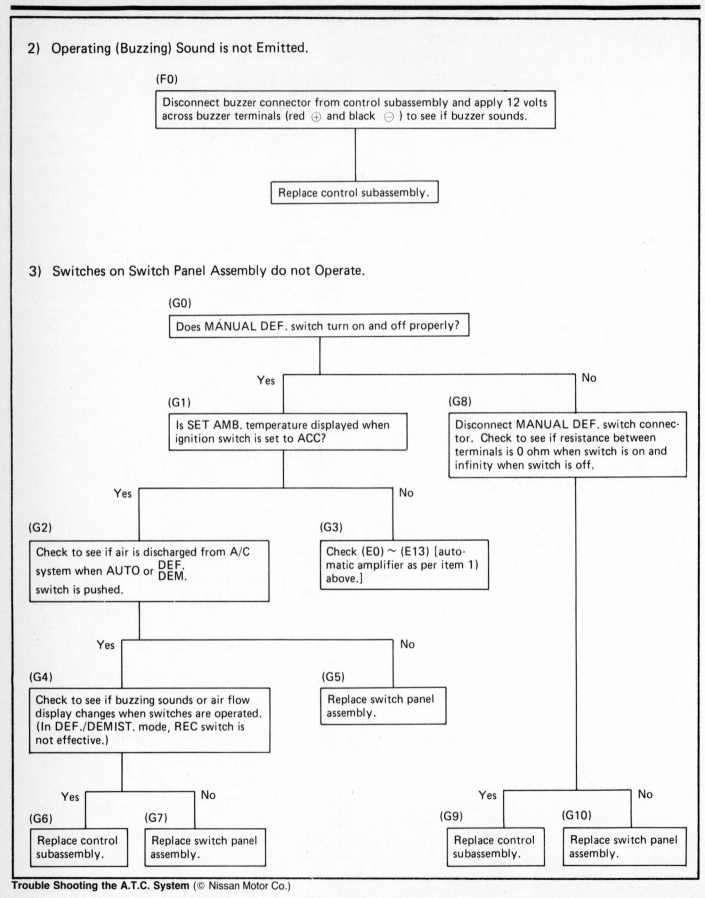

(F0)

Disconnect buzzer connector from control subassembly and apply 12 volts across buzzer terminals (red ⊕ and black ⊖) to see if buzzer sounds.

Replace control subassembly.

3) Switches on Switch Panel Assembly do not Operate.

(G0)

Does MANUAL DEF. switch turn on and off properly?

Yes / No

(G1)

Is SET AMB. temperature displayed when ignition switch is set to ACC?

(G8)

Disconnect MANUAL DEF. switch connector. Check to see if resistance between terminals is 0 ohm when switch is on and infinity when switch is off.

Yes / No

(G2)

Check to see if air is discharged from A/C system when AUTO or DEF./DEM. switch is pushed.

(G3)

Check (E0) ~ (E13) [automatic amplifier as per item 1) above.]

Yes / No

(G4)

Check to see if buzzing sounds or air flow display changes when switches are operated. (In DEF./DEMIST. mode, REC switch is not effective.)

(G5)

Replace switch panel assembly.

Yes / No

(G6)

Replace control subassembly.

(G7)

Replace switch panel assembly.

Yes / No

(G9)

Replace control subassembly.

(G10)

Replace switch panel assembly.

Trouble Shooting the A.T.C. System (© Nissan Motor Co.)

4) Erroneous Display during Inspection of the Input System

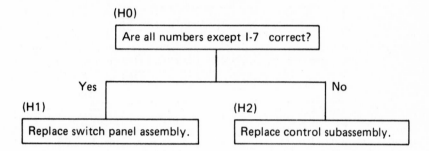

(H0) Are all numbers except I-7 correct?

Yes — (H1) Replace switch panel assembly.

No — (H2) Replace control subassembly.

5) Erroneous Operation during Inspection of the Output System

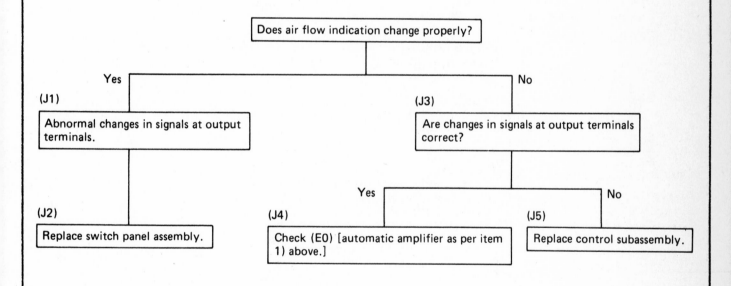

Does air flow indication change properly?

Yes — (J1) Abnormal changes in signals at output terminals.

(J2) Replace switch panel assembly.

No — (J3) Are changes in signals at output terminals correct?

Yes — (J4) Check (E0) [automatic amplifier as per item 1) above.]

No — (J5) Replace control subassembly.

6) MANUAL DEF. indicator does not come on.
   Replace switch panel assembly.
7) Escutcheon lamp does not come on.
   Check for burned-out lamp located at rear of switch panel assembly.

Trouble Shooting the A.T.C. System (© Nissan Motor Co.)

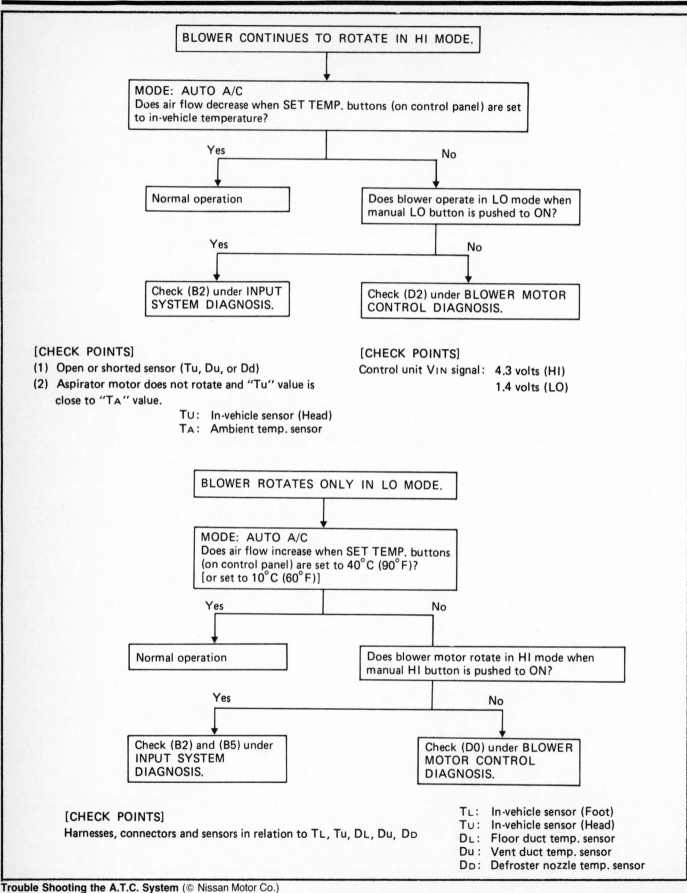

BLOWER CONTINUES TO ROTATE IN HI MODE.

MODE: AUTO A/C
Does air flow decrease when SET TEMP. buttons (on control panel) are set to in-vehicle temperature?

Yes — Normal operation

No — Does blower operate in LO mode when manual LO button is pushed to ON?

Yes — Check (B2) under INPUT SYSTEM DIAGNOSIS.

No — Check (D2) under BLOWER MOTOR CONTROL DIAGNOSIS.

[CHECK POINTS]
(1) Open or shorted sensor (Tu, Du, or Dd)
(2) Aspirator motor does not rotate and "Tu" value is close to "TA" value.

Tu: In-vehicle sensor (Head)
TA: Ambient temp. sensor

[CHECK POINTS]
Control unit VIN signal: 4.3 volts (HI)
1.4 volts (LO)

BLOWER ROTATES ONLY IN LO MODE.

MODE: AUTO A/C
Does air flow increase when SET TEMP. buttons (on control panel) are set to 40°C (90°F)?
[or set to 10°C (60°F)]

Yes — Normal operation

No — Does blower motor rotate in HI mode when manual HI button is pushed to ON?

Yes — Check (B2) and (B5) under INPUT SYSTEM DIAGNOSIS.

No — Check (D0) under BLOWER MOTOR CONTROL DIAGNOSIS.

[CHECK POINTS]
Harnesses, connectors and sensors in relation to TL, Tu, DL, Du, DD

TL: In-vehicle sensor (Foot)
Tu: In-vehicle sensor (Head)
DL: Floor duct temp. sensor
Du: Vent duct temp. sensor
DD: Defroster nozzle temp. sensor

Trouble Shooting the A.T.C. System (© Nissan Motor Co.)

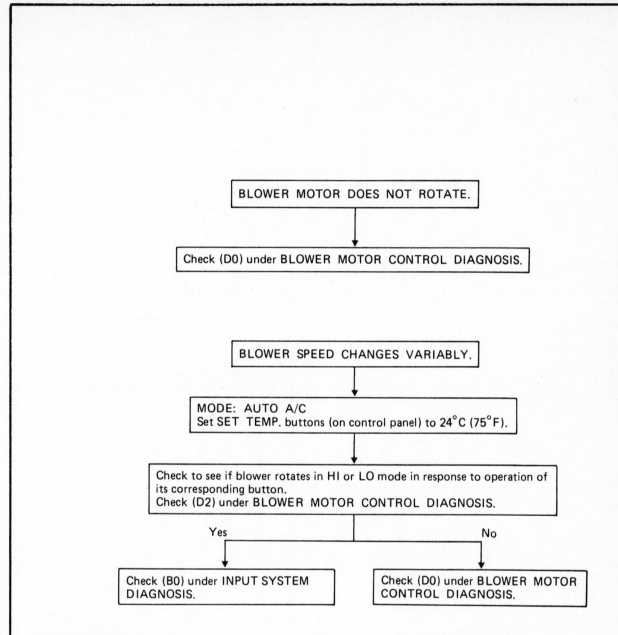

```
┌─────────────────────────────────────┐
│  BLOWER MOTOR DOES NOT ROTATE.       │
└─────────────────────────────────────┘
                    │
                    ▼
┌─────────────────────────────────────────────────┐
│  Check (D0) under BLOWER MOTOR CONTROL DIAGNOSIS. │
└─────────────────────────────────────────────────┘


┌─────────────────────────────────────┐
│  BLOWER SPEED CHANGES VARIABLY.      │
└─────────────────────────────────────┘
                    │
                    ▼
┌─────────────────────────────────────────────────┐
│  MODE: AUTO A/C                                   │
│  Set SET TEMP. buttons (on control panel) to 24°C (75°F). │
└─────────────────────────────────────────────────┘
                    │
                    ▼
┌─────────────────────────────────────────────────┐
│  Check to see if blower rotates in HI or LO mode in response to operation of │
│  its corresponding button.                        │
│  Check (D2) under BLOWER MOTOR CONTROL DIAGNOSIS. │
└─────────────────────────────────────────────────┘
         Yes                              No
          │                                │
          ▼                                ▼
┌──────────────────────────┐   ┌──────────────────────────┐
│  Check (B0) under INPUT   │   │  Check (D0) under BLOWER  │
│  SYSTEM DIAGNOSIS.        │   │  MOTOR CONTROL DIAGNOSIS. │
└──────────────────────────┘   └──────────────────────────┘
```

[CHECK POINTS]
(1) Poor or faulty connection of In-vehicle sensor (Foot), In-vehicle sensor (Head), Floor duct temp. sensor, Vent duct temp. sensor, Defroster nozzle duct temp. sensor, Ambient temp. sensor, Sunload sensor, Potentio Balance Resistor (AMl), Potentio Balance Resistor (AM2).
(2) Start-stop operation of aspirator motor and voltage measurements at sensors (Remove sensor assembly to gain access to sensors.)

Trouble Shooting the A.T.C. System (© Nissan Motor Co.)

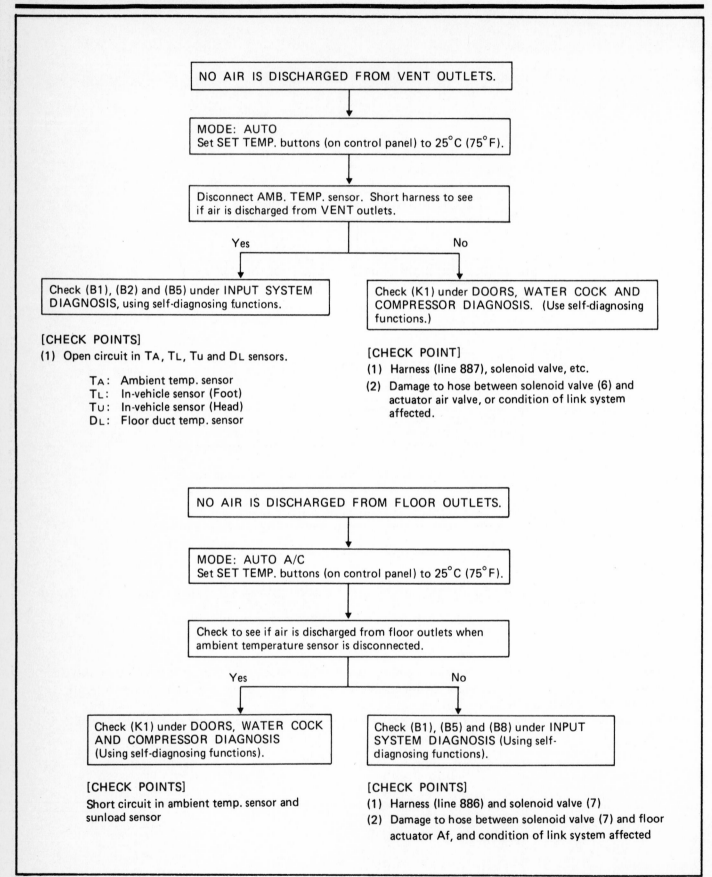

NO AIR IS DISCHARGED FROM VENT OUTLETS.

MODE: AUTO
Set SET TEMP. buttons (on control panel) to 25°C (75°F).

Disconnect AMB. TEMP. sensor. Short harness to see if air is discharged from VENT outlets.

Yes

No

Check (B1), (B2) and (B5) under INPUT SYSTEM DIAGNOSIS, using self-diagnosing functions.

Check (K1) under DOORS, WATER COCK AND COMPRESSOR DIAGNOSIS. (Use self-diagnosing functions.)

[CHECK POINTS]
(1) Open circuit in TA, TL, Tu and DL sensors.

- TA: Ambient temp. sensor
- TL: In-vehicle sensor (Foot)
- Tu: In-vehicle sensor (Head)
- DL: Floor duct temp. sensor

[CHECK POINT]
(1) Harness (line 887), solenoid valve, etc.
(2) Damage to hose between solenoid valve (6) and actuator air valve, or condition of link system affected.

NO AIR IS DISCHARGED FROM FLOOR OUTLETS.

MODE: AUTO A/C
Set SET TEMP. buttons (on control panel) to 25°C (75°F).

Check to see if air is discharged from floor outlets when ambient temperature sensor is disconnected.

Yes

No

Check (K1) under DOORS, WATER COCK AND COMPRESSOR DIAGNOSIS (Using self-diagnosing functions).

Check (B1), (B5) and (B8) under INPUT SYSTEM DIAGNOSIS (Using self-diagnosing functions).

[CHECK POINTS]
Short circuit in ambient temp. sensor and sunload sensor

[CHECK POINTS]
(1) Harness (line 886) and solenoid valve (7)
(2) Damage to hose between solenoid valve (7) and floor actuator Af, and condition of link system affected

Trouble Shooting the A.T.C. System (© Nissan Motor Co.)

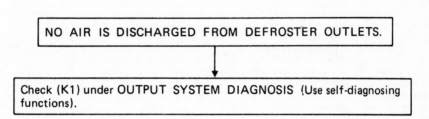

NO AIR IS DISCHARGED FROM DEFROSTER OUTLETS.

Check (K1) under OUTPUT SYSTEM DIAGNOSIS (Use self-diagnosing functions).

[CHECK POINTS]
(1) Harness (line 887) and solenoid valve 6
(2) Damaged hose/link between solenoid valve 6 and actuator Ad (DEF. door Actuator)

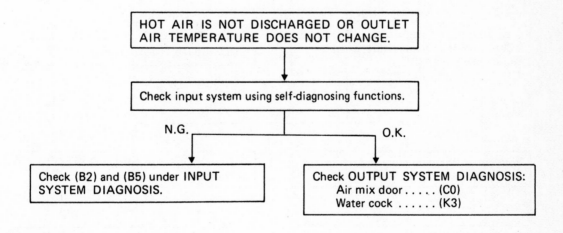

HOT AIR IS NOT DISCHARGED OR OUTLET AIR TEMPERATURE DOES NOT CHANGE.

Check input system using self-diagnosing functions.

N.G.

O.K.

Check (B2) and (B5) under INPUT SYSTEM DIAGNOSIS.

Check OUTPUT SYSTEM DIAGNOSIS:
Air mix door . . . . . (C0)
Water cock . . . . . . (K3)

Trouble Shooting the A.T.C. System (© Nissan Motor Co.)

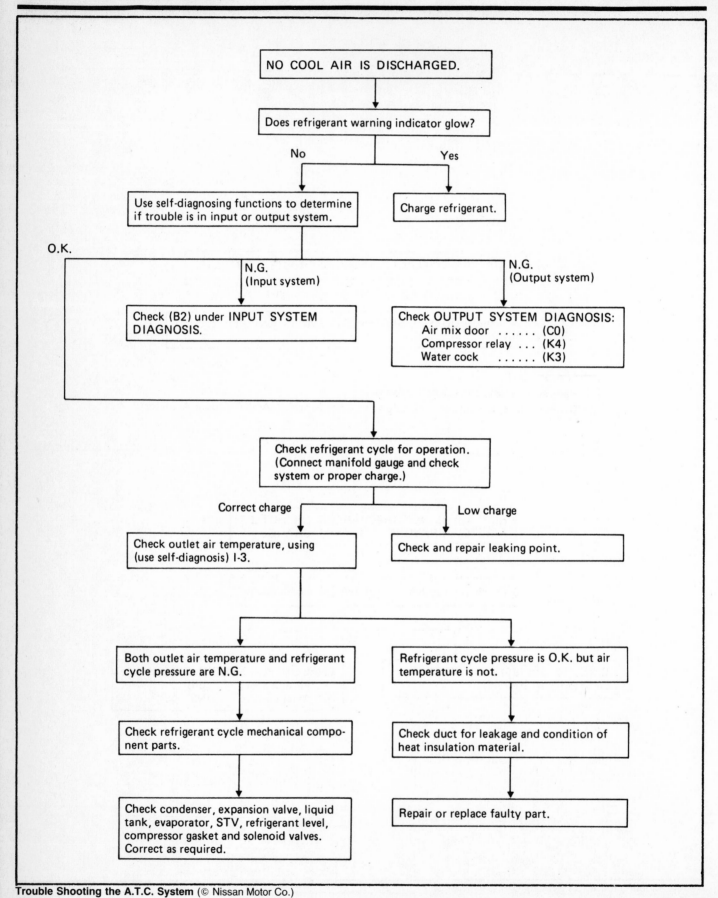

Trouble Shooting the A.T.C. System (© Nissan Motor Co.)

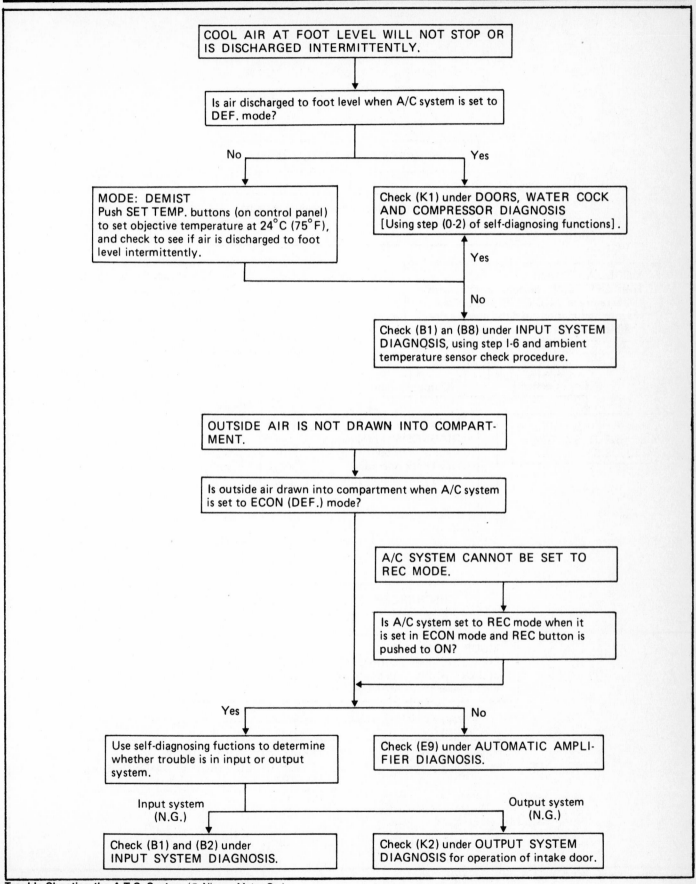

COOL AIR AT FOOT LEVEL WILL NOT STOP OR IS DISCHARGED INTERMITTENTLY.

Is air discharged to foot level when A/C system is set to DEF. mode?

No → **MODE: DEMIST**
Push SET TEMP. buttons (on control panel) to set objective temperature at 24°C (75°F), and check to see if air is discharged to foot level intermittently.

Yes → Check (K1) under DOORS, WATER COCK AND COMPRESSOR DIAGNOSIS [Using step (0-2) of self-diagnosing functions].

Yes

No → Check (B1) an (B8) under INPUT SYSTEM DIAGNOSIS, using step I-6 and ambient temperature sensor check procedure.

OUTSIDE AIR IS NOT DRAWN INTO COMPART-MENT.

Is outside air drawn into compartment when A/C system is set to ECON (DEF.) mode?

A/C SYSTEM CANNOT BE SET TO REC MODE.

Is A/C system set to REC mode when it is set in ECON mode and REC button is pushed to ON?

Yes → Use self-diagnosing fuctions to determine whether trouble is in input or output system.

No → Check (E9) under AUTOMATIC AMPLI-FIER DIAGNOSIS.

Input system (N.G.) → Check (B1) and (B2) under INPUT SYSTEM DIAGNOSIS.

Output system (N.G.) → Check (K2) under OUTPUT SYSTEM DIAGNOSIS for operation of intake door.

Trouble Shooting the A.T.C. System (© Nissan Motor Co.)

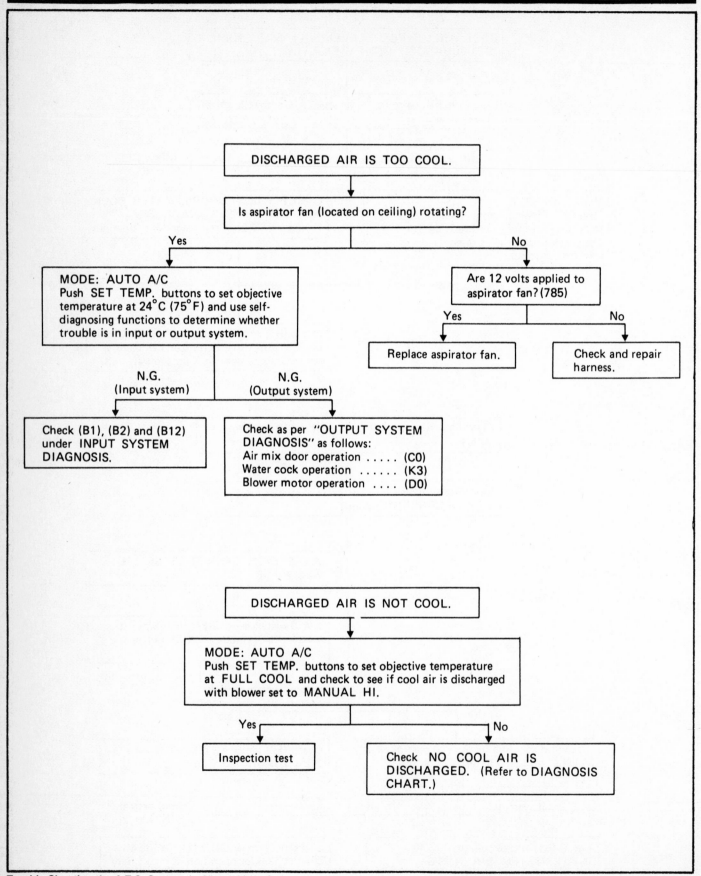

DISCHARGED AIR IS TOO COOL.

Is aspirator fan (located on ceiling) rotating?

Yes

No

MODE: AUTO A/C
Push SET TEMP. buttons to set objective temperature at 24°C (75°F) and use self-diagnosing functions to determine whether trouble is in input or output system.

Are 12 volts applied to aspirator fan? (785)

Yes

No

Replace aspirator fan.

Check and repair harness.

N.G.
(Input system)

N.G.
(Output system)

Check (B1), (B2) and (B12) under INPUT SYSTEM DIAGNOSIS.

Check as per "OUTPUT SYSTEM DIAGNOSIS" as follows:
Air mix door operation . . . . . (C0)
Water cock operation . . . . . . (K3)
Blower motor operation . . . . (D0)

DISCHARGED AIR IS NOT COOL.

MODE: AUTO A/C
Push SET TEMP. buttons to set objective temperature at FULL COOL and check to see if cool air is discharged with blower set to MANUAL HI.

Yes

No

Inspection test

Check NO COOL AIR IS DISCHARGED. (Refer to DIAGNOSIS CHART.)

Trouble Shooting the A.T.C. System (© Nissan Motor Co.)

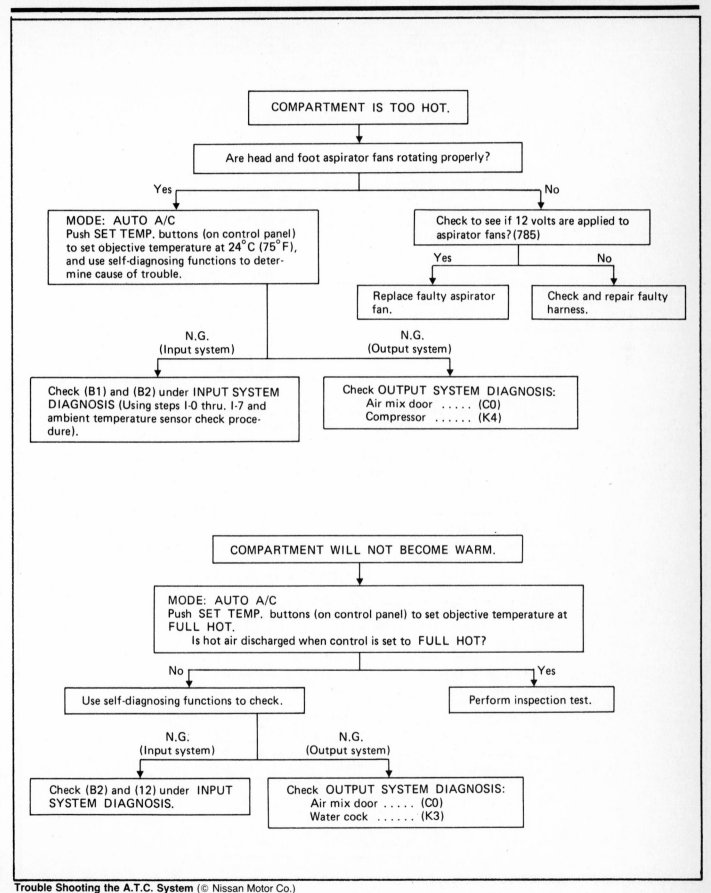

Trouble Shooting the A.T.C. System (© Nissan Motor Co.)

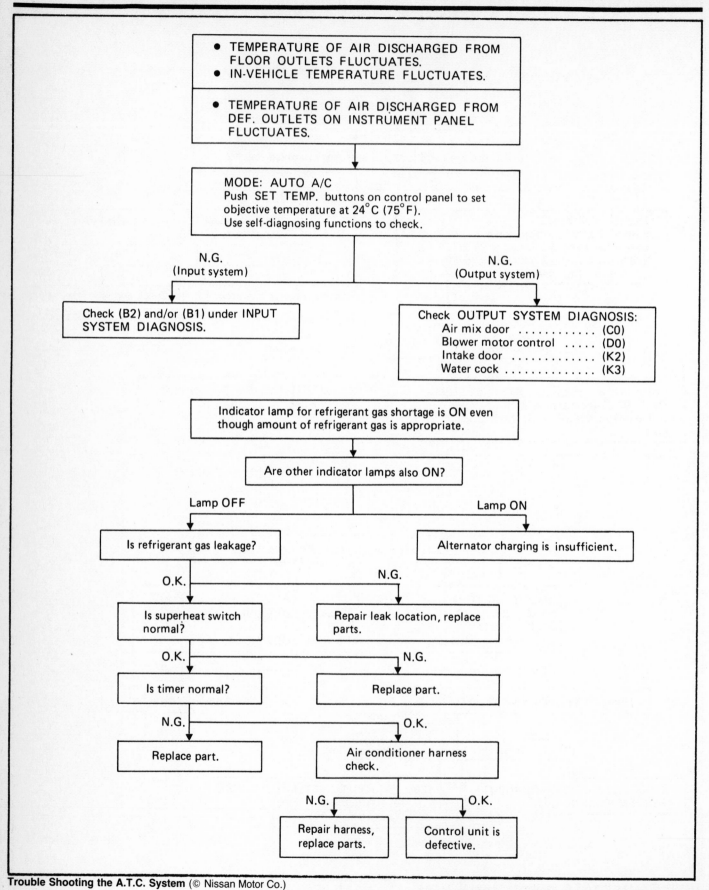

- TEMPERATURE OF AIR DISCHARGED FROM FLOOR OUTLETS FLUCTUATES.
- IN-VEHICLE TEMPERATURE FLUCTUATES.

- TEMPERATURE OF AIR DISCHARGED FROM DEF. OUTLETS ON INSTRUMENT PANEL FLUCTUATES.

MODE: AUTO A/C
Push SET TEMP. buttons on control panel to set objective temperature at 24°C (75°F).
Use self-diagnosing functions to check.

N.G.
(Input system)

N.G.
(Output system)

Check (B2) and/or (B1) under INPUT SYSTEM DIAGNOSIS.

Check OUTPUT SYSTEM DIAGNOSIS:
Air mix door .... (C0)
Blower motor control ..... (D0)
Intake door .... (K2)
Water cock .... (K3)

Indicator lamp for refrigerant gas shortage is ON even though amount of refrigerant gas is appropriate.

Are other indicator lamps also ON?

Lamp OFF

Lamp ON

Is refrigerant gas leakage?

Alternator charging is insufficient.

O.K.

N.G.

Is superheat switch normal?

Repair leak location, replace parts.

O.K.

N.G.

Is timer normal?

Replace part.

N.G.

O.K.

Replace part.

Air conditioner harness check.

N.G.

O.K.

Repair harness, replace parts.

Control unit is defective.

Trouble Shooting the A.T.C. System (© Nissan Motor Co.)

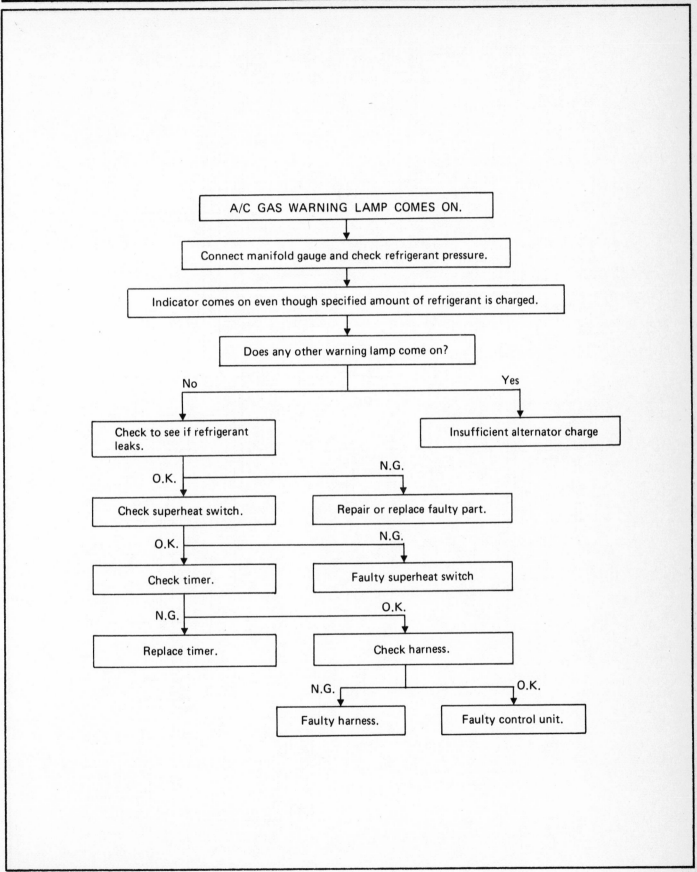

Trouble Shooting the A.T.C. System (© Nissan Motor Co.)

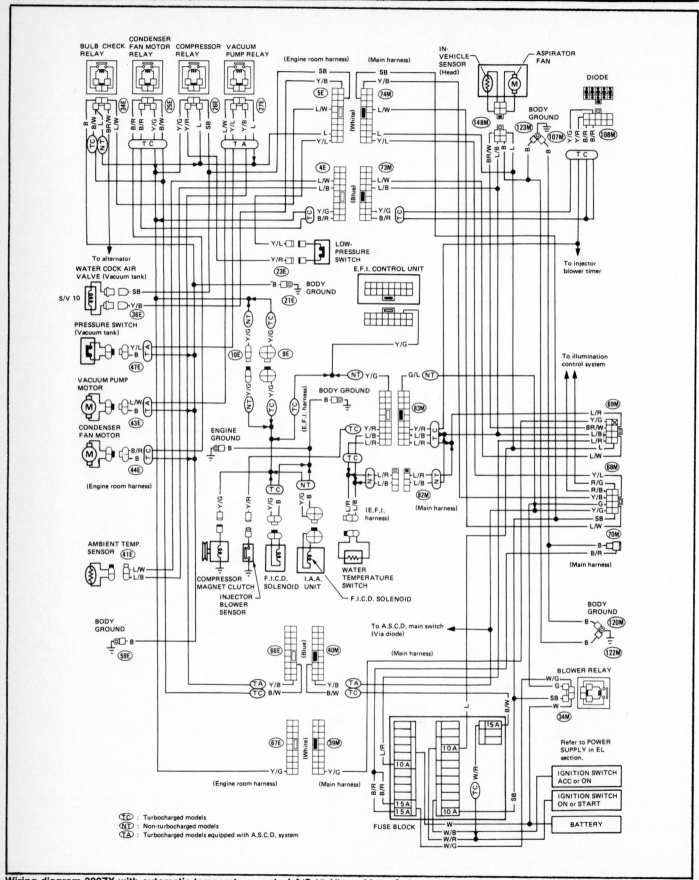

Wiring diagram-300ZX with automatic temperature control A/C (© Nissan Motor Co.)

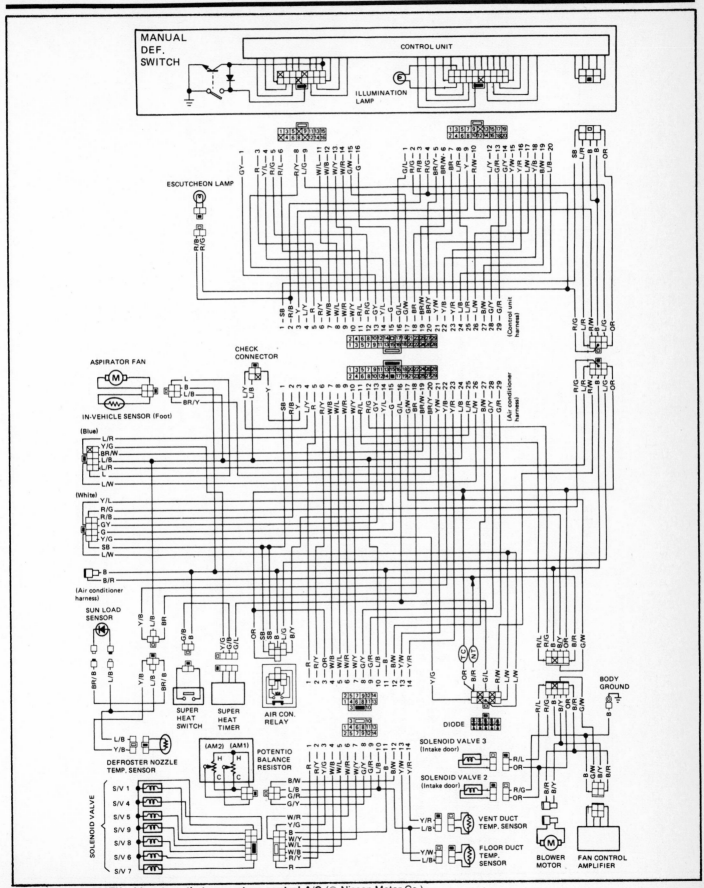

Wiring diagram-300ZX with automatic temperature control A/C (© Nissan Motor Co.)

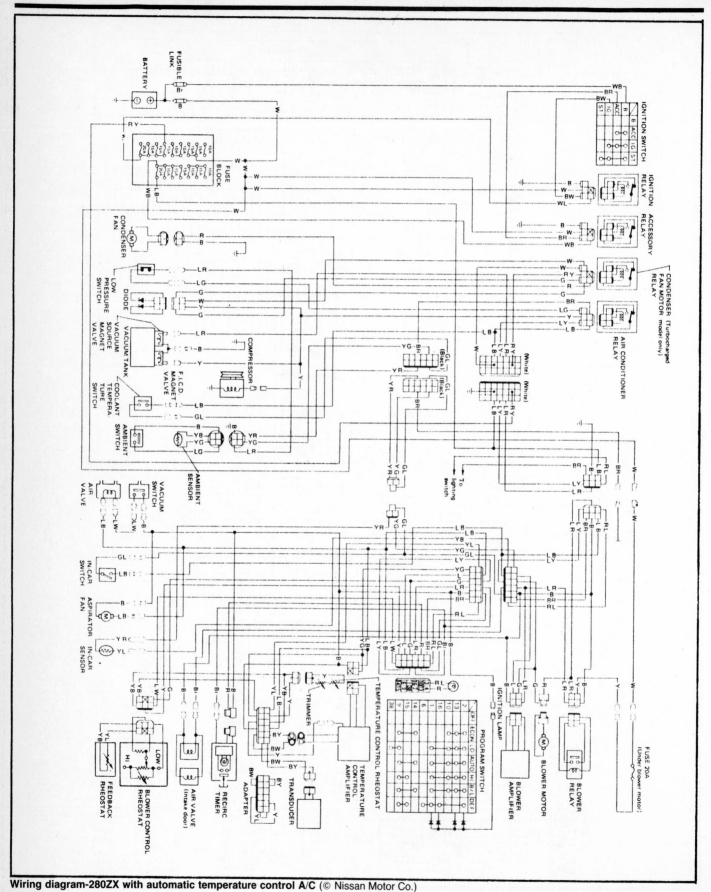

Wiring diagram-280ZX with automatic temperature control A/C (© Nissan Motor Co.)

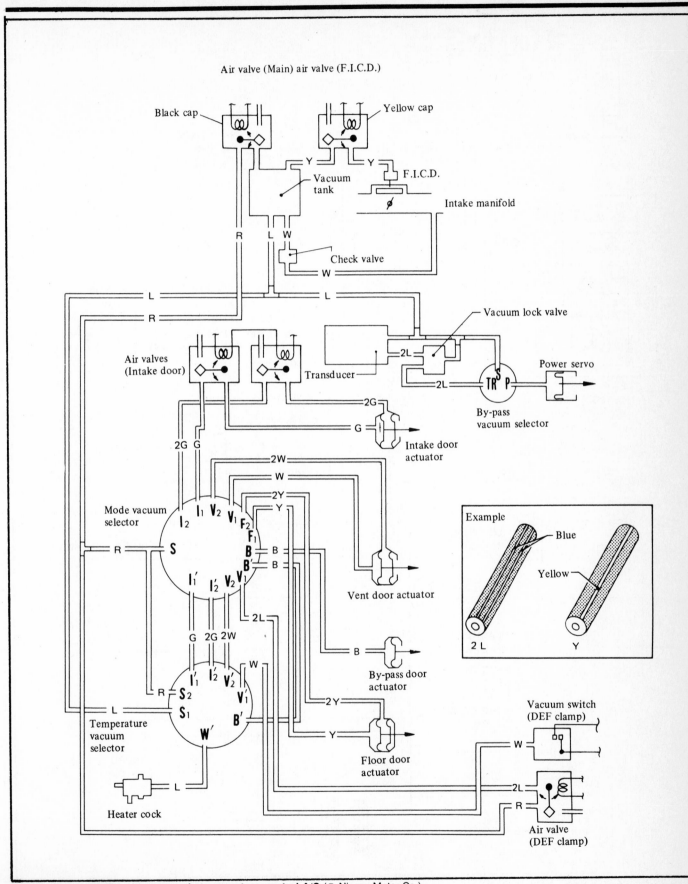

Air valve (Main) air valve (F.I.C.D.)

Black cap

Yellow cap

Vacuum tank

F.I.C.D.

Intake manifold

Check valve

Vacuum lock valve

Air valves (Intake door)

Transducer

Power servo

By-pass vacuum selector

Intake door actuator

Mode vacuum selector

Example

Blue

Yellow

2 L

Y

Vent door actuator

By-pass door actuator

Temperature vacuum selector

Floor door actuator

Vacuum switch (DEF clamp)

Heater cock

Air valve (DEF clamp)

Wiring diagram-280ZX with automatic temperature control A/C (© Nissan Motor Co.)

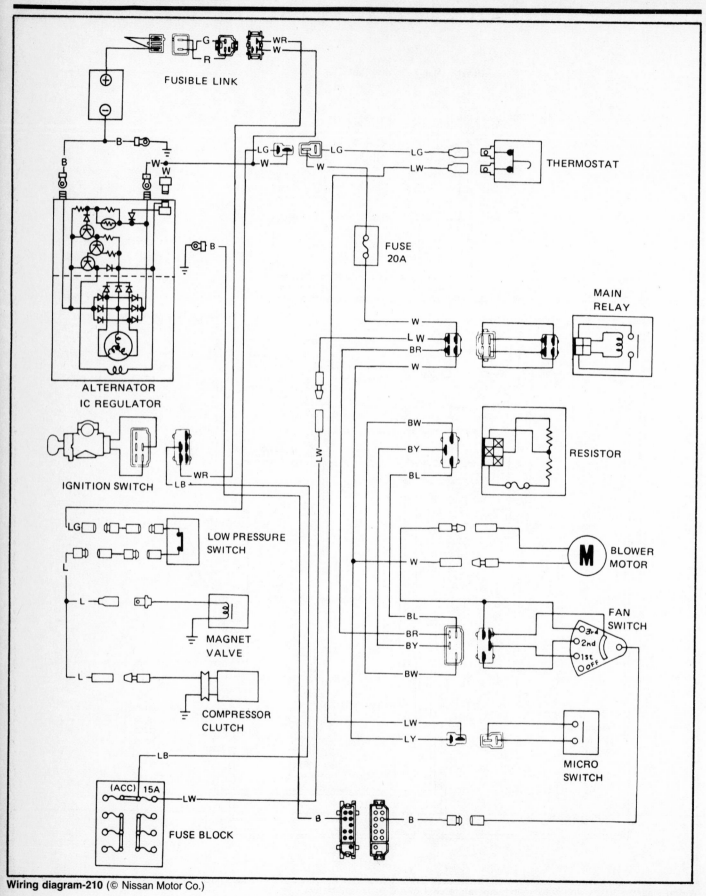

Wiring diagram-210 (© Nissan Motor Co.)

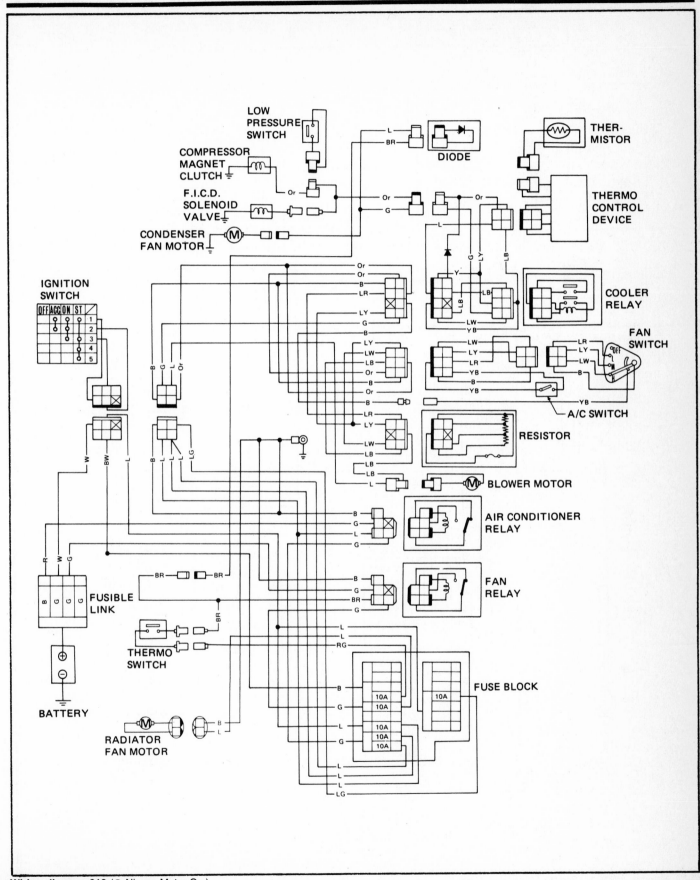

Wiring diagram-310 (© Nissan Motor Co.)

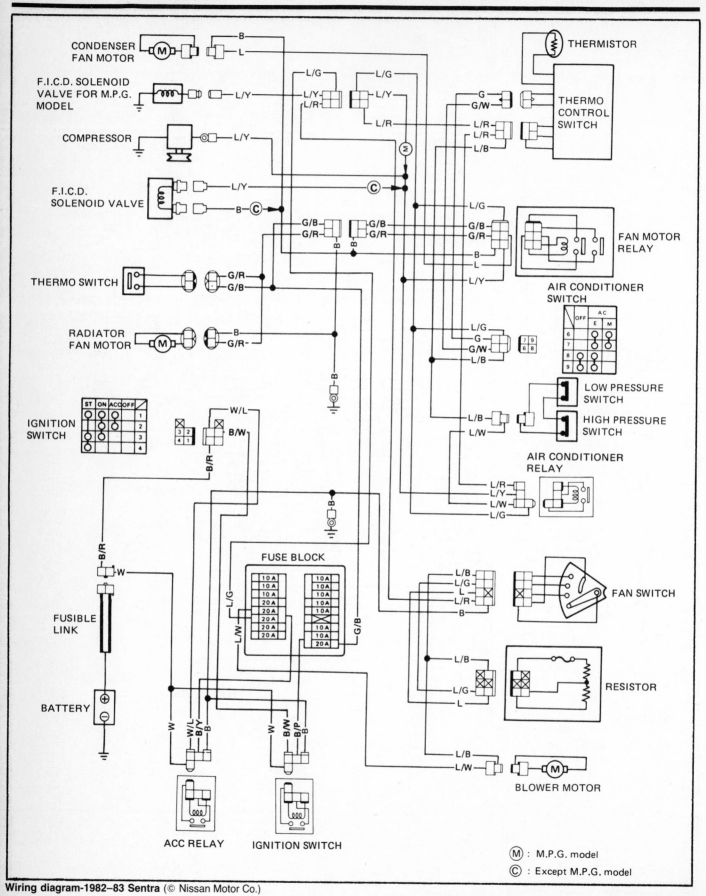

Wiring diagram-1982–83 Sentra (© Nissan Motor Co.)

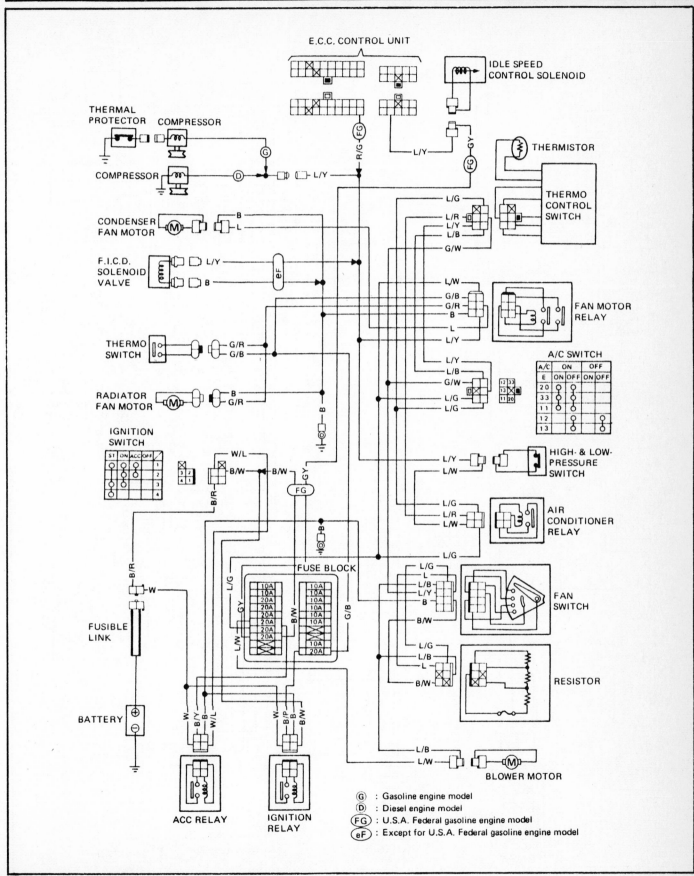

Wiring diagram-1984 and later-Sentra (© Nissan Motor Co.)

E.C.C. CONTROL UNIT

IDLE SPEED CONTROL SOLENOID

THERMAL PROTECTOR
COMPRESSOR
COMPRESSOR

THERMISTOR

THERMO CONTROL SWITCH

CONDENSER FAN MOTOR

F.I.C.D. SOLENOID VALVE

FAN MOTOR RELAY

THERMO SWITCH

RADIATOR FAN MOTOR

A/C	ON		OFF	
E	ON	OFF	ON	OFF
20				
33				
11				
12				
13				

A/C SWITCH

HIGH- & LOW-PRESSURE SWITCH

IGNITION SWITCH

	ST	ON	ACC	OFF
1				
2				
3				
4				

AIR CONDITIONER RELAY

FUSIBLE LINK

FUSE BLOCK

10A
10A
20A
20A
20A
20A
20A
20A
10A
20A

FAN SWITCH

RESISTOR

BATTERY

ACC RELAY

IGNITION RELAY

BLOWER MOTOR

G : Gasoline engine model
D : Diesel engine model
FG : U.S.A. Federal gasoline engine model
eF : Except for U.S.A. Federal gasoline engine model

433

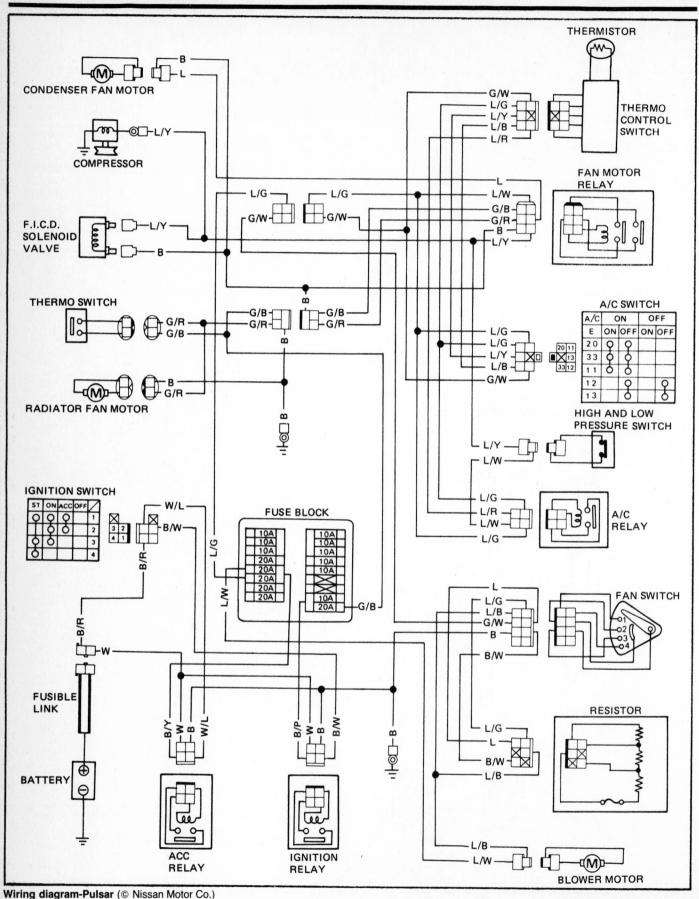

Wiring diagram-Pulsar (© Nissan Motor Co.)

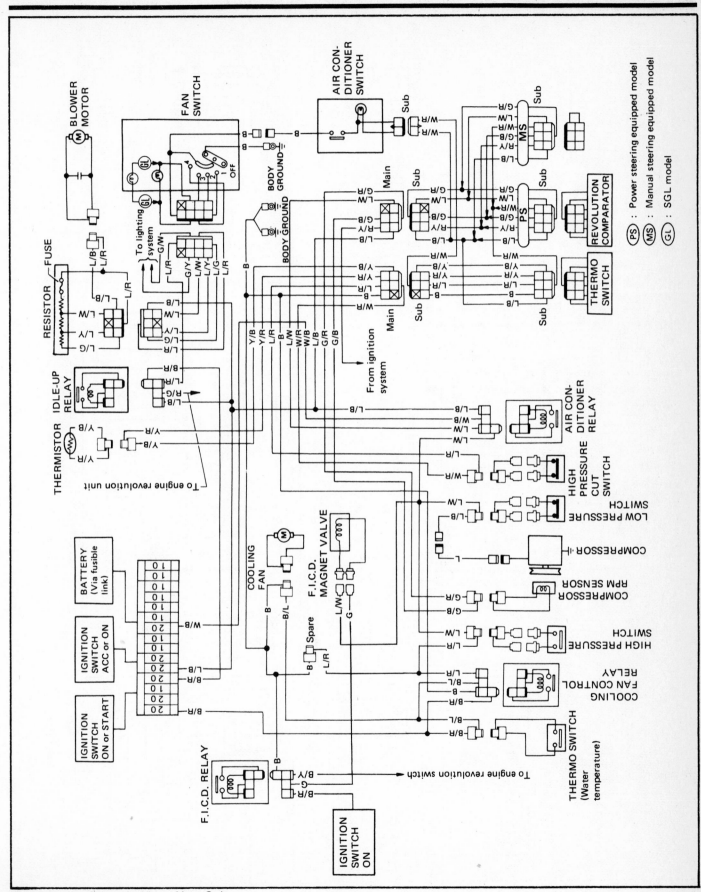

Wiring diagram-Stanza (© Nissan Motor Co.)

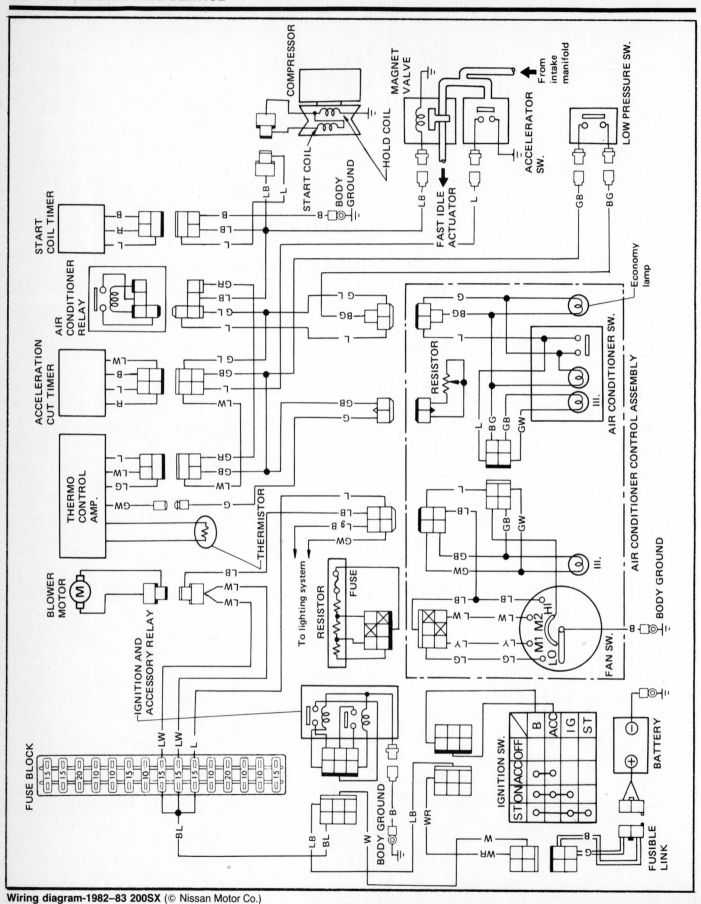

Wiring diagram-1982–83 200SX (© Nissan Motor Co.)

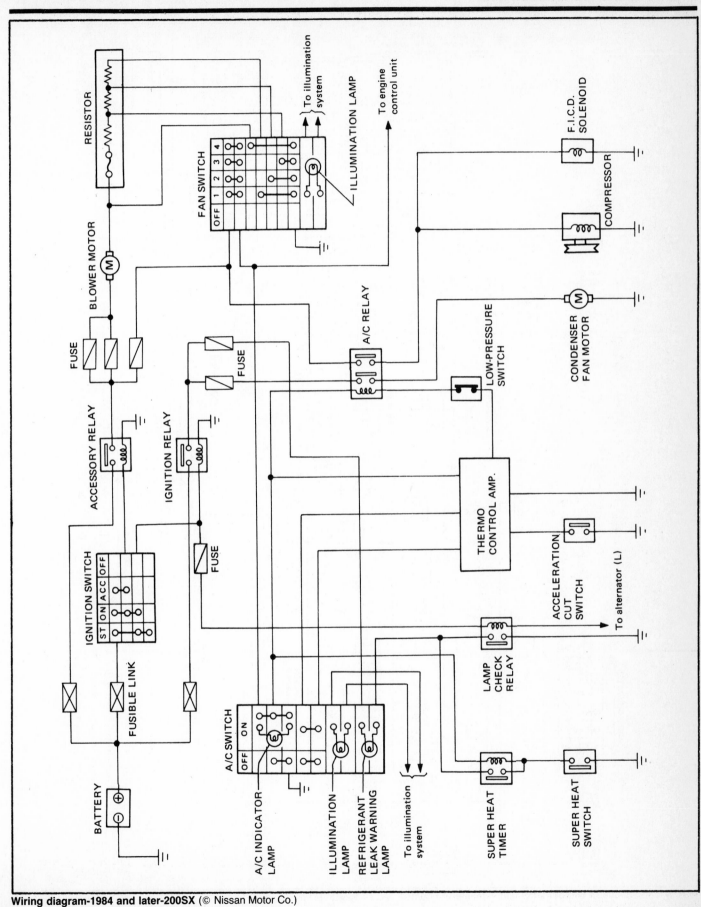

Wiring diagram-1984 and later-200SX (© Nissan Motor Co.)

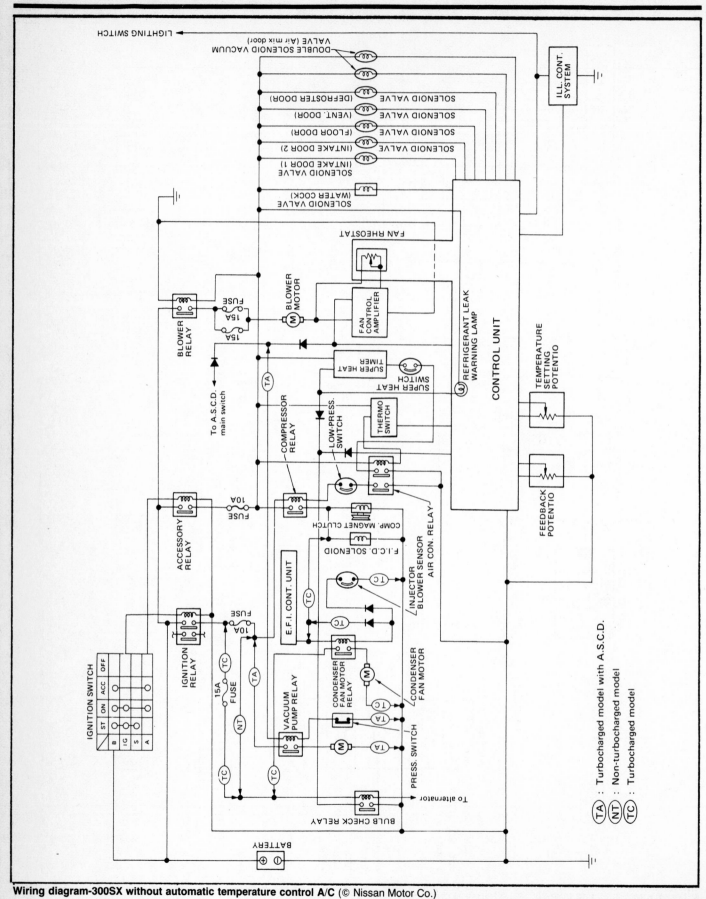

Wiring diagram-300SX without automatic temperature control A/C (© Nissan Motor Co.)

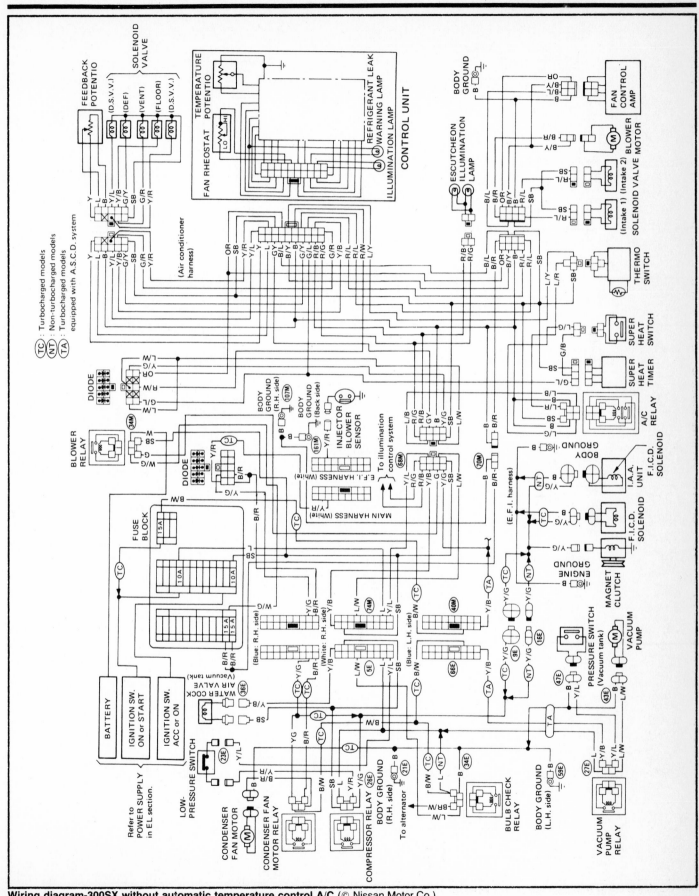

Wiring diagram-300SX without automatic temperature control A/C (© Nissan Motor Co.)

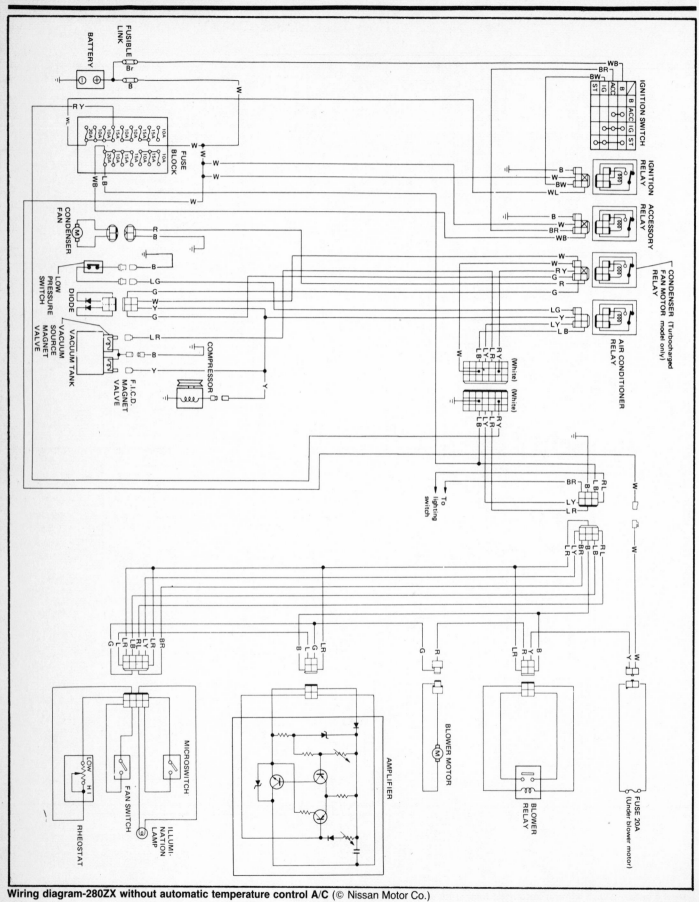

Wiring diagram-280ZX without automatic temperature control A/C (© Nissan Motor Co.)

AIR CONDITIONING DIAGNOSIS CHART
Except ATC

Condition	Cause	Correction
Compressor Noise	a) Broken valves	a) Replace valve plate
	b) Overcharged	b) Discharge, evacuate, and install correct charge
	c) Incorrect oil level	c) Isolate compressor and check oil level
	d) Piston slap	d) Replace compressor
	e) Broken rings	e) Replace compressor
Excessive Vibration	a) Incorrect belt tension	a) Adjust belt tension
	b) Clutch loose	b) Tighten the clutch
	c) Overcharged	c) Discharge, evacuate, and install correct charge
	d) Pulley misaligned	d) Re-align the pulley
Condensation Inside The Passenger Compartment	a) Drain hole plugged or improperly positioned	a) Check for proper installation and clean out drain hose
	b) Insulation improperly installed or removed	b) Replace insulation or expansion valve and hoses
Frozen Evaporator Coil	a) Faulty thermostat	a) Replace the thermostat
	b) Thermostat capillary tube improperly installed	b) Re-install capillary tube correctly
Low Side Low/High Side Low	a) System refrigerant low.	a) Evacuate, leak test, and charge system.
Low Side High/High Side Low	a) Internal leak in compressor—worn.	a) Remove compressor cylinder head and inspect compressor. Replace valve plate assembly if necessary. If compressor pistons, rings, or cylinders are excessively worn or scored, replace compressor.
	b) Head gasket leaking.	b) Install new cylinder head gasket.
	c) Expansion valve.	c) Replace expansion valve.
	d) Drive belt slipping.	d) Set belt tension.
Low Side High/High Side High	a) Clogged condenser fins.	a) Clean out condenser fins.
	b) Air in system.	b) Evacuate, leak test, and charge system.
	c) Expansion valve.	c) Replace expansion valve.
	d) Loose or worn fan belts.	d) Adjust or replace belts as necessary.
Low Side Low/High Side High	a) Expansion valve.	a) Replace expansion valve.
	b) Restriction in liquid line.	b) Check line for kinks—replace if necessary.
	c) Restriction in receiver.	c) Replace receiver.
	d) Restriction in condenser.	d) Replace condenser.
Low Side and High Side Normal	a) Air in system.	a) Evacuate, leak test, and charge system.
	b) Moisture in system.	b) Evacuate, leak test, and charge system.

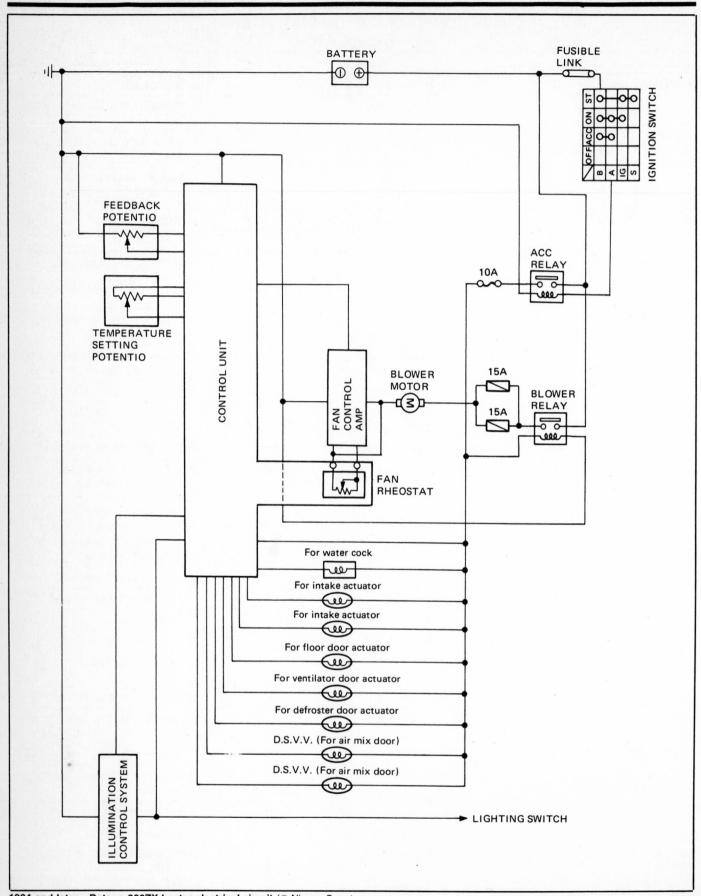

1984 and later—Datsun 300ZX heater electrical circuit (© Nissan Corp.)

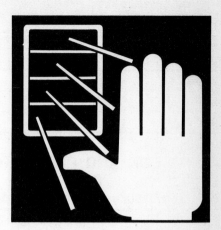

SECTION 7
IMPORT CARS
Mitsubishi

INDEX

SPECIFICATIONS

MITSUBISHI MOTOR CORPORATION

Year	Model
1983–85	Cordia & Tredia
1985	Mirage
1983–85	Starion

FREON AND REFRIGERANT OIL CAPACITIES
Mitsubishi Motor Corporation

Year	Vehicle	Refrigerant Capacity (Ounces)	Refrigerant Oil Capacity (Fluid Ounces)
1983-85	Cordia and Trediá	24	3
1985	Mirage	24	3
1983-85	Starion	24	3

BELT TENSION ADJUSTMENTS

There are different methods of air conditioning compressor belt tensioning adjustments used, involving the movement of one or more of the components within the belt span. These components are the air conditioning compressor, alternator, power steering pump and or an idler pulley if so equipped. When making belt adjustments be careful not to avoid any hidden bolts or nuts, so as not to cause any internal damage or misalignment of the pulleys, when applying tension pressure on the components.

--- CAUTION ---
Do not attempt to adjust the bell tension while the engine is running.

The methods for belt tension adjustments are as follows:

DEFLECTION METHOD

A predetermined location on the belt span or the center of its longest span between pulleys are used in the deflection methods adjustment. A straight edge or an imaginary line is used between the two pulleys involved, along the belt top surface. Either predetermined pressure or a moderate thumb pressure is used to depress the belt in the center of its span. The amount of movement measured and compares to specifications. Corrections are made with a wrench and all measurements are given in ft. lbs. or Nm.

After installing a new drive belt, push the belt with a force of 22 lbs (100N) at the midway point between the alternator pulley and the water pump pulley and adjust the belt deflection to ¼–⅜ in. (7–10mm) by moving the alternator. Tighten and torque the locking bolt to 9–10 ft.lbs. (12–14 Nm) and torque the pivot nut 15–18 ft.lbs. (20–24 Nm).

AIR CONDITIONING DIAGNOSIS CHART

Condition	Cause	Correction
Compressor noise	a) Broken valves	a) Replace valve plate
	b) Overcharged	b) Discharge, evacuate, and install correct charge
	c) Incorrect oil level	c) Isolate compressor and check oil level
	d) Piston slap	d) Replace compressor
	e) Broken rings	e) Replace compressor
Excessive vibration	a) Incorrect belt tension	a) Adjust belt tension
	b) Clutch loose	b) Tighten the clutch
	c) Overcharged	c) Discharge, evacuate, and install corret charge
	d) Pulley misaligned	d) Re-align the pulley
Condensation inside the passenger compartment	a) Drain hole plugged or improperly positioned	a) Check for proper installation and clean out drain hose
	b) Insulation improperly installed or removed	b) Replace insulation or expansion valve and hoses
Frozen evaporator coil	a) Faulty thermostat	a) Replace the thermostat
	b) Thermostat capillary tube improperly installed	b) Re-install capillary tube correctly
Low side low/ high side low	a) System refrigerant low	a) Evacuate, leak test, and charge system

Compressor

Removal and Installation

1983–85 CORDIA AND TREDIA
1985 MIRAGE

1. Discharge the refrigerant system.
2. Detach the high tension cable from the ignition coil and remove the distributor cap, air cleaner and air hose.
3. Loosen the tension pulley and remove the drive belt.
4. Remove the tension pulley from the bracket and disconnect the electrical harness for the magnetic clutch.
5. Remove the high and low pressure refrigerant lines.
6. Raise and support vehicle safely and from underneath the vehicle, remove the compressor with the magnetic clutch in the upright position.

NOTE: On some models it may be necessary to loosen the engine mounting bracket bolts and raise the engine to remove the compressor.

7. Installation is the reverse of the removal procedure.
8. Evacuate, charge and leak test the system after installation.

Removal and Installation

1983–85 STARION

1. Discharge the refrigerant system.
2. Loosen the idler pulley and remove the V-belt.
3. Disconnect the primary cord of the ignition coil.
4. Disconnect the magnetic clutch harness and remove the high and low pressure refrigerant lines from the compressor.
5. Remove the front and rear set bolts and remove the compressor.
6. Installation is the reverse order of the removal procedure.
7. Evacuate, charge and leak test the system after installation.

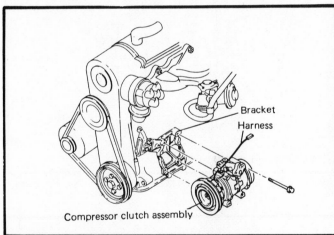

Compressor removal (© Mitsubishi Motor Sales of America, Inc.)

Expansion Valve

Removal

1983–85 CORDIA AND TREDIA
1985 MIRAGE

NOTE: In order to remove the expansion valve the evaporator must be removed.

1. Discharge the refrigerant system.
2. Remove the instrument panel under cover and glove box.
3. Remove the duct work and joints to the defroster.
4. Remove the connector to the control switch, connector to the power supply and the connector to the magnetic clutch of the compressor.
5. Remove the drain hose and disconnect the piping in the engine compartment.

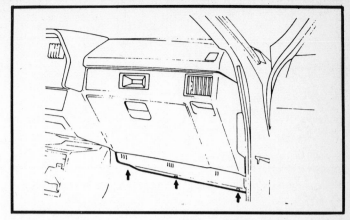

Instrument panel under cover removal (© Mitsubishi Motor Sales of America, Inc.)

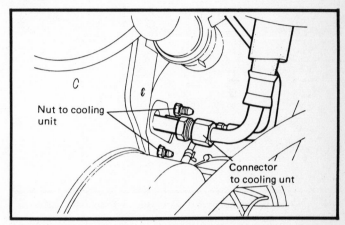

Disconnecting the cooling unit piping (© Mitsubishi Motor Sales of America, Inc.)

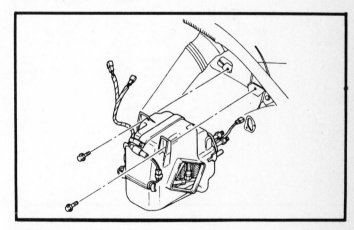

Removing the cooling unit assembly (© Mitsubishi Motor Sales of America, Inc.)

6. Remove the ducts on both sides of the cooling unit and remove the nuts on the cooling unit and lift the cooling unit out from under the dash panel.

Dissassembly

1. Disconnect the electrical harness from the cooling unit housing.
2. Separate the upper and lower housing by prying the clip off with a small prybar, after removing the clip, remove the upper housing first, then the lower housing side.

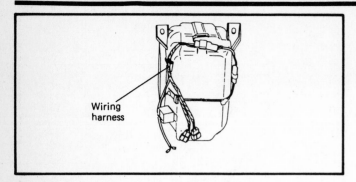

Removing the wiring harness (© Mitsubishi Motor Sales of America, Inc.)

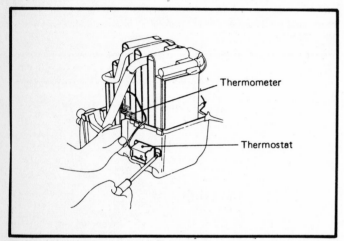

Removing the thermometer and thermostat (© Mitsubishi Motor Sales of America, Inc.)

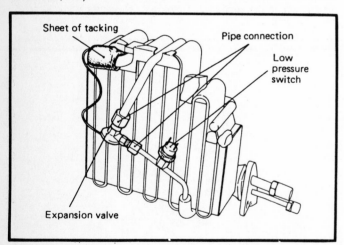

Expansion valve removal (© Mitsubishi Motor Sales of America, Inc.)

3. Remove the upper cooling case and remove the two screws that hold the thermstat to the cooling housing.

4. Remove the thermostat and remove the screws that secure the thermometer from inside the cooling unit fins.

5. Lift the cooling unit assembly from the lower cooling unit case to remove it. Be sure to hold the lower cooling unit case firmly when removing the evaporator coil (cooling unit).

6. To remove the expansion valve, peel off the sheet of tacking material and remove the capillary tube from the suction pipe.

7. Using two spanner wrenches or equivalent, loosen the flare nut on the pipe connection on both inlet and outlet lines of the evaporator and remove the expansion valve.

Installation

1. Installation is the reverse of the removal procedure.
2. Evacuate, charge and leak test the system after installation.

Expansion Valve

Removal and Installation

1983–85 STARION

1. Discharge the refrigerant system.
2. Remove the two screws attaching the right side console cover and remove the side cover.
3. Remove the screw from the lap heater duct, disconnect the duct and remove it.
4. Remove the glove box. The glove box should be removed with the lower frame attached.
5. Disconnect the glove box switch harness at the round top terminal.
6. Remove the lap heater duct and the under-tray stay.
7. Disconnect the duct joint and loosen the duct joint tightening bolt to free the duct joint.
8. Disconnect the A/C switch harness and air conditioner harness.
9. Disconnect the drain hose and the piping at the piping connection at the fire wall in the engine compartment.
10. Remove the cooling unit attaching nuts and the cooling unit top attaching bolts. Remove the evaporator coil (cooling unit).

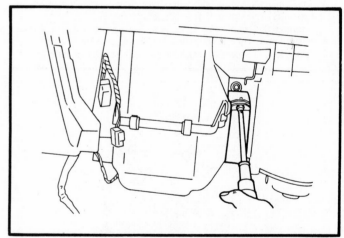

Disconnecting the duct joint (© Mitsubishi Motor Sales of America, Inc.)

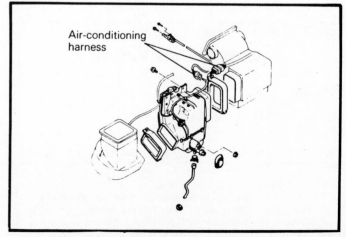

Disconnecting the air conditioner harness (© Mitsubishi Motor Sales of America, Inc.)

Disassembly

1. Remove the harness from the cooling unit case and remove the power relay.

2. Using a small prybar or equivalent, remove the upper and lower cooling case attaching clips.

3. Remove the upper cooling case.

4. Remove the thermostat and take out the capillary tube from inside the fin.

5. Lift the cooling unit assembly from the lower cooling unit case to remove it. Be sure to hold the lower cooling unit case firmly when removing the evaporator coil (cooling unit).

6. To remove the expansion valve, peel off the sheet of tacking material and remove the capillary tube from the suction pipe.

7. Use a spanner wrench or equivalent to loosen the expansion valve flare from the pipe connection and remove the expansion valve.

8. Installation is the reverse of the removal procedure.

9. Evacuate, charge and leak test the system after installation.

Condenser

Removal and Installation

1983–85 CORDIA AND TREDIA
1985 MIRAGE (W/O TURBOCHARGER)

1. Discharge the A/C system.
2. Disconnect the electrical harness for the electrical fan.
3. Remove the electric fan and fan shroud assembly.
4. Remove the bolts on the upper radiator and remove the radiator from the lower support. Tilt the radiator back towards the engine.
5. Remove the input and output refrigerant lines from the condenser.
6. Remove the upper bolts on the condenser and remove the condenser.
7. Installation is the reverse of the removal procedure.
8. Evacuate, charge and leak test the system after installation.

Removal and Installation

1983–85 CORDIA AND TREDIA
1985 MIRAGE (WITH TURBOCHARGER)

1. Discharge the A/C system.
2. Remove the bolts on the upper radiator and remove the radiator from the lower support.

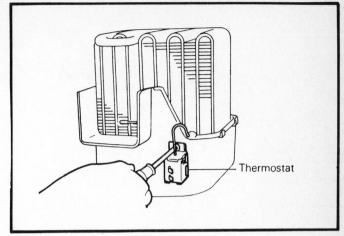

Thermostat removal (© Mitsubishi Motor Sales of America, Inc.)

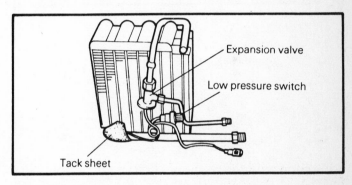

Removing the expansion valve (© Mitsubishi Motor Sales of America, Inc.)

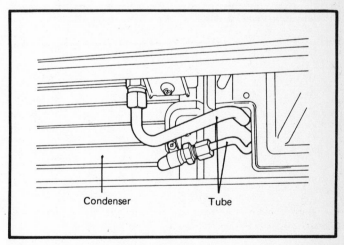

Disconnecting the condenser refrigerant level (© Mitsubishi Motor Sales of America, Inc.)

3. Tilt radiator toward the engine and disconnect the lower grill.
4. Disconnect the electrical harness for the fan and remove the electric fan and shroud assembly.
5. Remove the input and output refrigerant lines from the condenser.
6. Remove the upper bolts on the condenser and remove the condenser.
7. Installation is the reverse of the removal procedure.
8. Evacuate, charge and leak test the system after installation.

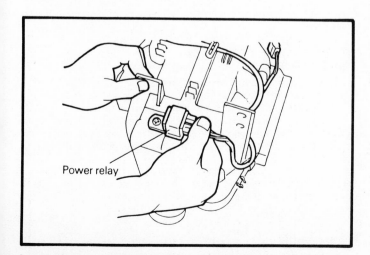

Removing the power relay (© Mitsubishi Motor Sales of America, Inc.)

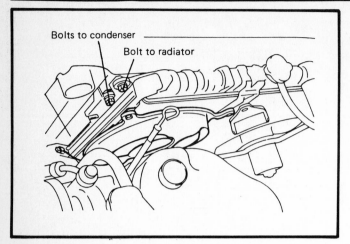

Condensor bolt location (© Mitsubishi Motor Sales of America, Inc.)

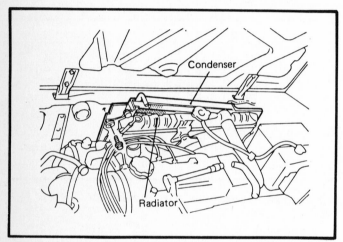

Condenser removal (© Mitsubishi Motor Sales of America, Inc.)

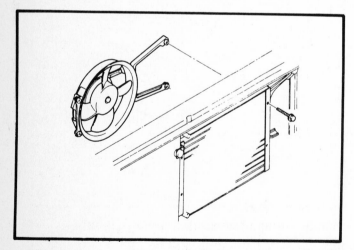

Removing the electric fan (© Mitsubishi Motor Sales of America, Inc.)

Condenser

Removal and Installation

1983–85 STARION

1. Discharge the A/C system.

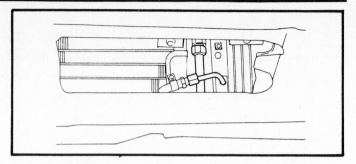

Condenser refrigerant lines—location (© Mitsubishi Motor Sales of America, Inc.)

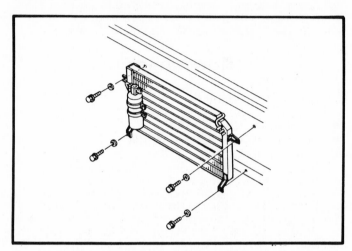

Removing the condenser (© Mitsubishi Motor Sales of America, Inc.)

2. Remove the center instrument brace, disconnect the receiver outlet and inlet refrigerant lines.
3. Remove the bolts from the top and the bottom of the condenser and remove the condenser.
4. Installation is the reverse of the removal procedure.
5. After installation, evacuate, charge and leak test the system.

Evaporator Assembly (Cooling Unit)

Removal

1983–85 CORDIA AND TREDIA
1985 MIRAGE

1. Discharge the refrigerant system.
2. Remove the instrument panel under-cover and glove box.
3. Remove the duct work and joints to the defroster.
4. Remove the connector to the control switch, connector to the power supply and the connector to the magnetic clutch of the compressor.
5. Remove the drain hose and disconnect the piping in the engine compartment.
6. Remove the ducts on both sides of the cooling unit and remove the nuts on the cooling unit and lift the evaporator coil (cooling unit) out from under the dash panel.

Disassembly

1. Disconnect the electrical harness from the cooling unit housing.
2. Separate the upper and lower housing by prying the clip off with

a small prybar. After removing the clip, remove the upper housing first, then the lower housing side.

3. Remove the upper cooling case and remove the two screws that hold the thermstat to the cooling housing.

4. Remove the thermostat and remove the screws that secure the capillary tube from inside the cooling unit fins.

5. Lift the evaporator coil (cooling unit) assembly from the lower cooling unit case to remove it. Be sure to hold the lower cooling unit case firmly when removing the evaporator coil (cooling unit) assembly.

Installation

1. Installation is the reverse of the removal procedure.
2. Evacuate, charge and leak test the system after installation.

Removal

1983–85 STARION

1. Discharge the refrigerant system.
2. Remove the two screws attaching the right side console cover and remove the side cover.
3. Remove the screw from the lap heater duct. Disconnect the duct and remove it.
4. Remove the glove box. The glove box should be removed with the lower frame attached.
5. Disconnect the glove box switch harness at the round top terminal.
6. Remove the lap heater duct and the under–tray stay.
7. Disconnect the duct joint and loosen the duct joint tightening bolt to free the duct joint.
8. Disconnect the A/C switch harness and air conditioner harness.
9. Disconnect the drain hose and the piping at the piping connection at the fire wall in the engine compartment.
10. Remove the evaporator coil (cooling unit) attaching nuts and the cooling unit top attaching bolts. Remove the cooling unit.

Disassembly

1. Remove the harness from the cooling unit case and remove the power relay.
2. Using a small prybar or equivalent, remove the upper and lower cooling case attaching clips.
3. Remove the upper cooling case.
4. Remove the thermostat and take out the capillary tube from inside the fin.
5. Lift the evaporator coil (cooling unit) assembly from the lower cooling unit case to remove it. Be sure to hold the lower cooling unit case firmly when removing the evaporator coil (cooling unit) assembly.

Installation

1. Installation is the reverse of the removal procedure.
2. Evacuate, charge and leak test the system after installation.

Low Pressure Switch

Removal and Installation

1983–85—ALL MODELS

1. Remove the evaporator assembly as previously outlined.
2. Disconnect the wiring at the round topped terminal.
3. Using a spanner wrench or equivalent remove the low pressure switch from the refrigerant piping.
4. Installation is the reverse of the removal procedure.

NOTE: For heater core removal, refer to the Mitsubishi heating section.

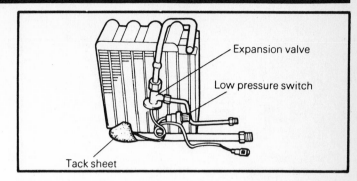

Low pressure switch on the Starion models (© Mitsubishi Motor Sales of America, Inc.)

Air Conditioning Control Switch

Removal and Installation

1983–85 CORDIA AND TREDIA
1985 MIRAGE

1. Remove the knobs from the control levers at the control head panel.
2. On the Cordia models, remove the meter hood of the control head panel.
3. Remove the light for the control head panel and then the control panel.
4. Remove the screws securing the air conditioning control switch to the dash panel, remove the electrical harness and the control switch.
5. Installation is the reverse of the removal procedure.

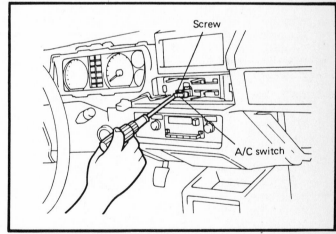

A/C switch removal (© Mitsubishi Motor Sales of America, Inc.)

Removal and Installation

1983–85 STARION

1. Remove the knobs from the control levers on the control head panel.
2. Remove the control head panel by pushing it out from behind the control panel.
3. Remove the screws securing the air conditioning control switch to the dash panel.
4. Remove the electrical harness from the air conditioning control switch and remove the switch.
5. Installation is the reverse of the removal procedure.

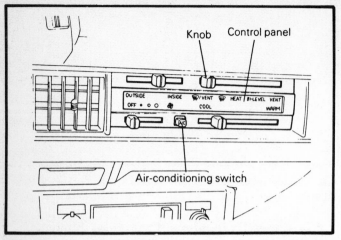

Starion control panel (© Mitsubishi Motor Sales of America, Inc.)

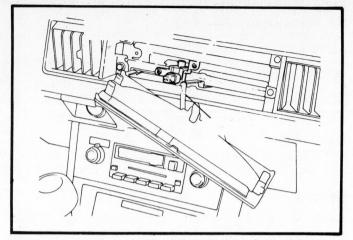

Starion A/C switch removal (© Mitsubishi Motor Sales of America, Inc.)

1. Vacuum pipe
2. Vacuum hose assembly
3. Harness assembly
4. Upper cooling case
5. Relay
6. Automatic temperature controller
7. Cooling unit assembly
8. Pad
9. Lower cooling case
10. Clip
11. Vacuum solenoid valve
12. Double vacuum solenoid valve
13. Relay
14. Low pressure switch
15. Expansion valve
16. Wire net
17. Vacuum diaphragm
18. Heater core
19. Hose
20. Water valve
21. Thermo switch
22. Servo motor
23. Vacuum diaphragm
24. Vacuum diaphragm
25. Heater case
26. Vacuum hose
27. Vacuum diaphragm
28. Blower case
29. Resistor
30. Fan
31. Blower motor
32. Control unit

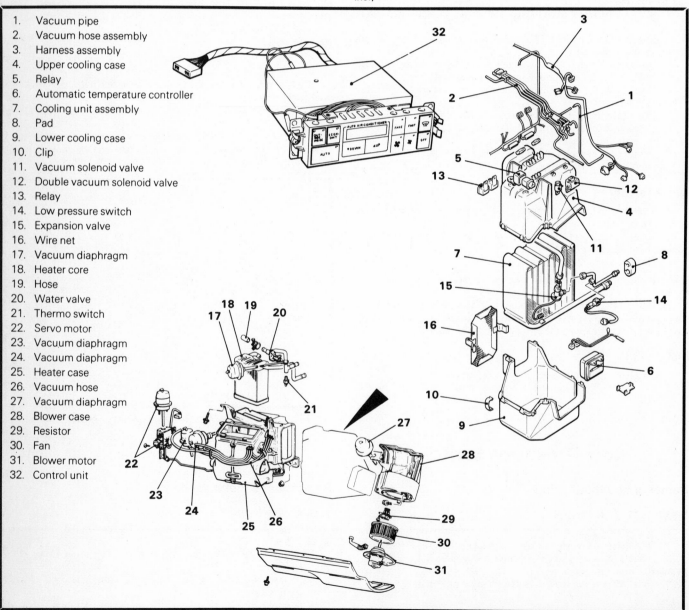

Exploded view of automatic air conditioning system, 1985 Starion models (© Mitsubishi Motor Corp.)

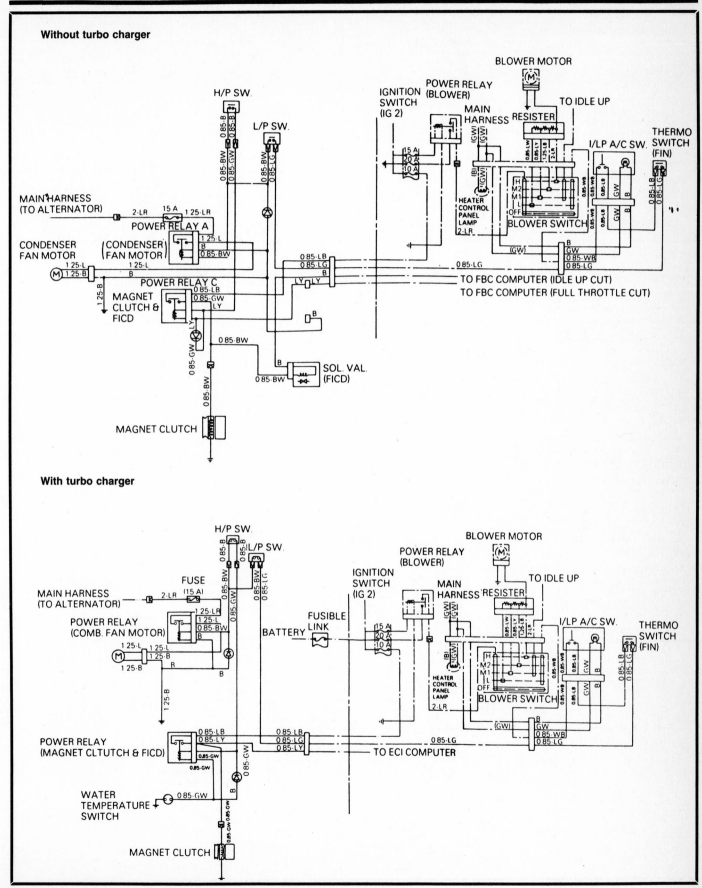

Without turbo charger

With turbo charger

A/C electrical schematics for 1985 Mirage (© Mitsubishi Motor Sales of America, Inc.)

Without turbo charger

With turbo charger

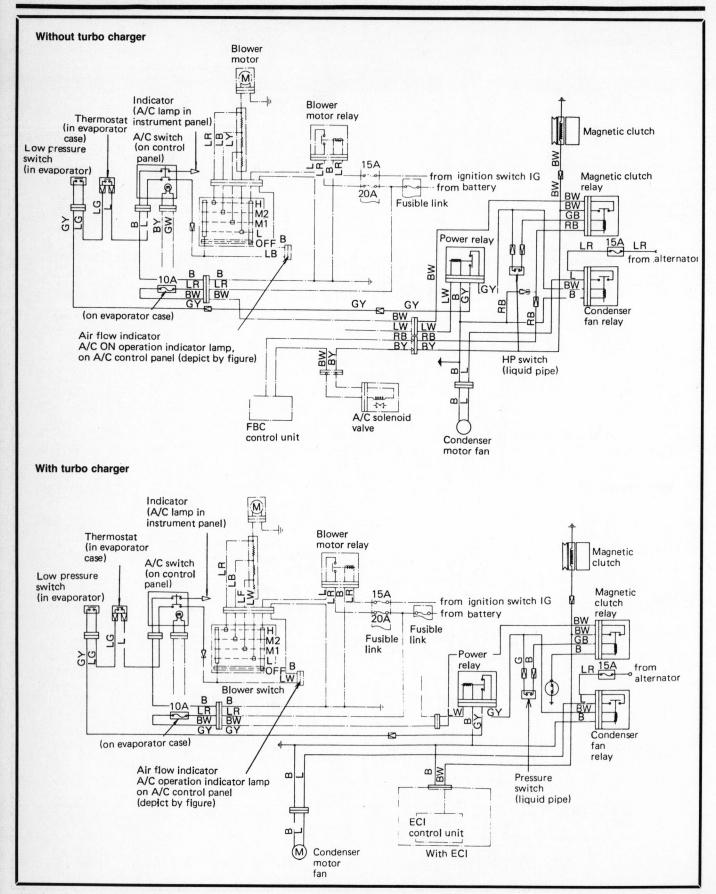

A/C electrical schematics for 1983-84 Cordia and Tredia (© Mitsubishi Motor Sales of America, Inc.)

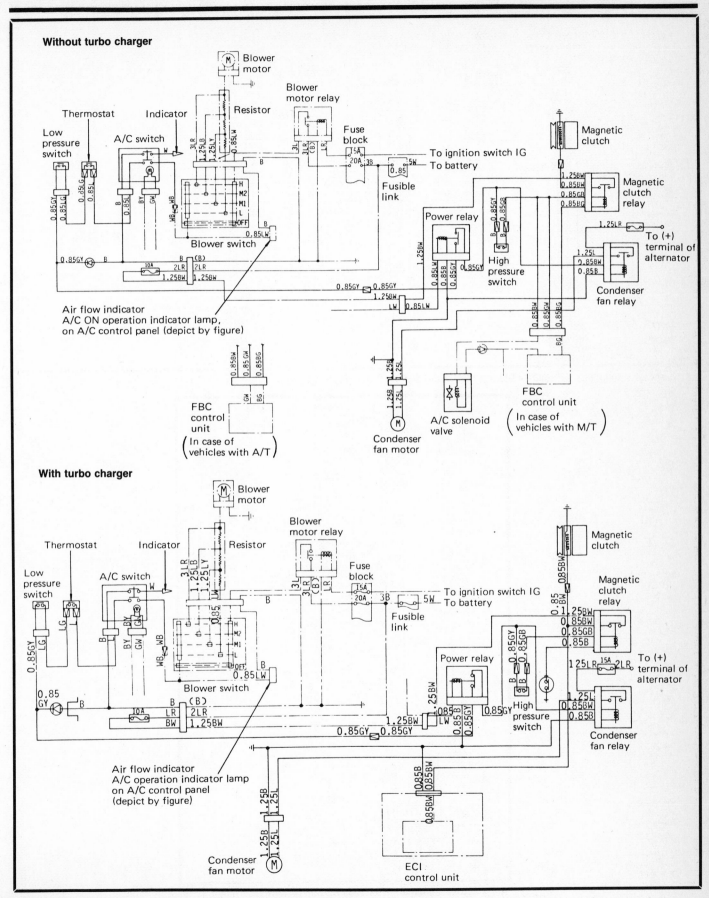

Without turbo charger

With turbo charger

A/C electrical schematic for 1985 Cordia and Tredia (© Mitsubishi Motor Sales of America, Inc.)

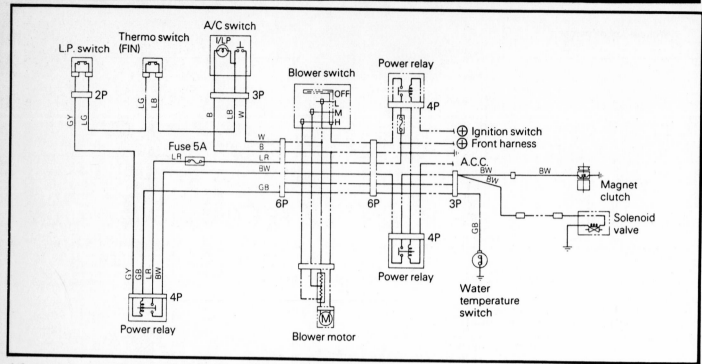

A/C electrical schematics for 1983-84 Starion (© Mitsubishi Motor Sales of America, Inc.)

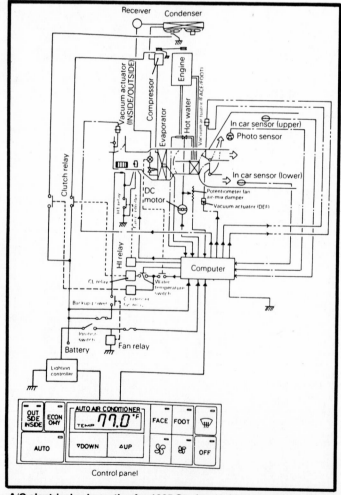

A/C electrical schematics for 1985 Starion (© Mitsubishi Motor Sales of America, Inc.)

SECTION 7
IMPORT CARS
Renault

INDEX

RENAULT/AMC—ALLIANCE AND ENCORE

SPECIFICATIONS

REFRIGERANT, REFRIGERANT OIL CAPACITY AND BELT TENSION SPECIFICATIONS

Year	Vehicle	Refrigerant Capacity, (Ounces)	Refrigerant Oil Capacity, (Fluid Ounces)	Compressor Drive Belt Tension (Ft. lbs)
1983	Alliance	28	6	90–115
1984–85	Alliance/Encore	28	6	90–115

Drive Belt Tension

Air conditioning compressor tension adjustment involves movement of one or more of the components within the belt span. Caution must be exercised to avoid missing hidden bolts and retaining nuts. No attempt should be made to adjust the drive belt tension while the engine is running.

Adjustment

1. Loosen the A/C compressor bolts and any adjustment bracket bolt.
2. Move the compressor against the drive belt until the proper tension is applied to the compressor.
3. Tighten the compressor bolts and the adjustment bracket.
4. Check the adjustment using a belt tensioning gauge.

AIR CONDITIONING SYSTEM

OPERATION

The air conditioning system is designed to cycle a compressor on and off in order to maintain the desired cooling within the passenger compartment. Passenger compartment comfort is maintained by the temperature lever on the control head. The system is also designed to prevent the evaporator from freezing.

The switch and the lever on the control head are used to control the operation of the A/C system.

When an air conditioning mode is selected, electrical current is sent to the compressor clutch coil. The clutch plate and the hub assembly are then drawn rearward which engages the pulley. The clutch plate and the pulley are then locked together and act as one unit. This in turn drives the compressor shaft which compresses low pressure refrigerant vapor from the evaporator into high pressure.

The compressor also circulates refrigerant oil and refrigerant through the A/C system.

On certain models, the compressor is equipped with cut-off solenoid. The solenoid will shut the compressor off momentarily under certain conditions. These include wide open throttle and low idle speeds.

Some A/C systems use a muffler to reduce the compressor noises and high pressure line vibrations. A malfunctioning muffler should be replaced.

SYSTEM PERIODIC MAINTENANCE

The system should be serviced at least yearly, preferably in the spring, before the warm weather. The following should be inspected and corrected as required:
1. Inspect the lines for damage or fraying.
2. Check the system for any freon leaks.
3. Check the refrigerant level and correct as required.
4. Remove the dirt, leaves or other foreign matter from the condensor.
5. Correct the belt tension as required.
6. Add only R-12 refrigerant and wax free 500 SUS (saybolt uniform seconds viscosity refrigerant oil to system.

Charging Locations

Charging locations will vary, but most of the time will either be located on the compressor or the refrigerant lines.

——————————— CAUTION ———————————
Always discharge, evacuate, and recharge the system at the low side service fitting.

Discharging, Evacuation and Charging

DISCHARGING PROCEDURE

1983 AND LATER

NOTE: Always discharge the air conditioning system at the low side service fitting with the engine off.

1. Connect the charging station to the low side service fitting on the accumulator. If the above mentioned charging station is not being used, a hose can be connected in its place and the oil discharged into a bottle.

2. Once the low side of the system is fully discharged, check the high side for any remaining pressure. If pressure is found, discharge using the same procedure as the low side.

NOTE: Pressure found in the high side of the system indicates a blockage and must be corrected prior to evacuating and charging the system.

3. Once the system is fully discharged, the amount of collected oil must be measured and replaced before attempting to evacuate and charge the system.

EVACUATING PROCEDURE

1983 AND LATER

Before charging any system it is necessary to purge the refrigerant and draw out the trapped moisture with a suitable vacuum pump. Failure to do so will result in ineffective charging and possible damage to the system.

Use this hook up for the proper evacuation procedure:

1. Connect both service gauge hoses to the high and low service outlets.
2. Open the high and low side hand valves on the gauge manifold.
3. Open both service valves a slight amount allowing any remaining refrigerant to discharge from the system.
4. Install the center charging hose of the gauge set to the vacuum pump.
5. Operate the vacuum pump for at least one hour.
6. Close the hand valves on the gauge manifold. Shut off the pump.
7. Observe the low pressure gauge to determine if the vacuum is holding. A vacuum drop may indicate a leak in the system.

CHARGING PROCEDURE

1983 AND LATER

1. Start the engine and allow it to reach normal operating temperature. Set the A/C control to "OFF".
2. Connect the charging station to the vehicle as prescribed by the manufacturer.
3. Open the R-12 source valve and allow one pound of refrigerant to flow into the system through the service fitting on the accumulator.
4. Set the A/C system to the "HI" mode on the control panel. This will draw in the remainder of the refrigerant charge.
5. After the remaining charge has been drawn into the system, close the R-12 source valve. Allow the engine to run for approximately 30–60 seconds to clear the gauges and lines.
6. While the engine is still running, remove the low side hose from the accumulator service fitting.
7. Replace any protective cap and check for leaks.

Blower Motor

Removal and Installation

1983 AND LATER

NOTE: Refer to Heater section

Compressor

Removal and Installation

1983 AND LATER

1. Disconnect the negative battery cable.
2. Discharge the air conditioning system as described earlier.
3. Tag and disconnect the electrical leads at the compressor.
4. Remove the refrigerant lines from the compressor.
5. Remove the air conditioner compressor retaining bolts from the brackets.

NOTE: Some vehicles may require the power steering pump, alternator or plug wires to be repositioned or removed. Other components may need to be removed depending on the optional accessories.

6. Remove the air conditioning compressor from the vehicle.
7. When installing the compressor, keep dirt and foreign material from getting into the compressor parts and system. Clean tools and a clean work area are important for proper service. The compressor connections and the outside of the compressor should be cleaned before the compressor is installed. If new components are being installed, note that they are dehydrated and sealed prior to shipping. All sub-assemblies are to remain sealed until use, with the sub-assemblies at room temperature before uncapping. This helps prevent moisture from the air entering the system due to condensation. Use a small amount of re-

frigerant oil on all tube and hose joints. Always use new O-rings dipped in refrigerant oil before assembling joints. This oil will aid assembly and help to provide leak-proof joints.

8. Install any accessories that may have been removed to make room for the compressor.
9. Evacuate, charge and leak test the system. Check for the proper operation of the system.

NOTE: For compressor overhaul, refer to the compressor section.

Expansion Valve

Removal and Installation

1983 AND LATER

1. Connect the manifold gauges and the service valves. Discharge the A/C system.
2. Disconnect the hoses from the expansion valve.
3. Remove the expansion valve from the evaporator.
4. Connect the replacement expansion valve to the evaporator.
5. Apply compressor oil to the threads of the hose connections. Attach the hoses to the expansion valve.
6. Evacuate, charge and check the system for leaks. Remove the manifold gauges.

NOTE: When an expansion valve is replaced, the evaporator unions must be plugged as soon as the hoses are removed.

Condenser

Removal and Installation

1983 AND LATER

1. Connect the manifold gauges to the service valves and evacuate the A/C system.

NOTE: Do not loosen the radiator draincock with the system hot and under pressure because serious burns from coolant can occur.

2. Drain the radiator.
3. Remove the radiator hoses and automatic transmission fluid cooler pipes from the heater.
4. Disconnect the A/C hoses from the condenser.
5. Remove the radiator and condenser as an assembly. Detach the condenser from the radiator.
6. Attach the replacement condenser to the radiator.
7. Install the radiator and condenser.
8. Connect the radiator hoses and automatic transmission fluid cooler pipes to the radiator.
9. Apply compressor oil to the threads of the hose unions and connect the hoses to the condenser.
10. Fill the radiator with coolant.
11. Evacuate, charge and check the A/C system for leaks.

Evaporator

Removal and Installation

1983 AND LATER

1. Remove the ignition coil.
2. Remove the attaching bolts from the plenum chamber cover panel.

NOTE: The air blower assembly must be removed before removing the evaporator housing.

3. The air blower assembly must be removed with the heater core.
4. Disconnect the battery cables.
5. Remove the instrument panel.
6. Remove the screws that retain the air blower assembly.
7. Disconnect the junction block.

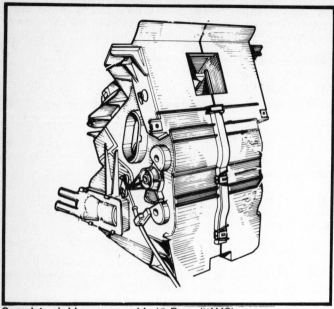

Complete air blower assembly (© Renault/AMC)

8. Clamp and disconnect the heater hoses.

9. Remove the air blower assembly by pulling it out to the right.

10. Bend out the tabs holding the heater core and remove the heater core.

NOTE: Use care to prevent damaging the heater core fins when separating the two halves of the casting.

11. Remove the bolts retaining the evaporator housing.

NOTE: Two of these bolts are accessible from inside the passenger compartment under the driver's side of the instrument panel.

12. Installation is the reverse of the removal procedure.

Heater Core

Removal and Installation

1983 AND LATER

NOTE: refer to heater section.

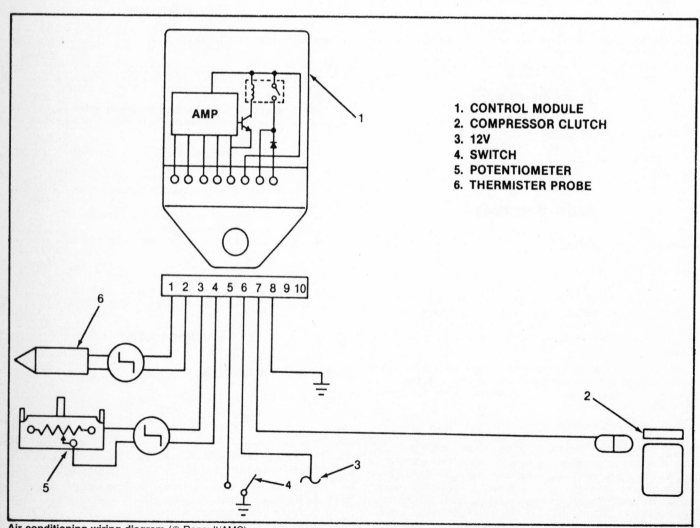

1. CONTROL MODULE
2. COMPRESSOR CLUTCH
3. 12V
4. SWITCH
5. POTENTIOMETER
6. THERMISTER PROBE

Air conditioning wiring diagram (© Renault/AMC)

Control Head

Removal and Installation

1983 AND LATER

1. Disconnect the negative battery cable.
2. Remove the necessary instrument panel trim to expose the control head retaining screws.
3. Remove the radio and/or knobs, radio speaker, ash tray, cigar lighter and the floor console trim plate if equipped.
4. After exposing the control head retaining screws, remove them and pull the control head away from the dash assembly.
5. Disconnect the bowden cable, electrical and/or vacuum connections. Remove the control unit.
6. Installation is the reverse of the removal procedure.

Thermister Probe Test

1983 AND LATER

Place the ohmmeter test probes across the control module wire harness connector pins 1 and 2.

Example: If the ambient temperature is 80°F, the probe resistance should be approximately 4,649 ohms ± 550 ohms.

NOTE: Thermister probe replacement can only be accomplished by removing the evaporator housing.

Potentiometer Test

1983 AND LATER

1. Place the ohmmeter test probe across pin 3 and pin 4 of the control module wire harness connector.
2. Temperature control lever in:
   a. Cold Position = 0 to 100 ohms
   b. Warm Position = Approx. 10,000 ohms
   c. Hot Position = ∞ (infinite) ohms

NOTE: If the resistance is not infinite in the hot position, check for a short circuit in the wires before replacing the potentiometer.

THERMISTER TEMPERATURE/RESISTANCE CHART

Ambient Temperature (°F)	Resistance (ohms)	Ambient Temperature (°F)	Resistance (ohms)
23°	21147	75°	5250
24°	20538	76°	5123
25°	19949	77°	5000
26°	19379	78°	4880
27°	18827	79°	4763
28°	18294	80°	4649
29°	17777	81°	4536
30°	17277	82°	4431
31°	16793	83°	4326
32°	16325	84°	4224
33°	15867	85°	4125
34°	15867	85°	4125
34°	15423	86°	4029
35°	14994	87°	3920
36°	14578	88°	3830
68°	6245	89°	3750
69°	6090	90°	3650
70°	5940	91°	3560
71°	5790	92°	3500
72°	5652	93°	3410
73°	5514	94°	3325
74°	5380	95°	3265

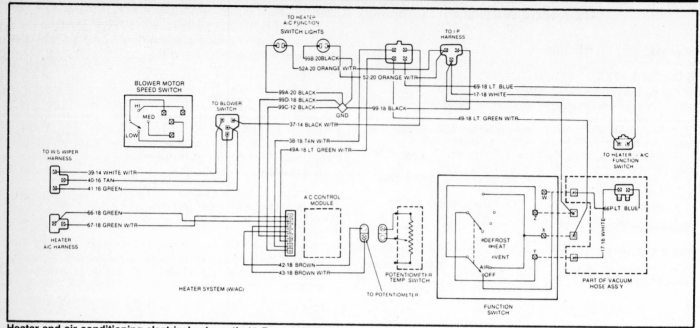

Heater and air conditioning electrical schematic (© Renault/AMC)

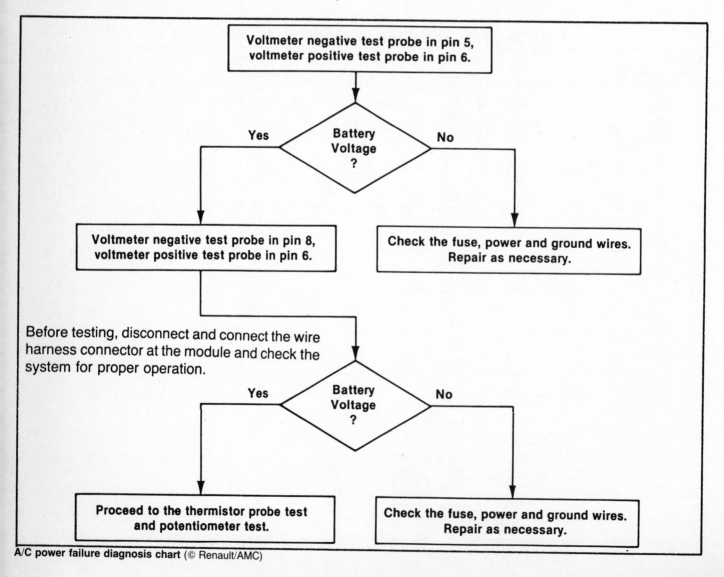

A/C power failure diagnosis chart (© Renault/AMC)

INDEX

SUBARU SPECIFICATIONS

Vehicle Models

1982–85

1600 SERIES STANDARD MODELS DL MODELS

1800 SERIES GL MODELS GIF MODELS

BRAT (OPEN MPV)

Freon and Refrigerant Oil Capacity

FREON

1.63 pounds minimum
1.74 pounds maximum

REFRIGERANT OIL

Type—Suniso 5GS or equivalent

CAPACITY

New Compressor—4.1 fluid ounces
Replacement compressor—Drain oil and add 2.4 fluid ounces.
Replacement evaporator—2.4 fluid ounces
Replacement receiver/drier—add no oil

7.5–8.5mm @ 98 N. depression pressure on mid to long belts

Replacement condenser   —1.7 fluid ounces
Replacement hose or tube   —1.7 fluid ounces
Quick freon leakage from system—1.7 fluid ounces

If no leakage is present, do not add refrigerant oil.

Drive Belt Tension

DEFLECTION METHOD

COMPRESSOR AND ALTERNATOR V-BELT
0.295–0.335 in. @ 22 pounds depression pressure on mid to long belt span

Blower Motor

Removal and Installation

1. Disconnect the negative cable from the battery.
2. Remove the package tray and the glove box assembly.
3. Disconnect the heater duct from the blower motor assembly.
4. Set the mode lever in the CIRC position and disconnect the vacuum hose from the actuator.

NOTE: If the mode lever is not set to the CIRC position, it is difficult to remove the vacuum hose.

5. Disconnect the electrical connector at the blower motor.
6. Remove the actuator from the blower motor assembly.
7. Remove the blower motor from the vehicle.
8. Separate the blower wheel from the motor, if necessary.
9. Separate the blower motor case into two separate parts, if necessary.
10. Reassemble the blower motor and wheel assembly.
11. Reverse the removal procedure to install the blower motor and fan assembly.

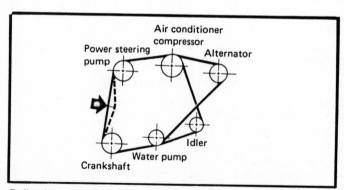

Deflection method of drive belt adjustment (© Fuji Heavy Industries LTD.)

Condition	Probable cause	Corrective action
INSUFFICIENT REFRIGERANT CHARGE Insufficient cooling. Bubbles appear in sight glass. Low-pressure gauge High-pressure gauge	Refrigerant is small, or leaking a little.	1. Leak test. 2. Repair leak. 3. Charge system. **NOTE:** **Evacuate, as necessary, and recharge system.**
ALMOST NO REFRIGERANT No cooling action. In sight glass appear a lot of bubbles or something like mist. Low-pressure gauge High-pressure gauge	Serious refrigerant leak.	**Stop compressor immediately.** 1. Leak test. 2. Discharge system. 3. Repair leak(s). 4. Replace receiver drier if necessary. 5. Check oil level. 6. Evacuate and recharge system.
FAULTY EXPANSION VALVE Slight cooling. Sweating or frosted expansion valve inlet. Low-pressure gauge High-pressure gauge	Expansion valve restricts refrigerant flow. <ul><li>Expansion valve is clogged.</li><li>Expansion valve is inoperative. Valve stuck closed. Thermal bulb has lost charge.</li></ul>	If valve inlet reveals sweat or frost: 1. Discharge system. 2. Remove valve and clean it. Replace it if necessary. 3. Evacuate system. 4. Charge system. If valve does not operate: 1. Discharge system. 2. Replace valve. 3. Evacuate and charge system.

Use of sight glass to determine refrigerant charge (© Fuji Heavy Industries LTD.)

Condition	Probable cause	Corrective action
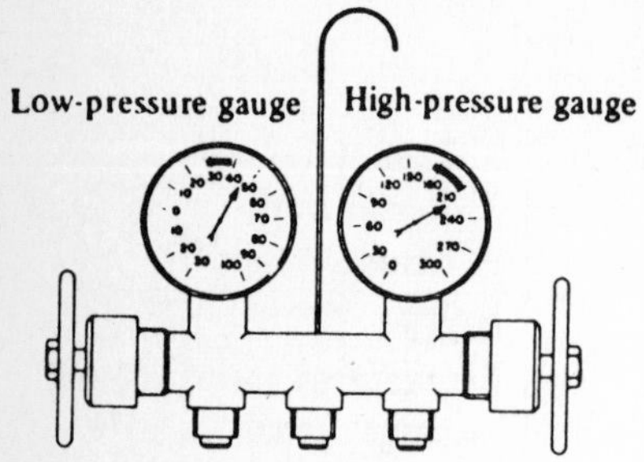 Insufficient cooling. Sweated suction line.	Expansion valve allows too much refrigerant through evaporator.	Check valve for operation. If suction side does not show a pressure decrease, replace valve.
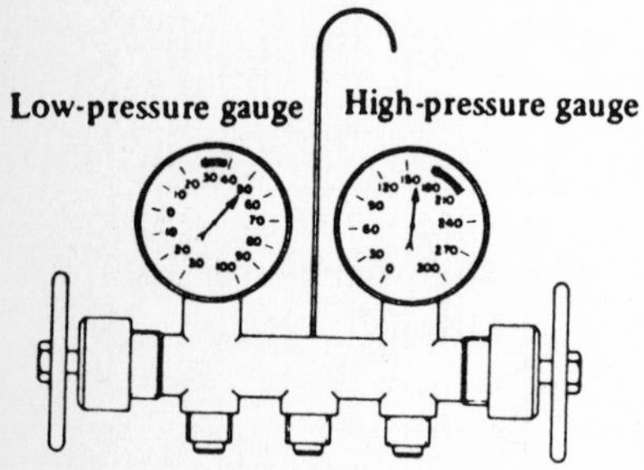 No cooling. Sweating or frosted suction line.	Faulty seal of O-ring in expansion valve.	1. Discharge system. 2. Remove expansion valve and replace O-ring. 3. Evacuate and replace system.

AIR IN SYSTEM

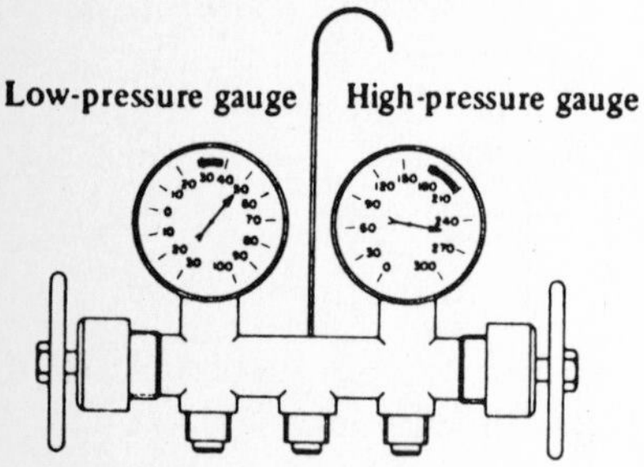 Insufficient cooling. Sight glass shows occasional bubbles.	Air mixed with refrigerant in system.	1. Discharge system. 2. Replace receiver drier. 3. Evacuate and charge system.

MOISTURE IN SYSTEM

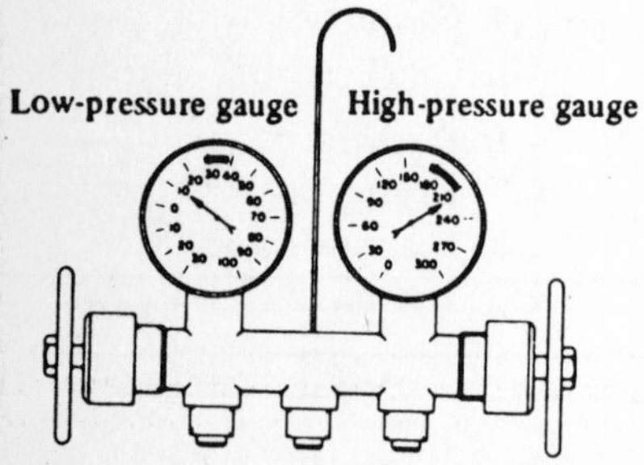 After operation for a while, pressure on suction side may show vacuum pressure reading. During this condition, discharge air will be warm. As warning of this, reading shows 39 kPa (0.4 kg/cm^2, 6 psi) vibration.	Drier is saturated with moisture. Moisture has frozen at expansion valve. Refrigerant flow is restricted.	1. Discharge system. 2. Replace receiver drier (twice if necessary). 3. Evacuate system completely. (Repeat 30-minute evacuating three times.) 4. Recharge system.

In each condition row, the left column also shows a gauge manifold illustration labeled "Low-pressure gauge" and "High-pressure gauge".

Condition	Probable cause	Corrective action
FAULTY CONDENSER Low-pressure gauge High-pressure gauge No cooling action: engine may overheat. Bubbles appear in sight glass of drier. Suction line is very hot.	Condenser is often found not functioning well.	• Check condenser fan motor. • Check condenser for dirt accumulation. • Check engine cooling system for overheat. • Check for refrigerant overcharge. **NOTE:** **If pressure remains high in spite of all above actions taken, remove and inspect the condenser for possible oil clogging.**
HIGH PRESSURE LINE BLOCKED Low-pressure gauge High-pressure gauge Insufficient cooling. Frosted high pressure liquid line.	Drier clogged, or restriction in high pressure line.	1. Discharge system. 2. Remove receiver drier or strainer and replace it. 3. Evacuate and charge system.
FAULTY COMPRESSOR Low-pressure gauge High-pressure gauge Insufficient cooling.	Internal problem in compressor, or damaged gasket and valve.	1. Discharge system. 2. Remove and check compressor. 3. Repair or replace compressor. 4. Check oil level. 5. Replace receiver drier. 6. Evacuate and charge system.

Performance test evaluation (© Fuji Heavy Industries LTD.)

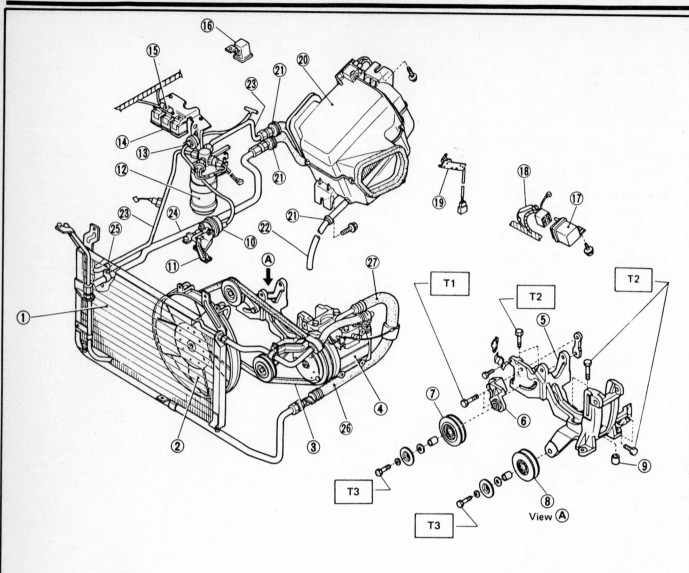

1	Condenser
2	Condenser cooling fan (Sub-fan)
3	Belt
4	Compressor
5	Compressor bracket
6	Tension pulley bracket
7	Tension pulley
8	Idler pulley
9	Spacer
10	Actuator (F.I.C.D.)
11	F.I.C.D. lever
12	Receiver drier
13	Air valve
14	Relay
15	Fuse (B)
16	Relay
17	Relay
18	Fuse (A)
19	Microswitch
20	Evaporator
21	Grommet
22	Drain hose
23	Pipe
24	Pipe
25	Clamp
26	Pipe and hose
27	Pipe and hose

Tightening torque N·m (kg-m, ft-lb)
T1: 24 - 39 (2.4 - 4.0, 17 - 29)
T2: 23 - 26 (2.3 - 2.7, 17 - 20)
T3: 22 - 25 (2.2 - 2.5, 16 - 18)

Air conditioning system for non-turbo models (© Fuji Heavy Industries LTD.)

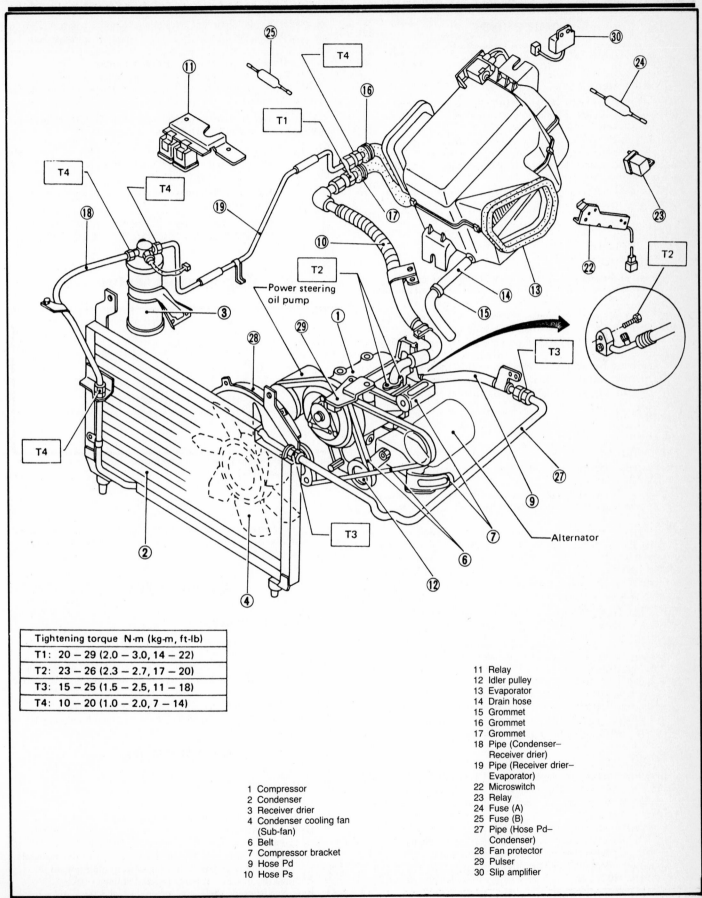

Power steering
oil pump

Alternator

Tightening torque N·m (kg-m, ft-lb)
T1: 20 — 29 (2.0 — 3.0, 14 — 22)
T2: 23 — 26 (2.3 — 2.7, 17 — 20)
T3: 15 — 25 (1.5 — 2.5, 11 — 18)
T4: 10 — 20 (1.0 — 2.0, 7 — 14)

1 Compressor
2 Condenser
3 Receiver drier
4 Condenser cooling fan
   (Sub-fan)
6 Belt
7 Compressor bracket
9 Hose Pd
10 Hose Ps

11 Relay
12 Idler pulley
13 Evaporator
14 Drain hose
15 Grommet
16 Grommet
17 Grommet
18 Pipe (Condenser–
    Receiver drier)
19 Pipe (Receiver drier–
    Evaporator)
22 Microswitch
23 Relay
24 Fuse (A)
25 Fuse (B)
27 Pipe (Hose Pd–
    Condenser)
28 Fan protector
29 Pulser
30 Slip amplifier

Air conditioning system for turbo models (© Fuji Heavy Industries LTD.)

Compressor

Removal

NON-TURBO MODELS

1. Disconnect the electrical wiring from the compressor.
2. Loosen the retaining bolts on the tension pulley and allow the drive belt to slacken.
3. Safely discharge the refrigerant from the system.
4. Disconnect the flexible hose from the compressor.
5. Loosen the compressor mounting bolts and carefully remove the compressor and bracket assembly.
6. With the compressor out of the engine compartment, remove the compressor mounting brackets from the compressor.

Installation

NON-TURBO MODELS

1. To install the compressor, reverse the removal procedure.
2. In addition to the reversal procedures, the following points must be followed.
    a. When attaching the compressor to the compressor bracket, push the upper bracket spacer 0.04–0.08 in. inward first.
    b. Be sure a gap of 0.79 inch exists between the flexible hose and the compressor.
    c. Adjust the belt so that a deflection of 0.295–0.335 in. at 22 pounds pressure, exists in a moderate length span between pulleys.
    d. Charge the air conditioning system and verify its proper operation.

Removal

TURBO MODELS

1. Disconnect the negative battery cable and safely discharge the air conditioning system.
2. Remove the pulser from the compressor bracket. Disconnect the electrical wiring connector. Temporarily re-install the bolt into the bracket.
3. Remove the fan protector from the radiator member.
4. After the air conditioning system has been safely discharged, remove the low pressure hose from the compressor. Immediately cap or plug the openings.
5. Remove the high pressure hose from the compressor. Immediately cap or plug the openings.

NOTE: The high pressure hose can be removed after the compressor and bracket assembly have been removed from the engine, if so desired.

6. Loosen the drive belt from the alternator. Disconnect the wiring and remove the alternator.
7. Remove the engine fan assembly.
8. Remove the compressor drive belt and adjusting pulley assembly.
9. Remove the compressor assembly with the brackets attached.
10. The brackets can be removed from the compressor when the assembly has been removed from the vehicle.

Installation

1. Install the brackets on the compressor. Temporarily tighten the upper compressor bracket bolt to which the pulser will later be attached. Install the adjusting bolt for the idler pulley assembly on the lower compressor bracket.
2. Connect the high pressure line to the rear of the compressor, or connect it after the compressor has been attached to the engine.
3. Install the compressor and bracket assembly to the engine.
4. Install the idler pulley and the drive belt. Adjust the belt tension to 0.24–0.31 in. at 22 pound tension on a moderate length span of the belt, between pulleys.
5. Install the fan assembly to the engine.

6. Install the alternator and drive belt assembly. Adjust the belt to obtain a deflection of 0.24–0.31 in. at 22 pounds pressure between pulleys.
7. Install the low pressure air conditioning hose.
8. Install the fan protector on the radiator member.
9. Install the pulser with the bolt used to temporarily install the compressor bracket.

NOTE: Be sure to provide a clearance of 0.12–0.04 in. between the pulser's sensor and the compressor clutch.

10. Complete the installation by attaching loose hose clamps, connecting wiring connectors, and evacuating, charging and testing the air conditioning system for proper operation.

NOTE: Compressor overhaul is covered in the Compressor Overhaul Section of this manual.

11. When replacing the compressor clutch assembly, the correct break-in procedure is to engage and disengage the clutch assembly some thirty times.

Expansion Valve

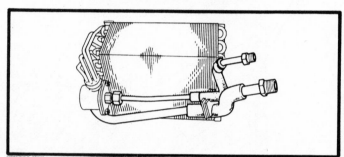

Location of expansion valve on evaporator core (© Fuji Heavy Industries LTD.)

The evaporator assembly must be removed and disassembled to expose the expansion valve. Refer to the Evaporator Removal and Installation outline of this section.

Condensor

Removal and Installation

1. Safely discharge the air conditioning system.
2. Remove the front grille and the lower stay.
3. Disconnect the pipe connections and cap or plug all openings.
4. Loosen the two mounting bolts from the radiator and remove the condensor.
5. To install the condensor, reverse the removal procedure.
6. Evacuate, leak test and recharge the air conditioning system.

Evaporator

Removal and Installation

1. Disconnect the negative battery cable.
2. Safely discharge the air conditioning system.
3. Disconnect the discharge pipe from the evaporator. Disconnect the suction pipe. Cap or plug the opening immediately.
4. Remove the grommets of the drain hose, vacuum hose, the evaporator outlet and inlet pipe connections from the firewall.
5. Remove the instrument panel top and storage pocket.
6. Remove the front shelf, the lower duct and the blower motor assembly.

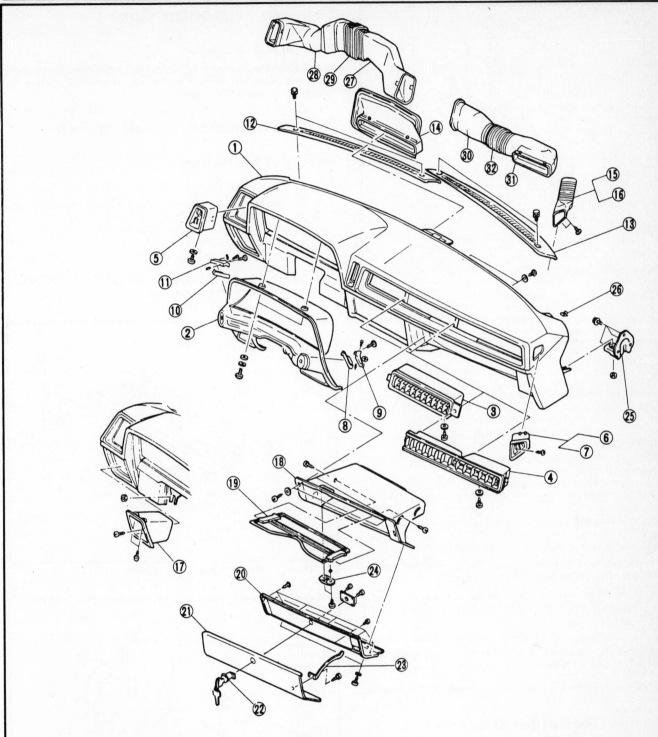

1 Pad and frame assembly
2 Visor and switch box
3 Center grille
4 Side grille
5 Side ventilation grille
6 Side defroster grille L.H.
7 Side defroster grille R.H.
8 Wiper plate
9 Wiper indicator lamp
10 Lighting plate
11 Lighting indicator lamp
12 Defroster grille L.H.

13 Defroster grille R.H.
14 Center duct
15 Side defroster duct L.H.
16 Side defroster duct R.H.
17 Coin box
18 Glove box
19 Shelf
20 Panel
21 Glove box lid
22 Lock assembly
23 Stay
24 Striker

25 Instrument panel bracket
26 Speed nut
27 Side ventilation duct A
   (L.H.)
28 Side ventilation duct B
   (L.H.)
29 Joint L.H.
30 Side ventilation duct C
   (R.H.)
31 Side ventilation duct D
   (R.H.)
32 Joint R.H.

Exploded view of dash assembly, typical (© Fuji Heavy Industries LTD.)

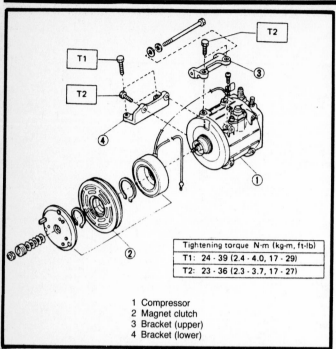

Tightening torque N·m (kg-m, ft-lb)
T1: 24 - 39 (2.4 - 4.0, 17 - 29)
T2: 23 - 36 (2.3 - 3.7, 17 - 27)

1 Compressor
2 Magnet clutch
3 Bracket (upper)
4 Bracket (lower)

Exploded view of compressor and bracket assembly, non-turbo models
(© Fuji Heavy Industries LTD.)

7. Disconnect the electrical wiring from the evaporator thermostat.

8. Loosen and remove the two retaining bolts of the evaporator housing. Carefully remove the evaporator from the vehicle.

9. With the evaporator out of the vehicle, the drain hose can be removed from the housing.

10. Using a pry bar, remove the seven retaining clamps and remove the top evaporator case.

11. Remove the lower case assembly.

12. Disconnect the connection between the expansion valve and the discharge pipe.

13. Remove the expansion valve from the header at the top of the evaporator.

14. Reassemble the evaporator in the reverse order of its disassembly.

NOTE: Be sure new O-rings are used as required and each is lubricated properly before installation.

15. Install the evaporator assembly into the vehicle in the reverse order of its removal procedure. Evacuate, leak test and charge the air conditioning system.

─── CAUTION ───
When installing the evaporator assembly into the vehicle, avoid pinching the electrical and/or vacuum hose between the evaporator and the firewall.

Receiver/Drier

Removal and Installation

1. Safely discharge the air conditioning system.

2. Drain the fluid from the w/s washer tank, remove the tank and set aside.

3. Disconnect the wiring from the receiver drier.

4. Disconnect the receiver/drier inlet and outlet pipes. Cap or plug the openings immediately.

5. Loosen the two mounting bolts and remove the receiver/drier.

6. The receiver/drier is replaced in the reverse of its removal procedure.

7. Evacuate, leak test and charge the system.

Heater Core

Removal and Installation

The removal and installation of the heater core is basically the same as the procedure outline for non-A/C equipped vehicle. Follow the outlined procedure in the Heater section.

Condensor Cooling Fan

Removal and Installation

NON-TURBO MODELS

1. Remove the clip on the electrical wiring and separate the connector.

2. Remove the retaining bolts and remove the shroud.

3. Remove the fan by removing the retaining bolts.

4. Remove the wiring from the shroud clip.

5. Remove the three screws to remove the motor bracket. Remove the motor from the shroud.

6. To install the fan and motor, reverse the removal procedure.

7. After the installation, operate the fan to be sure the motor does not make any unusual noises or vibrations.

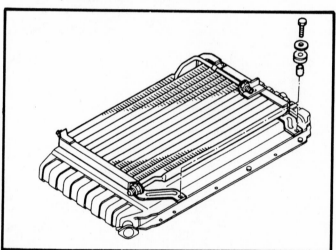

Condensor assembly (© Fuji Heavy Industries LTD.)

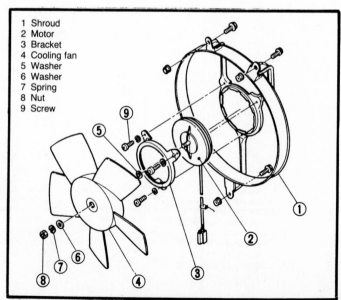

1 Shroud
2 Motor
3 Bracket
4 Cooling fan
5 Washer
6 Washer
7 Spring
8 Nut
9 Screw

Cooling fan, non-turbo models (© Fuji Heavy Industries LTD.)

TURBO MODELS

1. Remove the protector from the radiator assembly.
2. Remove the retaining bolts and remove the fan from the water pump pulley.
3. During the installation, fit the fan assembly to a pre-inserted bolt and then install the three remaining bolts.
4. Complete the assembly.

Fast Idle Control Device (FICD)

Adjustment

NON-TURBO MODELS

1. With the air conditioning off, check the clearance between the actuator hook and the lever on the Fast Idle Control Device.
2. Vehicles equipped with the HITACHI carburetor, the gap between the actuator hook and the lever should be 0.098, plus 0.04, or minus 0.059 inch (2.5, plus 1.0, or minus 1.5mm).
   a. If the clearance is incorrect, adjust it by loosening the lever's mounting bolts and resetting the clearance. Tighten the mounting bolts and recheck the clearance.
4. If the vehicle is equipped with the CARTER-WEBER carburetor, the clearance should be approximately 0.16 inch (4.0mm) when both the actuator and the lever are set in their normal positions.
   a. With the engine at normal operating temperature and the air conditioning system on, depress the accelerator pedal several times and turn the adjusting screw of the actuator to adjust the engine idle. The idle speed should be 950, (plus or minus 50) rpm.
   b. To adjust, loosen the locknut and turn the adjusting screw clockwise to decrease the idle and counterclockwise to increase the idle speed.
   c. The air cleaner must be installed and the air conditioning system on when adjusting the idle speed.
   d. After the adjustment is completed, be sure the lever of the Fast Idle Control Device is able to move to its full open position.

Relay and Fuses

Locations

The air conditioning fuse and relay harnesses are located in the engine compartment.

The blower motor fuse harness is located behind the instrument panel, while the blower motor relay is attached to the fuse box bracket.

Microswitch

Removal and Installation

1. Remove the package tray and the air duct assembly.
2. Remove the microswitch with the bracket which is installed on the right side of the heater/evaporator unit.
3. Install the microswitch in the reverse of the removal procedure.

Air Valve

Removal and Installation

NON-TURBO MODELS

1. Remove the vacuum hose.
2. Disconnect the connector of the electrical wires.
3. Loosen the two mounting screws and remove the air valve.

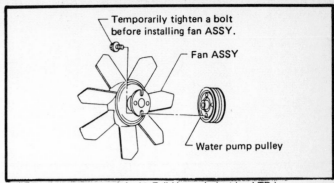

Cooling fan, turbo models (© Fuji Heavy Industries LTD.)

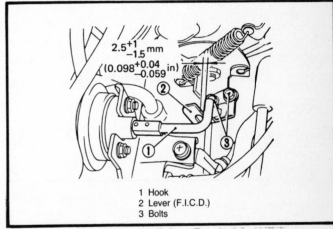

Clearance location for FICD on non-turbo models (© Fuji Heavy Industries LTD.)

1 Hook
2 Lever (F.I.C.D.)
3 Bolts

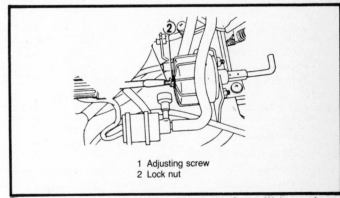

1 Adjusting screw
2 Lock nut

Adjustment of FICD unit when equipped with Carter-Weber carburetor (© Fuji Heavy Industries LTD.)

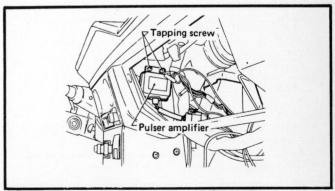

Pulse amplifier location (© Fuji Heavy Industries LTD.)

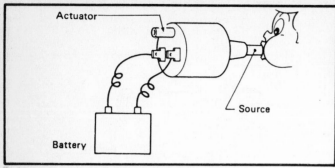

Testing air valve (© Fuji Heavy Industries LTD.)

4. To check the air valve, use a 12 volt battery to apply current to activate the unit. With the unit activated, air should be free to pass through the assembly. With the current disconnected, air passage should be blocked.

5. The installation is the reverse of the removal procedure.

Pulse Amplifier Unit

Removal and Installation

TURBO MODELS

1. Remove the instrument panel top and the storage box.
2. Remove the package tray.

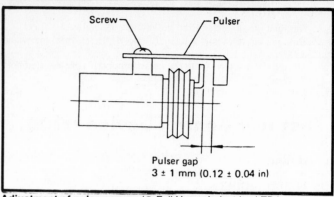

Adjustment of pulse sensor (© Fuji Heavy Industries LTD.)

3. Disconnect the body electrical harness from the amplifier.
4. Remove the amplifier from its bracket.
5. The installation of the amplifier is the reverse of the removal procedure.

Control Head

Removal and Installation

The removal and installation of the control head is basically the same as was outlined in the heater section. Refer to the appropriate outline for the correct procedures.

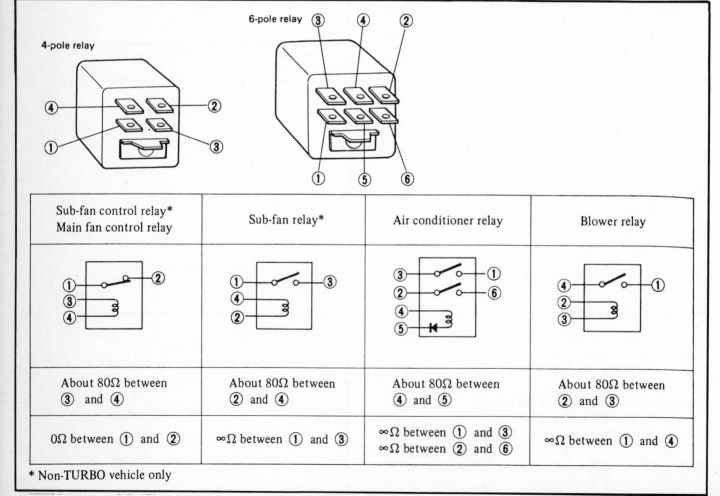

Sub-fan control relay* Main fan control relay	Sub-fan relay*	Air conditioner relay	Blower relay
About 80Ω between ③ and ④	About 80Ω between ② and ④	About 80Ω between ④ and ⑤	About 80Ω between ② and ③
0Ω between ① and ②	∞Ω between ① and ③	∞Ω between ① and ③ ∞Ω between ② and ⑥	∞Ω between ① and ④

* Non-TURBO vehicle only

Use and testing of relays, Turbo and non-turbo models (© Fuji Heavy Industries LTD.)

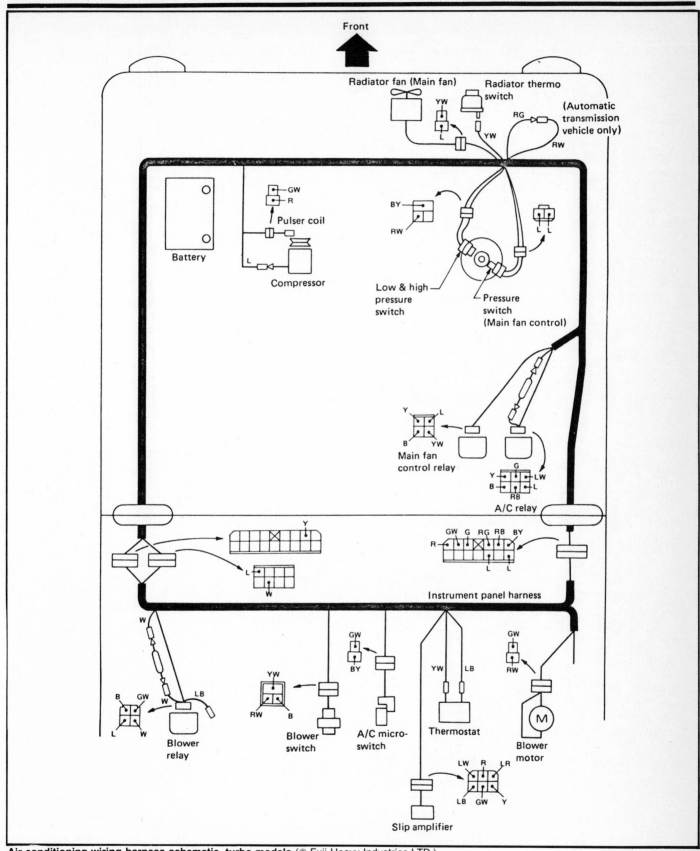

Air conditioning wiring harness schematic, turbo models (© Fuji Heavy Industries LTD.)

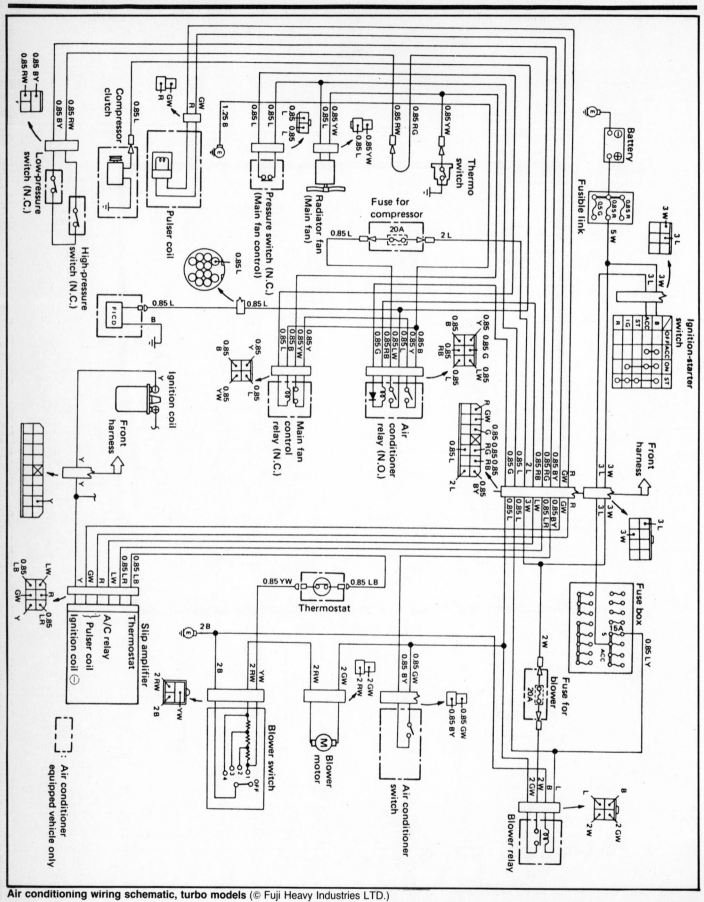

Air conditioning wiring schematic, turbo models (© Fuji Heavy Industries LTD.)

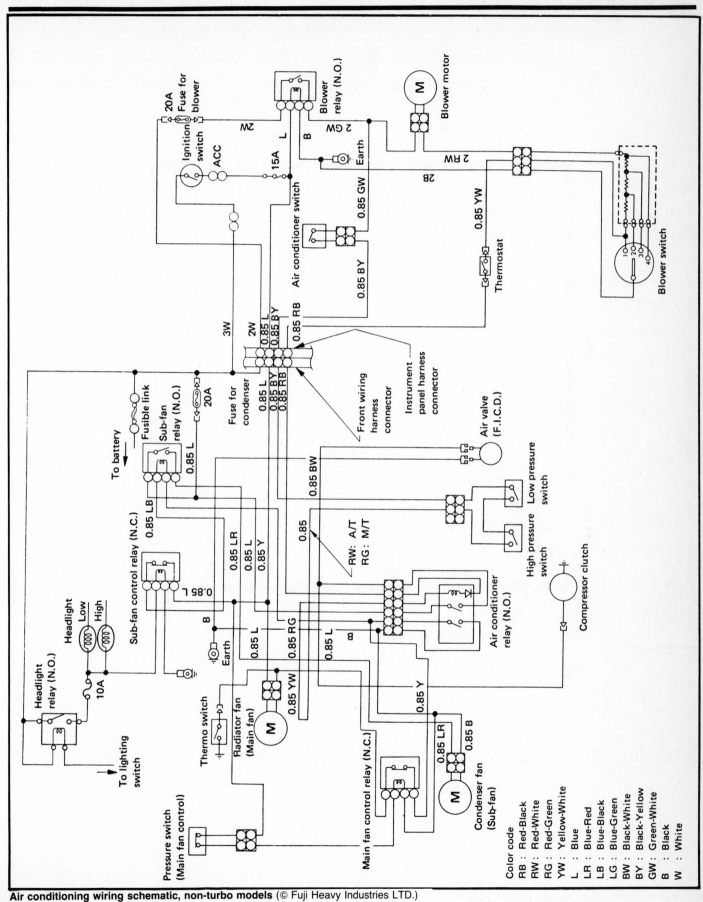

Air conditioning wiring schematic, non-turbo models (© Fuji Heavy Industries LTD.)

Color code
RB : Red-Black
RW : Red-White
RG : Red-Green
YW : Yellow-White
L : Blue
LR : Blue-Red
LB : Blue-Black
LG : Blue-Green
BW : Black-White
BY : Black-Yellow
GW : Green-White
B : Black
W : White

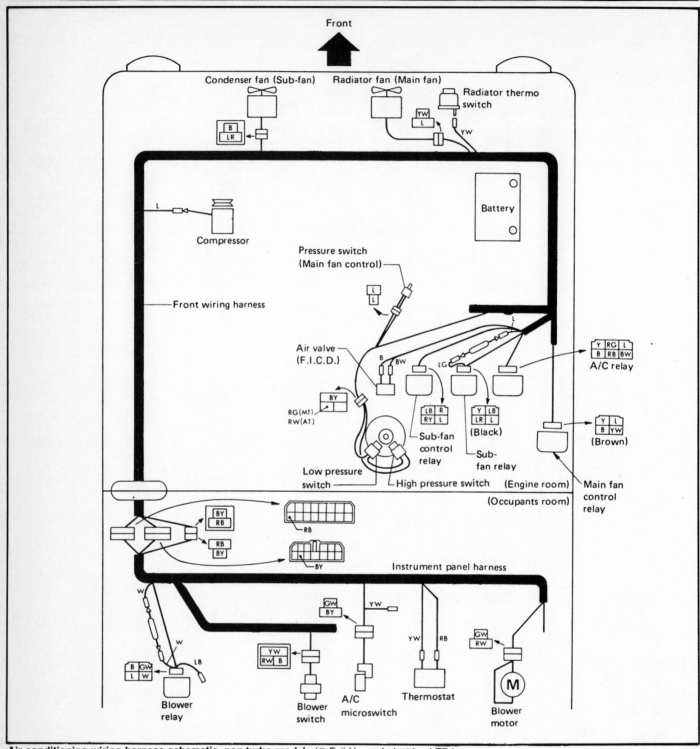

Front

Condenser fan (Sub-fan)   Radiator fan (Main fan)   Radiator thermo switch

B
LR

YW
L

YW

Battery

L

Compressor

Pressure switch
(Main fan control)

L
L

Front wiring harness

Air valve
(F.I.C.D.)

B   BW

LG

L

Y	RG	L
B	RB	BW

A/C relay

BY	

RG(MT)
RW(AT)

LB	R
RY	L

Sub-fan
control
relay

Y	LB
LR	L

(Black)

Sub-fan relay

Y	L
B	YW

(Brown)

Low pressure
switch

High pressure switch   (Engine room)

Main fan
control
relay

(Occupants room)

BY
RB

RB

RB
BY

BY

Instrument panel harness

W

GW
BY

YW

YW   RB

GW
RW

B	GW
L	W

W   LB

YW	
RW	B

M

Blower
relay

Blower
switch

A/C
microswitch

Thermostat

Blower
motor

Air conditioning wiring harness schematic, non-turbo models (© Fuji Heavy Industries LTD.)

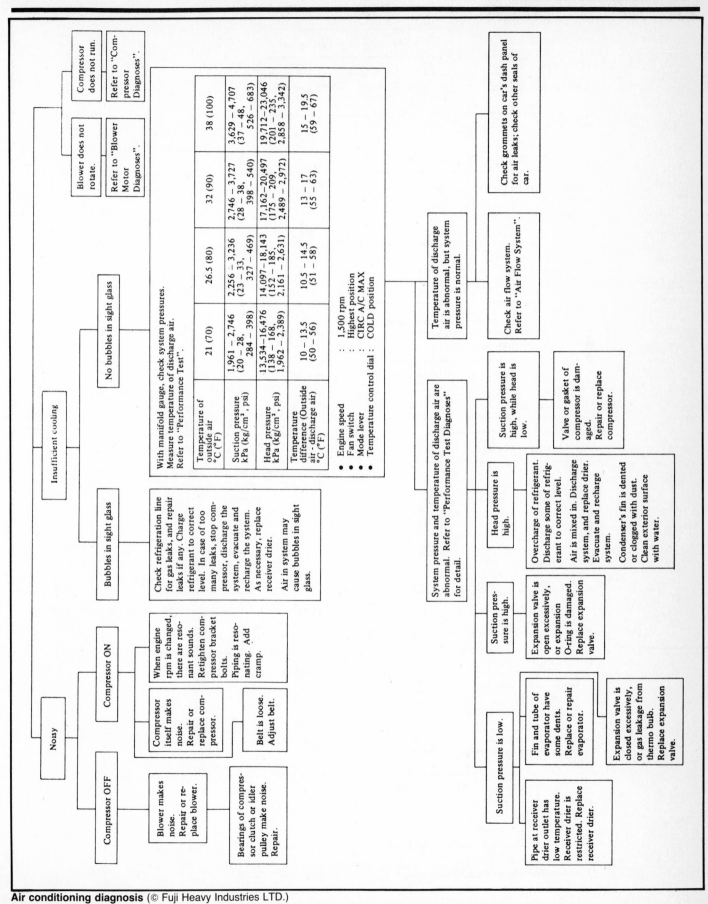

The flowchart contains the following elements:

Insufficient cooling branches:

- **No bubbles in sight glass** → With manifold gauge, check system pressures. Measure temperature of discharge air. Refer to "Performance Test".

Temperature of outside air °C (°F)	21 (70)	26.5 (80)	32 (90)	38 (100)
Suction pressure kPa (kg/cm², psi)	1,961 – 2,746 (20 – 28, 284 – 398)	2,256 – 3,236 (23 – 33, 327 – 469)	2,746 – 3,727 (28 – 38, 398 – 540)	3,629 – 4,707 (37 – 48, 526 – 683)
Head pressure kPa (kg/cm², psi)	13,534 – 16,476 (138 – 168, 1,962 – 2,389)	14,097 – 18,143 (152 – 185, 2,161 – 2,631)	17,162 – 20,497 (175 – 209, 2,489 – 2,972)	19,712 – 23,046 (201 – 235, 2,858 – 3,342)
Temperature difference (Outside air - discharge air) °C (°F)	10 – 13.5 (50 – 56)	10.5 – 14.5 (51 – 58)	13 – 17 (55 – 63)	15 – 19.5 (59 – 67)

- Engine speed : 1,500 rpm
- Fan switch : Highest position
- Mode lever : CIRC A/C MAX
- Temperature control dial : COLD position

- **Bubbles in sight glass** → Check refrigeration line for gas leaks, and repair leaks if any. Charge refrigerant to correct level. In case of too many leaks, stop compressor, discharge the system, evacuate and recharge the system. As necessary, replace receiver drier.

  Air in system may cause bubbles in sight glass.

Noisy branches:

- **Compressor OFF** → Blower makes noise. Repair or replace blower.

- **Compressor ON**:
  - When engine rpm is changed, there are resonant sounds. Retighten compressor bracket bolts. Piping is resonating. Add cramp.
  - Compressor itself makes noise. Repair or replace compressor.
  - Bearings of compressor clutch or idler pulley make noise. Repair.
  - Belt is loose. Adjust belt.

Blower does not rotate. → Refer to "Blower Motor Diagnoses".

Compressor does not run. → Refer to "Compressor Diagnoses".

Temperature of discharge air is abnormal, but system pressure is normal. → Check air flow system. Refer to "Air Flow System".

→ Check grommets on car's dash panel for air leaks; check other seals of car.

System pressure and temperature of discharge air are abnormal. Refer to "Performance Test Diagnoses" for detail.

- **Head pressure is high.**
  - Overcharge of refrigerant. Discharge some of refrigerant to correct level.
  - Air is mixed in. Discharge system, and replace drier. Evacuate and recharge system.
  - Condenser's fin is dented or clogged with dust. Clean exterior surface with water.

- **Suction pressure is high.**
  - Expansion valve is open excessively, or expansion O-ring is damaged. Replace expansion valve.

- **Suction pressure is high, while head is low.**
  - Valve or gasket of compressor is damaged. Repair or replace compressor.

- **Suction pressure is low.**
  - Pipe at receiver drier outlet has low temperature. Receiver drier is restricted. Replace receiver drier.
  - Fin and tube of evaporator have some dents. Replace or repair evaporator.
  - Expansion valve is closed excessively, or gas leakage from thermo bulb. Replace expansion valve.

Air conditioning diagnosis (© Fuji Heavy Industries LTD.)

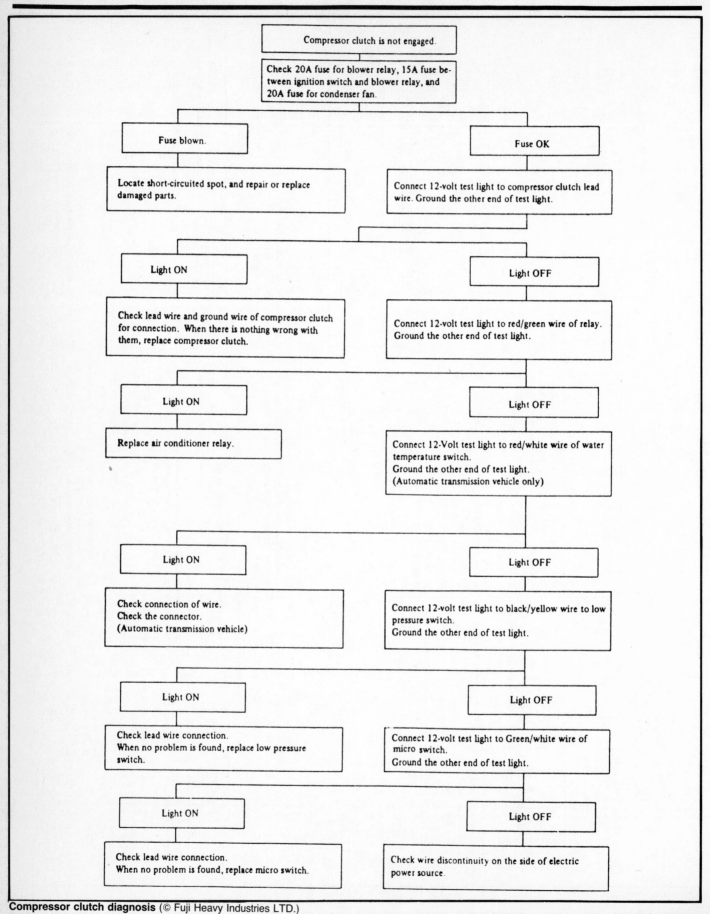

Compressor clutch is not engaged.

Check 20A fuse for blower relay, 15A fuse between ignition switch and blower relay, and 20A fuse for condenser fan.

Fuse blown.

Locate short-circuited spot, and repair or replace damaged parts.

Fuse OK

Connect 12-volt test light to compressor clutch lead wire. Ground the other end of test light.

Light ON

Check lead wire and ground wire of compressor clutch for connection. When there is nothing wrong with them, replace compressor clutch.

Light OFF

Connect 12-volt test light to red/green wire of relay. Ground the other end of test light.

Light ON

Replace air conditioner relay.

Light OFF

Connect 12-Volt test light to red/white wire of water temperature switch.
Ground the other end of test light.
(Automatic transmission vehicle only)

Light ON

Check connection of wire.
Check the connector.
(Automatic transmission vehicle)

Light OFF

Connect 12-volt test light to black/yellow wire to low pressure switch.
Ground the other end of test light.

Light ON

Check lead wire connection.
When no problem is found, replace low pressure switch.

Light OFF

Connect 12-volt test light to Green/white wire of micro switch.
Ground the other end of test light.

Light ON

Check lead wire connection.
When no problem is found, replace micro switch.

Light OFF

Check wire discontinuity on the side of electric power source.

Compressor clutch diagnosis (© Fuji Heavy Industries LTD.)

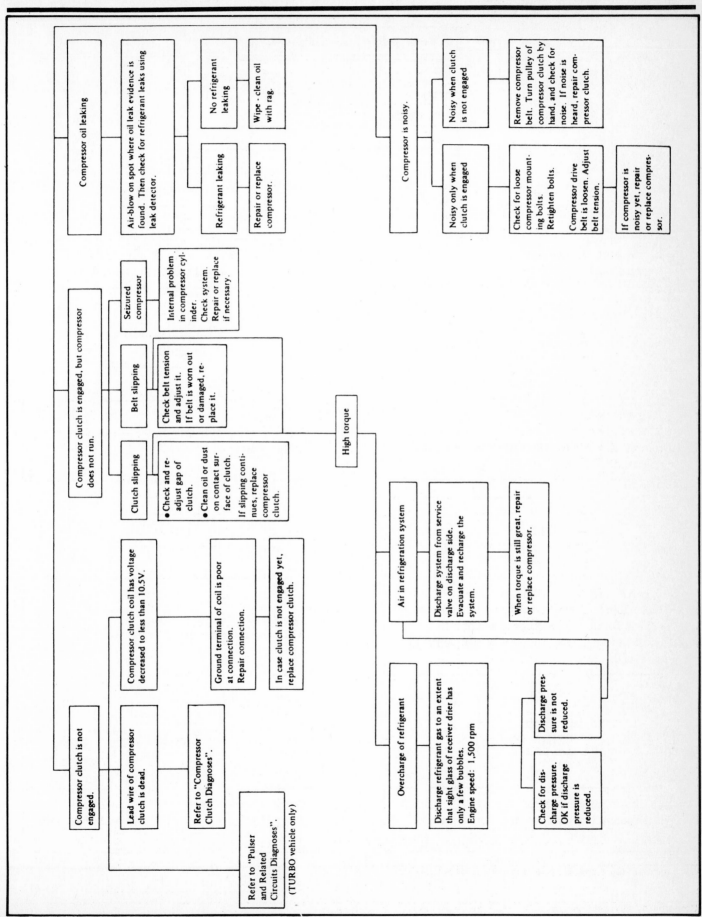

Compressor diagnosis (© Fuji Heavy Industries LTD.)

The flowchart contains the following boxes and connections:

Compressor oil leaking → Air-blow on spot where oil leak evidence is found. Then check for refrigerant leaks using leak detector.
- No refrigerant leaking → Wipe - clean oil with rag.
- Refrigerant leaking → Repair or replace compressor.

Compressor is noisy.
- Noisy when clutch is not engaged → Remove compressor belt. Turn pulley of compressor clutch by hand, and check for noise. If noise is heard, repair compressor clutch.
- Noisy only when clutch is engaged → Check for loose compressor mounting bolts. Retighten bolts. / Compressor drive belt is loosen. Adjust belt tension. → If compressor is noisy yet, repair or replace compressor.

Compressor clutch is engaged, but compressor does not run.
- Seized compressor → Internal problem in compressor cylinder. Check system. Repair or replace if necessary.
- Belt slipping → Check belt tension and adjust it. If belt is worn out or damaged, replace it.
- Clutch slipping → • Check and re-adjust gap of clutch. • Clean oil or dust on contact surface of clutch. If slipping continues, replace compressor clutch.

High torque
- Air in refrigeration system → Discharge system from service valve on discharge side. Evacuate and recharge the system. → When torque is still great, repair or replace compressor.
- Overcharge of refrigerant → Discharge refrigerant gas to an extent that sight glass of receiver drier has only a few bubbles. Engine speed: 1,500 rpm
  - Discharge pressure is not reduced.
  - Check for discharge pressure. OK if discharge pressure is reduced.

Compressor clutch is not engaged.
- Lead wire of compressor clutch is dead.
  - Compressor clutch coil has voltage decreased to less than 10.5V. → Ground terminal of coil is poor at connection. Repair connection. / In case clutch is not engaged yet, replace compressor clutch.
- Refer to "Compressor Clutch Diagnoses".
- Refer to "Pulser and Related Circuits Diagnoses". (TURBO vehicle only)

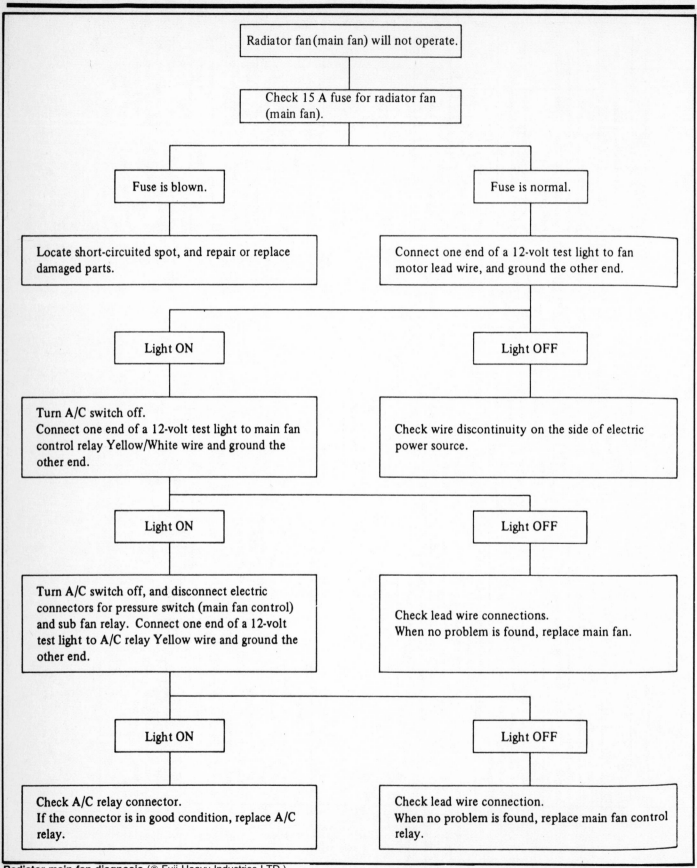

Radiator fan (main fan) will not operate.

Check 15 A fuse for radiator fan (main fan).

Fuse is blown.

Fuse is normal.

Locate short-circuited spot, and repair or replace damaged parts.

Connect one end of a 12-volt test light to fan motor lead wire, and ground the other end.

Light ON

Light OFF

Turn A/C switch off.
Connect one end of a 12-volt test light to main fan control relay Yellow/White wire and ground the other end.

Check wire discontinuity on the side of electric power source.

Light ON

Light OFF

Turn A/C switch off, and disconnect electric connectors for pressure switch (main fan control) and sub fan relay. Connect one end of a 12-volt test light to A/C relay Yellow wire and ground the other end.

Check lead wire connections.
When no problem is found, replace main fan.

Light ON

Light OFF

Check A/C relay connector.
If the connector is in good condition, replace A/C relay.

Check lead wire connection.
When no problem is found, replace main fan control relay.

Radiator main fan diagnosis (© Fuji Heavy Industries LTD.)

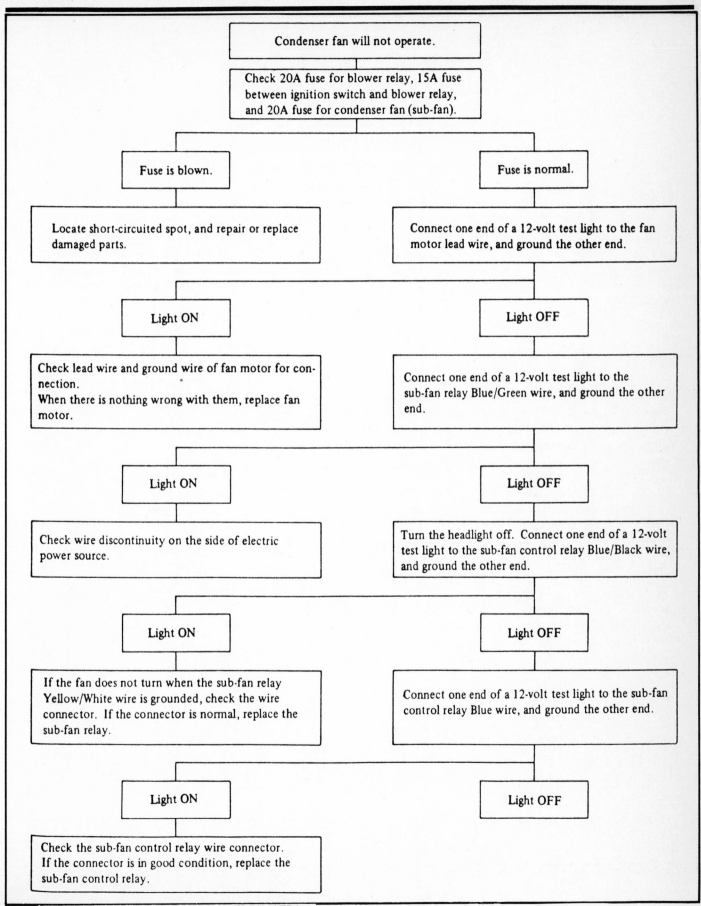

Condenser fan will not operate.

Check 20A fuse for blower relay, 15A fuse between ignition switch and blower relay, and 20A fuse for condenser fan (sub-fan).

Fuse is blown.

Fuse is normal.

Locate short-circuited spot, and repair or replace damaged parts.

Connect one end of a 12-volt test light to the fan motor lead wire, and ground the other end.

Light ON

Light OFF

Check lead wire and ground wire of fan motor for connection.
When there is nothing wrong with them, replace fan motor.

Connect one end of a 12-volt test light to the sub-fan relay Blue/Green wire, and ground the other end.

Light ON

Light OFF

Check wire discontinuity on the side of electric power source.

Turn the headlight off. Connect one end of a 12-volt test light to the sub-fan control relay Blue/Black wire, and ground the other end.

Light ON

Light OFF

If the fan does not turn when the sub-fan relay Yellow/White wire is grounded, check the wire connector. If the connector is normal, replace the sub-fan relay.

Connect one end of a 12-volt test light to the sub-fan control relay Blue wire, and ground the other end.

Light ON

Light OFF

Check the sub-fan control relay wire connector.
If the connector is in good condition, replace the sub-fan control relay.

Condensor sub-fan diagnosis (© Fuji Heavy Industries LTD.)

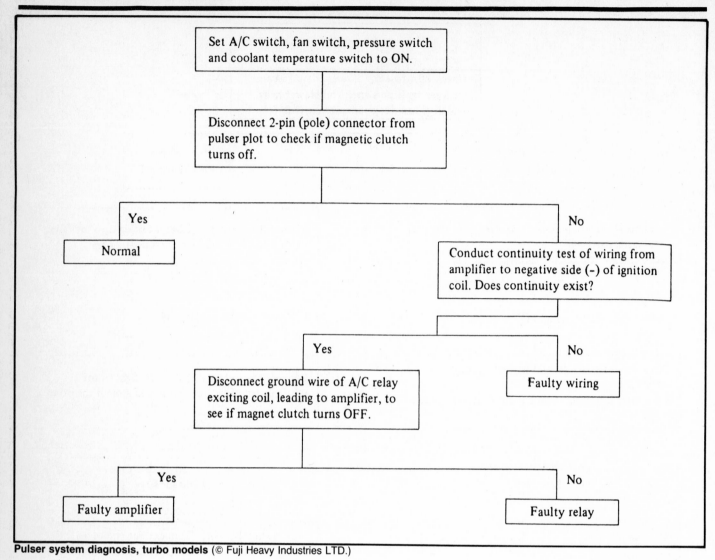

Pulser system diagnosis, turbo models (© Fuji Heavy Industries LTD.)

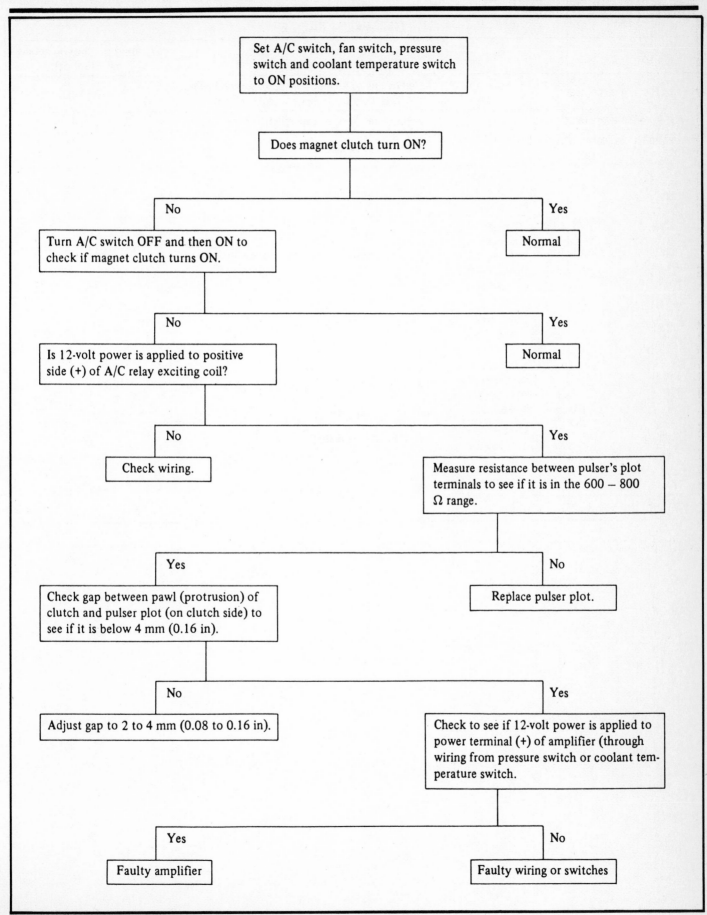

Set A/C switch, fan switch, pressure switch and coolant temperature switch to ON positions.

Does magnet clutch turn ON?

No → Turn A/C switch OFF and then ON to check if magnet clutch turns ON.

Yes → Normal

No → Is 12-volt power is applied to positive side (+) of A/C relay exciting coil?

Yes → Normal

No → Check wiring.

Yes → Measure resistance between pulser's plot terminals to see if it is in the 600 – 800 Ω range.

Yes → Check gap between pawl (protrusion) of clutch and pulser plot (on clutch side) to see if it is below 4 mm (0.16 in).

No → Replace pulser plot.

No → Adjust gap to 2 to 4 mm (0.08 to 0.16 in).

Yes → Check to see if 12-volt power is applied to power terminal (+) of amplifier (through wiring from pressure switch or coolant temperature switch.

Yes → Faulty amplifier

No → Faulty wiring or switches

Pulser system diagnosis, turbo models, continued (© Fuji Heavy Industries LTD.)

OIL CHARGE TABLE

Condition		Proper charging method	Amount of oil to be added ml (US fl oz)
Replacement of compressor		Remove all oil from new compressor and charge it with amount of oil shown in right column.	70 (2.4)
Replacement of evaporator		Add amount of oil shown in right column.	70 (2.4)
Replacement of receiver dryer (liquid tank)		Oil need not be added.	—
Replacement of condenser	There is no sign of oil leakage from condenser.	Oil need not be added.	—
	There are evidences of a large amount of oil leakage from condenser.	Add amount of oil shown in right column.	50 (1.7)
Replacement of flexible hose or copper tube	There is no sign of oil leakage.	Oil need not be added.	—
	There are evidences of a large amount of oil leakage.	Add amount of oil shown in right column.	50 (1.7)
Gas leakage	There is no sign of oil leakage.	Oil need not be added.	—
	There are evidences of a large amount of oil leakage.	Add amount of oil shown in right column.	50 (1.7)

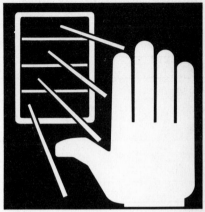

INDEX

SPECIFICATIONS

VEHICLE IDENTIFICATION CHART

1982	1983	1984	1985
Corolla	Corolla	Corolla	Corolla
Corona	Starlet	Starlet	Starlet
Starlet	Tercell	Tercell	Tercell
Tercell	Camry	Camry	Camry
Cressida	Cressida	Cressida	—
Supra	Supra	Supra	Supra
Celica	Celica	Celica	Celica

TOTOTA MOTOR CORPORATION
Freon and Refrigerant Oil Capacities

Year	Vehicle	Refrigerant Capacity, Ounces	Refrigerant Oil Capacity, Fluid Ounces
1982	Corona	18–25 oz.	2–3 oz.
1982–83	Corolla	24–26 oz.	4–5 oz.
1982–85	Starlet	24–26 oz.	2–4 oz.
1982–85	Tercell	24–26 oz.	2–4 oz.
1983–85	Camry	18–25 oz.	2–3 oz.
1982–84	Cressida	24–26 oz.	2–4 oz.
1982–85	Supra	24–26 oz.	2–4 oz.
1982–85	Celica	24–26 oz.	2–4 oz.
1984–85	Corolla	24–26 oz.	2–4 oz.

DRIVE BELT TENSION

Adjustment

1982 AND LATER

1. Loosen the A/C compressor bolts and any adjustment bracket bolts.
2. Move the compressor against the drive belt until proper tension is applied to the compressor.
3. Tighten the compressor bolts and the adjustment brackets.
4. Check the compressor for proper operation.

TROUBLESHOOTING

Condition	Cause	Correction
No warm air	a) Heater fuse blown	a) Replace fuse and check for short circuit
	b) Fan switch faulty	b) Check switch and replace if bad
	c) Wiring or ground faulty	c) Repair as needed
	d) Pressure switch faulty	d) Replace as necessary
	e) Faulty expansion valve	e) Replace expansion valve
	f) Low coolant level	f) Correct as required
	g) Low refrigerant level	g) Check refrigerant level, correct as required
Blower does not operate	a) Blower fuse blown	a) Replace fuse and check for short circuit
	b) Faulty blower switch	b) Replace blower switch
	c) Faulty blower motor	c) Replace blower motor
	d) Wiring faulty	d) Repair as needed
Failure of engine coolant to warm up	a) Defective thermostat	a) Replace thermostat
	b) Low coolant level	b) Correct fluid level
	c) Too large cooling system capacity	c) Match cooling system to engine
No coolant flow through heater core	a) Kinked heater hose	a) Straighten hose
	b) Blocked heater hose with foreign material	b) Clean or replace heater hoses
	c) Heater core blocked	c) Clean or replace heater core
	d) Defective heater shut off valve (if equipped)	d) Replace heater shut off valve
Cold air leakage	a) Missing or broken seals and/or grommets	a) Replace missing or broken seals or grommets
Air does not come through defroster nozzles	a) Obstruction in defroster nozzles	a) Remove obstruction in defroster nozzles
	b) Defroster door not operating	b) Inspect and repair door as required
	c) Inoperative blower motor	c) Check and repair blower motor or electrical circuits
Slow Heater Operation	a) Incorrect operation of controls	a) Explain proper operation of heater controls
	b) Low coolant level	b) Correct fluid level
	c) No blower operation	c) Correct blower operation
	d) Misadjusted control cable	d) Adjust control cable

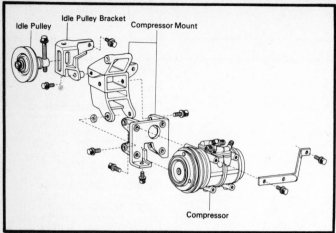

1982–1983 Tercel compressor mounting and related components
(© Toyota Motor Sales)

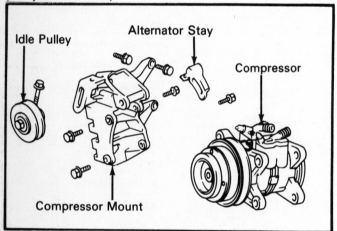

1984 and later Tercel compressor mounting and related components (© Toyota Motor Sales)

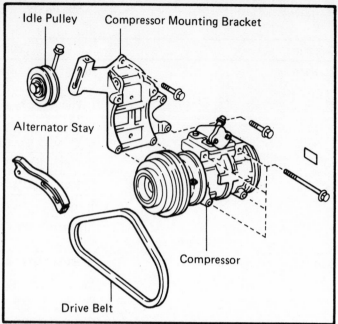

1984 and later Corolla compressor mounting and related components (© Toyota Motor Sales)

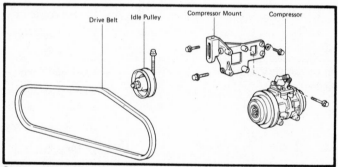

Supra compressor mounting and related components-typical (© Toyota Motor Sales)

Blower Motor

Removal and Installation

1982 AND LATER

1. Disconnect the negative battery cable.
2. Tag and disconnect the electrical connections from the blower motor assembly.
3. Remove the blower motor retaining screws. Remove any locking nuts from the motor assembly.
4. Remove the blower motor assembly from the vehicle.
5. Installation is the reverse of the removal procedure.

Compressor

Removal and Installation

1982 AND LATER

1. Disconnect the negative battery cable. Discharge the air conditioning system.
2. Remove any necessary components in order to gain access to the compressor. These may include the power steering pump and/or the alternator.
3. Tag and disconnect the electrical connections from the compressor.
4. Remove the air conditioning hoses from the compressor. Note their position on the compressor.
5. Loosen the compressor mounting bolts. Remove the compressor drive belt.

6. Remove the compressor mounting bolts. Remove the compressor from the vehicle.
7. Installation is the reverse of the removal procedure. Charge the A/C system. Check for proper operation and leaks.

Expansion Valve

Removal and Installation

1982 AND LATER

NOTE: The expansion valve is attached to the evaporator core. In order to service the expansion valve the evaporator core must be removed first.

1. Disconnect the negative battery cable and safely discharge the refrigerant system.
2. Disconnect the inlet and outlet refrigerant lines of the evaporator. Cap and plug all openings at once.
3. Remove the glove box, side air duct, air duct band and all electrical and vacuum connector as required.
4. Carefully remove all nuts and bolts securing the evaporator housing to the vehicle and remove the evaporator assembly from the vehicle.
5. On the later models remove the idling stabilizer amplifier and A/C wire harness from the evaporator assembly.

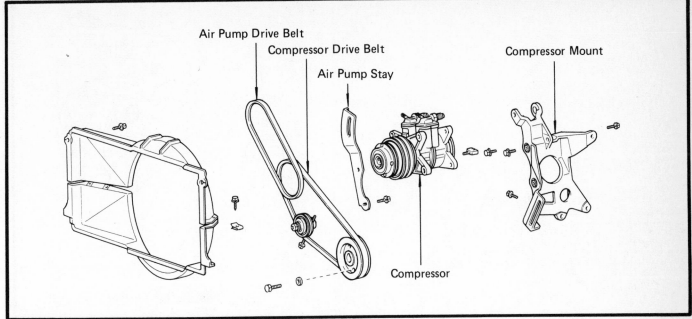

1982–1983 Corolla compressor mounting and related components (© Toyota Motor Sales)

6. Remove the thermister securing screws and remove the thermister.

7. Separate the evaporator housing by removing the retaining clips and screws that hold the two halves of the evaporator housing together.

8. Once the evaporator housing has been separated, remove the evaporator core.

9. Disconnect the refrigerant line from the inlet fitting of the expansion valve.

10. Using a suitable tool remove the expansion valve from the inlet fitting of the evaporator.

11. Installation is the reverse order of the removal procedure, also the torque for the expansion valve flare nut is 16–18 ft. lbs.

12. After installation is completed, evacuate, charge and leak test the system.

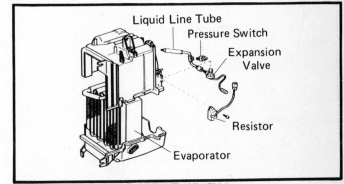

Expansion valve-exploded view (© Toyota Motor Sales)

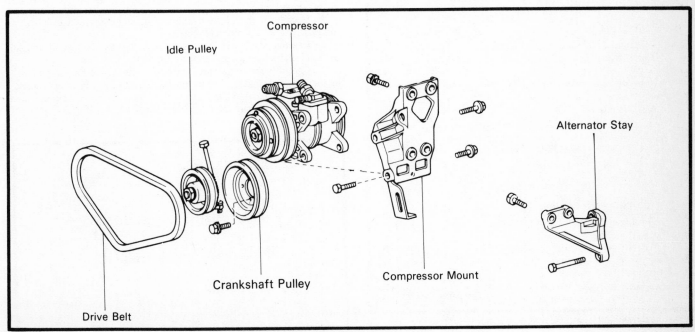

Starlet compressor mounting and related components (© Toyota Motor Sales)

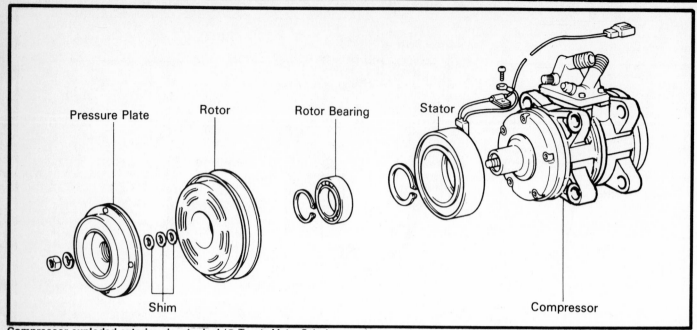

Compressor-exploded exterior view-typical (© Toyota Motor Sales)

Condenser

Removal and Installation

1982 AND LATER

1. Disconnect the negative battery cable. Discharge the air conditioning system.
2. Remove the front grille assembly as required.
3. Remove the flexible hose from the condenser inlet fitting.
4. Disconnect the liquid line from the outlet fitting on the condenser.
5. Remove the condenser retaining bolts. Remove the condenser.

6. Installation is the reverse of the removal procedure. Install the condenser making certain that the rubber cushions fit properly on the mounting flanges.

NOTE: When installing a new condenser in the vehicle, add 1.4–1.7 ounces of compressor oil to the compressor.

Evaporator Assembly

Removal and Installation

1982 AND LATER

1. Disconnect the negative battery cable and safely discharge the refrigerant system.
2. Disconnect the inlet and outlet refrigerant lines of the evaporator. Cap and plug all openings at once.
3. Remove the glove box, side air duct, air duct band and all electrical and vacuum connector as required.
4. Carefully remove all nuts and bolts securing the evaporator housing to the vehicle and remove the evaporator assembly from the vehicle.
5. On the later models remove the idling stabilizer amplifier and A/C wire harness from the evaporator assembly.

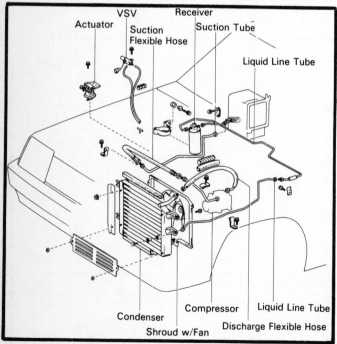

Condenser installation and related components-typical
(© Toyota Motor Sales)

Condenser retaining bolts location (© Toyota Motor Sales)

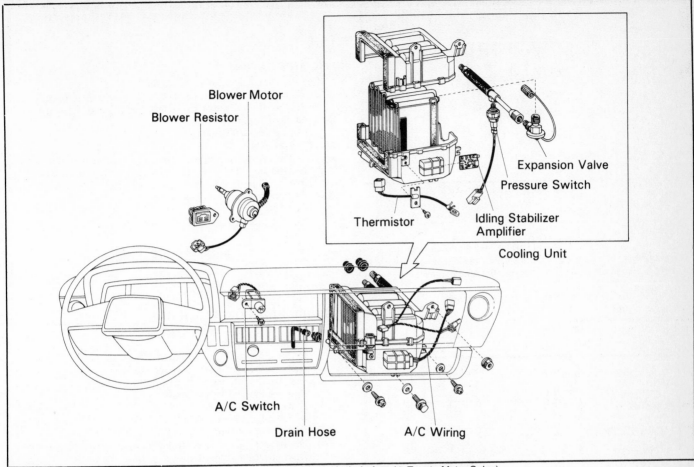

Air conditioning system components location with underdash exploded view (© Toyota Motor Sales)

6. Remove the thermister securing screws and remove the thermister.

7. Separate the evaporator housing by removing the retaining clips and screws that hold the two halves of the evaporator housing together.

8. Once the evaporator housing has been separated, remove the evaporator core.

9. Installation is the reverse order of the removal procedure.

10. After installation is completed, evacuate, charge and leak test the system.

Low Pressure Switch

Removal and Installation

1982 AND LATER

1. Disconnect the negative battery cable.

2. Remove the evaporator assembly as previously outlined.

3. Tag and disconnect the wiring at the round topped terminal.

4. Using a spanner wrench or its equivalent, remove the low pressure switch from the refrigerant piping.

5. Installation is the reverse of the removal procedure.

Thermistor

Removal

1982 AND LATER

1. Disconnect the negative battery cable and remove the glove box and undercover.

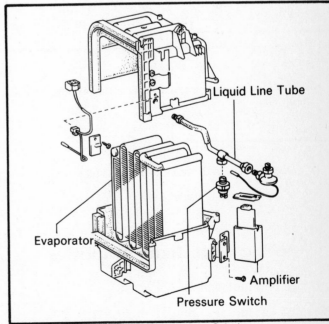

Pressure switch location (© Toyota Motor Sales)

2. With the thermistor still install, use an ohmmeter and measure the resistance at the connector (resistance 1,500 ohms at 77°F.).

3. Disconnect the thermistor connector and remove the thermistor securing screws along with the thermistor.

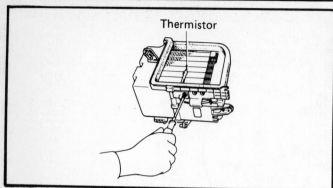

Thermister location on evaporator core (© Toyota Motor Sales)

Inspection

1. Place the thermistor in cold water and while varying the temperature of the water, measure the resistance at the connector with an ohmmeter, and at the same time measure the temperature of the water with a thermometer.

2. Compare the two readings on the chart below:
Resistance and Temperature Chart

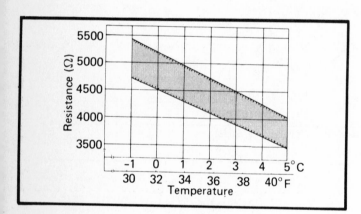

NOTE: If the intersection is not between the two lines, replace the thermistor.

Installation

1. Place the thermistor in position and install the thermistor securing screws.

2. Connect the electrical connector and install the glove box and undercover.

3. Connect the negative battery cable.

Idling Stabilizer Amplifier

Removal and Installation

1982 AND LATER

1. Disconnect the negative battery cable.
2. Remove the glove box and the glove box undercover.
3. Remove the electrical connectors to the amplifier and remove the securing screws.
4. Remove the idling stabilizer amplifier.
5. Installation is the reverse order of the removal procedure.

Idling Stabilizer Amplifier

Test

1982 AND LATER

Testing the engine speed detecting circuit:
1. Start the engine with the air conditioning system operating.
2. Inspect to verify that the magnetic clutch is disengages at the specified engine rpm.
   1982 Models: 700–800 rpm
   1983 and Later: 600–700 rpm
3. If the cut-off rpm is too high, adjust the rpm setting resister, located on the amplifier, to the specified rpm setting. If the cut-off rpm is too low, turn the rpm knob counterclockwise. If the cut-off rpm is too high, turn the rpm knob clockwise.

Heater Core

Removal and Installation

TERCEL AND COROLLA (FWD)

1. Disconnect the negative battery terminal.
2. Drain the radiator.
3. Remove the ash tray and retainer.
4. Remove the rear heater duct (optional).
5. Remove the left and right side defroster ducts.
6. Remove the under tray (optional).
7. Remove the glove box.
8. Remove the main air duct.
9. Disconnect the radio and remove it.
10. Disconnect the heater control cables and remove them.
11. Disconnect the heater hoses.
12. Remove the front and rear air ducts.
13. Remove the electrical connector.
14. Remove the heater bolts and remove the heater.

NOTE: Slide the heater to the right side of car to remove it.

15. Remove the heater core.
16. Installation is the reverse of removal.

COROLLA (RWD) AND STARLET

1. Disconnect the negative battery cable and drain the cooling system.
2. Disconnect the heater hose from the engine compartment side.
3. Remove the knobs from the heater and fan controls.
4. Remove the two securing screws, and take the heater control panel off.
5. Remove the heater control, complete with cables.
6. Disconnect the wiring harness.
7. Remove the three heater assembly securing bolts and remove the assembly.
8. Separate the core from the heater assembly.
9. Installation is the reverse of removal.

CELICA, SUPRA, CAMRY AND CRESSIDA

1. Drain the cooling system.
2. Remove the console, if so equipped, by removing the shift knob (manual), wiring connector, and console attaching screws.
3. Remove the carpeting from the tunnel.
4. If necessary, remove the cigarette lighter and ash tray.
5. Remove the package tray, if it makes access to the heater core difficult.
6. Remove the securing screws and remove the center air outlet on the Mark II/6.
7. Remove the bottom cover/intake assembly screws and withdraw the assembly.

8. Remove the cover from the water valve.
9. Remove the water valve.
10. Remove the hose clamps and remove the hoses from the core.
11. Remove the core.
12. Installation is the reverse of the removal procedure.

CORONA

1. Disconnect the negative battery cable.
2. Drain the cooling system.
3. Disconnect the heater hoses from the engine.
4. Remove the center console, if so equipped.
5. Remove the package tray and disconnect the heater air duct.
6. Unfasten the screws and take the glove compartment out of the dash.
7. Working through the glove compartment opening, remove the rear duct.
8. Detach the ventilation duct.
9. Remove the instrument cluster, as detailed below.
10. Remove the radio, if installed.
11. Remove the heater control assembly.
12. Take the defroster duct assembly out.
13. Tilt the heater assembly to the right and withdraw it from the package tray side.

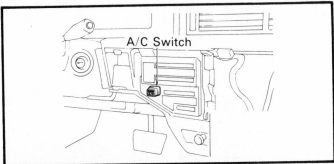

Air conditioning switch location on dash assembly
(© Toyota Motor Sales)

14. Remove the water valve and outlet hose from the heater assembly.
15. Take off the retaining band and remove the bolt.
16. Take out the core.
17. Installation is the reverse of the removal procedure.

Air Conditioning Control Switch

Removal and Installation

1982 AND LATER

1. Disconnect the negative battery cable.
2. Remove the air conditioning switch trim cluster from the instrument panel.
3. Remove the air conditioning switch retaining screws as required.
4. Tag and disconnect the electrical connections from the rear of the switch assembly.
5. Remove the switch from the vehicle.
6. Installation is the reverse of the removal procedure. Check system for proper operation.

Vent Control Switch

Removal and Installation

1982 AND LATER

1. Disconnect the negative battery cable.
2. Remove the necessary instrument cluster in order to gain access to the vent control switch.
3. Remove the heater control cables. Remove the vent mode switch connector.
4. Check the continuity between the terminal at the vent mode position using an ohmmeter. If there is no continuity, replace the switch.
5. Installation is the reverse of the removal procedure.

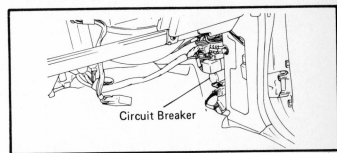

Typical circuit breaker in kick panel (© Toyota Motor Sales)

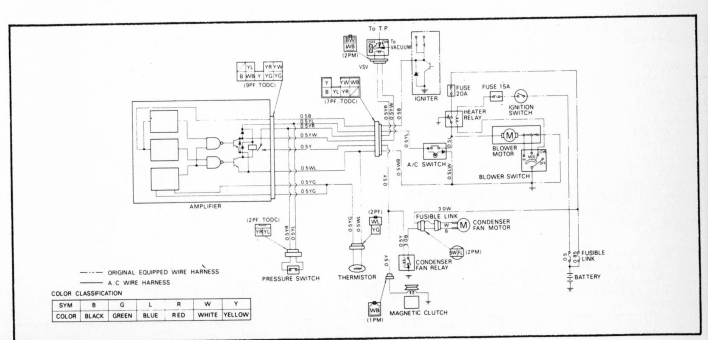

1982 Tercel A/C and heating electrical schematic (© Toyota Motor Sales)

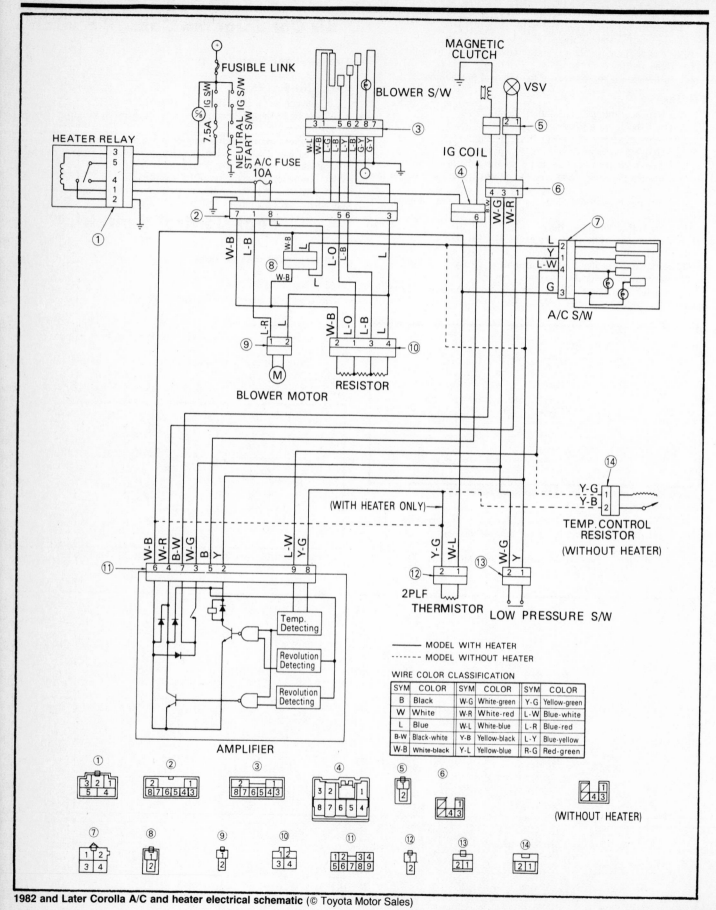

FUSIBLE LINK

IG S/W

7.5A

NEUTRAL IG S/W
START S/W

A/C FUSE
10A

HEATER RELAY

MAGNETIC
CLUTCH

BLOWER S/W

VSV

IG COIL

A/C S/W

BLOWER MOTOR

RESISTOR

(WITH HEATER ONLY)

TEMP. CONTROL
RESISTOR
(WITHOUT HEATER)

2PLF
THERMISTOR   LOW PRESSURE S/W

Temp.
Detecting

Revolution
Detecting

Revolution
Detecting

AMPLIFIER

—— MODEL WITH HEATER
------ MODEL WITHOUT HEATER

WIRE COLOR CLASSIFICATION

SYM	COLOR	SYM	COLOR	SYM	COLOR
B	Black	W-G	White-green	Y-G	Yellow-green
W	White	W-R	White-red	L-W	Blue-white
L	Blue	W-L	White-blue	L-R	Blue-red
B-W	Black-white	Y-B	Yellow-black	L-Y	Blue-yellow
W-B	White-black	Y-L	Yellow-blue	R-G	Red-green

(WITHOUT HEATER)

1982 and Later Corolla A/C and heater electrical schematic (© Toyota Motor Sales)

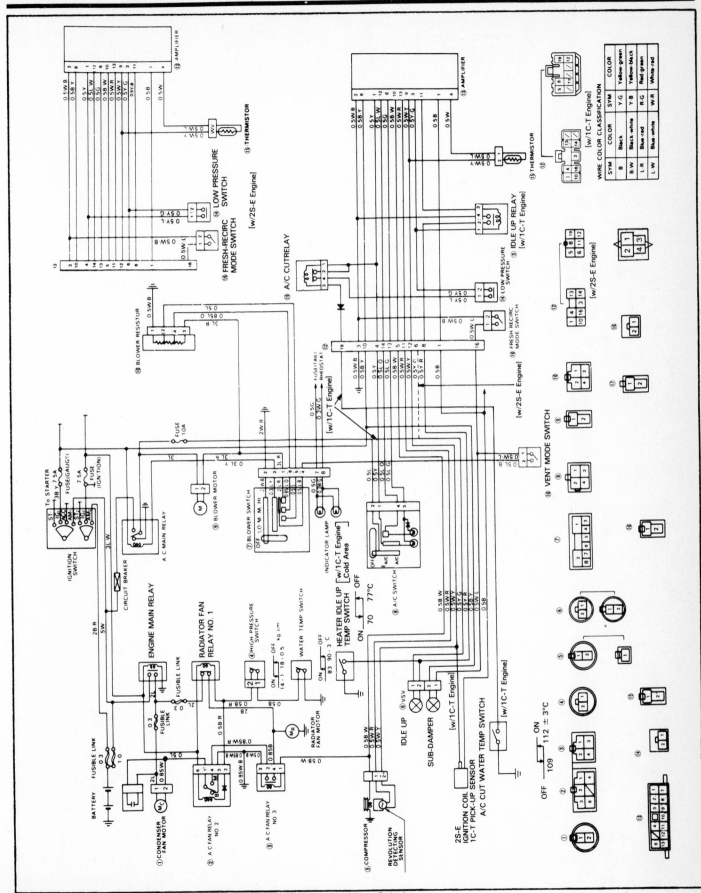

1983 and later Camry A/C and heater electrical schmatic (© Toyota Motor Sales)

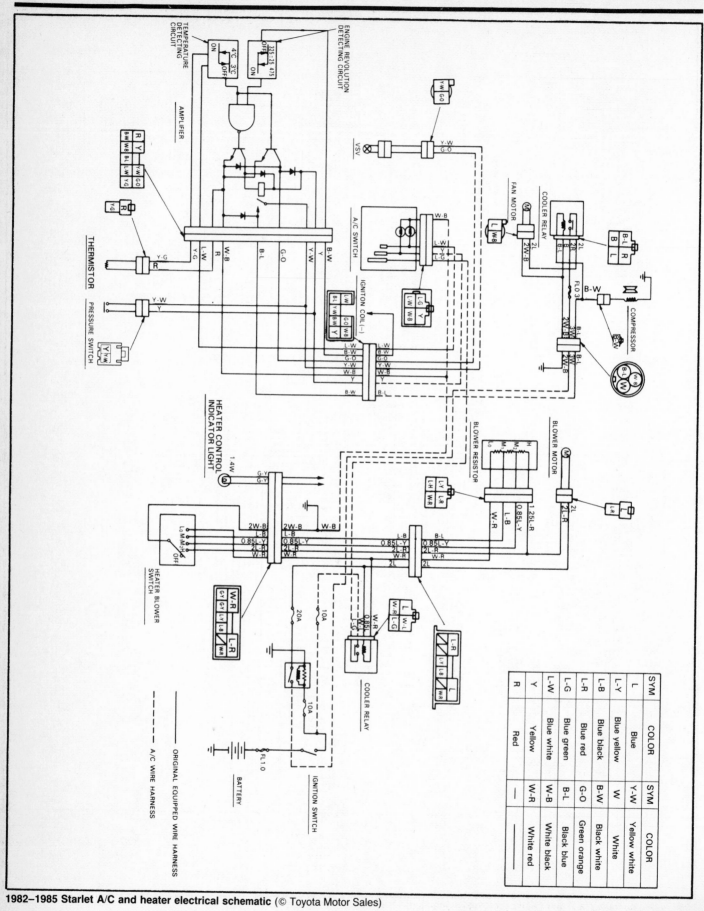

1982–1985 Starlet A/C and heater electrical schematic (© Toyota Motor Sales)

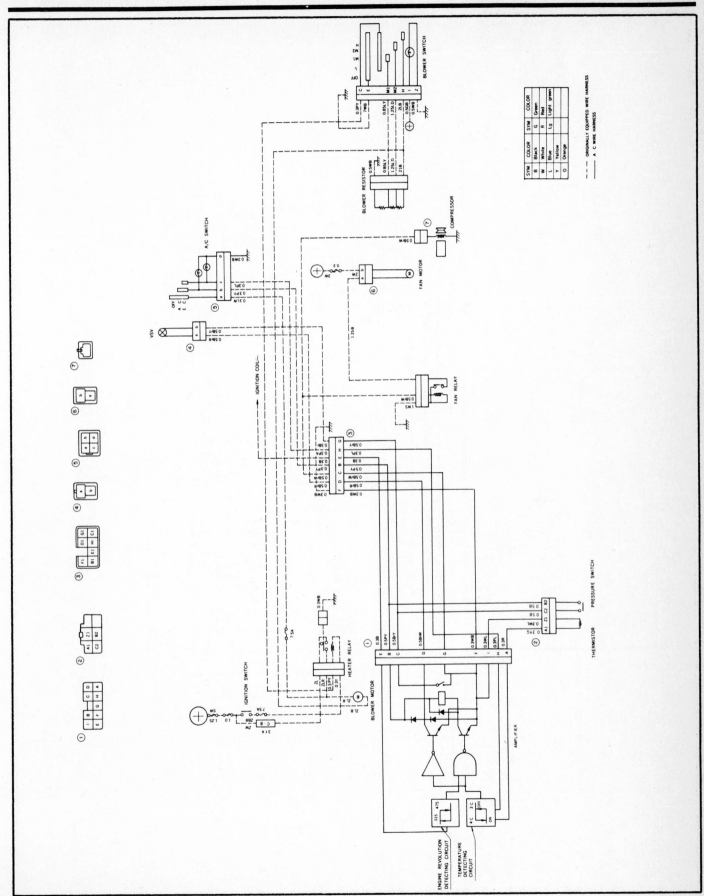

1983 and later Tercel A/C and heating electrical schematic (© Toyota Motor Sales)

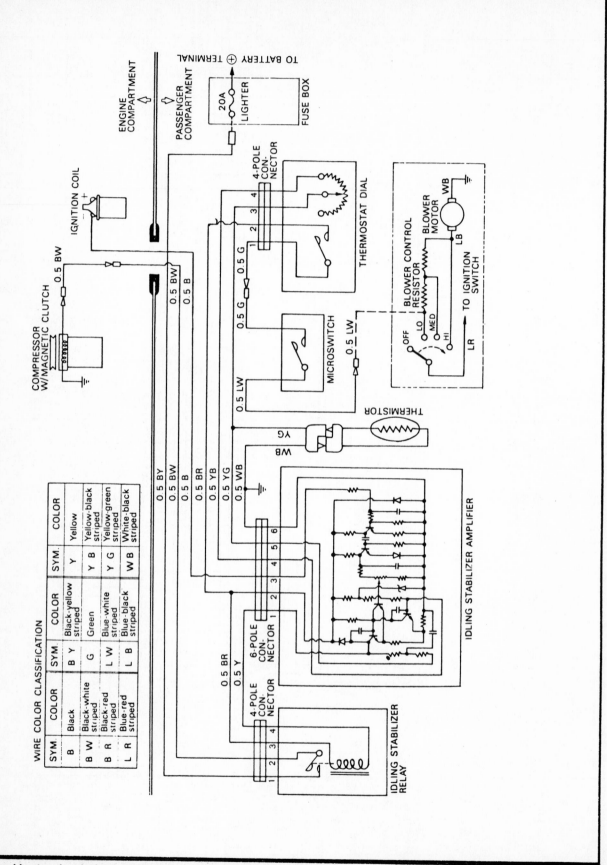

1982 Corona A/C and heater electrical schematic (© Toyota Motor Sales)

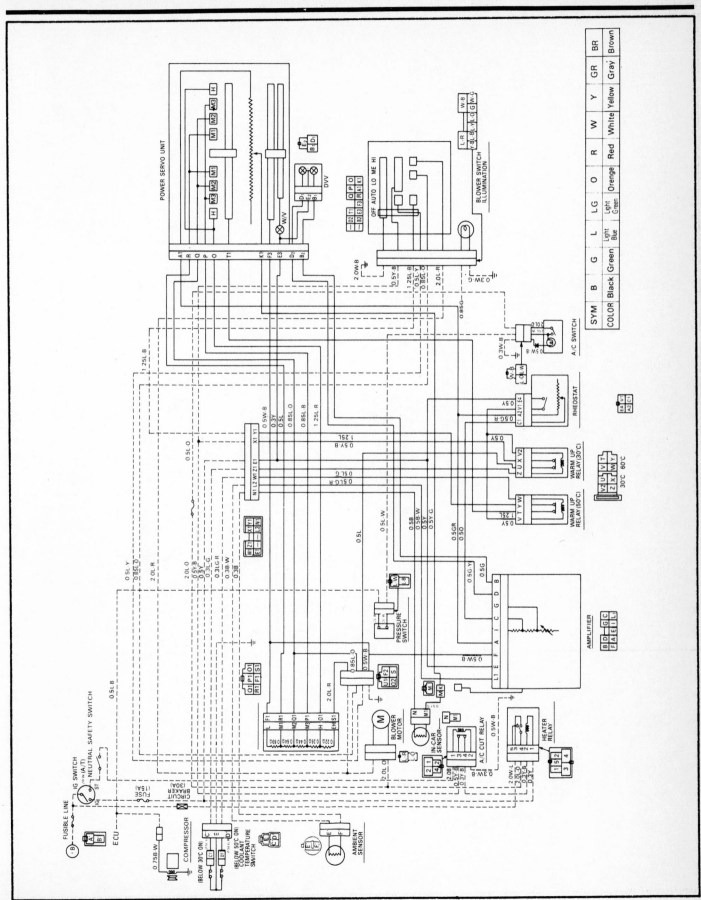

1982–1983 Cressida A/C and heater electrical schematic (© Toyota Motor Sales)

SYM	B	G	L	LG	O	R	W	Y	GR	BR
COLOR	Black	Green	Light Blue	Light Green	Orange	Red	White	Yellow	Gray	Brown

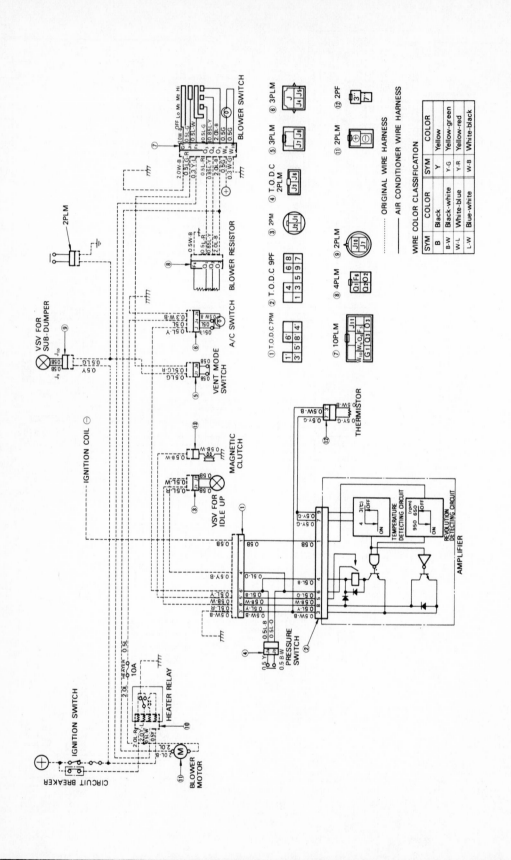

1982 and later Celica A/C and heater electrical schematic (© Toyota Motor Sales)

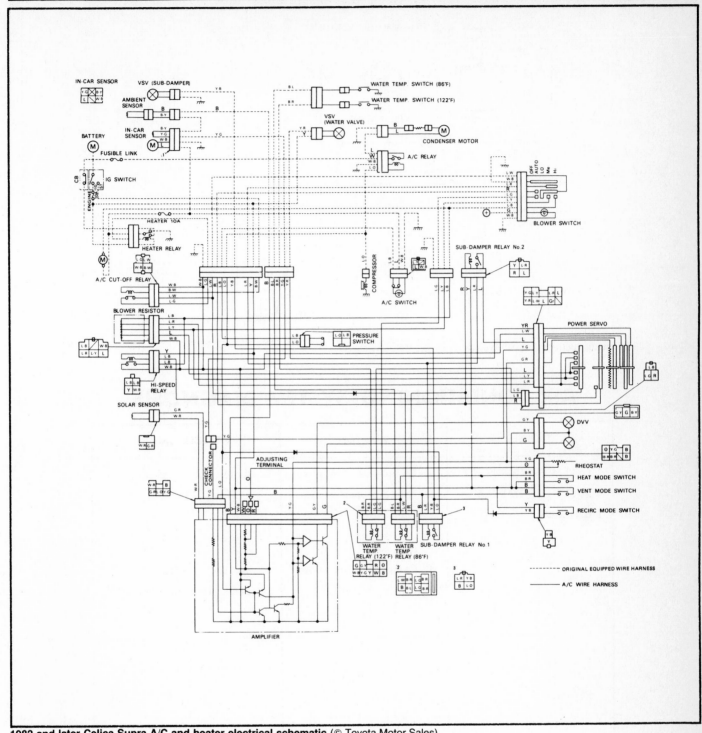

1982 and later Celica Supra A/C and heater electrical schematic (© Toyota Motor Sales)

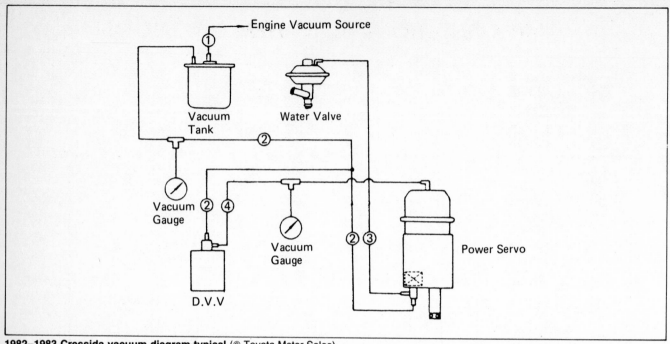

1982–1983 Cressida vacuum diagram-typical (© Toyota Motor Sales)

AIR CONDITIONING SYSTEM DIAGNOSIS

TROUBLE	SYMPTOM	POSSIBLE CAUSE
SYSTEM PRODUCES NO COOLING OR HARDLY PRODUCES.	I . Compressor does not rotate properly.	1. Loose or broken compressor belt
	II . Compressor and blower rotate normally.	1. No or insufficient refrigerant in system
		2. Defective expansion valve
		3. Choked dryer and strainer
		4. Defective compressor
		5. Defecive control system

AIR CONDITIONING SYSTEM DIAGNOSIS

INDICATION	REMEDY
1. a) The degree of depth at the center of belt is approx. 0.5 inches by pressing at 20 lbs. b) The belt is warmed abnormally.	1. Retighten or replace belt.
1. a) Sight glass shows bubbles or is cloudy.	1. Check the system for gas leakage. Recharge refrigerant.
2. a) Rotating compressor, low pressure gauge shows too low. This is caused by sticking freezed moisture on spray hole of expansion valve or by gas leaking in the remote bulb. b) Rotating compressor, low pressure gauge is too high. This is caused by opening widely spray hole of expansion valve due to loosen remote bulb holder.	2. a) Check and replace expansion valve. b) Replace or tighten remote bulb holder.
3. a) With rotating compressor, low pressure gauge indicates too low, and pipe near the strainer outlet is cooled down or becomes white with frost.	3. a) Check and replace the dryer and strainer.
4. a) High pressure gauge reading is not so different from low pressare one.	4. a) Check and disassemble compressor.
5. a) With rotating engine, dampers do not move when moving control knobs.	5. a) Check and disassemble control panel.

TROUBLE	SYMPTOM	POSSIBLE CAUSE
SYSTEM PRODUCES INSUFFICIENT COOLING	I. All dampers operate properly.	1. Defective ventilator
		2. Defective temperature control system
	II. Cool air comes out intermittently.	1. Compressor defective
		2. Defective magnetic clutch
		3. Insufficient or too much refrigerant
	III. Running at high speed, cool air comes out.	1. Condenser air passage clogged partially
		2. Compressor belt slipping
		3. Magnetic clutch slipping
	IV. When guessing trouble in the refrigeration system:	1. Expansion valve clogged
		2. Excessive moisture in system

AIR CONDITIONING SYSTEM DIAGNOSIS

INDICATION	REMEDY
1. a) Outside warm air comes in car interior through the side cowl ventilator.	1. a) Check and shut it completely.
2. a) Electrical parts in temperature control system are defective.	2. a) Check and replace them.
1. a) The pressure between discharge and suction is not so different.	1. a) Check and repair compressor.
2. a) The magnetic clutch is slipping due to oil on disc or too large gap.	2. a) Check and repair magnetic clutch.
3. a) If insufficient, bubbles can always be seen through sight glass, and if excessive, no bubble can be seen.	3. a) Check compressor discharge and suction pressure.
1. a) Condenser fins are clogged with dust or dirt.	1. a) Wash with water. Do not damage condenser fins.
2. a) Belt is loose.	2. a) Retighten the belt. Depth : 0.5 inch. (by 20 lbs.)
3. a) Clutch surfaces are fauled with oil. b) Clutch gap is too large.	3. a) Clean up clutch surfaces. b) Adjust the gap. Standard : 0.030 inch.
1. a) Low pressure gauge indicates too low or negative at engine speed of approx. 2000 r.p.m, and expansion valve outlet is covered with frost.	1. a) Check and replace the expansion valve.
2. a) After rotating compressor for a while, above phenomenon will present as if expansion valve is clogged, and when starting compressor, this trouble does not occur.	2. a) Replace dryer and receiver.

AIR CONDITIONING SYSTEM DIAGNOSIS

INDICATION	REMEDY
3. a) Pipe near dryer outlet is covered with frost.	3. a) Check and replace dryer.
4. a) Low pressure reading is too high. b) Compressor suction service valve is frosted. c) Remote bulb is loosen.	4. a), b), and c) Check and repair or replace expansion valve.
5. a) Between suction side and discharge side, the pressure is not so different.	5. a) Check and repair compressor.
6 a) If excessine both high and low pressure indicate comparatively high even if ambient temperature is not high, and no or a little bubbles can be seen through sight glass at any ambient temperature and compressor revolution. b) If short bubbles can be seen through sight glass at any ambient temperature and compressor revolution.	6. a), and b) Check refrigerant amount. Standard : 1.8 lb. in weight.
7. a) Even if the high pressure reading is high, a lot of bubble is observed in sight glass.	7. a) Purge air from air conditioning circuit.
1. a) When placing tempreature control knob at "HEAT" position, warmed air does not come out.	1. a) Check and replace control panel.
1. a) Belt is heated. Water pump does not run smoothly.	1. a) Restretch or replace belt.
2. a) Condenser fins are partially clogged with dirt and dust.	2. a) Check and wash condenser.
1. a) Pipe clamp is loosen.	1. a) Check and fix it, or use rubber seat.

AIR CONDITIONING SYSTEM DIAGNOSIS

TROUBLE	SYMPTOM	POSSIBLE CAUSE
NOISE IN SYSTEM		2. Defective blower motor
		3. Compressor
		4. Loosen belt
		5. Defective magnetic clutch

AIR CONDITIONING SYSTEM DIAGNOSIS

INDICATION	REMEDY
2. a) Blower touches to case. b) Motor shaft bearing lacks oil.	2. a) and b) Check and repair blower or motor.
3. a) A metallic sound is heard from compressor inside. b) Dull sound from whole compressor is resonance. c) Amount of compressor lubricant is not proper.	3. a) Check and repair compressor. b) Fix compressor bracket and retighten compressor belt.
4. a) When rotating compressor, belt sounds due to vibration.	4. a) Restretch as specified.
5. a) Bearings are worn out. b) The gap between the clutch disc and rotor ring face is too narrow.	5. a) Check and replace or repair. b) Exchange the number of washers.

AIR CONDITIONING SYSTEM DIAGNOSIS

TROUBLE	CHECK FOR	PROCEDURE
MAGNETIC CLUTCH DOES NOT ENGAGE	I . Fuse	Check "AIR C" fuse in fuse box and "15A" fuse in air conditioner wire harness.
	II. Magnetic clutch coil and power source.	Refer to wiring diagram. Measure terminal voltage of black-white striped wire to magnetic clutch rotor with circuit tester under following conditions : a) Run engine at 1,000 rpm. or more. b) Slide temp. control lever to coolest position c) Turn on blower switch.
	III. Air conditioner relay	Disconnect 4-pole connector from air conditioner relay. Apply 12V to ♀3 terminal and ♀4 terminal, then check contact points with circuit tester.

AIR CONDITIONING SYSTEM DIAGNOSIS

INDICATION	REMEDY
a) The fuse is blown b) The fuse is normal.	a) Replace fuse. b) Refer to wiring diagram and check electrical parts.
The circuit tester does not indicate 12V–14.5V.	Check for loose connection or open circuit of wire harness and examine other electrical parts.
a) The circuit tester indicates infinity (∞). b) The circuit tester indicates zero (0) ohm. AIR CONDITIONER RELAY #3 #2 #4 #1 Ω ⊕ ⊖ CIRCUIT TESTER BATTERY	a) Replace air conditioner relay. b) Relay is normal. Check for loose connection or open circuit and examine other electrical parts.

AIR CONDITIONING SYSTEM DIAGNOSIS

TROUBLE	CHECK FOR	PROCEDURE
MAGNETIC CLUTCH DOES NOT ENGAGE (Continued)	IV. Blower control switch	Disconnect 4-pole connector from idling stabilizer relay. Turn on ignition switch, and set blower control switch at "LO" position. Connect circuit tester ⊕ terminal to ⊂1 terminal and circuit tester ⊖ terminal to idling stabilizer relay body base.
	V. Idling stabilizer relay	Disconnect 4-pole connector from idling stabilizer relay. Apply 12V to ⊂3 and ⊂4 terminal of relay, then check contact points with circuit tester.
	VI. Microswitch for magnetic clutch on control panel.	Disconnect 6-pole connector from idling stabilizer amplifier, set blower control knob at "LO" position and air control lever at "COOL" position, then turn on ignition switch. Measure ⊂6 terminal voltage of connector with circuit tester.

AIR CONDITIONING SYSTEM DIAGNOSIS

INDICATION	REMEDY
Circuit tester does not indicate 12V–14.5V. AIR CONDITIONER WIRE HARNESS ⊕ ⊖ V TO RELAY BASE #1 TO IDLING STABILIZER RELAY	a) Check for loose connection or open circuit of wire harness. b) Replace blower control switch.
a) The circuit tester indicates infinity (∞). b) The circuit tester indicates zero (0) ohm. #4 #3 IDLING STABILIZER RELAY Ω ⊕ ⊖ CIRCUIT TESTER BATTERY	a) Replace idling stabilizer relay. b) Relay is normal. Check for loose connection or open circuit. Examine other electrical parts.
a) The circuit tester does not indicate 12V–14.5V. b) The circuit tester indicates 12V–14.5V. AIR CONDITIONER WIRE HARNESS #6 ⊕ ⊖ V TO IDLING STABILIZER AMP. TO AMP. BASE CIRCUIT TESTER	a) Check for loose connection or open circuit of wire harness. Replace control panel. b) Microswitch is normal. Examine amplifier and other electrical parts.

AIR CONDITIONING SYSTEM DIAGNOSIS

TROUBLE	CHECK FOR	PROCEDURE
MAGNETIC CLUTCH DOES NOT ENGAGE (Continued)	VII. Temperature control resistor and micro-switch for temp. control resistor in panel	Disconnect 6-pole connector from idling stabilizer amp. Connect circuit tester to ♯2 and ♯4 terminal of connector. Then, slide temp. control lever slowly from cool position to warm position.
	VIII. Idling stabilizer amplifier	Operate air conditioner. Set temperature control lever at coolest position and then increase engine rpm.
	IX. Thermistor	Disconnect 6-pole connector from idling stabilizer amp. Connect circuit tester to ♯2 and ♯3 terminal of connector. Measure resistance of thermistor.
MAGNETIC CLUTCH DOES NOT DISENGAGE	I. Magnetic Clutch	Turn off air conditioner. Check contact surface of rotor and pulley.

AIR CONDITIONING SYSTEM DIAGNOSIS

INDICATION	REMEDY
a) The circuit tester indicates infinity (∞) while moving control lever. b) The circuit tester indicates within 50–600 ohm. while moving control lever. 	a) Replace control panel. b) Temp. control resistor and microswitch for temp. control resistor is normal. Check amplifier or thermistor.
a) Cut-in rpm. is too high. b) Magnetic clutch does not engage.	a) Adjust or replace amplifier. b) Check for loose connection or open circuit. Check or replace amplifier and thermistor.
a) The resistance is too low. Standard : 330 $\pm$ 30Ω at 59°F b) The resistance is normal.	a) Replace thermistor or check for loose connection of wire harness. b) Check for loose connection of wire harness.
a) The contact surface is defective. b) There is normal gap between pressure plate of clutch pulley and rotor. Standard gap : 0.03 inch.	a) Repair or replace rotor and pulley or clutch bearing. b) Adjust gap with shim.

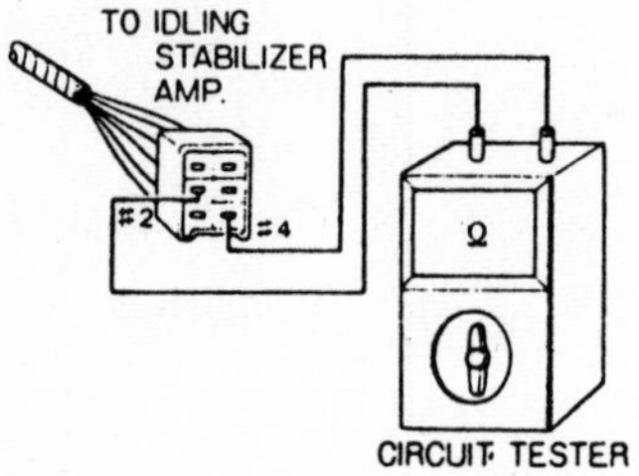

TO IDLING STABILIZER AMP.

#2 #4

Ω

CIRCUIT TESTER

AIR CONDITIONING SYSTEM DIAGNOSIS

TROUBLE	CHECK FOR	PROCEDURE
	II. Temperature control resistor and microswitch for temp. control resistor on control panel.	Disconnect 6-pole connector from idling stabilizer amplifier. Connect circuit tester to ♯3 and ♯4 terminal of connector and slide temp. control lever slowly from cool position to warm position.
	III. Idling stabilizer amplifier	1. Run engine, and turn on air conditioner. Measure cut-in and cut-off engine rpm. 2. Run engine, and turn on air conditioner. Disconnect 6-pole connector from amplifier.
	IV. Thermistor	Measure resistance of thermistor with circuit tester.
	V. Idling stabilizer relay	Run engine, and operate air conditioner. Disconnect 4-pole connector from relay.

AIR CONDITIONING SYSTEM DIAGNOSIS

INDICATION	REMEDY
a) The circuit tester indicates ZERO (0) ohm while moving control lever. b) The circuit tester indicates within 500-600 ohm while moving control lever. TO IDLING STABILIZER AMP. Ω CIRCUIT TESTER	a) Replace control panel. b) Temp. control resistor is normal. Check amplifier and thermistor.
1. Magnetic clutch engages at idling due to too low cut-in and cut-off engine rpm.	1. Adjust or replace to get specified cut-in and cut-off engine rpm..
2. a) Magnetic clutch disengages.	2. a) Check or replace amp., thermistor and temp. control resistor.
b) Magnetic clutch still engages.	b) Check or replace idling stabilizer relay and wiring.
a) The resistance is too high. Standard : $330 \pm 30\Omega$ at 59°F	a) Replace thermistor.
b) The resistance is normal.	b) Check for loose connection or open circuit of wire harness.
Magnetic clutch disengages.	Replace idling stabilizer relay.

AIR CONDITIONING SYSTEM DIAGNOSIS

TROUBLE	CHECK FOR	PROCEDURE
NO OR INSUFFICIENT COOL AIR COMES OUT	I. Fuse	Check "15A" fuse in wire harness of air conditioner.
	II. Blower motor	Disconnect a connector from blower motor. Connect battery ⊕ terminal directly to blue-black striped lead wire of blower motor.
	III. Air conditioner relay	Refer to item III
	IV. Blower control switch	1. Refer to item IV 2. Disconnect 3-pole connector from blower control resistor. Turn on ignition switch. Set blower control switch at "LO", "MED" and "HI" positions to measure each terminal voltage of 3-pole connector for control resistor with circuit tester.

AIR CONDITIONING SYSTEM DIAGNOSIS

INDICATION	REMEDY

1. a) The fuse is brown
   b) The fuse is normal.
	1. a) Replace fuse.
	   b) Check or replace other electrical parts.
	   Check for loose connection or open circuit of wire harness.

1. a) Blower motor does not rotate.
   b) Blower motor rotates smoothly.
	1. a) Replace motor.
	   b) Check air con. relay, blower control switch and blower control resistor.

1. a), b) Refer to item III	a), b) Refer to item III
1. a) Refer to item IV	1. Refer to item IV
2. a) Circuit tester does not indicate 12V–14.5V on each terminal. ORIGINAL WIRE HARNESS TO BLOWER CONTROL RESISTOR CIRCUIT TESTER	2. a) Check for loose connection or open circuit of wire harness. b) Replace blower control switch.

AIR CONDITIONING SYSTEM DIAGNOSIS

TROUBLE	CHECK FOR	PROCEDURE
	V. Blower control resistor	Turn blower control knob to "LO", "MED" and "HI" position.
	VI. Microswitch for magnetic clutch on control panel	Refer to item VI
	VII. Thermistor	Measure resistance of thermistor.
	VIII. Temperature control resistor and microswitch for temp. control resistor on control panel.	Disconnect 6-pole connector from idling stabilizer amp. Connect circuit tester to ☲2 and ☲4 terminal of connector, and slide temp. control lever slowly from cool position to warm position.

AIR CONDITIONING SYSTEM DIAGNOSIS

INDICATION	REMEDY
Blower speed does not change by changing knob.	a) Check for loose connection or open circuit of wire harness. b) Replace blower control resistor.
a), b) Refer to item VI	a), b) Refer to item VI
The resistance is lower than specified. Standard: $20 \doteq 2\,K\Omega$ at 77°F	Replace thermistor.
a) Resistance of temp. control resistor is too low.	a) Replace control panel.

	WARM	TEMPERATURE	COOL
TESTER READING	180Ω	500–600Ω	50–120Ω

TEMP. CONTROL LEVER

* The resistance will be changed from 500–600 ohms to 180 ohms by operating microswitch.

| b) Micorswitch for temp. control resistor does not operate. | b) Replace control panel. |

SECTION 7
IMPORT CARS
Volkswagen

INDEX

VOLKSWAGEN SPECIFICATIONS

Vehicle Base Models

1982–83
Rabbit
Jetta
Scirocco
Quantum
Vanagon
Pickup

1984
Rabbit
Jetta
Scirocco
Quantum
Vanagon

1985k
Golf
Jetta
Quantum
Scirocco
Vanagon

Freon Capacity

1982–1985
Rabbit/Golf
Jetta
Scirocco
Pickup .... 32 + 3 ounces
Quantum .... 34 ounces
Vanagon .... 42–46 ounces

Refrigerant Oil Capacity

During discharge of system, measure amount of refrigerant oil that has exited system with the refrigerant. Replace the exact amount. When compressor is being replaced, drain the replacement compressor and install six (6) fluid ounces. For replacement of major components, add no more than one (1) fluid ounce per major component.

Drive Belt Tension Adjustment

Adjust the belt so that with moderate thumb pressure, the belt can be deflected 3/16–3/8 inch between the compressor and the crankshaft pulleys.

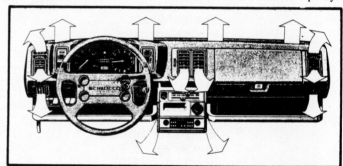

Scirocco ventilation/heating air flow with air conditioning (© Volkswagen of America, Inc.)

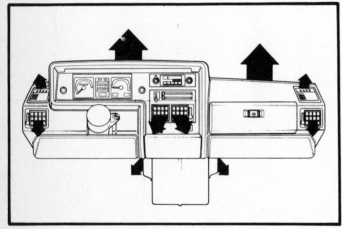

Rabbit ventilation/heating air flow with air conditioning (© Volkswagen of America, Inc.)

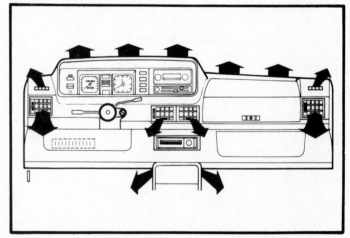

Jetta ventilation/heating air flow with air conditioning (© Volkswagen of America, Inc.)

Blower Motor

Removal and Installation

1982–84 RABBIT, JETTA AND PICKUP
1982–85 SCIROCCO
1. Drain the cooling system and discharge the air conditioning system safely. Remove the negative battery cable.

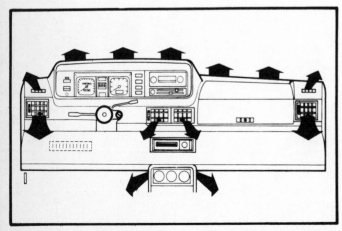

Rabbit convertible ventilation/heating air flow with air conditioning (© Volkswagen of America, Inc.)

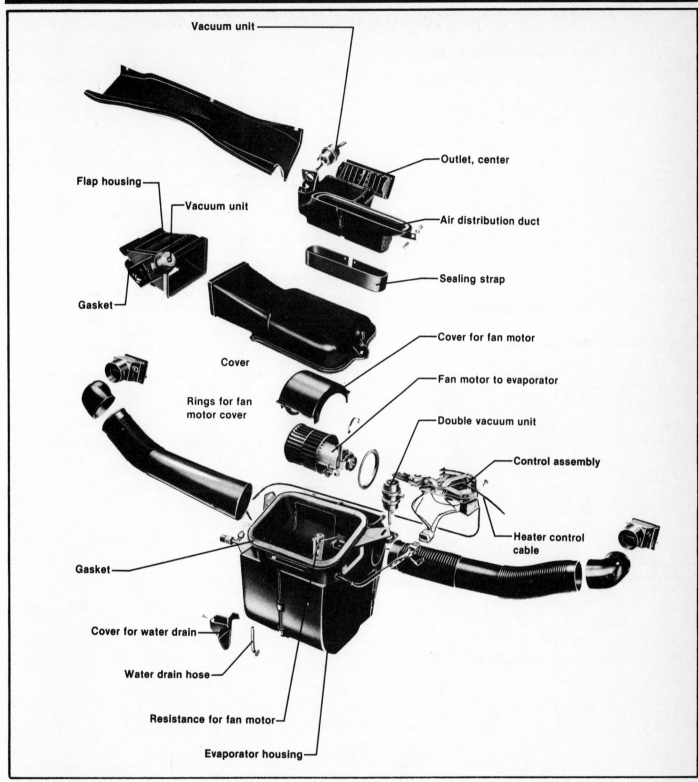

Vacuum unit

Outlet, center

Flap housing

Air distribution duct

Vacuum unit

Sealing strap

Gasket

Cover for fan motor

Cover

Fan motor to evaporator

Rings for fan motor cover

Double vacuum unit

Control assembly

Heater control cable

Gasket

Cover for water drain

Water drain hose

Resistance for fan motor

Evaporator housing

Location of blower motor, typical of Rabbit, Jetta, Scirocco and Pickup models (© Volkswagen of America, Inc.)

2. Remove the dash assembly, as required, remove the console, if equipped, disconnect the air ducts assembly and remove the assembly from the vehicle.

3. Remove the cover from the top of the heater/evaporator housing and remove the blower motor.

4. The installation of the blower motor, the heater/evaporator housing is the reverse of the removal procedure.

1982 QUANTUM

1. Remove the blower motor from the plenum chamber side of the housing.

2. Remove the cover from the blower motor, disconnect the wiring and remove the motor from the evaporator housing.

3. Reverse the procedure to install the motor.

1985 GOLF, JETTA AND GTI

1. Disconnect the wiring, disengage the locking lug and turn the motor assembly clockwise.

2. Remove the blower motor assembly from under the housing assembly.

3. Reverse the removal procedure when installing the motor to the housing.

4. During the installation, turn the motor assembly counterclockwise to engage the motor assembly to the evaporator housing. Engage the locking lug.

1984–85 VANAGON

1. The fan assembly is located in the evaporator housing, mounted to the front of the roof.

2. Carefully remove the retaining screws from the evaporator housing and lower the assembly to a working position.

3. Separate the housings and expose the blower motor and switches.

4. Remove the blower motor assembly.

5. To install the blower motor and the evaporator housing, reverse the removal procedure.

Compressor

REMOVAL AND INSTALLATION

NOTE: On some models, it may be necessary to remove both the compressor clutch and the water pump pulley in order to replace the compressor drive belt.

NOTE: On some models, it may be necessary to remove both the compressor clutch and the water pump pulley in order to replace the compressor drive belt.

All Models Equipped with York Compressor

1. Front seat service valves to prevent loss of refrigerant from the system.

2. Disconnect both the suction and the discharge service valves from the compressor head. Cap or plug the opening immediately.

CAUTION

Caution: A small amount of refrigerant will leak from the service valve connections during their disconnection. Observe safety precautions to avoid personal injury.

3. Loosen the compressor bolts or idler pulley, if equipped, to relax the tension on the drive belt. Remove the drive belt from the compressor pulley.

4. Disconnect the electrical connection from the magnetic pulley terminal.

5. Remove the compressor to bracket retaining bolts and remove the compressor from the engine.

NOTE: In some instances, to ease removal and installation, the brackets or part of the brackets can be removed with the compressor, taken from the compressor when on the bench and re-installed before installation of the compressor.

6. The installation of the compressor is the reverse of the removal procedure.

7. Verify oil level is correct in the compressor and charge the system as required.

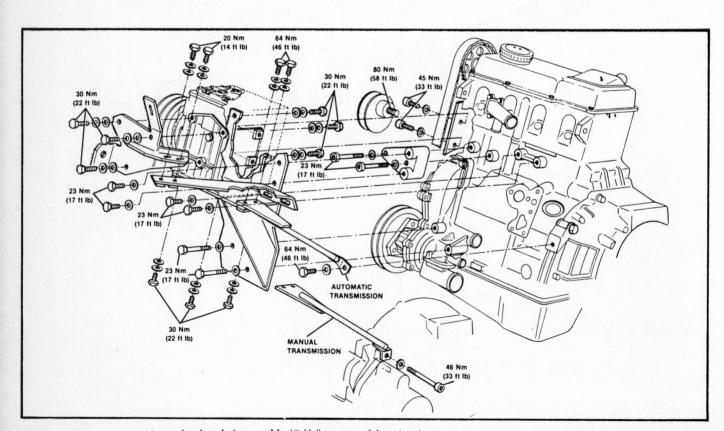

Typical York compressor to engine bracket assembly (© Volkswagen of America, Inc.)

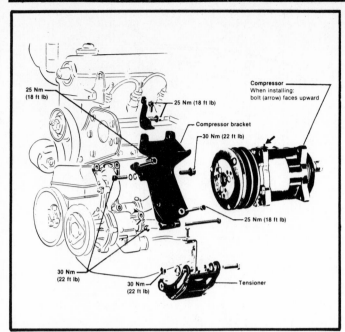

Typical Sankyo compressor to engine bracket assembly (© Volkswagen of America, Inc.)

All Models Equipped With Sankyo Compressor

1. If the compressor is equipped with the manually operated shut-off service valves, front seat the valves to prevent refrigerant from exiting the system.

2. If the system is equipped with Schrader type service valves, the system must be discharged safely.

— CAUTION —
Perform the service valve removal or the discharge of the system safely, to prevent personal injury.

3. Remove the electrical connection from the magnetic clutch terminal.

4. Loosen the adjusting bolts on the tensioner or idler pulley, if equipped, to provide slack in the drive belt. Remove the drive belt.

5. Remove the compressor retaining bolts to brackets. Remove the compressor from the engine brackets.

6. To install the compressor, reverse the removal procedure. Verify the compressor has the correct level of refrigerant oil.

7. Install the drive belt and adjust to a deflection of between 5/16 and 3/8 inch between the compressor and the crankshaft pulley.

8 If the system had been discharged, evacuate and charge the system as previously outlined.

9. Verify the system operates properly.

Expansion Valve

Removal and Installation

Refer to the evaporator removal and installation section for the expansion valve service. The expansion valve is located within the evaporator housing assembly with the evaporator core on most all models.

Condenser

Removal and Installation

ALL MODELS EXCEPT VANAGON

1. Drain the cooling system. Disconnect the upper and lower radiator hoses. Discharge the air conditioning system safely.

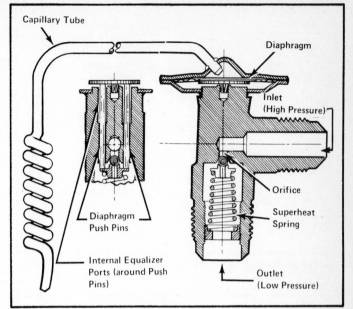

Cross section of typical expansion valve (© Volkswagen of America, Inc.)

2. Remove the shroud and electric cooling fan from the radiator and move towards the engine.

3. If the vehicle is equipped with automatic transmission, remove the fluid cooling lines at the radiator.

4. Remove the retaining bolts or nut from the top and bottom of the radiator and remove the radiator.

NOTE: The battery may be removed to gain more working clearance, if so desired.

5. Disconnect the inlet and outlet lines at the condenser. Cap or plug the openings immediately.

6. Remove the retaining bolts or nuts from the condenser and carefully lift the condenser from the front of the vehicle.

7. Upon repairs to the condenser or replacement, reverse the removal procedure to install the condenser.

8. Add the correct amount of refrigerant oil to the condenser. Evacuate and charge the air conditioning system. Verify the system operates correctly.

1984–85 VANAGON

The condenser is located at the front of the radiator, which is located behind the front grille. A special electric fan is used to aid in the cooling of both the radiator and the condenser, rather then to depend upon the ram air effect while driving and moving in traffic. A specific removal procedure is not available from the manufacturer at time of print. However, the grille can be removed to expose the condenser. Caution must be exercised to prevent personal injury during the removal and installation of the condenser.

Evaporator

Removal and Installation

1982–84 RABBIT, JETTA AND PICKUP
1982–85 SCIROCCO, QUANTUM

NOTE: The following Removal and Installation procedure can be re-sequenced to fit a particular model that may differ than the outline.

1. Drain the cooling system and discharge the air conditioning system safely. Disconnect the negative battery cable.

2. Remove the console, if equipped.

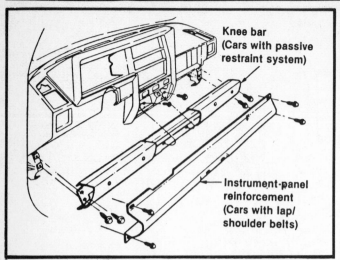

Removal or installation of dash components—typical (© Volkswagen of America, Inc.)

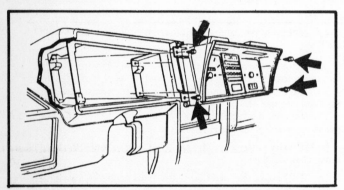

Removal or installation of instrument cluster—typical (© Volkswagen of America, Inc.)

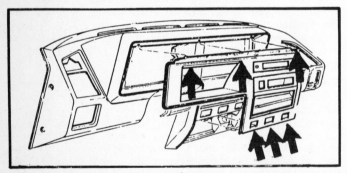

Removal or installation of instrument panel insert—typical (© Volkswagen of America, Inc.)

Location of right and left air ducts—typical (© Volkswagen of America, Inc.)

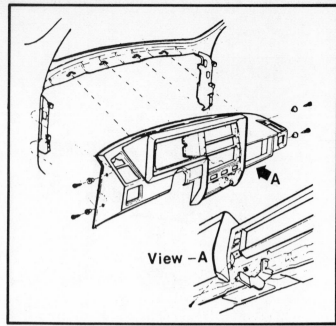

Removal or installation of dash assembly—typical (© Volkswagen of America, Inc.)

3. Remove the instrument panel top.

4. Remove the radio and the top and bottom glove boxes, if equipped with both.

5. Remove the dash completely. Disconnect the wiring connectors, vacuum connectors and speedometer cable from the dash panel components.

6. Disconnect the cables as required from the evaporator housing. Remove the retaining bolts, the heater core hoses, the evaporator inlet and outlet hoses and cap or plug the openings immediately.

7. Remove the evaporator housing from the vehicle. Separate the halves of the evaporator housing and remove the evaporator.

NOTE: The expansion valve can be removed and replaced from the evaporator at this time.

8. During the installation of a repaired or replacement evaporator core, position the expansion capillary tube on top of the evaporator pipe and secure with the special clip. Position the capillary tube from the thermostat into the evaporator at a depth of 5⅛ inch.

NOTE: The heater core can be replaced without the separation of the housing. A door is provided on the right side to allow the core to be removed and replaced separately.

9. After the assembly of the evaporator housing, install the assembly into the vehicle and complete the installation in the reverse of the removal procedure.

10. Install the coolant. Evacuate and recharge the air conditioning system.

11. Verify the cooling system and the air conditioning system is operating correctly.

Removal and Installation

1984–85 VANAGON

NOTE: The evaporator unit is mounted to the roof at the front of the vehicle. It is important to note that factory air conditioning is not available for the Vanagon when it is equipped with the factory installed electric sun roof.

1. Discharge the air conditioning system safely.

2. Remove the retaining screws holding the evaporator assembly to the roof.

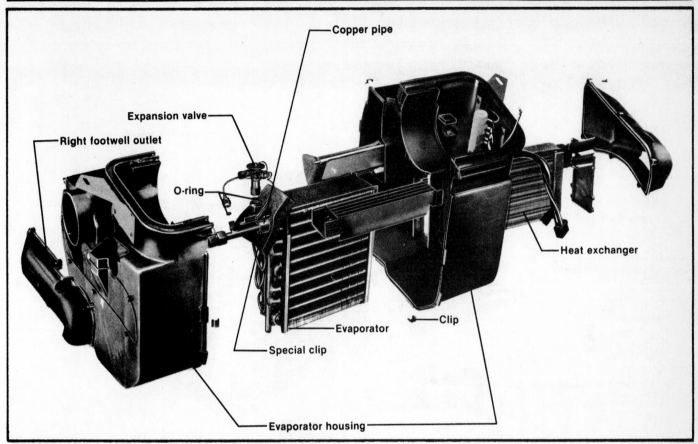

Exploded view of typical evaporator/heater housing (© Volkswagen of America, Inc.)

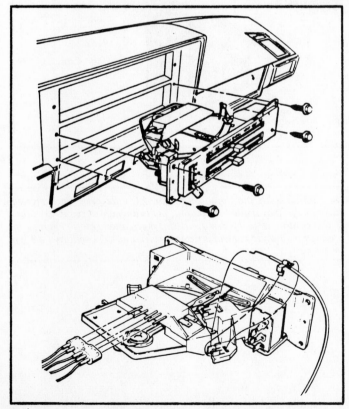

Removal or installation of control head from dash—typical (© Volkswagen of America, Inc.)

3. Carefully lower the unit and remove the inlet and outlet hoses from the evaporator. Cap or plug the openings immediately.

4. Separate the evaporator housing and remove the evaporator core from the housing.

NOTE: The expansion valve can be removed and replaced from the evaporator assembly at this time.

5. To install the evaporator, reverse the removal procedure. Evacuate and recharge the air conditioning.

6. Verify the air conditioning is operating properly.

Heater Core

Removal and Installation

The removal and installation of the heater core is outlined in the heater section. The heater core removal is made easier by the addition of a heater core cover door, which can be removed and the core slide from the housing. During the installation, sealers must be used to prevent air loss around the core. The heater core tube ends must be capped or plugged to prevent coolant from leaking onto the vehicle's interior floor covering during the removal procedure.

Controls

Removal and Installation

ALL MODELS

The control head of the air conditioning system can be removed from the dash by removal of the necessary trim panel, the removal of the

527

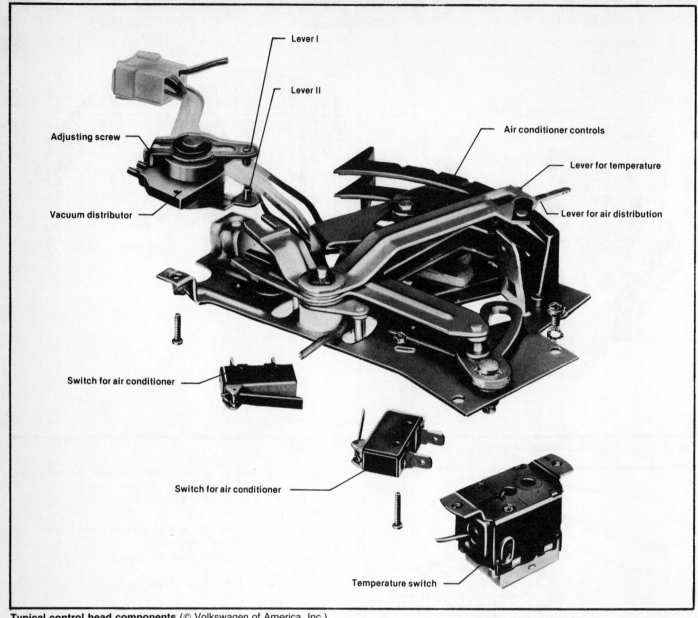

Lever I

Lever II

Air conditioner controls

Adjusting screw

Lever for temperature

Vacuum distributor

Lever for air distribution

Switch for air conditioner

Switch for air conditioner

Temperature switch

Typical control head components (© Volkswagen of America, Inc.)

retaining screws and pulling the control from the dash in order to expose the cables, vacuum connection and electrical wiring. On certain models, the radio and glove box(es) may have to be removed in order to obtain working clearance.

CAUTION

On controls with the thermostat attached, care must be exercised during the removal and installation, not to damage the capillary tube. If the control is to be removed, the thermostat can sometimes be removed before the control is disconnected and the capillary tube left in place.

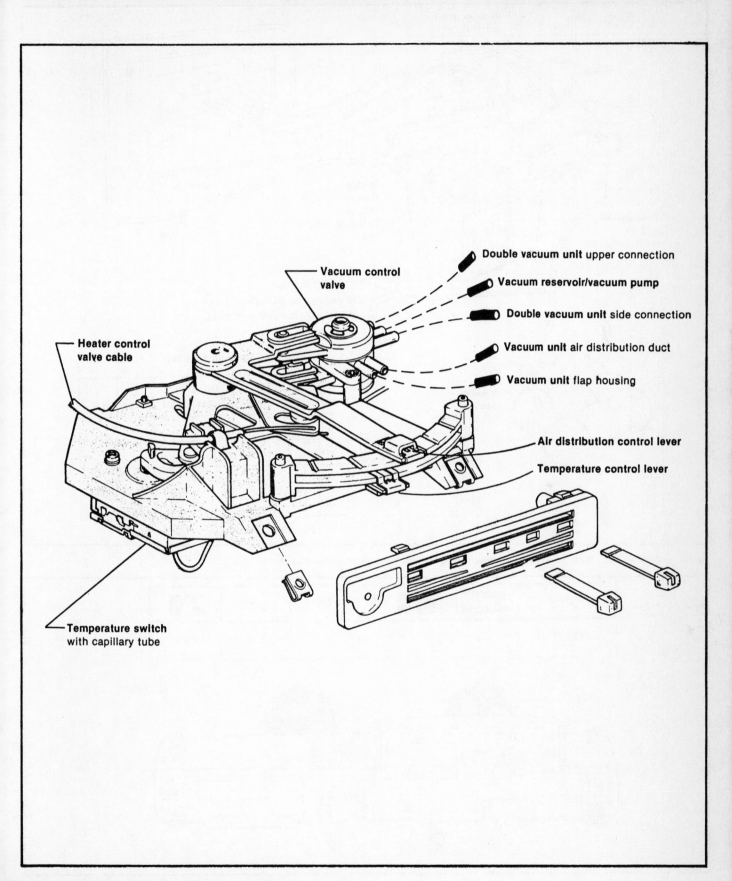

Vacuum control valve

Double vacuum unit upper connection

Vacuum reservoir/vacuum pump

Double vacuum unit side connection

Vacuum unit air distribution duct

Vacuum unit flap housing

Heater control valve cable

Air distribution control lever

Temperature control lever

Temperature switch with capillary tube

Vacuum routing from typical control head (© Volkswagen of America, Inc.)

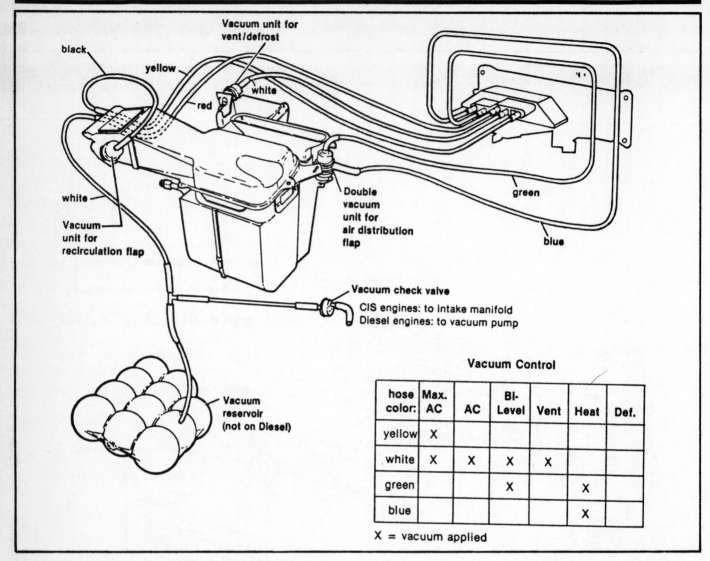

Vacuum Control

hose color:	Max. AC	AC	Bi-Level	Vent	Heat	Def.
yellow	X					
white	X	X	X	X		
green			X		X	
blue					X	

X = vacuum applied

Routing of vacuum lines and test procedure—typical (© Volkswagen of America, Inc.)

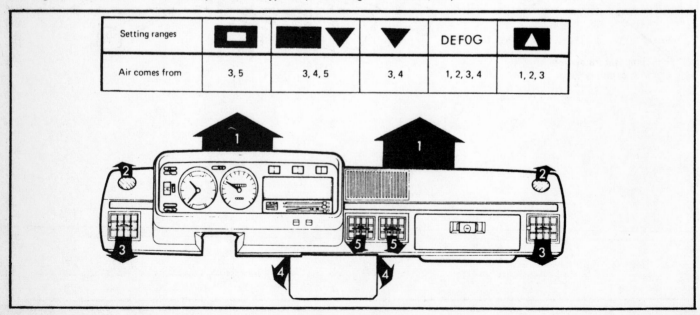

Setting ranges	▭	◼▼	▼	DEFOG	◣
Air comes from	3, 5	3, 4, 5	3, 4	1, 2, 3, 4	1, 2, 3

Air distribution troubleshooting—typical (© Volkswagen of America, Inc.)

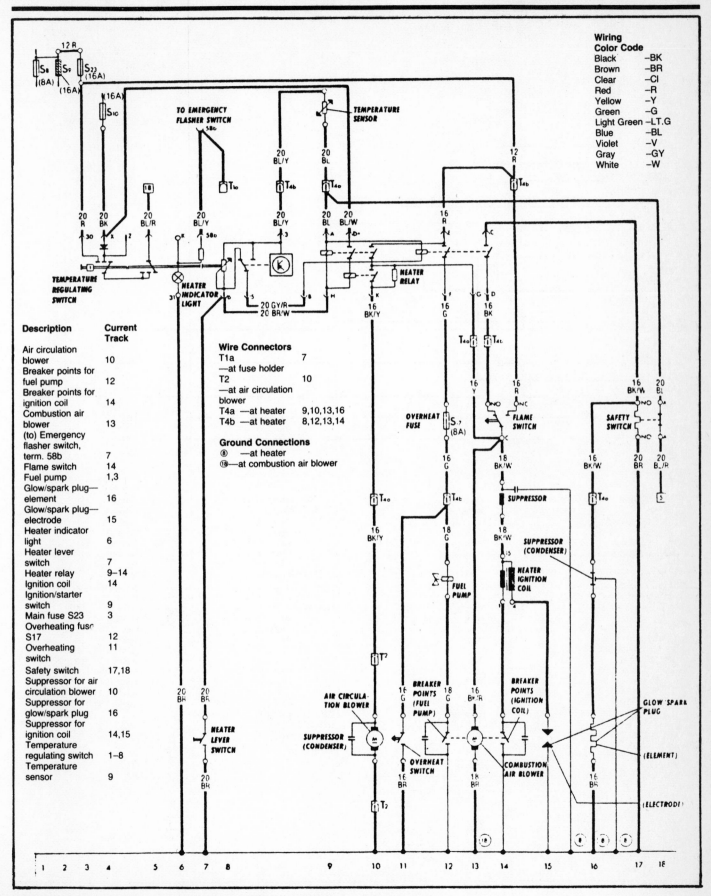

Description	Current Track
Air circulation blower	10
Breaker points for fuel pump	12
Breaker points for ignition coil	14
Combustion air blower	13
(to) Emergency flasher switch, term. 58b	7
Flame switch	14
Fuel pump	1,3
Glow/spark plug—element	16
Glow/spark plug—electrode	15
Heater indicator light	6
Heater lever switch	7
Heater relay	9–14
Ignition coil	14
Ignition/starter switch	9
Main fuse S23	3
Overheating fuse S17	12
Overheating switch	11
Safety switch	17,18
Suppressor for air circulation blower	10
Suppressor for glow/spark plug	16
Suppressor for ignition coil	14,15
Temperature regulating switch	1–8
Temperature sensor	9

Wiring Color Code

Black	–BK
Brown	–BR
Clear	–Cl
Red	–R
Yellow	–Y
Green	–G
Light Green	–LT.G
Blue	–BL
Violet	–V
Gray	–GY
White	–W

Wire Connectors

T1a	7
—at fuse holder	
T2	10
—at air circulation blower	
T4a —at heater	9,10,13,16
T4b —at heater	8,12,13,14

Ground Connections

⑧   —at heater
⑱—at combustion air blower

Wiring schematic for Vanagon heater booster system (© Volkswagen of America, Inc.)

531

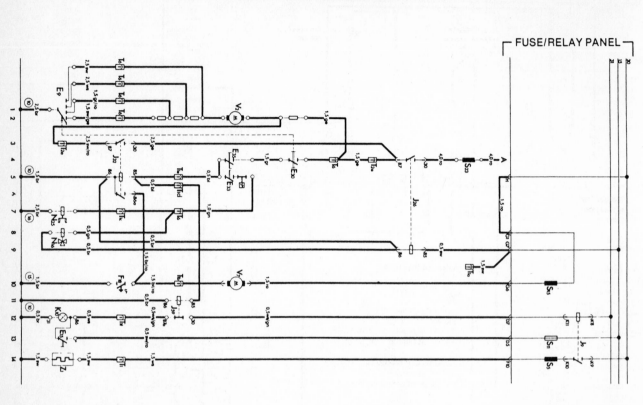

FUSE/RELAY PANEL

Description	Current track	J32 —A/C blower motor/rad. fan relay (on evap. housing)	3–6	Wire Connectors:	T2a —double, behind dash (center)

Description	Current track
A —to battery	4
E9 —A/C speed control	1,2
E15 —defogger switch	12,13
E30 —A/C clutch switch (on speed control)	4
E33 —temp. control	5
E35 —A/C clutch switch (on temp. control)	4
F18 —radiator fan thermo sw.	10
J9 —defogger relay	12–14
J26 —A/C on/off relay (on evap. housing)	4–9

J32 —A/C blower motor/rad. fan relay (on evap. housing)	3–6
J59 —defogger cut-out relay	11,12
K10 —defogger warn. light	12
N16 —two-way valve	8
N25 —compressor clutch	7
S5 —fuse (16A)	14
S11 —fuse (8A)	13
S15 —fuse (16A)	10
S23 —A/C fuse (25A—on evap. housing)	3

Wire Connectors:

T1 —single, in trunk	
T1a —single, vacant (on fuse/relay panel)	
T1b —single, in engine comp. (left)	
T1c —single, on compressor	
T1d —single, on evaporator	
T1e —single, behind dash (left)	
T1f —single, behind dash (center)	

T2a —double, behind dash (center)	
T6 —6 point, behind dash (center)	
V2 —A/C blower motor	2
V7 —radiator cooling fan	10
Z1 —rear window defogger	14
⑩ —grnd. conn., behind dash	
⑮ —grnd. conn., in engine comp.(left)	
⑯ —grnd. conn., in engine comp. (right)	

Wiring schematic for later Rabbit, Jetta, Scirocco and Pickup models (© Volkswagen of America, Inc.)

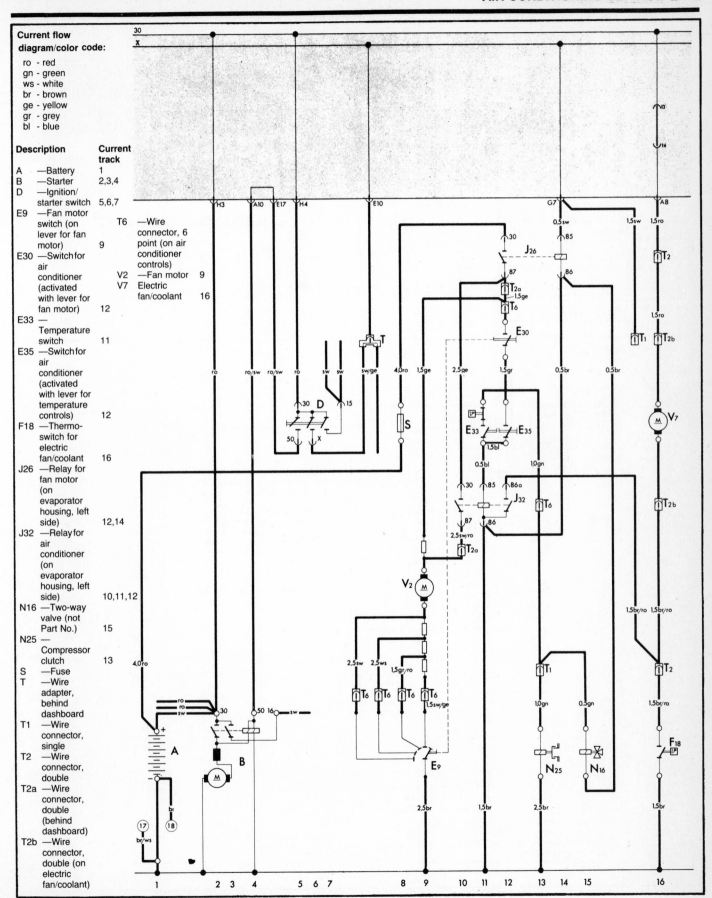

Current flow diagram/color code:

ro - red
gn - green
ws - white
br - brown
ge - yellow
gr - grey
bl - blue

Description		Current track
A	—Battery	1
B	—Starter	2,3,4
D	—Ignition/ starter switch	5,6,7
E9	—Fan motor switch (on lever for fan motor)	9
E30	—Switch for air conditioner (activated with lever for fan motor)	12
E33	—Temperature switch	11
E35	—Switch for air conditioner (activated with lever for temperature controls)	12
F18	—Thermo-switch for electric fan/coolant	16
J26	—Relay for fan motor (on evaporator housing, left side)	12,14
J32	—Relay for air conditioner (on evaporator housing, left side)	10,11,12
N16	—Two-way valve (not Part No.)	15
N25	—Compressor clutch	13
S	—Fuse	
T	—Wire adapter, behind dashboard	
T1	—Wire connector, single	
T2	—Wire connector, double	
T2a	—Wire connector, double (behind dashboard)	
T2b	—Wire connector, double (on electric fan/coolant)	
T6	—Wire connector, 6 point (on air conditioner controls)	
V2	—Fan motor	9
V7	Electric fan/coolant	16

Wiring schematic for early Rabbit, Jetta, Scirocco and Pickup models (© Volkswagen of America, Inc.)

TROUBLE SHOOTING CHART

ERRATIC OR INSUFFICIENT COOLING

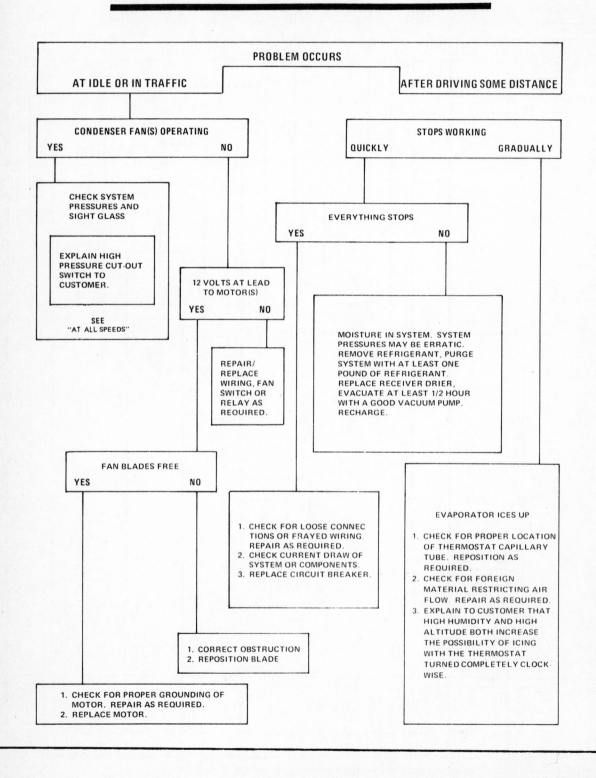

PROBLEM OCCURS

AT IDLE OR IN TRAFFIC — AFTER DRIVING SOME DISTANCE

CONDENSER FAN(S) OPERATING
YES — NO

STOPS WORKING
QUICKLY — GRADUALLY

CHECK SYSTEM PRESSURES AND SIGHT GLASS

EXPLAIN HIGH PRESSURE CUT-OUT SWITCH TO CUSTOMER.

SEE "AT ALL SPEEDS"

EVERYTHING STOPS
YES — NO

12 VOLTS AT LEAD TO MOTOR(S)
YES — NO

REPAIR/ REPLACE WIRING, FAN SWITCH OR RELAY AS REQUIRED.

MOISTURE IN SYSTEM. SYSTEM PRESSURES MAY BE ERRATIC. REMOVE REFRIGERANT, PURGE SYSTEM WITH AT LEAST ONE POUND OF REFRIGERANT. REPLACE RECEIVER DRIER, EVACUATE AT LEAST 1/2 HOUR WITH A GOOD VACUUM PUMP. RECHARGE.

FAN BLADES FREE
YES — NO

1. CHECK FOR LOOSE CONNECTIONS OR FRAYED WIRING. REPAIR AS REQUIRED.
2. CHECK CURRENT DRAW OF SYSTEM OR COMPONENTS.
3. REPLACE CIRCUIT BREAKER.

EVAPORATOR ICES UP

1. CHECK FOR PROPER LOCATION OF THERMOSTAT CAPILLARY TUBE. REPOSITION AS REQUIRED.
2. CHECK FOR FOREIGN MATERIAL RESTRICTING AIR FLOW. REPAIR AS REQUIRED.
3. EXPLAIN TO CUSTOMER THAT HIGH HUMIDITY AND HIGH ALTITUDE BOTH INCREASE THE POSSIBILITY OF ICING WITH THE THERMOSTAT TURNED COMPLETELY CLOCKWISE.

1. CORRECT OBSTRUCTION
2. REPOSITION BLADE

1. CHECK FOR PROPER GROUNDING OF MOTOR. REPAIR AS REQUIRED.
2. REPLACE MOTOR.

TROUBLE SHOOTING CHART

ERRATIC OR INSUFFICIENT COOLING

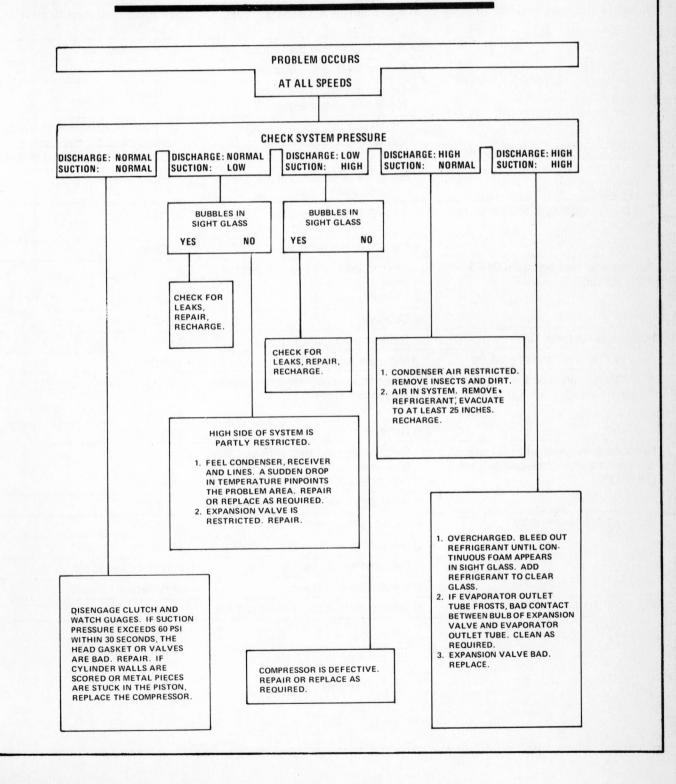

PROBLEM OCCURS

AT ALL SPEEDS

CHECK SYSTEM PRESSURE

| DISCHARGE: NORMAL | DISCHARGE: NORMAL | DISCHARGE: LOW | DISCHARGE: HIGH | DISCHARGE: HIGH |
| SUCTION: NORMAL | SUCTION: LOW | SUCTION: HIGH | SUCTION: NORMAL | SUCTION: HIGH |

BUBBLES IN
SIGHT GLASS

YES   NO

BUBBLES IN
SIGHT GLASS

YES   NO

CHECK FOR
LEAKS,
REPAIR,
RECHARGE.

CHECK FOR
LEAKS, REPAIR,
RECHARGE.

1. CONDENSER AIR RESTRICTED.
   REMOVE INSECTS AND DIRT.
2. AIR IN SYSTEM. REMOVE
   REFRIGERANT, EVACUATE
   TO AT LEAST 25 INCHES.
   RECHARGE.

HIGH SIDE OF SYSTEM IS
PARTLY RESTRICTED.

1. FEEL CONDENSER, RECEIVER
   AND LINES. A SUDDEN DROP
   IN TEMPERATURE PINPOINTS
   THE PROBLEM AREA. REPAIR
   OR REPLACE AS REQUIRED.
2. EXPANSION VALVE IS
   RESTRICTED. REPAIR.

1. OVERCHARGED. BLEED OUT
   REFRIGERANT UNTIL CON-
   TINUOUS FOAM APPEARS
   IN SIGHT GLASS. ADD
   REFRIGERANT TO CLEAR
   GLASS.
2. IF EVAPORATOR OUTLET
   TUBE FROSTS, BAD CONTACT
   BETWEEN BULB OF EXPANSION
   VALVE AND EVAPORATOR
   OUTLET TUBE. CLEAN AS
   REQUIRED.
3. EXPANSION VALVE BAD.
   REPLACE.

DISENGAGE CLUTCH AND
WATCH GUAGES. IF SUCTION
PRESSURE EXCEEDS 60 PSI
WITHIN 30 SECONDS, THE
HEAD GASKET OR VALVES
ARE BAD. REPAIR. IF
CYLINDER WALLS ARE
SCORED OR METAL PIECES
ARE STUCK IN THE PISTON,
REPLACE THE COMPRESSOR.

COMPRESSOR IS DEFECTIVE.
REPAIR OR REPLACE AS
REQUIRED.

HEATER/AIR CONDITIONING TROUBLESHOOTING

Condition	Cause	Correction
Air distribution incorrect	a) Vacuum system leaks	a) Vacuum system checking
	b) Vacuum distributor maladjusted	b) Vacuum distributor adjusting
No cooling output at any point throughout complete movement of control lever	a) V-belt broken	a) Replace
No voltage at compressor clutch	a) Fuse blown (on air conditioner relay)	a) Replace fuse, check for short circuit if fuse blows again
	b) Air conditioner relay does not operate	b) Check or replace
	c) Air conditioner switch defective	c) Replace
	d) Temperature switch has no through flow at ambient temperature	d) Replace
	e) Compressor clutch does not engage with voltage at T1c connector	e) Check clutch by connecting battery directly to clutch connection 1; if clutch does not engage, repair clutch
	f) Refrigerant circuit defective (suction line on compressor not cool)	f) Repair refrigerant circuit
With lever at left stop, no recirculating air operation	a) Vacuum distributor defective	a) Replace
	b) Vacuum system defective	b) Check
Air conditioner does not switch **OFF** in detent position	Air conditioner switch (on temperature lever) a) Incorrectly adjusted	a) Adjust
	b) Defective	b) Replace
Heater does not switch **OFF**	a) Cable incorrectly adjusted	a) Adjust
Fan motor not working in all positions	a) Multi-point connector loose	a) Repair
Air conditioner cannot be switched **OFF** (lever for fan motor in left stop position)	Switch for air conditioner (activated with lever for fan motor) a) Incorrectly adjusted	a) Adjust
	b) Defective	b) Replace
Fan motor does not run when fan lever is in position **I** with air conditioner switched **ON** or **OFF**	Switch for air conditioner (activated with lever for fan mottor) a) Incorrectly adjusted	a) Adjust
	b) Relay J32 for air conditioner defective	b) Replace
Vacuum gauge reading drops	a) Vacuum check valve leaking	a) Replace
	b) Grommet for vacuum reservoir leaking	b) Replace
	c) Vacuum distributor leaking	c) Replace and adjust
	d) Vacuum reservoir leaking	d) Replace
Vacuum unit pulled in	a) Vacuum distributor not working properly	a) Adjust

INDEX

VOLVO SPECIFICATIONS

Vehicle Models

1982
240 .... DL, GLT
260 .... GLF

1983
240 .... DL, GLT
760 .... GLE

1984–85
240 .... DL, GLT
760 .... GLE

Freon and Refrigerant Oil Capacity and Type

REFRIGERANT TYPE
R-12
REFRIGERANT OIL TYPE
Suniso 5
BP Energol LPT 100
Shell Clavus 33

Texaco Capella E 500
Or their equivalent

REFRIGERANT QUANTITY
240 .... 41 ounces
260 .... 51 ounces
760 .... 38 ounces

REFRIGERANT OIL QUANTITY
Compressor
Delco R-4 .... .36 pint
Delco 6 cylinder .... .65 pint
Sankyo SD 150 .... .50 pint
York A 210 .... .64 pint
Evaporator .... .15 pint
Drier .... .10 pint
Condenser .... .10 pint

Drive Belt Tension

It should not be possible to depress the belt by more than 0.04–0.08 in. (1–2 mm) at the middle of it longest belt span between pulleys.

240 AND 260 MODELS

Two Climate Units (CU) are used and are of common construction, one for the use of a heating system only and the other for the use of both a heating unit and an air conditioning unit combined. The removal

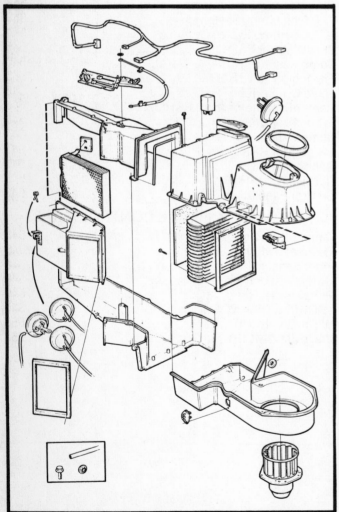

Exploded view of CU Climate Unit with air conditioning (© AB Volvo Car Corp.)

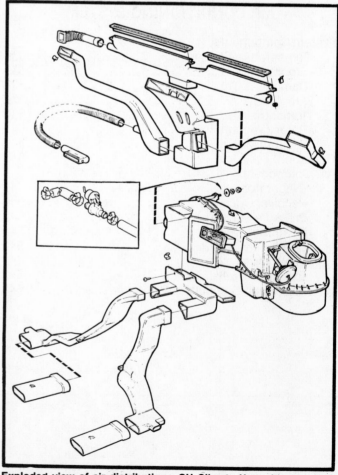

Exploded view of air distribution—CU Climate Unit with air conditioning (© AB Volvo Car Corp.)

and installation of the heating system components and the air conditioning/heating system components are basically the same for both CU units and the repair procedures are combined through-out the outline.

760 MODELS

Three different types of Climate Units (CU) are used and are of common construction. The difference in the units lies in the equipment used, such as with or without air conditioning and the manner in which the unit is controlled, either manually or automatic. The repair procedures are combined through-out the outline.

CLIMATE UNIT WITHOUT AIR CONDITIONING

This is a manually controlled heater and fresh air unit. The unit is prepared for the installation of an air conditioning unit. The panel vents and the water valve are controlled by vacuum and the air-mix shutter is controlled by a cable, connected to the temperature control lever. The same control panel is used on vehicles with manually controlled air conditioning systems.

CLIMATE UNIT WITH AIR CONDITIONING

This Climate Unit is identical to the heater only Climate Unit, but with air conditioning included. This unit has four A/C positions, MAX, NORM, B/L and DEFROST. The positions are controlled manually from the control panel where the mode, fan speed and temperature can be selected. The wiring, vacuum and the air flow schematics are the same as the CU unit without A/C. If the mode selector is in one of the A/C positions and the fan speed is in the O-position, the fan will operate automatically in speed 1 to prevent evaporator ice build-up.

AUTOMATICALLY CONTROLLED CLIMATE UNIT (ACC)

With this unit, the passenger compartment is kept at a preset temperature regardless of the ambient temperature. The unit is set at the control panel, but is controlled by a programmer located behind the instrument panel. The cooling system is the same as used with the manually controlled unit. However, the wiring, vacuum and air flow schematics are different from the other units.

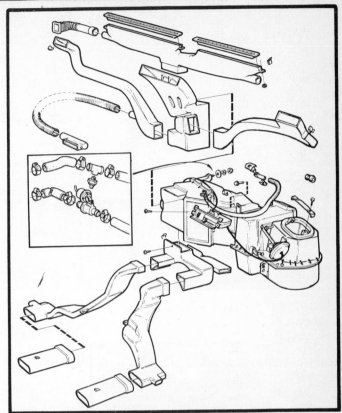

Exploded view of air distribution from CU Climate Unit with Automatic Climate Control (ACC) (© AB Volvo Car Corp.)

Components of the ACC System
TEMPERATURE SENSORS

Two temperature sensors and the temperature dial send signals to the programmer for the system operation. The sensors consists of two thermistors, the resistance of which varies with temperature. The sensors measure the temperature of the ambient air and the passenger compartment. The outer sensor is located in the fan housing and the inner sensor is located behind the instrument panel.

PROGRAMMER

The purpose of the programmer is to convert the incoming signals to the outgoing signals which control the fan speed, air mix shutter and etc. The programmer receives signals from the temperature dial and the two temperature sensors in electrical signals and vacuum signals from the mode selector. The programmer consists of the following components:

DAMPER

The damper consists of a feedback potentiometer connected to a gear wheel. Strong signals from the transducer are dampened here. The damper senses the position of the vacuum motor and compares it with the electrical signals from the amplifier. Without a damper, the vacuum motor would press against its stop position at all times.

AMPLIFIER

The amplifier does as its name implies, amplifies the electrical signals from the sensors and temperature dial.

TRANSDUCER

The transducer transforms electrical signals from the amplifier to vacuum signals for the vacuum motors.

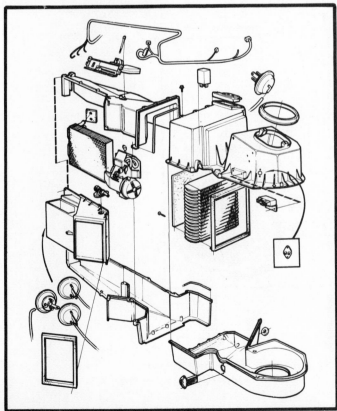

Exploded view of CU Climate Unit with Automatic Climate Control (ACC) (© AB Volvo Car Corp.)

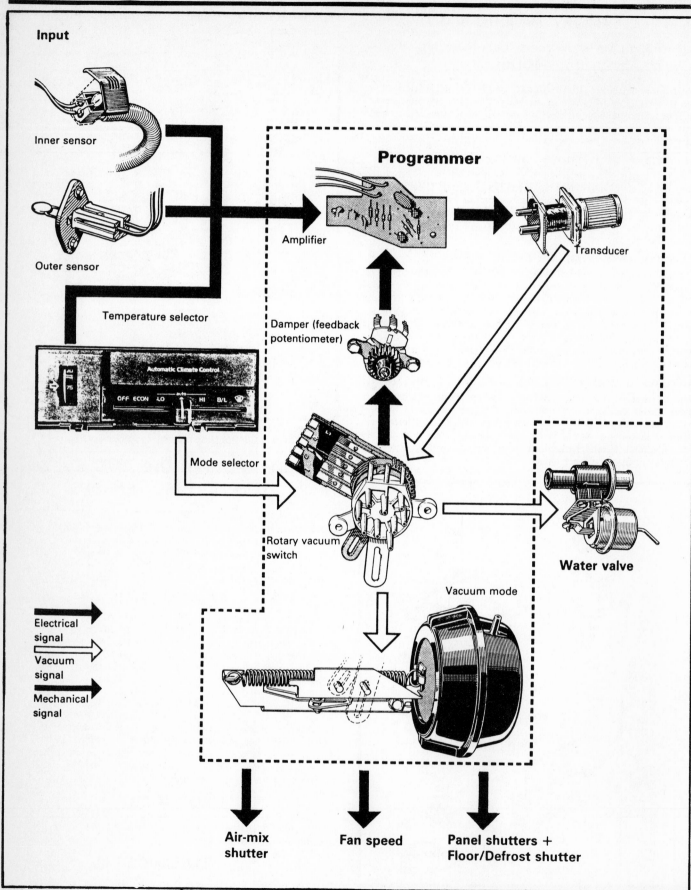

Input

Inner sensor

Outer sensor

Temperature selector

Programmer

Amplifier

Transducer

Damper (feedback
potentiometer)

Mode selector

Rotary vacuum
switch

Water valve

Vacuum mode

Electrical
signal

Vacuum
signal

Mechanical
signal

**Air-mix
shutter**

Fan speed

**Panel shutters +
Floor/Defrost shutter**

Mode of operation for the automatic climate control (ACC) (© AB Volvo Car Corp.)

ROTARY VACUUM VALVE

The rotary vacuum valve controls the various vacuum shutters and water valve by means of vacuum signals.

VACUUM MOTOR

The vacuum motor produces all mechanical motion within the programmer. It is spring loaded and infinitely adjustable. The motor controls, via a lever, the fan speed, the air-mix shutter and from which vents air is to be released.

Air Conditioning System Operation

The purpose of the air conditioning unit is to reduce the temperature in the passenger compartment to an acceptable level when ambient temperatures are high.

The unit operates on the principle that heat is always transferred from a hot medium to a cold one. In practice, warm air from the passenger compartments is circulated passed an evaporator which contains a cold liquid. Heat is therefore transferred from the air to the liquid, and the cooled air is then blown into the passenger compartment.

A direct relationship exists between the pressure, temperature and volume of the refrigerant. The refrigerant used is called freon 12. It boils at a very low temperature ($-30°C = -22°F$) at normal air pressure.

By allowing the refrigerant to circulate in a closed system and altering the pressure and volume conditions, it is possible to get the refrigerant to boil (evaporate). In the pressure conditions present in the system (approx. 1.7–3.2 bar = 23.7–44.6 psi), the refrigerant boils at approximately 0–4°C = 32–39°F. There must however be a heat source. For this purpose the warm air in the passenger compartment is directed thru an evaporator, in which the refrigerant circulates. Heat is taken up by the refrigerant and in doing so the warm air is cooled down and the refrigerant boils. It is this cold air which is then blown into the passenger compartment by the fan. The heat which is taken up by the

refrigerant in the evaporator is transferred to a condensor in the engine compartment where it is cooled by air flow with the aid of the engine and the electric fans.

A compressor is used to circulate the refrigerant within the system.

Air Conditioning Components
EVAPORATOR

The evaporator is made of aluminum, and consists of chambers which are separated by fins.

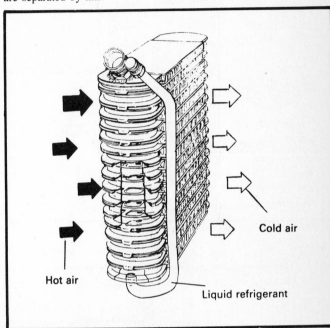

Hot air

Cold air

Liquid refrigerant

Evaporator air flow (© AB Volvo Car Corp.)

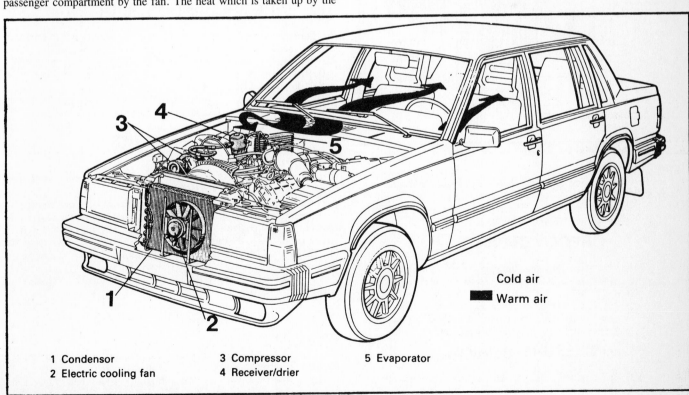

Cold air
▬ Warm air

| 1 Condensor | 3 Compressor | 5 Evaporator |
| 2 Electric cooling fan | 4 Receiver/drier | |

Air conditioning components and air flow (© AB Volvo Car Corp.)

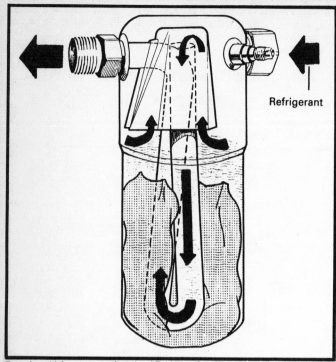

Receiver/driver operation (© AB Volvo Car Corp.)

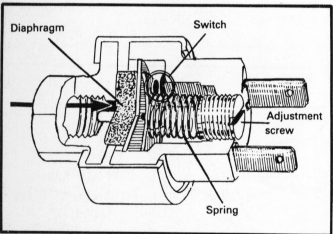

Pressure sensor operation (© AB Volvo Car Corp.)

The refrigerant flowing into the evaporator, expands and boils and consequently takes up heat from the surrounding air. As a result of this, water condenses on the fins. The water is drained off through a hose at the bottom of the evaporator housing.

RECEIVER/DRIER

The receiver/drier consists of two aluminum halves welded together. A drying agent is contained in the receiver to remove any moisture in the refrigerant.

The receiver has been designed in such a way that no, or hardly any, refrigerant can leave it in liquid form. This is because the outlet is located in a part which only contains gaseous refrigerant.

PRESSURE SENSOR

The pressure sensor senses the pressure of the receiver and engages/disengages the compressor accordingly. It works in the following way:

When the pressure in the receiver increases, and reaches 320 kPa (45 psi), a diaphragm in the pressure sensor is pressed against a spring loaded switch which engages the compressor. When the pressure drops to 110 kPa (24 psi), the compressor is disengaged.

COMPRESSOR B 28 F

The compressor contains 4 radially located pistons which lie in the same plane.

To keep the weight down, certain parts e.g. pistons, crankcase and cylinders have been cast in aluminum. The piston rings are made of teflon to provide a good seal against the cylinder walls.

A safety valve, located on top of the compressor, releases refrigerant if the pressure becomes too high (above 3.1 MPa, 441 psi). The compressor is belt driven through an electromagnetic clutch by the engine crankshaft pulley.

COMPRESSOR D 24 T

The compressor has 5 pistons placed in a ring-form around the input shaft. They move axially and compress against the cylinder head which is located at the end of the compressor opposite the input clutch.

Compressor and cylinder head are aluminum while cylinder liners are steel and are cast integrally with the housing. Pistons are also aluminum and are equipped with one ring.

The high pressure outlet from the compressor is equipped with a safety valve which releases refrigerant if pressure exceeds 3.1 MPa (441 psi). Compressor is driven, through an electromagnetic clutch, by a belt from the crankshaft pulley.

CONDENSOR

The condensor is made of aluminum and is constructed of tubes, shaped like coils and equipped with fins for cooling. The refrigerant flows through these tubes and is cooled by air flow.

FAN HOUSING—AIR INLET SHUTTER— (RECIRCULATION SHUTTER)

The fan housing contains a fan and an air inlet shutter which regulates the amount of incoming fresh air when the control lever is set at max AC. In this position a mixture of 85% passenger compartment air and 15% fresh air is drawn in. In this way the passenger compartment is cooled down quickly.

The automatic unit (i.e. ACC) is equipped with a sensor (thermistor) in the fan housing which senses the temperature of the inlet air.

FAN + MOTOR

760 MODEL

A drum type fan is used which can be balanced by fitting steel clips to the outer edge.

The motor, which is of the permanent magnet type, is located beneath the climate unit and is accessible from the passenger compartment. It needs to be well cooled to avoid overheating. For this reason a rubber hose is connected to the fan housing to supply cooling air. It is important that the hose is connected correctly at both ends to avoid damage to the motor.

A resistor, located above the motor, and to one side, regulates the fan speed.

EXPANSION VALVE

760 MODEL

The expansion valve is located in the evaporator inlet, and regulates the amount of refrigerant flowing into the evaporator.

The refrigerant is forced to flow through a small metal tube in the expansion valve. The rate of flow is decided by the condensor pressure and the temperature of the incoming refrigerant. The temperature and

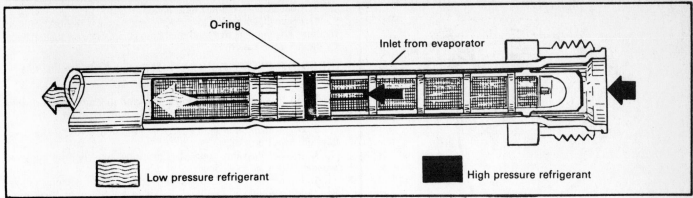

Expansion valve (fixed orifice tube) used with Automatic Climate Control (ACC) unit (© AB Volvo Car Corp.)

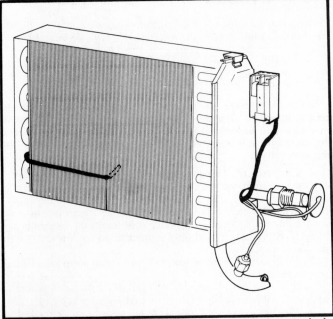

Expansion valve used with non-automatic air conditioning—typical (© AB Volvo Car Corp.)

pressure of the refrigerant are also lowered. The expansion valve is housed in a plastic sleeve.

IDLE SPEED COMPENSATION

760 MODEL

Vehicles equipped with B 28 F engine have idle speed compensation (when compressor is engaged) via the constant idle speed system (CIS-system). Vehicles with D 24 T engine do not require idle speed compensation.

WATER VALVE

The water valve is fitted to the inlet hose of the heater core, and is regulated by vacuum signals from the temperature control and/or mode selector.

The valve is closed at max AC or when the temperature control is set at Cool. In all other positions it is open.

HEATER CORE

The heater core is conventionally constructed with brass tanks, connecting tubes, and copper fins. The connecting tubes are routed to the engine compartment where they are connected to the engine cooling system.

On vehicles equipped with ACC (Automatic Climate Control), a thermal switch is located on the outlet hose from the heater core. It switches on and starts the fan motor only when the water temperature exceeds approximately 35°C (95°F). This prevents cold air from being blown into the passenger compartment during winter.

NOTE: The thermal switch is by-passed in the defrost position.

Locations of Charging Ports

240 AND 260 MODELS WITH YORK COMPRESSOR

High pressure at compressor DISCH valve. Low pressure at compressor SUCTION valve.

240, 260 AND 760 MODELS WITH DELCO AND SANKYO COMPRESSORS

High pressure service port located on compressor. Low pressure service port located on receiver/drier.

Discharging, Evacuation, Leak Testing and Recharging the Air Conditioning System

ALL MODELS

NOTE: If the York Compressor is used, the service valves must be mid-seated for manifold gauge operation during the discharge, evacuation and recharging of the air conditioning system.

DISCHARGING PROCEDURE

1. Attach the low gauge hose of either a charging station or gauge set to the low side service fitting on the receiver/drier.

2. Place the center hose (vacuum) into a container and open the low side valve. The refrigerant will be safely discharged into the container.

3. If no discharge occurs, check for missing or defective schrader valve in the service fitting or leakage within the system.

4. With the low side of the system completely discharged, check the high side for any remaining pressure.

5. If pressure is found, discharge the high side with the same procedure as was down when the low side was discharged.

NOTE: If pressure exists in the high side, a restriction on the high side is indicated. If such is the case, the cause must be diagnosed and corrected before evacuating and recharging the system is attempted.

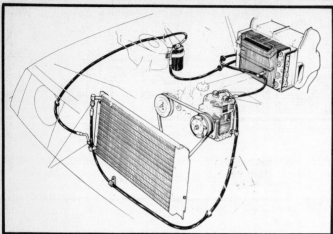

Typical air conditioning unit—equipped with york compressor (© AB Volvo Car Corp.)

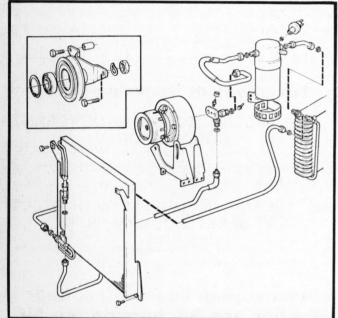

Typical air conditioning unit equipped with Sankyo or Delco compressor (© AB Volvo Car Corp.)

6. When the system is completely discharged, with no vapors present, measure and record the amount of refrigerant oil that has collected within the container. If the quantity is one half ounce or more, this amount of specified refrigerant oil must be added during the charging procedure, plus any quantity that may have been removed with a part that requires replacement. A specific procedure follows as to the introduction of refrigerant oil into the system.

COMPRESSOR SYSTEMS

COMPONENT REPLACEMENT WITH NO SIGNS OF EXCESSIVE OIL LEAKAGE

1. Compressor—Remove from engine, drain and measure the oil. Replace the same amount of new oil plus one fluid ounce.

NOTE: The R-4 and Sankyo compressors requires six fluid ounces of refrigerant oil while the A-6 compressor requires ten ounces of refrigerant oil.

2. Evaporator—Add three fluid ounces of oil.

3. Condensor—Add one fluid ounce.
4. Receiver/drier—Remove, drain and measure the oil. Replace the same amount plus two fluid ounces to compensate for that retained by the dessicant material.

SIGNS OF EXCESSIVE OIL LEAKAGE FROM SYSTEM

1. Remove the accumulator. Drain and measure the oil.

NOTE: It is not necessary to remove and drain the compressor, since the compressor retains a minimum amount of oil.

2. If less than three fluid ounces is measured, replace with three fluid ounces of new oil.
3. If more than three ounces is measured, replace with the same amount of new oil as drained.
4. If a new receiver/drier is being replaced to the compressor system, add an additional two fluid ounces to the system to compensate for the new dessicant material.

EVACUATING THE SYSTEM

1. Install the gauge set to the charging system by installing the low pressure side gauge hose to the receiver/drier low-side service fitting.
2. Connect the high pressure gauge hose to the vacuum pump.
3. Slowly open the low side and high side gauge valves. Start the pump operation and pump the system until the low side gauge reaches 28–29 in. Hg.

NOTE: The specification of 28–29 in. Hg. can only be reached at or near sea level. For each 1000 feet above sea level, specifications would have to be lowered by one in. Hg. An example would be if the procedure is being done at 5000 feet elevation, only 23–24 in. Hg. is required.

4. If the prescribed vacuum cannot be attained, close off the valves, stop the vacuum pump and check for vacuum leaks at connections or pump.
5. When the correct vacuum is reached, the system is fully evacuated. Close the high side gauge valve and turn off the vacuum pump.
6. If the vacuum is held for five minutes on the low side gauge, the system should be leak free.
7. If the vacuum holds, disconnect the vacuum pump and prepared for system charging.
8. If the system does not hold the vacuum for five minutes, charge the system with one-half pound of R-12 refrigerant and leak test.
9. If a leak is detected, discharge the system, repair the leak as required and repeat the evacuation procedure.

CHARGING THE SYSTEM

One of three standard methods of charging the air conditioning system can be used. The standard methods are as follows:
1. Charging station method.
2. Disposable can (14 oz.) method.
3. Drum method.

Charging Procedure

NOTE: If the charging station method is used, follow the manufacturer's recommended charging procedure for the station being used.

1. Attach the low gauge hose to the low-pressure fitting on the receiver/drier.
2. Attach the center hose to the R-12 refrigerant source.
3. Attach the high pressure hose.
4. Start the engine and run until normal operating temperature is reached. Set the A/C control lever to the OFF position.
5. Open the low side gauge valve and allow one pound or 14 ounces of R-12 to enter the system.
6. As soon as the refrigerant has been added to the system, immediately engage the compressor by setting the A/C control lever to the NORM position and placing the blower speed on HI, to draw in the remainder of the refrigerant charge.

NOTE: The charging operation can be speeded up by using a large volume fan to pass air over the condenser. If the condenser temperature is maintained below the charging cylinder temperature, the refrigerant R-12 will enter the system more quickly.

7. Close off the refrigerant source valve and run the engine for thirty seconds to clear the lines.

8. With the engine running, remove the low-side hose from the receiver/drier service fitting. Install the protective cap on service fitting.

NOTE: Unscrew the hose connector rapidly to avoid excessive refrigerant loss from the system.

——————————— CAUTION ———————————
Do not disconnect the gauge line at the gauge set while attached to the receiver/drier. This would result in rapid discharge of refrigerant from the accumulator due to the depressed schrader valve, causing possible personal injury.
————————————————————————————

9. Stop engine and check system with an approved leak detector.

10. Start the engine, operate system and test for proper system operation.

Blower Motor

Removal and Installation

240 AND 260 MODELS

1. Disconnect the negative battery cable.

2. Remove the sound insulation and side panels on both sides of the radio, if equipped.

3. Remove the control panel and center console.

4. Remove or disconnect as required, the center air vents, the cable and electrical connectors from the clock, the glove compartment and the air ducts for the center air vents.

5. From the right hand sde, remove the air ducts, disconnect the vacuum hoses to the shutter actuators.

6. Fold back the floor mat and remove the screw for the rear floor duct. Move the duct to one side.

7. Remove the outer fan casing and the fan wheel.

NOTE: It may be necessary to remove the support from under the glove compartment in order to remove the fan casing.

8. Disconnect the fan motor switch from the center console and the electrical leads from the switch.

9. From the left side, disconnect the air ducts and the vacuum hoses to the shutter actuators.

10. Fold back the floor mat and remove the screw from the rear floor air duct. Move the duct to one side.

11. Remove the outer fan casing and the fan wheel.

12. Remove or disconnect the inner fan casing, the vacuum hose to the shutter actuator for the rear floor, the fan motor and ground lead.

13. Should the blower motor need to be replaced, a modified replacement unit is available. Certain modifications must be done and instructions are included with the new assembly.

14. The installation of the assembly is the reverse of the removal procedure.

Removal and Installation

760 MODELS

1. Remove the panel below the glove compartment.

2. Remove the screws retaining the blower motor to the housing.

3. Lower the blower motor and remove the hose for air cooling.

4. Disconnect the wiring and remove the blower motor.

5. To install, use a sealer and coat the sealing flange to prevent air leakage.

6. Attach the wiring and the air cooling hose. Install the motor into position.

7. Install the retaining screws and the panel beneath the glove compartment.

Compressor

Removal and Installation

ALL MODELS

1. Attach manifold gauge assembly and discharge the refrigerant safely from the air conditioning system.

2. Disconnect the refrigerant lines at the compressor and cap or plug all openings immediately.

3. Loosen the mounting bolts on the compressor and mounting brackets. Disconnect the electrical connector at the compressor.

4. Remove the drive belt from the compressor and remove the mounting bolts.

5. Remove the compressor from the engine area. Drain the refrigerant oil from the compressor and measure so that the same amount can be installed in the rebuilt or renewed compressor.

NOTE: The compressor mounting brackets can sometimes be removed with the compressor and disassembled from the compressor when the assembly is out of the vehicle, much easier than trying to separate them in the engine compartment.

6. Upon installation of the compressor, mount the compressor on the mounting brackets and install the mounting bolts.

7. Immediately upon openng the service connection ports, attach the hoses and tighten securely.

8. Install the drive belt and tighten to specifications.

9. Evacuate, check for proper refrigerant oil level and charge the system.

10. Verify the system is operating properly.

NOTE: For Compressor overhaul and oil level checking procedures, refer to the Compressor Overhaul Section in this manual.

Expansion Valve/Fixed Orifice Tube

EXPANSION VALVE

Removal and Installation

240 AND 260 MODELS

1. Attach the manifold gauge set and safely discharge the air conditioning system.

2. Disconnect the negative battery cable.

3. Remove the right side sound proofing panel from under the glove box assembly.

4. Remove the console side panel from the right side.

5. Remove the evaporator cover and the evaporator outlet insulation.

6. Remove the expansion valve from the evaporator tube.

7. Carefully remove the capillary tube along with the expansion valve.

8. Carefully install the expansion valve and the capillary tube, using new O-rings lubricated with refrigerant oil.

9. Complete the installation in the reverse of the removal procedure.

10. Evacuate, check for proper refrigerant oil level and charge the system.

11. Verify the air conditioning system is operating properly.

FIXED ORIFICE TUBE (EXPANSION TUBE)

Removal and Installation

760 MODELS

The orifice tube is located in the evaporator inlet tube. The air conditioning system must be discharged and the tubing separated in order to remove the fixed orifice tube. Special tools are available to asist in the removal and installation of the orifice tube. Upon installation, the short filtered end (outlet filter) must be installed towards the evaporator. Evacuate and charge the system. Check the system for proper operation.

Heater/Evaporator Assembly

Removal and Installation

240 AND 260 MODELS W/COMBINED UNIT

NOTE: The heater/evaporator unit assembly is manufactured to accept both the heater system and air conditioning system or only the heating system. Thus, it is called a combined unit.

1. Disconnect the negative battery cable. Safely discharge the air conditioning system.
2. Move the heater—A/C controls to the closed position.
3. Remove the sound proofing and side panels on both sides of the center dash console.
4. Remove the radio, if equipped. Remove the center control panel. Disconnect any necessary cables and move the panel to one side.
5. Remove the glove box assembly and the strip below the right hand air vent by carefully prying it off with a screwdriver type tool.
6. Remove the steering wheel casing and disconnect the choke control with cover plate.

NOTE: Vehicles equipped with CI (Fuel Injection) system, remove the coverplate for the choke.

7. Remove the strip below the left hand air vent, the knob for adjusting the instrument panel lighting intensity and the light switch knob. Do not remove the switch.
8. Remove the extra instrument panel cover plate. The following procedures apply.
   a. Disconnect the speedometer drive cable and any electrical connections from the combined instrument panel.
9. After the extra instrument panel has been removed, remove the storage compartment, the center air vents and the instrument panel frame.
10. From the left side, unplug the windshield wiper connectors.
11. Disconnect the air duct between the heater—A/C and the center air vents.
12. Disconnect the lead to the glove box courtesy light and the rubber straps for the defroster vents.
13. Remove the dash board unit from the dash assembly.
14. Remove or disconnect the attachment screws for the rear floor air duct. Lower the duct slightly.

15. Remove or disconnect the following:
   a. the lower heater—A/C mounting screws.
   b. the vacuum hose to the vacuum tank.
   c. the cable to the control valve.
   d. the upper and lower screws for the center console.
   e. the screws for the center support that are located on the console.
   f. the fan motor ground lead.
   g. the inlet hose to the control valve.

NOTE: The radiator can be drained prior to the hose removal or the hose can be clamped to retain the coolant.

16. Disconnect the upper hose from the heater core tube.
17. Disconnect the vacuum hoses to the shutter actuators.
18. Loosen the upper mounting screws on the heater—A/C housing.
19. From the right hand side, disconnect the vacuum hoses to the shutter actuators.
20. Disconnect and remove, as required, the air ducts.
21. Remove or disconnect the hose from the vacuum tank, the screws securing the rear floor duct. Lower the duct slightly.
22. Disconnect the heater—A/C lower mounting and remove.
23. Remove the upper and lower mounting screws from the console and move the console to one side.
24. Remove the mounting screws for the right hand support and remove the support.
25. Disconnect the plug from the flower fan switch and the positive lead.
26. Disconnect the vacuum hose from the control panel for the REC shutter.
27. Disconnect the input vacuum hose from the T-connection to the floor shutter actuators. Remove the evaporator cover clips. Move the cover and free the evaporator slightly.

—————————— CAUTION ——————————
Do not damage the capillary tube when freezing the evaporator. Disconnect it from the evaporator, if necessary.

28. Remove the upper mounting screws and lift out the heater—A/C assembly from the vehicle.
29. When the assembly is out of the vehicle, it can be disassembled to remove the blower motor and components, the heater core and evaporator assembly and certain control components.
30. The installation of the heater—A/C assembly is the reverse of the removal procedure.
31. Before installation, be sure all sealing flanges are correctly sealed to prevent air leakage during the heater—A/C operation.

Evaporator Core

Removal and Installation of Evaporator Core Only

240 AND 260 MODELS

1. Safely discharge the air conditioning system.
2. From inside the vehicle, remove the right side panel from the center console. Remove the insulation panel and the glove box unit.
3. Remove the right side defroster nozzle and the air duct.
4. Remove the insulation compound from around the pipe connections for the evaporator.
5. Disconnect the hoses while holding the pipes so they do not turn. Cap or plug the openings immediately.
6. Remove the cover clamps and remove the evaporator cover.
7. Pull the evaporator out of the combined unit.
8. To install, place the necessary gasket on the new evaporator and install the evaporator into the combined unit.
9. Complete the installation in the reverse of the removal procedure.
10. Evacuate, leak test and recharge the air conditioning system.

NOTE: Be sure all insulation is replaced and correctly positioned.

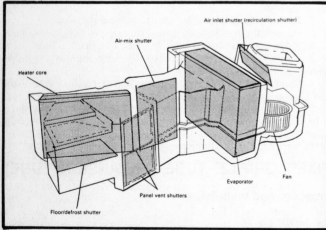

Air inlet shutter (recirculation shutter)

Air-mix shutter

Heater core

Evaporator

Fan

Panel vent shutters

Floor/defrost shutter

Construction of combined unit (© AB Volvo Car Corp.)

Heater Core/Blower Motor/Evaporator Core Assembly

Removal and Installation

240 AND 260 MODELS

1. The heater—A/C housing assembly must be removed from the vehicle. Refer to the Heater—A/C Assembly, Removal and Installation outline.
2. With the heater—A/C assembly out of the vehicle, set the assembly on a cleared area and remove or disconnect the following:
    a. The upper hose on the heater core.
    b. the air inlet rubber seal on the top of the housing.
    c. The REC-shutter clips, on the left side.
    d. The rubber seals for both defroster vents.
    e. All clips for both the outer fan casings and remove the casings from the assembly.
3. Remove the fan wheel locking clips from both sides and remove the fan wheels.
4. Remove the heater core drain hose, the vacuum tank assembly, the retaining screws for the vacuum tank bracket on the left hand side, the REC-shutter spring and all the heater housing clips.
5. Remove or disconnect the retaining screws for the fan motor, the heater control valve capillary tube from the attachment, and the shutter actuators vacuum hoses from the T-joint.
6. Pull the heater—A/C housing apart from the middle.
7. Remove the fan motor evaporator and the heater core assembly.
8. To install the heater core, evaporator and fan motor, reverse the removal and disassembly procedures. Be sure to seal the heater—A/C housing halves with sealer before housing assembly is done.

NOTE: If only the blower motor is to be removed for repairs or replacement, the heater—A/C housing does not have to be removed completely. The fan motor can be removed from the left side with the necessary components removed from the right and left sides of the housing. A modified motor is available for certain models and instructions for modifying the heater core would be included in the motor kit.

Climate Unit Assembly

Removal and Installation

760 MODELS

1. Drain the cooling system and discharge the air conditioning system safely. Disconnect the negative battery cable.
2. Remove the steering wheel and column casings.
3. Disconnect the speedometer and electrical connections behind the dash. Remove the instrument cluster and disconnect the remaining electrical and vacuum connections.
4. Remove the retaining screws for the instrument panel and remove it completely from the vehicle.
5. Disconnect the electrical and vacuum connections, both in the engine compartment and in the passenger compartment, for the climate control assembly.
6. Disconnect the evaporator lines and immediately cap or plug the openings.
7. Remove the holder for the central electrical unit, remove the screws and holders for the floor ducts, the screw for the distribution unit and the retaining screw on the cowl.
8. Lift the climate control unit assembly from the vehicle.
9. Upon installation, reverse the removal procedure and be sure all vacuum and electrical connections are correctly attached.
10. Install coolant into the cooling system and evacuate, leak test and recharge the air conditioning unit.

Evaporator

Removal and Installation

760 MODELS

1. Safely discharge the refrigeration from the air conditioning system.
2. Disconnect the evaporator connections in the engine compartment. Cap or plug the openings immediately.
3. From inside the vehicle, remove the panel beneath the glove compartment. Remove the glove compartment unit.
4. Disconnect the electrical terminals for the fan motor and the resistor.
5. Remove the retaining screws securing the lower fan housing cover.

NOTE: Two of the screws are hidden beneath the fan housing and evaporator housing.

6. Remove the cover and lift the evaporator from the housing.
7. Clean the sealer from the cover. Transfer the rubber seal and the filter to the new or repaired evaporator.

NOTE: Be sure the filter is clean.

8. To install the evaporator, lubricate the evaporator pipe connections, but do not remove the safety caps as yet.
9. To fit the evaporator tighter in the housing, apply a thick piece of butyl tape to the rear edge of the evaporator.
10. Apply sealer to the groove of the lower cover, install the evaporator and carefully insert the evaporator tube connections through the rubber grommets and into the engine compartment.
11. Complete the assembly and evacuate, leak test and charge the air conditioning system.

Heater Core

Removal and Installation

760 MODELS

1. Disconnect the negative battery cable.
2. Drain the cooling system or pinch the heater hoses to prevent coolant from leaking when the core is removed.
3. Remove the ashtray and holder, the cigarette lighter and storage compartment on the console.

NOTE: Two screws are located beneath the plastic cover.

4. Remove the console assembly from the gearshift lever and the parking brake.
5. Disconnect the electrical connector. Remove the rear ash tray, the console and light.
6. Remove the screws beneath the plastic cover in the bottom of the storage compartment and remove the parking brake console.
7. On the left side of the passenger compartment, remove the panel beneath the dashboard.
8. Pull down the floor mat and remove the side panel retaining screws, front and rear edge.
9. On the right side of the passenger compartment, remove the panel beneath the glove compartment and the glove compartment box with lighting.
10. Pull down the floor mat on the right side and remove the side panel retaining screws, front and rear edge.
11. Remove the radio compartment retaining screws.
12. Remove the screws around the heater control, the radio compartment console and the control panel.
13. Free up the central electrical unit and remove the mounting from the dash.
14. Remove the center dash panel, the screw retaining the distribution duct and all the screws holding the air ducts to the panel vents and to the distribution duct.

15. Remove the screws holding the air ducts top the rear seats and remove the air distribution duct section to the rear seat ducts.

16. Remove the vacuum hoses from the vacuum motors and the hose from the aspirator, if equipped with ACC unit.

17. Remove the distribution unit from the vehicle.

18. Remove the retaining clips and remove the heater core assembly.

19. If the vacuum motors must be replaced, remove the panel from the distribution unit and replace the vacuum motor.

20. The installation is the reverse of the removal procedure.

Condenser

Removal and Installation

240 AND 260 MODELS

1. Remove the grille and both headlamp outer rims.

2. Remove the grille center bracket. Remove the horn bracket.

3. Discharge the air conditioning safely. Disconnect the condenser lines and cap or plug them immediately.

4. Remove the condenser retaining bolts and remove the condenser from the radiator support.

5. To install the condenser, reverse the removal procedure.

6. Evacuate, leak test and charge the air conditioning system.

760 MODELS

1. Disconnect the negative battery cable.

2. Safely discharge the air conditioning system.

3. Remove the grille assembly and the air guide at the spoiler.

4. Disconnect the bracket in front of the condenser from the upper cover panel.

5. Disconnect the refrigerant hoses from the condenser. Cap or plug the opening immediately.

6. Remove the retaining bolts from the condenser and remove it from the vehicle.

7. Drain and measure the amount of refrigerant oil from the condenser and install the same amount of new oil in the replacement condenser.

8. To install the condenser, reverse the removal procedures. Evacuate, leak test and recharge the air conditioning system.

Receiver/Drier

Removal and Installation

ALL MODELS

1. Discharge the air conditioning system safely.

2. Disconnect the refrigerant lines to the receiver/drier assembly. Cap or plug all the openings immediately.

3. Remove the receiver/drier pressure switch connections.

4. Remove the receiver/drier from its bracket or remove the bracket assembly from the inner fender panel.

5. To install the receiver/drier assembly, reverse the removal procedures.

6. Evacuate, leak test and recharge the system.

NOTE: Before replacement of a new receiver/drier, drain the refrigerant oil from the old unit, measure the amount of oil and add the same amount of new oil into the new receiver/drier assembly.

Control Panel/Thermostatic Control

Removal and Installation

ALL MODELS

1. Remove the trim panel around the control panel head.

2. Remove the retaining screws from the control head and remove the control panel away from the dash.

3. Remove the retaining clip(s) from the rear of the control panel that maybe retaining the cables to the control head.

4. Remove any vacuum connections.

5. Remove the electrical connections.

6. Disconnect the light assembly and remove the control head.

7. The installation of the control head is the reverse of the removal procedure.

8. If the unit is equipped with a thermostatic control, the capillary tube must be handled carefully to avoid breaking it and rendering it inoperative.

NOTE: If a new thermostatic switch is installed, the capillary tube must be attached to the evaporator outlet tube.

Climate Control, ACC System

TEMPERATURE SENSOR

Removal

760 MODELS WITH ACC SYSTEMS

1. Remove the panel from around the control head. Free the control head and pull it away from the dash.

2. Disconnect the temperature sensor plug.

Testing

1. Using a volt-amp tester, check that current only flows through the sensor at temperatures above 65°F.

2. Check that the sensor cuts the current off at temperatures below 65°F.

NOTE: If necessary, cool sensor in refrigerator or by other means.

Installation

1. Install the temperature sensor and connect the wiring.

2. Install the control panel and the trim around it.

THERMAL SWITCH

Removal

760 MODELS WITH ACC SYSTEM

1. Remove the electrical lead and remove the thermal switch from the T-pipe.

Testing

1. Using a volt-amp tester, current should flow through the switch when the temperature of the switch is between 86–104°F. The current should be cut off when the temperature drops to 50°F.

Installation

1. Install new thermal switch into the T-pipe and attach the electrical lead.

INNER SENSOR

Removal

760 MODELS WITH ACC SYSTEM

1. Remove the panel beneath the glove box assembly.

2. Remove the glove box unit.

3. Disconnect the air hose and wiring from the sensor.

4. Remove the retaining clip and remove the sensor.

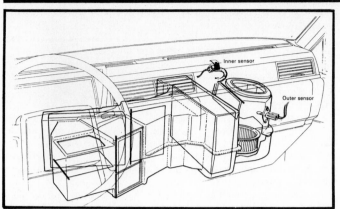

Location of inner and outer sensors—ACC unit (© AB Volvo Car Corp.)

Testing

1. Using a volt-amp tester, be sure current will flow through the sensor, if not, it must be replaced.

Installation

1. Secure the sensor with the clip.
2. Connect the air hose and wiring.
3. Install the glove box and panel below the box assembly.

OUTER SENSOR

Testing Without Removal

1. Remove the windshield wipers and the cowl upper panel.
2. Remove the cover from the air intake panel.
3. At room temperature, and the ignition switch off. Check the resistance with an Ohms meter. The resistance must be 30–40 ohms at temperature of 66–86 degrees F. If the ohms is 65–100, the sensor is defective and must be replaced.

NOTE: The higher the room temperature, the lower the resistance value.

Removal

1. The sensor is located in the fan housing and is replaced from inside the vehicle.
2. Remove the panel beneath the glove box and the glove box assembly.
3. Remove the outer panel vents and air ducts.
4. Free the control rod for the air inlet shutter from the vacuum motor.
5. Remove the vacuum motor from its mounting and let it hang.
6. Disconnect the sensor plug, remove the screws and remove the sensor from its seat.

Installation

1. The installation of the sensor is the reverse of its removal.

PROGRAMMER

Removal

760 MODEL WITH ACC SYSTEM

1. Remove the panel beneath the glove box and also the glove unit.
2. Remove the outer panel vents and the air ducts.
3. Free the rod for the air-mix shutter from the programmer.
4. Free and disconnect the plug on the left side of the programmer.
5. Remove the clips for the vacuum hose connections and disconnect the hose.

6. Remove the retaining screws and remove the programmer from the climate unit.

Installation

1. Install the programmer and secure it with the retaining screws.
2. Connect the plug on the left side of the programmer and connect the junction.
3. Install the air-mix rod and adjust as follows:
   a. Start the engine so as to obtain vacuum, if necessary.
   b. Set the temperature dial to MAX heat so that the programmer arm moves towards the passenger compartment.
   c. Pull the control rod until the end position is reached and secure it to the programmer arm.
4. Install the air ducts and panel vents.
5. Install the glove box unit and the panels underneath the glove box unit.

Troubleshooting The Air Conditioning System

All leaks must be rectified as soon as possible to prevent moisture or foreign particles from entering into the system. To reduce the risk of moisture ingress during repairwork, keep surfaces dry and clean.

The compressor lubricating oil should be stored in an air-tight container otherwise it will absorb moisture from the air.

Do not remove the protective plugs on new parts until just before the part is to be fitted. Leave one of the hose connections unconnected when fitting the component and flush the complete system with refrigerant for 15–20 seconds before connecting it. This removes any impurities and moisture. Do not however flush too strongly otherwise the lubricating oil will be flushed out as well.

In the event of a collision, check every component, which may have been damaged, very carefully. Check the soldered joints extra carefully. Deformed or split pipes must not be repaired.

RECEIVER/DRIER

The receiver/drier should be replaced after major repairs involving leakage or when fitting new components, or if moisture is suspected in the system. Normally under favorable conditions the receiver/drier need only be replaced every third time the air conditioning unit is serviced. Favorable conditions in this sense means e.g. a slow leakage repaired after 24 hours.

—————————— **CAUTION** ——————————
The system must be filled immediately after installation in order to prevent corrosion.

If the system is not filled within 24 hours it must be rinsed with approx 200 gram (0.5 lb) twice before final filling. Between rinses the system must be evacuated at least 10 minutes.

TOPPING UP WITH LUBRICATING OIL
—————————— **CAUTION** ——————————
Too much oil causes poor cooling. Too little will damage the compressor. Top up the compressor after repairing a leak or replacing one or more of the components in the system.

SLOW LEAKAGES (MORE THAN 24 HOURS)

Normally this does not involve any loss of lubricating oil. When replacing components observe:

COMPRESSOR

Drain and measure the oil from the old compressor. Also drain the oil from the new compressor. Then add the same amount of oil (new), as was drained from the old compressor to the new compressor.

OTHER COMPONENTS

Drain and measure the amount of oil. Add the required amount of oil to the new component before installing.

QUICK LEAKAGES (E.G. BURST HOSE)

This usually involves a loss of lubricating oil. The following volumes apply when fitting a new component.

Compressor	0.15 L, 5.0 fl. oz.
Evaporator	0.07 L, 2.4 fl. oz.
Drier	0.05 L, 1.7 fl. oz.
Condensor	0.05 L, 1.7 fl. oz.
Hose	0.05 L, 1.7 fl. oz.

INSTALLING A COMPLETE SYSTEM (NEW)

Make sure that there is the correct quantity oil in the compressor. The other parts do not contain oil but receive oil when the refrigerant is circulating.

SAFETY CAUTIONS

1. Use tap water to remove refrigerant from eyes.

2. Always wear tight fitting safety glasses when there is danger of refrigerant loss.

3. Safety glasses should always be worn when working with or near refrigerants. **Rubber gloves should be worn and all form of skin contact should be avoided since refrigerants cause frostbite.** If refrigerant should contact the eyes or skin, splash the eyes or affected area with cold water (preferably for 15 min) and treat the injury in the same way as for a frostbite.

4. Get in touch with a doctor if the injury does not heal, or sight is affected. Avoid working near open flames, cigarettes etc. High temperatures cause the refrigerant to form poisonous fumes which are toxic in high concentrations.

NOTE: The gases can cause serious lung damage even in low concentrations. The symptoms may not become evident for several hours or perhaps even a day later.

TROUBLE SHOOTING AIR CONDITIONER SYSTEM

Condition: No Cooling From System

1. Blown fuse.
2. Broken or disconnected electrical wire.
3. Broken or disconnected ground wire.
4. Clutch coil or solenoid burned out or disconnected.
5. Electric switch contacts in thermostat burned excessively, or sensing element defective.
6. Blower motor disconnected or burned out.
7. Ignition switch ground or relay burned out.
8. Loose or broken drive belt.
9. Compressor partially or completely frozen.
10. Compressor reed valves inoperative—indicated by only slight variation of both gauge readings at any engine speed.
11. Expansion valve stuck open—indicated by normal head pressure, high suction pressure and evaporator flooding.
12. Heater valve inoperative—indicated by hot water in heater and hot discharge air from evaporator.
13. Broken refrigerant line.
14. Leak in system.
15. Clogged screen or screens in receiver-dehydrator or expansion valve. Plugged hose or coil.
16. Compressor shaft seal leaking.

Condition: Noisy System

1. Defective winding or improper connection in compressor clutch coil or solenoid.
2. Loose or excessively worn drive belts.
3. Noisy clutch.
4. Compressor noisy—loose mountings or worn inner parts.
5. Loose panels on car.
6. Compressor oil level low—lower parts of compressor hot.
7. Blower fan noisy—excessive wear in motor.
8. Idler pulley and bearing defective.
9. Excessive charge in system—rumbling noise or vibration in high pressure line, thumping noise in compressor, excessive head pressure and suction pressure, or low head pressure.
10. Low charge in system—hissing in evaporator case at expansion valve, bubbles or cloudiness in sight glass, or low head pressure.
11. Excessive moisture in system—expansion valve noisy, suction pressure low.

12. High pressure service valve closed—compressor has excessive knocking noise, high pressure gauge reads above normal.

Condition: Insufficient Cooling From System

1. Blower motor sluggish.
2. Compressor clutch slipping.
3. Obstructed blower discharge passage.
4. Clogged air intake filter.
5. Insufficient air circulation over condenser coils (fins clogged with dirt or bugs).
6. Evaporator clogged.
7. Outside air vents open.
8. Evaporator pressure regulator, hot gas by-pass valve, suction throttling valve, or similar device defective or improperly adjusted—indicated by high pressure gauge reading normal, and low gauge reading too high.
9. Insufficient refrigerant in system.
10. Clogged screen in expansion valve— indicated by gauge pressures being normal or showing slightly increased head pressure and low suction pressure with discharge output temperature high.
11. Expansion valve thermal bulb has lost its charge—indicated by too high a low gauge reading and excessive sweating of evaporator and suction line.
12. Clogged screen in receiver—indicated by higher than normal reading on high pressure gauge, lower than normal reading on low pressure gauge, and receiver and liquid lines cold to touch with possible frost.
13. Excessive moisture in system—indicated by excessive head pressure gauge reading.
14. Air in system—indicated by excessive head pressure and possibly bubbles in sight glass.
15. Thermostat defective or improperly adjusted—indicated by low gauge reading high or clutch cycling at too high a reading.

Condition: Intermittent Cooling

1. Defective circuit breaker, blower switch, or blower motor.
2. Partially open improper ground or loose connection in compressor clutch coil or solenoid.
3. Compressor clutch slipping.
4. Insufficient control vacuum.
5. Unit icing up—may be caused by excessive moisture in system,

incorrect super heat adjustment in expansion valve, or thermostat adjusted too low.

6. Thermostat defective—indicated by low side pressure low or excessively high and adjustments will not correct.

7. Stuck hot gas by-pass valve or suction throttle valve—indicated by low pressures of both head and suction (indication of moisture in system).

8. Clogged evaporator.

Insufficient Cooling From Evaporator

COMPRESSOR AND CLUTCH (VISUAL INSPECTION)

Condition: Compressor Not Operating

1. Check system fuse.
2. Check belt tension. Tighten or replace belt.
3. Check for current at clutch coil. If present, check defective clutch coil or clutch.

SYSTEM PROCEDURES (INSTRUMENT TEST)

Condition: High Side Low, Low Side High
(= Defective Compressor)

1. Reed valves leaking.
2. Leaking head gasket.
3. Internal leak in compressor.
4. Replace compressor if cylinders or pistons are defective.

Condition: High Side Low, Low Side Low

A. BUBBLES IN SIGHT GLASS: REFRIGERANT IS LOW. MAY BE CAUSED BY SMALL LEAK
1. Check for leakage and correct.
2. Add refrigerant until bubbles disappear and both gauges show normal reading.

B. NO BUBBLES IN SIGHT GLASS, GAUGE READINGS ARE EXCESSIVELY LOW. POSSIBLY NO LIQUID IN SIGHT GLASS
1. A serious leak may be indicated.
2. Expansion valve screen may be clogged.
3. Expansion valve may be stuck closed. Replace valve.

Condition: High Side Normal, Low Side Normal
(= Moisture In System)

NOTE: low side reading may or may not drop into vacuum while reading.
1. Evacuate refrigerant.
2. Replace drier.
3. Vacuum pump system and recharge.

Condition: High Side High, Low Side Normal
(= Air In System)

NOTE: low side gauge reading may or may not drop into vacuum while reading.
1. Evacuate system.
2. Replace drier.
3. Vacuum pump system and recharge.

Condition: High Side High, Low Side High

A. REFRIGERANT OVERCHARGE
NOTE: Sight glass may show bubbles.
1. Bleed refrigerant until heavy stream of bubbles appear, then charge refrigerant until bubbles are eliminated from sight glass.

B. EXPANSION VALVE DEFECTIVE
1. Replace expansion valve.

C. CONDENSER DEFECTIVE
1. May be blocked and not have sufficient air flow. Clean condenser.

D. COOLING SYSTEM INCORRECT
1. Check belt tension and adjust if necessary.
2. Test radiator pressure cap and and cooling system thermostat.
3. Check all hoses.
4. Make sure the cooling system is filled with a 50% mixture of water and anti-freeze/summer coolant.

EVAPORATOR AND BLOWER CONTROLS

Condition: Evaporator Ices Over

1. Check air flow.
2. If there is no air flow, clean coils and repair or replace air duct.
3. If air flow is good, test system controls.

Condition: Evaporator Discharge Air Temperature High

1. Check evaporator pressure.
2. If pressure is too high, replace valve.
3. If pressure is normal, repair or replace heater valve or vacuum servo valve, as required.

Condition: Blower Does Not Operate

1. Check current flow at motor assembly. If current is present, replace motor.
2. If current is not present, check for faulty switch, broken wire, blown fuse or poor connector.

Condition: Blower Does Not Operate At All Speeds

1. Check blower switch and replace as necessary.

Air Flow Check For The CU And CU ± AC Units

1. When carrying out the following checks, make sure that the battery is fully charged and that there is sufficient vacuum in the system. The vacuum should be 35 kPa (10 inch hg).
2. If necessary use a separate vacuum pump.
3. The illustrations show the airflow in the different control positions. Note that the water valve is closed when the temperature control is set at Cool. The positions MAX and NORM are only available on the CU + AC system (i.e. air conditioning).

MAX (CU + AC ONLY)
The water valve is closed regardless of the position of the temperature control lever. Recirculation of air. Compressor operating. Air flow from panel vents.

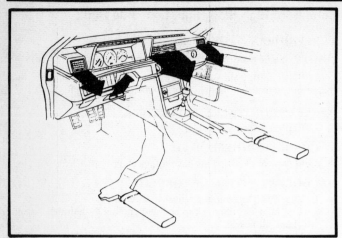

Air flow in MAX position (CU with air conditioning) (© AB Volvo Car Corp.)

NORM (CU + AC ONLY)

Compressor operating. Outside air admitted. Air flow from panel vents.

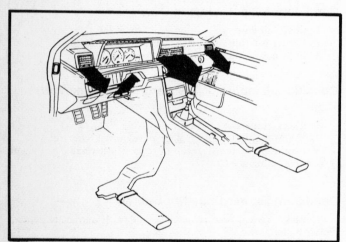

Air flow in NORM position (CU with air conditioning) (© AB Volvo Car Corp.)

B/L (BI LEVEL)

Air flow from panel and floor vents. Small amount of air from defroster vents. Compressor operating (CU + AC).

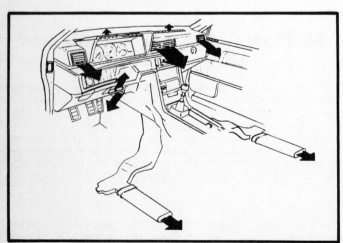

Air flow in the B/L (Bi-Level) position (© AB Volvo Car Corp.)

VENT

Air flow from panel vents. Compressor disengaged (CU + AC).

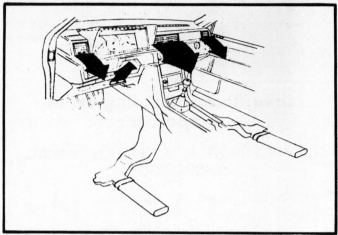

Air flow in the VENT position (© AB Volvo Car Corp.)

FLOOR

Air flow from floor vents. A small amount of air from defroster vents. Compressor disengaged (CU + AC).

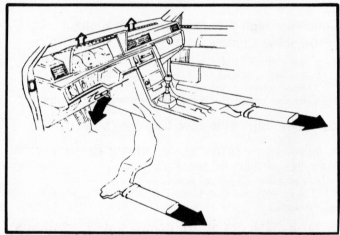

Air flow in FLOOR position (© AB Volvo Car Corp.)

F/D (FLOOR DEFROST)

Air flow from floor and defroster vents. Compressor disengaged (CU + AC).

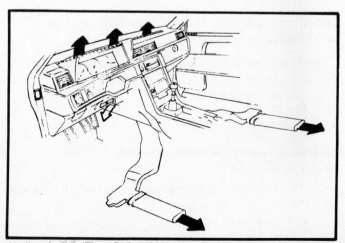

Air flow in F/D (Floor Defrost) position (© AB Volvo Car Corp.)

APPROX. TIME TAKEN FOR VACUUM CONTROL

Room temp. approx. 20–25°C

Temperature Lever	Mode Selector Moved From	Air From	Approx. Time Taken (Secs.)
Max cool (65°F)	OFF—ECON	Panel vent	10–12
	OFF—B/L	Floor & panel vents	5–8
	OFF—DEF	Defroster vents	3–6
	OFF—auto (without air recir)	Panel vents	15–20
	OFF—auto (with air recir above 20°C room temp)	Panel vents	15–20

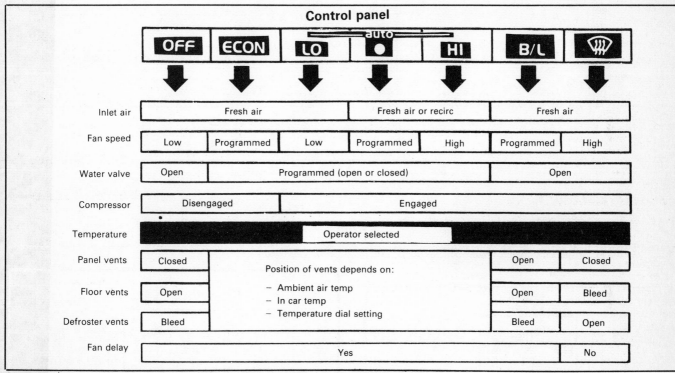

Control panel operation for Automatic Climate Control (ACC) unit (© AB Volvo Car Corp.)

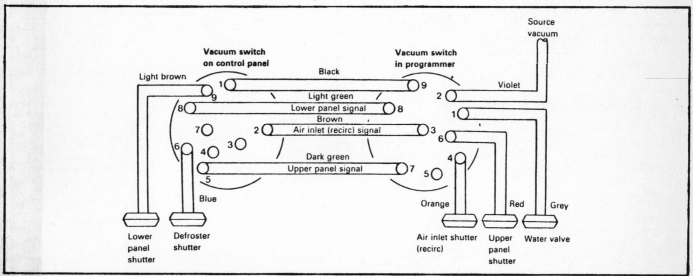

Vacuum schematic for Automatic Climate Control (ACC) unit (© AB Volvo Car Corp.)

7/4	Instrument connection 7 poles
8/1	Instrument connection 8 poles
10/D+	Alternator terminal D+
11/11	Fuse no. 11
11/14	Fuse no. 14
32	Glove compartment
38,42	Control panel light
43	Vanity mirror light
81	Pressure sensor
82	Thermal contact for fan motor
131	Relay for fan
132	Delay relay/compressor relay
165	Fan motor
169	Resistor, fan motor
176–7	Control unit, constant idle system
200	Control solenoid, AC compressor, 3.9A
202	Control panel for CU
203	Temperature dial
204	Outer air sensor
205	In-car sensor
206	Programmer
	Cooling fan (only D 24 T with AC and Tropic radiator)
11/6	Fuse no. 6
134/3	Relay for ignition advance B 28 F
156	Motor, elec. cooling fan 13 A
224	Thermal switch, Elec. cooling fan
236	Relay, pressure sensor, Tropic D 24 T
237	Pressure sensor, Tropic D 24 T

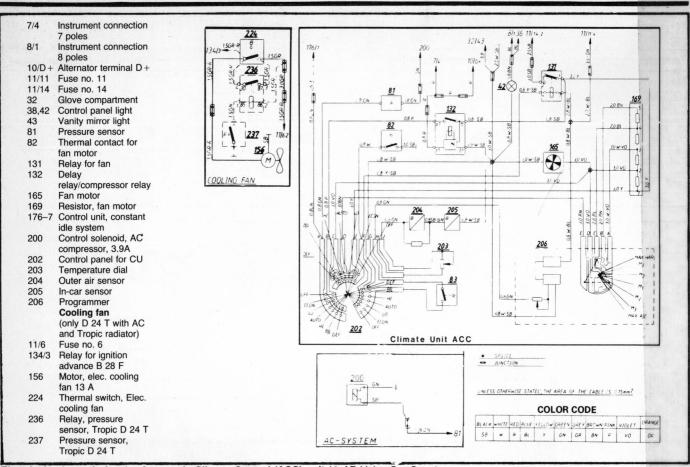

Electrical schematic for the Automatic Climate Control (ACC) unit (© AB Volvo Car Corp.)

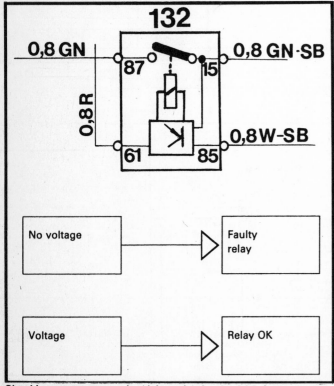

Checking compressor relay/delay relay for the ACC system (© AB Volvo Car Corp.)

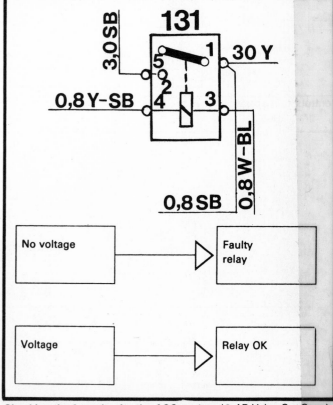

Checking the fan relay for the ACC system (© AB Volvo Car Corp.)